W9-BMO-914

AP* Achiever
Advanced Placement
European History
Exam Preparation Guide

to accompany

A History of the Modern World

Tenth Edition

R. R. Palmer
Joel Colton
Lloyd Kramer

Prepared by

Chris Freiler
Hinsdale Central High School

Mc
Graw
Hill

Boston   Burr Ridge, IL   Dubuque, IA   New York   San Francisco   St. Louis
Bangkok   Bogotá   Caracas   Kuala Lumpur   Lisbon   London   Madrid   Mexico City
Milan   Montreal   New Delhi   Santiago   Seoul   Singapore   Sydney   Taipei   Toronto

Higher Education

Published by McGraw-Hill, an imprint of The McGraw-Hill Companies, Inc., 1221 Avenue of the Americas, New York, NY 10020. Copyright © 2008. All rights reserved. No part of this publication may be reproduced or distributed in any form or by any means, or stored in a database or retrieval system, without the prior written consent of The McGraw-Hill Companies, Inc., including, but not limited to, in any network or other electronic storage or transmission, or broadcast for distance learning.

This book is printed on acid-free paper.

Printed in the United States of America.

11 12 13 14 QVS/QVS 17 16 15 14

ISBN: 978-0-07-325672-6
MHID: 0-07-325672-2

www.mhhe.com

ACKNOWLEDGMENTS

In writing this work, I have incurred numerous personal debts. First, I wish to thank my wife, Michele, for her outstanding editing skills, advice, and companionship in the completion of this project. My children, Megan and Kyle, waited patiently for their father to finish this or that paragraph before playing catch with them. I wish to recognize my colleague, John Naisbitt, for providing me with the most rewarding collaboration of my career over the past several years. Without the inspiration of Lloyd Kramer and Peter Hayes, my teachers at Northwestern University, I may not have pursued the field of history. To my parents I owe a strong work ethic and resilience in the face of adversity. Finally, I wish to thank my editor at McGraw-Hill, Mickey Cox, for her support and guidance.

ABOUT THE AUTHOR

Chris Freiler has taught Advanced Placement European History at Hinsdale Central High School in Hinsdale, IL, since 1993. Before that, he taught AP United States History and Political Science at Morgan Park Academy in Chicago, IL. He has also served since 1997 as a reader and table leader for the AP European History annual exam scoring. From 1998 to 2002, Chris served on the Test Development Committee (and later as an independent consultant) for AP European History, in the process acting as the primary author for three different document-based questions used on the national exam. Recently, he was appointed to the College Board Commission to reexamine the AP European History curriculum. Chris earned his B.A. in history and political science from Northwestern University in 1987, graduating with Highest Distinction, and an M.A. in history from the University of Virginia in 1989. Beginning with the 2007 exam scoring, Chris will serve as Assistant Chief Reader. He is currently working toward an M.A. in philosophy at Northern Illinois University.

PREFACE

You the AP student will find several products on the market designed to help prepare you for the Advanced Placement European History exam. All can be useful in reviewing the material for this course. The author, a former member of the AP Test Development Committee and a leader at the annual exam scoring, designed the volume you now hold to be the most realistic and comprehensive test preparation manual available. The following features make it stand apart:

- This book covers standard political, diplomatic, economic, and intellectual trends, but also makes a special effort to incorporate essential social and cultural history that is increasingly emphasized on the exam.
- Practice multiple-choice questions were developed to mirror both the content and types of questions you will encounter on the exam.
- Document-based and free-response questions follow the format and approach of those on the AP exam.
- The comprehensive content review follows the analytical yet accessible narrative of Palmer, Colton, and Kramer's *A History of the Modern World*, 10th edition. It covers nearly every conceivable topic on the exam in a manageable length.
- "Heads Up!" and "Sidebar" features throughout the guide are designed to connect important topics, clarify common misunderstandings, or add important information to assist in your preparation for the exam.

We recognize that you have a choice in selecting the right review guide for your study; we trust that you will find this volume the best available.

A NOTE FROM THE AUTHOR

Welcome to your study of Advanced Placement European History. You should find the course material challenging yet rewarding, as the curriculum covers some of the most significant developments and events that affect our lives still today. Though the sheer amount of material—the people, places, events, art works, and literature—can often seem overwhelming, you will not be expected to remember everything. More important than memorization is the development of your historical thinking skills—understanding cause and effect, making connections within historical eras, analyzing primary sources for point of view, noting comparisons across historical eras—and your ability to express this knowledge in writing.

My experience as a teacher has shown me that virtually any motivated student can succeed in the course and on the AP exam. Two keys to success are (1) a commitment to develop your skills in historical and written analysis and (2) a supply of proven strategies to prepare for the exam. You will supply the first key; this guide will provide you with the second.

This book is organized into three sections. In the first section you'll learn how the exam is structured and scored. Important terminology and recent developments in the test, keyed closely to the course outline provided by the College Board, will be covered. This section also surveys important strategies for increasing comprehension of your daily reading, meeting the tasks required by the document-based question (DBQ), and empowering your writing in response to the free-response questions (FRQs). The second section contains the crux of this review guide, with chapters surveying important content of different historical periods. Significant coverage is given to social and cultural developments, which have been increasingly stressed on the AP exam. Each chapter provides helpful study tips, a brief discussion of interpretive issues, and review questions. You will also find a concise list of suggested readings.

This review guide is keyed to the text by Palmer, Colton, and Kramer, *A History of the Modern World,* 10th edition; however, it can be used on its own or in conjunction with any textbook. In some cases, I have combined two chapters or added material to a topic, all in an effort to highlight important historical themes and make *A History of the Modern World,* or any textbook for that matter, a useful tool in your preparation for the Advanced Placement exam.

The final section provides two full practice examinations, complete with 80-question multiple-choice sections, a DBQ, and two sections of free-response questions. In all, you will find over 300 multiple-choice questions with substantial answer explanations, as well as sample DBQ and free-response essays. Sample essays have been included in the belief that seeing writing that succeeds, and also that which is lacking, serves as the best way to hone your own writing skills. Finally, in the belief that chronology is important for understanding the skills of historical thinking, I have included three different timelines in the appendix to this volume.

Good luck in your review of the course!

Chris Freiler

CONTENTS

SECTION II—*CONTENT REVIEW* 47

Chapter 3: *The Rise of Europe* 48

Chapter 4: *The Renaissance and Reformation* 58

Chapter 15: *Democracy, Totalitarianism, and World War II, 1919–1945*   **270**

Chapter 16: *The Cold War and European Recovery*   **296**

Section I

Studying for the Exam

CHAPTER 1
The Structure of the AP Exam

OVERVIEW OF THE TEST STRUCTURE

Each year's exam is designed by the AP European History Test Development Committee and covers the period from 1450 to the recent past. Because the exam is created several years before actual testing, it is unlikely that any recent events (i.e., within the past 5–10 years) will appear on the exam. However, increased attention has been given to the period following World War II; in fact, there is typically a free-response question (FRQ) focused on this period.

The exam consists of three parts. In Section I there are 80 multiple-choice questions. Once you complete Section I, you will not be able to return to it. Students are provided 55 minutes to complete this multiple-choice section. Section II is divided between the document-based question (DBQ—60 minutes) and two free-response questions (70 minutes). Thus, the total time you will have to work on Section II is 130 minutes. Of this time, 15 minutes are designated as a reading period in which you can look over the DBQ documents, select your FRQs, and outline your responses. However, you may not write anything scoreable in your pink booklets during this time. Overall, then, you will have no more than 3 hours, 5 minutes to complete the exam.

For many students, AP European history will be their first exam. If so, you will find it to be not only an intellectual test, but a physical and psychological one. It is important, therefore, to pace yourself and come to the exam well prepared.

Section	Number of Questions	Time
I	80 multiple-choice questions	55 minutes
Scheduled break of 5–10 minutes		
II	3 essay questions, including one document-based question	130 minutes 60 minutes recommended (includes 15-minute reading period)
	two free-response questions	70 minutes recommended
	Total	3 hours, 5 minutes

Part I: Multiple-Choice

The multiple-choice portion of the test counts as 50 percent of your composite score on the AP Exam. It is difficult to score well overall if you do poorly on this portion of the exam. Though this may give you pause if you tend to struggle with objective assessments, it is possible to improve your score with practice and the appropriate strategies. More will be said about this in Chapter 2.

There are 80 questions on the multiple-choice section of the exam, covering the period from 1450 to the recent past. "Recent past" generally means events prior to about 5 to 10 years before administration of the exam. Half of the questions cover the chronological period before 1815 and half after 1815. In addition, several cross-chronological questions may appear. Regarding topics, the exam is divided roughly into thirds: one-third of the questions on cultural/ intellectual themes, one-third on social/economic themes, and one-third on political/diplomatic themes. Questions can be of different types, such as identification of an important personality, event, or written work; interpretation of a visual stimulus (e.g., chart, map, art); or analysis of the effects of an historical event. Strategies for approaching these questions are covered in Chapter 2.

All questions will have a similar format—a "stem" that introduces the topic of the question and five answer choices, four of which will be "distracters" and one of which will be the "key," or correct answer. It is rare for "none of the above" or "all of the above" to appear as choices. Students must remember to read all the choices carefully and choose the *best* answer in response to the stem. Oftentimes, there will be two or three appealing choices, which you will become more skilled at narrowing down once you practice effective strategies. Do not be concerned if you find some of the questions highly difficult or topics unfamiliar. Few students will achieve a perfect score, and the questions are designed to range in difficulty from about 15 to 90 percent of students choosing the correct answer.

Part II: Essays

The written portion of the exam is composed of a document-based question, or DBQ, which is worth 45 percent of Part II (or 22.5 percent overall), and two free-response questions (FRQs), which are worth 55 percent of Part II (or 27.5 percent overall, 13.75 percent for each question). Part II counts as 50 percent of your total score.

The Document-Based Question (DBQ)

If this is your first Advanced Placement history class, you may be unfamiliar with the concept of a document-based question. Not to worry, as this portion of the exam requires no outside knowledge of the topic, simply a set of skills in historical interpretation learned primarily through practice and repetition.

Unlike the FRQs, there are no choices for the DBQ. All students will answer the same prompt. The topic is often specific and unfamiliar to most students. However, all the information you need to respond to the prompt is given in 10 to 12 accompanying documents. As you will see in Chapter 2, most DBQs first provide a brief historical background of no longer than a paragraph. Following this paragraph are the primary sources you will use to answer the question. These sources vary and may include a diary entry, speech, selection from a book, memoirs, chart, or political cartoon. Your task is to find patterns among the documents, group them logically, apply them to a thesis, and analyze them for bias and point of view. There is a specific rubric used to score the DBQ, much like a checklist, so your familiarity with the scoring system will help you address all the required tasks of the DBQ exercise (see p. 5).

As noted, the first 15 minutes of Part II is designated as a reading period. During this time, students will be reading through the DBQ documents, selecting their FRQs, and outlining their responses. However, you may not write anything in your booklet for a score. There are different ways to use this 15 minutes, one of which I recommend in Chapter 2. It is suggested that students take 60 minutes for the DBQ (which includes the time to read the documents and write the essay), though certainly if you finish early you may move on to the free-response questions.

Free-Response Questions (FRQs)

Free-response questions are designed to gauge your understanding of major developments, events, and trends in European history. Though some may be more specific than others, they are intended to assess your grasp of the "big picture" through the use of well-chosen examples. There are two sections (B and C) of three choices each. The Test Development Committee employs different approaches to the grouping of the essays, but in general you will find that the questions break down either chronologically (three pre-1800 and three post-1800) or topically (e.g., three social-cultural-intellectual and three political-economic-diplomatic).

At this point in the exam, it is easy to fall behind and find yourself short of time for these questions. Try to allow at least 30 to 35 minutes for each question, which includes 5 or so minutes to plan out your response, including your thesis and supporting evidence. AP Exam graders (known as "readers") will find a shorter, focused response preferable to a longer, rambling one.

HOW THE EXAM IS SCORED

All AP exams employ the same overall scoring system:

5 Extremely well qualified
4 Well qualified
3 Qualified
2 Possibly qualified
1 No recommendation

To calculate your overall total, a complex formula converts the raw score of each section of the exam. There are 180 possible points, 90 for each section. However, one should not think in terms of the standard 90-80-70-60 percent scale. "Break points" between each of the overall scores are determined after the test is administered based on historical standards and how well students performed that particular year on the exam.

Scoring of the Multiple-Choice Section

For the multiple choice section, keep in mind that the exam penalizes you for guessing. I often have students ask, "How did they know I was guessing?" The answer is simple: "If you got it wrong, you must have guessed." Each incorrect response will result in 1.25 points being taken off, compared with 1 point for a question left blank. As we will see in the strategies section, it will invariably be in your best interest to guess if you can eliminate even one of the choices. Let's say a student answered 52 of the multiple-choice questions correctly, left 8 blank, and thus marked 20 of them incorrectly ($52 + 8 + 20 = 80$). The student's raw score on this section of the exam would be $52 - (1.25 \times 20 = 5) = 47$.

Scoring of the Essays

The essays on the AP Exam are scored using a specific rubric, which for European History differs between the DBQ and the FRQs. For the DBQ, readers will apply a "core scoring" rubric centered on six analytical tasks. If you complete these six tasks on at least a basic level, you can earn additional points in the "expanded core." However, should you miss any one of the six tasks, you cannot earn a score higher than a 5, regardless of your proficiency overall on the essay. Therefore, your familiarity with this rubric is vital to your success on the DBQ. Though rubrics are tailored to specific questions, the generic standards are as follows.

The Document-Based Question

Generic Core-Scoring Rubric	Points
<u>Basic Core</u> 1. Thesis is explicitly stated and addresses all parts of the question. Does NOT simply restate the question. 2. The essay uses something specific from a <u>majority</u> of the documents. 3. Student understands the documents by using a <u>majority</u> appropriately (one major misinterpretation allowed). 4. Thesis is appropriately supported with a <u>majority</u> of documents; student does not simply summarize the documents. 5. Essay analyzes point of view or bias in at least THREE documents. 6. Documents are analyzed by placing them in at least THREE appropriate groups.	1 1 1 1 1 1 _____ 6
<u>Expanded Core</u> Essays may receive 0-3 additional points for the following: • Having a strong, analytical thesis • Using all or almost all of the documents • Addressing all parts of the question thoroughly • Using documents effectively as evidence • Showing an understanding of complexities in the documents • Analyzing bias or point of view in at least FOUR documents cited in the essay • Analyzing the documents in additional ways, e.g., additional groupings • Bringing in relevant historical context	0-3 _____ 9

For the European History DBQ, all that you will need to answer the question is directly in front of you—the documents, historical background, and instructions. If you can provide more powerful analysis or meaningful context to a document by referring to material outside what is contained in the document, then by all means bring your knowledge to bear on the response. If, however, you find that you are simply "name-dropping" and drifting from the documents, then this is unlikely to improve your score and may even detract from the primary task of the DBQ—analyzing historical evidence. First and foremost, your response should be driven by the material provided in the documents. Chapter 2 offers more detail on strategies for tackling the DBQ.

The Free-Response Questions

Free-response essays are scored "holistically," which means that readers will look at the essay "as a whole," unlike the checklist system employed in scoring the DBQ. Before assigning any score, a reader will read the entire essay, looking for features that tend to characterize an effective response. These indicators tend to be similar regardless of the question. Here is an example of a generic free-response rubric:

<u>Stronger Essays</u> 9-8-7-6

- Offers a clear, well-developed thesis in response to all parts of the question.
- Thesis is supported with relevant and substantial evidence.
- Essay is well-balanced in its treatment of the required tasks.
- May contain minor errors of fact or interpretation.

<u>Mixed Essays</u> 5-4

- Thesis attempted but may be incomplete, unfocused, or vague.
- At least some specific evidence provided in support of the thesis.
- Essay may be unbalanced or partially off-base in its treatment of required tasks.
- May contain some major and minor errors of fact or interpretation.

<u>Weaker Essays</u> 3-2-1-0

- Thesis is confused, misconstrues the question, or is absent.
- Little if any specific factual support, or if support is given, it is not explained.
- Essay may ignore one or more parts of the prompt or be primarily off-task.
- Contains major and minor errors of fact and interpretation.

As the rubric indicates, "job one" for you in receiving a high mark on your essay is to focus on addressing the question asked. Even if you find that time is running out, it may be possible for you to write a brief yet focused response that will earn a solid mark that adds to a high composite score.

REGISTRATION AND FEES

For most students, registering for the exam is fairly easy. It is generally handled by your school's AP coordinator, often someone in your guidance department. If you are unsure how to register and have not received any information by late winter, you may wish to ask your teacher or an administrator at your school. Should your school not administer the exam, contact AP Services at the College Board for a list of schools in your area that do. The current fee for taking the exam is $82, but if you have financial need, a $22 reduction is available. For more information about financial aid, contact your AP coordinator.

For more information on anything related to the AP program, visit <u>apcentral.collegeboard.com</u> or write to AP Services:

AP Services
P.O. Box 6671
Princeton, NJ 08541-6671
Phone: (609) 771-7300 or (888) 225-5427 (toll-free in the United States and Canada)

E-mail: <u>apexams@info.collegeboard.org</u>

WHAT TO BRING TO THE EXAM

To reduce any anxiety, it is important that you come prepared on the day of the exam. Here is a list of items you will need:

- Several sharpened No. 2 pencils with erasers, along with a separate eraser. To remove marks on scan sheets, white erasers often work most effectively.
- Several black or dark-blue ballpoint ink pens. Erasable ink or liquid ink can smudge and make it difficult to read your essays.
- Your school code.
- A watch (that makes no noise) to allow you to keep track of your time.
- Your social security number for identification purposes.
- A photo ID.

These items are prohibited or are best left at home:

- Books, dictionaries, or notes
- Highlighters or correction fluid
- Scratch paper
- Computers (unless you are a student with a disability who has prearranged for their use)
- Watches or other items that beep or have alarms
- Portable listening devices, such as iPods, MP3 players, CD players, and radios
- Cameras, beepers, personal digital assistants (PDAs), or cell phones
- Clothing with subject-related information

ADDITIONAL RESOURCES TO HELP YOU PREPARE

Using Your Textbook Effectively

For almost all students, the primary source of information is their textbook. Textbooks convey material in a standard manner, though they often differ in their areas of emphasis as well as the features they offer. Many texts now come standard with access to a Web site where you can get chapter summaries, take quizzes, find links to other useful resources, and even obtain feedback on practice essays that you write. In addition, your teacher may have had you purchase or may have provided a study guide that accompanies the text. These can often vary in quality, but you may find it useful to follow along with the text reading by consulting your study guide.

Just because a textbook is your main resource shouldn't prevent you from employing other useful resources, such as reference works, additional readings, periodicals, online materials, or even literature. Certainly, it is possible for you to succeed on the exam simply by making the most effective use of your textbook, but if you find other sources enlightening, convenient, or interesting, your teacher will probably not discourage and is likely to positively encourage them as a way to get a better feel for what you are learning.

AP Central

Your contact point for the latest information regarding the AP program is the official site of the College Board: apcentral.collegeboard.com. Any basic questions you have related to the administration of the exam, its scoring, policies, and others can be found at this Web site. In addition, you can purchase products that may help you in your review, such as free-response questions, sample essays, and a helpful CD-ROM for multiple-choice review. If you are a senior or would simply like to know policies of particular universities related to AP credit, the site features links to hundreds of colleges that can guide your decision making.

To get started, after you've accessed the site, simply create a user profile and password. You will also have to provide some basic information about yourself. If there are changes in the exam, you should be notified via e-mail. This Web site is a good way to keep up-to-date on anything AP related.

Internet Resources

Many students find that they are savvier Internet users than their teachers. Certainly, the Internet has opened new sources of information, particularly related to history, unknown to historians and students of history in years past. However, the Internet is a tool like any other and should be used judiciously to meet the appropriate need. Before you rely too heavily on any specific site—say one that you found using one of the major search engines like Google or Yahoo—you should ensure that the site is reliable and authoritative. Those sites affiliated with a known college or university, or perhaps sponsored by a teacher of the course, may prove useful to your studying. With that in mind, I have listed some Web sites that have been helpful to me and my students in the past. Keep in mind that your textbook publisher may also provide a Web site keyed to your textbook. This address is probably listed somewhere in the introductory materials for your text.

historyteacher.net/APEuroHomePage.htm—This site is one of the best by a teacher of the course—Susan Pojer, from Horace Greeley High School in Chappaqua, New York—and contains extensive review materials, practice DBQs, and links to other sources.

library.byu.edu/~rdh/eurodocs/—This site offers a thorough collection of primary sources organized by nation, and also includes a section titled "Europe as a Supranational Region."

www.fordham.edu/halsall/mod/modsbook.html—Perhaps the best resource for primary sources related to European history. You will find the site more user-friendly than the one above and the chronological organization easier to follow. The site carries classics, like Luther's "Ninety-Five Theses," but also interesting nuggets you're unlikely to find elsewhere.

www.historyguide.org/intellect/intellect.html—A scholarly yet accessible collection of college lectures on broad topics related to European intellectual and cultural history. Students may find it a welcome change of pace from their other materials.

bedfordstmartins.com/mapcentral/—This site offers historical maps that are keyed to some of the major textbooks in the field (try the maps accompanying Lynn Hunt et al., *The Making of the West*, 3rd edition). Maps like these will help you review the changing political landscape of Europe and assess shifts in the balance of power.

www.wga.hu/index.html—Regardless of whether art is one of your favorite areas, you will find this easily searchable site a treasure of visual images. You can search chronologically or alphabetically by artist for paintings, sculpture, or architecture. It is especially handy as you review the images that you wish to connect with particular historical eras.

Of course, this list is only a small sampling of sites available. As you read through the content review in Section 2, you will find additional suggestions for resources. With modern search engines at your fingertips, many more sites are waiting to be discovered for the motivated. Though these sites can be fun and useful, keep in mind that the rules of citation and rendering proper credit still apply. If you use one of these sites for research, make sure that you supply a bibliography and give proper credit—advice that applies to all of your studies and academic work. Help in formatting bibliographies can be found at **easybib.com.**

CHAPTER 2
Strategies for Success

HOW TO USE THIS REVIEW GUIDE

The review book you now hold is not intended as a replacement for whatever materials, including your text, your teacher has provided you. It is a supplement that should be consulted as frequently as you find useful. First, you should make sure that you are familiar with the structure of the curriculum and the AP Exam. Also, the study strategies covered here should improve your comprehension as you move through your daily reading and prepare for quizzes and exams. Another way you can employ this guide is to use Section 2 to review material prior to any assessment, particularly the AP Exam. After reading through content reviews, you may wish to try the multiple-choice questions at the end of each chapter. To help you develop your all-important writing skills, each chapter features a sample free-response question with an explanation of the score the essay received. As you try these, your skill in determining the score for each sample received should improve. This indicates that you are gaining an understanding of the features of a powerful essay response.

As you approach the exam, perhaps starting with your spring break or around late March, you should become more serious about breaking down what you have learned into more manageable chunks for review. Go back to those chapters that you have already covered and refresh your memory with some practice questions. As you near the test date, you should attempt a full practice test with only the scheduled 5- to 10-minute break after the multiple-choice section. This is important for you to get a feel for the emotional and psychological stresses of the test. Finally, one of the last items you should review is the full chronological scope of the course, including the timelines in the Appendix. Make sure you can place art movements, social developments, intellectual changes, wars, and so on in the appropriate chronological period. Like any resource, this review guide should prove as helpful as you are willing to make it. Realize, too, that it is one of many tools for the motivated student.

READING STRATEGIES

Your primary source of information for this course is likely to be your textbook. Chances are, you will find yourself spending about 30 to 60 minutes per day reading about 7 to 10 pages in it. It is important that you get the most out of the time you spend reading. My experience as a teacher has shown me that many students do not read as effectively as possible because they lack strategies that can increase their comprehension. Such strategies need not add significantly to your homework, but the extra 5 minutes or so that you spend with them will often pay dividends in the long run, both in your performance and in saving time later.

First, you will need to find a time and place that is conducive to your studying. For many students, this is a quiet place with few distractions, but not necessarily the most comfortable, such as your bed, where you are liable to become drowsy or lose concentration. Experiment with places and times of day when your brain is most active, so that you don't find yourself continually rereading passages because your attention has wandered.

One way for you to make reading and studying more interesting is to avoid reading passively, as if it were a story that "speaks for itself." Certainly there is element of story and drama in history, particularly at its best, but this is usually not the format of most textbooks. Most are written in a fairly standard format with a set of "cues," which, with some practice, you can pick up on and become adept at deciphering.

A textbook chapter often begins with a "hook"—a story, personality, event, work of art—that is designed to grab the reader's attention. Beneath the flowery language, the authors are trying to convey the themes, or main ideas, of the chapter. Challenge yourself to identify what the big picture is before you continue with your reading. Others texts, such as *A History of the Modern World*, begin with a more standard introduction to the chapter content and themes. Perhaps it would be helpful to write out one or two sentences based on this introduction that summarize the key points covered in the chapter. This could be done immediately after reading the introduction or after completing the entire chapter.

Though there are numerous strategies, not all work as well for each student. Find those that work well for you, and feel free to experiment until you discover what those are. Whatever you do, make sure that you are *actively* reading your text, much as a builder constructs a scaffolding or framework of a house, before moving on to the siding, roof, and interior. The difference is that your scaffolding acts as an analytical structure for your understanding of the entire chapter. To assist you in this process, several specific strategies follow to get you started. Keep in mind that there is nothing magical about these; their positive effect depends more on your perseverance in developing your skills of historical analysis and working at connecting the specific content of the course to the major ideas, themes, and concepts of each unit.

Scaffolding and Annotating

How do you get started with a scaffold? History is often more about asking productive questions than about always having the right answers. So begin your reading each night with an overarching question that you will attempt to answer when you've finished with the reading. This question will generally lead to further subquestions. Remember, you will invariably find the answers to your questions within the text itself.

Suppose that you are reading about the Italian Renaissance. The chapter begins with a vignette about Brunelleschi's creation of the dome over the Florence Cathedral and then moves into the following headings: "The Economic and Social Context," "Italian City-States," "Renaissance Humanism," and "The Artist as Hero." Each one of these headings is a clue to how the chapter fits together. Let's take a look at a section of the vignette about Brunelleschi.

This topic sentence establishes one of the key points of the introduction—the rise of Europe during the Renaissance, in contrast with its relatively weak position before then.	<u>In 1300 Europe was a relative cultural backwater.</u> China was more advanced intellectually and technologically. For centuries Europeans had borrowed Arab knowledge in mathematics, science, and medicine, and it was the Islamic world that had kept alive the classics of ancient Greece and Rome. In America the Aztecs had developed a modern sewage system to grace their capital city of Tenochtitlan, while Europeans sat in slop. <u>The fourteenth century seemed to offer little prospect for advance.</u> Not only did the <u>Black Death</u> and <u>Hundred Years' War</u> kill off 30–50% of Europe's population, but the Roman Catholic Church was racked by a decades-long <u>schism over papal succession.</u> <u>Class revolts</u> bred fear and violence. Yet <u>Europe was on the verge</u>
A sequence of sentences identifies those upheavals of the fourteenth century that set the stage for the Renaissance.	

of a breakthrough thanks to several major developments. There was an underlying dynamism present in European culture.

> To conclude the paragraph, the author returns to the theme of how the Renaissance indicates a new spirit in Europe.

In 1418, one hundred and thirty years after its ground-breaking, the cathedral of Santa Maria del Fiore stood incomplete, for few architects were willing to risk their reputations on roofing the massive structure with the largest dome in the world. To demonstrate the significance of their city, the center of the Renaissance, the Florentine city fathers had determined that their cathedral needed a dome—the perfect geometric shape—which would recall the greatness of Rome by imitating the famous Pantheon. Fillipo Brunelleschi had a daring and secret plan and suggested that whoever could make an egg stand upright on a flat marble surface should build the dome. When the last of Brunelleschi's competitors failed in his attempt, he handed the egg to Brunelleschi, who promptly cracked the end with a blow to the marble and made it stand. So it was resolved, and Brunelleschi drew up a brief outline of his plan.

> A major architectural achievement of the Florentine Renaissance.

> These statements refer to the importance of civic humanism, or the identification of each individual with the reputation of his/her city-state.

> The creator of "Il Doumo" and a major architect and intellectual of the Renaissance.

Architecture is the most public of the arts, for it requires not only the vision of a single person but a city's collective spirit and craftsmanship. That the cathedral of Florence was begun in the Middle Ages and completed in the Renaissance is telling. Brunelleschi drew on the elements of the Middle Ages' Gothic style while incorporating geometric principles and motifs from classical Greece and Rome to achieve a striking new design. Though the dome was completed before his death in 1446, Brunelleschi did not live to see the lantern, which holds the dome together and adorns it, publicly unveiled in 1482. The cathedral and the dome stand as a testament to the civic spirit of every Florentine citizen and the individual genius of one man— both powerful legacies of the Italian Renaissance.

> Perhaps these two sentences are the crux of the chapter's theme—the importance of both civic humanism and individual accomplishment as legacies of the Renaissance.

> A metaphorical link that shows how the Renaissance also built on the heritage of the Middle Ages.

> The concluding sentence returns to the theme of the topic sentence.

In this chapter introduction, I have underlined important terms and analytical statements that help clarify the main points of the chapter. Any introduction will include one or more of such statements. At first, these may be more difficult for you to locate, particularly if you are accustomed to thinking of history as "fact driven" rather than "analysis" and "interpretation driven" as historians do. Try to avoid simply highlighting your text obsessively in the hopes that you won't miss anything. You are unlikely to catch the embedded meaning of the chapter as you float by with your highlighter. Though the annotations to the introduction just given are fairly detailed, for purposes of economy try your hand at using simple phrases, such as "civic humanism" or "individual greatness," that will serve to remind you of these themes when later you return to study this material. Try to think of yourself as creating meaning rather than absorbing it. Comprehension depends, again, on asking productive questions and then seeking the answers to those questions.

Here are some questions you might ask about the previous vignette:

- Why was it so important for the Florentines to put a dome on their cathedral?
- How was the civic environment important to the culture of the Renaissance?
- How do Brunelleschi's achievements and corresponding status reflect the changing role of the artist during the Renaissance?
- To what extent and in what ways did the Renaissance differ culturally from the Middle Ages?
- How does this story illustrate the major themes of the Renaissance?

At first, it may be useful to write out such questions, and then jot down brief responses to them. As you progress with your analytical skills, prompts like these will come naturally to you, as will your skill in identifying responses to them as you read. Four basic questioning strategies can be easily applied to just about any unit of study:

1. What causes, both long- and short-term, led to the event or development in question?
2. How does this person, development, event, or work reflect the major ideas of this chapter or unit?
3. How is this development or area related to the other topics covered in this chapter or unit?
4. What was the impact, both short- and long-term, of this event or development?

Let's now take these general strategies and see how they might apply to the chapter headings listed earlier, which might roughly correspond to your own textbook, so you might wish to follow along with it in front of you:

Social and Economic Context:

- How did economic developments support the development of Renaissance culture?
- How appropriate is the term "Renaissance" as applied to social, family, and civic life?
- What was the connection between trade and the spread of humanistic ideas?

The Italian City-States

- Why was the city-state environment essential to the development of the humanism?
- How did the Renaissance city-states alter diplomacy?
- What happened to the Renaissance as the city-states declined in the sixteenth century?
- How do Machiavelli's ideas reflect both Renaissance humanism and the political situation in Italy?

Renaissance Humanism

- What factors led to the development of humanism first in Italy?
- Identify four or five concepts related to Renaissance humanism.
- How did humanism change attitudes toward the following: the individual, education, religion, society?

The Artist as Hero

- What new features characterized Renaissance art and architecture?
- Identify five or six important artists and analyze how their art reflected the ideals of Renaissance humanism.
- How had the social status of the artist changed as a result of the Renaissance?

These questions represent a high level of analysis and thinking for a student just beginning this course. Think of them as a goal at which to aim. Keep in mind that you need not specifically write out the answers to each question, though as you can see from the earlier annotation that questions of this nature were in mind as I marked up the text. As a general rule, you should spend 2 to 3 minutes prior to reading constructing such questions and about 5 minutes when you've completed the reading creating a brief outline to review what you have read. Simply rushing through the reading and flipping your book closed is of little use in the long run. Reviewing immediately after reading will reinforce what you have learned and help you more easily erect future scaffolding for the next reading assignment. As you've probably discovered when you try to remember an important meeting or errand without reinforcing it several times—usually immediately—that item is forgotten in the rush of your daily life. To assist you in your efforts at creating useful yet easily managed outlines, I have included a sample at the end of this imagined chapter section.

"Brunelleschi and His Dome"—civic humanism and individual accomplishment
Social and Economic Context
+ commercial recovery after Black Death
+ emergence of new elites—merchant and nobles merge
+ patriarchal family structure, marriage as economic arrangement
The Italian City-States
+ Five Major States: Florence, Venice, Milan, Papal States, Naples
+ Civic humanism
+ Renaissance diplomacy: balance-of-power and Machiavelli
Renaissance Humanism
+ concepts: secularism, individualism, classics, human-centered, power
+ figures: Petrarch, Bruni, Mirandola, Castiglione, Alberti
+ spread to North
Artist as Hero
+ from craftsman to genius
+ perspective, oil-based paints, portraits, classical themes, proportion
+ Donatello, Masaccio, Brunelleschi, da Vinci, Michelangelo, Raphael, Titian

An outline of this type can be completed briefly as you read, though you should avoid making it too extensive, because this can render it less effective as a study tool later, and, at some point, adding to it defeats its purpose as a distillation of what you have read. You may also wish to complete such an outline immediately after reading to briefly reinforce what you have learned.

Before we move on to other strategies, we need to address another often-neglected feature of most textbooks—visuals such as maps, charts, cartoons, and primary sources. Many students tend to view these items as pleasant breaks from the monotony of a full page of double-column text. Though they do offer such a break, they also serve an important purpose in reinforcing the major themes of the unit. It is a truism that we learn best by what we hear and see, rather than either by itself. Think of these nontext items as visual cues for the historical era under study. Again, you can ask useful questions and jot down the answers next to the sources themselves.

- How does this map represent the political situation of Europe in _____?
- What about this painting reflects the concerns of the era?
- How does this political cartoon illustrate conflicts or issues important to this period?
- What data in this chart helps me understand the developments of this chapter?
- Why was this primary source chosen as a representation of chapter themes?

About 20 percent of the multiple-choice questions on the exam include a visual stimulus. If you have embedded that work of art, map, quote from an important document, or map from an important era of diplomacy in your mind, you are much more likely to know and select the correct answer, not to mention improve your skills of critical thinking when it comes to the analysis of primary sources for the DBQ or should an FRQ begin with a visual prompt.

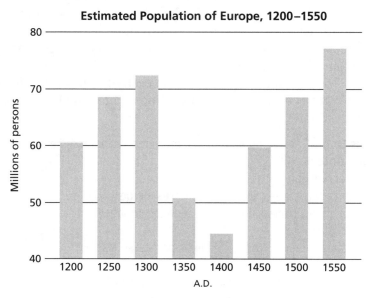

Estimated Population of Europe, 1200–1550

Source: M. K. Bennett, *The World's Food* (New York: Harper, 1954).

Consider what use you might make of the graph above. This simple population chart provides you with some essential information regarding demographic changes over several centuries. Population movements coincide with economic, political, and social developments. Try to identify and explain the factors that caused the decline and then recovery of population in this chart. By linking visuals to content in this way, you both hone your skills of visual analysis and reinforce your thematic understanding of a particular period in history.

Timelines and the Importance of Chronology

Perhaps like many of my students, one of the first questions you asked in your AP European history class was, "Do we have to know dates?" When I answer this question, I always choose my words carefully to make sure I convey my message accurately. There are two parts to the answer. First, the course and the exam do not test your knowledge of trivia. Dates and the events that occurred on them are generally not important in and of themselves. That's the easy answer. The second part is more nuanced. Chronology *is* essential to the understanding of history; in fact, without it, the fundamental historical tasks of analyzing cause-effect relationships, making connections across topic areas, and establishing interpretations would be impossible. So yes, you must have a strong grasp of chronology to perform well in the course and on the exam. This will involve knowledge of historical periods, as well as some dates.

To see why chronology plays this key role in your understanding, let's look at a free-response question:

Identify the features of European global trade and analyze its impact on European diplomacy and society in the period 1650–1763.

Clearly, if you have little or no knowledge of the developments in this period, you will be unable to address this question. There are few cues in the prompt itself, other than an assumption that economic developments influenced society and diplomacy. The dates in the question were chosen with a purpose, probably to encompass a particular historical era. What is the significance of 1650? This is approximately when the last of the religious wars (Thirty Years' War) ended, and it marks the beginning of the Age of Absolutism, also named after its dominant personality—the Age of Louis XIV. The latter date (1763) ends the Seven Years' War, the last of the major colonial conflicts prior to the French Revolution.

If you happened to remember that the seventeenth and eighteenth centuries roughly corresponded with the Commercial Revolution, then you would be off to a good start in being able to handle this prompt. This question, then, wants you to deal with the effects of the Commercial Revolution on diplomacy and society in the Age of Absolutism. With the competition for colonies and resources, along with the economic philosophy of mercantilism that emphasized scarcity, nations engaged in near-constant warfare to advance their power. These conflicts are often called the Commercial Wars. You needn't remember all of them, simply their nature and general results, for example, on the balance of power. For the second part of the question (effects on society), think in terms of demographics (the study of populations), classes, and standard of living.

Don't be concerned if you can't recall all of the details. It is enough for you to begin your essay with some specific historical context. This context serves as a useful way to begin your introductory paragraph and establish your control of the question. A good portion of your studying, then, should involve reviewing the events and developments that define historical eras. If someone asked, "What significant intellectual development occurred in the eighteenth century?" you should be able to respond with: "the Enlightenment." This knowledge will act as your key to entering any given free-response or multiple-choice question.

To assist you in your mastery of historical chronology, the Appendix includes three different timelines, one of which is divided into topic areas, so that you can see not only the important developments but also how these topics are connected. As you review the timelines, you will find it helpful to define the characteristics of an historical era (e.g., explain how Baroque art reflected the religious and political climate of seventeenth-century Europe). Remember that dates are markers—important primarily for how they delineate and define historical eras. Also keep in mind that many questions will refer to centuries rather than dates. A century refers to the hundred years numerically prior to the number of the century; for example, the sixteenth century covers the 1500s.

Following is a "slice" of chronology, about 70 years in length, that highlights developments in each of the topic areas addressed in the course. As you peruse the data, try to look across the chart to establish some themes, or threads, that tie together developments. Along with the dates and events, a row marked "themes" is provided for you to write out significant features of historical eras. The example that follows is already filled in to model the process, and as you make your way through the review section, you should improve your analysis and ability to make conclusions regarding historical periodization. Ultimately, the goal of a timeline is to help connect the "big picture" with the specific content of a unit, much like a tree trunk supports its branches. The latter are not possible without the former.

Topic	1450	1460	1470	1480	1490	1500	1510
Political/ Diplomatic	End of the Hundred Years' War (1453) Wars of the Roses (1455–1485) Fall of Constantinople (1453) Peace of Lodi (1454) Ferdinand and Isabella unite Spain (1479)			Military revolution RISE OF NEW MONARCHS Vasco de Gama reaches India (1498)	Columbus's discovery of New World (1492) Jews expelled from Spain (1492) *Reconquista* completed (1492) Cortez conquers Aztecs (1519–1521) Charles V as HRE (1519–1556)		
Religious	Spanish Inquisition established (1478) RENAISSANCE PAPACY (1417–1540s)					Martin Luther's "95 Theses" (1517)	
Social	Decline of feudalism			POPULATION INCREASE (to ca. 1600) Rise of nobility of the robe			
Cultural	Development of printing press (1450s) da Vinci born (1452)			Sistine Chapel built (1473) High Renaissance—centered in Rome Spread of Renaissance to northern Europe	Michelangelo's masterpieces		
Intellectual	Navigational and mapmaking advances				Machiavelli's *The Prince* (1513) Erasmus and More's works on Christian humanism		
Economic	Hanseatic League			Global trade begins with exploration Price Revolution			
Themes	Decline of feudal political structures, including medieval "imperial" Papacy, gives way to centralization under New Monarchs.	Political stability and commercial expansion returns, supporting population increase.		Height of Renaissance in Italy spreads to North, but threatened by invasion fed by rivalry among New Monarchs.	Secular concerns of Renaissance Papacy lead to calls for Church reform, Christian humanism, and ultimately, the Protestant Reformation.		

This timeline, which could be filled with more or less detail, provides cues that help you place the major events and developments in time and that characterize this particular slice of chronology. As is clear, the events and developments here mark those important movements that began your course—the Renaissance and Protestant Reformation. Just as you use landmarks and maps to guide your movement around geographical space, dates and timelines will assist you in marking historical eras, cause-and-effect patterns, and the themes of a historical period. You may find it helpful to make your own timelines, varying from general (perhaps for broad social developments) to more specific (the religious wars and French Revolution). Just keep in mind that the goal is always for you to see the big picture and how the trees make up the forest.

STRATEGIES FOR THE MULTIPLE-CHOICE QUESTIONS

Though Section I takes only 55 minutes of the exam's total time, the multiple-choice questions count for 50 percent of your grade overall. For some, this is a source of comfort, for others, fear. If you struggle with objective assessments, the goal of this review guide is not to persuade you that you prefer them to writing, only that you can create confidence and achieve improved scores with the right approaches. As you attempt the questions that follow, read through all of the choices before committing to one of them; though there will only be one correct answer, there will be several appealing choices. Always choose the *best* answer from the available choices.

First, let's look at the type of questions that appear on AP Exams. There are several basic types: identification, visual interpretation, quotation interpretation, and general analysis. In addition, you will likely encounter some cross-chronological and *"except"* questions, the latter of which can sometimes prove tricky to students.

Identification Questions

Identification questions are the most common type, accounting for somewhere between 40 and 50 percent of the test. These questions range from the most basic (e.g., naming the author of a famous work) to the somewhat more complex (e.g., identifying a tenet of a political ideology). You may be asked to identify the accomplishment of a historical figure, a major feature of an intellectual movement, or the result of a treaty. Simply because the question is specific and well defined does not mean that it is easy. Make sure you read *all* the choices before deciding on the key; there is often more than one appealing choice. Often, you will find two or perhaps three choices that you can eliminate quickly because they are (1) out of the time period, (2) involve absolute phrases ("never," "always," "complete"), or (3) have little to do with the question stem. Here is an example of an identification question:

What was the immediate result of World War I?
- (A) a return to normalcy and peace across Europe
- (B) the breakup of the Soviet Union
- (C) complete acceptance of peace terms by the defeated powers
- (D) dissolution of empires in Central and Eastern Europe
- (E) a United States boycott of the peace conference

The answer here is D. The situation in Europe at the end of World War I was chaotic and resulted in revolutions in several nations, most notably Russia. Thus, A is eliminated, as is C, because you might recall that the grievances left by the peace negotiations fed into World War II; Germany only grudgingly accepted the Treaty of Versailles. As the Soviet Union did not break up until 1991, we can eliminate B. If you chose B, perhaps you might have confused the break-up of Russia with its later counterpart. That's why you need to read the question carefully before choosing. Choice E is also incorrect because President Wilson played a central role at Versailles.

Analysis Questions

To assess your powers of historical understanding, about 20 percent of Section I consists of analysis-type questions. These tend to be somewhat more complex than the identification questions in that they ask you to make a conclusion or judgment about a particular topic. Often-times, you will be asked to assess the impact of a movement or judge the most important cause of a political event. Then again, the question may involve the most appropriate characterization of something—a political leader's policies, the features of a cultural movement, or how population changed over time. Unlike the previous sample question, which clearly had a correct answer and was narrow in scope, the analysis question that follows calls for you to pull in more historical context and understanding:

> Which of the following best characterizes the Enlightenment attitude toward organized religion?
> (A) a desire to eliminate all public religious practice
> (B) skepticism toward religious dogmatism
> (C) acceptance of its important role in morality
> (D) rejection of religious toleration for minority faiths
> (E) celebration of the progressive role of the Catholic clergy

Once again, we concentrate on avoiding those responses that involve overstated phrases, such as A. While some philosophés wished to maintain a natural religion ("deism") for purposes of public morality, most did not associate organized religion with improved morality, so choice C is eliminated. A major thrust of Enlightenment thinking was the extension of religious toleration to minorities; thus, D is incorrect. Choice E should obviously ring false, as philosophés such as Voltaire condemned the clergy in particular for their perceived fanaticism and support for tradition and hierarchy. We are left with B as the key. Please note that B is the virtual opposite of choices D and E. When you see two or more responses that are opposites, chances are one of those is the right answer. Why? When test-makers create multiple-choice questions, they first identify the right answer and then include at least one obviously wrong answer, often the opposite of the correct response. Though several of these choices may have appealed to you, this question aimed at the *characteristic* Enlightenment attitude toward religion.

Visual Interpretation

Here is where your increased attention to the visual supplements in your text pays off. About 20 percent of questions are of this type, and their numbers have increased over the years. You are provided with a visual stimulus—map, graph, chart, political cartoon, painting—and are asked to make some conclusion about it. The visual may seem obscure. Don't worry; the purpose of the question is not the picture itself. Most likely, the visual represents an important trend, conflict, or issue that was covered in your course. Put the visual in context and pay particular attention in cartoons to symbolism and irony. Try your hand at the following question. See the cartoon on page 19.

> This nineteenth-century British cartoon is a commentary on which of the following?
> (A) dangerous working conditions in textile factories
> (B) the improved standard of living produced by inexpensive cloth
> (C) the injustice of denying the working class the vote
> (D) British dominance of the Indian textile industry
> (E) the negative impact of a free trade treaty with France

Don't be fooled by the caption of the cartoon. Like many political cartoons, this one aims at a tone of ironic commentary on social issues. You might recall that a major issue for Great Britain in the nineteenth century was the negative side effects of industrialization. There are several choices that convey this criticism—A, C, and E. We can exclude D because the cartoon gives no indication relating to India. This is vital with visual interpretation. Even though there is some basis in fact for D, you must always choose an answer *that can be determined from the visual itself.* Choice B can also be excluded because the symbolism of the skeletons and the "fat-cat" over-

"Cheap Clothing" *Punch Magazine*

seer preclude this being a positive commentary. While C and E also have some basis in fact, they are not addressed directly by the cartoon. That leaves A, which is the answer. A cartoon like this was selected specifically to highlight an important theme of the course—the social cost of industrialization—not because the cartoon itself was important.

Recall this logic when it comes to other visual sources. If you find a map from a specific year, it should cue you to a significant treaty, situation prior to a war, or a shift in the balance of power. Further, should an area of the map be highlighted, expect it to be a nation or region that was important or contested during the period in question. The goal of the multiple-choice question is not to fool you or gauge your grasp of random facts, but rather to use specific content as a wedge into the significant concepts and themes of the course. Again, make sure that the answer you choose is not simply correct but is a correct reading of the visual.

Quotations

Approximately 5 to 10 percent of questions will employ a quotation for you to interpret or place in context. At first the quote may seem obscure or involve some complex wording. If you recall that the quotation represents some significant idea or development of the course, the correct choice should become clearer. Look for a significant phrase that might be associated with an important thinker or movement. For example, if you see some variation of the term "class struggle," chances are the question relates to Karl Marx or another socialist. Let's attempt one:

The quote below represents which of the following writers and contexts?
   (A) Darwin's concern for the "survival of the fittest"
   (B) Charles V's effort to combat the Ottoman Turks
   (C) Hitler's call for a racially pure Germany
   (D) Pasteur's explanation of the germ theory of disease
   (E) Mazzini's condemnation of foreign rule of Italy

"Blood mixture and the resultant drop in the racial level is the sole cause of the dying out of old cultures; for men do not perish as a result of lost wars, but by the loss of that force of resistance which is contained only in pure blood."

19

As you might have determined, this fairly straightforward question's correct answer is C. To arrive at this choice, all we need do is focus on the primary concept in the question: race. Of the writers and contexts listed above, which was motivated mainly by racial concerns? Though all might have addressed racial ideas, only Hitler placed it at the center of his (Nazi) ideology. Quotation questions on the AP Exam may be more difficult than this, but they will play on a central theme of the course and likely include a key phrase that should cue you to the correct answer.

Cross-Chronological and "Except" Questions

Both of these types of questions are rare but do comprise about 5 to 10 percent of the overall multiple-choice section. Cross-chronological questions involve choices that range across time periods; you are expected to have a broad enough grasp of topic to locate the trend in time. In fact, the quotation question given here is an example of a cross-chronological question. Here is another:

> In which two consecutive centuries did Europe experience first a decrease in population, and then in the next a steady population increase?
> (A) fifteenth and sixteenth centuries
> (B) sixteenth and seventeenth centuries
> (C) seventeenth and eighteenth centuries
> (D) eighteenth and nineteenth centuries
> (E) nineteenth and twentieth centuries

Only if you are familiar with general patterns in European population—a topic that does appear on the exam regularly—will you be able to handle this question. You can narrow your choices considerably if you can recall that only in one century covered in the course (1450–present) did Europe's population experience an overall decrease—the seventeenth. Therefore, the answer to this question is C.

Though the Test Development Committee has reduced the number of "except" questions in recent years, you can expect several to appear on the exam. If you are attuned to their structure, these questions shouldn't present you undue difficulty. When you see "except" in the stem that means all of the subsequent statements are true, except one. Keep that in mind for this question:

> All of the following helped cause the French Revolution EXCEPT:
> (A) a government budget crisis that the king was unable to resolve.
> (B) criticism by Enlightenment philosophés of the inequality of the Old Regime.
> (C) a subsistence crisis that led to high bread prices.
> (D) increased aristocratic opposition to royal absolutism.
> (E) the threat of foreign invasion by a British-led alliance.

The four distracters were chosen because they indicate major causes of the French Revolution, both long and short term. Long-term social, intellectual, and political causes are represented by choices B and D. Choices A and C constitute short-term economic and financial problems that drove Louis XVI to call the Estates General, setting in motion the events of the revolution. We are left with E as the key. France did face the threat of foreign invasion and opposition from Great Britain, but only after the revolution had commenced and European nations feared its spread.

Exam Organization, Pacing, and Guessing

As you attempt the practice multiple-choice questions at the back of this book, you may notice that they are organized roughly chronologically. This corresponds to the actual organization of the AP Exam. The exam usually begins with a question from the early part of the course and moves up to more recent history, then back again to an earlier period. As you proceed through the exam, you will process through about 7 to 9 of these groups, ranging from about 4 to 15 questions in a set. It is important to realize that this is only a *general* guideline, and you should not be thrown by a somewhat different organization. Knowledge of this organization may occasionally help you make more informed guesses. Let's see how:

11. Which of the following accurately describes a development in family life in the eighteenth century?
    (A) a rapid increase in the birth rate
    (B) a rise in the number of illegitimate births
    (C) decline of the nuclear family structure
    (D) a significant rise in the average age at marriage
    (E) the establishment of female equality in marriage

    • An emphasis on emotion
    • Interest in the unique individual
    • Themes of nationalism
    • Portrayal of nature

12. Which of the following artistic movements is best characterized by the list above?
    (A) Renaissance
    (B) Baroque
    (C) neo-Classical
    (D) Romanticism
    (E) Expressionism

13. Which of the following were major new industries that developed in the latter half of the nineteenth century?
    (A) textiles and electricity
    (B) petroleum and glassware
    (C) textiles and steel
    (D) bleaching and railroads
    (E) petroleum and electricity

Question 11 addresses an eighteenth-century topic, whereas question 13 deals with a late-nineteenth-century topic. Between these two is a cross-chronological question, with choices ranging from the fifteenth to the twentieth centuries. Knowing the general chronological organization of the exam may help you to narrow the period of question 12 to the early nineteenth century. If so, you may know that Romanticism (D) dominated the art world in the period 1800–1850. Keep in mind that this general guideline never replaces your understanding of history and should only be used when you find that you are forced to guess between two or more choices (note on answers: 11: B, 13: E).

Unlike many of the history tests you may have taken, the AP multiple-choice questions range significantly in difficulty level. Almost 95 percent of students will get the easiest questions correct, whereas only 10 to 15 percent will choose correctly for the most challenging questions. If you find that you must guess frequently or have little familiarity with some of the topics, it may help to know that very few students will achieve a perfect score on this section of the exam, and further, the usual 90-80-70-60 percent grading scale does not apply. The AP Exam is a standardized test, and the College Board wants to distinguish between smaller increments of understanding than a standard scale.

Most of the questions you encounter will be in the 40 to 70 percent difficulty range, or are of medium difficulty. As a general rule, the test tends to get somewhat harder as you move through the questions. Because of this, it is important that you pace yourself and also maintain your concentration. Factoring in 55 minutes for 80 questions gives you about 40 seconds for each question. You are likely to need more time on the second half of the test, so when you hit question 40, more than half of your time should be left.

As mentioned earlier, the AP Exam also employs a 1.25-point penalty for guessing. Statistically it is in your interest, then, to guess on any question in which you can eliminate even one of the choices. In the vast majority of the cases, you will be able to do this. Even if you get, say, only 30 percent of these questions correct, you are still ahead in the long run. At the same time, if you encounter a question of which you have no knowledge and all the choices look equally appealing, then don't think twice about leaving it blank. There is no magic number of questions to leave blank. Some students may feel confident enough to answer every single question; others may leave 5 to 10 blank. Both are fine. Just remember that the more you leave blank, the more you are denying yourself the opportunity to earn points overall.

Given the nature of the test, it is vital that you establish an appropriate pace and rhythm. Half of success on any test, particularly multiple-choice tests, depends on your confidence and mental approach (the other half being what you know and understand). As you attempt the multiple-choice practice questions in this book, keep in mind and try to follow these guidelines:

- Do not get bogged down or frustrated over any one question.
- Read the question carefully to make sure you understand what it is asking.
- Eliminate those choices you know to be incorrect.
- Look over the remaining choices, and then pull the trigger!
- Put that question out of your mind and move immediately on to the next.
- If you have time at the end, check over your previous responses.

Students often ask whether they should change answers they have already entered. There are differing views on this. My experience and, it seems to me, a majority of my students' is that one should not change answers already entered, *unless you find that you misread the question.* Think of your mind as having two parts—the instinctive part that knows the answer and the doubting part that fears getting it wrong. Trust yourself that you know the answer. Furthermore, do not confuse yourself by assuming the key is too easy. Many students overanalyze questions that are intended to be straightforward. Difficult questions are distinguished by the complexity of the concepts they test, not the trickiness of the choices. Confidence comes with success, so practice and establish an approach that works for you.

STRATEGIES FOR THE ESSAY QUESTIONS

Dissecting the Prompt: Answer the Question Asked!

Having read thousands of essays as a College Board consultant, I know first-hand that the primary reason for student underachievement in writing is the inability to address effectively the *question that was asked.* As your quivering hands grasp the newly opened green booklet of essay prompts, there is a tendency to fly right into the writing process. Resist this impulse. If planning a road trip, you would consult a map and only *then* decide on a route. Writing is no different.

Before writing, spend 5 minutes planning out your approach. First, make sure you understand what the question is asking you to accomplish, especially as it relates to (1) chronological scope, (2) geographic scope, and (3) topical scope (e.g., economics, politics, culture, etc.). The Test Development Committee employs standard essay-writing "prompt-tasks," which I list and explain as follows:

- *Analyze:* Establish how something is put together, how and why its elements relate to one another. Example: "Analyze the subject matter and style of modern art and how it reflected the political and intellectual concerns of the post-WWII period."
- *Assess* OR *evaluate:* Make a conclusion (*not* an opinion) about; weigh the pros and cons of; judge the value, success, or importance of. Example: "Assess the degree to which Napoleon I promoted the principles of the French Revolution."
- *Compare and contrast:* Address the similarities and differences between/among two or more things (make sure you do both if prompted!). Example: "Compare and contrast the participation of and impact on women in/of the Renaissance and Protestant Reformation."
- *Describe* OR *discuss:* Provide an account of; consider the varying arguments and positions regarding. Example: "Discuss the impact of the unification of Italy and Germany on the European balance of power in the period 1871 to 1914."
- *Explain:* Demonstrate the connection between related things; clarify the causes, effects, or reasons for. Example: "Explain how absolutism was evident in the political, economic, and religious policies of France under Louis XIV, 1650–1715."
- *Identify:* Give the features of; point out events, causes, effects. Example: "Identify the issues raised by industrialization in Great Britain and the responses to those issues in the second half of the nineteenth century."
- *To what extent:* Make a judgment regarding the scope or degree of. Example: "To what extent did the Enlightenment employ the methods of the Scientific Revolution in addressing issues of social and political in the eighteenth century?"

Let's take a closer look at one of these prompts:

<u>Assess</u> the degree to which <u>Napoleon I promoted</u> the <u>principles</u> of the <u>French Revolution.</u>

To ensure that you understand the tasks involved in the question, underline the relevant tasks and terms as I have done here. This should lead to the identification of a thesis and any appropriate examples as you take your 5 minutes to organize your approach. Recall that "assess" means to make a judgment or conclusion about, in this case regarding Napoleon's commitment to the ideals of the revolution. Though the chronological scope is not specified, it is implied—that is, the reign of Napoleon I (1799–1815). In addition, you will need to make reference to the French Revolution, if only broadly, to pick up the "principles" part of the question.

Organize Your Ideas

After you are sure you understand your goal, begin organizing the essay. Keep in mind that this is a brainstorming process of limited time, not a research paper. Think of all the examples and specifics related to the topic. If you end up with an unmanageable amount of information, select those most relevant to the prompt and consider how you can use them to support a thesis. Here is an example of what your notes might look like:

Principles of French Revolution
"Liberty, equality, fraternity"—the last can be construed as "nationalism."

Napoleon's policies
Liberty—secret police, censorship, manipulation of public opinion, allowed freedom of worship, conquest of foreign lands, ending of feudalism and serfdom in conquered lands. (*Assessment:* on balance, Napoleon did not promote liberty, ruled dictatorially posing as a "man of the people.")

Equality—Napoleonic Code, restricted rights for women, abolition of feudalism and serfdom, establishment of schools, creation of uniform bureaucracy, "careers open to talent," nepotism, reestablished slavery in colonies. (*Assessment:* in general, Napoleon's life and policies represent commitment to equality, but excluded women and compromised when it suited his power.)

Fraternity—Promoted nationalism in army, used revolutionary warfare, rewarded service with Legion of Honor, indirectly fed nationalism in conquered foreign lands. (*Assessment:* Napoleon used nationalism effectively to gain and maintain power, but his indirect promotion of nationalism in foreign lands led to his downfall.)

This outline may be more detailed than time or your immediately recalled knowledge will allow. Don't worry. A student could easily write a top-notch essay with less detail than is given here. More important than simply facts is that you demonstrate an understanding of the question and provide a clear and direct thesis in response to the prompt.

Start Strong: The Introduction and Thesis

You've probably heard it from your teachers before: "Make sure your essay has a thesis." "Where's your thesis?" "Your thesis needs to be clearer." An explicit thesis statement gives your essay direction and provides something on which to hang the evidence. A thesis is a (usually) one-sentence statement of the main arguments or points you will develop in your essay. Unfortunately, many essays lack such specificity and direction. As you practice your writing, work to develop your skills in articulating a thesis for your essays. What, then, makes for a powerful thesis?

First, a strong thesis does more than simply restate the question. Let's say you are responding to this essay prompt: "Identify and analyze the economic, geographic, and social factors that promoted the Industrial Revolution in Great Britain, 1750–1850." In their rush to get into the question with examples, many students will produce the following generic statement: "There were many economic, geographic, and social factors that led to the Industrial Revolution in Great Britain." This is merely a restatement of the prompt, and it adds little to your essay. Think of it this way: Imagine you watched the presidential debate last night between the Republican and Democratic candidates, while I missed it. Now I'd like you to tell me what each candidate stood for, so I have a better idea for whom to vote. If you simply say, "There were many issues discussed in the debate last night," that isn't going to help me much. In fact, I might think you were joking. Your essay is no place to play such a joke.

A strong thesis is specific in relation to the question. Because you were asked to *identify* factors in each area, you should be specific. If you characterize the British lead in each area, you would be on better footing. At this point, numerous examples are not necessary; save them for your body paragraphs. Stop and allow yourself time to recollect what you know about the topic. The following is more germane to the question:

Economic: Britain boasted important institutions that helped raise capital and promoted in-
    dustry—Bank of England; strong navy; commercial empire; productive agriculture
Geographic: abundant natural resources; easy access to the sea; security from invasion
Social: mobile and surplus labor force; elites open to money-making; strong inventive tradition
    from Scientific Revolution and Enlightenment

Make sure to allow time for this brainstorming process. Again, do not be concerned if you generate less in the way of examples. Try to identify for each area in one sentence *how* developments there contributed to Great Britain's advantage. Once this is done, you are ready to formulate your thesis. But first, let's look at how to structure an effective introduction.

No one strategy works like magic, yet there is a formula that can serve you well. Begin your introduction with one or two sentences of relevant historical context. Avoid philosophizing or taking your question too far outside the time period. For the question given here, you might begin like this:

> Prior to 1750, Great Britain was a major commercial power, passing rivals like the Dutch and Spain. While most of Europe, 1750–1850, was involved in revolutions, Great Britain used its advantages to become the major industrial nation.

This context serves as a trajectory into the question and establishes with solid chronological foundations that you have control of the question. Now you are ready to take the brainstorming topics generated and formulate a thesis—in this case, one that has three parts (economic, geographic, and social):

> The British used capitalistic economic institutions, such as the Bank of England, a secure geographic position with many resources, and a society that focused on invention and profit to become the world economic leader by 1850.

For added punch, finish off your introduction with a "clincher" that pulls the thesis together with a powerful interpretation. Consider the overall importance of the topic or its impact in the sweep of the course. In this case, Britain influenced other nations to adopt similar production strategies, leading eventually to Europe's economic dominance and imperial control of world trade:

> Over the next century, other European nations followed the British and developed their own economies to compete for trade and power all across the world.

Remember that this model is a process that you will need to hone in your class and as you use the practice questions in this book. The most important lesson you should take from our discussion is not that your thesis need be beautifully articulate (though that's an added bonus), rather that you are specific in addressing the question that is being asked. Avoid simply restating the question, which adds little to your essay and gives you no direction when you compose your body paragraphs.

The Body Paragraphs: Fleshing Out Your Thesis

Though an introduction provides direction and focus to your essay, the meat of it is the body paragraphs. As you write the body of your essay, however, you should always have one eye on your thesis. Often, students get caught up in telling a story or "data dumping," which has no relation to the ultimate point of the essay. All AP prompts are designed to gauge your *understanding,* not simply your factual recall. Keep focused on connecting your evidence/examples to the thesis, at the same time avoiding tangential issues and concerns.

An effective body paragraph always begins with a strong topic sentence that goes beyond restating the topic. If we take the essay on Britain and industrialization, our first body paragraph might be on economic factors. Keep in mind that you need to show *how* and *why* these factors assisted Britain in industrializing. Statements of this nature are insufficient: "Now I will talk about economics" OR "Economic factors also helped Great Britain to industrialize." Aim to capture the primary role that factor played: "Great Britain's supportive economic institutions provided the capital it needed to industrialize." This conclusion now gives the remainder of the paragraph, and your examples, the direction you need to analyze, rather than simply list or describe.

When it comes to support for conclusions, you must make selections. "More" is not necessarily better. Several well-chosen examples that are clearly and explicitly connected to the topic sentence, and ultimately the thesis, are preferable to an unorganized or unexplained catalogue. As you write, try to think of yourself as establishing connections between the examples and the concept. Schematically, the body paragraph will appear as follows, with explanations running along each line that connects the example to the topic sentence. For example, along the line from "strong navy" to the central idea of the paragraph, we might have: "England's strong navy allowed it to establish new colonies and defeat rival powers. The trade that resulted from England's colonial empire allowed entrepreneurs to finance industry back in the home country."

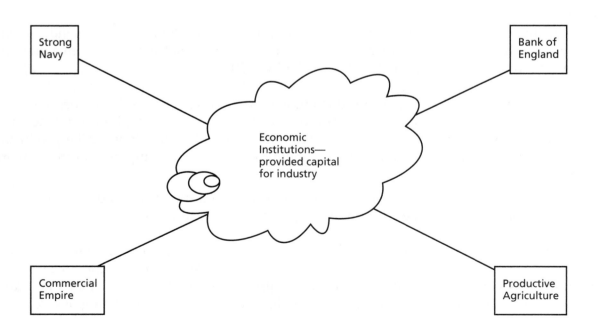

These four examples provide ample support for this paragraph. In fact, for each body paragraph, aim for approximately three or four examples as support. But always keep in mind that more is not always better. Fully explained examples show your control of the question and ability to develop a central idea, the thesis. Finally, to conclude your body paragraph, write a transitional sentence that sets up your next paragraph, such as: "While these institutions were important, perhaps they would not even have existed without Britain's favored geographic location." Sentences like this help take a reader systematically through an argument and show how each component part fits with the others. If you made it this far, sometimes, as with speaking, the most important task is to know when and how to stop.

The Conclusion: When and How to Stop Writing

Think of the conclusion of your essay as a dismount in a gymnastic routine—a last chance to influence the scorer positively. It is important here that you *add* to what you've already written. Therefore, avoid repeating the introductory paragraph or reiterating a point already made. If you follow a clear strategy and know exactly what you wish to accomplish with it, your conclusion will add significantly to your essay. In fact, a powerful conclusion will likely tip an AP reader in your favor who may be hovering between two scores.

Though your essay should be focused on the question asked, the conclusion is your opportunity to venture outside the bounds of the question slightly to make some additional analytical points. Remember that the test makers chose these questions because they believed them to represent some of the most important themes of the course. Now you can show that you recognize that importance.

Let's look at a specific example from another question:

Evaluate the economic and political factors that account for the failure of the German Weimar Republic, 1918–1933.

First, the dates in the question should cue you right into setting up both your introduction and conclusion. The year 1918 marks the end of World War I, and 1933, the appointment of Adolph Hitler as Chancellor of Germany. This chronological context will form the structure of our response: this topic is bracketed by the two world wars of the twentieth century. In fact, it was probably chosen as a question for the purpose of gauging your understanding of a significant theme of the course by examining a specific example.

Your recognition of the question's importance and place in the sweep of the course should make its way into your introduction and conclusion. Now, we'll focus on the conclusion, so we take our starting point as 1933 and consider how that date represents the failure of the Weimar Republic and context of the two world wars. Here is one way we might approach the conclusion of this essay.

> The Weimar Republic was born in a time of chaos and revolution after the First World War. Considering this, it never had much chance of success. Economic problems like reparations and the Depression, along with Germany's lack of a democratic history and anger over the Versailles Treaty, proved almost unsolvable. Weimar's failure was significant. Because Germany was unable to establish democracy, Hitler came to power in 1933 and quickly worked to undo the Treaty of Versailles. These policies led eventually to a conflict even larger and more violent—the Second World War.

At this point in the exam, you may feel pressed for time, so limit your conclusion to four to six sentences. There are, of course, several legitimate strategies to conclude your essay. I favor showing the importance of the topic because it allows you, the student, to demonstrate one final time your control of the question, as well as tells the reader that you grasp the importance of the topic as part of the AP European History curriculum.

How long should your essay be? As already mentioned, longer essays do not necessary equate with higher scores. With that in mind, most AP FRQ responses end up about two to three handwritten pages. Of course, this should serve as a guideline not a hard-and-fast rule.

MASTERING THE FREE-RESPONSE QUESTIONS

What Should I Expect?

"Expect the unexpected." Though this may be a cliché, it is good advice for the free-response questions. With a course as broad as AP European history, you will certainly encounter topics that will surprise you. Sure, there will likely be some old chestnuts as topics: the Renaissance, Protestant Reformation, French Revolution, and so on. However, these may be wrapped in unique packages. A question may focus on a particular feature of a wider and more familiar movement or event. One way to prepare for this is not to neglect particular areas of history. Simply because military history stimulates your interest—or perhaps the opposite, battles are a bore but family life fascinates you—doesn't mean you can ignore areas of little interest or focus exclusively on those of great interest. Though it applies to all areas, Leon Trotsky's quote is *apropos* here: "Just because you aren't interested in war doesn't mean that war isn't interested in you."

Even if you wouldn't have chosen any of the questions on the test yourself, the first rule is not to panic. Other students across the nation are experiencing the same feelings as you. Read the questions carefully and then decide, based on what you *do* know, which you are best equipped to answer. As noted previously, the questions will likely be divided either chronologically (three or so questions pre-1800 and three or so questions post-1800) or topically (three questions on political-diplomatic-economic topics and three questions on social-cultural-intellectual topics). Though it is difficult to predict which questions will show up on any given year (don't spend much effort on prophecy), there are some topics that seem to recur. Here are a few suggestions (in no particular order) to which you might dedicate some extra time and energy in your studies:

- Italian Renaissance or Protestant Reformation
- Women's or family history
- A significant intellectual or cultural movement, e.g., Scientific Revolution, Enlightenment, or the 1850–1914 period (Marx, Darwin, Freud)
- Post-1945
- Commercial or Industrial Revolutions
- Anything related to Russia
- Diplomacy or politics from 1789 to 1871

This is by no means intended to be an exhaustive list. You are best served by preparing for the entire sweep of the course and not counting on lucky guesses. If you prepare well, you will find a topic on which you can write effectively.

Selecting the Right Questions

Choose those questions you are best prepared to answer. Before you choose, however, make sure you read the question carefully. Though it may be on a topic you enjoy or know much about (say, the French Revolution), it may involve tasks for which you are not well-prepared. If so, avoid it and pick another. Make certain that you can devise a clear and focused thesis. Factual knowledge alone is not enough for an effective essay. Allow time to think before choosing. Perhaps your class completed a project or spent extra time on one of the topics. If so, try to recall what you learned from these extended activities and how you might incorporate them into your essay.

It's unlikely, but you may find that you are not confident about any of your choices. If that's the case, you should still try to choose the essay, of the ones you don't like, that you feel best equipped to answer. Brainstorm all the examples you can, and then try to make the most out of them. If you have learned some of the techniques of focused and clear writing from your course and this review guide, then you are in probably much better shape than you might fear.

Managing Your Time

When you get to the FRQs, you may feel fatigued, bored, or stressed. This is normal. Managing your time effectively can help immensely in reducing such feelings. Make sure you don't get bogged down in any one essay (especially the DBQ). Bring a watch and keep track of how much time is recommended for each essay question. Students often write much less on the second FRQ, as well as make more errors of fact and interpretation. A strategy that many students use can help you here. It's called the "5-5-5."

Remember that at the beginning of your 2 hours, 10 minutes on the essays there was a 15-minute reading period. The proctor might characterize this as time to read through the documents and develop your outline for the DBQ. Instead, consider spending the 15 minutes in the following way:

- 5 minutes to choose and organize your response for FRQ 1
- 5 minutes to choose and organize your response for FRQ 2
- 5 minutes to begin reading the documents for the DBQ (and then continue with DBQ until completed)

The purpose of this system is to account for your fatigue and stress at the end of the exam. If you have already chosen and outlined your two free-response questions, you are less likely to be rushed for time and make foolish or easily avoidable mistakes. If you do employ this system, keep in mind that your time will be "off" of the official timers a bit. For example, when the proctor recommends that you move from the DBQ to the FRQs, you will be 10 minutes behind. That is because you "gained' the 10 minutes at the beginning and will be "paying" for them by not taking the recommended 5 minutes to organize each FRQ (because you've already done that).

Final Tips for Writing an Effective Essay

Before moving on to the unique features of the document-based question, let's pull together the suggestions for effective writing, some of which apply to both the FRQs and DBQ. AP readers will think of your essays as a first draft, so spelling errors, grammar, and less-than-elegant penmanship generally do not detract from your score. With that said, there is no doubt that a clear, cogent writing style can only assist in conveying your understanding. It is in your interest to work at making your writing as tight as possible, that is, making every word count with no wasted motion. AP readers want to see your performance, not your warm-up routine. To assist in improving your writing style, a brief yet essential resource is William Strunk and E. B. White, *The Elements of Style* (Needham Heights, MA: Allyn & Bacon, 2000). This short primer on usage and style will give your writing power and clarity. So should the following suggestions:

- Allow yourself about 5 minutes (FRQ) to brainstorm and determine a clear direction for your essay.
- Get to your point as quickly as possible; avoid flowery prose, rhetorical questions, and dramatic scene-setting.
- Be specific in identifying your thesis; do not simply restate the question.
- Establish your control of the question with appropriate historical context (remember your chronology).
- Provide topic sentences to your body paragraphs that specifically relate to your thesis.
- *Apply* examples to the thesis, rather than simply mentioning or listing them.
- Steer clear of value judgments or opinions. Your role is as an impartial historian.
- Write directly and clearly. Try to avoid too many or needlessly complex prepositional phrases. Choose "action" verbs, such as *advanced, opposed,* and *established,* whenever possible.
- Manage your time effectively. Allow approximately equal time for both FRQs.
- Finish strong. Show that you understand the importance of the topic in the conclusion.

Even if you lose track of time or are rushed, don't panic. Several years ago, I had a student who found himself with only 12 minutes at the end of our final exam (a full AP Exam) to complete his last FRQ. He approached me and asked, "What should I do?" My response was, "Go back and write as much as you can in those 12 minutes." He complied and earned a 6 on his response. Not that I would recommend putting yourself under pressure, but it might boost your confidence to know that you don't have to be perfect on all components of the exam to score highly. However, you should try to make the most of your opportunities.

HOW TO APPROACH THE DOCUMENT-BASED QUESTION (DBQ)

Purpose of the DBQ

The document-based question is designed to test your skill in using historical sources—finding patterns among evidence, evaluating evidence for bias, noting multiple perspectives on an issue, detecting nuance, irony, and purpose in a document, and applying different techniques of analysis for different types of sources. In the current information age, we are bombarded by images, many connected to product sales, lofty advertising promises, high political rhetoric, and unsubstantiated claims by bloggers. As a citizen, you need to be able to sort fact from fiction, recognize the agendas behind the words, and appreciate that there can be many ways of looking at an issue. By practicing such skills with historical sources, it is hoped that you not only appreciate how historians arrive at interpretations and explanations, but translate these skills into whatever field you choose.

The Core Scoring Tasks

As noted earlier, it is unlikely a student could score well on the DBQ without knowing the scoring rubric. The rubric is not difficult to learn, and your continued practice with DBQs will build mastery and fluency. In fact, if there is one of area of the AP Exam where practice can do the most to improve your score, it is on the DBQ. Unlike U.S. history, the European history DBQ requires no "outside knowledge" (i.e., beyond what's in the documents themselves); everything you need to address the question will be directly in front of you. Though the topic may be one for which you have little or no knowledge, this need not concern you. It should actually help focus your attention on the documents. You may be tempted to wander off on tangents or name-drop from your studies. Resist that temptation, and *let the documents drive your essay.*

Before continuing, I urge you to refresh your memory on the core scoring rubric (see p. 5). Please remember that the rubric acts as a checklist, or gatekeeper. You MUST adequately address the six tasks in the rubric to be considered for additional points in the expanded core. What does this mean? Even if you perform admirably on five of the tasks, but neglect, say, to include three groups (perhaps two groups with another group that contains only one document or is inaccurate), the highest score you will receive is a 5. Should another student meet these core tasks at a barely minimal level, that student will score at least a 6. Inability to meet any of the six core tasks keeps one outside the "gate" and from the possibility of a higher score. You should also be aware that lapses in one core area can affect others; for example, if you fail to use a majority of the documents, you will not earn core points 2, 3, and 4. The only way to avoid slipping up on the core is practice, and more practice.

To assist you in mastering the core tasks, an extended example has been included here with a detailed analysis of how to approach it. In addition, you will find sample responses that illustrate the "do's" and "don'ts" of writing an effective response.

General Directions

1. You will have 60 minutes to complete the DBQ, of which 15 minutes is allotted for reading the documents and planning your response (if you use the 5-5-5 method).
2. Make sure that you read the question precisely, underlining key words and tasks you are charged to complete.
3. Read the documents completely and carefully; oftentimes, you will encounter a document that shifts tone or that outlines an argument with which the author *disagrees*, and then lays out his own perspective.
4. As you read, consider how each document helps you address the question. You should also begin formulating potential groups for the documents.
5. Pay careful attention to the authors and source attribution. Brainstorm approaches on how to use this information to address point of view and bias.
6. When you are finished reading the documents, make a brief outline that includes your (at least) THREE groups, along with the appropriate documents in support of that paragraph.
7. As you begin writing, keep referring back to the question to ensure that you are addressing it explicitly and by using the documents.

Practice DBQ Exercise

<u>Directions:</u> The prompt that follows is based on Documents 1-12 and will gauge your ability to comprehend and evaluate historical documents. Make sure in your essay that you:

- Provide an explicit thesis directly addressing all parts of the question.
- Discuss specifically a majority of the documents.
- Demonstrate a grasp of the essential meaning of a majority of the documents.
- Support your thesis with accurate interpretations of a majority of the documents.
- Analyze the sources by grouping them clearly and accurately in at least three ways.
- Take into account both the authors' points of view and biases.

You may refer to relevant historical context not addressed in the documents.

Analyze the views that affected the adoption of the potato as a major European crop and how these views changed in the period 1600–1850.

<u>Historical Background:</u> Following the period of European exploration, many New World crops were introduced into Europe. Among these was the potato, which was first cultivated in Spain and then gradually spread to the rest of Europe by the eighteenth and nineteenth centuries, becoming the major crop in several regions and nations. Its ease of cultivation, high caloric yield per acre, and complex nutritional value made it an important addition to the European diet wherever it was introduced. Ireland, in particular, relied heavily on the potato for nutrition, which resulted in a widespread famine there from 1845–1851 when blight destroyed the crop.

Document 1

Source: Town Council of Besançon, France, edict, early 1600s.

In view of the fact that the potato is a pernicious substance whose use can cause leprosy, it is hereby forbidden, under pain of fine, to cultivate it.

Document 2

Source: Tobias Venner, English physician and medical writer, *A treatise wherein the right way and best manner of living for attaining a long and healthful life is clearly demonstrated,* 1620.

The nutriment which potatoes yield is, though somewhat windy, very substantial, good and restorative, surpassing for nourishment all other roots and fruits. They are diversely prepared, according to every man's taste and liking—roasted in embers, sopped in wine which is especially good, but in whatever manner, they are very pleasant to the taste and do wonderfully comfort, nourish, and strengthen the body. They are very wholesome and good for every age and constitution, especially for the elderly.

Document 3

Source: William Salmon, English physician, *The English Herbal: or History of Plants,* 1710.

The Virtues of Potatoes

- They stop fluxes [diarrhea] of the bowels, nourish, and restore
- They increase seed and provoke lust, causing fruitfulness in both sexes
- They restore the lungs from atrophy [weakening], tuberculosis, and ulceration

Document 4

Source: Denis Diderot, French philosopher and writer of the Enlightenment, *The Encyclopedia,* 1751.

This root, no matter how much you prepare it, is tasteless and floury. It cannot pass for agreeable food, but it supplies a food sufficiently abundant and sufficiently healthy for men who ask only to sustain themselves. The potato is criticized with reason for being windy, but what matters windiness for the vigorous organisms of peasants and laborers?

Document 5

Source: Message from the town of Kolberg, to King Frederick II, upon being ordered by him to eat potatoes for relief of famine, 1774.

These things [potatoes] have neither smell nor taste, not even the dogs will eat them, so what use are they to us?

Document 6

Source: Arthur Young, English writer and agricultural reformer, *A Tour in Ireland,* 1780.

The food of the common Irish—potatoes and milk—have been produced more than once as an instance of the extreme poverty of the country, but this I believe is an opinion embraced with more willingness than reflection. I have heard it stigmatized as being unhealthy, and not sufficiently nourishing for the support of hard labor, but this opinion is very amazing in a country, many of whose poor people are as athletic in their form, as robust, and capable of enduring labor of any upon earth. The idleness seen among many when working for those who oppress them [English landlords] is a very contrast to the vigor and activity with which the same people work when they alone reap the benefits of their labor.

I will not assert that potatoes are a better food than the bread and cheese of the Englishman; but I have no doubt of a bellyful of the one being much better than half a bellyful of the other.

Document 7

Source: Guillaume-Charles Faipoult, prefect* for the Department of Escaut, memorandum to national government of France, 1801.

It is to the potato alone that the region owes the advantage of producing enough subsistence to feed its large population and also an abundance of grain for the distilleries and breweries, and sometimes even for export. However, abundance is less constant in potatoes than in wheat and rye. Two months of drought can reduce the harvest of a potato field to almost nothing.

Frequent periods of distress may result for a population that would exclusively base its means of subsistence on an uncertain crop. I am inclined to believe that by comparison with other crops, which should not be weakened too much, the cultivation of the potato has been carried about as far as sound judgment permits.

* a prefect is a local official representing the central government

Document 8

Source: Leopold Cuvier, French naturalist, *Elegy to Parmentier,* 1813.

Parmentier* looked forward to seeing full use made of the potato in France, notwithstanding the fact that some of the old-fashioned doctors still renewed the accusations of the seventeenth century against it. It was not of leprosy now but of 'fever' they complained. The famines in the south had produced epidemics, and these they had attributed to the one thing—the potato—which had proved the only means of preventing these disasters.

* Antoine Augustin Parmentier wrote a pamphlet and cookbook to promote potato cultivation in France.

Document 9

Source: John Christian Curwen, member of the British Parliament, businessman, agricultural reformer, *State of Ireland,* 1818.

The potato, which in some points of view, may justly be regarded as one of the greatest blessings to our species, is capable of operating the greatest calamities, when it exclusively furnishes the food on which a community is content to exist. The cultivation of a single statute acre may successfully and easily be attended by one individual, and its produce on average would give food for at least ten persons the year round, at 7 pounds each day, which may be considered as an abundant allowance. What chance, then, is there for manual exertion in such a society among whom an inherited aversion to labor and a habitual attachment to idleness rise above every other consideration?

Document 10

Source: William Cobbett, British journalist and social reformer, *A Year's Residence in America,* 1818.

Nor do I say it is filthy to eat potatoes. I do not ridicule the using of them as a sauce. What I laugh at is the idea of them as a salvation; of their going further than bread; of the cultivating of them in place of wheat as human sustenance of a country. As food for cattle, sheep or hogs, this is the worst of all the green and root crops; but of this I have said enough before; and therefore, I now dismiss the Potato with the hope, that I shall never again have to write the word, or see the thing.

Document 11

Source: Report of the Devon Commission to the British Parliament to Investigate Rural Conditions in Ireland, 1845.

The potato enabled a large family to live on food produced in great quantities at trifling cost, and, as a result, the increase of the people has been gigantic. There had, however, been no corresponding improvement in their material and social condition, but the opposite.

Document 12

Source: "A Potato Dinner" in Co. Kerry, Ireland, *The Illustrated London News*, February 22, 1846.

Interpreting the Question

As you probably noticed from this question, DBQ topics do not always address mainstream issues from the course. Don't let this alarm you. After all, your response will be guided primarily by the documents themselves. Any additional outside information you can include to put the documents in context or to understand the authors' potential biases is all to the good but is not necessary to earn a top score. Just remember: outside information should be related as much as possible to the documents. Avoid "name-dropping" figures or works that you studied if that takes you away from the primary task of analyzing the documents.

Notice that this prompt has two parts. You are to (1) analyze the views regarding the potato as a crop AND (2) show how these views might have changed over time. DBQ prompts will occasionally require this second intellectual task. This should not be surprising, as a major concern of historians involves interpreting patterns of change over time. For this prompt, you should be looking for the change as you read through the documents. It will not be enough simply to state in your introduction, "views changed over time." That is assumed by the question; your thesis and response should add new information. Try to be more specific than simply restating the question. Start thinking in terms of "pro" and "con" views. Don't stop there, though. The authors of these documents articulated bases for their views, whether good, bad, or ambivalent. See if you can be specific in identifying the ground of each author's position.

Interpreting the Documents

Most DBQs will include different types of documents: letters, speeches, books, articles, pamphlets, diaries, cartoons, charts, and illustrations. In one way your task is the same for each document: explain how it relates to your thesis. In another way, each document offers a different opportunity to address the author's bias, tone, or point of view. Often this will vary based on the type of document. For example, consider how you might address a teacher differently than a small gathering of your friends. In which situation—making a speech before a political gathering or writing a personal letter—would a politician more likely be forthright in explaining his true motives and intent? Political cartoonists boast a rich history of poking fun at the high and mighty. Illustrators and even photographers (in the manner of how they choose and compose their subjects) act as effective propagandists for and against political movements.

Each of the scenarios highlights an essential theme of your AP European history course: history is not simply "facts" but a contested story seen from multiple perspectives. Your job in the DBQ is to demonstrate that you can see through the smokescreen of bias, hidden motives, and between-the-lines motives. When addressing point of view, you may speculate as to the authors' motives and reliability. Just make sure that you explain the reasons for your assertions. Simply stating that "the author of Document 3 is biased" is insufficient and will not earn you credit for point of view. The document summaries below will give you an idea of different interpretations and ways to back those assertions.

Before we look at each document individually, let me add two more caveats. First, every document included is relevant to the exercise; there are no "trick" documents. Though the relevance of some documents may be harder for you to see than others, each can be related to the thesis and grouped with others, which leads to the next point. In any DBQ, two or three more subtle and nuanced documents will be included. Their purpose is to separate the average or above-average response from those that offer sharp and detailed insight into how the documents support the thesis. Take a moment to look through the following chart for ways in which the documents support the thesis or can be analyzed for bias/point of view. **(Note: if you wish to take the practice DBQ with less assistance, either skip down to "General Strategies" until after you've finished your response or read only one or two examples to get an idea of how to interpret documents and address point of view.)**

Document 1—Town Council of Besancon, France, edict, early 1600s: This document establishes an early negative view of the potato—from fear of the unknown, that it might cause disease. While you probably don't know anything about the council of this town, consider the job of local officials. Perhaps they are concerned about maintaining local order in the midst of fear and lack of information about this new crop.

Document 2—Tobias Venner, English physician and medical writer, *A treatise wherein the right way and best manner of living for attaining a long and healthful life is clearly demonstrated*, 1620: Now we get an almost opposite *positive* view. While the author notes the potato's tendency to cause gastric upset, he is more enthusiastic about its potential to "nourish and strengthen" the body. Moreover, the potato is easy to prepare and pleasant to the taste. How can you use the author's medical status for point of view? Perhaps this document is more reliable *because* the author is a physician and therefore would be in a better position to have direct knowledge of the potato's beneficial effects. On the other hand, the grandiose title of his treatise suggests that he is overdoing his endorsement of the potato. Either perspective would work.

Document 3—William Salmon, English physician, *The English Herbal: or History of Plants*, 1710: Salmon is another English physician, but in this case, he seems to convey folk wisdom rather than medical judgments. Certainly the claims in the document seem farfetched (potatoes provoking lust?!), so perhaps the author relies on word-of-mouth evidence rather than experiment. While the document promotes potatoes, it is similar to Document 1 in being unscientific.

Document 4—Denis Diderot, French philosopher and writer of the Enlightenment, *The Encyclopedia*, 1751: You will probably be familiar with Diderot and *The Encyclopedia*, which you can use to your benefit. Diderot notes the tendency for the potato to cause "windiness," but concludes this does not outweigh its benefits as a food for the lower classes. You may give added credence to Diderot as a philosopher or the editor of a major work of the Enlightenment. If so, you get credit for point of view. On the other hand, you could also note his high status and barely concealed scorn for the lower classes.

Document 5—Message from the town of Kolberg, to King Frederick II, upon being ordered by him to eat potatoes for relief of famine, 1774: This document can be seen from two perspectives: the continuing suspicion of common folk toward the potato OR the realization by rulers and others of the potential economic benefits of the potato. The rationale for bias in the document will be similar to that of Document 1.

Document 6—Arthur Young, English writer and agricultural reformer, *A Tour in Ireland*, 1780: Here is one of our more complex documents. Young notes the stereotype of the potato being associated with poverty, especially in Ireland, where it was widely adopted because of its ease of cultivation. Young rejects this notion, and claims that the Irish people are fit and robust, and further, if they are "idle," it is only because they are oppressed by their English landlords. When the Irish work for themselves, they are as industrious as any Englishman. For bias, you will be inclined to give credit for reliability to this document. The author visited Ireland and writes on agricultural issues as his profession. On the other hand, he is English—and thus perhaps biased in favor of the Irish and against his own country, which oppresses them. In addition, as a reformer, he would want to highlight issues of reform, and thus may exaggerate his account.

Document 7—Guillaume-Charles Faipoult, prefect for the Department of Escaut, memorandum to national government of France, 1801: This is another more complex document. Faipoult begins by acknowledging the benefits of the potato in producing an agricultural surplus, but then he warns of taking cultivation of the crop too far, as the potato is more susceptible to drought than traditional wheat or rye. In this way, the document foreshadows the later Irish potato famine. As a local official, the author is likely in a position to have direct information regarding the facts he reports. Moreover, the author's job is to provide impartial information to the national government so it can make intelligent policies. Finally, the tone of the document itself seems detached and impartial.

Document 8—Leopold Cuvier, French naturalist, *Elegy to Parmentier*, 1813: This document focuses on the work of another figure identified by an asterisk. It seems as if the author wishes to vindicate the reputation of Parmentier, who, we can assume, spent a lifetime advocating the benefits of the potato. Cuvier claims that while "old-fashioned" doctors (as in Documents 2 and 3?) continued to associate the potato ignorantly with disease, in reality, it was the only measure keeping France from famine. An "elegy" is a tribute to the deceased, so perhaps the author, though in a position to know about the potato as a naturalist, overstates his case in an effort to celebrate the work of a friend or colleague.

Document 9—John Christian Curwen, British member of Parliament, businessman, agricultural reformer, *State of Ireland*, 1818: While the author gives an initial boost to the potato, the remainder of the document focuses on what he considers its negative influence on the character of the Irish. Its ease of cultivation promotes idleness, which he sees as being an "inherited" and "habitual" condition of the Irish. This last comment clearly demonstrates bias, which might be expected as the author is an English politician and businessman, and therefore helps rule over the subdued Irish with a political and economic interest. In fact, the tone of the document toward the Irish suggests condescension.

Document 10—William Cobbett, British journalist and social reformer, *A Year's Residence in America, 1818*: This document suggests an intriguing tone of disgust and frustration with the grandiose claims that some apparently make for the potato. We infer from the author's references that he has written negatively about the potato before. If so, this indicates a bias the author may have. On the other hand, the document nicely prefigures the future troubles in Ireland for those who rely too heavily on the potato for their sole food source.

Document 11—Report of the Devon Commission to the British Parliament to Investigate Rural Conditions in Ireland, 1845: A short document that ties in well with the documents before and after. The major concern of the report is the effect of the potato on the population of Ireland: allowing it to support more people without improving their material condition. As a government report, the tone of the document is, again, detached and seemingly impartial, suggesting that it is reliable.

Document 12—"A Potato Dinner" in Co. Kerry, Ireland, *The Illustrated London News*, February 22, 1846: Now we encounter the only visual source. Portrayed is a small Irish family, seemingly poor, huddled around a fire, feeding along with their pig on a basket of potatoes. The scene suggests the negative effects on Ireland of reliance on the potato. In addition, you can use information from the historical background to connect the image to the Irish potato famine. Note that this is not a photograph, so it is impossible to determine if the image was fabricated to "illustrate" a national calamity, create pity for the Irish, or implicitly condemn the Irish way of life (it's an English publication)—any of these efforts at point of view would count to your advantage.

General Point-of-View/Bias Strategies

You may have noticed some strategies in addressing point of view in the previous examples. Here are some general questions to ask about the documents you encounter:

1. How might the author's identity (race, ethnic background, occupation, social class, age, nationality, religion) influence his/her position?
2. Does this source have first-hand knowledge about what it is he or she is reporting? In other words, how reliable is the source?
3. What is the context or occasion in which the author is writing? Is this a public or private document? This may affect whether the author's true intent or purpose is explicit. Does the document have a clear purpose, perhaps as propaganda (especially useful for visual sources)?
4. How close in time to the events being reported was this document written or published? Could the author's memory be faulty or idealized by nostalgic reflection?
5. What is the tone of the document? Are there strong words that suggest an explicit bias?

Tone Words

One way to demonstrate your mastery of point of view is to employ adjectives or verbs, other than "says" or "states," to capture the tone of the document. Try some of these to characterize the tone of the document:

condemned	doubted
encouraged	excoriated
praised	embraced
sarcastic	rejected
extolled	challenged
satirized	depicted
ridiculed	exalted
informed	claimed
patronizing	rationalized
dismissive	compared
speculated	exemplified
condoned	typified
mocked	implied
attacked	postulated
questioned	exhorted
idealized	showed
stereotyped	berated
generalized	modified
ignored	adapted
overlooked	issued
glorified	decreed
contrasted	suggested
recorded	categorized
noted	classified
observed	defended
criticized	

To receive credit on the core-scoring rubric for point-of-view analysis, you must provide THREE explicit examples. Again, avoid simply asserting bias without explaining your rationale. And remember, if you want to earn points in the expanded core, aim for *more* than three examples of point of view.

Grouping the Documents

To demonstrate your mastery of the document-based exercise, you must detect patterns among the documents. The core-scoring rubric requires that students "group the documents in as many appropriate ways possible." Almost always this will mean at least THREE groups. What should determine the logic of the grouping? There are many ways to earn credit for this point, though some strategies may be better or more convenient than others. First, one of the surest strategies is to divide the documents based on the types of arguments they advance. In our sample question, you may have noticed any of the following perspectives on the potato:

- as causing or preventing disease—Documents 1, 3, 8
- as providing important nutrition—Documents 2, 4
- as an appropriate food for the lower classes—Documents 4, 6
- ease of cultivation/uses—Documents 2, 4
- the "image" of the potato—Documents 5, 10
- its association with poverty—Documents 6, 9
- as affecting the character of those who rely on it—Documents 6, 9

- as a subsistence crop to ward off famine—Documents 7, 8
- overdependence on the potato—Documents 7, 9, 10, 12
- its effect on population growth—Documents 9, 11, 12

Of course, a straightforward grouping might also be: pro, con, and ambivalent. If you decide to group the documents according to positive and negative views, just ensure that you provide at least three groups. Remember that when you group as in the previous list, you will still discuss positive, negative, and ambivalent views *within* each of the paragraphs. Also notice that documents may fit in more than one group; this is more than acceptable, and in fact demonstrates your recognition that a particular perspective may be relevant to more than one interpretation or use. Finally, it is not necessary to include *all* of these groups. They are provided here to illustrate the many possible ways in which you can categorize the documents to yield at least three groups.

In addition to this fairly standard manner of grouping, it may also be appropriate to group the documents based on the common characteristics of the authors, which yields:

- French authors—Documents 1, 4, 7, 8
- English/British authors—Documents 2, 3, 6, 9, 10, 11, 12
- German authors—Document 5
- Physicians/doctors—Documents 2, 3
- Government officials—1, 5, 7, 9, 11
- Philosophers/scientists—Document 4, 8
- Reformers—Documents 6, 9, 10
- Journalists/writers/newspapers—Documents 2, 4, 6, 10, 12
- Businessmen—Document 9

A group is defined as having TWO or more documents, so "German authors" and "businessmen" would not count as a group were you to use them. You should avoid this type of grouping, however, if you are unable to find a common thread among these authors' views.

Let's not forget the other element of this question: change over time. When you see the word "change" in the prompt, look for a chronological evolution of views. This may produce another logic for your grouping. It may be that views proceeded in stages, and thus the documents could be grouped into, let's say, early, middle, and later perspectives. If you employ this approach, try to identify specifically the concerns about the potato at each stage. The first chart given here with the grouping based on views may suggest a chronological organization.

- early views—concerned with health effects, possible nutritional advantages
- middle views—more widespread adoption of the potato, usefulness as subsistence crop for lower classes, its image associated with poverty
- later views—inducing laziness in those who rely on it, concern with overdependence, and ultimately leading to disaster with the Irish potato famine

While reading through the documents, it may help your organization to create a chart. In keeping with the first organization choice, it may look like this:

	Positive Views	Negative Views
Medical/nutrition issues		
Subsistence/famine issues		
Poverty/population issues		

If you adopt this grouping format, don't forget to address the "change over time" issue *within* each body paragraph. Students often forget to address all parts of the prompt (Note: This is the first core-scoring task!).

To ensure that you address the chronological charge of the question, you may wish to adopt a chronological organization, which is simple enough to organize.

	Positive Views	Negative Views
Early period		
Middle period		
Later period		

Let me add one caution to the issue of chronology. Every DBQ places the documents in chronological order. Don't assume that the question calls for analysis of change over time unless that phrase appears in the prompt OR if you notice an explicit pattern in the documents. By no means should you simply list the documents in order ("Document 1 says," "Document 2 says," and so on) unless you have established a clear change-over-time format. A serial list, without analysis or a clear grouping logic, is a sure tip-off to the reader that the essay lacks a thesis and is simply summarizing the documents.

Writing the Introduction and Thesis

As with the FRQs, begin your introductory paragraph with one or two sentences of *brief* historical context, but avoid simply reiterating the information provided in the historical background. Move quickly into your thesis, which should identify your THREE explicit groups. At all costs, avoid simply restating the question or providing only vague descriptors, such as "some were for the potato, some against, and some were unsure." This would not count as an adequate thesis. For the change-over-time element of the question, use explicit cues to indicate your understanding of chronological development: "at first, many believed," "as time went on," "around the early eighteenth century," "by the end of this period."

Don't get bogged down in the introductory paragraph; it should be no more than five to seven sentences. Resist the temptation to provide extensive background or commentary on the topic. The focus of your essay will be the body paragraphs and treatment of the documents.

Effective Body Paragraphs Using the Documents

Begin your body paragraphs with a powerful topic sentence that indicates how that paragraph fits into your thesis. Avoid simply stating the topic: "Another argument had to do with economics." Give the reader more direction: "Observers were divided over the potato's nutritional value, though over time, it became accepted as an essential part of the European diet." Next, move into your documents. When you use a document, cite the author and the title or type of source. This is the first step toward addressing point of view. It is also a good practice to put the document number in parentheses after using it, for example (Doc. 4), to make it easy for the reader to count the documents should she be in doubt whether you used a majority.

Think of the documents as being part of a conversation or dialogue. Employ transition words to indicate (dis)agreement among sources: "this document is supported by," "on the other hand," "his view is directly contradicted by," "the author agrees, but for a different reason." For each document, you should (1) explain how it relates to the topic sentence of that paragraph and (2) potentially address bias or point of view. Though it is not necessary to address both with each document, and you probably won't have time, attempt at least four or five fairly substantial analyses. Conclude your paragraph by transitioning into the next paragraph; this is especially important if you are addressing change over time.

More so even than in FRQs, clear paragraphs are essential to an effective DBQ. Your paragraphs are your groups. If at the end of your response, you find that you have less than THREE body paragraphs and/or less than TWO documents per paragraph, the essay will not earn the core-scoring point for grouping. As you write, keep referring back to the question and your outline. There are a lot of tasks to juggle, but with practice, these will become hard-wired in your consciousness.

The "Ten Commandments" of DBQ Writing

1. Avoid long quotations from the documents. This adds little to the analysis and wastes time you could be spending on other higher-level tasks. Refer to specific information or use brief quotes and phrases.

2. The question is designed to gauge your skills of historical analysis, not articulating your own position on the issues. Avoid indicating your own opinion and using "I" words.

3. Make sure you address *all* parts of the question throughout your essay.

4. Cite the documents appropriately. Identify the author, source (this can be abbreviated if it's especially long), and put the document number in parentheses.

5. Make the structure of your argument clear by employing a direct thesis, strong topic sentences, and clear groupings.

6. Use the documents explicitly to advance your argument. Avoid simply quoting and paraphrasing without any connection to the thesis.

7. Be explicit in explaining your rationales for bias or point of view. Simply stating, "The author is biased," is insufficient. Aim for at least four or five examples of bias analysis.

8. Try to use all or almost all of the documents to support your response. It is acceptable to spend more time on a document that offers rich opportunities for analysis, but avoid getting bogged down with any particular document. Try to be efficient in using the documents to support your answer.

9. Include appropriate outside information, especially if it helps put the documents in context or assists with point of view. If you notice authors with whom you are familiar, exploit any knowledge to assist in your analysis of the document.

10. Think of the DBQ exercise as your reporting on a conversation or debate on an important topic. Identify the terms of the debate, the different sides, and, at the end (your conclusion), try to indicate the significance of this argument.

Practice Writing

Now you should be ready to begin writing the sample DBQ. Take 15 or so minutes to read through the documents and plan your response. To improve the focus and direction of your response, use one of the organizational charts provided. Once you begin writing (you have 45 minutes), stay focused on the question. When you are finished, compare your response to the samples that follow, which also have commentary included. Use the core-scoring rubric (on p. 5) to evaluate your essay. Remember that this is a first effort, so you may feel a time crunch. Don't worry, that's common and you will improve your efficiency with each effort.

Sample Essays

Sample A

During the period of European exploration, many new items and crops were brought to Europe. The potato was one of these crops that had a major impact on European life, especially in Ireland. During the years from 1600–1850, the potato gained an increasingly significant place in the daily life of Europeans, and effected how they lived daily, as many came to rely on it. Those who liked the potato were happy that it had become so prevalent in society, saying it was healthy and nutritious, abundant, and that it also had a good taste. Those opposed to the potato, however, thought that it was not healthy, overused, not dependable, had a bad taste, and, also, that it didn't improve the conditions of the people in Europe.

The potato had many benefits in European society. Tobias Venner, an English physician and medical writer, wrote that potatoes were a wholesome food, helping to "comfort, nourish, and strengthen the body" (Doc. 2). Document 3 also shows, in a book by William Salmon, an English physician, that potatoes have major health benefits. These men are trustworthy sources on the health effects of potatoes, because they are physicians and are experienced in the health field. Along with being healthy, potatoes were also very abundant and easy to cultivate. This helped the lower class avoid starvation. Guillaume-Charles Faipoult explained in a memorandum that the sole reason that the large population of its region was able to be sufficiently fed was the potato (Document 7). His point of view should be reflective of his town because he is a prefect in government. The French naturalist Leopold Cuvier explains in Document 8 that potatoes have helped cure famine in Europe. Also, the potato is good because along with being nutritious and preventing famine, it also tastes good, like Tobias Venner said in Doc. 2, which explained the diverse ways in which it could be prepared. Clearly, as more was learned about the potato from science and experience, people accepted it as a viable crop.

Although many people thought that the potato was a good crop for Europe, some people did not prefer to eat it. The Town Council of Bescancon in France issued an edict (Doc. 1) that forbid the cultivation of potatoes because they were *unhealthy*. However, this view at the time does not seem to have much medical backing. Denis Diderot, although in agreement that it was abundant and healthy, wrote that the potato could "not pass for an agreeable food" (Document 4). He probably had this point of view because he was a writer in France and did not need the potato to live off of. When ordered to eat potatoes to relieve famine, the townspeople of Kolberg sent a message (Document 5) that potatoes were no use to them because they had a bad taste. This shows that even though they had health benefits, people in some places refused to eat them because of their taste. These people might have a negative view of the potato because they were ordered to eat them and not given a choice. Finally, William Cobbett, in his, "A Year's Residence in America," expressed his tiredness of everything being about the potato in society. He thought that they were used too much and people considered them "salvation" (Doc. 10). By this time, many relied on the potato—mostly the poor—but some of the upper class still viewed it as a "lowly" crop.

Along with the strong supporters and criticizers of potatoes, there were some people who liked the potato but thought it had one major downfall. It was not reliable, but people still depended on it. Faipout explains in Document 7 that 2 months of drought can almost wipe out a potato field, and that, for this reason, they shouldn't be relied on. He is biased because he works for the government and is probably worried about possible crises in the regions of his government. More observers feared overreliance on the potato as time went on. Documents 9 and 10 also explain that people were only relying on the potato to feed them, and because of this, they were becoming lazy and their economic situations hadn't improved much. Potato famines, especially in Ireland, were a major consequence of the increasing reliance on potatoes.

The potato had benefits and downfalls. It was healthy, abundant, easy to prepare, and easy to harvest. However, it was also used in excess, and it was very unreliable. Finally, it made people lazy, because they just depended on one crop for everything. The potato was introduced during Europe's great period of exploration, and quickly caught on as a favorite crop throughout Europe. Between the years of 1600 and 1850, the potato was everywhere to be found in Europe. Whether it was believed to be good, bad or both, the potato had a significant impact on the lives of Europeans during this time period.

This essay meets all six core tasks. It addresses both parts of the question, by identifying specifically the views affecting the potato's adoption and how these views changed over time. Though the essay is not organized chronologically, the student efficiently incorporates references to change over time in each paragraph. Nine documents are referenced (Documents 7 and 10 are each used twice), which earns the student the core point, but none in the expanded core. Also, the response clearly employs the documents in support of the thesis and has no major errors. The student follows up the clear thesis with three explicit groupings based on the views toward the potato. As for point of view, the student provides five to six examples, depending on how these are counted. Documents 2 and 3 are addressed collectively (as physicians), which counts as one example. There are two separate treatments of bias related to Document 7 in two different paragraphs, which count as two examples. Point of view is also addressed with Documents 1, 4, and 5. In addition to the clear thesis, this extra point of view earns the students two additional points in the expanded core. Score: 8.

Sample B

From 1600 to 1850, the potato developed into the most prominent crop in Europe. The potato was always a very controversial crop—many people believed it saved numerous Europeans' lives. Others thought it caused their demise. Not only was there controversy on whether the potato should be grown, but also regarding its effect on society and the economy, which some people viewed as positive; however, others attributed Europe's despair to the potato. Over time, the potato came to be accepted but caused problems in places like Ireland.

An immense amount of people supported the prominence of the potato especially doctors. Tobias Venner, an English physician and medical writer, discussed all of the potato's benefits—they provide the most nourishment out of all the roots and fruits, they strengthen the body, and they are tasty especially because there are so many ways to prepare them (Doc. 2). Venner is a very credible source seeing as he is a physician; however, he may not know about the problem with later famines since he wrote this in 1620. In addition, William Salmon, another English physician, took a more professional stance regarding potatoes. He listed all the diseases and bodily functions that potatoes positively effect (Doc. 3). Salmon is even more credible than Venner because he wrote this in 1710, ninety years after Venner, during which time there were many scientific and medical advancements. In another field, Diderot discusses the practicality of the potato, saying that although it is tasteless, it helps people survive (Doc. 4). A French naturalist, Leopold Cuvier, discussed the lack of logic in blaming potatoes for leprosy or fever. He recognizes that potatoes saved people more than they hurt them (Doc. 8). He is a credible source because his job is to observe nature and its effects on people. Finally, the painting "A Potato Dinner" shows the appreciation of the people for potatoes (Doc. 12). The family is praying and thanking God for the food, a sign of how far the potato had come.

Moreover, there were a myriad of people on the opposite side of the fence. The town council of Besancon in France dubbed the potato as dangerous and the cause of leprosy (Doc. 1). The town council has no knowledge in this field of work (before the Scientific Revolution) and must come up with a scapegoat so the people of France don't panic. King Frederick II refused to eat the potatoes because he said they have no smell nor taste; he is a noble higher than all others and just refuses to eat potatoes because it is the food the commoners eat (Doc. 5). Arthur Young, an English writer and agricultural reformer, thinks the potato is very unhealthy and insufficient to provide nourishment for hard working laborers (Doc. 6). However, Young doesn't seem to understand that without potatoes, the laborers wouldn't have anything to eat. Cobbett agrees with Young saying that it is foolish to think potatoes can save people (Doc. 10). Cobbett's view is flawed because the potato did extend the lives of many Europeans from 1600 to 1845, but some grew angry with the excessive claims of the potato.

Not only is there controversy regarding whether or not potatoes should be grown but also on their effect. In France, a local official praised the potato saying it is the savior of their population. He also discussed its positive effect on breweries (allowed an abundance of grain) and its assistance in increasing exports, which thus, improved the economy (Doc. 7). Although he believes the potato also immensely helped France, he knows that if the potato is all France relies on there will be problems because of the frequent periods of distress that potatoes cause. On the contrary, two views from the Irish criticize the potato. Curwin, a member of Parliament, a businessman, and an agricultural reformer discussed the calamities caused by the potato. He said it caused an increased amount of laziness and corrupted the work ethic of Ireland's citizens (Doc. 9). His view is biased because he is Irish, and they experienced the worst famine of all. Other counties may view the effects differently. On the same note, a report to the commission to Parliament about an investigation in Ireland also criticized the social effects saying it didn't benefit the Irish at all (Doc. 11). His view is biased because he saw the effect only in Ireland, again the worst case scenario of potato famine in Europe occurred there. Concern over the effects of the potato is shown as we get closer to the potato famine in Ireland.

Many people debated over the potato in this period. Clearly, more people adopted the crop over time, though there was always concern over its taste, medical effects, and impact on the agricultural system. Supporters thought it was a nutritious crop that should be adopted just like traditional grains. Opponents at first claimed it caused disease but later tried to stop people from overusing it. The result was a disaster in Ireland.

There is much merit in this essay: it is clearly written, offers a strong thesis, and engages consistently in point of view. Clearly, the student deals with both parts of the question, and as with Sample A, the change over time is subtly embedded within the discussion of the documents. In addition, the response exploits all 12 documents explicitly in support of the thesis. Though the groups are somewhat awkward—positive and negative on adoption, effects—they work. The main issue with this response is errors. Mistakenly, the student refers to the source of Document 5 as Frederick II and attributes the negative views toward the potato to him, rather than the town of Kolberg responding to him. Also, the interpretation of Arthur Young (Document 6) mischaracterizes him as negative toward the potato, when in fact, he denounces the opinion that the potato has caused the poverty and idleness of the Irish. That's why it is important for you to read the *entire* document carefully before categorizing it. Finally, the author of Document 9 is mislabeled as being Irish, an error which negates the point of view also attributed to this document. In the context of this otherwise fine essay—with point of view provided for Documents 2, 3, 8, 1, and 11—these errors stand as a regrettable example of how missing even one of the core tasks can undermine your score. Score: 5.

Section II

Content Review

CHAPTER 3
The Rise of Europe

INTRODUCTION

The following chapters review the content of the AP European History course. You will find that they roughly correspond to the outline of your textbook. However, when warranted, I have added content deemed important to an understanding of the major themes and concepts of the course, particularly related to social and cultural topics. In addition, in the margins of the review are features titled "Heads Up!" and "Sidebar." Heads Up! comments connect the topic to review strategies and tips. Sidebars highlight topics or issues of special importance, or attempt to clear up common misconceptions and stereotypes. Safe travels on your journey through the exciting ride that is European History since 1450.

A NOTE ON GEOGRAPHY

Before we depart, it is important to know where we are and where we are going. Some claim that "geography is destiny." Though there is truth in this assertion, it is overstated. As with any geographic region, Europe has been tremendously influenced by its environmental context; economic activities, cultural practices, political forms, and even fashion have all been shaped by geographic and climactic circumstances.

Take note of the map on page 49. Several observations come to mind. First, Europe is an oddly shaped peninsula gouged with numerous inlands, seas, bays, and gulfs; punctuated by islands small and large; and narrowing toward the Atlantic and widening into the great plain leading to the vast Eurasian landmass. Second, Europe's location from north to south places it in the temperate climate zone—with wide variations between summer and winter temperatures, though this moderates in proximity to large bodies of water, such as the Atlantic Ocean and Mediterranean Sea. Third, a large variety of navigable rivers, mountain ranges, and plateaus indicate the tremendous diversity of landforms in such a small area (Europe is the second smallest of the seven continents).

What has been the impact of this geographic inheritance? For purposes of your course, two observations are offered. First, a wide variety of economic activities has marked the forward advance of European history. Europe's diverse climate and geography allow it to cultivate almost every important agricultural product—essential cereal grains, livestock, grapes for wine—and employ important natural resources for a wide range of manufacturing and industrial activities—mining, metallurgy, textile production. This geographic inheritance accounts largely for Europe's economic vitality and its outward reach to control markets and resources abroad, linking geography to the historical developments of exploration and imperialism, the Commercial Revolution, and industrialization.

Second, the European landmass has proved incredibly difficult for one political entity to control. Even the Romans were unable to subjugate all of it, and subsequent conquerors have repeated this failure. As a result, Europe's political and diplomatic history has been defined by a variety of political forms—nation-states, city-states, republics, empires, contested border regions—and multiple centers of power. Because of the inability of one entity—be it the Holy Roman Empire or Napoleonic France—to control the entire region, frequent warfare and shifts in

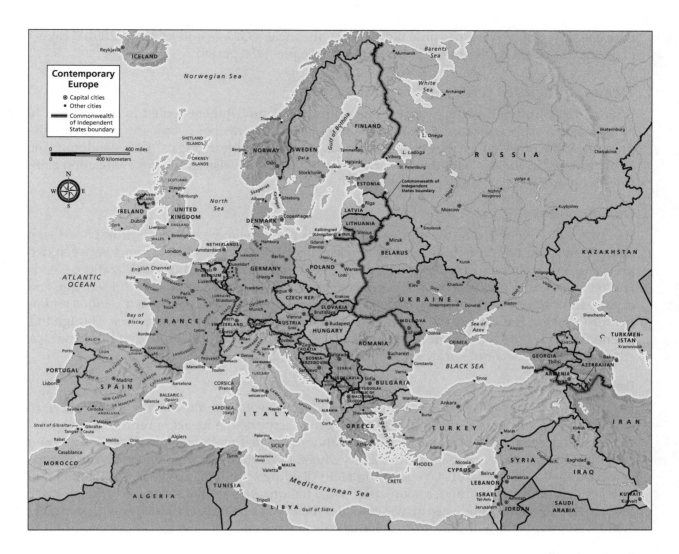

the balance of power define European political and diplomatic history. Though much common ground exists among the nations of Europe, until recent memory sufficient differences in language, culture, and history have prevented a strong enough shared identity to overcome conflicts that too often descended into warfare. Thus, we have a major theme of this course linked to the geographic context: the tension between the identities of the individual nations and the common heritage of "Europe."

As you study the content to follow, it is in your interest to keep a vigilant eye on the geographic context for these events and developments. You are advised to refer to the maps within this guide and in your textbook to connect the ever-changing political map of Europe to events that caused these shifts. Moreover, knowing the major regions and nations of Europe will provide a visual cue for grounding you in the historical content to follow. The time spent internalizing the map of Europe will pay off in your understanding and performance on the AP Exam.

THE ANCIENT AND MEDIEVAL INHERITANCE

Though the Advanced Placement European History Exam covers the period from 1450, some general knowledge of the ancient and medieval world will prove useful in your study of the material. For example, it is difficult to understand the fascination of Renaissance humanists with classical values if one has little familiarity with ancient Greece and Rome. With that caveat in mind, this brief chapter offers background on the pre-1450 period.

Trends Associated with the Rise of Europe

Prior to 1300, Europe's political power and cultural accomplishments paled in comparison to other major world civilizations. In 1300 the term "Europe" was not even used to describe the present continent. What we now call Europe was more likely referred to as "Christendom." The term "Europe" coincides with the modern age, just as Europe's rise as a major civilization coincides with modernity.

Globalization

As Europe has expanded outward and increased its power relative to other cultural hearths, it has helped spread important developments associated with modern life. Contact between two previous unknown hemispheres in 1492 (and after) initiated a period of globalization. Goods and resources from one area became accessible to all. Globalization marks our present age and involves the cultural and political penetration of previously remote or isolated regions by imperialist powers, multinational corporations, and telecommunications enterprises. Though this phenomenon is not synonymous with the rise of Europe, there is little doubt that European scientific, economic, technological, and political advances have fueled it.

Democratization

For much of Europe's history, elites held real political power. With the advent of the American and French Revolutions at the end of the eighteenth century, the ideals of representative government and guarantees of rights became a standard against which regimes were judged and provided an agenda for revolutionaries everywhere. Liberation movements starting in Europe spawned the first successful slave revolt in Haiti (leading to independence in 1804) and led to independence for Latin America soon after, while nationalism fed the Asian and African drive for self-rule in the twentieth century. Again, democracy is not a purely European concept, but is often stowed away with European colonial rule and culture.

Modernization

We tend to use "modern" as a short-hand term to mean "contemporary" or "up-to-date." Though the term comes into common usage during the Renaissance and leads historians to identify the modern age from about 1500, in fact, modernism is associated with a number of important trends in culture, intellectual life, and politics dating from the eighteenth century. Trends often associated with modernism include:

- A mass political culture based on appeals to popular will (if only indirectly)
- A secular and scientific view of the world
- Cultural movements associated with self-expression, the subconscious, and personal identity
- Economic systems based on mechanization, mass production, and marketing
- Global transportation and communication networks

Common historical terms, such as *ancient, medieval,* and *modern,* can be useful in identifying eras and associated trends, but you should not consider them as rigid lines dividing historical eras.

Heritage of the Ancient World

Greek Civilization

The Greeks are often called the founders of Western civilization, with justification. Greek civilization flourished from around 1000 B.C. until its conquest by Rome in 146 B.C., and its contributions in philosophy, science, architecture, drama, history, as well as other fields, became the standard and reference point for European civilization for years to come. There are moments and places whose greatness cannot be explained fully by an analysis of historical circumstances. One such place was Athens in the fifth century B.C. The Greek heritage of human accomplishment echoed through the ages and defined excellence in the following areas:

- *Philosophy*—Greek thinkers used reason in asking the most basic questions of nature and humanity, such as "What is the most real?" "What is the good?" "What is a just society?" Philosophers such as Plato and Aristotle established important principles and knowledge that dominated almost all academic fields until the sixteenth century.
- *Politics*—Though the political arena was restricted to free, property-owning males, democracy, as well as the active civic environment of the Greek city-states, inspired imitation among Renaissance humanists and created a model for future revolutionaries.
- *History*—Historians such as Herodotus and Thucydides emphasized the importance of social and political forces in historical causation. Moving away from mythology and divine explanations, Greek historians wrote history to edify and warn against human pride and stupidity.
- *Drama and Poetry*—Literary works in ancient Greece acted as mirrors held up to society's faults and the vanities of human nature. The tragedies of Aeschylus, Euripides, and Sophocles and the comedies of Aristophanes influenced later literature in their complex plots, rich characters, and thematic emphasis. Europe's great tradition of lyric poetry got its start with the ancient poets Pindar and Sappho.
- *Science and Mathematics*—Once again, Aristotle's ideas—wrong as they often were—defined the fields of physics, astronomy, zoology, and anatomy for centuries, later becoming the target of criticism during the Scientific Revolution. Borrowing much from surrounding civilizations, the Greeks contributed immensely to mathematics, particularly geometry, with the theorems of Pythagoras and Euclid.
- *Classical Aesthetics*—Perhaps the most lasting impact of Greek culture remains its emphasis in art and architecture on the virtues of balance, symmetry, and order. Whether the sculptural attention to the human form or the harmony of a great civic building, how Europeans ordered space and perceived human potential owes much to ancient Greek accomplishments.

Alexander the Great and the Hellenistic Age

Like all good things, ancient Greek civilization came to an end. The devastating Peloponnesian War between the Athenians and Spartans weakened the city-states, opening the way for conquest by the Macedonians from the north. Alexander the Great's armies swept through southeastern Europe, into the Middle East, and eventually halted near India. Alexander died in 323 B.C., but not before spreading Greek civilization to the areas he conquered. The subsequent two centuries witnessed the gradual synthesis of Greek ideas with those of surrounding regions. This period is known as the Hellenistic Age.

Roman Civilization

Rome began as a city in 753 B.C. and graduated into a far-flung empire ruling the entire Mediterranean basin by the second century A.D. This process did not involve a predetermined path, and was aided by luck, circumstance, and sheer determination. Certainly, the Romans deserve recognition for their contributions to many fields and the length of their rule, yet their initial importance lay in spreading Greek ideas to the remainder of Europe following the Roman conquest of the Balkan Peninsula in 146 B.C. With each conquest, Rome successfully integrated new ethnic groups and peoples into its realm, often by extending citizenship and conferring the benefits of Roman civilization upon those lands. While Rome built on Greek learning in many areas, its greatness tends to rest upon its practical accomplishments and enduring legacy.

- *Administration and Law*—As a republic, Rome survived by constantly adapting to shifting circumstances and making use of the patriotism it inspired in its citizens, whether fighting tenaciously in battle or drawing new citizens into its active political life. Internal social and political conflict, along with the rise of military despots, ultimately undid the republic and led to the creation of the empire. The empire's ability to centralize power and establish a uniform legal code across a vast expanse of territory became the touchstone and goal of many European rulers since the empire's fall in 476 A.D. (in the west; the eastern or Byzantine Empire continued until 1453).
- *Architecture and Infrastructure*—Rome thrived as a distinctly urban culture. Wherever Romans conquered, they brought roads, aqueducts, impressive public buildings, and other amenities previously unknown to their new subjects. Though much of this infrastructure eventually decayed owing to disrepair, even the ruins served as a legacy to be imitated. For example, Renaissance humanists scoured their Italian backyard searching for examples of Roman architecture, baths, and piazzas, not to mention sculptures and literary works for artistic imitation.
- *The* Pax Romana—During its almost half-millennium rule, the Roman Empire generally succeeded in providing a political order that allowed both an active public life and a thriving intellectual and cultural setting. Certainly the empire experienced turmoil—especially in the third century—due to barbarian invasions, military interference, and demographic decline, but resiliently rode further on the fumes of its nearly exhausted glory. Even after it fell, many looked to recover the peace and stability of the *Pax Romana,* or Roman peace.

Christianity

Though Christianity did not originate there, Europe has traditionally been the heartland of the Christian religion. After the fourth century, when it became the official religion of the Roman Empire, Christianity spread outward from the Mediterranean basin, reaching its final missionary outpost in the Eastern Baltic in the fourteenth century. Christianity's influence extends beyond the religious realm, into politics, ideas, culture, and the arts. Oftentimes, Christian dogma was reconciled and absorbed into pagan customs and beliefs, as can be seen with holiday practices during Halloween and Christmas. Nonetheless, the implications of Christian theology and practice held profound consequences for European society.

- *The Soul*—Belief in individual immortality and a moral structure that transcended the temporal ("material" or "earthly") world radically altered the perception of the human person.

Christianity holds that there is a spiritual reality, the "soul," that exists beyond the material world and is accessible only to the senses.

- *Individual Dignity*—The notion that each individual is "created in the image of God" has often acted as a check on absolutist tendencies in politics and provided a moral basis for law and society.
- *Monotheism*—Drawing from their Jewish roots, the Christian fathers of the early Church maintained a strong belief in one God, while at the same time articulating the doctrine of the Holy Trinity, or the three persons of God (Father, Son, Holy Spirit) who share the same substance.
- *St. Augustine (354–430)*—Perhaps the most influential of the early Christian saints, his writings emphasized the predominance of spiritual over temporal authority, the importance of the next world (the "City of God" vs. the "City of Man"), and the sovereignty and majesty of God.

> **Sidebar:** St. Augustine elaborated the idea of predestination and placed great emphasis on faith as a path to salvation, making him the primary inspiration for Martin Luther and other Protestant reformers in the sixteenth century.

- *Caesaropapism*—According to the traditions of the Roman Empire, political and spiritual authority were fused in the same person. While this tradition continued in the Eastern or Byzantine Empire, the two authorities developed separately in Latin Christianity. While this split caused repeated controversies between the Roman Catholic papacy and the Holy Roman Emperor during the Middle Ages, its positive effect was to carve out a zone between both authorities for political diversity and corporate (meaning "in groups") liberties where neither political nor spiritual power could reach, each being checked by the other.

Heritage of the Medieval World

The Early Middle Ages, 476–1050

The period following the fall of the Roman Empire is often termed "the Dark Ages." To some extent, this designation is true, as Roman cities became depopulated, roads fell into disrepair, trade dried up, and various barbarian tribes replaced the universal empire with a variety of Germanic kingdoms. In addition, the learning of ancient Greece and Rome was kept alive dimly by the candlelight of monastic scriptoria.

- *Barbarian Invasions*—Due to a "traffic jam" on the plains of central Asia, barbarian tribes poured into Europe in the waning days of the Roman Empire. Most of these tribes gradually assimilated into the empire, often being used for their military skills or to guard distant outposts. What had originally been a strength of the empire—the ability to assimilate various ethnicities—gradually diluted the culture and greatness of Rome. Thus, in 476 a barbarian leader deposed the last emperor in the West.
- *Latin vs. Greek Christianity*—Once the Roman Empire was divided in the fourth century between east and west for administrative purposes, the two parts drifted further apart culturally and religiously. After the fall of Rome, the Byzantine Empire, centered in Constantinople (today Istanbul) continued the legacy of the empire, but with a distinctly Greek cultural accent. Disputes throughout the medieval period over the authority of the pope, the use of religious icons in church, and other theological controversies led to a formal break between the Latin (Catholic) and Orthodox branches of Christianity that was formalized in 1054, and remains to this day.

Sidebar: Islam is the fastest growing religion in Europe today. Though many nations remain Christian in name, religious observance among European Christians has declined significantly in the past half-century. This shift has fueled concerns over the religious balance of power and has led to political parties geared toward restricting further immigration.

- *The Islamic World*—Islam came out of the desert in the 620s as the fastest growing religion in world history, quickly establishing political and cultural dominance of vast swaths of Asia, North Africa, and southern Europe. Arabs easily assimilated the intellectual legacy of the Greeks and Roman—keeping alive the learning of Aristotle and others more effectively than Europeans—at the same time making important contributions to mathematics (Arabic numerals, algebra), science (especially in astronomy and medicine), and literature. Since the early eighth century, Muslims have been a continuous presence in Europe, claiming a common religious heritage with Jews and Christians as "people of the Book," though believing Mohammad and the Koran to be the ultimate fulfillment of God's promise to His people.
- *Germanic Customs*—Unlike the Roman Empire, barbarian culture focused on loyalty to persons rather than institutions. Rather than adhering to abstract legal concepts or ideals, Germanic society revolved around tribal identities, which allowed in many ways for a greater amount of freedom than had existed in the Roman Empire. However, this freedom came at the cost of political unity, economic vitality, and an active civic culture.
- *Monasteries*—Monasteries acted as more than houses for religious orders. Beginning in the fifth century when they adopted the discipline of St. Benedict (c. 480–543), monasteries retreated from the chaos of political life to concentrate on the life of the spirit and the mind. This meant that monks kept alive ancient Greek and Roman texts, at the same time inventing—everything from champagne to pretzels.
- *Charlemagne*—A Frankish king (from the tribe of the Franks, later France), Charlemagne, provided a short-lived period of unity and intellectual revival in central Europe. Crowned emperor by the pope in 800, Charlemagne drove out rival barbarian chieftains and established a seat of government in Aix-la-Chapelle (Aachen in German) in imitation of the Roman ideal. Though he could not himself read, Charlemagne led a mini-Renaissance of learning, which faded when his successors fought among themselves over the political spoils after his death in 814.
- *Second Wave of Invasions (Ninth Century)*—Following the rule of Charlemagne, Europe once again was beset by a period of instability and foreign invasion. During the ninth century, tribes from the north, east, and Muslim pirates from the south threatened to overrun the weak kingdoms of the European heartland. As before, the Norse from Scandinavia and the Magyars from Asia were gradually incorporated into European political culture and converted to Christianity. By 1000, Europe had settled into relative political stability, with the map now filled in with virtually all of the major ethnic groups, though borders would continue to shift and evolve according to war, conquest, and migration.

The High Middle Ages, 1050–1300

As a historical era, the Middle Ages gets a bad rap, whether being spoofed by Monty Python or being associated with terms such as "Dark Ages" or "gothic." A more appropriate way to view this millennium is as a gradual synthesis of the major strands of European culture, politics, and society—ancient Greek and Roman, Christianity, and barbarian. In fact, the High Middle Ages was a period of dynamic developments in ideas, economics, technology, politics, and society. Simply because medieval life looks different to our contemporary eyes doesn't mean it was backward or uncivilized. Perhaps the brief review that follows will convince the skeptic of this validity.

- *Agriculture*—Improvements in agriculture, such as three-crop field rotation, the iron plow, horse collar, and use of windmills, supported an increasing population. More land was brought under cultivation, in places producing a surplus, which helped to stimulate an increase in trade. By 1300, Europe had reached an all-time (up to then) population high of 75 million, which represented a doubling from the level of 1000.

Sidebar: One might make a convincing case that the thirteenth century was the greatest of all centuries, with universities founded, innovative cathedrals built, a revival of commerce, technological breakthroughs (clocks, compass, gunpowder, glasses, etc.), Scholasticism, and the Magna Carta. Yes, the Middle Ages was less tolerant than our present age; however, recall that the recent twentieth century stands by far as the most destructive age in human history.

- *Feudalism*—Based on the decentralized nature of Germanic political culture and the insecurity of the Early Middle Ages, the system of feudalism emerged during the High Middle Ages. Relationships between lord and vassal were based on specific contractual obligations of loyalty and protection. In return for protection, peasants provided labor and gave loyalty to feudal elites, who controlled peasants and serfs through an intricate set of obligations, fees, rituals, and taxes. As warfare required continuous training and expensive equipment (a result of the invention of the stirrup allowing heavy mounted warriors), only an elite few could engage in the practice. Society became divided, at least in theory, into those who fought (nobles and knights), those who prayed (the clergy), and those who worked (peasants and artisans).

- *Towns and Commerce*—As the economy improved throughout the High Middle Ages, its effects were felt most strongly in the growth of towns. Medieval towns were not the teeming urban centers of the industrial era, but did act as magnets for skilled labor, ideas, and goods. Towns lay outside the feudal structure and jealously guarded their liberties, which were generally confirmed by charters. Towns often banded together in leagues to protect their independence or promote their commerce, as with the Hanse, the German trading centers in the Baltic. A central institution of most towns was the guild, which controlled the production of goods in a particular craft. Not only did the guild ensure a minimum quality of goods and license its members' skills, it also acted as a civic institution, reflecting the corporate (small, organized groups) nature of medieval society. With the continued growth and attraction of cities in western Europe, feudalism, especially serfdom, declined in importance, to be replaced by a more commercial and money-oriented economy.

- *National Monarchies*—The states of the Middle Ages lacked the complexity and administrative tools of more modern forms of government. Nonetheless, kings and queens of this era worked diligently to establish hereditary claims to their thrones. In fact, the beginnings of bureaucracy (government agencies) and representative government can be seen in several nations. First, monarchies established some power to tax their subjects to support the state, though this often required the approval of other bodies. A well-known example demonstrating the trend is the English nobles limiting the power of the king in 1215 with the Magna Carta, which eventually led to the formation of the Parliament. Royal councils and representative bodies confirmed limits on the power of monarchs and mandated that traditional liberties must be respected.

- *The Church*—During this period, the Catholic Church reached the height of its political, spiritual, and cultural influence. Throughout the High Middle Ages, the pope and the Holy Roman Emperor continuously vied for power in central Europe, generally over the issue of clerical control, with the result that each checked the power of the other. For a time, popes were successful in establishing their claims to make and unmake kings. The climax of these grand ideals came with the papacy of Innocent III (1198–1216), who attempted to unify the entire Christian world under his authority. At the same time, there was growing criticism of the behavior of the clergy and the lack of regularity in church doctrine and practice. The result was a revival of the monastic ideal (termed the Cluniac movement) and the calling of an exceptional Church council in 1215—the Fourth Lateran—that established new regulations for the clergy and formalized many church doctrines related to the sacraments, which stand to this day.

- *Gender Roles*—As with many periods in history, women's roles in the Middle Ages were bound by legal and economic prescription. However, medieval women of different classes often found ways to express autonomy, initiative, and talent within these parameters. The nature of medieval warfare often left noblewomen to manage large manors, engage in politics, and organize the defense of castles. Younger noblewomen often joined convents, where they could pursue intellectual and spiritual interests outside the control of men. Women also played major roles in movements of religious change or in so-called heresies. Further, the ideal of courtly love and chivalry placed women at the center of an important cultural tradition. Cities and towns relied on the labor of women in artisan families, often as guild members in food preparation, brewing, and cloth production. Peasant and serf women labored alongside their husbands in mowing hay, tending to vegetable gardens, or in harvesting. Since peasant homes were simple, domestic chores actually played more of a minor role for women.

> **Sidebar:** Much of the Renaissance was directed against what was perceived as the Scholastics' focus on stale logic and impractical learning.

- *Universities and Scholasticism*—With the rise of towns came a quickening of intellectual life. Informal meetings of students and teachers evolved into the formal founding of the first universities in the early thirteenth century. Universities taught a variety of subjects in their various faculties, but our current separation of spiritual and material subjects did not exist in the medieval worldview. In fact, theology stood as the "queen of the sciences," and liberally borrowed from other disciplines to elaborate its truths. The best example of this practice was the creation of Scholasticism. During the thirteenth century, a mini-Renaissance, or revival, of Aristotle's philosophy took place. Pagan ideas governing logic and the natural world were synthesized into Christian dogma, especially by scholars such as St. Thomas Aquinas, to explain divine truths. This intellectual system came to dominate the universities until well into the eighteenth century, though with growing criticism after 1500.

- *The Crusades*—A sign of the increasing power of Europe was the Crusades. Due to the expansion of commerce, population, and political organization, Christian Europe was able to go on the offensive against Islamic rule of the Holy Land. The first crusade was launched in 1095, and subsequent efforts succeeded in establishing kingdoms in Palestine and surrounding areas. However, many of these efforts were driven by prejudice (against Jews, for example) and sheer bloodlust, often producing atrocities and tragic consequences, like the needless sack of Constantinople in 1204 (during the Fourth Crusade). Despite some of the baser motives, the Crusades demonstrated Europe's newfound assertiveness and interest in the outside world, stimulating a spirit of exploration.

Expanding Europe

As of 1300, Europe had become one of several important civilizations on the Eurasian landmass and Africa that came into increasing contact with one another. By this time, Europe stood in a much more advantageous position than it had only a century earlier, able to withstand the onslaught of the Mongols and Ottoman Turks in upcoming centuries. Despite its successes, Europe's technological and cultural accomplishments still paled in comparison to China's, yet in the next 600 years it was Europe that successfully projected its power abroad, not China. Why? Though it invented printing and gunpowder, China did not exploit these technologies in pursuit of global commerce and power. Ironically, Europe's lack of central political power, separation of secular and religious authority, and disorderly conflict among various nations (none of which existed in China) acted as the engine that fed technological and scientific innovation, yielding a strange mix of conflict and war along with freedom and dynamism.

ADDITIONAL RESOURCES

Bridenthal, Renate et al., *Becoming Visible*—Valuable collection of essays on women's history from ancient times to the present.

Cantor, Norman, *The Civilization of the Middle Ages* (rev. 1993)—Straightforward and helpful review of all things medieval.

Diamond, Jared, *Guns, Germs, and Steel* (1997)—An impressive work arguing for the importance of environmental factors in explaining the rise of Europe.

Grant, Michael, *The Founders of the Western World: A History of Greece and Rome* (1990)—A popular writer surveys the topic in an accessible manner for students.

Hart, Michael, *The 100: A Ranking of the Most Influential Persons in History,* 2nd ed. (1992)—The title gives the book's premise, and this volume is always good for sparking interesting debates. Many figures covered in the course can be found here.

Riley Smith, Jonathan, *The Crusades: A Short History* (1987)—A good place to start for an understanding of this fascinating and tragic era.

Times Atlas of European History (1994)—Clean maps and brief text take the reader through a tour of European history.

CHAPTER 4
The Renaissance and Reformation

Note: Many terms in these review chapters have been bolded to draw your attention to their importance. Before an exam, you may find it useful to scan down the page for these terms as a final review.

If the High Middle Ages represented dynamic growth, then the fourteenth century acted as the stick in the spokes of this runaway medieval cart that brought it crashing to the ground. Sometimes, however, tragedy can pave the way for the emergence of new cultural trends. In the wake of social, religious, cultural, and economic crisis, there emerged two defining movements of early modern European history—the Renaissance and the Protestant Reformation.

THE UPHEAVALS OF THE FOURTEENTH CENTURY

Sidebar: Large areas of eastern Europe were relatively unaffected by the Black Death, which ironically spared the feudal system there. Serfdom and the manorial system continued to define a major difference between east and west.

Europe's peak population of 75 million in 1300 was already pushing up against its natural boundaries when the continent was hit by the **Great Famine of 1315–1317** and the cataclysmic **Black Death** of 1348–1351. The latter represents perhaps the greatest natural disaster in world history, costing Europe upwards of 40 percent of its people. More important than sheer numbers was perhaps the psychological and social cost of the disease. Caused by fleas traveling on rats, the bubonic plague spread quickly along trade routes and especially devastated urban areas. No one could explain the cause of the pestilence. **Flagellants** took the calamity to be God's wrath upon man and whipped themselves in atonement. Many blamed Jews for poisoning wells, which led to a notorious persecution of that minority in Nuremberg. Art reflected the obsession with death; paintings featured skeletons performing the *danse macabre*. The Catholic Church could offer little solace, especially since the disease killed off well over 60 percent of the top clergy. Perhaps most significantly, the Black Death caused a labor shortage that undermined the feudal structure, as peasants bargained for improved labor conditions, winning lifetime tenures and converting other obligations to cash payments.

Improved peasant conditions did not last long. Governments and nobles reasserted their power throughout the century, which led to the *jacquerie* rebellion in 1358 in France and Wat Tyler's revolt in 1381 in England. Urban revolts also occurred in Florence; each of these revolts was eventually overturned, often with great violence. Of more lasting import was the blow delivered to the feudal system in the west.

National monarchies were young creations, and therefore fragile. Dynastic instability (e.g., the inability to produce male heirs) plagued many states throughout the fourteenth century and led most seriously to the **Hundred Years' War** (1337–1453). Really a series of wars, this conflict between France and England over the French throne (and the cloth trade in the Low Countries) also dealt a fatal blow to the medieval idea of warfare. Time and again, English longbowmen demonstrated the power of massed infantry against France's heavily mounted feudal knights. French fortunes revived upon the back of a divinely inspired peasant girl. In 1429, **Joan of Arc** believed the voice of God called her to break the siege of Orleans. Despite her success, Joan was tried for witchcraft and burned at the stake (later made a saint in 1920). Yet the tide had turned, and by 1453, England held only the city of Calais on the continent. Each nation then turned inward to resolve pressing political conflicts.

The Catholic Church also stood in the midst of crisis. Since 1307, the papacy had lived in exile in France during the so-called **Babylonian Captivity.** Though not really a captive of the French monarch as many assumed, the papacy's prestige declined in proportion to the increase in its administrative apparatus and material wealth. When an Italian crowd forced the mostly French cardinals to elect one of their own, the church plunged into the **Great Schism** (1378–1417), with rival French and Italian popes forcing the nations of Europe to choose sides. Advocates of **conciliarism** attempted to use church councils (unsuccessfully) to solve the crisis *and* to check the power of the papacy. Reformers such as **John Wyclif** (the Lollards) in England and **John Huss** in Bohemia (part of the Holy Roman Empire) attacked the institutional power and wealth of the church and called for a simpler Christianity. Though Huss was burned at the stake in 1415 at the Council of Constance, his and Wyclif's ideas set the stage for the Protestant Reformation of the sixteenth century.

THE SETTING OF THE RENAISSANCE

Italy was the first area of Europe to experience the Renaissance. Several reasons account for this early lead.

- *Geography*—Italy was not only the center of the Mediterranean, which made it a crossroads of trade, it also boasted centers of ancient culture. After all, if artists wanted to imitate classical motifs, they need look no further than their own Roman backyard. Ideas followed in the wake of trade, particularly as humanists escaped the declining Byzantine Empire, being besieged by the Turks (and falling in 1453).
- *Urbanization*—While in most of Europe only 10 percent of the population lived in cities, up to 25 percent of Italians partook directly of the civic culture so essential to Renaissance humanism. Cities often act as magnets for trade, ideas, and culture; this was no less true during the Renaissance.
- *Social Factors*—Nobles played a vital role in Italy, just as they did in every European nation, though their attitudes tended to be more oriented to money-making and cultural accomplishments than elsewhere. A common blending of families in Italy involved a cash-strapped aristocrat and an up-and-coming wealthy merchant, thus creating a new elite, where wealth and worldly achievement mattered more than simply status.
- *Political Variety*—In the fourteenth century, Italy was a collection of small and large city-states. No centralized authority existed to stamp out potentially threatening ideas. If artists or intellectuals found difficulty in one place, they could simply move to another and continue their work. This disunity later became a liability, but at that time, Italy benefited from the multiplicity of competing political centers.

With its thriving city-states, Italy imitated the ancient *poleis* of Greece and the Roman Republic. Citizenship and freedom acted in the ancient world as the sparks of intellectual and cultural life, and the same held true of Renaissance Italy. A major concern of Renaissance thinkers was a life of active civic engagement. The life of the mind (*otium*) must eventually contribute to the bettering of one's city-state (*negotium*). Reflection *and* action promoted *virtú*, or excellence, in the true Renaissance man or woman.

As with today, family acted as a central social institution of the Italian Renaissance. Renaissance families were patriarchal, placing a

Sidebar: As in the ancient world, not all residents could take part in the civic culture of the Italian city-states. Citizenship was generally reserved for adult males, who often had to be members of the guilds. Slaves, women, aliens, or those who did not own property were excluded and could partake in the Renaissance only indirectly.

Sidebar: Gregorio Dati, a fourteenth-century Florentine merchant, recounts in his diary his 5 marriages and 19 children in the space of less than 25 years.

great deal of power in the male head of the family, or *patria potesta*. Before a man could achieve legal autonomy, his father must officially liberate him before the appropriate authorities. Oftentimes, men were not able to establish an independent existence until their late 20s or early 30s. At the same time, families commonly married off their daughters as early as their midteens. Marriages were frequently arranged to the benefit of both families. Economic concerns predominated; compatibility of the couple came second, and often not at all, given the significant age difference between man and woman. As a result of this marriage-age gap, Italy experienced some predictable side effects. First, prostitution was rampant, and since it was almost impossible to eliminate, it was generally tolerated and even regulated by governments. Second, the incidence of rape and sexual violence was high, though lower-class men were punished more severely if their victim was from the upper classes. Finally, men often died before their spouses, who remarried quickly due to the difficulties involved in living an independent existence. This led to remarriage, numerous blended families, and an abundance of stepparents. Though the nuclear family (mother, father, and children) acted as the norm, Renaissance Italy also depended on African **slavery,** a result of the labor shortage created by the Black Death. Slaves lived with families and often performed domestic work. Though as much as 10 percent of Italy's population in 1400 was made up of slaves, the practice in Europe declined with the recovery of the population in the fifteenth century.

RENAISSANCE HUMANISM AND ART

The term "Renaissance" is the creation of the modern Swiss historian **Jacob Burckhardt** (his *Civilization of the Renaissance in Italy* was published in 1860). Though the average layperson will tend to view the Renaissance, or "rebirth" of classical culture, as a distinct break from the Middle, or "Dark," Ages, historians often disagree over how useful this term is in describing a particular time period. One of the difficulties involved is periodization. That is, when do we date the beginning of the Renaissance? **Petrarch** (1304–1374), the father of humanism, already argued for a new age as early as the 1340s. However, this is before the Black Death. Does that mean the Black Death stands as a feature of the Renaissance? In addition, one of the great painters of the late medieval period, **Giotto,** acted as a powerful influence on later Renaissance painters. So where do we put Giotto? Even if there is much wisdom in viewing the Renaissance as a continuation of medieval trends, there is little doubt that a new self-consciousness regarding human beings and a new self-assertion is evident in Italy by 1350.

Heads Up! The Catholic Church continued to play a major role on the peninsula, often as a patron of the arts, and 90 percent of paintings continued to employ religious subject matter. Indeed, the Church continued as a focal point of most people's lives. Be careful of overstating the degree to which the Renaissance expressed a secular view of the world.

As the name suggests, humanists were fascinated by humans and their potential. The fabric of **humanism** is woven of several important strands:

• *Secularism*—Humanists encouraged humans to focus their attention on the here-and-now, and less on the afterworld, as had been the tendency during the Middle Ages. Education, self-help manuals, and treatises on civility all reinforced the notion that humans stood to gain rewards—wealth, status, prestige, fame—in the temporal world. Even in religious paintings, humans take on increased significance, while painting itself becomes more of an exercise to glorify the artist than to glorify God.
• *Classics*—Ancient Greece and Rome acted as the moral center of many humanists' outlook. Collectors of manuscripts, such as

Poggio Bracciolini, scoured monasteries, ruins—anywhere—to find evidence of the ancient way of life. For example, the ancient Roman Vitruvius's *On Architecture* provided a guide to the creation of buildings that imitated the coherent system of columns, arches, and pillars. Also, the recovery of the long-lost Hellenistic sculpture *Laocoön* in the early sixteenth century inspired Michelangelo to create his masterpiece, **David**. Ancient values and aesthetics, as pre-Christian, told a captivating story with humans at the center, from which humanists took inspiration.

- *Individualism*—By "individualism," humanists meant not a narrow, selfish conception of human actions, but rather that the focus on learning and human affairs should concern the individual. It was as if humanists had just discovered mankind and could not tear themselves away. This attitude can be seen in the self-consciousness of Petrarch's verse as well as Castiglione's suggestions for achieving fame, wealth, and position.

- *Power*—Amid the inspiring philosophy and mesmerizing art, it is easy to forget that the Renaissance was at its heart about human control of the environment. Machiavelli preached this message in politics, but is taken to be the odd man out. In fact, much of what humanists aimed to do was provide society with intellectual tools that could be used to master everything from the globe (cartography), to sound (musical notation), to abstract space (three-dimensional perspective in painting), to business (double-entry book-keeping), and finally politics. It's no coincidence that along with the great works of art came exploration/colonization, the centralization of the New Monarchs, and urban planning.

Humanism experienced many expressions—literature, philosophy, education, politics, and, of course, art. As you review the list of representative figures that follows, keep in the mind the principles just noted that their work demonstrates.

The Writers and Philosophers

Leonardo Bruni (1369–1444): Bruni studied under Chrysoloras, a Greek scholar who had escaped from the faltering Byzantine Empire, and translated ancient Greek texts into Latin. In addition, Bruni served Florence in various political capacities and later wrote a Latin history of the city. He is most famous for his admiration of Cicero, the Roman statesman and model of civic virtue.

Lorenzo Valla (1406–1457): Valla excelled in the discipline of **philology**, or study of ancient languages. Even though a member of the clergy, Valla demonstrated through textual analysis that the "Donation of Constantine," which supposedly granted the pope authority over political bodies, was a forgery.

Pico della Mirandola (1463–1494): A revival of Plato's philosophy occurred during the Renaissance, and there is no better example of this than Mirandola's "Oration on the Dignity of Man." Many consider it the classic statement of human potential. **Neo-Platonism** held that humans had once shared a divine nature and though they had freely chosen to enter the material world, they retained a spark of divinity, which could be recaptured through intellectual and spiritual regeneration.

Lorenzo de'Medici (1449–1492): Known as "the Magnificent," Lorenzo ruled Florence during its Golden Age. A strong advocate of **civic humanism** and a man of diverse interests, Lorenzo is most famous for this patronage of intellectuals and the arts. His untimely death in 1492 led to the invasion of Italy by foreign powers, as well as the decline of Renaissance culture in Florence.

Niccolo Machiavelli (1469–1527): One of the most famous figures of the Renaissance, Machiavelli's claim to fame is **The Prince**. Dedicated to the Medici family, the book serves as a manual for the realistic ruler who must appear virtuous, wise, and courageous (like a "lion"), at the same time ready to be ruthless and cunning (like a "fox"). Machiavelli denies the traditional notion that the political realm must uphold the laws of God. Politics expresses its own logic in the hard-headed rules of power, or **raison d'etat** (reason of state), which is why *The Prince* is often considered the first modern work of political science. It is important to remember the context for Machiavelli's writing—the invasion of Italy and its subsequent domination by foreign powers. *The Prince*, as well as Machiavelli's other writings endorsing citizen militias and republican government, can be seen collectively as patriotic appeals for a free and united Italy. After being tortured and losing his position in government, Machiavelli tried desperately to win back his influence, with little success. What is certain is that, fairly or unfairly, Machiavelli's name is associated with a brand of amoral politics both condemned and practiced since the sixteenth century.

Petrarch (1304–1374): Often called the "Father of Humanism," Petrarch helped popularize the notion that Italy was entering a new age of learning and individualism, distinct from the age of "ignorance" characteristic of the Middle Ages. Petrarch concerned himself with reviving a more pure form of Latin and, as such, spent most of his literary energies composing verse in the language, much of it related to a psychological portrait of humans and the theme of love, where he wrote of his beloved Laura.

Baldassar Castiglione (1478–1529): Castiglione first gained fame as a diplomat, but is most known for his **Book of the Courtier**, a how-to manual on winning fame and influence among the rich and powerful. To gain position and fortune, Castiglione counsels the "Renaissance Man" to be widely read in the classics, including history, poetry, music, and philosophy, as well as know how to conduct himself in public. The courtier will be skilled in the military arts, not to mention cultured and polished. In addition, Castiglione advocated education for women, but of a particular kind: a musical instrument, poetry, and literacy. Abstract subjects such as math and science were reserved for men.

Works in Oil, Marble, and Stone

Perhaps the Renaissance is most famous for its amazing production of renowned works of art. Several developments mark the upward trend of Renaissance art:

- *Oil-based paints*—Historically, artists had used tempera paints with an egg base, but with oil-based paints (from the Low Countries), artists could achieve more startling effects with light and shadow by applying layer after thin layer of paint.
- *Perspective*—For centuries, artists had attempted to achieve a realistic effect of three-dimensional space, but their methods tended to be haphazard and approximate. With the rediscovery of theories of optics and perspective geometry, Renaissance painters were able to achieve a strikingly realistic view of a visual plane.
- *Naturalism*—The Renaissance focus on the human body was reflected in its portrayal on canvas and in stone. Painters and sculptors gave increased attention to musculature and movement of the human body. This emphasis is clearly seen in Michelangelo's **Sistine Chapel**, where the master achieves a heroic view of humans, and also da Vinci's sketches from anatomical dissection.

- *Subject Matter*—While artists continued to focus on religious paintings, human beings, natural landscapes, and classical architecture play a more central role in these works.
- *Order and Symmetry*—In all three artistic media, Renaissance creators placed great stock on orderly composition. Architects employed proportion in their use of classical motifs such as the column, dome, and arch.
- *Status of the Artist*—Many artists of the Middle Ages are unknown, primarily because they were considered craftsmen. As patronage by wealthy merchants and the church increased, the reputation of artists as creative geniuses—people set apart—became the standard.

> **Heads Up!** To understand any artistic movement and its context, visual touchstones are essential. Try to find an art book and identify the features you see described here and in your text.

Donatello (1386–1466): Donatello revived the free-standing sculpture. His depiction of **David** is the first full-size statue cast in bronze since ancient times. The sculptor imbued his forms with psychological detail and expression, representing Renaissance naturalism.

Masaccio (1401–1428): Masaccio employed perspective geometry for the first time in his **Holy Trinity**, and also realized a depth of realism and three-dimensional space in a series of frescoes in the Brancacci Chapel, of which the "Expulsion of Adam and Eve from the Garden" is a highlight for depicting the agony and shame of the couple. Unfortunately, this master died young.

Fillipo Brunelleschi (1377–1446): Though an architect, Brunelleschi expressed interest in all the arts, including cast bronze and painting— it was he who helped develop the use of perspective geometry in painting. By far, Brunelleschi's primary achievement is the massive dome (**Il Duomo**) he created on the Cathedral of Florence, an amazing feat of artistic vision and engineering.

Leonardo da Vinci (1452–1519): Perhaps the foremost "Renaissance Man," da Vinci gained fame for just a few paintings—**Mona Lisa, The Last Supper,** and *Madonna of the Rocks*. His diverse interests led him into science, engineering, and anatomy. Da Vinci introduced the notion of systematic observation, which he tracked in his notebooks, written backwards to make it difficult for imitators to steal his ideas.

Michelangelo Buonarroti (1475–1564): With a name synonymous with genius, Michelangelo excelled in all the artistic media—sculpture (*David*, **Pieta**), painting (*Sistine Chapel*, **Last Judgment**), and architecture (**St. Peter's Basilica Dome**, *Laurentian Library*). The master's nudes offer a heroic vision of the human form influenced by neo-Platonic philosophy, though his later works express a darker vision. In addition, Michelangelo composed poetry and was working on another Pieta at the age of 89 when he died.

Raphael (1483–1520): The youngest of the great masters, and considered a rival of Michelangelo's, Raphael often sought artistic patronage in Rome, where the Renaissance refocused after about 1490. Raphael's **School of Athens** stands as a tribute to the ancient world and his fellow artists, as the Greek philosophers take on the physical appearance of his contemporaries. In addition, Raphael painted numerous portraits of the Madonna, the Mother of Jesus.

Education and the Printing Press

Renaissance humanism spurred education. Humanists founded schools for both boys and girls, though the latter tended to focus more on keeping appearances rather than mastery of abstract subject matter. **Latin** and **Greek** were prized by scholars of the fifteenth and sixteenth centuries, yet a truly well-rounded person needed to be conversant in all the liberal arts—grammar, music, arithmetic, geometry, astronomy, rhetoric, and logic—not to mention poetry, horsemanship, and military arts. Renaissance schools included structure and regular promotion of pupils from one level to the next, and in that sense, have influenced the values and curricula of schools today.

Sidebar: Though the focus of Renaissance publishing early on was Latin and Greek works, the printing press played a major role in helping to establish modern vernacular dialects. For example, the Tuscan dialect evolved into modern Italian as a result of the works of Dante and Boccaccio, which, while predating the press, inspired other authors to write in a similar style.

Though the Chinese invented printing, they did not capitalize on their success. Johann Gutenberg and his colleagues perfected the skill of movable type in the 1450s, publishing their famous Gutenberg Bible, of which several dozen still exist. Books continued to be expensive luxury items for the upper classes, but the dye had been cast. No longer could church or state exercise a monopoly on education or intellectual life. Certainly, the **printing press** assisted in the spread of the Renaissance and helped to establish standard versions of texts, but its most important impact was to secure the success of the Protestant Reformation. Few would deny that the invention of the printing press stands as one of the most, if not *the* most, significant technological developments of the past millennium.

WAS THERE A RENAISSANCE FOR WOMEN?

Though there were several well-regarded female humanists, women faced significant barriers to their intellectual pursuits. For the most part, the accepted notion was that women's focus lay in the domestic sphere. More enlightened humanists favored education for women, but even this never equaled the type of learning available to men. Nonetheless, women often played key political roles, especially when their statesmen husbands were off at war, and several gained fame for sponsoring the forerunners to the salons of the Enlightenment. In some ways, the status of women declined from the Middle Ages, as they came to be viewed as objects of art or pawns in marriage alliances, a fact accentuated by the gap in average ages between husband and wife. Some famous humanists and early feminists did leave a mark:

Christine de Pisan (1364–1431): A French noblewoman, de Pisan is believed to have published one of the first modern statements of feminism, *The City of Ladies*, which defends women's intellectual capabilities against antifemale bias. After her husband's death, she fought to retain her property and turned to writing to support her family; she may have been the first woman in European history to make a living through her writings.

Isabella d'Este (1474–1539): Often called the "First Lady of the World," d'Este married into the famous Gonzaga family of Mantua. After her husband departed for war, d'Este conducted diplomacy on his behalf (and sometimes behind his back). She also found time to establish schools for girls, attract humanists to her court, and write hundreds of letters of literary quality.

Laura Cereta (1469–1499): Cereta's life again illustrates the importance of marriage and early mortality. Her husband died after 18 months of marriage, and rather than enter a convent or remarry, Cereta wrote works advocating equality of opportunity for women. She, too, died young, however.

RENAISSANCE POLITICS AND THE NEW MONARCHS

Lest you forget, the Renaissance expressed concerns beyond paint and page. Politics was central to Renaissance views regarding power, status, and values such as civic humanism. As noted previously, Machiavelli's ideas played a major role in introducing a secular conception of politics, and historians such as Guicciardini emphasized impersonal social and political forces, rather than divine providence, in recounting the diplomacy and great events of the day. Given the divided nature of the Italian peninsula, regular diplomacy emerged to maintain the balance of power. Ambassadors no longer served Christendom generally, but instead patriotically—and often deviously—represented their city- or nation-state. To ensure that no one power gained dominance, the five major city-states continually jockeyed for position, thus the concept of **balance-of-power** politics, which would come to play such a central role in European diplomatic thinking, emerged. Perhaps the best example of this attitude is the **Peace of Lodi,** signed in 1454, which created a fairly stable arrangement that ensured 40 years of peace. Furthermore, the so-called **New Monarchs** aimed to reassert strong dynastic claims with centralizing techniques after the disasters of the fourteenth century.

Sidebar: Certainly other city-states played a role on the peninsula, but their power tended to be absorbed by their larger neighbors throughout the fifteenth century.

Though it is not necessary to have a detailed knowledge of each city-state, you should be passably familiar with the general characteristics.

City-State	Government	Key Figures	Assessment
Florence	A republic led by members of each of the many guilds, but really dominated behind the scenes by the Medici family, which made a fortune in banking.	***Cosimo de' Medici** (1389–1464)—Patriarch of the family. Wealthy patron of humanism who helped found the Florentine Platonic Academy. (See Lorenzo, his grandson, discussion earlier in this chapter.) ***Savanarola** (1452–1498)—Preached against the secular focus on art and pagan philosophy, eventually taking over the city before being burned at the stake.	Florence was the center of banking and textiles on the peninsula, and one of the richest of the city-states. This wealth helped make it the "Queen City of the Renaissance" before the invasion of Italy by the French in 1494. Many of the great names associated with Renaissance culture made their name in Florence.

City-State	Government	Key Figures	Assessment
Milan	A military dictatorship ruled by the **Visconti** family for centuries.	***Francesco Sforza** (1401–1466)—Seized control of the city in the 1450s, providing a good example of how reliance on mercenary soldiers—*condottiere*—helped to undermine Italy's independence.	Of the city-states, Milan was most closely tied to trading interests in central Europe. Strategically located, disputes over its control led to the invasion of foreign armies, and the ultimate end of the Renaissance.
Papal States	Technically ruled as a despotism by the papacy, it was really an elective monarchy that had difficulty managing the noble factions in its diverse territories.	***Alexander VI** (1492–1503)—From the Borgia line, he represents the height of corruption in the Renaissance Papacy. Used his children to cement marriage alliances and regain power on the peninsula. ***Julius II** (1503–1513)—Known as the "Warrior Pope," he led armies into battle and also sponsored grand art projects, such as the Sistine Chapel.	The period from 1417 to the 1540s is known as the **Renaissance Papacy,** and it is not a proud moment in the history of the Catholic Church. Popes were deeply involved in politics and seemed to the faithful more focused on luxury, art, and rebuilding Rome, which became the center of the **High Renaissance** after 1490. Because a line of popes ignored pleas for reform, the problems that would lead to the Protestant Reformation festered.
Venice	Technically a republic, but really an oligarchy ruled by wealthy merchant families. Nicknamed the **"Serene Republic"** for its stability throughout the era.	***doge**—Leader of the Venetian government chosen by the Great Council and Senate, two bodies consisting of wealthy merchants. ***Book of Gold**—Registry of the leading families in Venice; membership implied full citizenship rights.	The major trading power of the Italian city-states due to its contact with the Byzantine Empire and later the Ottoman Empire. Its arsenal represents one of the first factories in history. Finally, Venetian artists, such as **Titian** and Bellini, stressed light and color over line and composition.

City-State	Government	Key Figures	Assessment
Naples	Relatively backward feudal monarchy claimed and eventually won by Ferdinand of Aragon.		Though the city of Naples was Europe's largest in 1500, the kingdom participated little in the intellectual and artistic Renaissance.

The state as we know it today did not exist in 1500, yet the New Monarchs of this era were laying the foundations for the modern nation. To rebuild after the devastation of the fourteenth and early fifteenth centuries, monarchs engaged in similar policies, while at the same time addressing problems unique to their geographic location with more focused policies. General strategies of centralization consisted of the following:

1. **Taxation**—Securing access to consistent revenue.
2. **Taming the aristocracy**—Monarchs established that they were more than "first among equals" with other aristocrats by forming alliances with the middle class in towns and creating new nobles as officials, called the "**nobles of the robe**" (because their status came from their official capacities).
3. **Codifying laws and creating courts**—Most nations were still a patchwork of customs, dialects, and legal traditions in 1500, so monarchs attempted to establish royal courts that applied more uniform laws.
4. **Controlling warfare**—Medieval armies were private affairs, and thus less than reliable. The New Monarchs worked to make armies and war the sole preserve of the state, which made sense given the increasingly complex nature of war.
5. **Early bureaucracy and officials**—Early states lacked the mechanisms to enforce their will, let alone keep track of the affairs of government. To remedy this, monarchs began to employ agencies, committees, representative bodies, and councils to assist in implementing royal authority.
6. **Religious control**—The medieval tension between religious and secular authority began to tilt in favor of the latter, even before the Protestant Reformation, as monarchs attempted to assert increased authority over the clergy and the functions of religion within their national boundaries.

Now let's look briefly through the following chart at how these general strategies were applied in specific instances. Throughout this review guide, I will use a straightforward conceptual device to assist you in keeping track of nations, rulers, and policies: Challenges (what issues and problems did the nation/ruler face) → Response (what policies the ruler/nation enacted to address these issues) → Result (what impact these policies had on the nation's strategic position).

Nation	Challenges	Response	Result
England	Following the Hundred Years' War, England was plunged into the **Wars of the Roses,** a civil conflict between two factions of nobles. When the war ended in 1485, the **Tudors** set about rebuilding the power of the state.	* **Henry VII** (1485–1509) and **Henry VIII** (1509–47) tamed the nobles, reducing the number of dukes from 9 to 2, and created a new aristocracy. * **Star Chamber**—royal system of courts established. * Ended livery and maintenance, the private armies of the nobles. * Built England's first state navy. * Henry VIII took control of the Catholic Church in England and confiscated its lands.	The Tudors established the basis of English political and commercial power. However, Henry VIII's obsession with producing a male heir demonstrated the continuing fragility of royal rule and also created a religious issue that would not be easily resolved.
France	France had experienced warfare on its soil for over 100 years, while its eastern neighbor Burgundy aimed to replace French leadership on the continent.	* **Louis XI, the "Spider"** (1461–1483) added new territory to the royal domain through strategic marriages and by conquering part of Burgundy. * **Francis I** (1515–1547), a Renaissance king, gained control of the French clergy by agreement with the pope (**Concordat of Bologna**) * Established taxation with *taille* (direct tax) and *gabelle* (government salt monopoly). * Claimed lands in Italy.	France extended its territory, laid a secure foundation for taxes, and created the largest army in Europe. This represents a strong recovery from the Hundred Years' War, but the kingdom continued to face encirclement by the Habsburgs.
Russia	The truncated duchy of Muscovy barely resembled the Russia of today, as it was threatened by powerful neighbors such as the Mongols and Poland.	* **Ivan III, the "Great"** (1462–1505) drove out the Mongols, claimed Moscow as the "**Third Rome**" by marrying niece of last Byzantine emperor, and created the *streltsy*, a military service class. * **Ivan IV, the "Terrible"** (1547–1584)—so nicknamed because of his hatred of the *boyars* (nobles), also continued Russian expansion.	Russia emerged as a great power, yet continued to face issues of cultural and technological backwardness. When Ivan IV killed his heir in a fit of rage, it plunged Russia into civil chaos and foreign invasion for 30 years.

Nation	Challenges	Response	Result
Spain	Spain did not even exist until the marriage of Ferdinand and Isabella in 1469, and even then, Spain needed to complete the *reconquista* of the Moors and establish a national identity among its diverse kingdoms.	* **Isabella of Castile's** (1479–1504) and **Ferdinand of Aragon's** (1479–1516) marriage did not create a unified nation. * Made alliances with towns (*hermandades*) to establish law and order. * Personally visited each area of the country. * Completed *reconquista*. * Established strict religious orthodoxy with **Spanish Inquisition** (from 1478) and **expelled Jews** in 1492. * Sponsored voyages of exploration. * **Charles I** (aka Charles V in the Holy Roman Empire, 1516–1555) inherited diverse lands and became the most powerful monarch in Europe.	Spain emerged as the strongest nation in Europe. Access to the wealth of the New World and Charles's inheritance of numerous lands established Spain's Golden Age. However, its crusading mindset, heavy taxes, and persecution of talented minorities had already sapped some of its strength by the end of Charles's rule.

NORTHERN RENAISSANCE AND CHRISTIAN HUMANISM

Renaissance culture began in Italy but quickly spread via the new printing press and along trade routes to the rest of Europe. It was particularly strong in the Low Countries (today's Netherlands and Belgium), France, England, and Germany, though almost every nation experienced some manifestation of humanist learning and classical revival.

Though northern humanists employed the same tactics of textual analysis and criticism as their Italian neighbors, their emphasis tended to be on Christian readings, such as the Bible, but also included the writings of the early church fathers (St. Augustine, for example). For this reason, northern humanism is often called **Christian humanism.** In general, Christian humanists were critical of many of the Catholic Church's abuses, but wished to maintain the unity of Christianity by reforming from within. Many intelligent observers recognized that the ark of the church was listing badly and desperately needed repairs. The split that occurred in the sixteenth century revolved around this issue—whether the ship could be saved or should simply be abandoned in favor of a more stable vessel. Years before Luther, Christian humanists urged a reform, primarily through education, that would rescue the church from its worldliness and corruption. Though numerous Christian humanists labored to save the church, two clearly stand out for their literary accomplishments and clear teachings.

Before we address Erasmus and Thomas More, we need to paint a picture of late medieval spirituality. Perhaps the best word to describe the mindset of the fourteenth and fifteenth centuries is "anxiety." Amidst the death and upheaval of the plague, Great Schism, and political breakdown, European Christians became obsessed with securing eternal life. On one hand, this fear fed the mechanical exercises of **indulgences,** relic veneration, and pilgrimages. In a positive sense, many Christians deeply desired a meaningful experience with God. Some turned to **mysticism**—the belief that the Christian can bridge the gap between himself and the Almighty through meditation, prayer, and other acts of devotion. A popular book in this regard was Thomas à Kempis's *Imitation of Christ*, which provided daily exercises to commune directly with God. In the Low Countries and Germany, an organization of laypersons (not members of the clergy) called the **Brothers and Sisters of the Common Life** ministered to the poor, founded schools for the education of character, and supported each other in living a Christian life. Clearly, religion remained dearly important to many; if it had not, the influence of the Catholic Church might have faded slowly without any disruptive spread of a new and vibrant Protestant theology.

Desiderius Erasmus (1466–1536) stood as the most famous intellectual of his day, and his name today remains a symbol of tolerance and scholarship. Raised in a monastic environment, he never took vows, claiming he had "a Catholic soul but a Lutheran stomach" (and thus was not able to withstand the church's demand for ritual fasting). With humor and style, Erasmus poked fun at the clergy and its abuses in works such as the *Praise of Folly*, which was eventually placed on the Index of Prohibited Books. Erasmus's primary message, as seen in *Handbook of the Christian Knight* and *On Civility in Children*, lay in the power of education to promote true reverence for God and in living out the Gospel message. Protected by powerful patrons, Erasmus condemned fanaticism of all kinds, and while his reputation remained undiminished by his death, his voice of moderation had been drowned out by extremists on all sides. He might have opposed the sentiment, but it is often said that "Erasmus laid the egg that Luther hatched."

> **Sidebar:** More's life has been forever memorialized in the brilliant play (and movie) *A Man for All Seasons.* While great drama and doing justice to More's intellect, it tends to portray More as a modern martyr to freedom of conscience. In fact, More had on occasion presided over the execution of Lutheran "heretics" in England and died for his *specific* belief of the primacy of spiritual authority, not for modern civil liberties. More was canonized (made a saint) in 1935.

Perhaps no intellectual better represents the bridging of the medieval and modern worlds than **Thomas More** (1478–1535). A man of deep piety (More wore a hairshirt—a rough and painful undergarment made of goat's wool–to mortify his flesh throughout much of his life), More well understood the "game" of life in this world, where one sought fame and position, but always kept a careful eye on the next. More's talents brought him to the attention of the monarchy, where he served in Parliament and as the first nonclerical Lord Chancellor (the highest judicial position in England). More's literary fame rests primarily on *Utopia*, a satire of sixteenth-century European society, and vision of a better life based on communal living. A friend of Erasmus, More possessed less of his comrade's moderate tendencies. More *was* willing to die for his beliefs, which occurred when he opposed Henry VIII's takeover of the Catholic Church. The scholar's last days were spent in the Tower of London, before his beheading in 1535, another victim of the growing rift between religious and political authority.

CAUSES OF THE PROTESTANT REFORMATION

We have already hinted at several causes of the Protestant Reformation—Christian humanism, late medieval spirituality, and the state of the Catholic Church—but now it is time to focus on the last of these. Simply put, the Catholic Church in 1500 stood amidst a crisis. Desperate to recapture its former glory and influence, the papacy seemed to focus more on artistic patronage and Machiavellian politics than the spiritual state of its flock. Abuses that began during the Babylonian Captivity festered and produced a general cry for reform, a cry generally ignored by corrupt popes fearful of limits on their power by church councils. These abuses were:

- **Simony**—The buying and selling of high church offices, which often produced a revenue (annates) for the holder
- **Nepotism**—The granting of offices to relatives (e.g., Pope Alexander VI conferred a cardinal's hat upon his 16-year-old son)
- **Pluralism**—The holding of multiple church offices
- **Absenteeism**—Not residing in one's spiritual domain because one held multiple positions
- **Indulgences**—The most controversial, the belief that a believer could draw on Jesus' and the saints' previous stock of grace to reduce the sinner's or a relative's time in **purgatory** (that region between heaven and hell reserved for the final "purging" of sinful souls)

It was this last abuse that sparked the Reformation, but prior to this spark, recall that a goodly pile of tinder had been accumulating for generations.

THE PROTESTANT REFORM MOVEMENTS

Luther and Lutheranism

The Protestant Reformation began with one man's spiritual crisis. This crisis revolved around a nagging but central question in Christianity: "How can I be saved?" It is common to think of Luther as attacking the abuses of the church, but his critique went well beyond that. Luther questioned not only the practices of the church, but condemned it for *teaching* wrongly, ultimately calling into question the entire sacramental system of Catholicism as it related to salvation.

In a complex transaction, **Pope Leo X** (1513–1521) allowed in 1517 the sale of indulgences by the monk **Johan Tetzel** (a sort of medieval used-car salesman) to finance the building of St. Peter's Basilica in Rome. Luther responded almost immediately with the **Ninety-Five Theses,** wherein he condemned indulgences as twisting the central mystery of Christianity—Jesus' crucifixion as a once-and-for-all sacrifice wiping the human slate clean of sin and death. Previous to the indulgence controversy, Luther had been working out in his reading and lecturing a different conception of salvation. The decisive break only became clear to him (and eventually to the Catholic Church) over the next few years, as Luther continued to publish pamphlets elaborating his ideas and denouncing what he considered false teachings. Luther's new theology can be summarized in three Latin phrases:

> **Sidebar:** It is one of the ironies of history that the church most associated with the spiritual home of Catholicism and a paragon of High Renaissance architecture (the dome was designed by Michelangelo and inspired the Capitol dome in Washington, D.C.) helped to drive a wedge into Christian unity.

- **Sola scriptura**—The only authority in Christianity is the Bible. While the Catholic Church had based authority on Scripture *and* the teaching function of the church (the magisterium) in the persons of the bishops, cardinals, and popes, Luther argued that doctrine or practice needed to be supported by the revealed word of God *alone.*
- **Sola fide**—Salvation comes from faith alone. As Luther put it, "Good works do not make a good man, but a good man does good works." Faith is a free gift of God and cannot be "earned" through any human activity, such as pilgrimages, relic veneration, or indulgences.

- **Sola gratia**—Salvation comes by the free gift of God's grace. Grace is the spiritual quality that gives the sinner merit in the eyes of God. Since humans are incapable of acquiring this merit through their own sinful efforts, it must be God's free gift. In contrast, the Catholic Church held that the primary instruments of grace were the sacraments; in short, that grace was mediated through the clergy.

In some ways, Luther's attack only echoed many of the critiques made by Hus, Wyclif, and even Erasmus. What made Lutheranism successful was the urgency and passion with which Luther conveyed his message, and, more important, the printing press. It is hard to imagine the Protestant Reformation's success without the tremendous propaganda instrument of the cheaply printed word. To illustrate, in the first 10 years of the Reformation, one-quarter of the books published in Germany were by Luther. In addition, many of the publications were not designed to appeal to intellectual theologians. Songs, sermons, and woodcuts mocking the Pope all appealed to a mass audience. Several of Luther's publications with which you should be familiar include:

- "On the Freedom of the Christian" (1520)—A short pamphlet in which Luther rejects the notion of free will when it comes to salvation. Why, Luther asks, would I want to be in charge of my salvation when God can do it so much better? The work prompted Erasmus uncharacteristically to reply to Luther by defending free will.
- *On the Babylonian Captivity of the Church* (1520)—This is a longer work, in Latin, for theologians. Here Luther condemned the Catholic conception of the sacraments as holding the faithful "in bondage" to the earthly power of the clergy. In addition, Luther retained only two sacraments—**baptism** and the **Lord's Supper**—because these had scriptural justification.
- *An Address to the Nobility of the German Nation* (1520)—Recognizing he needed political support in the Empire, Luther patriotically appealed to the German princes to support his cause and thereby resist Roman taxation and power.
- German translation of the Bible (1530s)—Traditionally Bible reading had been reserved for theologians or clergymen. By rendering the Bible into his native tongue, Luther made clear that the Bible was to be read by all, including women, and placed it front and center as an act of Christian worship.

It is often said that Luther demonstrated the fire of a theological revolutionary but the caution of a social and political conservative. No doubt, Luther was a complex figure who recognized that his attack on the Catholic Church held the potential to rip the whole of society apart. For Luther, the "real" church was the spiritual one of the next world; because perfection could not be reached on earth due to the sinful nature of humans, social and political revolution was self-defeating.

Luther's message inspired a gaggle of other reformers, many of whom interpreted it in more radical ways. German firebrands, such as Andreas Carlstadt and Thomas Müntzer, applied Luther's idea of the "**priesthood of all believers**" more literally, to indicate a move toward social equality. These leaders supported the **Peasants' Revolt of 1524–1525,** the product of long-standing economic grievances and the new religious ideals. Luther was incensed, denouncing the firebrands and the peasants in "**Against the Murdering and Robbing Horde of Peasants,**" wherein he called for the death of all who challenged legitimate authority and who perverted the true Christian message, which was spiritual not political. Ultimately, the peasants were crushed at the cost of 100,000 lives, and Luther gained a reputation for intolerance that might have spent some steam from his movement in the 1530s. Another reason for Luther's attitude toward social upheaval lies in his need for support among the German princes, the only force standing between him and Charles V, the Holy Roman Emperor, before whom Luther in 1521 stood in defiance at the **Diet of Worms.** As a result, wherever Lutheranism became the dominant religion (much of Germany and Scandinavia), the church was placed under the control of the state.

Through a series of timely marriages and untimely deaths, **Charles V** (1516–1556) stood in 1519 as the most powerful ruler in Europe, controlling Spain, the Low Countries, the Holy Roman Empire, significant parts of Italy, and the Spanish Empire in the New World. Charles recognized the need for reform in the church and continually pressured the pope to call a general council (unsuccessfully until 1545). At the same time, Charles believed it his duty to maintain the political unity of Catholicism. Unfortunately for him, Charles's entire reign was spent on horseback attempting to keep his far-flung possessions together in the face of his many enemies:

- **Ottoman Turks**—The Ottomans killed Charles's brother-in-law Louis in battle in 1526, taking Hungary, and moved to besiege Vienna (the capital of the Habsburg dominions) in 1529.
- **France (Valois)**—Francis I represented Charles's most consistent rival. The perennial goal of France aimed to avoid encirclement by the Habsburgs and prevent the centralization of power in Germany. The **Habsburg-Valois Wars** (1494–1559) began in Italy but eventually intruded into the outcome of the Reformation in Germany, as Francis, though a Catholic, took the side of the German Protestants.
- **Algerian pirates**—Spain's interests in the Mediterranean were continuously threatened by piracy based in North Africa. Charles launched an expedition in 1541 that temporarily helped the problem.
- **The Papacy**—Though both Charles and the pope shared an interest in salvaging Catholicism, they differed over tactics and political goals, especially when Charles's troops **sacked Rome in 1527,** effectively bringing the Renaissance to an end.
- **German Lutherans**—Because of other preoccupations, Charles was forced to compromise with Lutherans early in his reign. An imperial diet in 1529 at Speyer attempted to impose a religious settlement but failed when Lutherans protested (which accounts for the term "Protestant"). By 1546, Charles was prepared to solve the issue through force. The Lutheran princes had formed the **Schmalkaldic League** and were prepared to resist with the aid of outside powers. After an initial victory in 1547 at Muhlberg, Charles was unable to follow on his success.

To settle the religious conflict in Germany (sometimes termed the "First Thirty Years' War"), Charles agreed in 1555 to the **Peace of Augsburg,** which employed the compromise formula *cuius regio, eius religio* ("Whose rule, his religion") to divide the Empire between Lutheran and Catholic areas, to be determined by the individual rulers. It is important to note that this settlement did *not* endorse religious toleration, only to recognize the relatively even balance of religious power in Germany. In addition, Charles V abdicated in 1556, splitting his realm between his brother Ferdinand (as HRE) and his son Philip II, who took everything else.

> **Sidebar:** A future result of this split was that two Habsburg lines emerged—one Spanish, one Austrian—with the two lines continually intermarrying to maintain diplomatic unity. Eventually this caused problems genetically, culminating with the last Habsburg king of Spain, Charles II, whose mental and physical debilities, including sterility, precipitated a major succession war.

Calvin's Second Wave

By 1540, the Protestant Reformation already required a boost; **John Calvin** (1509–1564) provided just that. A second-generation reformer, Calvin was born in France and received a strong humanist education. Unlike Luther, Calvin studied to be a priest but switched to the legal profession, which may account for the strong images in Calvinism of God as the omnipotent sovereign and law-giver. Calvin set up his reform movement in Switzerland, and after some initial turmoil was recognized as the unquestioned leader of **Geneva.**

Calvin accepted much of Luther's reformed theology (justification by faith alone, two sacraments) but placed more emphasis on **predestination,** the notion that God foreknows and forejudges each individual prior to birth. Those who were saved ("the elect") did not suffer from spiritual complacency, as one might expect, but a zealous determination to create the "Most Holy City on Earth." In *Institutes of the Christian Religion*, originally published in 1536 but succeeding through numerous editions, Calvin synthesized a generation of reformed theology, while providing tactics for organizing a reformed movement. Genevan politics were guided by the **Ecclesiastical Ordinances,** which divided the church into doctors (who studied scripture), pastors (who preached the word of God), deacons (who administered charity), and elders (who ensured discipline). Elders employed the **Consistory** to practice "Christian watchfulness" and punish those who violated laws on public morality, against public drunkenness, gambling, and so on. Compared with Luther, Calvin believed the fundamental purpose of the political system was to fulfill the moral law of a Christian community. Though not a theocracy, church leaders played a major role in ensuring that public affairs were governed by church teachings.

Calvinism spread quickly among the nobility and the middle class, many of whom likely believed themselves to be the elect and who resented the privileges of the clergy. To promote the spread of the Reformation, Calvin founded the **Genevan Academy** in 1559, designed to train leaders who would sow the seeds of Calvinism in other locales. Perhaps the most famous graduate was **John Knox** (1505–1572), who brought Calvinism to Scotland. Taking their cue from their leader and minority status in most nations, Calvinists represented the forefront of a militant Protestant movement dedicated to battling the still-strong power of Catholicism.

Evangelical Reformers

Some historians divide the Reformation into evangelical and magisterial branches. The former refers to the grassroots movement of individual persons, towns, and communities spreading the new reform gospel through preaching, conversion, and town disputations. In this last, advocates of both the established Catholic faith and the new reformed faith would debate, with the town voting as a whole whether to adopt the reformed faith. Some reform, however, was imposed from the top down, by magistrates, princes, and monarchs. We'll discuss the most famous example of this magisterial reform in the next section, but now let's look at some of the more radical reformers.

Ulrich Zwingli (1484–1531) claimed to preach a reformed message prior to Luther, but there is little evidence for this. Zwingli did serve as a chaplain to the many Swiss mercenaries who were often forced by poor economics to sell their services to a variety of nations. It was in his native Zurich where Zwingli established a reformed movement more radical in style than Luther's. Like Luther, Zwingli accepted two sacraments but disagreed with him over the meaning of the Lord's Supper. While Luther argued a real presence of Jesus coexisted with the bread and wine (called **consubstantiation**—"two substances together"), Zwingli held Luther's position to be illogical. Jesus was in heaven at the right hand of the Father and could not be present in body and blood during services; the sacrament was symbolic only. In the context of the mounting power of the emperor, Luther and Zwingli met to attempt to settle their disagreement. The subsequent **Marburg Colloquy** failed miserably, and as a result, Zwingli was killed in 1531 in the Swiss Civil War. Before he died, however, Zwingli had laid the basis for a different style of worship. Followers of Zwingli broke organs, smashed statuary, and painted churches white, all in an effort to focus the believer's attention on the Word of God.

The first 20 years of the Reformation was a period of great ferment and experimentation. In many areas, it was women who first accepted the reform message, spreading the gospel and converting their husbands, father, and brothers. A famous example is **Catherine Zell** (1498–1562), who, along with her husband Matthias, preached, wrote, and ministered to the poor. One movement most associated with this trend toward equality was the Anabaptism. **Anabaptists** believed membership in a Christian community was an adult choice, and therefore practiced adult baptism. More important, they tended to take the Bible more literally when it came to living a life apart from worldly temptations. Because they practiced adult baptism—thereby putting the souls of unbaptized babies in peril—and advocated the total separation of church and state, Anabaptists were hated by Catholics and other Protestant denominations. For the most part, Anabaptists lived in small, peaceful communities and posed little real threat to the state. An exception is the movement established in the 1530s in Munster, Germany, where a mystical personality—Jan of Leiden—declared himself King of Munster, introduced polygamy, burned all books but the Bible, and proclaimed the imminent end of the world. Jan and his followers were captured by a joint Catholic-Lutheran army in 1536. One matter Catholics and Lutherans could agree on was that movements like Munster's went too far: Jan of Leiden was tortured and executed.

Magisterial Reform in England

The most well-known example of magisterial reform occurred in England. Though Lutheran ideas had gained a few adherents in the kingdom, **Henry VIII** (1509–1547) tolerated little opposition to the Catholic faith, having earned the title "Defender of the Faith" for penning a response to Luther's attack on the sacraments. However, matters of state intervened. Henry had no male heir, and blamed his marriage to Catherine of Aragon. Normally Henry's appeal for a divorce would have been granted by **Pope Clement VII** (1523–1534), but he was under the control of Charles V, who happened to be the nephew of Catherine.

After years and numerous appeals, Henry was desperate, having fallen in love with Anne Boleyn, whom he had impregnated. In 1533, Henry acted with the support of the Parliament. First, the Parliament declared Henry the head of the Catholic Church in England with the **Act of Supremacy.** Further, the **Act of Succession** legitimated the offspring of Henry and Anne (the future Elizabeth I). With the aid of his primary minister, **Thomas Cromwell,** Henry also moved to confiscate the lands of the church. However, Henry held no interest in religious reform, getting Parliament to confirm distinctive Catholic practices such as clerical celibacy in the **Six Articles.** Many English reformers, such as the new Archbishop of Canterbury **Thomas Cranmer,** wished to take the reform further. They would have to wait until Henry died and his sickly teenage son, **Edward VI** (1547–1553), succeeded him in 1547.

Under Edward, the reform moved in more of a Zwinglian direction, with a new **Book of Common Prayer** and **Act of Uniformity** providing a simpler interpretation of worship. Edward's early death in 1553 turned England back once again into the Catholic camp, under **Mary I** (1553–1558), the daughter of the scorned Catherine of Aragon and wife of the Most Holy Catholic **Philip II** (1556–1598), king of Spain. Mary's persecution of Protestants, memorialized in the famous *Foxe's Book of Martyrs,* and pro-Spanish foreign policy earned her the nickname "**Bloody Mary**" and did little in the long run to reestablish Catholicism in England.

It was **Elizabeth I** (1558–1603) who met with the most success in establishing a compromise, often called the **Elizabethan Settlement.** Under house arrest for much of her youth, Elizabeth

Sidebar: Mary married into a powerful French noble family (the Guises) and was raised in France while the reformation brewed in her homeland. Though vivacious and educated, Mary was hated by reformers like John Knox for her defense of Catholicism and the scandalous nature of her love relationships. After her execution, Mary's son, James, became the rule of both Scotland and England, initiating the Stuart line in the latter.

learned the dangers of religious dogmatism. In fact, Elizabeth represented a new type of leader, termed a *politique*, or one who places political unity above conformity to religious dogma. During her reign, Elizabeth had many suitors but ultimately played the role of matriarch of the nation, never marrying. She refrained from persecuting religious minorities—with the exception of Catholics—and engineered a new Book of Common Prayer, vague enough in its language to satisfy all interpretations. These compromises were cemented in the **Thirty-Nine Articles.** At the same time, Elizabeth could play the "lion," as she demonstrated by executing her cousin, Mary of Scotland, for plotting against her, and defending England in 1588 against the impending **Spanish Armada.** By the end of her reign, often called the Golden Age, Elizabeth had established England as the leading Protestant power in Europe.

SOCIAL IMPACT OF THE PROTESTANT REFORMATION

The Protestant Reformation was primarily a religious movement, yet it led to profound consequences for social life. Movements of intellectual or cultural change often attract those—women, peasants, workers, minorities—who wish to change other features of society. Invariably, these movements eventually come to formalize and institutionalize new forms of life to avoid more wrenching changes. In that sense, the Protestant Reformation can be viewed as a significant shift but also a lost opportunity for many groups. We now look briefly at several affected areas:

- **Family and gender**—As a result of the Protestant Reformation, family was placed at the center of social life. Celibacy was abolished, and many former clergy, like Luther, took spouses and glorified the marital bond as the most natural and God-like. For women, the results were mixed. Though women preached early on and earned limited rights of divorce, as well as education, Luther, Calvin, and other reformers preached that women's natural sphere was the domestic. Further, religious vocations and female religious images were removed from churches.

- **Education**—There is no doubt that the Protestant Reformation spurred education. With the emphasis on Bible-reading, it was important to ensure literacy for boys *and* girls. Luther's colleague and defender, **Philip Melancthon** (1497–1560), earned the nickname *Praeceptor Germanie* (Teacher of Germany) for advocating a system of basic schooling called the *Gymnasia*. After the establishment of the Jesuits, Catholic nations began to place increasing importance on education.

- **Social classes**—Other than the firebrands, few reformers explicitly argued for social equality. However, some historians have argued that a "**Protestant work ethic**" spurred the development of capitalism, and thus strengthened the middle class. Supposedly, the emphasis on deferring gratification and building a godly city on earth led to an ethic of hard work and capital accumulation. (This interpretation is problematic, but you probably will earn points in an essay for mentioning it.)

- **Religious practices**—For centuries, European religious life had centered around the church calendar, with its saints' feast days, **Carnival** and **Lent,** sacraments, rituals, and clerical importance. In many lands, these practices were either abolished or modified. Protestant nations placed more emphasis on Bible-reading and sought to eliminate externals, such as relics, pilgrimages, and festivals. Even many Catholic nations attempted more rigorously to monitor excessive practices and curb long-accepted "sins" such as prostitution.

CATHOLIC REVIVAL AND REFORM

Even before 1517, many Catholics recognized the need for reform. In fact, reform was already under way if we consider the lay piety movement and the writings of Christian humanists. Under **Cardinal Ximenes de Cisneros** (1436–1517), Spain had already addressed many clerical abuses and had tightened regulations for the training of priests. However, the institutional church, led by the papacy throughout the early sixteenth century, "fiddled while Rome burned." Finally, under the pontificate of **Paul III** (1534–1549), the hierarchical church finally responded to the challenge of the Protestant Reformation. The Catholic response to the reformation was multipronged and complex. Those actions designed to revive Catholic spirituality are often termed the **Catholic Reformation,** while those designed negatively to stop the spread of the Protestant Reformation are called the **Counter-Reformation.** Following is a list of the actions, positive and negative, taken by the Catholic Church in response to the Protestant Reformation.

- **New religious orders**—For most Catholics, their connection to the church was their parish priest. Thus, a major element of reform involved the revival of religious orders and the establishment of new ones. The most important of these was the Society of Jesus, or **Jesuits,** founded by **Ignatius Loyola** (1491–1556) in the 1540s. Like Luther, Loyola underwent a spiritual conversion. After being injured in battle, Loyola practiced rigorous acts of self-discipline and recommitted himself to the mysteries of the church. His important book, *Spiritual Exercises*, contains the famous phrase, "If I see a thing to be white but the institutional church commands it to be black, I will see it as black." Jesuits had no national base, seeing themselves as the "troops of the Pope" and missionaries to those who did not know Christ. Jesuits worked primarily through education and argument, and their efforts paid off by re-Catholicizing large parts of Eastern Europe, including Poland and Hungary after 1560.Other religious orders focused on charitable works and education. **Angela Merici** (1474–1540) founded the Ursulines to bring education to girls. The Spanish mystic, **Teresa of Avila** (1515–1582), saw mystical visions of Jesus and founded the discalced (without shoes) Carmelites dedicated to a life of contemplation and service. Also, a group of clergy and laypeople formed the **Oratory of Divine Love** to push for reform in the church and assist one another in leading lives of simply piety. Finally, a new breed of austere and hardworking bishops emerged, such as **Gian Matteo Giberti** (1495–1543) of Verona and **Cardinal Charles Borromeo** (1538–1584) of Milan.
- **Council of Trent (1545–1563)**—Though rather tardy and poorly attended, the council finally got the church's house in order. First, the Cardinals (most from Italy and Spain) eliminated many church abuses and provided for better education and regulation of priests. Second, the church refused to compromise on religious doctrines, reaffirming distinctive Catholic practices such as clerical celibacy, the importance of good works, the authority of the papacy, and **transubstantiation.** According to the last, the bread and wine, though retaining the "incidents" of bread and wine such as taste and texture, are truly transformed into another substance (the body and blood of Jesus) during the **Mass.**
- **Strengthening the Papacy and Inquisition (1542)**—To better meet the challenge of unorthodox belief, the Papal bureaucracy was centralized and strengthened. A major feature of this revamping was the creation of the **Roman Inquisition** (not to be confused with the

Spanish Inquisition), designed to root out perceived heresies. In the long run, the Inquisition had a chilling effect on intellectual life in Italy, as can be seen by the Galileo incident in 1633.

- **Index of Prohibited Books**—Under the conservative pontificate of **Pope Paul IV** (1555–1559), the church decided to clamp down on any printed materials that threatened to mislead the faithful away from the orthodox interpretations of the magisterium. Though of limited impact, the Index continued until the twentieth century.
- **Baroque Art**—In an effort to revive Catholic spirituality, the church patronized an artistic movement that emphasized grandeur, illusion, and dramatic religiosity. In music, Palestrina composed numerous masses and sacred pieces geared toward arousing strong religious emotion. Multitalented artists such as **Giovanni Lorenzo Bernini** (1598–1680) helped rebuild Rome as a showplace of Catholic piety.

How successful was the Catholic response? By 1560, the religious divide in Europe was an accomplished fact; in that sense, the Catholic response came too little and too late. On the other hand, some parts of Europe had been re-Catholicized, and the church emerged from its reforms stronger and more militant than in 1500, before the Reformation. One fact is sure: after the completion of the Council of Trent's work in 1564, no religious compromise was possible. With a militant Calvinism and revived and rearmed Catholic Church, an extended period of religious conflict lay on the horizon.

ADDITIONAL RESOURCES

Bainton, Roland, *Here I Stand: A Life of Martin Luther* (1994)—Considered the classic account of an important figure.

Burke, Peter, *The Renaissance: Culture and Society in Italy* (1999)—Explains the concept of the Renaissance and offers a complex account of how applicable the term is.

Crosby, Alfred W., *The Measure of Reality: Quantification and Western Society, 1250–1600* (1997)—Explores the development of quantitative thinking in the later Middle Ages and Renaissance—a challenging but fairly brief and interesting read.

Erikson, Erik, *Young Man Luther: A Study in Psychoanalysis and History* (1962)—One of the first biographies employing psychoanalytic methods; by a noted psychiatrist, and controversial in its conclusions.

Mattingly, Garrett, *Renaissance Diplomacy* (1971)—Still considered the standard work on the subject.

Rabb, Theodore K., *Renaissance Lives: Portraits of an Age* (1993)—Brief and vivid biographies of representative and leading figures.

Rice, Eugene F., and Anthony Grafton, *The Foundations of Early Modern Europe, 1460–1559* (1993)—The first volume in the accessible Norton History of Modern Europe provides a solid and well-written overview of the period.

Tuchman, Barbara, *A Distant Mirror: The Calamitous Fourteenth Century* (1978)—Readable account of a difficult century by a popular historian.

McNeill, William H., *Plagues and Peoples* (1976)—Examines the impact of disease in world history.

PRACTICE QUESTIONS

1. A major impact of the Black Death (1348–1351) in European social life included which of the following?
    a. a period of increased creativity and spirituality in art
    b. a revival of confidence in the Catholic Church
    c. a successful overthrow of the social order
    d. the decline of manorialism in western Europe
    e. the strengthening of family bonds

2. When the papacy returned in 1417 to Rome to end the Great Schism, popes were criticized most strongly for which of the following?
    a. focusing too much on secular and worldly concerns
    b. continuing to promote Scholastic learning
    c. attacking new developments in art and philosophy
    d. intervening in conflicts between France and Spain
    e. sponsoring Christian humanist writings

3. All of the following account for the Renaissance occurring first in Italy EXCEPT:
    a. its location on major trade routes in the Mediterranean.
    b. its proximity to centers of classical culture.
    c. its centralized monarchy able to promote art.
    d. its high degree of urban development.
    e. its active culture of the city-states.

4. The building pictured below, the Pazzi Chapel, best demonstrates the Renaissance architectural interest in which of the following?

    a. vertical lines, to demonstrate an upward ascent toward God
    b. classical principles of order and symmetry
    c. humble and human-centered spaces
    d. a focus on the achievements of the single individual
    e. the dominance of secular over religious concerns

5. In which area did women experience the greatest increase in opportunities during the Renaissance?
   a. education
   b. religion
   c. politics
   d. art
   e. philosophy

6. The New Monarchs of the sixteenth century attempted to accomplish which of the following?
   a. the reduction of war as an instrument of foreign policy
   b. toleration of religious minorities in order to gain support
   c. an alliance with the nobles to tame the independent towns
   d. deference to the papacy in matters of public policy
   e. the centralization of power and direction of armies

7. Which of the following is the best explanation for Martin Luther's condemnation of the German Peasants' Revolt, 1524–1525?
   a. Luther feared that the emperor would use the revolt as an excuse to reassert his control.
   b. The peasants' attack on Jewish communities violated Luther's support for religious toleration.
   c. Luther did not wish his ideas of spiritual equality to be used to overthrow the existing social order.
   d. Luther was a pacifist and believed that all violence contradicted the direct teachings of the Bible.
   e. The revolt threatened to spread into Switzerland and harm Luther's newly formed alliance with Zwingli.

8. Which of the following groups was most likely to allow women to preach and spread the message of the Reformation?
   a. Lutherans
   b. Calvinists
   c. Anglicans
   d. Anabaptists
   e. Zwinglians

9. Of the following, which is the most accurate characterization of the Catholic response to the Protestant Reformation?
   a. By 1560, most areas of Europe had returned to the Catholic faith.
   b. At the Council of Trent (1545–1563), the Church refused compromise with Protestants.
   c. The power of the clergy was greatly diminished and religious orders disbanded.
   d. The power of the papacy was weakened and given over to church councils.
   e. The Catholic Church did little if anything to respond to the Protestant Reformation.

10. Which of the following best describes Henry VIII's motives for his break with the Catholic Church?
    a. Henry wished to control the church but leave doctrine untouched.
    b. Henry had been deeply influenced by Lutheran theology.
    c. Thomas More had convinced Henry of the political advantages of such a break.
    d. Henry needed the support of the nobility, many of whom were Protestant.
    e. Henry's aggressive foreign policy in Italy led to his excommunication.

SAMPLE ESSAY

To what extent did women improve their status as a result of the Renaissance and the Protestant Reformation?

Throughout history, women have often been treated less than men. Women were made to be in charge of the domestic sphere and given few chances for education or political power. All of this changed with the Renaissance and Reformation. Many famous women, such as Isabella d'Este and Elizabeth of England, played a major role in these movements. Not all changed for the better, because women were still inferior to men, but they were definitely better off.

The Renaissance was all about humanism, and a big part of that was education. Many intellectuals of this period thought that even women should receive an education. One of these was Castiglione in his *Book of Courtier.* Though this education was not the same as men's, it still was important because before this, women were usually illiterate. Also, there were even some famous women humanists. One of these was Isabella d'Este, a ruler of a city-state on the Italian peninsula. She gathered other thinkers at her court, a bit like a salon, and also wrote treatises about women having more rights. However, women had drawbacks as well. Since men were often much older than women when they were married, they were not always treated well. To escape the control of their husbands, women had affairs and exercised some power "behind the scenes." All in all, women gained an important role in the Renaissance, but this did not always apply to poor women, many of whom turned to prostitution just to survive.

Women also gained some from the Reformation. In fact, many important rulers of this period were women, such as Elizabeth and Mary Tudor. These rulers showed that politics was not just for men. Elizabeth may have been the best ruler in England's history. Why? She helped solve the religious conflict left over from her father, Henry VIII, and got the Protestants and Catholics back together again. In addition, she was able to fight off the Spanish and their armada in 1588, a great victory that made England the new sea power. Some women even played a role in religious issues, such as Catherine Zell. Catherine was an Anabaptist—people who were radical and practiced adult baptism—and preached in churches with her husband. Catholic women even played a role, such as Teresa of Avila. She had visions of Jesus and created a new group of nuns who helped the poor. So, as you can see, women did not just let men control politics and religion. They got involved and proved that they were up to the task.

Women's rights really came later in the twentieth century, but the Renaissance and Reformation got the ball rolling. Some famous women played major roles in spreading both movements. Of course, not all women gained, especially lower classes, but that doesn't take away from the strides women made. Perhaps if women stand up for their rights, they will continue to gain equality with men.

This is a strong though not top essay. First, the student is "in control" of the question—she addresses it directly, offers a thesis (if simplified), and provides relevant support. Second, the essay is balanced, in that there is roughly equal treatment of both the Renaissance and Reformation. Third, the response is clearly organized and contains no glaring errors of fact. What might improve this essay? Though the thesis is evident, it is simplified. In fact, the student often relies on clichés ("get the ball rolling," "up to the task," "got involved") rather than a more specific analysis of specifically how women's status changed or stayed the same. Perhaps the student might follow up her good insight regarding the lack of change for poor women with further analysis, especially for the Reformation, of how average women were affected, not simply famous rulers. Moreover, while the essay avoids major factual errors, it does fall into some interpretive ones, for example, Elizabeth getting "Protestants and Catholics together." Finally, for your response, try to do more with the conclusion—placing the topics in more specific historical context, or explaining what makes them important. The present conclusion reiterates several points from the essay, and then engages in some "cheerleading" for women's rights. Score: 7.

CHAPTER 5

Economic Expansion, Social Change, and Religious Wars, 1550–1650

One of the most significant events in world history is the European encounter with the Americas as a result of exploration and colonization. Not only were Europeans forced to rethink cultural and intellectual assumptions, they gained access to untold wealth, which shifted the balance of power politically in Europe and caused widespread destruction to the colonized cultures. The resulting global economy, what is often termed the Commercial Revolution, altered economic and social structures in Europe. Moreover, this era also saw the effects of the Protestant and Catholic Reformations played out in a century of religious wars, never free from political and economic considerations. A major result of these developments was to shift the locus of European power from the center of Europe to those nations on the Atlantic.

THE OPENING OF THE ATLANTIC

Motives and Means

Europe's expansion really began with the Crusades in 1095 and continued throughout the Middle Ages, with the *reconquista* in Spain, Marco Polo's journey to China, and the first tentative Portuguese steps to explore the coastline of Africa. What accounts for the burst of exploration in the fifteenth and sixteenth centuries? The usual explanation is "**God, gold, and glory**," a mantra that captures the missionary impulse, economic incentives, and personal motives of the conquistadores. However, we should not overlook the role that technological developments played as well as the sponsorship provided by competitive states eager to reap the political advantages of this exploration.

For centuries, Europe's access to the coveted goods of the East was provided by Arab and Ottoman middlemen. Direct control of spices, silks, sugar, porcelain, precious metals, gems, and strategic minerals would reduce costs and ensure a ready supply of profit-making goods. With the growth of towns and commerce in the Middle Ages, merchants and governments were keen on exploiting opportunities to fill their private and state coffers with newfound wealth. And missionaries considered the lands of the East rich ground for spreading the Gospel message. Though many viewed religion as more of a rationale than a motive for exploration, others were genuinely motivated by piety, even if it was misplaced. In fact, once the Reformation was under way, religious groups such as the Jesuits viewed the new colonies as a proving ground of religious commitment. Motives, then, for exploration were clearly in place; now all that was needed were the means.

The fifteenth century served as the culmination of a long chain of navigational and intellectual advances that supported overseas exploration. Ironically, the Chinese had already made contact with Africa and the Indian Ocean basin in the early fifteenth century but did not follow up their successes. China considered itself culturally and economically superior and thus in no need for the goods or ideas of other cultures. However, China's ingenuity served Europe well, as its **compass** and axial rudder allowed Columbus and others the ability to conduct voyages far from their homelands. In addition, the **quadrant** (and more sophisticated **astrolabe**) allowed explorers to measure the angle of the Pole Star to determine latitude. New maps, called *portolani,* provided detailed information about headlands and direction, though little information regarding the open ocean. New ship designs, such as the **caravel** (a light maneuverable craft) and **lateen** (or triangular) **sail,** which allowed a crew to "tack" against the direction of the wind, made blue-water voyages possible. Finally, perspective geometry and the rediscovery of Ptolemy's (a second-century Greek astronomer) *Geographica* provided for the gridlike structure found on most modern maps, even if Ptolemy had overestimated the size of Asia (a fact that Columbus would use to his advantage).

Many knew of these developments, but not all were able to exploit them. Keep in mind that a key factor supporting colonization was the strong, centralized state. Because Portugal and Spain were the first to establish monarchical control over their diverse realms, they became the first nations to sponsor long-distance sea voyages. Setting up and administering colonies on far-flung lands required resources, bureaucratic mechanisms, and sustained political energy.

Though many early explorers hailed from Italy (Columbus, Vespucci, Verrazano, the Cabots), the country sponsored no overseas voyages; it couldn't, because it was divided and preoccupied with foreign invasion. Also, centralized governments had gained a monopoly on violence and were thus able to employ new techniques and technologies in warfare, such as cannons, steel weapons, and plate armor, which simply overwhelmed colonial opponents.

The Development of Colonial Empires

One nation that experienced a substantial economic boost from exploration was Portugal. In retrospect, Portugal's rise is amazing. A nation lacking natural resources with only about 1 million inhabitants, tucked in the southwestern corner of Europe, Portugal by 1510 had established a worldwide trading empire. Prince Henry (1394–1460), nicknamed "The Navigator," founded a school for seafarers at Sagres, which trained the first generation of sailors who settled the Azores Island chain (a basing area for transatlantic voyages) and explored along the west coast of Africa. Though the Portuguese plucked the gold, pepper, and slaves of Africa, they still had not found the coveted sea route to the East. Then Vasco de Gama (c. 1469–1524) in 1498 made it around the Cape of Good Hope and to the riches of India. The single returning boat earned a 1000 percent profit for its investors!

De Gama followed up his success by returning with cannons, which overwhelmed the advanced civilizations of the Indian Ocean basin. By 1510, the Portuguese had established control of several strategic "choke points" in the East, which allowed them to extract trade concessions and radically reduce the cost of luxury products. Though Portugal lacked the population and resources to maintain extensive settlements, its maritime empire fed Europe's appetite for trade with the East until it was taken over by the Dutch at the end of the sixteenth century.

Not far behind the Portuguese were the Spanish. Though Christopher Columbus (1451–1506) completed four voyages to the Americas, he never recognized his miscalculation of the earth's circumference. Subsequent explorers welcomed the prospect of exploiting two previously unknown continents, and in the decades that followed, the Spanish monarchy sponsored expeditions that would lead to the subjugation of an entirely "New World."

Before describing the Spanish empire, let's review the accomplishments of several major figures in the history of exploration, keeping in mind that for this topic the AP Exam will focus less on personalities and more on motives and effects:

- **Hernando Cortés** (1460–1547)—*Conquistador* who overwhelmed the advanced Aztec civilization through use of horses, cannons, and diplomacy. He helped establish the Spanish presence in North America.
- **Ferdinand Magellan** (1480–1521)—Skilled Portuguese seaman who sailed under the flag of Spain. He led his men through the treacherous straits at the tip of South America, now named for him, before perishing in the Philippines. Magellan is credited with the first successful circumnavigation of the earth.
- **John Cabot** (c. 1450–1499)—Italian who along with his brother Sebastian helped claim parts of North America for England. He was lost at sea on his second voyage.
- **Jacques Cartier** (1491–1557)—Laid claim to part of North America for the French.
- **St. Francis Xavier** (1506–1552)—Jesuit missionary who used wit and zeal to establish Christianity in India, Indonesia, and Japan.
- **Francisco Pizarro** (c. 1475–1541)—Brutal conqueror of the Incas in the Andes. He was aided by disease, as he and his less than 300 men laid claim to South America.
- **Vasco Nunez de Balboa** (c. 1475–1519)—Stowaway who hijacked a ship and led an expedition across the Isthmus of Panama to discover the Pacific Ocean.

Following Columbus's discovery, the Portuguese and Spanish negotiated the **Treaty of Tordesillas** (1494) whereby they divided the world in half for purposes of colonization. Eventually Portugal laid claim to Brazil in South America, but the primary presence in the Americas proved to be Spain, a presence that had profound consequences for both the colonizer and the colonized.

Soon after the Spanish conquest of the Americas, the exploitation of native peoples began. To provide for the orderly development of the new continents, the Spanish introduced the *encomienda* system. According to this system, settlers were given grants of land and native labor, in return providing for the Christian instruction and protection of their workers. In reality, the indigenous people were brutally exploited in mining and other operations, beginning the rapid decline in their population. The Potosi mine in present-day Bolivia stands as a fearful example of how the system quickly went awry. Though the mine became the primary supplier of Spanish silver, this wealth came at the expense of the native civilization.

The indigenous population found a defender in the Dominican monk **Bartolome de las Casas** (1484–1566), whose *Brief Account of the Devastation of the Indies* (1542) highlighted the issues of abuse and devastation. De las Casas's account eventually led to the New Laws, which reformed the *encomienda* system. Unfortunately, it was too late; most of the native population had been decimated by neglect and disease. The resulting labor shortage led to another negative legacy from exploration: African slavery. Though the slave trade dated back to the early fifteenth century, it didn't take off until the meeting of three cultures (European, American, and African). In all, approximately 12 million Africans suffered the horrors of the so-called **Middle Passage** across the Atlantic in Portuguese, Spanish, and ultimately Dutch and English ships. Though Africans were able to create new cultures in a new land, the issue of African slavery has left a deep imprint on the history of four continents.

> **Sidebar** Ironically, the writings of de las Casas led to the so-called "Black Legend," which was used by the English and others to portray the Spanish as especially cruel and violent in their colonial ventures. In fact, the English were little better in their treatment of the indigenous peoples, and were less tolerant of mixed-race relationships.

Of all the colonial empires, Spain's acted in the most centralized fashion. Policies were administered directly, if sometimes slowly, by the **Council of the Indies,** under the control of the Spanish monarchy. Imperial administrators tended to be loyal to Spain rather than to the Spanish Americans they governed. The New World was divided into two **viceroyalties**—New Mexico and Peru—which were subdivided into captaincies-general for more direct control. To assist and oversee royal governors, *audiencias* acted as advisory bodies and de facto courts. To settle in Spanish America, one was required to adhere to the Catholic faith. Over time, remaining native peoples were converted to Catholicism, and the hierarchical structure of the Church was transferred to Spanish America, resulting even today in the largest concentration of Catholics in the world.

THE MEETING OF TWO WORLDS: EFFECTS

Intellectual and Cultural Impact

A key impact of exploration was the **Columbian Exchange,** the cultural and economic diffusion of practices and goods across the Atlantic. Exploration efforts were richly rewarded with a bounty of new crops and goods from the Americas, such as potatoes, tobacco, tomatoes, cocoa, gold and silver, beans, corn, peanuts, and possibly syphilis. Many of the crops and animals now considered "natural" to the Americas were, in fact, originally from the Old World: horses, cattle, sheep, pigs, honey bees, rice, wheat, sugar cane, and, most notoriously, diseases. These last, including measles, smallpox, typhus, and malaria, acted as the largest destroyer of native peoples, who lacked immunity to such infectious pestilences. Along with abusive treatment, by the end of the sixteenth century, the thriving population of the Americas had been reduced by 90 percent, though historians disagree sharply on the pre-1492 population levels (from 20 to 70 million).

> **Heads Up!** AP European history is seen increasingly from a global perspective. Thus, the Columbian Exchange represents the kind of topic likely to be more emphasized on future exams.

Colonization also reoriented Europe's intellectual world. Contact between two previously unknown civilizations was bound to make all parties rethink at least some of their cultural assumptions. First, Europeans set about creating new maps that more accurately depicted the world in precise, scientific, and abstract space (e.g., with grids and keys). The pioneer in this field was **Gerardus Mercator** (1512–1594), a Flemish mapmaker who succeeded in mass-producing the first globes and also rendering a three-dimensional space (the earth) on a two-dimensional surface—the still-standard map that continues to bear his name. Also, even though Europeans approached indigenous peoples with little regard for their cultures, some used the encounter to reevaluate and even critique European society. Probably influenced by de las Casas, **Michel de Montaigne** (1533–1592), a French lawyer and inventor of the essay, introduced a new skeptical attitude toward European customs, even suggesting that native cannibalism was no worse than many of the atrocities of Europe's religious wars. A final legacy of 1492 was the creation of entirely new cultures in the New World from the mixing of the old. From the racial blending of the *mestizos* to the religious practices of voodoo to the Gullah and Creole dialects and finally to the music of jazz, the Americas continue to bear the legacy of exploration and colonization.

The Commercial Revolution, Phase I

Europe's colonization of the Americas and its creation of maritime empires led to significant changes within Europe. We examine some of the economic and social changes here; in a later chapter, we'll take a turn at the diplomatic and political results.

The economic result of exploration and colonization is termed the **Commercial Revolution**—an acceleration in global trade involving new goods and techniques. Often underestimated as an important topic by students, the Commercial Revolution fed many of the changes leading to the growth of modern society. Two of these changes were an increase in Europe's population (to about 90 million in 1600, finally surpassing the preplague level) and a steady inflation, or rise in prices. This latter development aided in the creation of a money-oriented economy, which further undermined the feudal system in Western Europe. Though traditionally the **Price Revolution** was attributed to the importation of precious metals from New World, more recent interpretations have stressed population growth as the source. Quite simply, with more demand chasing a supply of goods not keeping pace, inflation was the inevitable result. Landowners benefited from the inflation, unless they had leased their land via long-term rents, and many turned to the production of "cash crops." A new class of independent farmers, outside the feudal structure and focused on producing for the market, began to arise. In England, they were called the **gentry,** or gentlemen, and they attempted to imitate the lifestyles of the lords and nobles. Like the bourgeoisie, they were resented by those below and scorned by those above.

Traditionally the **guilds** dominated the production of goods in towns and cities; workers owned the capital and performed the labor. With the increase in profit from trade, merchants began to invest their earnings in long-distance business ventures, often ending up in banking, like the Medici in Italy or the **Fuggers** in Germany. Families such as the Fuggers often formed close relationships with monarchs, as with Charles V, loaning money for state enterprises such as mining. Eventually larger banks were formed from the resources of numerous investors. One of the more prominent, the **Bank of Amsterdam** (founded in 1609), funded the commercial dominance of the Netherlands. By this time, bankers ignored the traditional Christian prohibition against usury (the charging of interest on loans); the profits were just too great to ignore.

The separation of capital and labor is a major feature of **capitalism,** and the divergence became more pronounced beginning in the sixteenth and seventeenth centuries. Entrepreneurs began investing in their own manufacturing enterprises. To sidestep the guild structure, they provided (or "put out") the raw materials to rural families eager to supplement their marginal incomes by finishing goods. This was especially pronounced in the textile industries, where the various steps of manufacture—spinning, carding, weaving—were mechanized at different times. The **putting-out system** signaled the decline of the guild structure and served as a halfway house toward factory production in the late eighteenth century. Other industries did not fit neatly into the guild structure and also received stimulus from the new capital—printing, bookmaking, mining, shipbuilding, and weapons manufacture.

During the late sixteenth and into the seventeenth centuries, Europeans gained a strong appetite for luxury and staple items from overseas. As the goods became more common, such as tea and coffee, they gradually established a cultural influence on European styles and diet, often beginning with the aristocracy and seeping down through the bourgeoisie into the lower classes. The New World tomato and potato took a strong hold on European diets, though the latter had to overcome resistance to its appearance and taste. Eventually, however, the potato became the salvation of many nations, especially Russia, Germany, and Ireland, because of its versatility and ease of cultivation. Coffee- and tea-drinking provided opportunities for socializing outside more traditional networks and also gave workers a jolt of energy midday, particularly when combined with the largest profit-maker of the era—sugar.

A status-conscious upper class and their middle-class imitators craved symbols of style and status. This meant silks and porcelain from China, calicoes (light, brightly colored cotton cloth)

Sidebar For centuries, Europeans coveted Chinese porcelain but could not figure out how to make it, despite governments locking up the occasional alchemist to "force" the issue. Legend has it that the European discovery occurred in Dresden, when a soil with kaolin accidentally found its way into some ceramics. When the creators noted the shiny and translucent character of the "china," they attempted to lock down the factory for the next 20 years to protect their monopoly. Word eventually got out and Europe had its own porcelain industry.

from India, and spices from the East Indies. Hunger for luxury goods fed the Commercial Revolution and competition among nations to establish techniques and colonies that would secure access to raw materials and facilitate the amount of goods carried in their merchant marines. New techniques arose out of mercantile ingenuity as well as state sponsorship.

To pool financial resources and share risk, investors created **joint-stock companies.** Of these, the **Dutch** and **British East India Companies** (both founded in the first decade of the seventeenth century) were the most famous and profitable. Such companies gained monopoly status from government charters and were expected to provide an increase in trade as well as incoming gold and silver. Gradually the Dutch pushed the Portuguese out of the East Indies and, along with England, began to challenge the dominance of the Iberian empires. Colonial competition among the Netherlands, England, France, and Spain accelerated throughout the seventeenth and eighteenth centuries, culminating with a series of decisive commercial wars (see Chapters 6 and 8).

Global trade on a large scale fed the rise of commercial capitalism in Europe. The credit, financial, and mercantile systems described earlier defined the nature of capitalism until the rise of mechanized mass production in textiles in the late eighteenth century. In an effort to exploit fully the potential for wealth, European nations adopted the economic theory of **mercantilism.** This theory—which generally guided the policies of most nations until the laissez-faire ideas of Adam Smith—was based on three essential tenets:

- **Scarcity**—The total amount of global resources and wealth is limited. Therefore, any advances by one nation come at the expense of another; trade is a "zero-sum game."
- **Wealth = specie (hard money)**—Mercantilists held that real wealth equaled the amount of gold and silver flowing into a nation. Given this assumption, governments attempted to promote exports through trade monopolies, acquisition of colonies, and subsidies at the same time that they limited imports via tariffs, trade restrictions, and war aimed at an enemy's mercantile potential.
- **Government intervention**—Though governments did not generally own the means of production, they did actively intervene to promote national objectives. Governments provided incentives to key industries, sought new colonies, and worked to establish national markets by building roads and canals and abolishing localism. The ultimate goal of these efforts proved to be a favorable balance of trade, that is, more specie flowing into the nation than flowing out. In the next chapter, we'll examine the mercantilist policies of specific nations.

CHANGING SOCIAL STRUCTURES, 1500–1700

Early modern society (defined as the period from 1500 to 1700) experienced both significant change, which altered the lives of many, and also much that remained the same. Many of the social structures of this period seem alien to contemporary students. As you read through this section, try to step outside your assumptions and judgments. Capturing the mentalities of early modern Europeans requires sensitivity to historical context, aided by a vivid imagination. This period serves as a rich area for essay questions on the AP Exam, though it is often overlooked by students. As you study the period, try to establish a strong grounding in *specific* developments that influenced the lives of Europeans. When addressing any period, locate it clearly in time and place. Avoid expressions such as "throughout history" or "women have always cooked and cleaned," as they reveal an anachronistic ("out of time") understanding of the past.

Demographic Changes and Social Structures

As noted previously, a major structural change in early modern European society proved to be an increase in population. Until about 1550, this increase helped bring fertile land under cultivation as Europe recovered from the Black Death. After 1550, however, Europe's population began to strain existing resources, resulting in the Price Revolution described earlier. Population continued to increase throughout the rest of the century, but poor weather, war, lack of resources, and periodic famine caused a decline in population throughout the seventeenth century. In fact, some nations, such as Spain, experienced a rapid drop in population, which seriously hampered its economy and threatened its great power status. Though governments did not keep accurate census data until the late eighteenth century, local studies have noted the serious negative impact of poor economic conditions on daily life, as revealed by a serious drop in marriages and births during hard times. For the big picture: Europe's population maxed out at 100 million about 1550, dropped to around 80 million by 1650, and had recovered to 100 million again by 1700.

Economic developments rippled through the class structure. Though the traditional system was not overturned, some changes were evident by 1700. First, the aristocracy continued to maintain its primary position through the addition of "new blood." This "new blood" was those members of the middle class who were able to acquire noble status through the purchase of an office, which often became hereditary with a payment of a tax (called the *paulette* in France). Sometimes resented by the older nobles ("**nobles of the sword**"), these new nobles were termed the "**nobles of the robe**" and played a more important role as governments expanded their bureaucratic functions.

Below the nobles were the *bourgeoisie,* or burghers, meaning those who lived in towns. Technically outside the feudal structure, the middle class made their livings in a variety of economic activities. In fact, the middle class was by no means a monolithic group. Some owned large amounts of land and lived off of rents, others traded goods as merchants, and still others filled out the growing professions, such as physicians, clergy, and attorneys. In addition, towns also thrived on the labor of the lower middle class or *petit bourgeoisie,* who acted as shopkeepers, artisans, grocers, and store owners. As the money economy and world trade expanded in the sixteenth and seventeenth centuries, the numbers of the middle class increased, though they were not as yet able to translate these numbers into political power.

Agriculture and the Countryside

The lives of the vast majority of Europeans were dictated by the seasons and the paces of agricultural life. Agriculture was generally practiced in a village setting, with decisions made communally. This **subsistence agricultural system**—growing enough to feed the village with little left over for export—was defined by the **three-field crop rotation** system in the north and the **two-field** system in the south. In these systems, one section of land was left fallow (uncultivated) to allow for replenishment of the soil, clearly not a full use of resources. Each village included a **commons** area, used for livestock grazing, wood-gathering, hunting, or eking out a marginal existence for the landless. Throughout the sixteenth century, England began selling off common land to allow for its purchase by wealthy landowners. The practice had the double effect of creating a new nonaristocratic class of wealthy landowners, the gentry, as well as increasing the numbers of landless poor, who either had to contract out their labor or move to the cities. Between these two groups stood the **"yeomanry,"** or small freeholders who owned their land. As often occurs with economic changes, some took advantage and improved their status while others found their already marginal existence threatened further.

> **Heads Up!** Often European history is construed as western European history. It would be a mistake to ignore the importance of eastern Europe in shaping the continent. For purposes of the seventeenth century, you can think of the Elbe River in Prussia as a dividing line between free and unfree peasants.

The paths of western and eastern Europe began to diverge more during the seventeenth century. As most of the peasants of western Europe became freed from **serfdom** and other feudal obligations, those of eastern Europe were drawn more tightly into a highly codified system of laws governing an individual's life. While western peasants continued to owe their lords **manorial obligations,** such as the payment of taxes, fees for the use of ovens and mills, and the hated labor service (called *corvée* in France, *robot* in the east), they were generally free to leave the land and could call on a set of traditional prerogatives to protect themselves against excessive landlords. Such was not the case in eastern Europe as, for example, serfdom became state law in the mid-seventeenth century in Russia. Large manors, often exploiting the labor of up to 100,000 serfs, dominated nations such as Poland and Hungary, where nobles made up 10 percent of the population, compared to 2 to 3 percent in France or England.

The Life of the Towns

Though only 10 to 20 percent of Europeans lived in towns or cities, urban centers played an economic and a cultural role out of proportion to their numbers. Compared with our strong individualistic spirit, early modern Europeans were embedded in a web of social relationships—guild, village, neighborhood, church, city, class, family. In fact, popular metaphors for society construed it as a great organism, with each group playing the appropriate role assigned to it—the **Great Chain of Being** or the **Body Politic.** Institutions tended to be hierarchical in theory, though traditions and the desire to avoid social conflict often prevented social superiors from becoming arbitrary. In this period, cities acted as magnets for the countryside, attracting both landless laborers and those seeking opportunity. By the end of the sixteenth century, most cities could no longer adequately handle the influx of new residents. The majority of city dwellers were the working poor, who survived by finding odd jobs (e.g., unloading ships, hard manual labor, or domestic service) or by begging.

By 1550, when the economy was stressed, poverty reached crisis proportions in many European nations. Many of the poor resorted to begging; some even maimed themselves to garner sympathy. Traditional religious and charitable institutions were overwhelmed, so governments began to enact strict regulations that distinguished between the **"deserving"** (disabled, elderly, children) and **"undeserving"** (able-bodied males) **poor.** England's Poor Law of 1601, for example, provided charitable relief but also seriously punished those who violated its regulations.

Crime acted as the ever-present companion to poverty. Both property and violent crime increased in the period from 1500 to 1700. Because governments lacked modern police forces and prisons, they tended to inflict cruel and often hideous punishments on captured criminals to make an example out of them. Public executions were common, even for property crimes such as theft. Not until the eighteenth century did reformers call for the changes in the legal and penal system.

Family and Communal Life

As today, the most basic institution in European life was the family. In western Europe, the **nuclear family** (parents, children, and perhaps an elderly grandparent) predominated. Because taxes in nations such as Russia and Hungary were assessed on households, extended families proved more common. Unlike Renaissance Italy, the average age of marriage for men was mid- to late-20s and early- to mid-20s for women, though these averages increased in hard economic times. Women of the aristocracy tended to marry somewhat earlier and, on average, experienced eight to nine live births, whereas women of the middle and lower classes experienced on average six to seven live births. Part of this disparity can be explained by the use of **wet nurses** among the upper classes (breast-feeding tends to dampen fertility). Old age was rare because of high infant mortality and low life expectancy (around 30 to 35 in most nations). Because of this, remarriage and blended families were common. Despite the common stereotype of female labor as primarily domestic, women proved, in fact, integral to the family economy, and a wife's death often drove a widower to remarry as soon as possible. In artisan households, for example, women supervised the workers, kept the books, and marketed the products.

By standard interpretation, the concept of childhood did not exist until its invention during the Enlightenment. In fact, evidence indicates that in the early modern period, parents did love their children and considered the loss of a child a tragedy. Nonetheless, children were expected to contribute labor to the family unit—often overseen by the father—and were subjected to corporal punishments for disobedience. Also, keep in mind that society or parents did not provide compulsory schooling or age-appropriate toys, reading materials, or clothing for children. In most nations, children did not earn full legal rights at a specific age, but only when they established their own residences. Female children were expected to bring a **dowry** into a marriage (land, furniture, personal property, cash), though in Germany, for example, tradition protected a father from arbitrarily depriving a daughter of her inheritance.

Early modern leisure differs significantly from our contemporary diversions. Whereas our forms of amusement tend to be consumptive (shopping, amusement parks, dining, etc.) and in small groups, Europeans of the sixteenth and seventeenth centuries engaged in **communal leisure.** The rhythms of life in early modern Europe were governed by the seasons; periods of extended labor were followed by those of extended celebration. In Catholic nations, the church calendar, with its cycle of saints' feast days and rituals, dictated the pace of work and leisure. **Carnival,** the period right before Lenten fasting and penance, served as the largest of these festivals. For over a week, villagers and townspeople consumed large amounts of food and alcohol, while playing traditional games and engaging in a higher-than-normal amount of sexual activity. In addition, classes and genders switched roles for the **"world turned upside down,"** which served the important function of letting off discontent in a ritualized way before returning to the normal hierarchy. With the Reformation, many Protestant and even some Catholic areas tried to restrain what they considered the excesses of the practice. Finally, to ensure social conformity, many localities imposed rituals of public humiliation on those who stepped outside of community standards, such as a husband who could not "control" his wife or a woman who committed adultery. In France, this practice was called *charivari* and in England **skimmington.**

Witchcraft Persecution

One of the most notable social phenomena of early modern Europe was the persecution of witches. The height of the scare was from about 1580 to 1700, in which approximately 100,000 people, mostly women, were executed for being in league with the devil. To our modern sensibility, the practice seems backward and barbaric. We should also try to understand what beliefs and socioeconomic conditions gave rise to the hysteria. First, almost all Europeans, even the educated, believed in witches and demons. Increased Bible-reading because of the Protestant Reformation emphasized both the reality of the devil and the supposedly weak and credulous nature of women. Second, the early modern period experienced rapid social and economic change that tended to undermine or challenge traditional practices—enclosure, religious wars, poverty, crime, and overpopulation. Third, religious passions were inflamed by the Protestant and Catholic Reformations and resulting religious wars, creating suspicion among communities, especially in regions divided by religious belief. Finally, those targeted for accusation tended to exist on the margins of the community—the poor, older women, those living alone—and thus seemed potentially beyond the reach of social norms. Women, in particular, were believed to have special knowledge of and powers over the body (because of their role in childbirth) and often did supplement family income by preparing traditional "cures" or potions. In fact, some may have even considered themselves to be practicing "white magic." With the general acceptance of scientific explanations by elites, the witch trials declined markedly after 1720 and were almost gone by 1750.

> **Sidebar:** Witch persecution is often associated with the Middle Ages. Indeed, Europeans were executed for this supposed crime in the Middle Ages, but it was the modern state that regularized the judicial procedures for witch interrogations and trials, inadvertently turning what might have been local incidents into a continental phenomenon. Ironically, one of the bestsellers off the new printing press in the 1480s was *Malleus Maleficarum,* a handbook on the examination of witches.

THE RELIGIOUS WARS

One of the more complex and challenging topics you will study this year is the religious wars. Amidst the numerous personalities and rapidly changing motives, try to keep your eye on the key issues: the causes, nature, and end results of the wars. Though historians term these "religious" wars, each conflict was influenced by political and territorial ambitions.

Philip II: Catholic Protector

At the center of the religious conflicts of the second half of the sixteenth century stood **Philip II** (1556–1598), ruler of Spain and the **Low Countries,** parts of Italy, and the New World. Like his Habsburg father, Charles I (V as Holy Roman Emperor), Philip saw himself as the political protector of Catholicism in Europe, though Philip lacked Charles's more cosmopolitan background. Philip was a Spaniard and was influenced by that nation's strong Catholic tradition and crusading mentality. **El Escorial,** Philip's palace on the barren plains outside Madrid, reflected the ruler's personality. Part residence, part monastery and religious retreat, the Escorial acted as the central governing point of a huge empire stretching across oceans. Philip insisted on overseeing even the minutest details of government, earning him the nickname the "**King of Paper,**" after his habit of reviewing each document from his diverse realm. Philip's first area of concern was France, even though he did not directly rule that nation.

The French Wars of Religion

France's long series of religious conflicts (1560–1598) grew from religious and political roots. Despite **Francis I**'s (1516–1547) attempts to stamp out the spread of Protestant faiths, Calvinism continued to grow in his kingdom, often indirectly aided by the patronage of his sister, **Marguerite of Navarre** (1492–1529), a deeply religious woman and author of several controversial stories and religious works. Calvinism found fertile ground among the French aristocracy in particular, perhaps because members already believed themselves as "the elect." By 1560, fully 40 percent of French nobles advocated the **Huguenot** faith (as French Calvinists were called), which, because nobles held important positions in the government and military, posed a threat to the Catholic **Valois** monarchy. These religious causes were exacerbated when the strong French king **Henry II** (1547–1559) died tragically in a jousting accident. His death plunged France into a civil conflict over control of the throne *and* over France's religion.

The conflict in France is best viewed as a three-sided struggle. In the middle was the Catholic Valois family, now led by Henry's widow, the moderate yet cunning **Catherine de' Medici** (1519–1589). Like the future Henry IV and Elizabeth I of England, Catherine advocated political stability over religious orthodoxy, being known as a *politique*. In addition, Catherine attempted to maintain the throne for her three weak sons—Francis II (1559–1560), **Charles IX** (1560–1574), and **Henry III** (1574–1589). Against the Catholic Valois on one side stood a faction of Protestant nobles who laid claim to the throne through **Henry Bourbon** (of Navarre) and wished free worship for those of the Huguenot faith. Also opposed to the Valois and with the backing of the Jesuits, the papacy, and Philip II were the **Guise** family, or **ultra-Catholics**. The ultra-Catholics viewed the Valois monarchy as weak in the face of the Protestant threat and wished to restore a more strongly Catholic king.

Religious conflict in France was really played out in a series of 13 short wars, with numerous attempts at compromise by Catherine and her sons. One of these attempts at compromise led to one of the worst atrocities during this violent period. In 1572, Henry Bourbon agreed to marry Catherine de' Medici's daughter as a sign of reconciliation. However, during the wedding celebration in Paris, rumors flared that Protestants were plotting to take over the government. What followed was a slaughter of the Protestant nobles, in Paris and throughout France, known as the **St. Bartholomew's Day Massacre.** In all, approximately 10,000 French Protestants were killed, though Henry Bourbon escaped by converting to Catholicism (a conversion he quickly renounced). The event seemed to show the corruption of the Valois monarchy and deepened resistance to it.

The final stage of France's civil war is called the **War of the Three Henries.** In 1588, Henry Guise (leader of the ultra-Catholics) took the city of Paris, threatening the Valois hold on the nation. Henry III, of Valois, felt he had no alternative but to form an alliance against the ultra-Catholics with Henry Bourbon, whom he promised to make next in line to the throne. On the pretext of compromise, both Henries invited Guise to the palace and had him assassinated. In reprisal, a fanatical monk killed Henry III in 1589, making Henry Bourbon (IV) ruler of France. However, **Henry IV's** (1589–1610) way to Paris was barred by Spanish troops, and he would spend the next decade winning control of the nation. To bring peace to the France, Henry converted back to Catholicism (the majority religion of France), supposedly saying "**Paris is worth a mass,**" and then engineered the **Edict of Nantes,** which allowed Huguenots to practice their religion outside Paris and fortify towns to protect their hard-won liberties. Over the next several years, Henry IV became one of the most beloved monarchs in French history and established a strong Bourbon dynasty, laying the foundations for absolutism.

The Wars of Spain

An important part of Philip's inheritance was **Burgundy,** the 17 provinces known as the Low Countries, where his father Charles had been raised. Philip was an outsider to those in the Low Countries, who wished to maintain their traditional decentralized political structure and relative religious liberty. Philip's policies eventually sparked a revolt, which had at its base religious, political, and economic causes. First, Philip attempted to increase taxes to fund the cost of the Spanish empire, thus alienating many in the middle classes. Next, Philip determined to stamp out "heresy" by tightening the church structure in the Netherlands (another name for Burgundy) and by employing the Inquisition. Because the 17 provinces stood astride important trade routes and had a tradition of religious tolerance, they had attracted many adherents of Calvinism.

In response to Philip's tax policy, discontented Burgundians in 1566 directed their ire against the symbols of Catholicism, smashing statues and church decorations, in what was known as the **iconoclast revolt.** Philip played "hard ball" by sending the **Duke of Alba** to the Netherlands. Alba established the so-called **Council of Blood** and executed a number of leading Protestant nobles, which only had the effect of further inflaming the provinces. Soon a leader of the revolt emerged—**William "the Silent"** (1533–1584)—from the House of Orange in Holland), so-called because of his reluctance to discuss his strategies with others. William was aided by the **"sea beggars,"** ships that engaged in acts of piracy against the Spanish. When Spanish troops pillaged the city of Antwerp in 1576 (they had not been paid because Spain lacked funds), all 17 provinces called for the end of Spanish rule in the Netherlands, an event known as the **Pacification of Ghent.** This action caused Philip to change tactics and overshadowed the great Spanish naval victory over Ottoman forces in 1571 at **Lepanto,** which cleared the western Mediterranean of the Muslim threat.

Philip appointed his nephew **Alexander Farnese** (1545–1592), the Duke of Parma and a brilliant military leader, to subdue the Netherlands through the "carrot and the stick." Farnese succeeded by 1578 in prying away the southern 10 provinces from the revolt and winning their allegiance to Spain with the **Union of Arras.** These provinces were populated primarily by the French-speaking Walloons. In response, the northern, mostly Dutch-speaking Flemish seven provinces formed the **Union of Utrecht** in 1581 with the intent of separating from Spain. Throughout the conflict, Elizabeth I of England quietly assisted the Dutch with financial and naval aid, including attacks on Spanish shipping by the **"sea dogs"** such as **Sir Francis Drake** (c. 1540–1596). By 1588, Philip was determined to end English meddling and teach Elizabeth, his one-time sister-in-law who had spurned his offer of marriage, a lesson. Philip's **"Spanish Armada"** did not have a chance against the more maneuverable English ships and because his plan for an invasion was too complex, Spain's "confident hope of a miracle" turned into a rout in the "Protestant wind," which signaled the rise of England and the relative decline of Spain as maritime powers, though Philip would raise other armadas and continue to fight on.

Though Philip never admitted defeat in the Netherlands, his successor Philip III signed a **Twelve Years'** truce in 1609 with the Union of Utrecht, which all but granted the Dutch independence. The southern 10 provinces remained loyal and became known as the **Spanish Netherlands.** Once the strongest nation in Europe, Spain slowly declined throughout the seventeenth century. There were several reasons for this loss of power. First, the Spanish had overextended themselves politically and militarily, taxing their subjects excessively and allowing the nation to fall behind economically. Second, the Iberian crusading mentality led the Spanish to persecute talented minorities, such as the *moriscos* (Muslim converts to Catholicism), who were driven out in the early seventeenth century. Finally, internal revolts over high taxes and government centralization, combined with population decline, sapped Spain's internal energy. By the end of the Thirty Years' War, to which we now turn, Spain's *siglo de oro* (Golden Age) was over, an important lesson for those who believe that power entails invincibility.

The Thirty Years' War, 1618–1648

Prior to the world wars of the twentieth century, the most devastating conflict in European history was the Thirty Years' War. The conflict began as a civil war over religion in Germany but escalated into a continental conflagration involving territorial and political ambitions. Years before war started, German Catholics and Protestants geared up for battle by forming alliances with outside powers. These alliances—the **Protestant Union** and **Catholic League**—ensured that when war did come, it would involve the great powers of Europe.

Following the Peace of Augsburg (1555), Germany stood divided between Lutheran and Catholic states. However, the treaty did not take into account the fastest growing denomination after 1560—Calvinism. When the ruler of the Palatinate, **Frederick V** (1610–1623), converted to Calvinism, the delicate religious balance in Germany was threatened. It became apparent that neither Protestant nor Catholic leaders had any intention of treating Augsburg as a permanent settlement to Germany's religious division. What complicated matters was the elective nature of the Holy Roman Emperor, nominally the political leader of Catholicism and still a position of importance. According to the **Golden Bull of 1356,** the emperor was elected by seven states, three of which were controlled by Catholic rulers and three by Protestants. To gain control of the last electoral state (Bohemia), the next Habsburg in line (the traditional imperial ruling house)—**Ferdinand II** (1620–1637)—promised the Bohemian nobles he would respect their religious liberties if they would elect him the king of Bohemia (whereby he could in turn vote for himself as emperor). After Ferdinand was elected king in 1618, he betrayed his promise to the Bohemian nobles, thus initiating the conflict.

The event that set off the conflict was the so-called **Defenestration of Prague** (1618), in which the Bohemian nobles tossed two imperial officials out of the Prague castle. Following this act of rebellion, the nobles elected Frederick V of Palatine as their new king. Subsequent fighting is usually divided by historians into four distinct phases, which are outlined as follows:

Phase	Events	Groups/Leaders	Results
Bohemian, 1618–1625	The Protestant forces under Frederick V were defeated soundly at **White Mountain.** Once Ferdinand II of Habsburg was elected emperor, he confiscated the lands of the rebellious Bohemian nobles, redistributed them, and then brought the Counter-Reformation to Bohemia.	* Frederick V of Palatine * Ferdinand II (Habsburg) and Holy Roman Emperor	Catholic forces emerged victorious as Bavaria, leader of the Catholic League, took over much of the Electorate Palatine.
Danish, 1625–1629	Christian IV, the Lutheran king of Denmark, entered the conflict both to support the Protestant cause and to gain territory in the Baltic. Wallenstein defeated Christian, thus giving imperial forces the upper hand.	* **Christian IV** (1588–1648) of Denmark * **Albrecht von Wallenstein** (1583–1634)—unpredictable leader of imperial forces who funded his own war machine	Ferdinand confidently issued the **Edict of Restitution** (1629), which returned all confiscated Church lands since 1517, angering Protestant and Catholic nobles alike who had gained from this confiscation. The Habsburgs appeared on the verge of completing a centuries-old dream of centralizing power in central Europe.
Swedish, 1629–1635	Sweden's great military leader, Gustavus Adolphus, entered the conflict to revive the Protestant cause and to secure trade in the Baltic. At **Breitenfield** and **Lutzen,** Gustavus succeeded in defeating the imperial forces and bringing the war to the Catholic south. In an example of the war's horrifying effect, the city of **Magdeburg** was sacked and burned, killing thousands of civilians.	* **Gustavus Adolphus** (1611–1632) * **Cardinal Richelieu** (1585–1642)—advisor under **Louis XIII** (1610–1643) who brought France into the conflict to reduce the power of the Habsburgs. * Wallenstein was assassinated with the okay of the emperor for negotiating independently with the Swedes.	To end the war, the emperor (now Ferdinand III— 1637–1657) revoked the Edict of Restitution and signed the **Peace of Prague** with the other German states in 1635. However, this did not end the fighting, as the conflict had devolved into a continental struggle between the Spanish Habsburgs vs. the Swedes and French (also supported by the Dutch).

Phase	Events	Groups/Leaders	Results
Franco-Swedish, 1635–1648	In the most violent phase of the war, Germany became the battleground for the territorial and political ambitions of its neighbors. At the battle of **Rocroi** (in the Spanish Netherlands) in 1643, the French soundly defeated the Spanish, signaling the rise of the former as the major military power in Europe.	* **Philip IV** (1621–1665) of Spain—continued to use Spain's dwindling resources to fight against France, despite facing internal rebellions by Portugal (which regained its independence in 1640) and the province of Catalonia.	By the end of the conflict, all sides were exhausted. However, peace negotiations dragged on for years before the war was finally ended in 1648.

The **Peace of Westphalia** (1648) marks an important turning point in European politics and diplomacy. After this point, the Holy Roman Empire no longer played a major role in the affairs of central Europe, though the Austrian Habsburgs turned to the east in subsequent years to revive their imperial fortunes. The treaty formally recognized the independence of Switzerland and the Dutch Republic, as well as reflected a shift in the balance of power. Emerging as stronger powers were France, Sweden, Prussia (in Germany), and the Dutch. Losing energy were the Holy Roman Empire and Spain, which now fell into the ranks of the second-tier beset by a declining population and economy.

Historians often view the Westphalia settlement as the "final nail in the coffin of the Middle Ages" because it recognized the internal sovereignty of each nation over its own religious affairs and ended any hopes of the future religious unity of Europe. Indeed, the papacy was virtually ignored in the peace negotiations and would play a sharply reduced role in future diplomacy. Though Europe could rest easier now that the last of its wars primarily motivated by religion was over, Germany was not so lucky. Estimates vary, but Germany's population may have declined by 20 to 33 percent. In areas of heavy fighting, entire towns ceased to exist and economic life was severely curtailed. Central Europe represented a vacuum of power that would soon be filled by the emergence of two competing German powers—Prussia and Austria—whose fortunes will be traced in the next chapter.

As a result of the Thirty Years' War, Europe underwent a **military revolution.** Gunpowder and the mounted foot-soldier (pikemen and musketeers) played a major role, as the infantry square employed massed volleys (firing at the same time). Tactics became more flexible, with the use of lighter and more mobile cavalry, pioneered by Gustavus Adolphus. In addition, to fund the increasing costs of war and oversee its complexity, governments grew larger and more centralized. Warfare had become the primary function of European states, who often spent up to 80 percent of their budgets on fielding, training, supplying, and of course, using armies (to meet their political objectives). As we'll see in the next chapter, this trend caused a further expansion of the state's power in the age of absolutism.

ADDITIONAL RESOURCES

Burke, Peter, *Popular Culture in Early Modern Europe* (1994)—A vivid and interesting study of the topic.

Cipolla, Carlo, *Before the Industrial Revolution: European Society and Economy, 1000–1700* (rev. 1994)—A wealth of information and data on every major feature of economic activity prior to the eighteenth century.

Crosby, Aldfred, *The Columbian Exchange: Biological and Cultural Consequences of 1492* (1972)—For those of a scientific bent, this book explains how colonization affected the world exchange of plants, animals, and diseases.

Dunn, Richard S., *The Age of Religious Wars, 1559–1715* (1979)—Another fine survey from the Norton History of the Modern World.

Elliott, J. H., *Europe Divided, 1559–98* (rev. 2000)—Fast-paced and informative introduction to European politics during the period.

Fernandez-Armesto, Felipe, *Columbus* (1991)—Interesting study of a complex figure, includes up-to-date interpretations.

Laslett, Peter, *The World We Have Lost: England Before the Industrial Revolution* (1983)—A study of family life in England.

Levack, Brian, *The Witch-Hunt in Early Modern Europe* (1987)—Surveys the many explanations for the phenomenon.

Manchester, William, *A World Lit Only by Fire* (1993)—Presents a rather stereotyped view of the Middle Ages, but the final chapter on Magellan's voyage makes for great reading.

Mattingly, Garrett, *The Armada* (rev. 1989)—The standard and exciting account of how 1588 changed European history.

Ozment, Steven, *The Burgermeister's Daughter: Scandal in a Sixteenth-Century German Town* (1997)—Told like a novel, this book shows how the historian works to recreate the features of everyday life.

Parker, Geoffrey, *Europe in Crisis, 1598–1648* (1979)—Comprehensive overview of the many complex developments in European politics during this period.

Parry, J. H., *The Age of Reconnaissance: Discovery, Exploration, and Settlement, 1450–1650* (rev. 1981)—Brief introduction to the voyages of exploration and their effects.

Stearns, Peter N., ed., *Encyclopedia of European Social History, 1350–2000* (2000)—If you can find it at a nearby library, these volumes are a wonderful resource on all areas of social history.

PRACTICE QUESTIONS

1. All of the following technological or educational developments supported overseas voyages of exploration EXCEPT:
   a. the use of the quadrant and astrolabe to calculate latitude.
   b. improved maps (*portolani*) that provided headlands and direction.
   c. the lateen sail, which allowed for maneuverability on the open seas.

    d. accurate marine chronometers to determine longitude.

    e. steel weapons and gunpowder, which allowed for dominance of native populations.

2. Which of the following caused the greatest number of deaths of American Indian populations after the conquest of the Americas?

    a. exploitation and overwork

    b. infectious diseases

    c. enslavement

    d. economic breakdown

    e. suicide

3. As a result of the voyages of exploration and colonization, the balance of power in Europe shifted toward:

    a. the Mediterranean.

    b. Central Europe.

    c. the Atlantic states.

    d. Scandinavia.

    e. England.

4. The primary reason for the gradual inflation in sixteenth-century Europe (Price Revolution) was:

    a. the importation of precious metals from the Americas.

    b. a shortage of goods due to guild restrictions.

    c. a decline in trade due to commercial competition.

    d. government establishment of trade monopolies.

    e. steady population growth throughout the century.

5. The accompanying illustration suggests which of the following about early modern European families?

    a. Families often worked under the same roof as an economic unit.

    b. Poverty caused parents to rely on child labor for additional income.

    c. Work was strictly divided based on gender.

    d. Lack of appropriate tools limited productivity.

    e. An economic recession forced many to labor in factories.

(Giraudon/Art Resource, NY)

6. Mercantilism can best be defined as which of the following?

    a. an economic system based on free competition and private property

    b. a focus on labor as the main source of value

    c. government efforts to obtain specie through favorable trade balances

    d. the rejection of colonies as a drag on the economy

    e. a plan by government to support the policies of local guilds

7. Which of the following is the best explanation for the prevalence of accusations against women as witches in early modern Europe?
    a. Women often accused other women to increase their social status.
    b. Men feared female leaders of a growing women's rights movement.
    c. Most men were off at war and thereby shielded from accusations.
    d. Popular attitudes held that women had special powers over the body.
    e. Governments targeted women as a form of population control.

8. The Edict of Nantes (1598) finally ended the French religious conflict by accomplishing which of the following?
    a. tolerating the Huguenot religion
    b. abolishing the practice of Catholicism
    c. ensuring Valois control of the monarchy
    c. forming an alliance with the Spanish
    e. eliminating state involvement in religion

9. A major goal of Philip II (1556–1598), king of Spain, was to:
    a. form an alliance with Protestants in England.
    b. grant gradual independence to the Americas.
    c. reduce Spanish dependence on specie from the New World.
    d. establish strong relations with the papacy.
    e. support the cause of European Catholicism.

10. The following illustration, *The Hanging Tree* (1633) by Jacques Callot, shows which of the following regarding the Thirty Years' War?
    a. The war represented a glorious victory for the French.
    b. Germany experienced violence and social breakdown.
    c. Mercenary soldiers arbitrarily killed civilians.
    d. Though violent, the war produced a unified Germany.
    e. Religion no longer played a role by the end of the war.

Anne S. K. Brown Military Collection, Brown University Library

SAMPLE ESSAY

Analyze the economic and cultural impact of the colonization of the Americas on Europe in the sixteenth and seventeenth centuries.

Europe went on many missions of exploration after 1492 and discovered many important lands. After Columbus, there was Cortés and other conquerors who created a large empire for Spain. With all the wealth and goods flowing into Europe, it could not help but be changed, and often for the better. Of course, these changes harmed the native peoples; for them, it simply wasn't worth it.

Economically, Europeans colonized in pursuit of luxury goods, such as spices and silks. The saying was "God, gold, and glory," but the middle one was really the most important. Both the Portuguese in India and the Spanish in the New World pursued gold, silver, and other important products. Their dreams came true. From the Americas, Europeans benefited from sugar, tobacco, rice, tomatoes, and potatoes. These products helped the European diet, so many people began to live longer. Also, there was an impact on the class system of this exchange of goods. Merchants gained in wealth and played a larger role in social life. States enjoyed this new-found wealth as well, because the empires and colonies made them stronger.

Cultural causes of exploration were important too. If it wasn't for new maps, ships, and navigation advances, Europeans would never have been able to explore overseas. From the Chinese, Europe got access to the compass and rudder, which allowed them to know where they were going. Arabs used the astrolabe, which was a fancy device to tell the latitude of the night sky, and then Europe navigated with it. The Portuguese developed the caravel. This ship was both sturdy and maneuverable on the open sea. Triangular sails made it possible to sail into the wind, which wasn't possible with the square sails. Without all of these cultural developments, Europe could not have established a presence in the New World.

Exploration obviously had many causes and effects. But it was the effects that were the most important. After 1492, there really was a whole new world, because before, the world was only half its current size—at least from the perspective of Europe, who now became the new masters of colonization. This conquest gave Europe many new goods, like corn and cocoa, which played a major role in Europe's diet and also expanding the economy.

Here is a clear example of a student who is not fully in control of the question. Though there is some relevant evidence, much of the essay is off-task. The student confuses causes and effects, which is apparent in the introductory paragraph. If there is a thesis, it seems accidental and confused. The student nearly falls into a narrative mode, tracing the voyages of exploration.

Though a few factual errors are embedded in it, the first body paragraph does provide a relevant if uneven discussion of the new goods as well as the impact they had on European society. The second body paragraph is almost completely tangential, as the student discusses cultural *causes* instead of *effects*. It doesn't matter that the discussion is relatively intelligent and cogent, because the student misses the point of the question.

In the conclusion, the student offers several solid insights regarding the effects of colonization, as if he has recalled the focus of the prompt. As it is, this response only partially responds to the question, though the relevant part is reasonably focused and factual. Score: 4.

CHAPTER 6

Absolutism and the Balance of Power in West and East, 1640–1740

This chapter covers a wide array of nations and rulers. To assist your comprehension, try employing the framework discussed earlier for each nation: Challenge → Response → Result. In response to the devastation of the religious wars and the general upheaval in the period 1550–1650, rulers increasingly justified their power based on absolutist or divine-right theories of monarchy. As we'll see in this chapter, not all accepted such theoretically expansive powers and worked to limit monarchical authority. Rulers also exploited developments in commerce to enhance their nations' power. The resulting competition led to nearly continuous warfare in this period over colonies, trade, and territory. To prevent the predominance of any one power (usually France), European diplomacy relied on the **balance of power.** Both of these trends—development of strong centralized monarchies and balance-of-power diplomacy—played out in eastern and western Europe against the backdrop of various political forms and the differing geographic and social imperatives of east and west.

> **Note:** To users of Palmer, Colton, Kramer, *A History of the Modern World,* this chapter combines Chapters 4 and 5 from your text.

POLITICAL THEORIES AND THE AGE OF CRISIS

To understand the drive for centralized power in European states, it is useful to recall the context of the period 1550–1650. This period is often referred to as the **Age of Crisis,** owing to the cumulative effect of the following forces:

- Religious warfare
- Climate change involving poor weather
- Resulting shorter growing seasons, crop failures, and famines
- High taxes
- Internal rebellion
- Witchcraft accusations
- Intellectual changes in explaining natural phenomena (the Scientific Revolution)
- Economic changes: Price Revolution, enclosure, increase in poverty/begging
- Increase in violent and property crime

Though we prize our liberties today, this fact might be a function of our relative political and social stability. Often in times of chaos and crisis, people willingly sacrifice rights in the interests of security and order. Such was the case for advocates of absolutism in the early seventeenth century. To provide for stability, some political theorists developed justifications for the enhanced power of rulers. Not all agreed, and such opponents provide counter-theories justifying limits on monarchical power.

Given the strong religious beliefs of the period, arguments based on the authority of God carried a natural resonance. Divine-right arguments were new only in the expansive powers with which theorists attempted to imbue them. The most famous advocate of **divine-right rule** was the French clergyman **Bishop Bossuet** (1627–1704), and his views are not known for their subtlety. Quite simply, kings derive their power from God directly and rule on earth in his behalf. Once this view is understood, the resulting magnificent displays of power by Louis XIV and his imitators become clearer as a ruling strategy, as well as the abhorrence with which rebellion and treason were viewed in this era. Some resisted the general trend toward absolutism, such as the Huguenots who endorsed resistance by local officials against what was perceived as a repressive monarchy. The most important theories for and against absolutism will be covered in the next chapter.

THE AGE OF LOUIS XIV IN FRANCE

Foundations of French Absolutism: Henry IV and Louis XIII

Absolutism reached its highest expression in France during the reign of **Louis XIV** (r. 1643–1715). The previous two Bourbon monarchs laid the foundation for the sparkling but flawed edifice that was the Age of Louis XIV. **Henry IV** (r. 1589–1610), the first in the Bourbon line, after bringing the religious conflict to an end with the Edict of Nantes (1598), turned his attention to putting France's financial and economic house in order. Under Henry and his primary advisor, the Duc de Sully, the French state balanced its budget and established a firmer basis for taxation. In addition, Henry promoted economic development through the building of roads and canals, draining swamps, and promoting colonization. His strong rule allowed France to survive his assassination in 1610 and the regency of his wife, Marie de Medicis, on behalf of their son, Louis XIII.

Louis XIII (r. 1610–1643) relied strongly on the advice of his talented and shrewd advisor, **Cardinal Richelieu** (1585–1642), who increased direct *(taille)* and indirect (*gabelle*—government salt monopoly) taxes. Louis and Richelieu concerned themselves with curbing the power of the nobility. To this effect, Richelieu banned dueling (which suggested violence independent of the state), employed spies to monitor the provincial nobility, and appointed *intendants,* or local officials, whose job it was to be the "eyes and ears of the monarchy." In addition, while allowing Huguenots to maintain their religious practices, Richelieu forced them to relinquish their fortified towns. Though Richelieu was a prince of the Catholic Church, under his guidance France supported the *Protestant* forces during the Thirty Years' War. Like Machiavelli before him, politics was for Richelieu about *raison d'etat,* or "reason of state," as he expressed it in his *Political Testament.* According to Richelieu, it was in France's interests to limit the growing power of the surrounding Habsburgs (the political leaders of the Catholic cause), regardless of the religious allegiances of Richelieu, or France more generally.

Louis XIV and French Absolutism

When Louis XIV inherited the throne in 1643, France was once again faced with the prospect of a boy king (Louis was 5). Discontent over high taxes and foreign influence in government led to a series of rebellions in Paris and the countryside known as the **Fronde** (1648–1652). In fact, the young Louis's first memory may have been fleeing from his capital in a carriage surrounded by an angry mob. The event convinced him to build his seat of government in the nearby suburb of Versailles and to establish an iron-fisted rule that could overwhelm any potential future opposition.

Early in Louis's reign, the real ruler of France was **Cardinal Mazarin** (1602–1661), who continued many of the policies of his predecessor, Richelieu. Upon Mazarin's death in 1661, Louis at the

> **Heads Up!** Louis XIV stands certainly as one of the more important figures of the course. As you study, keep in mind not only his policies and goals, but how he reflects the larger trend toward absolutism AND how his rule set the stage for the later French Revolution (1789).

age of 23 took personal control of government and never relinquished it until his death in 1715. A major concern for Louis was to overcome the provincialism and feudal remnants of the French state. Seventeenth-century France was divided by linguistic dialects, provincial customs and **estates,** and by a variety of political bodies that potentially limited monarchical power. One of these political bodies was the 15 regional *parlements,* or courts, controlled by the nobles, and who by tradition had to register the king's decrees to give them effect. To control these bodies, Louis wielded threats of exile and confiscation of property, or involved nobles in court patronage and intrigue at the glittering palace of Versailles.

The Palace at Versailles

Perhaps no greater symbol of royal absolutism exists than Louis's palace at **Versailles.** Originally a hunting lodge, Versailles became under Louis not only a seat of government but a teeming city of patronage-seekers and the backdrop for the drama of Louis's kingship. Looking over the palace itself, the manmade canal, lush gardens, and grandiose out-buildings, one begins to understand the importance of Louis's expression "**I am the state.**" The palace was constructed over several decades, and though the records were deliberately destroyed, it is estimated that the palace absorbed as much as 60 to 80 percent of the state's revenues during the years of its construction. Versailles was more than a royal residence. Nobles were encouraged to live on the grounds and participate in the pageantry of Louis's rule. **Court etiquette** and seeking royal favor deliberately occupied the energies of thousands of the French aristocracy, safely under Louis's gaze and unable to make trouble in the provinces. All of Louis's activities were infused with almost religious solemnity; nobles competed to participate in the ceremonies of the king's waking, dining, and retiring to bed *(lever, dîner,* and *coucher).* French culture and the grandeur of Louis's Versailles became the envy of Europe, as elites across Europe sharpened their French language skills and rulers built their own mini-Versailles.

Economic Policies

Reflecting a continental trend, France under Louis practiced mercantilism to enhance its economic position. Under **Jean-Baptiste Colbert** (1619–1683), the minister of finance and Louis's primary advisor until his death in 1683, France developed a unified internal market and also expanded its commercial presence around the world. Like many nations, France's economy was limited by internal tariffs; though Colbert did not eliminate these, he did create a free-trade zone, known as the **Five Great Farms.** In addition, Colbert continued to enhance France's infrastructure with roads, a postal system, and the establishment of **manufacturing codes.** Industries were organized into corporations, which fell under the guidance of the state, a process that helped the nation earn a reputation for high-quality luxury goods. To promote commerce, Colbert established the **French East India Company** (to rival Britain's and the Netherlands') and built a royal navy. High **tariffs** (taxes on imports) limited foreign goods and, along with the high taxes imposed to finance Louis's many wars, had the effect of increasing the burden on the lower classes (especially peasants) by raising prices and taking much of their hard-earned subsistence. Members of the nobility had negotiated exemptions from many direct taxes over the years, creating a regressive and inefficient system that increased discontent as time wore on.

Religious and Cultural Policies

Though Louis was a committed Catholic, he often clashed with the papacy over the issue of controlling the clergy in France. Louis even drafted a "**Declaration of Gallican Liberties,**" which asserted a semi-independent stance toward Rome, but the conflict was eventually resolved. During Louis's reign, the **Jansenist** controversy divided those in French intellectual circles. Jansenists opposed the Jesuits' strong version of human free will in favor of a Calvinist predestination view of salvation. Perhaps this controversy convinced Louis that he could no longer tolerate "heretics" in an absolutist system that theoretically expressed "**one king, one faith, and one law.**" Thus the very presence of Huguenots was perceived by Louis as a threat to these theoretical powers, so in 1685 Louis revoked the Edict of Nantes (known as the **Edict of Fontainebleu**) and attempted forcibly to convert French Protestants back to Catholicism. Rather than convert, most simply took refuge, along with their property and skills, in those lands that welcomed them, such as the Dutch Republic and Brandenburg-Prussia.

The grandeur of Louis's France was often associated with its artistic and intellectual achievements. In the 1660s, Louis established the **French Academy of Arts** and the **French Academy of Sciences.** The former created works of painting, sculpture, architecture, music, and drama under clear aesthetic guidelines—artists should glorify Louis and France, and link France's greatness with classical subjects and style. Much of this patronage revolved around Versailles, which featured an opera house/theater for the playwrights **Moliere** (1622–1673), **Racine** (1639–1699), and **Cornielle** (1606–1684) to express their comic or tragic commentaries on classical themes. Under the painter **Charles Le Brun** (1619–1690) and the sculptor/architect **Jules Hardouin-Mansart** (1646–1708), who assisted in the design of Versailles, France achieved a continental reputation for combining the scale of the Baroque (see following discussion) with the restraint of the neoclassical. In the area of science, Louis hoped to exploit advances in astronomy, medicine, and navigation to enhance France's prestige as well as its economic and military potential.

> **Sidebar:** Though Louis succeeded in controlling the nation of France through his personality, he never did dismantle its feudal structure of estates, *parlements,* and regional law codes and dialects. The theory of absolutism was grandiose, and one could argue it was never fully realized in France. Rationalization of France's antiquated tax system and administrative structure would await the work of the French Revolution and Napoleon.

The Army

During the seventeenth century, France replaced Spain as the leading military power on the continent and the nation most often threatening the balance of power. Louis XIV considered his and his nation's greatness tied to the army. Under the **Marquis de Louvois** (1641–1691), Louis's minister of war, France's army became the largest in Europe at 400,000 men. Despite Louvois's skill and the addition of territory on France's eastern border, the wars of Louis XIV (see following discussion) drained the treasury and severely taxed the country's manpower and resources.

A COMMERCIAL REPUBLIC: THE DUTCH

For all of France's greatness, its small neighbor to the northeast posed a challenge by being different in almost every possible way. The seven northern provinces of the Netherlands (or United Provinces, officially the Dutch Republic after 1648) became Europe's leading commercial power in the first half of the seventeenth century. How did this nation of about 1 million people with few natural endowments threaten powerful France? First, the Dutch made efficient use of their resources. Land was recovered from the sea by use of dams and dikes and was then organized into *polders* for purposes

> **Sidebar:** Keep in mind that the southern 10 provinces remained loyal to Spain and were known as the Spanish Netherlands. They were primarily Catholic and French-speaking.

of diverting water. After 1580, the Dutch moved into Portuguese markets in the East Indies and South America, establishing colonial outposts and reaping huge profits with their joint-stock companies. Second, the Dutch set themselves up as the "middlemen of Europe" by ignoring the prevailing mercantilist philosophy and using their fleet of maneuverable **flyboats** (or *fluyts*) to trade with all nations and their colonies. It didn't hurt that the Netherlands lay astride important trade routes in the Baltic and Atlantic. **Amsterdam** served as an *entrepot* city, where ships were efficiently uploaded and offloaded with goods (much like a modern computer file server), as well as the financial center of Europe, with its **Bank of Amsterdam** and the **Stock Exchange.** Merchants played a key role in the Netherlands, and their activities drew investment and trade from all over Europe. Finally, the Netherlands practiced religious toleration, attracting Huguenot refugees from France, Jews, small Protestant denominations, and those fleeing the Inquisition in Spain. These talented minorities lent their business acumen and craftsmanship to the flourishing Dutch economy.

The period from 1550 to 1650 marked the Dutch Golden Age. Its "embarrassment of riches" fueled an outpouring of cultural activity, which, unlike in France, focused on themes of middle-class domestic life, nature, and science. Talented painters, such as **Jan Vermeer** (1632–1675), **Judith Leyster** (1609–1660), **Frans Hals** (1588–1666), and **Rembrant von Rijn** (1606–1669), reflected the Dutch preoccupation with light and shadow, natural landscapes, still lifes, domestic scenes, and group portraits. **René Descartes** (1596–1650) and **Baruch Spinoza** (1632–1677) found a home for their unorthodox philosophies in the Netherlands when they couldn't elsewhere. Such economic and cultural achievements attracted the envy of the Netherlands' larger neighbors.

Internal strife and external threat posed a problem for the Dutch. In religion, disagreement over the issue of predestination continued to cause conflict within the Dutch Reformed church. Constitutionally, the Netherlands was a loosely connected federation of seven provinces that often jealously guarded their liberties, but in times of war relied on leadership from the House of Orange in Holland. Because of continual threats to their security, the other six provinces elected **William of Orange** (later king of England) in 1673 as the hereditary *stadholder* of the Netherlands, though the House of Orange never succeeded in creating a strong centralized monarchy. Given its inherent limitations, it was probably only a matter of time before the Netherlands was surpassed by its rivals. A major turning point proved to be the **Anglo-Dutch Naval Wars,** fought in three phases between 1652 and 1674 over the **English Navigation Acts** (1651, 1660), which attempted to restrict Dutch trade with England's colonies. Though the Dutch survived the onslaught, it seriously undercut their commercial power and set the stage for their later conflict with Louis XIV.

BRITAIN: CIVIL WAR AND LIMITED MONARCHY

Causes of the Conflict

Like the so-called religious wars, the English Civil War was both religious and political in nature. The political component revolved around a conflict over sovereignty (ultimate authority) between the new **Stuart** line of monarchs and the **English Parliament.** Religiously, **Puritans** wished to purify the state **Anglican Church** of what they perceived as the residue of Catholic doctrine and worship, which the Stuarts seemed to endorse. Lasting almost a century (from 1603 to 1689), the conflict ultimately laid the foundations for England's unique system of government that combined elements of monarchy, oligarchy ("rule by a few"), and democracy.

Heads Up! The English Civil War is one of the more complex events you will study this year. To avoid getting bogged down in the details, keep bringing yourself back to these essential causes.

Elizabeth I left England without an heir, but she died the most beloved monarch in its history. In 1603 the throne went to the son of Mary, Queen of Scots, **James I** (VI of Scotland, 1603–1625). James would not prove so beloved. As a Scottish outsider, James did not seem to understand the important legislative role played by the English Parliament, whom he continually lectured about his divine-right powers and foolishly laid out in a book, *The True Law of Free Monarchies* (1598). In addition, James antagonized Puritans with the hierarchical structure he retained for the Anglican Church. To control the clergy and religion in general, James believed such an episcopal ("of bishops") structure was necessary; hence, his saying, "**No bishop, no king.**" The growing number of Puritans in Parliament preferred a loose church configuration that allowed individual congregations to control local affairs but cooperate through regional governing boards—a **Presbyterian** structure. James's policies fueled anti-Catholic sentiment, which was only heightened when radical Catholics failed in 1605 to blow up the Parliament, an event known as the **Gunpowder Plot.**

The English Civil War

These issues came to head during the reign of James's son, **Charles I** (1625–1649). When Charles demanded revenue, Parliament issued the **Petition of Right** (1628), an assertion of its prerogatives regarding taxation and liberties from arbitrary arrest and imprisonment. This latter issue had arisen due to the Stuarts' use of the **Star Chamber,** a royal court where the usual judicial procedures were ignored, in favor of secrecy and allegedly arbitrary judgments. Frustrated with Parliament, Charles decided to rule alone from 1629 to 1639, relying on revenues from the royal domain and the use of **ship money**—in which coastal towns were required to contribute either ships or money for defense. This latter policy had the effect of alienating the growing mercantile elite. Further, Charles's religious policies, guided by Archbishop of Canterbury **William Laud** (1573–1645), seemed to Puritans little different than Catholicism. Laud *was* an Anglican, but of the "High Church" variety, and when he attempted to impose uniformity on the realm in 1640 with his **Book of Common Prayer,** the Scots, who favored a Presbyterian church structure, rose in rebellion.

Now Charles had to call the Parliament back into session in order defend against a Scottish invasion. Rather than grant Charles his requested taxes, the so-called **Long Parliament** (because it sat in one form or another for 20 years, until 1660) once again asserted its liberties and placed two of his top officials on trial for treason. When Charles attempted in 1642 to arrest the parliamentary leaders of the Puritan cause, his action misfired and plunged England into civil war. The war between the forces of the king (**Cavaliers**) and those of Parliament (**Roundheads**—due to their short haircuts) resulted in the capture of Charles in 1645. This conflict brought the brilliant and zealous leader of Parliament's **New Model Army** to the fore—**Oliver Cromwell** (1599–1658). Not only an outstanding military leader who employed many of the new more flexible tactics, Cromwell was a devout Puritan who believed, along with his men, in religious toleration for all Protestant denominations and a democratic church structure.

Oliver Cromwell and the Protectorate

When Parliament refused to take action against the captured king, who continued to live in luxury and refused to negotiate, Cromwell surrounded the Parliament and drove out its more moderate members, an action known as **Pride's Purge.** The remaining **Rump Parliament** of **Independents,** who favored independent control by church congregations themselves, placed the king under arrest and executed him for treason in 1649. Soon Cromwell had disposed of even the Rump Parliament and named himself **Lord Protector** under the only written constitution in England's history, the **Instrument of Government** (1653). Eventually Cromwell imposed military

Sidebar: When the Stuarts were restored, Charles II held a posthumous execution of Cromwell, digging up his body and having it drawn and quartered, then dumped in a pit. Cromwell was not formally reburied until 1960. By many, Cromwell is viewed as a righteous defender of Protestantism and English liberties; to others (like the Irish), he is a tyrant and a brutal conqueror.

rule and pursued vigorous policies aimed at reforming English morals (by banning plays, gambling, and the celebration of Christmas, which smacked of Catholic "idolatry"), promoting English commerce via mercantilism, and violently subduing rebellion in Ireland and Scotland. After Cromwell's death in 1658, the English aristocracy, weary of military rule and Cromwell's Puritanism, agreed to restore the Stuart monarchy.

The Stuart Restoration and Glorious Revolution

With the **Restoration** of **Charles II** (1660–1685) as monarch, the same issues of religion and political control did not take long to reassert themselves. Charles did prove wilier than his father, Charles I, and though he was privately inclined toward Catholicism (he was said to have converted on this deathbed), he hid his sympathies behind a façade of religious tolerance. Charles issued a **Declaration of Indulgence** for dissenting faiths, and even more maddening, continued to appoint Catholics as justices of the peace (local officials). In 1673 Parliament responded with the **Test Act,** which required all officeholders to take communion in the Church of England. Further, Charles's pro-French policy ran counter to years of English diplomacy. In fact, Charles had signed in 1670 the secret **Treaty of Dover** with Louis XIV, in which he gained an annual subsidy from the French king while agreeing to reintroduce Catholicism in England at the first opportunity. With these funds, Charles was able to rule without Parliament in the last years of his reign.

Sidebar: The Irish continued to support the Catholic James II, who was finally defeated in 1690 at Boyne, Ireland. Thereafter, Ireland was treated as a subjugated colony, stripped of its religious liberties and subjected to harsh rule by English landlords. These policies fueled resentment between Catholics and Protestants, which survives to this day in the religiously divided northern counties of Ireland, known as Ulster.

What caused the end of the Stuart monarchy was the prospect of a Catholic dynasty for the foreseeable future. Charles's brother, **James II** (1685–1688), ascended to the throne in 1688, despite the division in Parliament between those who supported his legitimate succession—the **Tories**—and those who opposed him—the **Whigs.** James was an avowed Catholic, which might have been tolerable, until his aging wife gave birth to a male heir in 1688. Faced with this prospect, Whig members of Parliament invited James's daughter Mary, a Protestant, and her husband, William of Orange, stadholder of the Netherlands, to invade the nation and claim the throne as co-rulers. The resulting **Glorious Revolution** proved a success, and **William III** (1689–1702) and **Mary II** (1688–1694) agreed to respect parliamentary sovereignty and English liberties with the **Bill of Rights** (1689). In addition, Parliament passed a **Toleration Act** (1689), which allowed Protestant dissenters to worship but excluded them from public service, and the **Act of Succession** (1701), which prohibited the English monarchy from ever being held by a Catholic. Finally, to cement ties formally with Scotland, the English Parliament agreed in 1707 to create the **United Kingdom** of Great Britain, whose people now called themselves "British." The Glorious Revolution and this series of acts laid the foundation for Britain's unique but stable government and commercial dominance in the eighteenth century.

ART: FROM MANNERISM TO BAROQUE

Due to foreign invasion and economic decline, the Italian Renaissance style of symmetry, order, and classical themes gave way to a style based on complex composition, distortion, and elongated human figures. This late sixteenth-century genre was known as **Mannerism,** meaning those who painted in the "manner" of the later Michelangelo, such as his "Last Judgment" (completed in 1542). The most famous Mannerist painter, who accomplished his greatest work during the Spanish Golden Age, was **El Greco** (1541–1614). Known for introducing yellows and grays into the painter's palette, El Greco expressed in his "Burial of Count Orgaz" and "Landscapes of Toledo" a complex psychology toward a Spain on the verge of decline. To get an impression of the Mannerist style, you might also check out **Tintoretto's** (1518–1594) version of "The Last Supper" and compare it with da Vinci's. Clearly, Catholic Counter-Reformation mysticism had replaced the classical style and three-dimensional emphasis of Leonardo's version.

Mannerism gradually evolved into the **Baroque** style, which dominated art and music from 1600 to about 1730. A major theme of the Baroque is power—expressing the rising absolute monarchs and the reviving Catholic Church, both of whom were the major patrons of Baroque artists. The figure most associated with the rebuilding of Rome in the age of the Counter-Reformation is **Gianlorenzo Bernini** (1598–1680), an accomplished painter, sculptor, and architect. Bernini designed the magnificent altar in St. Peter's Basilica, the papal throne, and the welcoming arms of **St. Peter's Square** outside. In addition, Bernini's version of the "David" demonstrates the Baroque style eloquently: Unlike Michelangelo's static psychological portrait, Bernini provides the viewer with the action of David flinging his slingshot. Bernini's most famous work—**"The Ecstasy of St. Teresa"**—combines sculpture and architecture to recreate an ecstatic religious vision.

Absolute monarchs like Louis XIV needed artists to assist in conveying their grandeur. Court painters, such as **Velazquez** (1599–1660) of Spain, managed to win patronage by not only glorifying monarchy but also creating rich and complex commentaries on their subjects, as with **"The Maids of Honor."** Another outstanding painter of the Baroque style who attracted many patrons was **Peter Paul Rubens** (1577–1640). Rubens was one of the first studio painters, employing a team of assistants, to help him complete his many muscular and energetic compositions of both religious scenes, such as **"The Raising of the Cross,"** and the political, such as his **"Portraits of Marie de Medicis"** (wife of Henry IV of France). In addition, the painter popularized a full-figured female body style, in both women and angels, known as Rubenesque. There is little coverage of music on the AP Exam (unless you can use your knowledge in a relevant essay prompt), but it bears mentioning the musical compositions of J. S. Bach, Antonio Vivaldi, G. F. Handel, and the operas of Claudio Monteverdi, all of which expressed the Baroque fascination with ornate, complex structure as well as religious and secular themes of power.

> **Heads Up!** An outstanding resource for students to use to analyze this and other masterpieces of art is Robert Cumming, *Annotated Art* (1995).

THE WARS OF LOUIS XIV

To understand European diplomacy, you must understand the importance of the balance of power. Balance-of-power politics developed during the Italian Renaissance but reached its most explicit form during the Age of Louis XIV. Louis's desire to extend France to its "**natural frontiers**" (the Rhine River) and also accrue glory to himself led him into nearly constant warfare during his reign. As Spain continued its decline under the Habsburgs, France rushed in to exploit the vacuum of power in the Western Europe. In each of these wars, Louis animated a coalition of powers against him to prevent his threat to the balance of power, or the dominance of one nation over the rest. As you read over the wars discussed next, focus on how the balance of power operates and shifts with each phase of conflict.

The first targets of Louis's ambitions were the Spanish Netherlands and Dutch Republic, the latter whose commercial success he envied. Louis struck in two phases, first in 1667 and again in 1672, now with England as an ally. This **Dutch War** earned Louis the strategic province of **Franche-Comté,** or the former Burgundy, which gave France substantial territory on the Swiss border and also outflanked Alsace-Lorraine, his next target. Taking advantage of the growing weakness of the Holy Roman Empire, Louis in 1689 then invaded Alsace-Lorraine. The subsequent **Nine Years' War** resulted in an anti-French alliance, also known as the **League of Augsburg.** Now both the stadholder of the Netherlands and king of England, William III (of Orange) pieced together this coalition to prevent Louis's bid for continental domination. Famines, sieges, and high taxes marked this desultory conflict, which ended practically where it started with the **Treaty of Ryswick** in 1697, Louis gaining only a few towns along his border. Bigger game awaited, as the Spanish monarch, Charles II, continued to decline in health, with no heir to the throne.

European royal houses had waited decades for the death of poor **Charles II** (1665–1700), the last Habsburg ruler of Spain and sad result of generations of interbreeding between the Spanish and Austrian Habsburg lines. Complicating matters, Louis XIV and the Holy Roman Emperor claimed the throne through family marriages to Charles's sisters. Both contenders signed a treaty in 1700 to partition the Spanish Empire and thus maintain the balance of power. These plans fell to naught when Charles left a will in 1700 after his death granting his entire possessions to his nephew, Philip V, the Bourbon grandson of Louis XIV. Louis decided to press his claim to the Spanish throne via his grandson. The resulting **War of Spanish Succession** (1702–1713) proved to be the most costly, important, and last of Louis's wars for continental domination. France and Spain faced off against England, the Netherlands, the Holy Roman Emperor, and a few smaller states. Warfare in the eighteenth century tended to revolve around elaborate and slow movements designed to outmaneuver opponents or capture strategic fortresses. The French were stunned at the battle of **Blenheim** (1704) in Bavaria, when **John Churchill, the Duke of Marlborough** (1650–1722), marched his English troops over 300 miles to meet up with the emperor's forces and surprise Louis. Nonetheless, the war dragged expensively on, as each nation—large and small—exploited the conflict to meet long-held territorial and political goals.

> **Sidebar:** Churchill also served as Queen Anne's primary advisor. In honor of his great victory, the English built the duke a palace named Blenheim. Winston Churchill, a distant relation, spent time in the palace as a youth.

With the **Peace of Utrecht** in 1714 the conflict finally came to a close. Louis's grandson, **Philip V** (1700–1749) did become the Bourbon ruler of Spain, but it was a truncated empire that could never be united with its northern Bourbon neighbor of France. To recognize the weaker position of Spain, the 10 southern provinces of the Netherlands were given to Austria (now the Austrian Netherlands), as were former Spanish territories in Italy. The big winner of the conflict proved to be England, which gained **Gibraltar,** a fortress at the opening of the Mediterranean, new territory in North America, and the privilege of trading with the Spanish Empire, known as the *asiento.* Britain's Protestant succession was also confirmed, and it was now poised, with a stable government and enhanced commercial position, to become the leading maritime power in Europe. As we'll see in the following discussion, other nations emerged from the conflict with either newfound or curtailed power. However, the major consequences of the war and the treaty were to block Louis XIV's last effort to impose French domination on the continent and to confirm the European state system of sovereign nations constantly shifting positions to maintain or create a balance of power. On his deathbed in 1715, Louis told his heir and great-grandson (the future Louis XV) that he feared he "had loved war too much."

AGING EMPIRES IN THE EAST

Central Europe in the seventeenth century was dominated by three aging states—the Holy Roman Empire, Poland, and the Ottoman Empire. The weakness of these "soft states"—so-called because of their loose organization—allowed for the emergence of a new constellation of powers.

Following the Thirty Years' War (1648), the Holy Roman Empire's status as a loose confederation of over 300 German states was confirmed. The traditional rulers of the empire, the Austrian Habsburgs, turned east over the next century to enhance their power, particularly at the expense of the declining Ottoman Empire. Though Austria was able to gain significant swaths of land in east-central Europe, these conquests continued to bring more non-German minorities (Slavs, Poles, Italians, Romanians, and Ukrainians) into the empire, which later proved a centrifugal force, as nationalism took hold in the nineteenth century.

Poland was the weakest of the European kingdoms. Ironically, in 1500 Poland had been the largest nation in Europe. Throughout the sixteenth century, the powerful nobles of Poland—the *szlachta,* who made up almost 10 percent of the population—succeeded in limiting the power of the Polish kings. Eventually, the Polish monarchy evolved into an elective position, and one that was fought over by rival European powers, who bribed the noble-electors with promises of religious toleration and respect for their "liberties." Starting with the reign of **Sigismund III** (1587–1632) from Sweden, who embroiled Poland in a needless war to recapture the Swedish throne, until 1795, the nation was ruled by only two native-born monarchs. Further, any single noble could block the actions of the **Sejm,** Poland's representative body, by using the *liberum veto.* Poland's experience ran counter to the larger trend toward absolutism, and unable to establish permanent taxes or a standing army, Poland fell prey to larger rivals. The tragic result of this failure to centralize for the formerly great kingdom was its final partition in 1795.

After the Turks captured Constantinople in 1453, the Ottoman Empire periodically sent shockwaves of fear throughout central Europe as it went through an ebb and flow of expansion. In 1529, the Turks had nearly captured Vienna, but eventually fell back into internal turmoil for over a century. Once again, **in 1683 the Turks besieged the Habsburg capital,** which was rescued triumphantly by a multinational Holy League (led by the last great native Polish king, Jan Sobieski). Never again would the Turks pose a major threat to central Europe. What had once been Ottoman strengths now decayed; the empire simply did not keep up with rest of Europe. First, the Turkish rulers, the sultans, grew corrupt from court intrigue, assassination plots, and sensuous living. Second, the once-great **Janissaries,** the elite fighters comprised of former Christians, became a static force opposed to technological and strategic change. Finally, though the Ottoman rulers tolerated religious minorities (more so than most European nations), the resulting tradition of local rule made it difficult to draw effectively on the resources of the empire's far-flung provinces. Many states, such as France, desired the continued existence of the Ottoman Empire as a counterweight to the Austrian Habsburgs, but only if the Islamic state could be influenced and indirectly controlled from the outside.

AUSTRIA TURNS EAST

Once the Austrian Habsburgs held off the Turkish invasion in 1683, they were able to turn the battle back toward their long-time enemies. Employing the talents of a castoff from the court of Louis XIV, **Eugene of Savoy** (1663–1736), the Austrians defeated the Turks at the battle of Zenta (1697) and eventually gained back Hungary and added Transylvania, as well as territory in the

Balkan Peninsula, via the **Treaty of Karlowitz** (1699). Austria needed to end the Turkish conflict so as to turn its attention to the impending War of Spanish Succession (see previous discussion). Though the Austrians were unable to reunite the two Habsburg branches (Spanish and Austrian) during the conflict, the Peace of Utrecht (1713–1714) granted them territory in the Netherlands and Italy.

The reign of Emperor **Charles VI** (1711–1740) was dominated by one issue: ensuring the succession of his daughter and heir, Maria Theresa (1740–1780), to the many Habsburg lands. To this effect, Charles negotiated the **Pragmatic Sanction** with Europe's rulers, whereby they agreed to respect the Habsburg inheritance to a female ruler. Given the circumstances, Austria adjusted effectively after its losses in the Thirty Years' War, but as we'll see in the next chapter, the succession issue would ultimately cost the Habsburgs their dominant position in central Europe.

THE RISE OF PRUSSIA AND ITS ARMY

The rise of Brandenburg-Prussia (later simply Prussia) in the seventeenth century was a surprise. A scattered nation with a small population (2 million in 1650) and few natural resources, Prussia relied heavily on three factors for its amazing rise to power: (1) skillful and resolute leadership from the **Hohenzollern** dynasty, (2) efficient use of resources, and, most important, (3) an outstanding military tradition. As was often joked, "Prussia is not a state with an army, but an army with a state." For no other nation was the military so closely associated with its power and prestige, perhaps a link to the tradition of the crusading Teutonic Knights.

Brandenburg stood in the middle of north-central Germany, of importance only as an Elector of the Holy Roman Emperor. However, in 1618 the Hohenzollerns inherited the Duchy of Prussia, so far east that it was surrounded by Poland. During the Thirty Years' War (1618–1648), Brandenburg experienced widespread devastation, its capital city of Berlin reduced to a village of rubble. Nonetheless, Brandenburg-Prussia gained territory in the west along the Rhine and in Pomerania as a result of the Peace of Westphalia (1648). **Frederick William, the "Great Elector"** (1640–1688) resolved that his nation would never again be overrun by invading armies.

Frederick William was the first in a line of great Prussian rulers. To gain the support of the Prussian nobility—the **Junkers**—Frederick William gave them important positions in the army and allowed them almost complete power over their serfs. In exchange, the aristocracy agreed to accept Hohenzollern leadership and an excise tax to fund the activities of the state. With these funds, Frederick William erected the skeleton of the Prussian state. To collect the taxes, Frederick William created the **General War Commissariat**, which at first provisioned the army but which evolved into a state bureaucracy, famous for its punctuality and efficiency. The Hohenzollern rulers generally lived a Spartan existence, allowing most of the state's revenues to flow into the army. Though Frederick William enhanced the army to 40,000 men, his goal was not to use it for conquest, but for security and as the glue that held scattered Prussia together. In addition, Frederick William practiced mercantilism by establishing monopolies, raising tariffs on imported goods, and promoting economic development. When Louis XIV revoked the Edict of Nantes, the Prussian state welcomed the persecuted Huguenots, eager to cash in on their economic skills.

During the War of Spanish Succession, the Habsburg emperor called on the support of Brandenburg-Prussia to drive out the French from Germany. As a reward for his support, the duke of Brandenburg-Prussia earned himself a new title—king of Prussia. The first great king of Prussia proved to be **Frederick William I** (1713–1740), not to be confused with Frederick William, the Great Elector. Frederick William's personality and approach to governing were strict, paternalistic, and austere. The ruler could often be seen patrolling the streets of his realm with a walking stick, admonishing government officials or wayward citizens. Efficiency and duty took precedence over all else. State funds were used judiciously to augment the size of the army (up to 83,000 at Frederick William's death) and often came at the expense of the royal household budget. Frederick William also introduced merit to government service, often promoting the middle class, though this by no means challenged the primary position of the Junkers or the army. Another curiosity of Frederick William's was his penchant for tall soldiers; he formed the **Potsdam Regiment** of men 6 to 7 feet in height, perhaps to intimidate potential enemies. However, Frederick William fought no wars in his reign. This feat he left for the son with whom he never got along, Frederick II.

PETER AND THE WESTERNIZATION OF RUSSIA

Russia's Unique Position

Much of Russia is *in* Europe, but Russia has not always been *of* Europe. Many of the trends we have addressed thus far—Renaissance, Reformation, Scientific Revolution (see Chapter 7)—did not touch the Russian state or its people. For many in the west, Russia was a mystery, more closely tied to the political and religious traditions of Asia. It is not as difficult, however, to identify the thrust of Russia's experience, as the themes of (1) expansion and (2) relative backwardness define its role in European history.

As we've seen, Russia made strides in establishing a larger and more modern state under both Ivan III and Ivan IV in the sixteenth century. These rulers succeeded in driving the Mongols from much of central Asia, establishing some semblance of an administrative structure and creating a military class *(streltsy)*. Unfortunately, Ivan IV killed his heir to the throne in a fit of rage, causing Russia to enter a difficult period of internal instability and foreign invasion known as the **Time of Troubles** (1604–1613). The situation was not resolved until the feudal estates, known as the Zemsky Sobor, elected **Michael Romanov** (1613–1645) as the tsar of Russia. Romanov rule would last in Russia until the Russian Revolution in 1917 led to the end of the family line.

Russia now had some stability but continued to lag behind the rest of Europe. First, it was during the seventeenth century that Russia's oppressive system of **serfdom** was put into legal form. Though other nations in eastern and central Europe practiced serfdom, only in Russia could serfs be bought and sold like chattel. This slavelike existence often provoked massive rebellions. Such was the case with the revolt led by **Stephen Razin** (1630–1671), who gathered together discontented serfs and Cossacks (a warrior tribe) proclaiming the overthrow of landlords and those in authority. Though the movement was crushed in 1671, Russia's rulers imposed an even more rigorous serfdom on the nation, fearful of another uprising. Furthermore, Russia's dominant religion was the tradition-bound Orthodox Church, which tended to oppose social and religious changes. When the Russian patriarch Nikon (head of the Russian Orthodox Church) undertook reforms in the Bible and worship, a group called the **Old Believers** opposed the reforms and threatened to break away from the church. These represent only two issues facing Russia during this period, but they demonstrate well the divide between Russia's people and its government, as well as the conflict between tradition and modernization.

The Reforms of Peter the Great

One of the greatest and most amazing figures in Russian history is **Peter I, the Great** (1682–1725). On one hand, Peter was attracted by all that was modern—technology, science, industry; on the other, he could be brutal and ruthless in the pursuit of his goals. By the sheer force of his personality and vision, Peter hoped to bring Russia into the European state system and within a generation render his nation a great power. Though Peter did succeed in making the rest of Europe take note of Russia's might, his reforms did not seep down to the common person and often created divisions within Russian society.

> **Heads Up!** When studying a major figure such as Peter, try to go beyond simply committing his policies to memory. Consider how he/she reflects the issues and conflicts of the period. For example, Peter demonstrates the tension in Russian history of being in Europe geographically but not always taking part in all of its cultural or intellectual developments.

As a boy in Moscow, Peter enjoyed the company of westerners who lived in the so-called German suburb of the city. Here he learned about engineering and manufacturing. When Peter took the throne, he decided to embark on a **Great Embassy** (1697–1698) to the west with hundreds of technical advisors. Peter attempted to travel incognito, but it was hard to miss the nearly 7-foot-tall Russian leader as he visited shipyards, manufactories, and colleges. The trip was cut short as Peter faced a rebellion at home by the *streltsy,* who opposed his trip and his reforms, viewing them as a threat to their power. Upon his return, Peter personally interrogated and executed many of the leaders of the rebellion, hanging their bodies on the city gates as a warning to others. With this storehouse of new technical skill, however, Peter helped build Russia's first navy and a more modern army. During his reign, Peter was nearly continuously at war, generally with the Ottoman Turks and Swedes.

Internally, Peter set out to strengthen the nation as well as reform the habits of his people. Taxes were imposed on a variety of items, including "heads," known as the **poll tax.** With these funds, Peter pursued mercantilist policies aimed at making Russia a commercial nation, with its own joint-stock companies, merchant fleet, and monopolies. Peter even employed serf labor in mining, metallurgy, and textile manufacture. Russians also needed to look modern, so Peter banned the wearing of long coats, beards, and the veiling of women. To promote loyalty to the state, Peter required all members of the landowning class to engage in state service. This later evolved into a system of merit, known as the **Table of Ranks,** whereby subjects could rise in status based on contributions to the state. To make governing the vast Russian expanse more effective, Peter eliminated the feudal organs of self-government and divided the nation into 10 governing units, with a senate of advisors to assist him in day-to-day administration. Finally, to resolve the conflict within the Russian Orthodox Church, Peter simply eliminated the position of patriarch and instead placed the church under the control of the state, a power that was exercised through a **Holy Synod** of bishops.

The Great Northern War

The primary goal of these changes was to gain territory at the expense of Russia's neighbors. At first, Peter directed his attention toward the Black Sea, hoping to gain a port city (Azov) there. His campaigns failed to achieve much, except to demonstrate the backwardness of the Russian military. However, Peter's main rival was Sweden, whose territory and dominant position in the Baltic he wished to replace. At this time, Sweden was ruled by the militarily talented but unpredictable **Charles XII** (1697–1718), who was able to defeat a vastly superior Russian force in 1700 at the battle of **Narva,** which kicked off the **Great Northern War** (1700–1721). As usual, Peter learned from his mistakes and changed his tactics and technology, all while Charles became bogged down in Polish politics. Again in 1709, the two armies faced off. This time Peter used the traditional Russian tactic of drawing the enemy into the Russian interior to face its brutal winter. Then at **Poltava,** Peter struck at Charles's army, crushing it and forcing him into exile in the Ottoman Empire. By the **Treaty of Nystadt** (1721), Russia gained significant territory in the Baltic, which allowed Peter to build a new capital city, St. Petersburg, which represented his "**window to the west.**" Never before had Russian influence extended so far into Europe.

No doubt, Peter accomplished much in his forced modernization of Russia. Prior to his reign, Russia was a large but backward entity relatively unknown to the rest of Europe. When Peter died in 1725, he left Russia a great power of Europe, feared for its sheer size and military potential. Many elites in Russia eagerly adopted Peter's reforms, as they saw in them the potential for individual gain and national power. Nonetheless, most of Peter's reforms came at the expense of the masses—serfs, Old Believers, lower classes. While Russia had adopted a veneer of technological and industrial might, its autocratic (rule by one person) system of government was fastened more tightly on the nation than ever before. In the short run, Russia was now a major power and always posed a threat of expansion; in the long run, these perennial issues of backwardness and autocratic rule contributed to the Russian Revolution in the twentieth century.

ADDITIONAL RESOURCES

Burke, Peter, *The Fabrication of Louis XIV* (1992)—Studies the man and myth that was the Sun King.

Cameron, Euan, *Early Modern Europe: An Oxford History* (1999)—Provides recent interpretations by leading historians on a variety of relevant topics.

Cromwell (1970)—Fast-paced film portrayal of the English Civil War, starring Richard Harris (Albus Dumbledore in the first two Harry Potter films) as Oliver Cromwell.

Davies, Norman, *Europe: A History* (1998)—This massive history places Poland at the center of Europe. The appendices and anecdotal "boxes" are alone worth the price of the book.

Fraser, Antonio, *Cromwell, the Lord Protector* (1973)—Well-known biographer of English rulers tackles a complex subject.

Goubert, Pierre, *Louis XIV and Twenty Million Frenchmen* (1970)—A readable volume that places political history in social context.

Massie, Robert K., *Peter the Great: His Life and World* (1980)—Fascinating character study. A lengthy book that could be used in sections. Also recommended is the outstanding miniseries based on the book, which can be purchased at Amazon.com.

McKay, Derek, and H. M. Scott, *The Rise of the Great Powers, 1648–1815* (1983)—Detailed account of how and why the balance of power shifted during this period; useful in sections for research on specific nations.

http://www.classical.net/—For those interested in classical music, this site offers biographical sketches of important composers.

PRACTICE QUESTIONS

1. Which of the following best indicates the importance of the Peace of Utrecht (1713–14)?
   a. It confirmed the dominance of Spain and reduced the power of England.
   b. It ended Louis XIV's bid for dominance and reaffirmed the balance of power.
   c. It resulted in the union of the Spanish and French crowns by the Bourbons.
   d. It demonstrated the growing power of Russia in the east.
   e. It halted the decline of Sweden, the Netherlands, and Poland.

2. What does the accompanying painting by Jan Vermeer reveal about Dutch society in the seventeenth century?
   a. The Dutch valued aristocratic status and prestige above all else.
   b. Most Dutch people had difficulty surviving the difficult economic times.
   c. Single parents became common as out-of-wedlock births increased.
   d. The Dutch prized domestic comfort and middle-class values.
   e. Baroque themes of power and ornamentation predominated.

Erich Lessing/Art Resource, NY

3. Which of the following expresses a basic cause of the English Civil War?
   a. Conflict between aristocratic landowners and middle-class merchants increased.
   b. The English people resented the efforts of the Stuarts to reimpose Catholicism.
   c. Parliament and the Stuart kings clashed over which had ultimate authority.
   d. A serious economic depression and rising prices led to popular riots.
   e. Government overspending led to a takeover of the state by wealthy banking families.

4. All of the following resulted from the Glorious Revolution EXCEPT:
   a. parliamentary sovereignty was affirmed.
   b. religious toleration was extended to Protestants.
   c. a bill of rights was enacted and signed by the monarchy.
   d. Catholics could not hold the throne of England.
   e. the House of Lords was abolished.

5. Why did Louis XIV (1643–1715) revoke the Edict of Nantes in 1685?
   a. Louis believed the Huguenots' existence threatened the unity of the state and religion.
   b. Huguenots were captured plotting on overthrowing Louis's monarchy.
   c. Louis fulfilled an agreement with the papacy to persecute the Huguenots.
   d. Economic Minister Colbert convinced Louis that the Huguenots harmed the economy.
   e. Louis wished to support the Jansenist movement, rivals of the Huguenots.

6. The palace at Versailles was built primarily to:
   a. provide a means for Louis XIV to control the nobility.
   b. absorb excess revenues from French tariffs.
   c. intimidate foreign nations with France's greatness.
   d. provide public works jobs for landless peasants.
   e. house the extended family of the French monarchy.

7. With the Pragmatic Sanction, Charles VI (1711–1740) of Austria hoped to accomplish which of the following?
   a. assure Habsburg control of the Spanish crown
   b. form an alliance against the emerging Prussia
   c. ensure the inheritance of Habsburg lands for his daughter
   d. create a coalition to combat French threats
   e. reform the practice of serfdom in the empire

8. Which of the following is most closely associated with the rise of Prussia as a major power?
   a. the army
   b. the civil service
   c. Hohenzollern monarchy
   d. commerce
   e. a strong navy

9. Which of the following resulted from Peter the Great's (1682–1725) policies in Russia?
   a. a general reform of the habits and attitudes of the masses
   b. widespread opposition and attempts to overthrow the government
   c. the abolition of serfdom and modernization of agriculture
   d. victory in the Great Northern War (1700–1721), making Russia a major power
   e. a strong governing alliance between the monarchy and the growing middle classes.

10. Which of the following best accounts for the weakness of Poland in the seventeenth century?
    a. factionalism among the nobility
    b. lack of economic development
    c. a declining tax base and periodic famine
    d. lack of a strong, centralized monarchy
    e. religious conflict between Catholics and Protestants

SAMPLE ESSAY

Choose any TWO of the following rulers and compare and contrast their success in addressing the challenges to their nation's power in the period 1640–1740.

Louis XIV (1643–1715) in France
Frederick William, the Great Elector (1640–1688) in Prussia
Peter I, the Great (1682–1725) in Russia

In the period 1640–1740 Europe experienced an increase in absolutist monarchy. Many nations had to deal with instability and rebellion, so a strong divine-right ruler seemed a way to strengthen the political system. Two of greatest of these rulers were Peter the Great of Russia and Louis XIV, the Sun King, of France. They used similar policies, like controlling the nobles, building up armies, and putting the church under the state, but they did have to deal with different issues based on their geographies. In all, Peter was the more successful than Louis in taking his nation to a higher point.

When Peter took the throne, Russia was a backward nation. Most people in the rest of Europe didn't even know anything about it. Peter made Russia a nation to be feared. First, he traveled to the west to gain new technology and industry, which he brought back to Russia. These technologies were used to build up the army and navy, not to mention the economy. Peter practiced mercantilism, which was based on increasing a nation's commercial position. However, Peter had a problem: no ports or trading areas. To resolve this, Peter went to war against Sweden and conquered large territories in the Baltic. This allowed him to build St. Petersburg, his "window to the west." Also, Peter wanted his people to be modern, so women could take off their veils and nobles were required to cut their beards. If they didn't, Peter cut them off for them. Finally, Peter made the nation easier to govern, with a Senate and geographic regions. He even introduced a system of merit called the Table of Merit. With all these policies, Russia was now a great military power. Nonetheless, Russia had no democratic traditions, so Peter ruled with an iron fist and shoved these changes down his nation's throat.

Louis XIV was certainly a dazzling monarch. His palace at Versailles was the envy of Europe. The reason he built it was to keep track of the nobles, who had risen in rebellion early in his reign. Aristocrats came to the great palace—which had an opera house, orange trees, and fancy fountains—to seek Louis's favor and get easy positions at court. There was even a waiting list to live in a small apartment there. France had many traditions of local rule, especially with the parlements, courts that could limit the king's power. Though Louis did not dismantle these, he was able to dominate them with his royal glory. Moreover, Louis really loved war; he fought about five in his reign, all to gain territory and glory for himself. In the end, these wars proved costly and bankrupted the treasury. The Huguenots had existed in France for over a hundred years, but Louis did not want their presence in his kingdom, because he was a firm Catholic. He drove them out, and this hurt the economy because many of them were talented with trade. Like Peter, Louis practiced mercantilism through his advisor Colbert. This did help France's economy, but they still were not as strong as the Dutch or English. No doubt, Louis was powerful and reigned a long time. But you could argue that France was worse off after his reign: with debt, discontent, and angry nobles.

There were many great monarchs in this Age of Absolutism. But if we look at where Russia and France started when Peter and Louis took power, clearly Russia was at a lower point. France was already pretty powerful. Louis XIV's policies were mostly for show; you could even say he didn't make France more powerful, just more famous. On the other hand, Peter took a backward nation and made it a great world power. That's the real test of a ruler, and Peter wins.

This is a strong essay. The student clearly addresses all parts of the question in the introductory paragraph: She identifies similarities and differences and offers an explicit response to the issue of who proved more effective. Both body paragraphs are well-balanced and provide both internal and foreign policies. More important, the examples support the thesis. A minor error ("Table of Merit" instead of "Table of Ranks") certainly does not detract from an otherwise strongly argued and focused response. If an AP reader were debating between an 8 and 9, the strong conclusion, which returns to thesis and sharpens it, would lean him or her toward the higher score. This response is an effective model of a clear, cogent writing, even if the student engages in some informalities. Score: 9.

CHAPTER 7
The Scientific View of the World

It would be difficult to overestimate the importance of the Scientific Revolution to the history of humanity. For many historians, the advent of a mathematical, scientific view of the world marks the beginnings of our modern age. For centuries, the achievements of ancient Greece and Rome had established the standard of excellence and reference point for all knowledge. However, during Europe's "Age of Genius" in the seventeenth century, scientists and philosophers demonstrated that this classical heritage could be surpassed through the application of the scientific method. Scientific thinking has come to infect almost all intellectual disciplines; the result has been not only improvements in technology but the challenging of traditional religious, political, and intellectual perspectives. Modern science represents an intellectual tool of great power, though a power that can also be used to destroy.

THE OLD SCIENCE

Prior to the sixteenth century, scientific thinking about motion, the cosmos, and the human body was dominated by **Aristotle** (fourth-century B.C. philosopher), **Ptolemy** (second-century Greek astronomer), and **Galen** (second-century Greek physician). In essence, the worldview of these ancient Greeks was qualitative—humans could employ their logical and rational capacities to determine the nature of objects, and from there, describe their behavior. Greek thinking was absorbed into Christianity in the thirteenth century with **Scholasticism,** which thereafter dominated the investigations of natural philosophy, as science was usually called. Scholastics dealt first with definitions and general propositions and went on to deduce further structures of knowledge from these.

Systematic observation, experimentation, and mathematics played little role in the Scholastic system. Therefore, the **Aristotelian-Ptolemaic view** of the cosmos relied on the "logical" view that the earth lay at the center of the universe with the moon, sun, other planets, and stars revolving around it along crystalline spheres in perfect circles. The "heavens" were made of a separate substance (the "quintessence," or fifth substance, to distinguish it from earth, air, fire, and water) and moved in circles, because the sphere represented the perfect geometric shape, reflecting the perfection of the heavens. Earthly objects moved along straight lines and fell toward earth, not because of a mysterious force called gravity, but to be at one with the substance from which they were made. Each object demonstrated properties unique to its nature; thus, heavy objects were believed to fall faster because they contained more matter and thus moved more quickly to their natural resting place. Though the ancient Greek philosophers Pythagoras and Plato did believe mathematical harmonies underlie all of nature, ancient and medieval scientific thought did not contemplate the notion of universal laws that could be expressed through mathematical *equations.*

Ancient cosmology was reflected in views of human anatomy. Galen postulated that the human body contained **four humors**: blood, phlegm, yellow bile, and black bile. Each of these humors was associated with a particular temperament, so individuals dominated by blood, for example, tended to be "sanguine," or optimistic and cheerful. Bodily disorders arose from an imbalance of humors. Treatment involved correcting this imbalance through **purging** (inducing vomiting) and **bleeding.** Regardless of these treatments' failures, such ideas held sway among physicians for centuries, whose studies revolved more around reading ancient texts than anatomical study or clinical work with patients. Church prohibitions on dissection probably hindered anatomical knowledge in this regard; though Leonardo da Vinci violated this taboo, his detailed sketches of the human body, as well as other amazing diagrams of flying machines, led to few practical consequences, as they were not pursued systematically or taken up by future scientists.

Several stimuli account for the development of new scientific approaches in the sixteenth century: the Renaissance interest in nature, the need for celestial navigation to support exploration, and the Catholic Church's interest in an accurate calendar. Though the old model had worked well for centuries, the discrepancy between its theories and actual observations grew, and could not be explained satisfactorily by continued reference to its assumptions.

ADVANCES IN ASTRONOMY AND PHYSICS

There are moments when ideas can change the world—literally. Such was the case with **Nicholas Copernicus's** (1473–1543) *On the Revolutions of the Heavenly Spheres,* published just before the author's death in 1543. A Polish Catholic priest, Copernicus was called on by the church to develop a more accurate calendar. He presented the notion of a heliocentric, or sun-centered, universe as a mathematical supposition. Though Copernicus retained many features of the Ptolemaic **cosmology** ("view of the universe"), this radical notion that God's special creation—humans and their terrestrial home—were no longer the center of the universe served to spark criticism and further astronomical inquiry. The developments that follow in astronomy and physics represent the primary field of advance during the Scientific Revolution; as you review, consider the relationship between new *ideas* and new *methods*.

> **Sidebar:** One of the first figures to criticize the theory was Martin Luther, who reportedly said, "that fool wants to turn the entire science of astronomy upside down!" At first the Catholic Church did not denounce heliocentrism, as long as it was treated as only a mathematical hypothesis, not an actual fact.

The work of Copernicus demonstrates how a mathematics-driven astronomy could lead to and support new theories of planetary motion. Copernicanism temporarily stood as a theory without support from observations. Danish astronomer **Tycho Brahe** (1546–1601) provided these observations, as he spent over 20 years staring at the night sky on the isolated island of Hven off the coast of Denmark—all without the aid of a telescope! In 1577 Brahe charted the path of a comet that seemed to be traveling in an irregular (not circular) path as it passed through the supposed crystalline spheres, something that wasn't supposed to happen under the Ptolemaic system. While Brahe never fully accepted the heliocentric theory, his massive collection of data aided future scientists.

One of history's greatest scientists, **Johannes Kepler** (1571–1630), put Brahe's data to good use. Formerly Brahe's assistant, Kepler became court astronomer to the Holy Roman Emperor, despite being Lutheran. He used his mathematical genius to make a conceptual leap regarding planetary motion: Many of the anomalies in the Copernican system were eliminated if the planets traveled in **elliptical paths.** Further, Kepler articulated **three laws of planetary motion,** all of which could be expressed precisely using equations. For example, Kepler demonstrated that the closer a planet orbited to the sun, the faster it moved, which fit with observations. Nonetheless, not all Kepler's views would be regarded as scientific today. Somewhat of a religious mystic, Kepler believed that the orbits of the planets expressed a cosmic harmony, which could be heard in the "music of the spheres."

Galileo Galilei (1564–1642) combined interests of wide scope with an ability to attract patronage and attention, not all of which was positive. First, the Italian scientist's correspondence with Kepler demonstrates the emergence of an international scientific community. Second, based on repeated experiment, Galileo devised one of the first mathematical formulas to explain and predict natural phenomena, the law of accelerating bodies: 32 ft/sec/sec. Providing **empirical** ("based on the senses") support for the heliocentric theory represents Galileo's most famous contribution to science. In 1609 Galileo built one of the first telescopes and trained it on the heavens. The resulting *Starry Messenger* (1610) depicted the moon with an imperfect and rough surface, sunspots, millions of stars, and moons orbiting Jupiter—all of which contradicted the notion of "perfect" heavenly bodies, the limited and static size of the universe, and that all bodies rotated around the earth. Despite an agreement with the papacy to teach heliocentrism as only a theory, Galileo later published a clear endorsement of it with *Dialogue Concerning the Two Chief World Systems: Ptolemaic and Copernican* (1632), which landed him before the Roman Inquisition in 1633. Galileo remained a committed Catholic who believed in the unity of truth—scientific and spiritual—and that any conflict between them required a reappraisal of biblical passages in light of new discoveries. In the midst of the Thirty Years' War, the Catholic Church silenced Galileo (placing him under house arrest for the next nine years) and thereby stifled intellectual life in Italy for the foreseeable future.

> **Sidebar:** The Newtonian view of the world remained dominant until the late nineteenth century when quantum physics and relativity theory revealed its limitations. While Newtonian mechanics works effectively to explain most of the phenomena we experience, you should recall that science does not deal in "truth," but in theory and fact.

Galileo's ideas could not be silenced, and his death in 1642 also marks the birth of the last great thinker of the Scientific Revolution—**Isaac Newton** (1642–1727). Truly one of the greatest geniuses in history, Newton combined profound conceptual insights, precise mathematical expression, and systematic observation. Newton synthesized the work of over a century into a coherent view of the world, based on universal laws, as expressed in his *Principia Mathematica* (1687); as he later said, "If I have been able to see so far, it is only because I stood on the shoulders of giants." All objects behave similarly, according to Newton, because they all obey the same **three laws of motion.** What previous astronomers had observed piecemeal and speculated about, Newton synthesized into a cosmic machine, held together with the **universal law of gravitation.** In addition, to explain infinitesimal changes in motion, Newton invented a new form of mathematics—**calculus.** With these tools, the universe could now be viewed as a finely calibrated watch that obeyed natural laws with mathematical precision, which allowed it to be explained and controlled by human reason. Though Newton was a deeply religious man who retained the image of God's will behind all, his cosmology helped separate the world of matter from that of spirit, setting the stage for deism in the future (see Chapter 9).

ADVANCES IN ANATOMY AND MEDICINE

In the same year that Copernicus introduced his heliocentric theory (1543), Flemish anatomist **Andreas Vesalius** (1514–1564) published the landmark book in his field—*The Structure of the Human Body.* Based on dissections and precise drawings, Vesalius contradicted many of Galen's ideas regarding the human body, again by employing direct empirical evidence. Building on this success and working for years in a laboratory, the English physician **William Harvey** (1578–1657) developed the modern theory of blood flow, with arteries and veins circulating oxygen through human tissue.

Further discoveries in anatomy were greatly assisted by the development of the **microscope,** which became the basis for the investigations of a Dutch nobleman, **Anton von Leeuwenhoek** (1632–1723). For his discoveries of blood corpuscles, sperm, and bacteria (it was not linked to disease until later), Leeuwenhoek is often given the title "The Father of Microbiology." Leeuwenhoek also corresponded with a secretary of the Royal Society of London (see following discussion), Robert Hooke, who had published his own book on the subject, *Micrographia* (1665), and who worked with the chemist **Robert Boyle** (1627–1692). Boyle's book, ***The Sceptical Chemist*** (1661) criticized the blending of alchemy (the art of attempting to turn metals into gold) with chemistry, which represented the scientific investigation of nature's most basic substances—the elements. In addition, Boyle articulated his famous law whereby the temperature, pressure, and volume of a gas can be related according to a mathematical formula.

Though these developments provided a more modern understanding of the human body and its functions, they did not translate into improved medical care for some time. In fact, many physicians continued to receive their training in the traditional classical style—reading Galen and Hippocrates, rather than through experimentation and clinical practice. Hospitals in the seventeenth and eighteenth centuries were as likely to house vagrants as the sick. Given the lack of understanding regarding bacteria and germs, hospitals generally served as places for the sick to die, not to be cured. Faith healers, midwives, and **barber-surgeons,** who engaged in the traditional bleeding and purging regimen, continued to provide medical care for the vast majority of Europeans.

THE SCIENTIFIC METHOD: BACON AND DESCARTES

Modern scientific thinking was the product of two differing intellectual temperaments—the English **Francis Bacon** (1561–1626) and the French **René Descartes** (1596–1650). Both shared a disdain for the Scholastic tradition and skepticism toward knowledge claims that had not been demonstrated through a rigorous system of thought. Bacon, from a noble family and occupying important positions in government, advocated a scientific approach based on **inductive thinking.** As opposed to the Scholastic tradition of working first with definitions and propositions, Bacon called for systematic investigation and observation of nature, as well as experimentation, before articulating theories or general laws. In his uncompleted three-volume work, ***Instauratio Magna*** ("The Great Renewal"), Bacon called for a new start to human knowledge, for humanity to put aside ancient preconceptions and prejudices and look at nature with fresh eyes. For Bacon, science should be useful to human beings; it should make their lives longer, more secure, and more comfortable. To demonstrate the great potential of science, Bacon published his *New Atlantis* (1627), which portrayed a scientific utopian and prefigured many modern technological developments. Though his ideas proved influential, Bacon himself did not fully appreciate the importance of theory and mathematics in scientific investigation.

A brilliant mathematician, René Descartes initiated the modern movement in philosophy. Descartes deliberately rejected Scholastic notions; his intellectual project involved subjecting every single assertion of human knowledge to systematic doubt. The goal of this skepticism was not to reject knowledge *per se*, but to build a surer foundation for it. Descartes even doubted that he existed. However, though he could doubt the existence of his body (because his senses often deceived him), Descartes could not doubt the existence of his mind, for in the very process

Heads Up! Though Bacon and Descartes are usually credited with articulating theories of scientific inquiry, other scientists such as Galileo and Newton contributed to the development of the method as they developed their ideas. As you study, consider how scientific ideas (content) and methods were connected.

of doubting, he affirmed that he had a mind—**"I think; therefore, I am."** From this thought experiment, Descartes argued for **dualism,** the idea that nature is made of two basic substances—an intangible, thinking substance known as mind and a tangible, extended (taking up space) substance known as matter. Descartes also demonstrated the power of mathematics in scientific thinking. With *Discourse on Method* (1637), he argued for a **deductive approach** to knowledge, much like a geometric proof, moving from general principles to more particular cases by steps of reason. With his Cartesian coordinate system (x, y, and z axes), Descartes provided a precise abstract depiction of space useful for engineering, architecture, and the military arts. Some of Descartes's ideas were later proved wrong—he speculated that animals were like machines and felt no pain—and his unorthodoxy almost landed him in hot water with the Catholic Church. Nonetheless, Descartes stands as one of the great philosophers in history and initiated the separation of matter and spirit that marks the path of secularism in subsequent centuries.

WOMEN AND SCIENCE

Women contributed to science and, in turn, were affected by scientific thinking. Given social constraints, it is a wonder that any women were able to contribute to science. Women were excluded from universities, scientific societies, and generally received an inferior education. Opportunities were available, however. In Germany, for example, the craft tradition allowed women to work alongside fathers and husbands; as a result, 15 percent of German astronomers in the seventeenth and eighteenth centuries were women. One such was **Maria Winkelmann** (1670–1720), who discovered a comet before her husband and helped to prepare the astronomical calendar for the Berlin Academy of Sciences. Despite these contributions, she was not allowed admission into the academy. **Maria Sybilla Merian** (1647–1717) traveled to South America to study insects, and her subsequent text and illustrations, *Metamorphosis of the Insects of Surinam,* became a standard in the field of entomology. Women such as Emilie du Chatelet (1706–1749) translated Newton to make his abstract works accessible to a mass audience, while Dorothea Erxleben (1715–1762) became one of the first women to earn a medical degree from a university.

Unfortunately, these women proved exceptions. Institutional barriers remained strong, though attitudes served as an even more effective roadblock. Throughout the seventeenth century, philosophers and scientists debated the *querelle de femmes*—the "women question." Ironically, some of science's greatest doubters—Spinoza, for example (see following discussion)—could not extract themselves from long-held prejudices when it came to women. Studies of anatomy seemed proof that women's smaller skulls and wider hips demonstrated their intellectual inferiority and fitness only for domestic roles. Investigation into human reproduction affirmed the greater importance of males in providing the "life force," with women providing only the matter or location of conception. It was not until 1823 that the ovum was discovered, proving otherwise. Did women, then, experience a Scientific Revolution? On one hand, women did participate in scientific discoveries despite the obstacles, but on the other, "science" was used to corset women even more tightly in limited social and intellectual roles. When it came to women, science in the seventeenth century proved most *un*revolutionary.

RELIGION AND SKEPTICISM

Though most scientists of the seventeenth and eighteenth centuries were religious and saw no conflict between scientific inquiry and spirituality, the Scientific Revolution resulted in an increased skeptical and secular attitude among European elites. At first, many scientists blended (what would today be considered) superstitious beliefs in alchemy and astrology with materialist and mathematical perspectives. As time wore on, educated Europeans demanded empirical evidence or conformity with natural laws for claims of knowledge. This new standard is reflected in the decline of witchcraft persecutions after about 1650, which no longer received the support of those in positions of power. New standards of evidence eliminating torture and hearsay testimony, especially in England, provided a more scientific basis for legal proceedings. Furthermore, European colonization stimulated **travel literature,** which, in revealing the diversity of human societies and customs, suggested the possibility of cultural relativism. Following in the path of the French humanist and skeptic Montaigne (see Chapter 5), **Pierre Bayle (1647–1706)** examined beliefs from a wide range of human endeavors in the *Historical and Critical Dictionary,* only to conclude that most owed more to human credulity than to rigorous and rational thought. Bayle's work forms a bridge from the Scientific Revolution to the eighteenth-century Enlightenment (see Chapter 9).

More common than straightforward criticism of religious beliefs was an attempt to reconcile new scientific discoveries with them. A new field of biblical scholarship attempted to retain the essential truths of Christianity along with a more critical look at the evolution of scripture as a product of human creation, not simply the revealed word of God. This scholarship also involved the dating of the earth. Archbishop James Usher famously calculated the "actual" date of the beginning of the world (in 4004 B.C.) based on a recreation of Old Testament genealogies. Many scholars did not accept such precise determinations. In addition, the papacy introduced an entirely new (and more accurate calendar) in 1582 under the patronage of Pope Gregory XIII, this all despite the Catholic Church rejecting the notion of a heliocentric universe. This **Gregorian calendar** remains the system of dating in most nations today, gradually replacing the old and less accurate Julian calendar of Roman times.

Two thinkers stand out in their attempts to create a synthesis of the scientific and the spiritual. **Baruch Spinoza** (1632–1677) came from a family of Portuguese Jews forced to immigrate to the Netherlands as a result of the Inquisition. Beginning in the Cartesian tradition of dualism regarding substances, Spinoza came to reject Descartes's understanding of God and substance. For Spinoza, all of nature was ultimately one substance: All that we experience is simply a modification of that substance, which is God. We can conceive of this substance with the attribute of extension (taking up space) or of thought (mind), but these attributes are ultimately manifestations of the same substance. Spinoza's substance **monism** made little sense to the Jewish community from which he was excommunicated, or to orthodox Christians who thought it no better than atheism. Spinoza's rejection of an anthropomorphic God (in the form of humans) led him to a naturalistic view of human affairs and ethics. Even the title of his most famous work, *Ethics as Determined in a Geometric Manner* (1677), illustrates his rigorous rationalist style. In

Sidebar: While the sixteenth century saw widespread experimentation in religion, it spawned few thoroughgoing skeptics. The terms "atheist" and "agnostic" were not coined until the eighteenth and nineteenth centuries. By the eighteenth-century Enlightenment, many had embraced these labels as a sign of their rejection of Christianity and endorsement of skeptical open-mindedness.

rejecting miracles, holy books, rituals, dogma, and even free will, Spinoza left human beings primarily with their minds to offer consolation, guidance, and whatever freedom comes from putting oneself in accord with the laws of nature.

Blaise Pascal (1623–1662) was a child prodigy of true mathematical genius. It is said that he independently discovered several theorems of Euclid's geometry at the age of 9. In addition, he later invented the first successful adding machine, developed Pascal's Triangle to show the pattern of ascending exponential functions of algebraic equations, and developed the geometry of solids as well as modern probability theory. After experiencing a profound religious conversion in 1654, Pascal gave up his work in science and mathematics for religion and philosophy. Pascal fell under the influence of the Jansenist movement (see Chapter 6) in France, which rejected the Jesuits' strong view of human freedom. In his famous work the *Pensées* ("The Thoughts"), Pascal set out to show the proper relationship between reason and faith. Though the scientific discoveries had demonstrated the insignificance of humans in the cosmos, Pascal nonetheless looked at human reason as a distinct capacity in the universe, or as he wrote, "Man is a reed, but he is a thinking reed." When it comes to religious faith, we will always want for evidence and arguments, said Pascal. Therefore, humans can weigh the alternatives—for example, the promise of eternal reward versus sacrifice of earthly pleasures—according to **Pascal's Wager** and gamble on belief, for we have much to gain and little to lose with faith.

A SCIENTIFIC VIEW OF HUMAN AFFAIRS: LAW AND POLITICAL THEORY

Inevitably, scientific thinking crept into human affairs. If matter followed natural laws, why could human behavior not also be explained according to the same laws? The birth of "**natural law**" philosophy and the concept of "**natural rights**" have grounded much of modern political development toward democracy and equality. Natural law holds that humans can discover what is fair, just, and "natural" in the political and social realms by consulting reason. Custom, tradition, or the edicts of kings cannot override natural rights, which inhere in human beings because of their unique capacities. For example, the ability of humans to speak, write, and create symbols suggests that they have a natural right to freedoms in these areas. In diplomacy, several seventeenth-century jurists, such as Hugo Grotius in *Law of War and Peace* (1625) and Samuel Pufendorf in *Law of Nature and of Nations* (1672), attempted to define rules for commerce and war based on the common good of nations rather than simply the might of the strongest. Even with international organizations such as the United Nations today, the world continues to struggle with winning adherence by all nations to a code of international law.

Thomas Hobbes

Natural law can also be used to justify absolutism. A sophisticated and secular justification (compare with Bossuet's divine-right account in Chapter 6) of absolutism comes from **Thomas Hobbes** (1588–1679). Hobbes wrote his *Leviathan* (1651) amidst the Scientific Revolution and the English Civil War, both of which left their mark on his political philosophy. According to Hobbes, humans are born into a "**state of nature,**" in which life is a continual war of "every man against every other man" for gain, glory, and security. If humans are equal, it is only in their ability to destroy one another. Hobbes viewed human society as akin to a closed system of energy, which tends to dissipate (into anarchy) over time. The only solution to this insecurity and chaos is for each individual to leave the state of nature by agreeing to a **social contract** with one another and with the **sovereign,** who will absorb the wills and power of each member of society into an all-powerful ruler. In the resulting **commonwealth,** the will of the sovereign (which could be a group of rulers) stands as law. Rebellion is prohibited, as it would only return society to the chaotic state of nature. Hobbes's justification is secular and "scientific," and though it would be rejected by many in his native England, his notions of the state of nature and the social contract influenced subsequent thinkers.

John Locke

The most important defense of limited government based on natural law was written by the Englishman **John Locke** (1632–1704) to justify the Glorious Revolution. Locke's *Second Treatise on Government* (1689) takes Hobbes and stands him on his head. In Locke's state of nature, man freely enjoys his natural rights of life, liberty, equality, and property. These **inalienable rights** come *before* the development of human society. Though humans are basically rational, they still conflict in the state of nature over property. Such disputes create insecurity and reduce the enjoyment of one's liberties. Thus, individuals enter into a social contract and leave the state of nature to better secure those rights. Governments are limited by their original purpose—arbitrating disputes and providing order and public goods. Should governments become abusive toward these ends, society can invoke the **right of rebellion** to secure those rights anew. In all, governments are made by people and must display features of the limiting social contract—representation, guarantees of rights, respect of property. Locke's ideas helped promote the unique development of England in this era, though it should *not* be viewed as an endorsement of modern mass democracy.

> **Sidebar:** Locke's ideas influenced American political thought. In fact, Locke viewed America as fertile ground for his conception of the state of nature. As he said, "In the beginning, all the world was America." If one holds Jefferson's "Declaration of Independence" aside Locke's *Second Treatise*, the former's intellectual debt to the latter becomes apparent.

Like Pierre Bayle, John Locke forms a bridge between the Scientific Revolution of the seventeenth century and the Enlightenment of the eighteenth century. Locke looked at the world from an empirical perspective, yet he believed that Christianity was a "reasonable" religion. At the same time, he supported religious toleration (except for the Catholics and atheists, whom he viewed as a threat to the state) as part of the settlement surrounding the Glorious Revolution. The ideas of Francis Bacon and John Locke form bookends to the seventeenth century regarding the importance of an empirical approach to the world. Locke became the foremost advocate of an empirical approach to knowledge in his philosophical writings. In *Essay Concerning Human Understanding* (1690), Locke rejected Descartes's notion of innate ideas, in favor of the mind as a *tabula rasa,* or "blank slate." Humans learn primarily from experience, which writes upon their minds and character their personality and knowledge. These ideas held radical implications when it came to education, as Locke argued in *Some Thoughts Concerning Education* (1689); children learn best *not* from rote memorization but from experience and from "praise and esteem." In all, Locke's wide-ranging interests and writings sparked new thinking in several fields, including child-rearing, education, politics, and philosophy.

SCIENCE APPLIED: SOCIETIES AND TECHNOLOGY

Governments saw great promise in science. Certainly, prestige accrued to nations that sponsored great scientific discoveries, but, more important, states hoped to exploit theoretical advances for navigational and military purposes. To this end, the first great scientific societies were formed in the 1660s. In England, the privately run **Royal Society of London** received a government charter in 1662; eventually, Sir Isaac Newton served as its president. Not to be outdone, Louis XIV chartered, under more strict government supervision, the **French Academy of**

Sciences in 1666. Smaller or more regional societies, academies, and universities for the study and perpetuation of science were also founded in the century. These organizations held meetings, published journals, established research projects, and shared their results with scientists across the continent. Even if governments wished to monopolize science for their narrow national interest, it would not have been possible given the modern printing press. An international scientific community seemed necessary to the very nature of modern science; to ensure reliability, experiments had to repeated, data shared, and theories confirmed.

Science can be of the most abstract nature; at the same time, all humanity shares an interest in its practical results. New scientific equipment and machines—telescopes, microscopes, barometers, globes, marine chronometers, pendulum clocks, improved cannons, early steam engines—all held out the promise of greater human control of the environment. In subsequent centuries, Europeans would exploit these advances to the fullest. The results have been both the greatest period of human technological creativity and the most destructive conflicts in history.

ADDITIONAL RESOURCES

Applebaum, Wilbur, *The Scientific Revolution and the Foundations of Modern Science* (2005)—Accessible to high school students, this work comes from the Greenwood Guides to Historic Events.

Henry, John, *The Scientific Revolution and the Origins of Modern Science* (2002)—From the Studies in European History series, this brief account provides the political, religious, and cultural background to the Scientific Revolution.

Shapin, Steven, *The Scientific Revolution* (1996)—An excellent and brief, but challenging, overview of the topic.

Sobel, Dava, *Galileo's Daughter: A Historical Memoir of Science, Faith, and Love* (2000)—A popular history that shows the trial of Galileo against the backdrop of his relationship with his daughter, a nun.

Sobel, Dava, *Longitude: The True Story of a Lone Genius Who Solved the Greatest Scientific Problem of His Time* (1996)—Tells the story of how John Harrison created the first successful marine chronometer.

http://galileo.rice.edu/—Outstanding resource at Rice University related to Galileo's life, investigations, and accomplishments.

PRACTICE QUESTIONS

1. Prior to the sixteenth century, scientific ideas were based primarily on which of the following sets of thinkers?
   a. St. Thomas Aquinas, St. Augustine, Galen
   b. Aristotle, Ptolemy, Galen
   c. Copernicus, Aristotle, Plato
   d. Pythagoras, Plato, Cicero
   e. Newton, Copernicus, Ptolemy

2. Of the following astronomers, which did *not* accept the heliocentric theory?
   a. Copernicus
   b. Kepler
   c. Brahe
   d. Galileo
   e. Newton

3. Bacon and Descartes agreed in their thinking regarding on the scientific method in which of the following ways?
   a. that science should begin with systematic observation
   b. that science was fundamentally mathematical
   c. that science should respect traditional authority
   d. that science need not produce practical benefit
   e. that science needed clear standards of proof

4. New discoveries in the understanding of the human body during the seventeenth century produced which of following effects?
   a. Few practical changes occurred in medicine until the nineteenth century.
   b. Infectious diseases were effectively understood and curbed.
   c. Vesalius's anatomical drawings led to the founding of new medical schools.
   d. European life expectancy increased markedly in the seventeenth century.
   e. Church authorities effectively banned further dissection of cadavers.

5. Which of the following is the most accurate characterization of the relationship between religion and science in the seventeenth century?
   a. Spinoza's monism created a widely accepted synthesis of the two.
   b. Most scientists expressed skepticism and hoped to reduce religion's influence.
   c. The Catholic Church effectively silenced unorthodox scientific ideas.
   d. Though secularism grew, many thinkers attempted to reconcile the two.
   e. Religion and science inhabited separate spheres and had little contact with one another.

6. This quote below best reflects the ideas of which of the following?
   a. Thomas Hobbes
   b. Bishop Bossuet
   c. John Locke
   d. René Descartes
   e. Isaac Newton

   "The supreme power cannot take from any man any part of his property without his own consent: for the preservation of property being the end of government, and that for which men enter into society, it necessarily supposes and requires, that the people should have property."

7. Women's relationship to the Scientific Revolution is best expressed in which of the following statements?
   a. Though women participated in scientific discoveries, science was used to reinforce female ideas of inferiority.
   b. Through their scientific discoveries, women were able to demonstrate their equality and earn equal rights.
   c. Women were effectively banned from any participation in science and received no scientific education.
   d. Most scientists supported equal participation and rights for women, but believed the time was not yet right.
   e. The scientific accomplishments of women tended to center on the practical, such as engineering and technology.

(*Giraudon/Art Resource, NY*)

8. What does the accompanying picture, "The Founding of the Academy of Sciences" (1666), convey about the state's primary goal related to science in the seventeenth century?
   a. to demonstrate the state's openness to new ideas
   b. to undermine religious orthodoxy and control the church
   c. to promote international cooperation and sharing of scientific ideas
   d. to control the nobility by involving them in state-sponsored activities
   e. to oversee scientific exploration for the betterment of the state

9. Newton's synthesis of scientific thought expressed which of the following views of the universe?
   a. The universe was essentially an unknowable mystery.
   b. God's hand was actively present and could be seen in supernatural events.
   c. The universe functioned like a machine, obeying fixed laws.
   d. Motion was more apparent than real, but could be expressed mathematically.
   e. The effects of natural forces could be observed but were only an illusion.

10. All of the following were reasons for the Catholic Church's silencing of Galileo before the Inquisition EXCEPT:
    a. The Church believed that Galileo had broken an agreement to teach the heliocentrism as a theory only.
    b. In the midst of the Thirty Years' War, the Church feared a further loss of its spiritual and temporal power.
    c. Galileo's ideas seemed to contradict biblical passages that described the earth as the center of the universe.
    d. Martin Luther had openly supported the heliocentric theory, and the Church wished to decrease the influence of Lutheranism.
    e. The Church believed Galileo's observations and experiments were not in accord with a rigorous scientific method.

SAMPLE ESSAY

Analyze how the Scientific Revolution affected the relationship between the state and science AND ideas about politics in the seventeenth century.

The Scientific Revolution radically changed how politics worked and also how people thought about politics. Many rulers wanted to take advantage of new scientific ideas; they liked having great scientists in their nations and also wished to make their states more powerful. Also, thinkers like Hobbes and Locke used scientific concepts like natural law to devise differing theories of government.

Science seemed like a good activity for states to be involved in. Whether it was astronomy, physics, or medicine, states felt like they could use the ideas of science and its technologies. States hired scientists to do research and publish their findings. Galileo, for example, worked for the Duke of Tuscany and other scientists received patronage. This is why England founded the Royal Society and France the Academy of Sciences. They wanted famous scientists and also hoped that they could use their discoveries to make better weapons and better ships. If new medical care occurred, this might also make their subjects live longer and give them further support.

Hobbes was for absolutism and Locke was for constitutional government, but they both used natural law to justify their ideas. Both believed that humans lived in a state of nature; it's just that Hobbes thought this state was nasty and Locke thought it was pretty good, with rights and freedoms. For Hobbes, people left the state and formed a social contract because they feared other people. As a result, the ruler was strong and had to be obeyed. He described it all like a scientific experiment. Locke had people leave the state of nature to have more secure rights. Because of this, the government had to protect those rights and be limited. If it didn't, the people could overthrow it. All this was based on supposedly observing nature, just like with science.

Science had a big impact on society in the seventeenth century. Since all the states of Europe were always competing, they wanted to use science in their competition. And they would continue to do this as they waged wars with each other. At the same time, theorists used science to understand how politics worked; this gave birth to "political science." This would continue into the Enlightenment, when more philosophers tried to become more scientific in their view of politics.

This response does address the question clearly, and the student demonstrates control of the question. Starting with the introduction, the student is focused on the tasks of the question and provides a strong thesis in response. In addition, the essay provides balance between the two topics, along with some specific examples. What keeps this essay from a top score is the use of examples. First, there could be a few more specific examples to support each body paragraph. More important, these examples could be more explicitly connected to the thesis. For example, the paragraph on political theory is generally accurate, but it is left unclear exactly how Hobbes's and Locke's ideas represent a scientific perspective. One or two more precise analytical statements in each body paragraph might have raised this essay by 1 to 2 points. Score: 7.

CHAPTER 8

The Struggle for Wealth and Empire

Note: to readers of the Palmer, *A History of the Modern World,* this and the next chapter have been slightly modified in order to consolidate the discussion of intellectual and cultural developments around the theme of the Enlightenment in the next chapter.

The eighteenth century represents a turning point in the history of Europe. Many of the developments of previous centuries—the Scientific Revolution, centralized states, commercial advance—reached their full flower during the eighteenth century. Hope for change and optimism regarding the future took hold, particularly among the upper classes. At the same time, this period was one of immense contradictions: tradition versus progress, privilege versus equality, wealth versus poverty, elite versus popular culture. In this chapter, we review the social structure of the Old Regime (on the eve of the French Revolution), recount the continuing advance of commerce, and show how competition over wealth and trade led to a major conflict in two phases that altered the European balance of power.

SOCIAL STRUCTURE OF THE OLD REGIME

Demographic Changes

Prior to the eighteenth century, Europe experienced periods of healthy population growth; inevitably, however, this was followed by decline. Such declines usually resulted from scarcity of resources, warfare, and disease. The eighteenth century represented a shift in this trend, though it was not apparent at the time, in that Europe's population continued a steady and even significant growth in following centuries. From 1720, when the growth became evident, until the French Revolution (1789), Europe's population increased from about 120 to 180 million. What factors account for this growth?

- **Diet**—As a result of the Agricultural (see following discussion) and Commercial Revolutions, Europeans secured access to increased amounts and a wider variety of food supplies. Malnutrition and famine became rarer.
- **Transportation improvements**—The building of roads and canals made it easier for national governments to address local shortages of grain and make good on crop failures.
- **Decline of the plague**—Despite a few minor outbreaks, the dreaded bubonic plague, which every generation seemed to wipe out 10 to 15 percent of the population in certain regions, mysteriously disappeared from the continent.
- **Weather**—Europe's **Little Ice Age** was coming to an end, especially after 1750, which meant a longer growing season and more reliable crops.

- **Medical improvements (?)**—Though Edward Jenner introduced the smallpox vaccine in the eighteenth century, medical improvements actually played only a minor role in the population increase. Hospitals, medical training, and the understanding of disease remained woeful.

All of Europe took part in the population growth, but the increase tended to be more gradual in eastern than western Europe, except for Russia, which surpassed France as the most populous nation in Europe around 1780. Urban areas grew the fastest, often straining their still-primitive infrastructure of roads, housing, waste removal, and charitable relief.

> **Sidebar:** Even seemingly small annual increases in population of, say, 2%–3%, can quickly lead to a doubling of overall levels. A shorthand rule is $70/x =$ years to double, where x represents that rate of population growth. For example, a 5% annual increase $(70/5)$ yields a doubling in approximately 14 years!

The Class System

In the eighteenth century, European society continued to be divided into "estates," or legally defined classes, which determined one's status. Though change was evident with the increasing importance placed on wealth, most nations continued to grant privilege for those who claimed hereditary descent from noble blood. Wealthy merchants and cash-strapped nobles often saw the benefit of blending families, fulfilling the twin purpose of raising the status of the merchants while infusing wealth into a threadbare aristocratic line. The following chart provides you with a snapshot of the class system in the eighteenth century. Keep in mind that this data represents a baseline for comparison's sake to evaluate the social impact of the French Revolution, which began in 1789.

Class	Activities	Status/Standard of Living	Developments/ Assessment
Nobility	* Lived primarily off of their estates, which varied considerably in size. * Pursued mercantile ventures to provide wealth for their ostentatious lifestyles.	* Wealth varied among nobles; it was common for the middle class to exceed the lowliest nobles in means. * Noble status was defined by a set of legal and social **privileges**—the right to hunt, to be tried in special courts, to hold certain offices, to claim **exemptions** from taxes.	* Aristocrats of the eighteenth century experienced a revival of power following the great age of absolutism. * Remarkably adaptable, nobles used investments and strategic marriages with merchants to "marry" their noble status with new wealth.

Class	Activities	Status/Standard of Living	Developments/ Assessment
Nobility	* To be viewed as "seeking wealth" was considered a characteristic of the "vulgar bourgeoisie." * Often monopolized positions in the military as well as government and judicial offices. * Nobles often had more in common with those of the same class in other nations than they did with peasants in their homelands. * Often received a classical education, spoke French (the language of philosophy and culture in the eighteenth century), and if male, ventured on a grand tour. * A rite of passage, the **grand tour** allowed male aristocrats to experience European art and ideas, as well as gam-bling and prostitution.	* Aristocrats enjoyed Europe's best diets, with plenty of meat and wine, fresh fruits, and sweets/nuts. * With advances in commerce, nobles prided themselves on acquiring the newest fashions, carriages, art, and luxury items. * In England, to keep lands intact, families practiced **primogeniture** and **entail,** or granting all lands to the eldest son and prohibiting him or his heirs from ever breaking them up. Such laws forced younger sons into business or the clergy and became a hated symbol of privilege. * In imitation of Louis XIV, many nobles built gracious **country houses,** especially in England. With the grandeur of a palace and the comfort of home, such residences expressed classical style and the need for increased **privacy.** Servants now often lived in separate wings, green spaces established distance between nobles and commoners, and rooms divided public from private functions.	* To support a more luxurious lifestyle, nobles tried to wring out of the peasantry whatever taxes, fees, dues, and obligations could be justified from the remnants of the feudal system. * The continued existence of this system of unequal privileges came under increasing attack by Enlightenment *philosophés* (see next chapter).

Class	Activities	Status/Standard of Living	Developments/ Assessment
Peasants	* The great majority of Europeans (about 80–85%) continued to work the land as either peasants or **serfs.** * **Free peasants,** who lived primarily in western and some parts of central Europe, often owned their own land or had the right to work the land of a lord. * Villages governed the lives of peasants. Decisions regarding agriculture, local disputes, public order, and religion were made by village leaders according to customs and the needs of the community.	* Standards of living for peasants varied significantly, depending on the degree of freedoms, soil/climate conditions, and strength of the nobility. * Those living east of the Elbe River or in southern Italy and the Iberian peninsula often faced more difficult burdens. * Nobles in eastern Europe and Russia were larger in number and exercised greater power over their peasants and serfs. * Peasant diet was simple and consisted primarily of black breads, which were high in nutrients, gruels, and the occasional meat. New crops such as potatoes and corn provided additional nutrition. Since water was often of unreliable quality, peasants drank diluted beer and wine. * Despite improvements in diet and transportation, peasants still fell prey to famines and diseases (because of greater susceptibility due to malnutrition).	* In some ways, little changed in peasant life from the sixteenth to eighteenth centuries— nobles still held sway, customs dictated everyday life, and fate seemed to rule one's destiny. At the same time, changes were evident. * Peasant life was marginally more secure because of improved diet and better weather. * Discontent over a lingering feudal system often sparked revolts. The most famous of these was the **Pugachev Revolt** in the 1770s in Russia, the largest peasant uprising in European history. Eventually the revolt was crushed and its leaders executed, but the incident underscored the growing dissatisfaction with the unequal class system.

Class	Activities	Status/Standard of Living	Developments/ Assessment
Townspeople/ Bourgeoisie	* Towns acted as magnets for both people and wealth. * Cities produced wealth through manufacture and trade. * The middle class often owned land in the countryside, living off rents and dues. * Peasants resented the parasitical role of the towns, which seemed to absorb the wealth of the countryside but provide nothing in return.	* Cities technically existed outside the feudal structure and jealously guarded their liberties. * Standards of living varied widely between the **merchant oligarchs** who dominated political and social life, and the **petty bourgeoisie** of artisans and shopkeepers, down to the occasional laborers, beggars, and prostitutes. * Many wealthy merchants and entrepreneurs imitated the tastes and styles of the nobility, often intermarrying with them or gaining noble status through purchase of an office. * As commerce expanded, cities grew in size and eventually became overwhelmed with the problem of **poverty.** Charitable institutions still existed to address needs, but attitudes hardened against professional beggars. Many nations passed laws to house the poor in "hospitals" or workhouses.	* "Cities" in the eighteenth century paled in comparison with today's teeming industrial metropolises. Europe's largest city was London with around 1 million people. Many towns had only 10,000 to 50,000 inhabitants. * Towns played an important economic and cultural role, attracting migrants from the countryside, capital from investors, and ideas from all over Europe. * Cities found their infrastructure of streets, houses, and waste removal inadequate to the problem of growing population. * Belief in a "**moral economy**" led city-dwellers to demand "fair prices" for grains. * Monarchs tapped into wealth of towns, especially in western Europe, through taxation and regulation. * To avoid bread riots, governments also stored grain to provide reasonable prices.

Family Life and Child-Rearing

The eighteenth-century European family remained predominantly nuclear, with the exception of parts of eastern Europe where the tax system promoted extended families living under one roof. Average ages at first marriage in Europe remained high compared with other civilizations in the eighteenth century—often mid- to late-20s for both men and women. Couples delayed wedlock until they were able to support themselves economically and provide for children.

Families generally labored together as an economic unit. In agricultural settings, tasks tended to divide based on gender, with men generally involved in heavier work such as plowing, while women assisted with harvesting, mowing hay, and preparing food. Children were expected to contribute productive labor at an early age. In towns, boys were apprenticed to a local shop or filled any job that augmented the family income. Young women often found themselves in domestic settings as servants and maids, their goal being to earn a sufficient **dowry** to guarantee a favorable marriage partner. Theoretically, servants were to be treated as members of the family, with the heads of the household responsible for their well-being and moral upbringing. In fact, young women often found themselves subject to verbal abuse and the sexual advances of male family members.

Strong community controls in early modern Europe had ensured that couples avoided having children out of wedlock. As long as the couple was married prior to the birth of the child, little social stigma was attached to premarital sex. However, between 1750 and 1850 a rapid increase of illegitimacy occurred. It is unclear what caused this trend. One explanation is that the new opportunities provided by **cottage industry**—earning money at home by finishing products—allowed couples to earn income without access to land or regular employment. Additionally, small children could contribute to the family income quickly as part of this system. Furthermore, migration to cities tended to disrupt traditional patterns of arranged marriages and enforcement of marriage promises by men.

The unfortunate consequences of the out-of-wedlock births were the related problems of **infanticide** and child abandonment. Though Europeans used traditional methods to limit population, these techniques proved unreliable and dangerous, as in the case of abortion. Unwanted children were often "accidentally" smothered in bed during the night. Some nations even outlawed the common practice of parents and children sharing a bed to discourage these actions. Given the extremes of poverty and inequality that existed in eighteenth-century cities, it was not surprising that young women felt driven to infanticide. An illustration of this sad practice occurred when the city of Rennes, France, opened a storm drain in 1721 only to find the skeletons of 80 infants within.[1] Rather than the extreme measure of infanticide, many couples or mothers abandoned their children on the steps of a church or hospital. Wealthy philanthropists and Catholic religious orders established **foundling homes** to care for this burgeoning population. However, such homes were often overwhelmed, and the vast majority of the children under their care died before reaching maturity.

Traditionally, children were viewed as sinful "sprigs of Adam," and parents were warned that "to spare the rod was to spoil the child." The modern expression **"rule of thumb,"** in fact, derives from the limitation on the width of a stick a husband was allowed to reprove both children and wife. Children were tightly swaddled to restrict their natural impulsive movements, as

---

[1]Isser Woloch, *Eighteenth-Century Europe: Tradition and Progress, 1715–1789* (New York: Norton, 1982), p. 162.

parents worked to instill discipline from the earliest ages. Upper-class women relied on **wet nurses** to provide nutrition for their children, which often meant they went undernourished or neglected. Perhaps these attitudes were a function of the high rate of infant mortality, which might have decreased emotional attachment to children among some parents.

Heads Up! This theme of child-rearing practices will continue in later chapters. Please note that childhood is an *idea*—certainly it is clear to the senses that children age into adults, but the notion that childhood is a *distinct* phase of life, with unique physiological and psychological characteristics, seems to be a product of the Enlightenment.

Such views of children began to change slowly in the eighteenth century. A result of the ideas of John Locke (see Chapter 7) and the educational writings of Jean-Jacques Rousseau (see next chapter), new attitudes began to stress the view of children as innocent creatures who needed tender love and guidance through progressive stages of development. Rousseau and others denounced the practices of wet-nursing and swaddling. Children, they argued, should be insulated from the adult world of violence, vulgarity, and cruelty. Among the upper classes, parents began to provide their children with age-appropriate clothing, reading materials, and games. Books and toys were designed to stimulate children's interest and moral development. Simplified scientific ideas found their way into books such as Tom Telescope's *Newtonian System of Philosophy*, probably written by **John Newbery** (1713–1767). Newbery, also famous for *The Pretty Little Pocket Book,* richly illustrated his books to appeal to children's eyes. Along with the jigsaw puzzle, parents lavished children with dolls, *camera obscuras* (a simple machine for projecting images), and tops. New family practices were also reflected in more government attention being given to primary education (see next chapter).

THE DYNAMIC ECONOMY OF THE EIGHTEENTH CENTURY

At the center of the significant social, cultural, and intellectual developments occurring in eighteenth-century Europe stood an expanding and changing economy. More than ever, Europe became enmeshed in a global system of trade; while at the same time, the continent reaped the fruits of incremental advances in manufacturing and agriculture. Ultimately, the national pursuit of wealth and empire fueled a series of midcentury wars that altered the European balance of power and set the stage for the French Revolution.

Cottage Industry

For centuries, European manufacturing had taken place in towns under the restrictions of the guilds. During the eighteenth century, the system of cottage industry expanded, whereby a merchant capitalist paid wages to rural families to finish raw materials. Due to its lack of internal tariffs and weak guild structure, England experienced the most rapid expansion of this "putting-out" system. Though the British Isles later gained the reputation for industrial ingenuity, their manufactures in 1750 were easily surpassed by several other nations. However, England could boast an expanding base of textile production, one of the most basic of consumer goods. The many and varied steps of textile production lent themselves to the decentralized nature of cottage industry. Entrepreneurial expansion of manufacturing in the countryside allowed merchants to reinvest profits from trade and later provided sufficient capital for investment in large-scale industrial enterprises. In addition, cottage industry provided rural families the opportunity to supplement a livelihood often threatened by changes in the nature of agriculture.

The Agricultural Revolution

An inefficient agricultural system acted as a traditional brake on European population growth. The open three-field system wasted a large proportion of useful land, and primitive techniques offered little margin for error, often plunging regions into famine, as had happened in the 1690s. Much of this insecurity was relieved by the Agricultural Revolution of the eighteenth century. The movement began in the Netherlands and England and primarily involved the introduction of new crops and the application of new techniques. Some have given the label "**scientific agriculture**" to the bundle of changes in crop and livestock farming.

To combat the waste of allowing fields to lie fallow, agricultural reformers such as **Charles "Turnip" Townsend** (1674–1738) supported the use of nitrogen-replenishing crops such as turnips, clover, and alfalfa. Such **fodder crops** also proved useful as feed for livestock, whose manure was in turn used to further increase the output of fields. One of the more important crops for human use proved to be the **potato.** Easy to grow, rich in vitamins, and versatile, the crop became a staple of the peasant diet in Ireland, Prussia, and Russia. A large family could subsist on as little as an acre of potatoes.

Increasing production also involved solutions as simple as clearing more land. Using new drainage techniques, such as **terracing,** the Dutch and English were able to reclaim swamps and bogs. **Jethro Tull** (1674–1741) was another reformer concerned about increasing yields. His advocacy of soil aeration through use of the hoe and invention of the **seed drill,** which pushed the seed safely beneath the soil, demonstrate Tull's use of Enlightenment reason and empirical study in service of practical solutions. Improvements in livestock, through **selective breeding,** served as a natural next step. The English government granted awards to those who could produce the fattest and meatiest cattle, providing additional meat for the average person's diet.

Efficiency often requires doing things in a big way, or what is known as economies of scale. In agriculture, this meant that the traditional open-field system of scattered strips of land had to be abandoned. This process had already been under way in England since the sixteenth century with enclosure. Advances in agricultural techniques in the eighteenth century acted as additional spur, as Parliament passed **enclosure acts,** which allowed wealthy landowners to buy up common land and enclose it within large manors. This destruction of the commons produced an unequal system of landholding in England, with a few large landholders at the top, some independent yeoman and enterprising tenant farmers in the middle, and a mass of landless laborers on the bottom. For this last group, the loss of land rendered them dependent on earning wages, driving them into the newly expanding and industrializing cities as an unskilled labor force.

> **Heads Up!** Britain's advance in scientific agriculture represents an important cause of the Industrial Revolution, which will be covered in chapter 11. Increased productivity "liberated" small farmers from the land, though the victims of enclosure viewed themselves as "thrown from the land" into "hellish factories."

The Commercial Revolution, Phase II

Though the Dutch remained important traders, they had been surpassed by the French and the English, both of whose commerce ballooned in the eighteenth century. East India companies, pooling the resources of numerous investors, were established by numerous nations who exploited the European taste for a whole range of new consumer goods. **Triangular trade** facilitated the exchange of goods between the continents of Europe, Africa, and the Americas, also promoting the human trafficking in slaves. Europe's sweet tooth caused untold suffering for Africans forced to work in the horrifying conditions of Caribbean sugar plantation "factories."

Europeans continued to demand spices from the East—cinnamon, nutmeg, cloves, pepper, and saffron. The new beverages of **coffee** and **tea** could now also be added to the menu, making the East Indies, India, and Ceylon focal points for colonial interest. These areas were also known for the production of fine cloth and rugs. Light, brightly colored **calicoes,** muslins, and chintzes poured into the homes of Europe's upper classes, as signs of status and cosmopolitanism. Goods from overseas, as well as porcelain and cloth now produced within Europe, promoted a **consumer revolution** in tastes, as the well-to-do stocked their drawing rooms, boudoirs, and eating areas with genteel finery.

The biggest money-maker of all was **sugar.** Small sugar islands in the Caribbean easily outpaced the entire North American mainland in value to the British Empire. Throughout the eighteenth century, sugar production skyrocketed. As sugar increased, so did slavery. Over 600,000 slaves were brought from Africa to the island of Jamaica alone from 1700 to 1786. Originally dominated by the Portuguese then the Dutch, the **slave trade** became the preserve of English trading interests after the War of Spanish Succession. Because much of the profit from the slave trade and sugar went directly to England's industrial expansion, it would be fair to conclude that British capitalism resulted directly from the enslavement of Africans. What's more, because profits were so easy to come by on these sugar islands, plantation owners possessed little incentive to invest in the humane treatment of their slaves, thus causing one of the highest mortality rates in the world.

Global trade produced a myriad of important results. Let's focus on three for right now:

- The profits from commerce promoted the development of a **capitalist system** of private property. Governments became much more dependent on entrepreneurs as a source of taxation and to underwrite state borrowing of funds, through banks and other credit institutions.
- As noted earlier, the accumulation of wealth by the **middle class** tended to facilitate its **merging with the aristocracy,** as both stood to gain from intermarriage.
- The potential for great riches naturally led to an **intensification of commercial rivalries** that resulted in war. Often the conflict over territory within Europe coincided with overseas competition for colonies and markets, thus producing the first world wars in history.

DIPLOMACY AND WAR

Commercial competition invariably led to war in the eighteenth century. Soon after the Peace of Utrecht (1713–1714), one old rivalry (England vs. France) reasserted itself while another arose between Prussia and Austria over predominance of German affairs. These two rivalries stood at the center of diplomacy and war in the middle of the century. Spain experienced new life under the Bourbon monarchy of **Philip V** (1700–1749), and the Netherlands remained important financially, though neither was able to exert influence equivalent to that enjoyed before 1715. In the east, Russia demonstrated that its modernization under Peter the Great left it a force to be reckoned with in the system of European diplomacy.

Before moving on to the wars, we take a quick snapshot of Britain and France after 1715. For purposes of the AP Exam, this review is helpful in the case of Britain to note how that nation developed a unique constitutional system following the Glorious Revolution, and in the case of France to lay the foundations for the long-term causes of the French Revolution.

France—Louis XV and Cardinal Fleury

When **Louis XV** (1715–1774), great-grandson of Louis XIV, ascended to the throne in 1715, he was only 5 years old. For decades, France was ruled by a regency, which was forced to grant concessions to the various *parlements* that Louis XIV had succeeded in taming. The **Parlement of Paris** in particular claimed the power to assent to legislation and taxes, representing a theme of French politics leading up to the fateful year of 1789—the emerging political conflict between a supposedly absolutist monarchy and a newly assertive nobility. Making matters worse was the attitude and habits of Louis XV. Louis relied heavily on advisors such as **Cardinal Fleury** (1653–1743), an elder statesman more interested in conciliating the propertied classes and avoiding war than in vigorously pursuing clear policies. The king himself proved lazy and rather than govern preferred the hunt and company of his mistresses, one of whom, **Madame de Pompadour,** was believed to exercise undue influence in the affairs of government. Such rumors, combined with Louis's weak rule, undermined support for the monarchy.

The landed and commercial classes (they were not always separate) both increased their power in France between 1715 and 1789. The government's need to fund the debt left over from its many wars along with the constant desire of investors to profit from the Commercial Revolution led to an unintended crisis in public finance. Under the influence of a Scottish investor, John Law, the monarchy chartered the Mississippi Company in the hopes that its issuance of stocks would underwrite the government's debt, reform the tax system, and make money for its investors. However, speculation in the company stock led to the "**Mississippi Bubble**" in 1720, which bankrupted thousands and forced the state to repudiate its debt. Unlike England, France never developed the notion of a **public debt** funded by banks—the debt was considered the king's *personal* debt—and as a result France lagged behind in the development of credit institutions and the ability to borrow money. Not surprisingly, the issues that forced the French monarchy to concede limits on its theoretically absolutist powers in 1789 were government debt and taxation.

Great Britain—the "King in Parliament" and Prime Minister

Following the Glorious Revolution in 1688, Britain developed a unique form of government known as the "**king in parliament.**" In short, English monarchs continued to play an important political role, but worked through Parliament and a **Prime Minister** to pass legislation and govern. After the last Stuart monarch, Queen Anne (1701–1714), died without an heir, England turned to a related German dynasty—the **Hanoverians.** Many Tories would have preferred to recall the son of the last Stuart monarch, James III, who attempted to lead an uprising in 1715 by landing an army on Scotland, as did his son in 1745. However, the Whig influence in government would not countenance another Catholic monarchy, and each of the potential threats was crushed with wide public support. So despite the unpopularity of the first Hanoverian, George I (1714–1727), who did not speak English, the dynasty was able to establish a functioning government system by relying on a prime minister and the cabinet system.

A major reason for Britain's commercial success in the eighteenth century involved the close relationship between government finance and private enterprise. The Bank of England issued stock to finance government debt and also allowed investors to draw on a larger amount of capital than in other nations. As in France, this system almost led to disaster in 1720. The South Sea Company purchased government bonds (debt) and issued stock based on the hope of profits trading with Spanish America. When the stock became overvalued, the **South Sea Bubble** burst, causing significant loss to its investors. Unlike France, Britain was able to save the South Sea Company, as well as other credit institutions involved in the scandal. Under the leadership of a new prime minister, Britain was able to continue the development of its public finance.

Sidebar: Britain was by no means a democracy in the eighteenth century. Parliament was controlled by large landowners and wealthy commercial interests. Burgeoning cities like Manchester and Liverpool had no representation in government. So-called "pocket boroughs" (districts that elected members to Parliament) were often controlled by a few wealthy individuals. Also, Walpole's system seemed to endorse corruption and bribery in government. These criticisms led to calls for reform and merged with the American Revolution.

The man largely responsible for the development of Britain's **cabinet system** of government was **Robert Walpole** (tenure, 1721–1743), also considered the first prime minister. Walpole appointed ministers to head up government agencies who also served in the Parliament. Moreover, Walpole carefully selected commercial-oriented Whigs personally loyal to him, creating the notion of the cabinet as a group bound to each other with a common goal. By carefully managing his parliamentary majority through issuance of government stocks, promises of patronage, and the like, Walpole was able to steer legislation through the **House of Commons** (the more important of the two houses of Parliament). Throughout his tenure, Walpole worked diligently to advance Britain's commercial interests abroad while avoiding war (to keep taxes down), a task he was able to accomplish except for a naval war with Spain (1739–1742) forced upon him by public opinion, that would soon merge with larger European conflicts.

Eighteenth-Century Warfare

For those students who enjoy playing games of strategy and war, it is eighteenth-century warfare that you have in mind. War was waged between highly trained and professional armies for specific strategic objectives. Soldiers were drawn from the underclass and less productive groups in society, perhaps "recruited" after a drunken night in a tavern. Their aristocratic army officers often ruled them through harsh discipline. Because conflict proved less destructive to civilians and land than the religious wars of an earlier age, states entered into it more lightly and also withdrew from it more quickly. Questions of war tended to be practical and rational in nature. Armies were expensive to maintain, train, and supply, so generals were reluctant to risk them carelessly in battle, often making warfare a game of movement and securing supply lines. Infantry played the major role in war, their inaccurate **smoothbore muskets** and bright uniforms imparting a parade-ground atmosphere to battles. Nonetheless, eighteenth-century warfare was brutal, destructive, and disruptive; it only seems less so in comparison with the conflagrations of the twentieth century.

The War of Austrian Succession, 1740–1748

The War of Austrian Succession began with a cynical attack by **Frederick II "The Great"** (1740–1786), king of Prussia, on Austria in defiance of the Pragmatic Sanction. Like a swarm of vultures, other nations (Bavaria, Saxony, Spain) rushed in to claim territorial prizes from the threatened empire. In continuance of their longtime opposition to the Habsburgs, the French joined the assault in alliance with Prussia. To prevent the dismemberment of Austria and maintain the balance of power on the continent, Britain joined the fray on the side of the new Habsburg ruler, **Maria Theresa** (1740–1780). In this way, the two primary rivalries in European politics merged into a complex conflict, which would be fought in two phases (see the following Seven Years' War discussion).

Frederick the Great experienced a difficult youth. More interested in learning French and playing the flute than war, Frederick often feuded with his stern father, Frederick William I (see Chapter 6) who intended to break his son. The young Frederick attempted to escape the kingdom with a friend, whom Frederick William I had executed right before his son's eyes to teach him a lesson. All of Europe expected the new king to drive Prussia into the ground as vengeance against his father. On the contrary, Frederick proved to be one of the great rulers in German history and a true military genius. The primary target of Frederick's aggression was the resource-rich province of Silesia, which he was able to win and hold until the end of the conflict.

Frederick was almost equally matched by Maria Theresa. In an act of political theater, Maria Theresa held aloft her newborn son (the future Joseph II) before the Hungarian nobles in 1741 to appeal for their support, which they gave in a spasm of chivalric fervor. Though Maria eventually lost Silesia, she did well to hold onto most of her other possessions by the **Treaty of Aix-la-Chapelle** (1748). The treaty reflected an Anglo-French agreement in which the Habsburg ruler had little say.

Britain and France waged war in several theaters in pursuit of their commercial and colonial objectives. Each side made advances against the other, with the British taking the North American fortress of Louisburg and squeezing the Caribbean, and the French grabbing Madras in India and holding Belgium (long a concern of the British) after their victory at Fontenoy in 1745. The antagonists were thus content to return to the situation as it had existed before the war, with the British happy to cede Silesia to Frederick in order to keep Belgium under Austrian rather than French control. Though the map had changed little beyond Silesia, the War of Austrian Succession had highlighted two issues: (1) France sat in an unfavorable strategic position, hamstrung between major continental commitments with its large army and a growing commercial empire in need of naval defense, and (2) Austria and Prussia now uneasily coexisted as two relatively even powers in Germany, with the latter immensely enhanced by its capture of Silesia, which had doubled its population to 6 million and strengthened its economic base. Maria Theresa was just as determined to regain the territory.

The Reforms of Maria Theresa and Diplomatic Revolution of 1756

Maria Theresa embarked on a wide-ranging series of reforms after 1748. To reduce inefficiency, Maria Theresa centralized the collection of taxes and combined the chancelleries (administrative offices) of the various territories of her empire. The army was tripled in size, while a military academy and engineering school were also founded. Later in her reign, Maria Theresa promoted primary education in the interests of economic productivity, promoted smallpox vaccination, outlawed torture and capital punishment, and eased the burdens of serfdom. Though many of these reforms benefited her subjects, her primary goal was to strengthen the state so as to recapture Silesia.

In 1756, the great Austrian diplomat and advisor to Maria Theresa, **Count von Kaunitz** (1711–1794), engineered one of the great diplomat coups of all time. Von Kaunitz convinced France to give up its traditional opposition to the Habsburgs and enter an alliance against the "greater threat" of Prussia, an alliance that Russia also joined. This **Diplomatic Revolution of 1756** forced Britain onto the side of Prussia to prevent another continental disruption to the balance of power (and a threat to Hanover, the ancestral home of Britain's

Sidebar: Maria Theresa deserves the reputation as one of the great Habsburg monarchs. While ruling, she found time to act as matriarch to her sixteen children. Though a reformer, Maria is not usually classed as an "enlightened" despot because of her strong Catholic loyalties (see next chapter). As part of the new French alliance, her youngest daughter, Marie Antoinette, was married to the French heir, Louis XVI, another unhappy result of the Austrian alliance for the French.

monarchy) and helped reignite the worldwide colonial conflict between France and Great Britain. Once again, despite the switch in alliances, the two key rivalries had merged, this time to produce a true world war with profound consequences for three continents.

The Seven Years' War, 1756–1763

The Seven Years' War stands as Frederick II's darkest and finest hour. Though outnumbered by his enemies almost 10 to 1, Frederick fought brilliantly, even when his capital Berlin was burned to the ground and all seemed lost. Britain provided primarily financial support in order to concentrate its energies on the colonial conflict with France. Frederick was aided by the disorganization of his opponents, who never seemed able to coordinate their attacks, and the French lack of enthusiasm for their new Austrian alliance. Despite his sometimes desperate situation and aging seemingly 20 years in 7 years' time, Frederick once again was able to hold onto Silesia by the **Treaty of Hubertusburg** (1756).

Fighting between France and Great Britain proved more decisive. Under the brilliant leadership of **William Pitt the Elder** (1708–1778), Britain won victories on land and sea in North America, the Caribbean, and in India. France found itself again depleted by fighting major wars on the continent of Europe and overseas. France and Britain both used their East India companies to exploit the decaying Mogul Empire in India, enlisting local rulers and warlords in pursuit of their interests. However, with its superior naval forces, Britain emerged victorious on balance, a fact that was reflected in the peace treaty.

By the **Treaty of Paris** (1756), Great Britain secured sole access to North America east of the Mississippi River and gained the dominant position in India, which became the "crown jewel of the British Empire." France was, however, able to win back its profitable sugar islands in the Caribbean. Though Britain clearly came out the dominant maritime power, French commerce continued to grow after 1763 and may have even outpaced Britain. The Treaty of Paris stands as one of the most important four or five treaties you will study this year. Why? It set the stage for major events on three continents. In North America (where the conflict was called the French and Indian War), British colonists were now free of the perennial French threat while the British were determined to make them pay for the costs of empire, a difference in outlook leading directly to the American Revolution. For Europe, the Seven Years' War confirmed the dualism in Germany of Austria and Prussia, but, more important, set the stage for the French Revolution by increasing the debt of and criticism against the French monarchy. On the Indian subcontinent, Britain oversaw the further dissolution of the Mogul Empire and established a strong colonial presence that would change both civilizations.

ADDITIONAL RESOURCES

Anderson, M. S., *Europe in the Eighteenth Century, 1715–1783*, 3rd ed. (1987)—Provides a useful overview of political developments in each country.

Black, Jeremy, *The Cambridge Illustrated Atlas of Warfare: Renaissance to Revolution, 1492–1792* (1996)—For those students interested in the details of warfare, this book offers excellent maps, concise text, and worldwide coverage.

Doyle, William, *The Old European Order, 1660–1800,* 2nd ed. (1992)—Explains the persistence of privilege in a changing century.

Flandrin, Jean-Louis, *Families in Former Times* (1979)—Overview of family life and structure of the household.

Hufton, Olwen, *The Prospect Before Her: A History of Women in Western Europe* (1996)—Strong history of women, especially the chapters on the eighteenth century.

Mintz, Steven, *Sweetness and Power: The Place of Sugar in Modern History* (1985)—For those interested in the European fascination with the sweet tooth.

Woloch, Isser, *Eighteenth-Century Europe: Tradition and Progress, 1715–1798* (1982)—A helpful survey in the Norton History of Europe that nicely combines political and social history.

http://www.bampfa.berkeley.edu/exhibits/newchild/—Uses art to show the changes in childhood in Great Britain.

PRACTICE QUESTIONS

1. Which of the following is the best interpretation of the accompanying eighteenth-century engraving?
   a. It reflects the new attitudes of love and tenderness toward children.
   b. It demonstrates the expansion of the cottage industry system of manufacturing.
   c. It shows the movement toward independent female labor unions.
   d. It highlights the poor working conditions of the new textile mills.
   e. It illustrates the increasing poverty and poor living conditions of the period.

© SSPL/The Image Works

2. In the quote below by Daniel Defoe (1726), which of the following ideas does he support?
   a. Nobles should dominate trade to maintain their privileged position in society.
   b. Commerce provided opportunities for poor peasants to rise in class.
   c. Trade is a respectable pursuit for elites and a way of social advancement.
   d. Trade was beneficial to the state by providing taxable income.
   e. Commerce attracted the lowest classes and should be avoided by gentlemen.

   "As so many of our noble and wealthy families are raised by and derived from trade, so it is true that man of the younger branches of our gentry, and even of the nobility, have become tradesmen. Thus, our tradesmen in England are not, as in other countries, always the lowest of our people. Nor is trade itself in England, as in other countries, the meanest thing men can turn their hand to; on the contrary, trade is the readiest way for men to raise their fortunes and families."

3. Which of the following best describes the position of the nobility in France from 1715 to 1789?
   a. tamed by a resurgent monarchy under Louis XV (1715–1774)
   b. surpassed in status by a rising bourgeoisie
   c. impoverished by high taxes and the costs of private warfare
   d. appealing to the peasants for support against the monarchy
   e. reviving in power and determined to check absolutism

4. New attitudes toward children and child-rearing were advanced by which of the following pairs?
   a. Jethro Tull and Charles Townsend
   b. Frederick William I and Maria Theresa
   c. Thomas Hobbes and Voltaire
   d. John Locke and Jean-Jacques Rousseau
   e. Madame de Pompadour and Maria Winkelmann

5. All of the following played a major role in supporting an increased population in eighteenth-century Europe EXCEPT:
   a. improved diet and nutrition.
   b. advances in understanding of disease.
   c. better weather and fewer famines.
   d. scientific agriculture and livestock breeding.
   e. virtual disappearance of the plague.

6. Which is the best characterization of the British political system in the eighteenth century?
   a. a growing trend toward democratization and male suffrage
   b. dominance of the government by landed interests
   c. reassertion of the dominant role of the monarchy
   d. emergence of the prime minister and cabinet as key roles
   e. gradual abandonment of common law in favor of a written constitution

7. Which of the following goods in the eighteenth century became a leading commercial profit-maker and also resulted in the enslavement of millions of Africans?
   a. sugar
   b. tea
   c. tobacco
   d. cotton
   e. spices

8. The best characterization of warfare in the period 1715–1789 is:
   a. standing armies pursuing limited strategic objectives
   b. large citizen armies fighting for their liberties
   c. private mercenaries living off the land and through pillage
   d. targeting of civilians and use of propaganda
   e. limited use of war due to effective collective security measures

9. From 1748 to 1780, Maria Theresa of Austria embarked on a series of political, social, and economic reforms. Which best describes the primary motive behind these policies?
   a. She was inspired by Enlightenment philosophy and wished to promote equality.
   b. Her Catholic piety influenced her belief that the state must better its subjects.
   c. She wished to strengthen the state so as to meet the challenge of Prussia.
   d. She wanted to impress her new ally France with her determination.
   e. She hoped that the reforms would quiet a rebellious peasantry and nobility.

10. Which of the following resulted from the Treaty of Paris (1763), which ended the Seven Years' War?
    a. France's commercial position continued a century-long decline.
    b. Spain reemerged as the leading military power on the continent.
    c. Austria succeeded in regaining Silesia from Prussia.
    d. India gained independence from both Britain and France.
    e. Britain established itself as the leading commercial power.

SAMPLE ESSAY

Analyze the social and diplomatic consequences on Europe of the expansion of global trade in the period 1700–1763.

Europe experienced a major increase in its trade in the eighteenth century. After the voyages of discovery and colonization, European powers like France, England, Spain, and the Netherlands, continued to seek trade and colonies throughout the world. This led to new methods of trade, like joint-stock companies and triangular trade. One of the more important effects was the increase in new goods, such as sugar, coffee, tea, spices, cloth, and porcelain. As a result, society experienced changes, like increased population and more middle-class influence. Diplomatically, commercial expansion led to one result: war.

All of the new goods that came to Europe changed people's lifestyles. More people desired goods that had been luxury products. These included spices from the East Indies, silks from China, tea from India, and coffee from Java. Wealthy people enjoyed expressing their status by decorating their homes with fancy rugs, fine china, and other trinkets from the "Orient." Even the lower classes benefited from this trade. New crops like potatoes, corn, and tomatoes helped the European diet. This made the diet better and increased the population, which really increased in the period 1700–63.

Competition for colonies seemed to lead to conflict among the European powers. At first the Dutch were the "kings of commerce," but they were eventually surpassed by the English, with whom they fought a naval war. Many of the wars revolved around France's goals under Louis XIV, like the War of Utrecht over Spain. Though Spain and France were not united, the Bourbons did come to the throne in Spain, even if Louis got stopped from dominating Europe. Later there were wars between Austria and Prussia over Silesia. This was fought in two phases, the second of which involved France and Britain. This Seven Years'

War was also called the French and Indian War in America, because North America was a major area of competition. Each side wanted the goods and commerce from the Americas, as well as India.

Overall, the expansion of goods and commerce in the eighteenth century had positive and negative effects. On the plus side, it gave European consumers more goods to buy and fill up their homes with luxuries. Without the improved nutrition, there probably would not have been a major increase in the population. On the down side, all of this competition for colonies created huge wars between the commercial powers. These wars tended to make Britain stronger and France weaker. Also, the Seven Years' War led to the way to the French and American Revolutions.

This response begins with an effective introductory paragraph and a clear thesis that specifies both social and diplomatic results. The two body paragraphs include support, though the one on social effects seems more focused and applies the examples more directly to the thesis. Perhaps two or three more examples would help in clarifying the thesis and would demonstrate further understanding of the prompt. Though the body paragraph addressing war offers plenty of detail, it tends to lose its focus on the question. Recall that the prompt asked for how commerce produced diplomatic changes; the response falls into a narrative mode, rather than demonstrating the commercial *cause* of the wars. Referring to the War of Spanish Succession (ended by the Peace of Utrecht) acts as a minor error, though it reinforces that the student is not fully in control of this part of the question. As for the conclusion, there is some reiteration of previous points, but it is on target with the prompt. I like the reference to how the Seven Years' War set up the French and American Revolutions; perhaps a sentence of explanation is in order. Overall, this is a strong but flawed essay—needs a few more examples in places, has a few errors, and includes some loss of focus on the question. Score: 7.

CHAPTER 9

The Enlightenment and the Dynamic Eighteenth Century

The great philosopher Immanuel Kant wrote of the eighteenth-century Enlightenment: "We live in an age of Enlightenment, but not an enlightened age." Kant considered the eighteenth century a time of significant reform and a questioning of established traditions, optimistically pointing toward progress. At the same time, Kant realized how far Europe still had to go toward the ideals of reason, equality, individualism, and secularism—all principles of the Enlightenment. The Enlightenment, its principles, and its adherents act as the central focus on this chapter, but we also examine cultural and political manifestations of Enlightenment thought. As an intellectual movement, the Enlightenment ranks as one of the most important you will study this year and a frequent subject of AP Exam questions. In your review, try to keep two central interpretive questions in mind: (1) How does this thinker/book/topic reflect the principles of Enlightenment thought? AND (2) To what degree was this area of life (medicine, education, law, etc.) reformed in line with Enlightenment principles?

> **Note:** to users of Palmer, Colton, and Kramer's *A History of the Modern World,* this chapter includes material from Chapter 7 of your text in an effort to link cultural developments to the Enlightenment.

ELITE AND POPULAR CULTURES

Despite differences in station and outlook, peasants and nobles partook of similar cultural experiences in early modern Europe. This changed during the eighteenth-century Enlightenment as elite and popular culture began to diverge. Those in the upper classes inhabited a culture of print, reading the latest novels, periodicals, newspapers, and perhaps philosophical treatises. Congregating in salons, coffeehouses, reading clubs, and libraries, members of the aristocracy and bourgeoisie acquired an appreciation for scientific knowledge and secular learning. Peasants and poor townspeople, however, lived within an oral culture, with knowledge and stories transmitted through story-telling, legend, or perhaps the symbolic imagery of a religious service. Once again, we are faced with a paradox of the eighteenth century—the Enlightenment gaining a strong cultural foothold, while many if not most Europeans remained relatively untouched by and unaware of it.

The Reading Public

If your life had spanned across eighteenth-century Europe, you would have witnessed a huge increase in the amount of printed material available—newspapers, periodicals, books, and novels. The phenomenon was both a cause and a result of an increase in the literacy rate, which in turn was supported by improved access to primary education. All classes and groups took part in this increase, though it was strongest among males and the middle classes.

By 1780 most European cities supported publication of at least one daily or weekly newspaper. It is easy to see how this phenomenon fed interest and concern regarding public affairs, including government policies. Publishers often catered to specific segments of the population. One of the more notable, though short-lived, publications was Richard Steele and Joseph Addison's *Spectator,* which featured articles of public interest and inspired the *Female Spectator,* focusing on domestic topics such as child-rearing and household management. Though books remained expensive, more members of the upper classes willingly invested resources in their purchase. Popularized scientific accounts, history books, and philosophical works all competed for shelf space. These works often reflected a secular focus or took a more critical view of religion. **Edward Gibbon's** (1737–1794) ***Decline and Fall of the Roman Empire,*** an immense chronicle of its subject, argued that the adoption of Christianity had sapped the Stoic energy of Rome.

Novels proved to be the biggest sellers. England pioneered the development of these works, which featured complex plots, character development, and ultimately, a strong moral message. For example, Samuel Richardson's (1689–1761) *Pamela: Or, Virtue Rewarded* recounts the tale of a serving girl who resists the sexual advances of her master, who then comes to understand her worth and eventually proposes marriage to her; thus her chastity is rewarded. Reflecting the eighteenth-century theme of child abandonment, Henry Fielding's *The History of Tom Jones, a Foundling* traces the adventures and ultimate success of the title character, a wily orphan who in traveling around England allows the author to satirize the hypocrisy of the age. Such works illustrated a growing "**cult of sentiment,**" the belief that open emotional displays equated with sincerity, and that humanitarian impulses elevated society by sustaining reform movements.

> **Sidebar:** Not surprisingly, when Americans revolted against British authority, they cited Enlightenment writers in support. When French revolutionaries expressed grievances with the Old Regime, they articulated these in the language of the Enlightenment. In both instances, one might credit the Enlightenment with turning revolts into revolutions.

Governments did attempt to censor works they deemed threatening to public order or blasphemous to organized religion. Efforts at **censorship** rarely succeeded in the long run, due partly to the decentralized nature of intellectual life in Europe and because states lacked the enthusiasm or manpower to enforce them adequately. To illustrate, the French government at one time or another banned publication of the famous *Encylopédie* as well as works by Voltaire, yet these publications eventually saw the light of day in other nations or the authors went into temporary hiding only to reappear when the circumstances had shifted.

Other than the sheer increase in knowledge, why is this increase in reading material important? Two words: **public opinion.** It is hard to imagine the American and French Revolutions occurring without the political energy generated by a reading public who was both informed and concerned about politics.

Education

Even in this age of Enlightenment, education remained the preserve of the well-to-do. Secondary schools reinforced the hierarchy of European society and focused on a curriculum of classical languages unlikely to provide practical advantages to an aspiring member of the lower classes. Educational reformers also criticized the stale education of the universities, slow to change in their adherence to Greek and Latin and often ignoring the scientific advances of the previous two centuries. Nonetheless, changes were evident. In Germany, *Realschule* were founded, which focused on practical skills to prepare young men for business. Furthermore, if a modern-minded scholar wished to learn the new science, he could attend one of the following universities: Leiden in the Netherlands, Halle in Germany, or Edinburgh in Scotland.

Art and Music

Though the Baroque style in the arts and music continued well into the eighteenth century, by the 1720s the Rococo style had taken hold, especially in France. Whereas the Baroque expressed power, illusion, and movement—the art of popes and kings—**Rococo** concentrated on light-hearted and pensive themes of romance and the transitory nature of life. Paintings by **Antoine Watteau** (1684–1721) and **Jean-Honoré Fragonard** (1732–1806) employ rich creams and golds, subtle curves, and lush settings to portray the graceful material pleasures of the aristocracy. To gain an appreciation for the Rococo style, particularly in contrast to the Baroque, find an image of **Balthasar Neumann's** (1687–1753) pilgrimage church *Vierzehnheiligen* ("The Fourteen Saints") set in southern Germany. Its lush detail and opulent ornamentation provide the pilgrim with an earthly view of heaven.

Nearer the middle of the century, Rococo gives way to another renewal of classical subject matter and motifs. Reflecting the increased attention paid to civic culture in an enlightening age, artists, such as **Jacques-Louis David** (1748–1825), in their **neoclassical** style drew from stories of ancient Greece and Rome. The David masterpiece "**Oath of the Horatii**" (1785) recounts the story of three brothers pledging to their father the patriotic sacrifice of their lives. Male figures stand firmly and starkly drawn with straight lines and bold colors beneath masculine Doric columns, while the emotionally prostrate women await the action in their muted colors and passive curves.

With the works of **Joseph Haydn** (1732–1809) and **Wolfgang Amadeus Mozart** (1756–1791), we move into the great Age of Classical Music (1750–1830). Composers experimented with full orchestration, writing symphonies of several movements that developed simple themes into complex musical patterns. Operas, such as Mozart's *Don Giovanni* or *The Magic Flute*, allowed composers to demonstrate mastery of several artistic forms—drama, music, and set design. Haydn wrote over a hundred symphonies in a prolific and long career. Mozart, on the other hand, was a child prodigy who wrote his first symphony at the age of 9 and first opera at 12. Though he only lived to be 35, Mozart's graceful style and appealing melodies set the standard for future composers.

Crime and Punishment

Governments of the eighteenth century lacked modern police forces and prisons. When criminals were captured, punishments tended to be public and harsh in order to set an example. An Italian jurist, **Cesare Beccaria** (1738–1794), condemned the traditional approach in his ***On Crimes and Punishments*** (1762). According to Beccaria, reason and the certainty of punishment (not its severity) should act as guides to law and the penal system. Torture, breaking on the wheel, and drawing and quartering all served as horrifying spectacle but tended to excite people's bloodlust and fear of power rather than respect for the law. Beccaria's ideas promoted penal reform and the building of prisons, beginning in the United States, which aimed at rehabilitation of inmates through discipline. Many enlightened monarchs further reflected humanitarianism by working toward the rational codification of laws to replace the patchwork of local customs and the elimination of torture and even capital punishment (see following discussion).

Medicine

Despite slight improvements, the medical care given to most Europeans remained inadequate and based either on outmoded classical ideas or dubious folk remedies. Life expectancy remained low, even with gradual improvements in urban hygiene and the beginnings of **vaccination,** first developed to address the scourge of smallpox in the 1770s. Most prospective physicians continued to train by attending universities that emphasized classical learning and paid little heed to a scientific or clinical approach, an exception being the University of Leiden in the Netherlands, famous as the setting for Rembrandt's paintings of human dissection. To improve standards and training, British physicians formed the first professional group, the Royal College of Physicians, and were followed by surgeons who broke away from barbers to create the Royal College of Surgeons. **Professionalization** aimed to exclude traditional practitioners, such as **midwives** and folk healers, as outside the circle of expertise and knowledge of medicine. Though these developments created a more favorable setting for medical study and practice, the general improvement in Europeans' standard of living in this period owed more to better diet and nutrition than to medicine.

Religious Revival in a Secular Age

Enlightenment *philosophés* hoped to improve European society through a secular and scientific approach. Many Europeans did not share this goal and clung to a religious worldview. Secular thinking advanced during the eighteenth century, but AP students often overstate the degree to which ordinary people were affected by this trend. Strong evidence to the contrary is offered by several movements of religious revival. **John Wesley's** (1703–1791) **Methodism** in England represents the most famous of these movements. Wesley appealed directly to the lower classes, many of whose lives had been negatively affected by economic changes or alcoholism, with a warm spirituality that emphasized huge open-air meetings highlighted by dramatic stories of conversion. In Germany, Count von Zinzendorf (1700–1760) initiated the **Pietist revival** within a Lutheran religion that many perceived as stale and overly institutional. Revivalism acted as a transatlantic phenomenon as Wesley's conversion tactics were employed liberally on the American frontier, and German Pietists immigrated to the American colonies to practice their religious faith.

Unlike in previous centuries, many enlightened monarchs approached religious matters with skepticism and attempted to create a barrier between private religious belief and public expressions of religion, which were of concern to the state. At the insistence of several governments, the papacy in 1773 banned the Jesuit order, which was perceived as beholden to a foreign power, though it was later reinstated in 1814 following the French Revolution. Furthermore, monarchs began to extend religious toleration to minorities. Going furthest in this regard was Joseph II of Austria, whose **Edict on Toleration** (1781) even granted toleration to Jews, allowing them to practice their religion freely, own land, and hold titles of nobility. The process of **emancipation** for Jews continued into the French Revolution, allowing them to assimilate more fully into economic and intellectual life. However, it should be noted that Jews continued to be subjected to scorn by Enlightenment thinkers and prejudice by popular opinion.

Popular Culture and Leisure

Literacy increased among all classes in eighteenth-century Europe; however, literate lower-class members generally shunned the novels, histories, and treatises of the elites. Many poor townspeople and peasants favored the 24-page cheaply printed **chapbooks,** as well as **almanacs,** both of which carried chivalric romances, religious stories, folk wisdom, and information about weather. Oral culture remained strong among the illiterate, who often told folk and fairly tales to understand their condition and warn the young about the harsh world outside. One artist who both reflected and influenced mass culture was the British illustrator **William Hogarth** (1697–1764). Hogarth's sets of prints told diverging stories of success and failure, depending on the character and moral attributes of his protagonists. His humorous satires and moral message played well with all groups.

Carnival celebrations played a key role in the cycle of seasonal work in early modern Europe. Despite government efforts to curtail them following the Protestant Reformation, many clung to the tradition of concentrated indulgence and riotous behavior that the festival offered. The masses could turn to other amusements even if Carnival was restricted. Drink has always played a major social and dietary role in the lives of Europeans. During the eighteenth century, many of the lower class turned to stronger (and often cheaper) spirits such as gin and whiskey for escape. **Taverns** in Great Britain advertised "drunk for a penny, dead drunk for two." Alcoholism became a major social problem for the first time. For further escape, peasants and poor townspeople turned to the **bloodsports** of bare-knuckle fisticuffs, cockfighting, and bearbaiting (chaining a bear taken from the woods and "siccing" ferocious dogs upon it). These popular leisure activities serve to remind us of the growing divergence between popular and elite cultures and that the Enlightenment ethos clearly did not reach all members of society.

ENLIGHTENMENT THOUGHT

Enlightenment philosophy took its cue from the Scientific Revolution of the sixteenth and seventeenth centuries. Given this, remember the following brief and useful definition of the Enlightenment:

An effort to apply the methods and principles of the Scientific Revolution to issues of political, economic, and social reform.

In other words, Enlightenment thinkers believed that just as laws guided the movements of the planets or workings of the human body, human reason and observation could discover the same laws of human affairs—for example, in law, politics, or even religion. We have already seen how the skeptical mindset liberated by the Scientific Revolution laid the foundations for the eighteenth century. Now we look at the social setting in which this philosophy gained currency.

The Setting of the Enlightenment and the Role of Women

To experience the Enlightenment in its full flower, one needed to live in Paris. Many of the greatest *philosophés* hailed from France, and French served as the unifying language of intellectual discourse, particularly among the elite. Scotland, Britain, Germany, and America—these all contributed to the Enlightenment, but the movement took its tone and spirit from the salons of Paris. The women who ran the **salons**—known as *salonnières*—attracted philosophers, economists, and writers from all over Europe in an effort to stimulate an ongoing conversation regarding the key issues facing Europe. For 25 years, **Madame de Geoffrin** (1699–1777) hosted intellectuals at her dinners, acted as mediator and financial patroness, and invited foreign thinkers and rulers to her famous Parisian salon. Many writers chose the salons of Julie Lespinasse or Suzanne Necker as the settings to introduce newly published works or discuss new theories.

Women clearly participated in the culture of the Enlightenment. Some women and even a few male *philosophés* such as Condorcet advocated the equality of women. Importantly, **Mary Wollstonecraft** (1759–1797), a writer and collaborator in radical political movements, penned the first modern statements of the feminist movement. Wollstonecraft's *Thoughts on the Education of Daughters* took issue with Rousseau's gender-based educational philosophy, arguing that only if women were trained for intelligence and self-reliance could they raise children who exhibited these same characteristics necessary for republican government. Later, during the French Revolution, Wollstonecraft defended the movement for equality with *A Vindication of the Rights of Woman* (1792), which held that no legitimate basis, other than physical strength, could be devised to discriminate between men and women. Though these works set the feminist agenda for the next century, women gained few tangible benefits from their participation in a movement that aimed more at religious superstition and intellectual suppression than gender inequality.

For those who could not participate in the salons, other venues provided opportunities for the exchange of new ideas. The middle classes congregated in **coffeehouses** and reading clubs to discuss the New Science or the latest novel. Though most *philosophés* hailed from aristocratic status, the bourgeoisie often imitated noble fashions and intellectual interests, including Enlightenment philosophy. An additional if more secretive setting for the spread of the Enlightenment was the Freemason lodges, founded in the early 1700s. **Freemasonry** attracted many famous intellectuals, including Mozart and many early U.S. presidents, with its emphasis on tight-knit camaraderie, select membership, and betterment through education and technology.

The Philosophés and Their Ideals

Heads Up! These principles represent the kind of material it is helpful to commit to memory. If you are asked in an essay prompt about the main features of the Enlightenment, reference to concepts like these will start your response with an explicit direction and avoid the kind of vague generalizing that often dooms weaker efforts.

Who were the *philosophés*? The majority were not, in fact, professional philosophers, though several, such as Hume and Kant, were. Most acted as writers, social critics, and publicists for new ideas. Just as an engineer or political leader uses a plan to guide his actions, the *philosophés* expressed an intellectual project: to subject all of human custom and tradition to a systematic criticism using reason and the methods of science. Revolution was far from their thinking; progress should occur through gradual acceptance of the Enlightenment message of reform. As you review the important *philosophés* discussed next, consider how their works reflect the following important principles:

- **Reason**—Perhaps the concept most associated with the Enlightenment, belief in human reason's ability to discover the relevant laws of nature and humanity expresses the assumption that the world itself is inherently "knowable" to the human mind and an **optimism** in the advance of human understanding.
- **Secularism**—Not all *philosophés* demonstrated hostility to organized religion or advocated atheism. Most Enlightenment thinkers did believe that the dogmatism often accompanying organized religion should not be allowed to intrude into public life. Science and rational inquiry should replace theology as the authorities in public affairs. In place of organized religion, many intellectuals adhered to belief in God based on reason, not revelation. This **deism** portrayed God as a kind of Newtonian "clockmaker" who designed the world with scientific natural laws and then simply allowed it to function. With

this "natural religion," the prophets, holy books, dogma, clergy, and rituals of organized religion were considered unnecessary.

- **Equality**—Though many *philosophés* noted the crushing inequality present in European institutions, few trusted the masses to rule. Belief in the betterment of the lower classes did not necessarily translate into support for democracy.
- **Progress**—A natural byproduct of belief in human reason, the notion of progress lay at the heart of the Enlightenment project. According to the foremost American advocate of the Enlightenment, Benjamin Franklin, the pursuit of knowledge should ultimately yield practical benefits for humankind.

Brief biographical and intellectual sketches of the most important figures of the Enlightenment follow.

Denis Diderot (1713–1784)—Diderot, one of the first outspoken atheists, achieved fame for his editing of the *Encylopedié*, a 17-volume reference work that ambitiously set out to arrange the sum total of human knowledge alphabetically, without deference to ecclesiastical (religious) or political authority. Many of the articles created controversy by taking a critical perspective on organized religion or by revealing the trade secrets of the guilds. In addition to print articles, the *Encylopedié* provided illustrations designed to convey practical knowledge of science, the military arts, and manufacturing. Diderot possessed an expansive mind, which led him to write in a variety of genres, including drama and education for the deaf, making him a favorite in the salons and at courts such as Catherine the Great's of Russia.

David Hume (1711–1776)—A down-to-earth, jovial leader of the Scottish Enlightenment, Hume conveyed a radically empirical approach to human knowledge. According to Hume (see *Enquiry Concerning Human Understanding* [1748]), it was a fallacy of reasoning to say that we *experience* the "laws of nature" or even that personal identity persists through time. Stable knowledge arises from our immediate observations (what Hume called perceptions); the further removed from these we become by forming "ideas," the less reliable is our knowledge. Further, in his *Dialogues Concerning Natural Religion* (1779), Hume articulated a skeptical and an agnostic attitude toward miracles and the intelligent design argument for God's existence. Finally, Hume argued that the "oughts" of morality cannot arise from the "is'es" of nature; ethics, then, could only be based on our moral sense, or sentiments, not our reasoning.

Immanuel Kant (1724–1804)—Kant stands as one of the most brilliant and incomprehensible philosophers of the modern age. Rarely traveling outside his home town of Königsberg, Prussia, Kant never married and dedicated his life to developing a complete system of philosophy. Kant's "Copernican revolution" in philosophy combined the empirical and rationalist traditions into one coherent system of knowledge. Our rational intuitions about time, space, and causation (rationalism) do provide us with knowledge about what we experience (empiricism), Kant held, but they can never tell us about the "things in themselves," for these lay beyond our experience. Kant's system is called constructivism, because the perceptual "lenses" of our intuitions construct the world out of our experiences. When it came to ethics, however, Kant rejected Hume's moral-sense ideas in favor of a purely rationalist approach—the ethical act is objectively determined by testing whether it could be applied universally without contradiction.

Baron de Montesquieu (1689–1755)—Montesquieu's experiences as a French Protestant and member of the Bordeaux *parlement* influenced his writings. Keeping with the new travel literature, Montesquieu in 1721 penned the **Persian Letters,** a satirical account of two foreign visitors' adventures through France as they encounter what seem like strange and often ridiculous beliefs and customs. By far, Montesquieu's most important work was *The Spirit of the Laws* (1748). Based on his investigation of history and contemporary nations, Montesquieu concluded that geography, climate, and history tended to determine the forms of government and laws of each nation. Large nations tended toward despotism (like Russia), medium-sized nations toward monarchy (like France), and smaller nations toward republics (like Switzerland). Montesquieu favored a government like Britain's, which incorporated **checks and balances** to restrain the vices associated with each major political interest: monarchy—tyranny, oligarchy—factionalism, democracy—anarchy.

Physiocrats and Adam Smith (1723–1790)—Adam Smith (Scottish) built off the ideas of the French **Physiocrats,** both of whom criticized mercantilism for violating the natural laws regarding economics. Whereas mercantilists held specie (hard money) to be the true source of wealth, the Physiocrats believed it to be land, as that resource provided society with its agricultural sustenance and mineral resources. To produce a higher standard of living, Physiocrats argued, one must free land from the inefficient feudal restrictions placed upon it and promote the development of commercial agriculture. It was the Physiocrats who coined the expression **"laissez faire"** ("let it be") to argue against the kind of continuous government supervision of the economy associated with mercantilism. Adam Smith agreed with Physiocracy's analysis of mercantilism, but provided a somewhat different analysis of the natural laws of economics in his "bible of capitalism," *Inquiry into Nature and Causes of the Wealth of Nations* (1776). Many of his ideas still guide economic thinking today and can be summarized as follows:

1. Labor is the ultimate source of value, as it is labor that mixes with raw materials to make useful products.
2. Economic activity is too complex to be guided by the blunt instrument of government. The **"invisible hand of the marketplace"** or the laws of **supply and demand** should determine what is produced, how much is produced, and at what price.
3. Nations should allow the free flow of goods across borders and concentrate on producing those goods for which they possess a **comparative advantage** (e.g., Guatemala produces coffee more efficiently than computers). Mercantilism's assumption of scarcity will be rendered false, as all nations will benefit from this practice of **free trade,** without artificial tariffs that protect inefficient producers and harm consumers.
4. Opposing the traditional guild system, Smith argued for a higher **division of labor** to produce larger quantities of goods and lower costs. When the production process is broken into its component steps, worker specialization yields greater efficiency.

Voltaire (1694–1778)—The middle-class François-Marie Arouet later took the famous pen name "Voltaire" and came to represent the ideals of the Enlightenment. Voltaire's sarcasm, witty style, and commitment to intellectual freedom won him admiration and resentment. Wide ranging in his interests, Voltaire took aim at religious fanaticism and hypocrisy. During the **Calas Affair**—when a Protestant father was falsely accused of killing his son to prevent his conversion to

Catholicism—Voltaire argued for religious toleration and claimed that "revealed" religion made people stupid and cruel. His famous battle cry resounded "crush the infamous thing!," meaning organized religion. Like many *philosophés,* Voltaire held instead to a rational belief in God, or deism. In ***Philosophical Letters on the English,*** Voltaire expressed his admiration for England's balanced government and relative religious tolerance. Voltaire spent two years at the court of Frederick II of Prussia, with whom he shared a belief in enlightened top-down reform and a distrust of the ignorant masses. In response to the stupidity and shallow optimism Voltaire believed to be a part of human nature, he wrote the novelette ***Candide,*** which recounts the misadventures of a young man who ultimately learns the best we can hope for is "to tend our own garden," or develop our intellectual capacities without interference.

The Later Enlightenment

Some historians believe that after about 1760, the Enlightenment entered a new phase. According to this interpretation, some *philosophés* grew more insistent and radical in their criticisms of existing society and called for the adoption of an explicitly mechanistic and materialist view of the world. Though he is difficult to categorize, Jean-Jacques Rousseau is often associated with this more radical view of the Enlightenment.

Jean-Jacques Rousseau (1712–1778)—Unique among the *philoso-phés,* Rousseau came from the lower middle class. His life represents a tale of misfortune, as he was neglected as a child, lived from job to job, found patronage among older women, and eventually married a local barmaid, with whom he had five children, whom he later abandoned. In his many writings, Rousseau developed several themes. Early on, in *Discourses on the Arts and Sciences* and *Discourses on the Origin of Inequality Among Men,* Rousseau portrayed civilization as corrupting to humans' natural inclination for mutual association, leading to exploitation and artificial divisions. Rousseau glorified the life of the **Noble Savage,** exemplified by Native Americans, for whom there was no need of reason, as instinct

> **Sidebar:** Rousseau's ideas became highly influential during the radical phase of the French Revolution. The vagueness of Rousseau's institutional arrangements in *The Social Contract* seemed to justify governments ranging from direct democracy to totalitarian dictatorship.

and emotion more reliably produced happiness. Concerned with the moral dimension of human experience, Rousseau wrote in ***The Social Contract*** (1762) that the fundamental dilemma of any political system was to find a form of political association in which the **General Will** of the entire society could be realized through pursuit of the common good. Rousseau left the institutional structure of this republican state ambiguous, for the General Will could not be expressed through representative bodies or legal formalities. With *Émile* (1762) and *La Nouvelle Heloise* (1762), Rousseau completed his presentation of the "cult of sentiment." In the former, Rousseau laid out a new approach of child-rearing and education with a focus on the child's positive experiences, rather than rote memorization or an early focus on reason. Within this system, Rousseau viewed women as naturally fitted for the domestic sphere, where their duties lie with breast-feeding and nurturing their children. For the latter work, a sentimental novel, Rousseau showed how artificial boundaries between two lovers can lead to tragedy. In imitation of Rousseau, many began to weep openly, speak emotionally, and glorify nature. Overall, Rousseau stands as one of the most creative and controversial of the *philosophés,* but also the first figure of the later Romantic movement.

Though many *philosophés* wished to retain a veneer of spirituality in the world with deism, others were content to push a scientific view of the world to its further limits. **Baron d'Holbach** (1723–1789) of Germany contributed to the *Encylopedié* articles attacking Christianity as preventing humanity from reaching its full moral development. In *The System of Nature* (1770), he boldly asserted that all of existence consisted of no more than particles in motion, guided by built-in natural laws. God, souls, angels, and spirits could not exist since they did not possess a material nature. From this, d'Holbach concluded that human behavior itself was subject to the same material forces and was therefore determined, even if actions *seemed* the result of free choice. Not only churches, but even thinkers such as Voltaire found d'Holbach's ideas repugnant to the spirit of human progress and improvement characteristic of the Enlightenment.

Marquis de Condorcet (1743–1794), an aristocratic mathematician and political scientist, wrote passionately in his life for equality (including women), justice, constitutional government, and individual liberty. His most famous work, *Progress of the Human Mind* (1795), portrays human civilization as the advance toward scientific thinking and science's connection to greater freedom and happiness. Condorcet's idealism could not save him from the radicalism of the French Revolution, as he was arrested because of his aristocratic lineage and later died in prison, an example of how the forces unleashed by the Enlightenment could not always be controlled by its creators.

ENLIGHTENED DESPOTISM

Monarchs recognized the potential of Enlightenment methods for the rational ordering of the state. While rulers patronized the Enlightenment and attracted *philosophés* to their courts, their focus remained on the realities of power. Several rulers in the eighteenth century fit the label "enlightened despot," but three stand out, as discussed next.

Prussia and Frederick II "the Great" (1740–1786)

We have already seen how Frederick established the greatness of Prussia through his military exploits and winning of Silesia (see Chapter 8). A strong skeptic, Frederick practiced religious toleration, as did his Hohenzollern ancestors, but did not offend the religious sensibilities of his people by ridiculing their faith. While Louis XIV said "I am the state," Frederick believed himself to be "the first servant of the state." In *Forms of Government* (1781), Frederick laid out how each element of society played a specific and necessary function for the operation of the machinery of state. His ideal of efficiency and reason did not produce equality, however. Prussian social classes remained legally defined, with little or no social mobility between them. Frederick also reversed many of his father's policies related to merit, once again favoring the Junker nobility above others. In addition, outside of Frederick's own crown lands, serfdom grew worse during his reign. Nonetheless, Frederick achieved a greater degree of centralization, **codifying the laws** of his diverse lands and enforcing them with Prussia's renowned bureaucracy. Frederick invited the likes of Voltaire to his court, but their egos were too large for close company. Despite such displays of enlightenment and Frederick's early interest in music and philosophy, the aging monarch often cynically put the interests of state above principles, as with his calculated invasion of Silesia in 1740 and the Polish Partition of 1772.

Austria and Joseph II (1780–1790)

Of all rulers, Joseph II most thoroughly believed in and upheld Enlightenment principles during his brief 10-year reign. Building on the reforms of his mother, Maria Theresa, Joseph pursued reform systematically and often recklessly. Genuinely concerned with the plight of the lower classes, Joseph abolished serfdom, granted religious toleration to minorities (**Edict on Toleration,** 1781), granted liberty of the press, and introduced legal equality. Though nominally

Catholic, Joseph clashed with the pope and insisted on greater control over the church in Austria. His **Edict on Idle Institutions** disbanded unproductive monasteries and diverted the funds for the establishment of secular hospitals. Joseph also attempted to promote economic development in his empire by advocating a version of Physiocracy. Despite issuing over 10,000 edicts in his life for the betterment of the people, when Joseph died at 49, many of his reforms were reversed. In his effort to centralize his diverse lands and improve the lives of his people, Joseph offended local traditions and alienated important segments of society, such as the clergy and nobility. No one can doubt Joseph's commitment to the Enlightenment principles, but his fast-paced reform and disregard for opposition ultimately proved too much for many in the empire.

> **Sidebar:** To see a humorous portrayal of Joseph, combined with a tragic portrayal of Mozart, you might rent the popular film *Amadeus*. Like many films, it makes for good entertainment but not always good history.

Russia and Catherine II (1762–1796)

Catherine may have been the most famous and admired woman of her era. Between Peter the Great's death in 1725 and Catherine's accession in 1762, Russia had been led by a series of weak and unstable rulers, which allowed the nobility to resurrect their power. In addition, Catherine hailed from Germany and gained power via a palace coup against her weak husband. Despite these obstacles, Catherine proved a strong ruler, though one who continuously compromised her adherence to Enlightenment principles in favor of practical political realities. The "philosopher on the throne," Catherine attracted Voltaire and Diderot to her court, wrote a famous **Instruction to the Legislative Commission** (1767) expressing her belief in reason and equality, established schools for girls, and even abolished torture and capital punishment. On the other hand, she gained a reputation for leaving grandiose projects unfinished and acting ruthlessly when it suited her interests. She allowed serfdom to worsen by selling off crown lands, brutally crushed the subsequent Pugachev Revolt in the 1770s, and liberated the nobles from state service with a **Charter of the Nobility** (1785) while never following up with the proposed constitution for all Russia's people. Perhaps her greatest accomplishment, Catherine added more territory to Russia than any ruler in its history, both by defeating the weakening Ottoman Empire and by partitioning neighboring Poland out of existence. Reflecting a double standard toward women, Catherine earned a reputation for sexual promiscuity by taking lovers of her advisors and political allies. One of these, Grigori Potemkin, lends his name to the fake villages set up to impress foreign dignitaries with Russia's greatness. Like the Potemkin Villages, Russia appeared immense and powerful to the outside world, but in Catherine's Russia much suffering and unfinished reform hid behind this façade.

The Realities of Enlightened Despotism and the Partitions of Poland

Enlightened despotism allows us to gauge and assess the ideals and realities of the larger movement, which makes it a helpful topic of study for the AP Exam. With the failed exception of Joseph II of Austria, enlightened monarchs viewed enlightened ideals primarily as a *tool* to exercise power. When push came to shove, most rulers chose the path of power and compromised on ideals. Even so, enlightened despotism laid the groundwork for the revolutionary movements of the late eighteenth and early nineteenth centuries. By promoting centralization and calling into question traditional authorities, enlightened monarchs provided an agenda and a method for future changes, even if in the future by way of revolution. Since the Middle Ages, monarchy had generally acted as a progressive force for change; by 1780, the enlightened despots had taken their reforms about as far as they could without undermining their hereditary dynasties. Not surprisingly, after the French Revolution, monarchies looked backward instead of forward, attempting to avoid change while supporting tradition.

Poland represented an outlier among European monarchies. Its elective monarchy and powerful nobility never allowed the kingdom to achieve centralized institutions such as a tax system, bureaucracy, or standing army. As a result, the three great eastern powers—Austria, Prussia, and Russia—saw it in their interests to take advantage of internal instability in Poland to eliminate its independent existence. Though each of the three partitions (in 1772, 1793, and 1795) was prompted by differing circumstances, each stemmed from the collusion and cynicism of Poland's great power rivals. The **Partitions of Poland** maintained the balance of power in eastern Europe, but at the expense of the old international order, which had often upheld the existence of weaker states like Poland. The enlightened despots who helped carve up Poland once again demonstrated how power politics under the guise of enlightened reform held the potential of upsetting the basis for traditional government.

REALIZING THE ENLIGHTENMENT IN POLITICS

Reform in Britain

Prior to the great revolution in France (1789), clouds of change wafted across the Atlantic World. Let's look first at Britain, before traveling to its colonies in America. As part of the humanitarian impulse borne out of the Enlightenment, reformers targeted slavery as one of greatest violations of the principles of equality and freedom. In 1783, the **Quakers,** who believed all humans possessed an "inner light," founded the first abolitionist society in Europe. Soon after, another British group targeted the slave trade itself for elimination, which resulted in success with both Britain's and America's abolition of the practice in 1807.

Within Britain, the system of "rotten boroughs" and patronage came under increasing criticism. Many cities lacked representation, and only the wealthy exercised the vote. Voices for democratic reform rallied around the case of John Wilkes, a radical journalist and member of Parliament who criticized the king's policies. Though the "king's men" excluded Wilkes from Parliament until 1774, his cause animated the crowds of London with cries of "**Wilkes and Liberty!**" Calls for reform echoed throughout Britain's empire; however, attempts at change in Ireland resulted only in an Act of Union in 1801, which bound it more tightly to Britain. As for India, the rule of the British East India Company grew more centralized under parliamentary supervision. Of these trends toward democratization and centralization, the American colonists took up the first and defied the second.

The Promise of the Enlightenment—The American Revolution

The United States appears on the AP Exam only in its relation to European history, which means only sporadically until World War I. It is not necessary to recount the American Revolution here, but a word is in order to place the Enlightenment in proper context.

First, the American colonists followed events closely in Britain, particularly the Wilkes affair. Such events, as well as the reading of British critics of the king-in-parliament system (called commonwealthmen), inspired America in its own rebellion against British efforts at centralizing the empire. These protests resulted in American independence and, later, the first written constitution in the modern age expressing Enlightenment principles. Enlightenment thinking stretched across the Atlantic Ocean, and, indeed, several Americans contributed to the movement:

- **Benjamin Franklin**—(1706–1790)—Franklin discovered electricity; invented bifocals and the Franklin stove; negotiated the Treaty of Paris that ended the War for American Independence; founded the American Philosophical Society; published one of America's first newspapers; and founded the postal service, first library, first hospital, first fire company, and the University of Pennsylvania. Franklin retired at 48 and thereafter lived out his credo that knowledge should be useful to the human race.

> **Sidebar:** Both Franklin and Jefferson lived in France as American diplomats and were quite popular. Franklin played up the "backwoods" American role by wearing a coonskin cap, even though he came from Philadelphia. During the opening phase of the French Revolution, French leaders consulted in Paris with Jefferson, who was a lifelong supporter of revolution.

- **Thomas Jefferson**—(1743–1826)—Jefferson gained fame for this writing of the **Declaration of Independence,** one of the greatest expressions of Enlightenment thought, justifying natural law, inalienable rights, and the right of revolution. One of the only presidents who openly espoused deism, Jefferson promoted religious toleration and sponsored numerous scientific endeavors. Of course, Jefferson's ownership of slaves demonstrates the limitations of his enlightened philosophy.

- **Thomas Paine**—(1737–1809)—Born in Britain, Paine set sail for America in 1774 just in time for the revolution. Paine's *Common Sense* (1776), which criticized monarchy as unnatural, sparked the movement for independence. Later involved in the French Revolution, Paine defended the radical movement for equality and liberty with *The Rights of Man* (1791) as well as deism with *The Age of Reason* (1794).

As we see in the next chapter, the American Revolution inspired belief that Enlightenment principles could be realized politically, and also indirectly led to revolution in France by bankrupting that nation's treasury through its support for American independence.

ADDITIONAL RESOURCES

Darnton, Robert, *The Great Cat Massacre: And Other Episodes in French Cultural History* (1985)—Through the author's retelling of fascinating vignettes, we come to understand how historians recreate the mental worlds of the past.

Hampson, Norman, *A Cultural History of the Enlightenment* (1969)—A challenging read, but provides strong insight in one focused volume.

Jacob, Margaret C., *The Enlightenment: A Brief History with Documents* (2000)—This slim volume in the Bedford Series provides primary sources with brief analysis.

Krieger, Leonard, *Kings and Philosophers, 1689–1789* (1970)—This volume in the Norton History Series offers useful sections on enlightened absolutism.

Smith, Bonnie, *Changing Lives: Women in European History Since 1700* (1988)—Good resource that begins with useful chapters on the Enlightenment and French Revolution.

http://andromeda.rutgers.edu/~jlynch/18th/—This site provides links for anything related to eighteenth-century culture.

PRACTICE QUESTIONS

1. Which of the following is most associated with the increase in literacy rates in eighteenth-century Europe?
    a. Monarchs adopted universal compulsory schooling.
    b. Nobles hoped educating the masses would forestall revolution.
    c. The amount of printed materials rose significantly.
    d. Women agitated for better schooling and more rights.
    e. A changing economy required more skilled workers.

2. What contemporary issue is highlighted by this William Hogarth print below?
    a. the decline in economic productivity caused by class conflict
    b. the negative influence of traditional child-rearing practices
    c. the lack of democratic development in British politics
    d. the uproar caused by radical Enlightenment principles
    e. the moral decline caused by alcoholism among the working class

The Metropolitan Museum of Art, Harris Brisbane Dick Fund, 1932 [32.35 (124) Image © The Metropolitan Museum of Art

3. Which of the following issues was of primary concern to the Italian *philosophé* Cesare Beccaria?
    a. child-rearing
    b. legal reform
    c. technology
    d. religion
    e. agriculture

4. All of the following are accurate statements regarding European religious life in the eighteenth century EXCEPT:
   a. religious practice in Catholic nations declined dramatically.
   b. monarchs extended toleration to minority religious groups.
   c. John Wesley led the Methodist revival in England.
   d. Jews became more assimilated into European society.
   e. agnosticism and atheism attracted open support.

5. Which of the following best characterizes how the *philosophés* viewed human nature?
   a. essentially selfish and in need of strict controls
   b. guided by reason and capable of progress
   c. naturally social and spontaneously cooperative
   d. driven by animalistic impulses and drives
   e. emotionally intense and sentimental

6. The passage below conveys an idea central to the work of which Enlightenment figure?
   a. Voltaire
   b. Diderot
   c. Montesquieu
   d. Rousseau
   e. Hume

   "Let moralists say what they will, human understanding is greatly indebted to the passions, which likewise are greatly indebted to human understanding. It is by the activity of our passions that our reason improves. We covet knowledge merely because we covet enjoyment, and it is impossible to conceive why a man exempt from fears and desires should take the trouble to reason."

7. Which of the following most directly led to the rise of deism in the eighteenth century?
   a. the religious wars of the seventeenth century
   b. decrease in the number of witchcraft accusations
   c. return of economic stability in western Europe
   d. the influence of the Freemasons
   e. the mechanistic cosmology of Newton

8. All of the following were policies of the eighteenth-century enlightened despots EXCEPT:
   a. promoting democratic movements abroad.
   b. codifying laws and eliminating torture.
   c. gaining control over religious affairs.
   d. centralizing government bureaucracies.
   e. patronizing intellectual figures.

9. A major result of Poland's inability to create a strong, centralized monarchy in the eighteenth century was:
   a. the creation of an alliance between the nobility and powerful merchants.
   b. a successful effort at internal reform guided by Stefan Poniatowksi.
   c. a diplomatic agreement between France and Britain to maintain Polish neutrality.
   d. the eventual partition of the Polish state by its powerful neighbors.
   e. the decline of the Polish economy and its absorption by Russian commerce.

10. Which of the following best characterizes the impact of the American Revolution on Europe?
    a. It led to a serious decline in British commerce and dismemberment of its empire.
    b. It demonstrated that Enlightenment ideals could be realized politically.
    c. The American Revolution was little-known in Europe and thus had small impact.
    d. Trained revolutionaries traveled to Europe to foment a similar revolution in France.
    e. The antislavery movement spread and succeeded in abolishing slave trade by 1800.

SAMPLE ESSAY

In what ways and to what extent did Enlightenment thought affect the practice of religion and the exercise of politics prior to the French Revolution (1789)?

The Enlightenment had many new ideas about society, religion, and politics. For the first time, many people were atheists and religion went down. There were also political figures who tried to use the ideas of the movement to help their states. In the following essay, I will examine these areas and show how the Enlightenment affected them.

First, before 1700 most people in Europe were very Christian. This all changed with the Enlightenment. When Diderot wrote his Encyclopedia, he showed atheism. Hume was another *philosophé* who questioned miracles and whether you could really ever know God. Also, countries began practicing religious toleration for minority groups, like Jews. This created more peace and secular thinking in nations. Then there was Deism. Building off of Newton and the Scientific Revolution, Deists believed that God created the world and just stood back and watched. He didn't do miracles, and the clergy was unnecessary. Voltaire was one, and many of his writings criticized the church.

Enlightenment thinkers wanted more equality. Rousseau wrote in *The Social Contract* how each person needs to feel equal for the state to run well. Montesquieu had his system of checks and balances, which also affected the United States. Then there were the enlightened absolutist monarchs like Frederick the Great and Catherine of Russia. They really believed in the Enlightenment and making their nations' better with reform. Laws were made more consistent, reforms were enacted, and they tolerated religions. However, Joseph II of Austria shows how many monarchs just manipulated the Enlightenment ideals. He made serfdom worse and even though he had many intellectuals at his court, he mostly just cared about getting more power, usually from Poland.

So, as we can see, the Enlightenment was a very important intellectual group. Religion and Christianity declined but politics got better. People began questioning all that they had known before and doing things in different ways. This was what the Enlightenment was all about, and it eventually led to the French Revolution.

This rather simplistic student response scores a bit better than it reads. While the thesis is overstated and lacks sophistication, it is responsive to the question. The body paragraphs, again, do not indicate a strong understanding of the topic by the student, yet she is able to convey four or five relevant examples in each, as well as apply them to the thesis to some degree. A major error in the paragraph on politics related to Joseph does detract from the response. To portray Joseph as cynically manipulating the Enlightenment is a misinterpretation that costs the student at least a point. Finally, the conclusion adds little to the essay and seems hurriedly tacked on. Despite its obvious flaws, this essay could easily have entered the stronger category with any of the following: a clearer sentence of analysis in each body paragraph, a stronger conclusion, avoidance of a major error. Score: 5.

CHAPTER 10

The French Revolution and Napoleonic Era, 1789–1815

When asked in the 1950s about the importance of the French Revolution, Chinese revolutionary Mao Zedong responded, "It's too early to tell." The revolution that gripped France, the European continent, and ultimately the world stands as the crossroads of your course. It is generally considered the model for all revolutions; it gave us our modern ideologies and our political geography of "left" and "right." Unlike the American Revolution, which today in the United States is considered an accomplished and successful fact, the French public still debates the significance and meaning of this defining event in their nation's existence. This chapter examines the causes and phases of the revolution and also traces its development through the Napoleonic Era. As you study this complex event, you should focus on the following issues: (1) What interaction of factors brought about the French Revolution? (2) What were the accomplishments of the various phases of the revolution? (3) How and why did the revolution become more violent after 1791? (4) To what extent did Napoleon uphold the ideals of the French Revolution?

> **Note:** To users of Palmer, Colton, and Kramer, *A History of the Modern World*, this chapter combines Chapters 9 and 10 in your text.

> **Sidebar:** Historians term the literature of historical interpretation on a topic *historiography*. For the French Revolution, it might take a dedicated scholar a lifetime to familiarize herself with it, especially since it grows every year. Though you need not be familiar with particular "schools" of interpretation for the AP Exam, you may find some of these issues instructive and interesting. Please consult the Additional Resources for suggestions.

CAUSES OF THE FRENCH REVOLUTION

Observers and historians have debated the causes and meaning of the French Revolution since it began. This debate often revolves around which factors keyed the revolution—political, social, intellectual—as well as the overall legacy of the revolution—positive or negative. The revolution grabbed the attention of Europe and the world because France itself was important. After Russia, France was Europe's most populous nation, the center of Enlightenment culture, and, despite the problems of its monarchy, considered basically well-governed and stable. For most, the revolution came as a surprise, though it certainly could have been predicted given the constellation of circumstances facing France in the 1780s.

Social Causes: The Three Estates

France remained separated into **three estates,** each with its own legal status and privileges. The First Estate, the clergy, amounted to less than 1 percent of the population, or about 100,000 religious clergy of different types. Though the position of the church had declined in previous centuries, it remained a social, cultural, and economic force. The church owned about 10 percent of the land in France and collected the **tithe,** a tax that amounted to about 3 to 5 percent of individual income. In an age of increasing secularism, many resented the privileges and high social status of the upper clergy—bishops and cardinals—even if many sympathized with their parish priests, known as *curés.*

Nobles comprised about 2 percent of the population, about 400,000 members, though they often differed widely in income, and owned approximately 25 percent of France's land. Counter to Marxist interpretations, which emphasize the rigidity of the class structure, bourgeois members of the Third Estate could ascend into the Second Estate, often by purchase of a government office. In fact, about 40 percent of nobles in 1789 had earned their status in the previous 150 years. Aristocratic status depended on inherited privilege (right to hunt on common land, separate courts, right to wear distinctive clothing, etc.) and exemptions from certain taxes. Members of the nobility monopolized positions in government and the military. After the death of Louis XIV in 1715, nobles reasserted their power and as part of a "feudal reaction," attempted to support their increasingly extravagant lifestyles by reviving feudal dues and strictly enforcing their collection. Some members of the nobility, particularly the old "nobles of the sword," attempted to limit the further entry of the middle classes into their privileged station with the Segur Law (1781), which restricted military positions to those who could trace their noble lineage back four generations.

The vast majority of French people (about 24 million) belonged to the Third Estate, obviously not a monolithic group. Members of the Third Estate varied from the wealthiest merchant down to the few serfs or landless laborers still existing in France. The bourgeoisie increased in numbers and economic power significantly in the seventeenth and eighteenth centuries with the growth of commerce. In addition to their mercantile and professional interests, the bourgeoisie owned about 25 percent of the land in France. Many resented the privileges of the aristocracy while at the same time envying their status and imitating their fashions and interests. The **petty bourgeoisie** of artisans, shopkeepers, and small business owners felt the pinch of, on one hand, rising prices for goods, while on the other, stagnant wages. These *sans-culottes* ("without breeches," worn by the well-to-do) favored equality and played a major role in the radicalization of the revolution. Peasants formed the largest social class. Most were small landowners who wished to be free from the plethora of service obligations, taxes, tithes, and feudal dues that could eat away over 50 percent of their livelihood. Owning about 40 percent of the land, peasants tended to be conservative in outlook, wishing simply to be free of the feudal system.

France's social inequality is taken to be the most fundamental cause of the revolution. It would be a mistake, however, to portray the revolution as simply a drama of class struggle, with a discontented lower class overthrowing its oppressors. In fact, aristocrats and bourgeoisie often shared similar lifestyles and outlooks. Further, some members of the nobility influenced by the Enlightenment criticized the inequities of the **Old Regime** and led the initial phases of the revolution. Also, during the radical phase of the revolution, nobles and peasants shared distaste for the radical policies of Paris. Even with these caveats, the social inequality of the three estates drove the revolution forward and accounts for the depth of its radicalism.

Political Causes

The conflict between the resurgent nobility and a theoretically absolute monarchy constitutes the fundamental political cause of the revolution. French aristocrats accepted and often admired the monarchy, but wished it to evolve along English lines. To limit Bourbon pretensions to absolutism, nobles asserted the powers of the *parlements*, the 15 regional law courts, to check the king's ability to tax and legislate arbitrarily. During the weak reign of Louis XV (1715–1774), some progress was made in this regard. However, near the end of his reign in 1771, Louis decided to get tough and dissolve the **Parlement of Paris.** As a gesture of goodwill, the young Louis XVI reconvened the body in 1774. This move only emboldened the nobility in their efforts to move France toward a constitutional monarchy.

Many condemned the capricious nature of the monarchy. Hated symbols of arbitrary government were the *lettres de cachet,* which allowed the king to arrest and imprison any individual without judicial procedures. No doubt the stories of an army of political prisoners rotting in the Bastille proved to be exaggerated, but Enlightenment principles of equality and justice spoke against the practice. Additionally, the personalities of **King Louis XVI** (1774–1793) and his Austrian wife, **Marie Antoinette** (d. 1793) acted as a magnet for discontent with the regime. By all accounts, Louis was a pious, well-meaning family man. However, he also had difficulty consummating his marriage, which, when combined with Marie's promiscuous reputation, earned the couple ridicule and scandal. As events unfolded, it became clear that Louis lacked the energy and purpose to see his nation through its crisis. The king's behavior during key moments of the revolution often escalated conflict and fueled radicals' demands for a republic.

Intellectual Causes

The Enlightenment did not directly cause the French Revolution; however, it ensured that unfocused discontent and class anger crystallized into a more fundamental criticism of the Old Regime. Ideas from Voltaire, Rousseau, Montesquieu, and other *philosophés* provided systematic tools for the expression of grievances, though most people gravitated more to the salacious underground press with stories of the scandals of the royal couple. Even if readers for high-minded philosophy were lacking, a century of enlightened thought helped create public concern over political issues, awareness of the larger world, and a strong spirit of criticism. Though hard to trace exactly, all of these influenced the nature and tone of the French Revolution.

Economic and Financial Causes

Economic and financial causes for the revolution were distinct but related. France did not fall into revolution because of economic stagnancy; more accurately, the French state and legally defined social system coped poorly with rapid economic change. Between 1714 and 1789, French commerce expanded tenfold, faster than Britain's, and fed the wealth of the nation. However, this wealth was unequally distributed. Though France stood out as one of the wealthiest nations in Europe, it was as if it had one hand tied behind its back.

Due to its semifeudal nature, the French state never tapped effectively into the nation's wealth. We have already seen how France, unlike Britain, did not develop an extensive credit network. More important, France was plagued by an inefficient and regressive tax system. Tax rates varied widely based on geography, the highest class claimed exemptions, and the task of collecting the taxes was franchised out to the **Farmers General.** This group of wealthy financial families legally skimmed off as much as half of state tax revenue.

Louis XVI realized the dire need for tax reform. The debt of the French monarchy accumulated from numerous wars—most recently the American War for Independence (1778–1783)—threatened to choke the state budget. By 1785, the French treasury was bankrupt, and half of the budget went simply to pay the interest on the debt! Louis attempted several far-reaching efforts at reform but was blocked by restive nobles who insisted on more fundamental changes in the political structure before they would agree to new taxes. If Louis had pursued his plans more consistently or resolutely, he might have staved off disaster. Each time one of his finance ministers (see following list) encountered opposition, he was dismissed by the king.

- **Turgot**—(1774–1776)—Advocate of Physiocracy, Turgot mercilessly attacked privilege. He proposed converting the *corvée* labor service of the peasantry into a cash payment, eliminated numerous government positions and pensions, attacked government monopolies, slashed spending, advocated free trade, and moved to adopt a single direct tax on land to replace the multitude of confusing indirect taxes. Turgot pursued his plan ambitiously and, as a result, sparked wide opposition.

- **Jacques Necker**—(1776–1781)—A talented Swiss Protestant banker, Necker published a complete accounting of the state budget, the *compte rendu,* which revealed the incredible waste therein. Necker's plans for economy proved too much for some, so he was dismissed in 1781. This well-respected symbol of reform was recalled by the king during the early phase of the revolution in 1789.
- **Charles de Calonne**—(1781–1787)—Realizing that the parlements of Paris would never agree to reforms, Calonne handpicked an **Assembly of Notables** in 1787 to approve new taxes. When they refused, Calonne's reputation plummeted and he was forced to leave the country.
- **Archbishop Brienne**—(1787–1788)—Brienne convinced Louis temporarily to play hardball and intimidate or subdue the *parlements,* which would not consent to reform of the financial system. His policies fomented organized opposition to the monarchy and ultimately led to the fateful calling of the Estates General in 1788.

By 1787, the situation in France turned desperate, for two reasons. First, France stood at the verge of bankruptcy, and the efforts at financial reform were stalled by growing opposition across the nation. Second, during the years 1787 to 1789, which coincided with the early stages of the revolution, France suffered from the last great subsistence crisis of the century. Poor crops led to high bread prices, sending urban crowds into the streets. Louis sat upon an explosive situation, and little seemed left to do but call the Estates General.

THE LIBERAL PHASE, 1789–1791

Labeling the first phase of the French Revolution "moderate" or "liberal" makes sense only if we keep in mind that the violence inherent from the outset paled only in comparison to what came later. From the calling of the Estates General in 1788 until the onset of war in the spring of 1792, the revolution accomplished a major reordering of French state and society. Unfortunately, the revolutionaries' inability to address major economic issues and ideological divisions increased violence and strengthened the hand of radicals. For ease of study, the following three sections will provide a timeline with commentary.

Prior to the meeting of the Estates General, Louis XVI asked all French people to write down their grievances in notebooks, called the *cahiers de doléances,* most of which expressed moderate demands for tax equality and the gradual abolition of feudalism. The subsequent national election was France's first since 1614, and both the election and grievances helped politicize the entire country with the expectation of change. As the Estates General convened in 1789, immediate disagreements broke out over two issues: (1) whether to double the number of delegates to the Third Estate, seeing as it represented 98 percent of the nation, and (2) whether the delegates should vote as individuals ("heads") or by orders, with each of the three estates getting one vote. The first issue was easy enough to resolve, but the Third Estate and many liberal nobles, known as the **Committee of Thirty,** refused to budge on the second. The pamphlet *What Is the Third Estate?* by clergyman **Abbé Sieyès** (1748–1836) stoked discontent by arguing that the Third Estate *was* the assembled will of the nation and that the noble caste could simply be abolished.

June 17, 1789—Unable to reach agreement on the issue of voting, the Third Estate declares itself the **National Assembly.**

June 20, 1789—Finding themselves locked out of their meeting place, the National Assembly adjourns to a nearby tennis court and pledges not to disband until they have written a new constitution for France, an event known as the **Tennis Court Oath.**

Unsure what to do next, the king begins raising an army possibly to disperse the National Assembly. In addition, he dismisses Finance Minister Jacques Necker in July, signaling his movement away from reform.

Sidebar: Those who led the attack on the Bastille were not discontented peasants but solid members of the middle class. Contrary to popular belief, the assault on the Bastille was well planned and did not result in the liberation of thousands of prisoners, but five insane inmates and two forgers.

July 14, 1789—Fearing the king's military power, the crowds of Paris march to the Bastille, a symbol of royal despotism, but also an armory. After accidentally firing on the crowd, the defenders are captured and many are executed by beheading. The **fall of the Bastille** saves the National Assembly and demonstrates the power of mob violence. Soon after, revolutionaries form the **National Guard** to protect the revolution, appointing the **Marquis de Lafayette** (1757–1834), called the "hero of two worlds" for this support for the American Revolution, as head.

The king is forced to recognize the National Assembly and orders the other two estates to sit with the new legislative body. However, rumors spread in the countryside regarding events in Paris and of plots to undermine the revolution, leading to attacks on nobles.

June–August 1789—In the **Great Fear,** peasants attack manorial courts and noble manors, clearly directing anger against the feudal system. To reestablish order, the National Assembly on the famous "**night of August 4**" dismantles the entire feudal system. In one blow, feudal privileges, the tithe, noble hunting rights, labor service, and serfdom are all destroyed.

August 26, 1789—The National Assembly completes the **Declaration of Rights of Man and Citizen,** an expression of Enlightenment principles such as legal equality, freedom of religion, judicial rights, and "liberty, property, security, and resistance to oppression."

October 1789—Angry over high bread prices and fearing the king's opposition to the Declaration of Rights of Man (and August 4 decrees), the women of Paris march on Versailles and break into the queen's chamber, killing several guards and forcibly bringing the royal family back to Paris, where they would remain as virtual prisoners of the revolution. The actions of women to protect the revolution are termed the **October Days.**

By the end of 1789, the revolutionaries succeeded in radically restructuring the French state. One of the more important but underestimated actions the assembly took was the abolition of all feudal institutions, *parlements*, estates, provincial law codes, and tariff and tax bodies, to be replaced by **83 equal departments,** subdivided into cantons and communes. As a result, France became a centralized national government based in Paris in a way it never had been under royal absolutism.

November 1789–July 1790—In a fateful move that divided the revolution, the National Assembly attacks the privileged position of the Catholic Church. First, the revolution **confiscates the lands owned by the Catholic Church** and issues paper currency, *assignats,* based on the value of the land, which results in rapid inflation. Later, the church is brought under control of the state—bishops are to be elected and paid by the state, their numbers reduced to 83, and the pope's influence over the clergy eliminated. In addition, after the pope condemns the revolution, the **Civil Constitution of the Clergy** requires all priests to swear an oath of loyalty to the revolution. About half ultimately swear the oath, while the **nonjuring clergy** (those who would not swear allegiance) later become a rallying point for counterrevolution.

June 1791—The National Assembly completes the **Constitution of 1791,** a conservative document that creates a single legislative body with a constitutional monarchy possessing only the power to delay legislation. "Active" citizens are those who own substantial property (about half a million men), while those less well-to-do and women are deemed "passive" citizens. The document indicates that the revolution still rests in the hands of the wealthy bourgeoisie. Nonetheless, the king, under influence from his wife and *émigrés* who had escaped the revolution, decides to flee France. His **"flight to Varennes"** is stopped just short of safety, and he is brought back to the **Tuileries Palace** in Paris.

July 17, 1791—A crowd gathers in a public park to demand the overthrow of the king and the declaration of a republic. The National Guard under Lafayette disperses the crowd with gunfire, killing 50. The **Champs de Mars Massacre** radicalizes public opinion and leads to further distrust of the monarchy.

Political culture in France now openly embraces symbols of the revolution—"liberty trees," "liberty caps," *citoyen* and *citoyenne* as forms of address, and the replacement of religious with revolutionary icons. Citizens join in clubs to discuss issues and agitate for change. The **Jacobins Club** grows in influence and later produces many of the most important leaders of the radical phase of the revolution.

By the summer of 1791, the revolution has achieved much. However, its laissez-faire policies have not solved the rapid inflation or government debt. Complicating matters are the behavior of the king and growing divisions over how far the revolution should go. The debate extends across Europe as writers, citizens, and governments choose sides. English conservative **Edmund Burke** (1729–1797) condemns the radical destruction of France's traditions and predicts in *Reflections on the Revolution in France* (1790) that the revolution will end in military dictatorship. Thomas Paine responds (see Chapter 9) with *The Rights of Man* (1791) in defense of the revolution. *Émigrés* from France heighten tensions by working against the revolution from abroad, a situation that seems ripe for war.

Sidebar: The French Revolution helped create the American political party system. Along with the differences over America's future, events overseas forced early political leaders and common citizens to choose sides. The Federalists under Hamilton opposed the revolution and were pro-British, while the Democratic-Republicans under Jefferson favored the French and were anti-British.

THE RADICAL PHASE, 1792–1794

Why did the revolution become more radical after 1792? Several answers present themselves:

- **Economic problems**—Rapid inflation continued and the laissez-faire policies of the revolution angered workers stung by high prices and policies directed against union activity.
- **The royal family**—The king clearly had reservations regarding key events of the revolution, such as the Civil Constitution of the Clergy. His effort to flee the revolution undermined much of his remaining support.
- **Counterrevolution**—By now, several groups actively opposed the revolution—provinces jealous of the power of Paris, nonjuring clergy, *émigrés*, religious peasants—and worked to thwart it.
- **War**—War tends to radicalize politics. When France declared war in the spring of 1792, it strengthened the hands of those who called for an even more violent break with the past.

August 1791—The Austrian emperor (brother of Marie Antoinette), along with the Prussian king, issue the **Declaration of Pillnitz,** promising to restore order in France if other nations provide support.

This declaration, as well as the actions of the king and *émigrés*, convince the **Girondins** party that the only way to save the revolution is to spread it across Europe by force of arms. To the strains of *La Marseillaise,* the revolutionary anthem, the first citizen-soldiers in modern European history depart for the front.

Sidebar: The Girondins hailed from the provinces and represented the solid middle class. Though they favored war at this point, they were divided over the issue of executing the king. Eventually they were outflanked on the left by the more radical Mountain (or Montaguards) led by Robespierre. *Both* arose out of the radical Jacobins Club.

April 20, 1792—France declares war on Austria. The king supports the declaration because he believes France will *lose,* and thus his power would be restored.

July 25, 1792—With the war going badly for France, Austria and Prussia stand on the verge of invading France. Together the nations issue the **Brunswick Manifesto,** threatening the revolutionaries with violence if any harm comes to the king and queen. The manifesto produces the exact opposite intended effect by inflaming violence against the monarchy.

By now, the working people of Paris, known as *sans-culottes,* and other cities oppose the half-measures of the Girondins and are ripe for persuasion by radical leaders. The vehement journalist **Jean-Paul Marat** (1743–1793) with his *L'Ami du peuple* (The Friend of the People) demands the deaths of traitors and for heads to roll. The skilled politician **Georges Danton** (1759–1794) works to create a revolutionary government in the capital, the **Paris Commune,** which would play a major role in forcing moderates to adopt more aggressive measures.

August 10, 1792—In an event known as the "**Second French Revolution,**" an armed mob storms the Tuileries Palace and forces the arrest of the king. The Constitution of 1791 is abrogated and a more radical **National Convention** is elected to govern France.

September 1792—Fearing that political prisoners will aid the advancing Austrian-Prussian army, revolutionaries break into prisons across France and massacre thousands, many of them innocent bystanders (**September Massacres**).

Sidebar: The guillotine was named for its primary advocate Joseph-Ignace Guillotin. Invented as a humanitarian gesture, it was believed that the device would more quickly dispatch the condemned. Also, all classes were to be executed by the same method, a symbol of equality, even in death. Thus, the guillotine came to symbolize the terror and justice of the revolution. France last used the device publicly in 1977 and abolished the death penalty in 1981.

September 20–21, 1792—After victory in the battle of **Valmy,** which stopped the invading armies, the National Convention abolishes the monarchy and **declares France a republic,** with 1792 as Year I of the new era.

January 21, 1793—The king is placed on trial for treason and after being found guilty by the Convention and at the insistence of the Mountain, is executed by **guillotine.** With the execution, France enters the Reign of Terror.

May–June 1793—Under pressure from the *sans-culottes,* the Paris Commune arrests and executes the leaders of the Girondins. The Mountain (a faction of the Jacobins), under the leadership of the radical **Maximilien Robespierre** (1758–1794), comes to dominate the Convention. The democratic **Constitution of 1793,** which calls for universal male suffrage, is passed, though is never put into effect because of the crisis situation.

Over the next year, France is ruled by the **Committee of Public Safety,** a 12-member executive body elected each month by the

Convention, which steers France through the **Reign of Terror.** It is aided by the **Committee of General Security,** the police arm of the revolution. A major province of France, the **Vendée,** rises in counterrevolution against the centralizing and anti-Catholic policies of Paris. War continues and justifies further radical measures.

Robespierre emerges as the dominant personality. An ambitious lawyer from northern France, Robespierre served in the National Assembly, gaining some notoriety with his calls for universal male suffrage and the abolition (ironically) of capital punishment and slavery in the colonies. Obsessed with creating a new political culture, Robespierre argues that virtue must be combined with terror. Even if they condemn his methods, most historians consider Robespierre sincere in his beliefs; indeed, he earns the nickname "The Incorruptible" in his lifetime. Robespierre is aided by his young protégé, **Louis de St. Just** (1767–1794). As a result of the Mountain's policies, **revolutionary tribunals** arise across France, executing about 50,000 over the course of the terror, and **"representatives on mission"** ensure that the policies of Paris are followed. Though members of the clergy and aristocracy represent the largest segment of victims as a percentage of their numbers, in absolute terms it is the peasants and the working class who make up 70 percent of the victims.

Many view the Reign of Terror as a period of unnecessary and bloodthirsty excess. Others believe that the radicals enacted many creative reforms that helped see France through its time of crisis. As you review the policies in the following list, consider where you stand on this interpretive issue.

- *Levée en masse*—All French citizens are required to contribute to the war effort. Never before in European history has a nation marshaled so many citizens in arms, raising an army of over 1 million men who fought with passion for *"liberté, égalité, fratenité."*
- **Law of General Maximum**—Abandoning free-market policies, the Convention establishes maximum prices for key commodities and punishes severely those who break the law. However, this battle against inflation is difficult to enforce.
- **Abolition of slavery**—Ratifying the massive **slave revolt in Saint-Domingue** (Haiti) led by Toussaint L'Ouverture, the Convention abolishes slavery in all French colonies. Napoleon was later unable to subdue the revolt, and Haiti gained its independence in 1804.
- **Revolutionary calendar**—As part of a campaign of **de-Christianization,** the Convention devises a new calendar with months and days renamed after weather conditions and agricultural products. Months are divided into 30 days of three *décade,* allowing for only 1 day of rest in 10, rather than 7. The new republican era begins with 1792 as Year I.
- **Cult of the Supreme Being**—De-Christianization leads to the elimination of saints' names on streets and Notre Dame becoming a Temple of Reason. Robespierre opposes these excesses and wishes to create a new deistic civic religion, which culminates with a **Festival of the Supreme Being** in June 1794.
- **Standardization of weights and measures**—Following a trend of the moderate phase and reflecting Enlightenment reason, the Convention advances use of the metric system and, as with the calendar, restructures time along the same principles.
- **Military victories**—With these policies, France turns around its fortunes on the battlefield, invading the Netherlands in June 1794 and creating a sister Batavian Republic to replace the old Dutch provinces.

March 1794—The Committee of Public Safety do not tolerate extremism on the left either. Radicals who advocated complete equality and terror, known as Hébertists, or *enragés,* are sent to the guillotine.

May 1794—Danton, the popular leader of the Paris Commune and a growing critic of Robespierre, is executed along with his supporters, known as Indulgents.

By the summer of 1794, France seems to have emerged from it crisis. Counterrevolution has been defeated, French armies are advancing on the battlefield, and the worst of the inflation seems to have passed. Despite these successes, the pace of executions quickens in the summer of 1794. When Robespierre announces in the Convention the **Law of 22 Prairial,** which allows looser standards for proof of treason and a new list of proposed executions, fearful opponents ally against him.

July 27, 1794—The Convention arrests Robespierre and his supporters. After a failed attempt at suicide, Robespierre, along with his associates, is guillotined. This event ends the Reign of Terror.

THERMIDOR AND THE DIRECTORY, 1795–1799

The period following Robespierre's fall is known as the Thermidorian reaction (Thermidor, or "heat," was the revolutionary month of Robespierre's execution). Revolutionary violence takes a breather as the Reign of Terror subsides and extreme policies are reversed. Jacobins Clubs are closed and a "white terror" instigated against former radicals. To provide order while maintaining republicanism, the Convention once again writes up a plan of government, the **Constitution of Year III** (1795). Though all males can vote, their votes are filtered through well-to-do electors who in turn choose representatives for the two-chamber assembly. For day-to-day governing, this assembly appoints five directors as an executive body. The regime known as the **Directory** rules France for four years. During this time, aristocratic fashions return as French politics remain divided over the future course of the revolution. These divisions plague the weak Directory, which faces opposition from both the left and the right.

Spring–Summer 1796—Extremists led by Gracchus Babeuf attempt to establish a socialist government with the **Conspiracy of Equals** but are arrested, tried, and executed.

September 4, 1797—After free elections create a majority for royalists, the Directory, assisted by **Napoleon Bonaparte** (1769–1821), annuls the results and maintains power in the *coup d'état* of **Fructidor.**

With little popular support, the Directory remains dependent on battlefield victories to maintain itself in power. The situation seems ripe for an ambitious and successful military leader to overthrow the government and restore order.

THE RISE OF NAPOLEON

Some have labeled Napoleon Bonaparte the "first modern man." His rise to power owed nothing to traditional ecclesiastical, aristocratic, or political institutions. Napoleon was a self-made man of immense talent and ambition, qualities that account for both his stunning successes and his crushing defeats. Born into a minor Italian noble family on the island of **Corsica,** which the French had annexed in 1768 (a year before his birth), Napoleon set out to prove he was the equal of every Frenchmen he encountered in his military academy and the army. Napoleon combined a quick mind that excelled in practical subjects, such as engineering, history, law, and administration, with supreme confidence in his talents and destiny.

Napoleon earned his first fame with the Italian campaign. Defying traditional rules of warfare, the general outmaneuvered and outfought the larger Habsburg army, and then proceeded to negotiate with the Austrian emperor on his own. The **Treaty of Campo Formio** (1797) established several new Italian republics and spread revolutionary ideas throughout the long-divided peninsula. Napoleon followed up his success with a bold move—the invasion of Egypt in 1798–1799. Though his strategic goals were unclear, Napoleon initially defeated the Ottoman army at the Battle of the Pyramids. However, the British fleet cut off the French army's supply lines with the naval victory at Aboukir. With bigger stakes in mind, Napoleon abandoned his men in Egypt and found his way to France, in time to take part in an overthrow of the moribund Directory. Joined by two other conspirators, Napoleon's *coup d'état* of **Brumaire** succeeded in creating a new government, the **Consulate** (with three Consuls). Chosen as First Consul, Bonaparte quickly outmaneuvered the other two consuls and in 1801 proclaimed himself First Consul for life. At the age of 32, Bonaparte commanded France and set out to institutionalize the principles of the revolution.

> **Sidebar:** Though a military defeat, Napolean's Egyptian campaign proved a cultural success. The general brought along numerous scholars, who not only discovered the Rosetta Stone (to decipher ancient hieroglyphics) but published dozens of volumes, creating the modern field of Egyptology.

NAPOLEON'S DOMESTIC POLICIES, 1799–1814

Soon after being named First Consul, Napoleon consolidated his power, culminating with his proclamation of the French Empire in 1804 and his crowning as emperor. It is generally believed that Napoleon promoted equality and nationalism during his rule; however, he implemented his policies from the top down with little democratic input and disregarded individual rights, such as freedom of the press or privacy, whenever it suited his interests. The following provides an idea of the nature of Napoleon's domestic policies in several areas. As you read, consider the extent to which Bonaparte either fulfilled or twisted the ideals of the revolution.

- **Governance and administration**—Keeping with the tradition of the revolution, Napoleon created a constitution for the Consulate and then the Empire. In reality, Napoleon concentrated power in his own hands. Laws were enacted by the **Legislative Corps** but could not be debated. The body acted in effect as a rubber stamp for the emperor's will. Unlike absolute monarchs, Napoleon succeeded in centralizing administration through the creation of a **professional bureaucracy. Prefects** ran each of the 83 departments but reported directly to Paris. To present himself as a man of the people, Napoleon used **plebiscites,** or referenda, on specific issues, often after the fact, such as whether the people agreed with Napoleon's proclamation of the empire (they did, by a large majority). However, Napoleon would not countenance opposition to his rule. The press was censored, and under the watchful eye of **Joseph Fouché** (1763–1820), a **secret police** infiltrated intellectual circles to identify opposition to the regime. Eventually Napoleon became occupied with the trappings of imperial rule, which was reflected in the nation at large with a new **Empire Style** of architecture and décor.
- **Legal and social policies**—Napoleon announced *"careers open to talent"* for those like himself who came from middling or lowly stations but wished to rise through talent and ambition. Napoleon created a **Legion of Honor** to recognize the contributions of those who served in the revolutionary wars. It is the **Napoleonic Code** that represented the revolution's ideals of merit and equality and perhaps Napoleon's single most significant accomplishment. Guided by the enlightened impulse toward rational systemization, Napoleon created a single legal code for all of France, as well as the many nations he conquered, which stands to this day. However, the Civil Code reinforced patriarchy in the home and limited the rights of women related to divorce, property, and male infidelity.

Heads Up! Future rulers of the nineteenth century, such as Napoleon III, Cavour of Italy, and Bismarck of Germany, imitated the style and methods of Napoleon's rule, something to consider as you study their policies and methods. Though he ruled in an authoritarian manner. Napoleon presented himself as a "man of the people" and manipulated his public image and nationalism to gain support.

- **Economic and financial policies**—To enhance industry, Napoleon modernized the infrastructure of France—building/ repairing roads and bridges, beautifying the nation with monuments, and establishing the **Bank of France.** The bank helped in finally eliminating the budget deficit and modernizing the tax system. Napoleon's efforts at industrial simulation—tariffs, loans, public works—proved less successful, as his failed Continental System (discussed later) against Great Britain hindered French trade.
- **Educational policies**—In an effort to modernize France and promote opportunity, Napoleon established a nationwide system of secondary schools, called the *lycée,* open to all social classes. A national system of **technical universities** was also begun, reflecting the emperor's interest and belief in scientific progress.
- **Religious policies**—Napoleon finally ended the war between the revolution and the Catholic Church with his signing of the **Concordat of 1801** with Pope Pius VII (1800–1823). By the agreement, the pope regained some control of the French clergy, and Catholicism was recognized as the majority religion of France. However, the Church acknowledged the loss of its properties, and the French government retained a veto power over clerical appointments. Of skeptical mindset himself, Napoleon manipulated popular religious belief to his advantage, proclaiming in Egypt, "I am a Muslim," but also extending religious toleration to those in conquered nations.

NAPOLEONIC WARFARE, 1796–1814

Regardless of how Napoleon is viewed politically, he certainly revolutionized the practice of warfare. It will not be necessary for you to grasp the complexities of Napoleonic battles and shifting coalitions, except in general outline, but you should understand the role of warfare in Napoleonic diplomacy and the legacy it left in the nineteenth century.

Though Napoleon met ultimate defeat and made several strategic blunders, he did not lose a battle on land until 1814. What accounts for his stunning success?

- **Movement**—Conventional military wisdom emphasized maneuvers to conserve manpower and guard supply lines and fortresses. Napoleon turned this wisdom on its head and made the enemy army his target by striking quickly.
- **Defying traditional limits**—Napoleon's armies ignored customs regarding when to fight: Sundays, winter, night—all were fair game. The French army learned to live off the countryside, cut off from supplies.
- **Offensive**—With no patience for drawn-out campaigns, Napoleon aimed to defeat his opponents in a decisive battle, by concentrating force at the enemy's weakest spot.
- **Propaganda**—Napoleon always presented himself as a liberator. He liberally issued proclamations to conquered nations establishing a republican government and ending feudalism.
- **Citizen armies**—The French Revolution helped establish, and Napoleon advanced, the notion that warfare was an affair primarily for free and equal citizens, not paid mercenaries—an idea that remains to this day.

In the period 1792–1815, France fought a number of different coalitions of nations. Despite the general agreement among rulers that the French Revolution should be quarantined, great power politics continued. Nations continued to pursue traditional territorial and political objectives, even if in a more complex revolutionary environment. Britain most consistently opposed French designs, expressing its traditional objective of preventing the emergence of a dominant power on the continent.

France emerged victorious against the first two coalitions, which failed to stop the advance of the French Revolution and its expansion into neighboring nations. In 1802, Napoleon negotiated the **Peace of Amiens** with Britain, the final holdout from the Second Coalition. It would not last, as Napoleon's expansionist designs inevitably clashed with British mercantile interests. During the War of the Third Coalition (1805–1807), Napoleon masterfully defeated each of his continental opponents in turn—Austria, Prussia, and Russia—and with the **Treaty of Tilsit** (1807) had established himself as master of the continent. All major continental nations were either annexed to France, allied with it, or a friendly neutral. Napoleon's plans to defeat Britain outright were thwarted at the **Battle of Trafalgar** (1805), as a Franco-Spanish invasion fleet was destroyed by the British navy under Horatio Nelson.

To subdue Britain, Napoleon forced the nations on the continent to embargo British goods, known as the **Continental System.** The plan proved difficult to enforce, harmful to continental trading interests (including France), and highly unpopular. By 1810, Russia had withdrawn from the system, compelling France to launch the fateful Russian campaign. Though many of Napoleon's policies within conquered nations proved popular, his actions also aroused nationalism, especially in Germany. These factors, in addition to a decline in Napoleon's tactical skill, led to his final defeat. The **Grand Army's retreat from Moscow** cost it 90 percent of the men who had set out. Though Napoleon was able to raise another army, he was defeated again in Germany at the **Battle of Nations** in 1814 (the largest battle prior to the twentieth century) and ultimately at **Waterloo** in 1815.

NAPOLEON'S FOREIGN POLICIES, 1799–1814

In foreign policy, Napoleon pursued two basic goals: (1) institutionalize the ideals of the Enlightenment and French Revolution in conquered lands and (2) gain territory and influence for the French nation. At first, Napoleon captured the imagination of intellectuals across Europe, such as Beethoven and Goethe, as well as the support of the common people for his abolition of the Old Regime. However, his exploitation of subject lands and ruthless imposition of "French values" alienated a critical mass of nations bent on stopping him. In the last analysis, Napoleon was done in by the same superabundant ego that had led to his amazing rise to power. As you review Napoleon's policies listed next, again consider his adherence to revolutionary principles.

- **Reforms**—Napoleon proclaimed the liberation of conquered nations and implemented many of the revolution's policies. To win over peasants, he announced the **abolition of feudalism** and the end of the Old Regime, including the end of guilds, old town charters, internal tariffs, and local weights and measures. In their place, Napoleon promoted rational government based on enlightened principles of religious toleration, efficient centralized government, and equality under the Napoleonic Code. Among progressives, such policies gained support, at least until opinion against Napoleon turned.
- **Creation of new diplomatic system**—Napoleon paid little respect to diplomatic traditions. As he conquered, he **created republics** in Italy, the Low Countries, and Switzerland, often appointing his relatives to ruling positions (a practice of nepotism seemingly at odds with his ideas of merit). After defeating Austria again in 1806, Napoleon simply **abolished** the

long-standing **Holy Roman Empire,** replacing it with the 35-state **Confederation of the Rhine.** To gain the support of Polish leaders, Napoleon recreated a smaller version of Poland, the **Duchy of Warsaw.** Once Napoleon felt secure in his domination of the continent, he attempted to wrap himself with dynastic legitimacy. In 1804, he convinced the pope to attend his coronation as emperor, and when he and Josephine were unable to produce an heir, he married a young Habsburg princess, Marie Louise (which made him by marriage the nephew of the deceased Louis XVI).

> **Sidebar:** Napoleon's policies drew the United States, one of the few neutral and large trading nations, into European conflict. First, Napoleon's inability to crush the Haitian slave revolt convinced him to sell the Louisiana Territory to the United States. Then the Continental System helped foment the War of 1812 between the United States and Britain.

- **Continental System**—As noted, Napoleon attempted to cut the continent off from British trade. This proved difficult because Britain's colonial products could not be easily replaced. Transportation difficulties and differing tariffs among the member states prevented continental trade from taking up the British slack. Not only did the Continental System fail in its objective, it aroused opposition toward a French-dominated Europe.
- **Peninsular war**—In 1808, Napoleon coerced the Bourbon king of Spain to abdicate and then replaced him with his brother Jerome. The Spanish resented Napoleon's high-handed tactics and toleration of religions other than Catholicism. With British support, the Spanish bogged the French down in a guerilla war, sapping resources and men.

CODA: WOMEN AND THE REVOLUTION

Women played a central role in the French Revolution. But did this participation yield tangible results? It was during the "moderate" phase that women gained the most—the right to divorce, inherit property, and child custody. Also at this time, **Olympe de Gouges** (1748–1793) published the **Declaration of Rights of Women and the Female Citizen** to counter the similarly titled document by the National Assembly, but she was guillotined in 1793 for her revolutionary activities. During the radical phase, some women formed the **Society for Revolutionary Republican Women,** which agitated for equal rights. The club was banned by the Mountain, because they believed it violated Rousseau's ideals regarding women's domestic role. Finally, the Napoleonic Code, often viewed as a blow for equality, generally excluded women from the principle. The code limited female property rights, restricted divorce, and reinforced the sexual double-standard for adultery. Most women who participated in the revolution probably did so on behalf of their class rather than their gender. Nonetheless, it seemed that once again a movement promising change and equality left women excluded from the revolutionary application of its principles. Taken together, the Enlightenment and the French Revolution, however, established the agenda for the feminist movement over the next century.

ADDITIONAL RESOURCES

Brinton, Crane, *The Anatomy of Revolution* (1965)—Famous account of how revolutions follow similar paths—examines the English, American, French, and Russian examples.

Censer, Jack, and Lynn Hunt, *Liberty, Equality, and Fraternity* (2001)—A wonderful resource for students, this book is concise, focused, and includes a CD-ROM of images, songs, and documents. Also see the related Web site: http://chnm.gmu.edu/revolution/.

Danton (1982)—Interesting film depicting the conflict between Danton and Robespierre. Provides a good sense of the atmosphere of the revolution, though students are to be cautioned about nudity and violence.

Doyle, William, *Origins of the French Revolution* (1980)—Provides an account of the events leading up to the revolution, concentrating on the financial crisis and political conflict.

Empires—Napoleon (2000)—A four-hour PBS documentary that traces the entire life of Napoleon. Offers a helpful companion Web site: http://www.pbs.org/empires/napoleon/.

The French Revolution (2005)—This History Channel special is available on DVD. It is a suitable overview of the topic, but it tends to overstate the role of Robespierre early on and engages in much melodrama.

Furet, Francois, and Mona Ozouf, eds., *A Critical Dictionary of the French Revolution* (1989)—For those who need a comprehensive resource for further study and research.

Lefebvre, Georges, *The Coming of the French Revolution* (1967)—This is considered the classic Marxist explanation of the revolution's origins in terms of class struggle.

Palmer, R. R., *Twelve Who Ruled: The Year of the Terror in the French Revolution* (1989)—Classic study that examines the personalities of the 12 men on the Committee of Public Safety.

Schama, Simon, *Citizens: A Chronicle of the French Revolution* (1990)—Well-written but challenging work focusing on the new civic culture and the use of violence.

Schom, Alan, *Napoleon Bonaparte* (1997)—For those wanting more about one of the fascinating personalities in world history.

PRACTICE QUESTIONS

1. The influential interpretation below by historian Georges Lefebvre emphasizing class conflict is considered flawed today because:
   a. the division between nobility and bourgeoisie is not as clear as once believed.
   b. the clergy actually maintained much of their power during the revolution.
   c. the revolution was an intellectual struggle between the *philosophés* and the king.
   d. the bourgeoisie actually held most of the power in society before 1789.
   e. such Marxist interpretations have been discredited since the fall of communism.

   "The role of the nobility had declined; and the clergy found its authority growing weaker. These groups preserved the highest rank in the legal structure of the country, but in reality economic power, personal abilities, and confidence in the future had passed largely to the bourgeoisie. Such a discrepancy never lasts forever. The Revolution of 1789 restored the harmony between fact and law."

2. All of the following represent significant accomplishments of the so-called Liberal Phase of the French Revolution (1789–1791) EXCEPT:
   a. the writing of a constitution.
   b. fall of the Bastille.
   c. *Declaration of Rights of Man.*
   d. abolition of feudalism.
   e. elimination of government debt.

3. Which of the following resulted from the National Assembly's passage of the Civil Constitution of the Clergy in 1790?
    a. An accommodation was reached between the revolution and the papacy.
    b. The Catholic Church was brought under control of the French state.
    c. Rebellious members of the clergy were given amnesty for antirevolutionary actions.
    d. All religious activities and members of the clergy were outlawed.
    e. Religious toleration was extended to Protestants for the first time in France's history.

4. All of the following were reasons the French Revolution became more radical after 1792 EXCEPT:
    a. the threat of invasion from nations threatened by the revolution.
    b. vicious attacks against the king by army officers led by Napoleon.
    c. uncontrolled inflation that harmed workers in Paris and other cities.
    d. counterrevolutionary efforts by *emigrés*, refractory priests, and provinces.
    e. fear that the king did not support and sought to undermine the revolution.

5. Which of the following best demonstrates the participation of women during the French Revolution?
    a. *The Declaration of Rights of Man*
    b. the Civil Constitution of the Clergy
    c. the Tennis Court Oath
    d. the October Days (march on Versailles)
    e. the Napoleonic Code

6. Which of the following policies during the Reign of Terror (1793–1794) caused the greatest amount of internal opposition?
    a. the universal mobilization of the nation for total war
    b. laws that regulated the price of grain
    c. the abolition of slavery in French colonies
    d. a campaign of de-Christianization
    e. restricting women's involvement in politics

7. What accounts for the success of French armies during the revolutionary wars, 1792–1815?
    a. French generals returned to simple tactics easily mastered by large armies.
    b. The opponents of the revolution were divided and often fought over strategy.
    c. The citizen armies of France believed they were fighting for the cause of mankind.
    d. Soldiers were strongly motivated to avenge the death of Louis XVI.
    e. French armies made use of female soldiers, giving them a numeric advantage.

8. Which of the following is the best description of the Napoleonic Code?
    a. an effort to institutionalize the revolutionary principle of equality
    b. a public relations effort to win over conquered territories
    c. an event that increased anti-French German nationalism
    d. return to hierarchy of the Old Regime in law
    e. a strict system of punishment for those who opposed Napoleon

Erich Lessing/Art Resource, NY

9. The accompanying painting by the Spanish artist Francisco Goya illustrates which of the following events of the French Revolution and Napoleonic Era?
   a. reprisals by counterrevolutionaries against those who attacked the Bastille
   b. popular violence attending the initial meeting of the Estates General in 1789
   c. executions of the leaders of the Mountain by supporters of the king
   d. atrocities by the French army during the Peninsular Campaign
   e. actions by the British government to eliminate pro-French parties

10. Which of the following important events during the French Revolution and Napoleonic Era are in the correct chronological order?
    a. calling of the Estates General, declaration of republic, storming of Bastille
    b. storming of Bastille, Napoleon's Russia campaign, Reign of Terror
    c. execution of Louis XVI, Reign of Terror, Civil Constitution of the Clergy
    d. Constitution of 1791, Continental System, abolition of feudalism
    e. calling of Estates General, Reign of Terror, Napoleonic Code

SAMPLE ESSAY

Which of the following labels most accurately characterizes the rule of Napoleon Bonaparte (1799–1814)—enlightened despot, preserver of the revolution, modern dictator? Choose ONE of the labels and analyze how it applies to Napoleon's domestic and foreign policies.

Napoleon Bonaparte certainly stands as one of the most influential rulers of all-time, both within and outside of France. Napoleon portrayed himself as a man of the people, and in many ways he was. Born in Corsica, Napoleon had to prove himself through his talent and ambition, one of the major ideals of the French Revolution. When he came to power in 1799, Napoleon set out to bring order back to revolutionary principles. Though sometimes his policies seemed dictatorial or imperial, his ultimate goal was always to preserve the revolution for the people, and in this, he succeeded.

Equality was a major principle of the revolution. Napoleon made sure that opportunity was available for all people in France and in other nations. When he liberated a nation, he proclaimed the abolition of feudal privileges and all the features of the Old Regime. What's more, he did this all with his military and intellectual talent. His actions won him the support of great intellectuals like Beethoven (who dedicated the Third Symphony, Eroica, to Napoleon), as well as citizens who wanted to rise in society. In France, Napoleon created schools, universities, and a Legion of Honor, all for the benefit of those who really contributed to society, unlike the old sponging nobles. The culmination of this was his Napoleonic Code. It threw out all the old feudal and backward legal codes and made one rational equal system for all, including for taxes. If Napoleon overlooked some liberty, it was only because France was in chaos and someone needed to provide reform and order. Even then, Napoleon had a constitution and allowed people to vote in plebiscites.

Napoleon promoted another great ideal of the revolution—nationalism. The reason his soldiers fought so strongly was because they believed they were fighting for their own nation and their equality and liberty. Many foreign nations saw how powerful nationalism could be in their own nations. After Napoleon brought his equal law code and promoted equality, many believed that their nations also could benefit from nationalism. One place where this was especially important was Germany. Many German intellectuals found Napoleon a great figure who showed how a nation could be united, which Germany was not. Herder and Fichte wrote of the power of the united state, and how old feudal hierarchies needed to be eliminated. Just because Napoleon inadvertently promoted the kind of nationalism that led the Germans to get rid of the French does not change the point— Napoleon did promote nationalism!

People who say that Napoleon was a dictator or that he twisted the ideals of the revolution don't understand the situation at the time. France had swung back and forth between royalism and Jacobinism and needed a break. Napoleon was that break—someone who took a mass of rhetoric and grand ideas and made them into something tangible. If you don't believe this, just try this thought experiment. Imagine the French Revolution without Napoleon . . . would its ideals have spread to other nations? Would it be something that French people admire? I say no!

Clearly our student is an admirer of Napoleon, which for the most part, he uses to his advantage. The essay offers a strong thesis, strong factual support, and clear organization. On one hand, the student acknowledges the ways in which Napoleon failed to fulfill revolutionary ideas (liberty), but provides an explanation for this anomaly. The body paragraphs focus on the prompt and provide a fairly wide but relevant range of examples. Finally, the conclusion employs a somewhat novel but effective way of making its point—the thought experiment works to convince the reader once more of the student's thesis, and his passion for his point. However, this same passion may blind the student to some obvious counterexamples to his strong thesis. In promoting equality, Napoleon clearly left out half of the population (women) in the Napoleonic Code; the student makes no mention of this fact, or further, how his policies in conquered areas were not always met with approval and/or failed to promote revolutionary ideas. In attempting to uphold Napoleon's reputation, the student seems too willing to overlook the obvious and extensive violations of liberty, Napoleon's imperial trappings, and his ultimate downfall due to his ego and scorn for humanity. All in all, the response is very strong but the caveats noted here prevent it from being a top essay. Score: 8.

CHAPTER 11
Industrial Society and the Struggle for Reform, 1815–1850

The Industrial Revolution in economic production and the French Revolution in politics combined to transform every facet of European life in the nineteenth century. Moving on parallel but often intersecting tracks, these two movements are often termed the **Dual Revolution.** Many historians consider the revolution in production, transportation, and marketing of goods identified with the Industrial Revolution the single most significant event in human history. In this chapter, we address the growth of industry in Great Britain, its spread to the continent, the effort to restore the Old Order at the Congress of Vienna, the development of political ideologies as a response to the Dual Revolution, and the revolutionary echoes rebounding through the first half of the nineteenth century from the French Revolution, culminating with the revolutions of 1848. This period lays the foundation for modern society, politics, and production, and, as such, represents a rich and detailed area for AP Exam questions.

> **Note:** To users of Palmer, Cohen, Kramer, *A History of the Modern World,* this chapter includes material on the Congress of Vienna from Chapter 10 and on the revolutions of 1848 in Chapter 12 to provide thematic focus on the Dual Revolution.

GREAT BRITAIN'S INDUSTRIAL EXPERIENCE

Definitions and Great Britain's Advantages

Before exploring the reasons for Britain's industrial lead and dominance, let's define what is involved in the term "Industrial Revolution." Each of the following three definitions expresses an essential feature of the process:

1. **An assault on the scarcity of the Old Regime, leading to a revolution in access to the means supporting human life.**
2. **The substitution of mineral and mechanical energy (theoretically inexhaustible) for animal and human energy (which tires or wears out).**
3. **Rising output per capita (per person) at declining unit cost; in other words, each worker produces more goods at a cheaper cost, supporting a rising standard of living.**

Of course, Europe had enjoyed commercial growth in the past and at times a rising standard of living. Inevitably, these periods of growth ran up against the limits of natural resources or the primitive nature of technology. Britain's accomplishment seemed unique in applying new production **techniques and technologies** to exploit the full potential of nature's bounty. Owing to the following package of advantages, Great Britain, first among European nations, realized the processes expressed above:

- **Geographic advantages**—Britain's unique **island status** insulated it from continental strife, freeing it from supporting a standing army while at the same time promoting an **overseas empire.** No place in Britain was more than 70 miles from the ocean. Profits from trade could be reinvested in manufacturing enterprises. In addition, Britain possessed **natural resources,** such as coal and iron ore, necessary for industry.
- **Economic advantages**—Promotion of the **Agricultural Revolution** allowed for a larger population and the resulting **mobile labor force** to man the new factories. Also, no nation

could boast a better financial network of **banks** and **credit institutions** able to supply entrepreneurs and nascent businesses with the capital necessary for industrial enterprises.

- **Political advantages**—Even if many nations mirrored Britain's industrial potential, chances are those inclined toward industry exercised little influence over government policy. Not so in Britain. Through Parliament, mercantile and industrial interests enacted laws such as the **enclosure acts** to promote commercial agriculture and laissez-faire policies to protect **private property.** These groups supported development of the British **navy** and the acquisition of **colonies,** the source of **raw materials** and **markets** for British products.
- **Social advantages**—In traditional European societies, the pursuit of profit (to be distinguished from the accumulation of wealth) was frowned upon by elites as characteristic of the "vulgar bourgeoisie." In Britain, aristocrats and the middle class instead shared an **interest in commerce and profit accumulation.** Though Protestant dissenters experienced religious toleration, their exclusion from the paid clergy, the university system, and government positions drove them into commercial and industrial pursuits. Their "**dissenting academies**" emphasized practical and technical training, and, indeed, many of the early inventors derived from this group.

The Classical Economists

Many of the features just outlined correspond with the term "capitalism," but note that industrial development can occur within a command or socialist economic model. The so-called Classical Economists articulated the nature of a laissez-faire capitalist economic order, though not always with our contemporary positive view of its potential. Of the three figures associated with capitalism, one (Adam Smith, "the father of capitalism") was addressed in Chapter 9; now we look at two other important figures:

Sidebar: Malthus's ideas also influenced the evolutionary theories of Darwin related to species struggle for resources. Environmentalists concerned with population growth today still cite Malthus's ideas in support of measures to limit it.

<u>Thomas Malthus (1766–1834)</u>—Malthus believed that food supplies, which increase only incrementally, could never keep up with natural population growth, which occurs exponentially. Even today, Malthus's *Essay on Human Population* (1798) represents the classic statement of concern for population growth and the need for limits. Malthus was pessimistic about the prospects for birth control and technological advance, though he did underestimate the productive capacity unleashed by both the Agricultural and Industrial Revolutions.

<u>David Ricardo (1772–1823)</u>—Taking Malthus's ideas regarding population, Ricardo introduced the concept of the **Iron Law of Wages.** In the short run, Ricardo argued, if the poor gain increased wages, they will simply produce more children, increasing the labor supply and driving down incomes. Thus, in the long run, humanity could not produce a higher standard of living. Once again, Ricardo miscalculated the potential of new technologies and techniques to generate wealth and the human desire for smaller families within this capitalist, consumerist regime.

Textile Innovations

Textiles led the way in the early Industrial Revolution. The many processes of textile production lent themselves to the development of cottage industry, which took hold in Britain in the eighteenth century. Several simple technological breakthroughs, beginning in the 1730s, paved the way for the mechanization of spinning under one roof, or the first factories. It is important to keep in mind that production processes such as mechanization and the putting-out system often complemented each other in industries with multiple steps, such as textile production. Further, mechanization did not penetrate production in other industries for several generations. As you review the textile innovations that follow, focus more on the incremental nature of technological change rather than the names of the inventors.

Flying shuttle, 1733: John Kay halved the time of the weaving process and allowed a single loom operator to work with wider cloth by creating a shuttle that could be operated with one hand. The invention created a demand for more spun yarn, stimulating the next round of inventions.

Spinning jenny, 1768: Improving on the traditional spinning wheel, James Hargreaves developed the spinning jenny, which allowed the operator to spin eight or more threads with the additional spindles.

Water frame, 1771 and "mule," 1780: Richard Arkwright added water power to the principle of the jenny, allowing for the development of factories near rivers, which could harness this natural resource. Samuel Crompton combined the mechanical principles of the jenny and the water frame to create the spinning mule.

Power loom, 1785: Edmund Cartwright's power loom took several generations to perfect, and when it finally became cost-effective in the 1830s, it quickly drove the many handloom weavers out of business.

By the middle of the nineteenth century, then, the entire textile industry had become mechanized. Demand for raw cotton jumped exponentially, which, along with the new **cotton gin** (1793), provided a new lease on life for American slavery. Britain thus established dominance in a key consumer item with its cheap, sturdy cotton cloth.

Steam Power, Coal Mining, Iron, and Railroads

These four industries or technologies were closely connected. Developments in one tended to feed demand in the others, like a feedback loop. The first steam engines in the early eighteenth century pumped water out of coal mines, but did so inefficiently, using more energy than they produced. **James Watt** (1736–1819), in partnership with the entrepreneur Matthew Boulton, perfected the **steam engine** by employing a separate condenser to cool the steam and later added rotary motion, essential to the development of locomotion. Watt's invention provided a much-needed source of power for factories, which could now be located anywhere.

Coal mining expanded significantly in Great Britain in the eighteenth century, driven by the energy needs of the new steam engines and for metallurgical processes. Traditionally, **iron smelting** employed charcoal (fuel produced from burning wood), but this had led to the depletion of English forests. In 1709, Quaker Abraham Darby developed the first blast furnace using **coke** (a by-product of coal) to heat iron ore, which burned cleaner and allowed for the production of greater amounts of iron. Later in the century, Henry Cort pioneered the puddling and rolling processes that enabled factories to produce higher-quality wrought iron and to shape it more easily for industrial purposes. Soon, all processes were consolidated under one roof, vastly increasing British production of iron in the first half of the nineteenth century. Metallurgy, in turn, required vast amounts of coal, stimulating both industries.

Eighteenth-century Britain witnessed a great age of **canal building**. Water transportation proved more reliable and cut the costs of bringing goods to market. Many of the first canals were privately funded, earning huge profits for their investors. With the advent of cheaper iron and the power of the steam engine, **railroads** replaced canals as the most efficient form of transportation. At first, railways consisted of horse-drawn wagons over wooden rails, used to transport coal out of mines to foundries. In 1804, Richard Trevithick designed and built the first steam-powered locomotive. Soon after, engineer George Stephenson created a faster engine, "The Rocket," which could travel at the (for-the-time) amazing speed of 24 mph! Stephenson developed his engine specifically for the first railroad, the Stockton and Darlington, which opened in 1825. Other railroads soon veined across Britain, providing cheaper goods and a new form of reliable passenger transportation. Railroads decreased isolation and allowed for geographic and social mobility, making them one of the most important inventions of the nineteenth century.

The great age of railroad building energized the production of iron, steam engines, and the mining of coal. In addition, **machine tools,** made of more refined and flexible **steel,** enabled engineers to shape, mold, bore, drill, cut, and saw materials with great precision. Together, these industries formed the "spine" of the British economy and fed other industrial processes.

The Factory System and Other Industries

History's first industrialists combined the roles of inventor, entrepreneur, and manager. Early businesses grew out of limited partnerships and fed off borrowed funds from Britain's extensive credit network. These industrialists eventually realized the benefits of standardization and specialization by combining industrial processes in one locale—a factory. The first **factories** appeared in textile spinning in the 1780s in the new industrial towns of the north, such as Manchester and Liverpool. **Josiah Wedgwood** (1730–1795) stands as a fine example of the new entrepreneur who extended the factory principle to new industries. Lacking an academic background in chemistry, Wedgwood nonetheless used trial and error to develop new styles of pottery and porcelain. Wedgwood not only centralized and standardized his industrial processes, he also marketed his products with a keen eye to consumer tastes. His Queens' Ware gained fame throughout Europe for its delicate style and refinement.

Like petroleum later, coal processing led to the development of important by-products. Mauvine, the first synthetic dye, was extracted from coal tar in the middle of the century. **Synthetic bleaches and dyes** replaced laborious traditional processes and opened up new fashion opportunities. Certain colors, such as purple, were associated with aristocratic status; with cheap textiles and dyes, fashion could now be democratized.

By the mid-nineteenth century, Britain had established its industrial preeminence. To celebrate the nation's accomplishments, British leaders organized the first world's fair in 1851 in London called the **Crystal Palace Exhibition.** Symbols of technology and progress took center stage and stood as examples for the continent to imitate.

INDUSTRIALIZATION ON THE CONTINENT

Continental European nations wished to copy Britain's industrial success. Some succeeded; others seemed unable to overcome institutional barriers or a lack of resources. In some ways, the British lead proved beneficial, as that nation's engineers, technicians, and inventors might be enticed by continental powers to share their industrial secrets. Often, however, governments needed to take a more active role in promoting and overseeing industrial development. This government intervention stands in contrast to Britain's laissez-faire approach. Let's see how this worked with several brief examples.

France and Gradual Change

Like Britain, France experienced industrialization, but more gradually and without the disturbing side effects. As a legacy of the revolution, France continued a tradition of small, family-based agriculture without the destabilizing impact of enclosure and the Agricultural Revolution. Also, France's large internal market and skilled labor force allowed it to focus on higher-end products, such as silks and intricately patterned textiles. Without extensive reserves of coal and iron ore, France did not develop Britain's level of heavy industry. As a result, French industrial cities were smaller in number and did not grow as rapidly, avoiding some of the worst effects attending those in Britain. It was not until after 1850 that French finance, railroads, and communications were able to bring about a fuller modernization of attitudes and habits related to production and consumption.

Germany: A Shackled Giant

Remember that there was no such nation as Germany in 1815. "Germany" remained divided among several dozen states, each with its own tariffs, tax systems, and state priorities. Though Germany boasted a strong supply of coal and iron ore, a rich agricultural sector, and a strong craft tradition, its disunity hindered its full economic potential. In the 1830s, Prussian economist **Friedrich List** (1789–1846) argued for the development of a *national* economic system, beginning with a customs union that would create a free trade zone among the member German states. This Prussian-led *Zollverein* not only promoted economic integration but laid the basis for Germany's later political unity. In addition, List recognized that Britain's method would not work in Germany, so he suggested government building of railroads, subsidies for key industries, and protective tariffs. Germany's economic "take-off" would await its political unity in 1871, but it was already establishing strength in key industrial sectors such as iron, coal mining, and chemicals.

> **Sidebar:** List's economic nationalism represents an alternative model of industrialization to Britain's laissez-faire approach. After World War II, many East Asian nations (Japan, Taiwan, South Korea) borrowed List's ideas to promote rapid economic development.

Other Lands

While other regions of Europe, such as Belgium and northern Italy, as well as the United States, had built an industrial base by midcentury, many nations languished in the inertia of resource poverty, backward agriculture based on serfdom, and elitist attitudes that discouraged the profit motive. For example, Spain lacked many resources necessary for industry and faced geographic obstacles with a barren plain dominating the center of its nation. However, the most important barriers proved to be the continuing influence of aristocratic privilege and religious otherworldliness. After 1848, Russia remained the only major nation continuing to practice serfdom, an enormous waste of labor and land that effectively hindered its economic development despite its strong resource base. In some cases, underdeveloped nations adopted outward manifestations of industry, such as a "show" railroad or a model factory, but the essential economic attitudes and the legal and educational infrastructure needed to secure private property or supply technical skills were sadly lacking.

SOCIAL EFFECTS OF AND RESPONSES TO INDUSTRIALIZATION

The Industrial Revolution profoundly influenced first British and later European society. Problems such as overcrowding, pollution, worker discontent, and inequality compelled governments, reformers, and radicals to devise a range of contending responses to such issues.

Population Increase

Industrialization supported a marked increase in population. From 1750 to 1850, the population of the British Isles rose 200 percent, from 10 to 30 million. What's more, most of this humanity found itself crowded into the new industrial cities of Lancashire and the Midlands, north of London. **Manchester** came to symbolize the problems of the new industrial city, growing from 20,000 people in 1750 to almost half a million by 1850, making it the second largest city in Britain. Many migrants to the cities were driven by famine in Ireland or landlessness in the countryside. Though many found work in the new cotton mills, urban problems followed closely behind.

Working and Living Conditions

It is easy to dramatize the conditions in the first factories or urban areas, and even though basis exists for these facts, you should incline toward analysis and specifics for any essay prompts on the Industrial Revolution. Initial factory conditions were deplorable. Workers were expected to labor up to 14 hours per day with inadequate light and ventilation. Strict rules punished tardiness and fraternization among workers. Owners often preferred **children as laborers,** for their small hands able to reach into machinery, as well as women, considered more docile and willing to work for lower wages than men. In coal mines and factories, laborers were exposed to toxic substances and particulates, causing lung and other **diseases.** Finally, because machines often determined the pace of labor, workers found themselves living by a regimented schedule and subject to fatigue that could be deadly if they should fall into the moving parts of machines.

Living conditions mirrored those in the workplace. Because of their rapid growth, cities found that their infrastructure of streets, housing, and sewage disposal could not keep up with the onslaught of new residents. Cramped housing and diseases, such as cholera, dysentery, and typhoid, reduced life expectancies by half compared with rural areas. Air and water pollution rendered even breathing and drinking dangerous activities. In addition to sanitary and environmental problems, there was crime, prostitution, alcoholism, and family breakdown.

As a consequence of the mechanization of labor, the family was transformed from a unit of production to a unit of consumption, that is, gathering only for activities related to eating and leisure. It is easy to exaggerate how quickly and commonly this occurred; nonetheless, mechanization of labor set the precedent of moving work from the home, where workers exercised control over the pace and conditions, to a process managed by the owners of capital seeking profit by squeezing out costs through lower wages and sacrificing on basic safety conditions. Once the British Parliament passed legislation protecting women and children in the 1830s and 1840s, family life was further altered by separating male "productive" work outside the home from female domestic labor completed in the home.

New Industrial Classes

Industrialization created new classes. At the top, the **industrial middle class** gained wealth and status from the profits of industry. Though they were still few in number, this growing bourgeoisie set a social tone of frugality, respectability, and hard work, exemplifying the ideal of social mobility through self-help. The growth of the unskilled working class, or **proletariat,** paralleled that of the industrial middle class. Owning no capital or personal property of which to speak, unskilled workers were forced to sell their labor at a disadvantage, as the supply of workers continued to grow and employers freely dismissed those deemed unproductive or troublesome. Industrial workers remained a relatively small segment of the population in Europe until after the middle of the nineteenth century, and therefore could exercise little influence on politics through union activity or political pressure.

Responses: Reform, Rebellion, and Rejection

It is helpful to think of responses to these problems as existing on a continuum from open acceptance of the new industrial system on one side to complete rejection on the other. We explore this topic further in the section that follows on "isms," but for now focus on immediate and practical responses to those issues. You may find the following diagram helpful in imagining how these varying responses relate to one another.

Sidebar: As a result of these class distinctions, urban areas became more segregated based on income and occupation. Revolutionary outbreaks by the working class convinced middle-class reformers to support the development of the first modern city police forces, which became professionalized in the mid-nineteenth century, and played a role in both combating crime and maintaining order. In addition, states built modern prisons with the aim of long-term incarceration of criminals and with the goal of rehabilitation.

rejection   acceptance

Luddism   revolutionary socialism   utopian socialism   Chartism/unions   reform legislation   laissez faire

We have already examined the laissez faire approach of the classical economists. Many laypeople recognized the obvious problems with industrialization but believed that these "evil side effects" naturally attended all economic systems. To tamper with the workings of the free market, in their minds, would only create more suffering in the long run. Eventually the problems became too pronounced for any but the most hardened capitalist to ignore. Reformers feared that if nothing were done to ameliorate the horrid working and living conditions, moral breakdown or, worse, revolution would occur. In 1832, Parliament appointed the **Sadler Commission** to investigate child labor in mines and factories. The appalling testimony of workers convinced Parliament to pass the **Factory Act of 1833,** which provided for inspection of factories, a limitation on hours, and at least two hours of education per day for children. Sanitary reformer **Edwin Chadwick's** (1800–1890) publication of *The Sanitary Condition of the Laboring Population* (1842) highlighted the need for improved sewage and sanitary conditions in the crowded and polluted cities. Soon after, Parliament again responded with the **Public Health Act of 1848,** providing for the development of sanitary systems and public health boards to inspect conditions. Further acts are discussed in the section "Reform in Great Britain."

Sidebar: Cholera outbreaks in Manchester and other cities laid the foundations for the modern trend of gathering population statistics. To track the disease, the British government located each incidence and gathered further data on the characteristics of the individual and neighborhood. States found this data, along with that gathered from censuses, useful in identifying and addressing problems from a rational and technical perspective.

Despite the first tentative steps toward reform, workers voiced a more fundamental need for change, one that involved greater control over the workplace and political power. It became clear that, as individuals, workers could do little to blunt the capitalist system. To exert collective power, laborers formed unions. Skilled engineers formed a trade union, later called the Amalgamated Society of Engineers, in 1851 to bargain for better working conditions and higher wages, much like medieval guilds. The more radical **Grand National Consolidated Trade Union,** encouraged by the industrialist Robert Owen (see following discussion), attempted to organize all industrial workers for strikes and labor agitation. The British government looked with hostility on efforts at worker organization, passing the **Combination Acts** in the early nineteenth century to prevent much union activity. Many workers favored more direct political activity. The **Chartists,** named after the founding document of their principles, employed petitions, mass meetings, and agitation to achieve **universal male suffrage** and the payment of salaries to members of Parliament. Chartism became associated with violent disturbances and petered out as a movement after 1848, even though many of its goals were later reached.

Since socialism developed into a coherent ideology, it is covered more extensively in the section on "isms." **Luddism** represented an outright rejection of the principle of mechanization of labor. Named for a mythical figure, Ned Ludd, the supporters of the movement met in secret throughout the early 1810s to plan the destruction of knitting frames and spinning devices they perceived as taking their skilled jobs. Many viewed the perpetuation of an artisan culture of sturdy skilled craftsmen as trumping any supposed benefits from industrial specialization and efficiency. The British government crushed the movement by exiling or executing those involved. Today, those who oppose technological change are often dubbed by their detractors as Luddites.

THE CONGRESS OF VIENNA AND CONCERT OF EUROPE

The Vienna Settlement, 1814–1815

After the French Revolution and Napoleonic Wars, the great powers of Europe met in Vienna to rebuild a stable diplomatic order. Twenty-five years of violent upheaval and warfare had convinced conservatives of the need to reestablish "legitimate" governments and create mechanisms to subdue revolutionary movements. Negotiations were interrupted by the escape of Napoleon from Elba and his 100 Days campaign culminating with his defeat at Waterloo. In general, the victorious powers treated France leniently—though somewhat less so after the 100 Days—wanting to avoid saddling the restored Bourbon monarchy with a harsh treaty. The Congress of Vienna, then, was guided by the following three principles:

- **Legitimacy**—"Rightful" monarchs were restored to those nations that experienced revolutions. This meant the Bourbons back in France (Louis XVIII, brother of the executed king), Spain, and Naples. Though some monarchs conceded constitutions in deference to public opinion, power remained in the hands of conservative interests—**"throne, altar, and estate"**—that is, monarchy, church, and aristocracy.
- **Compensation**—Nations that lost territory in one area received compensation in another. For example, Austria surrendered possession of the Austrian Netherlands (Belgium) but gained control of several states in northern Italy.

- **Balance of power**—Key to the Congress's deliberations, balance-of-power considerations led to the creation of a series of buffer states to quarantine France should revolution break out there again. The new Kingdom of the Netherlands combined the former Dutch republic and Austrian Netherlands, Prussia gained extensive territory on the Rhine, and Piedmont-Sardinia in Italy was strengthened on France's southern border.

The following chart provides an overview of the key players and their nations' goals.

Nation	Leader	Goals
Austria	**Klemens von Metternich** (1773–1859)—The dominant personality at the Congress.	As the most multiethnic of the great powers, Austria wished to repress nationalism and build a system of collective security to maintain the status quo. Owing to Metternich's association with the Congress of Vienna, the period 1815–1848 is sometimes termed the "Age of Metternich."
France	**Talleyrand** (1754–1838)—Wily "survivor" who represented revolutionary France, Napoleon, and then the restored Bourbons.	France wished to be readmitted into the "family of the great powers" by demonstrating its return to legitimacy. Talleyrand won over Metternich by exposing the plan of Prussia and Russia to take all of Saxony and Poland (the **Polish-Saxon Question**) without consulting the other powers.
Great Britain	**Castlereagh** (1769–1822)—Poor speaker but represented Britain with integrity.	Britain saw the Congress primarily as reestablishing the balance of power on the continent, its long-time goal. Britain did not wish to be involved in a kind of international police force to crush revolutions.
Prussia	**Prince von Hardenberg** (1750–1822)—Older leader often outmaneuvered by Metternich.	Least influential at the Congress, Prussia generally followed the lead of Austria, the other German power. Prussia also desired to incorporate its long-time enemy, Saxony, into its territory.
Russia	**Alexander I** (r. 1801–1825)—Began as a reformer, but grew conservative and more religious in response to revolution.	The largest of the powers and growing in influence, Russia under the once-Liberal Alexander wanted to control Poland and also gain support for a **Holy Alliance** of powers committed to stopping "godless" revolution.

The resolutions of the Congress of Vienna reflect the traditional diplomacy of elites of the great powers redrawing the map of Europe to meet their goals. After almost nine months of deliberations and another war against Napoleon, the great powers finally completed their work in June 1815, with the following decisions:

Territorial adjustments: Some have been addressed in the previous discussion. The Polish-Saxon question almost led to war among the powers, but as a compromise, the Prussians gained 40 percent of Saxony and the Russian tsar was named King of Poland, though in reality ruled "**Congress Poland**" directly. To ensure stability in central Europe, a 39-state **German Confederation** was created with Austria as the dominant power. France relinquished any conquests from the revolutionary wars.

Alliances: To ensure peace and stability, the great powers formed the **Quadruple Alliance,** which was termed the **Quintuple Alliance** with the inclusion of France after 1818. In addition, the three conservative central and eastern European powers—Austria, Prussia, and Russia—created the **Holy Alliance,** envisioned by Alexander I as a brake on revolutionary movements.

Indemnities: After Napoleon's return and the 100 Days, the victorious powers placed some moderate sanctions on France. The nation was required to return the art Napoleon had stolen from conquered lands and had to support an occupation army, which was removed in 1818.

Collective Security: To ensure peace and stability, the great powers agreed to meet periodically to discuss issues of mutual concern, especially related to war and revolution. This **Concert of Europe** provided a degree of informal security in the first half of the nineteenth century; however, Britain disagreed with Metternich's vision of collective security as committing the members to the suppression of revolutionary movements.

The Congress System

Several times after the meeting in Vienna, the great powers invoked the Concert of Europe to address revolutionary situations. The details of these meetings follow:

Congress of Aix-La-Chapelle, 1818: Based on France's "good behavior," the army of occupation was removed and France was admitted to the Concert of Europe and Quintuple Alliance.

Congress of Troppau, 1820: Revolutionaries in Spain and Naples forced the kings of those nations to admit to constitutional limits on royal power. Metternich perceived the act as the beginning of revolutionary violence and urged the other powers to sign a protocol committed to united action. When France and Britain demurred, Austria (with Prussian and Russian backing) subdued the revolt in Italy.

Congress of Verona, 1822: Two situations preoccupied the great powers—the continuing instability in Spain and **Latin American revolts** against Spanish control. On the first question, the great powers, excluding Britain, authorized a French army to subdue the threats to the Spanish monarchy and punish the revolutionaries, which was successfully done. Britain strongly objected to any armed intervention in Latin America, as it wished to exploit the breakup of the Spanish empire to enhance its own trade. More important, the United States issued the Monroe Doctrine in 1823 warning against any further European colonial ventures in an American "sphere of influence."

No congresses met after Verona, demonstrating the differing visions of the Concert of Europe among the "Big Five." Even if the great powers failed to create an institutional structure of collective security, a spirit of cooperation lingered until 1848. In assessing the Vienna settlement, some historians point out how its failure to recognize the forces of Liberalism and nationalism led to over 30 years of continuous revolution. On the other hand, the great powers did provide a framework that avoided a general war among all of the great powers for almost a century (until 1914). Regardless of interpretations, clearly the Congress of Vienna fundamentally shaped the political and diplomatic climate for the first half of the nineteenth century.

> **Heads Up!** The Congress of Vienna represents one of the most important diplomatic settlements in the AP curriculum. Consider both how it shaped the politics and diplomacy of the nineteenth century and how its tasks and security settlement compare with the Versailles settlement after World War I, a topic that has appeared on the AP Exam several times.

RESTORATION AND REACTION

The following is a quick review of domestic developments related to the post-1815 theme of how governments attempted to restore traditional arrangement and ensure stability. For purposes of the AP Exam, focus on the theme and general outline for each nation, not the details. France and those nations that experienced revolutions are covered in the section "Revolutions and Reform."

Great Britain

Conservative Tories controlled British politics after 1815 and were intent on clearing away latent radicalism in the kingdom, often with censorship. Parliament remained unrepresentative, as none of the new industrial towns in the north elected members. Landed interests passed the **Corn Laws,** protecting British grain from competition but at the same time harming consumers with higher prices. Democratic movements agitated for reform; one such peaceful gathering in 1819 in Manchester was met with armed forces, killing 11 and wounding hundreds. Opponents of the government derisively dubbed this event the **Peterloo Massacre.** A gradual loosening of repression in the 1820s paved the way for Liberal reforms in the 1830s.

Germany

The personality of Metternich dominated politics through the German Confederation. Idealistic young student nationalists formed the *Burschenshaft* to celebrate German culture and discuss political issues. Viewing the movement as a threat, Metternich convinced the Confederation to issue the **Carlsbad Decrees** (1819), forcing the dissolution of the *Burschenshaft*, censoring the press, and placing government officials to supervise universities.

Russia

With its small middle class and autocratic tradition, Liberalism proved a thin reed in Russia. Nonetheless, army officers influenced by revolutionary ideology had formed the Decembrist Society to push for a constitutional government. When Alexander I died in 1825, the **Decembrist Revolt** agitated for the accession of Constantine, considered a Liberal, rather than his reactionary brother, Nicholas. **Nicholas I** (1825–1855) crushed the revolt and ruled Russia in succeeding decades with the motto "Autocracy, Orthodoxy, and Nationality," as he relied on a new secret police, religious uniformity, and the imposition of Russian language and culture.

THE "ISMS"

The period 1815–1850 can be termed the Age of Ideologies. In response to the issues raised by the Dual Revolution, many Europeans adhered to a set of ideas that provided both a systematic view of human affairs as well as a blueprint for changing the world. Such ideologies or "isms" influenced how people viewed events and motivated them to action.

Conservatism

Conservatism should not be equated with complete rejection of change (such adherents are known as reactionaries). Defying the optimistic views of human rationality associated with the Enlightenment and French Revolution, Conservatives believed that human nature was driven primarily by the passions. **Edmund Burke** (1729–1797) became a leading advocate for **change through adaptation,** not violent revolution, with his statements against events in France (see Chapter 10). Humans are capable of reason, he argued, but often employ it as an excuse for self-interested actions. Customs and traditions, which have evolved over time to meet the needs of particular human societies, act as checks on the passions and should not be discarded lightly. Along with Burke, French philosopher **Joseph de Maistre** (1753–1821) demonstrated how once the revolution in France broke from its traditions of church, monarchy, and nobility it descended into violent chaos. Burke and de Maistre were not opposed to constitutions per se—as Burke supported the American Revolution—only those based on abstract and supposedly universal principles not in keeping with a society's experiences. Conservative philosophy supported the restoration governments of the post-1815 order.

Liberalism

Heads Up! Today when we use the term "conservative," we generally mean a classical Liberal, who favors a more laissez-faire economic philosophy. The term "liberal" in contemporary politics usually indicates someone who supports income redistribution to aid the poor, but the first welfare programs in European history were initiated by conservatives. Why the switch in meaning of the terms? Liberal movements found their laissez-faire approach challenged by the problems of industrialization, and around the turn of the twentieth century came to support government intervention to assist the working class.

Classical Liberalism of the nineteenth century is distinguished from the way the term "liberal" is used today. Based on Enlightenment and revolutionary ideals of reason, progress, and individual rights, Liberalism acted as a powerful philosophy of change throughout the nineteenth century. Economically, Liberals embraced the **laissez-faire** principles of Adam Smith's capitalism and strong protection of private property. Politically, Liberals favored the social contract theory of limited government advocated by John Locke and the French revolutionaries as the surest guarantee of **religious toleration** and **individual rights.** Many if not most Liberals came from the middle class and supported a more representative government and an expansion in suffrage, though only for property holders. British philosopher **Jeremy Bentham** (1748–1832) articulated the related approach of **utilitarianism,** wherein "good" was defined as providing pleasure and "evil" as causing pain. Holding that the purpose of government was to promote the "**greatest good for the greatest number,**" Bentham argued for separation of church and state, women's rights, and the end of slavery. Beginning in the utilitarian tradition, **John Stuart Mill** (1806–1873) later provided in his *On Liberty* (1859) one of the most eloquent defenses of freedom of expression and the dangers of the "tyranny of the majority." Mill also collaborated with his wife, Harriet Taylor, and defended the cause of female suffrage in Parliament.

Socialism, Republicanism, and Feminism

Self-proclaimed radicals and republicans embraced the "principles of '93" from the French Revolution. Many were drawn from intellectual circles or the working class and favored equality and **universal male suffrage** while opposing the influence of organized religion, as well as monarchy and aristocracy. Republicanism shaded off into socialism. Socialists believed the capitalist system was unequal and unjust, and wished to replace it with **social and economic planning.** One of the first socialists, ironically, was a textile entrepreneur, **Robert Owen** (1771–1858). Owen built a model factory in **New Lanark,** Scotland, to better provide for his workers' needs, with high wages, improved conditions, and provision for schools and other amenities. The industrialist also attempted to export his **utopian socialism** to the United States, constructing an experimental colony in New Harmony, Indiana, which, like many such communes in the United States, failed soon after its founding. Most other early socialists were French, reflecting the legacy of the revolution. **Henri de Saint-Simon** (1760–1825) and **Charles Fourier** (1772–1837) embraced an ethos of **cooperation** and shared property to realize human needs beyond merely the economic. Additionally, the socialist Louis Blanc's idea of "national workshops" for the working class played a key role in the revolution in 1848 in France. Despite the creativity, utopian socialism led to few practical successes and gave way after 1850 to the more militant Marxian version of socialism.

Many advocates of women's rights, such as Mary Wollstonecraft and John Stuart Mill, drew from the Enlightenment tradition of individual rights and social equality. Socialists combined their criticism of the class system with that of gender roles. French female socialist **Flora Tristan** (1803–1844) argued that the oppression of women, whether as factory workers or in domestic roles, sprung from the unequal ownership of property. Numerous famous female writers of the period, such as Jane Austen, George Sand, and Germaine de Staël, once again demonstrated that women could exercise independent creative voices. By 1850, many feminists had established a clear agenda for the movement, obtaining greater access to education along with legal, property, and political rights.

Nationalism

Nationalism proved the most combustible ideology of the nineteenth century, and it is essential to your understanding of political and diplomatic events after 1800. Spread by the example of the French Revolution, nationalism initially consisted in a cultural revival and celebration of traditions. Long-divided Germany in particular experienced a wave of cultural nationalism fed by the Napoleonic Wars. **Johann Gottfried Herder** (1744–1803) replaced the political-judicial conception of state with an organic folk-nation best represented by the term *Volksgeist,* or "spirit of the people." Germans celebrated their music and folklore, as with Beethoven's symphonies or the Grimm Brothers' fairy tales. Such cultural nationalism eventually took on political overtones. The German philosopher **Hegel** (1770–1831) glorified the national state as the march of destiny through history. History itself consisted of a clash of opposing ideas, called the dialectic, which pointed the way to a new synthesis—the idea of German national unity.

Given the atmosphere of repression and reaction during the post-1815 period, many nationalists formed secret societies to promote their agendas of unity. The Italian **Giuseppe Mazzini** (1805–1872) first joined the secretive **Carbonari,** who aimed to expel the Habsburgs from the peninsula, before forming **Young Italy** in 1831. Mazzini worked to foment nationalist uprisings in his native land, while in his writings argued that the overthrow of the Concert of Europe would lead to the founding of free, independent states based on linguistic and ethnic identity. States constituted along national lines would eliminate the need for wars and create true brotherhood and peace. Eastern Europe also experienced a revival of national traditions. Intellectuals representing the diverse group of Slavic speakers—Poles, Serbs, Croats, Czechs, Slovaks—looked to common linguistic and cultural traditions and advocated **pan-Slavism,** or the unity of all Slavs. Pan-Slavism inspired uprisings in the 1815–1850 period, but given the power of the Habsburg and Ottoman Empires over the Slavs, the subsequent failures of these revolutions demonstrated the need for the patronage of an outside power—namely Russia, the "protector of the Slavs."

Romanticism

Romanticism was a literary, musical, and artistic movement dominating European culture in the first half of the nineteenth century. Romantics reacted to the Enlightenment's emphasis on reason and science, instead stressing the following:

- **Emotions**—Taking their cue from Rousseau, Romantics emphasized feeling and passion as the wellspring of knowledge and creativity.
- **Intuition**—Science alone is not enough to understand the world; imagination and the "mind's eye" can also reveal its truths.
- **Nature**—Whereas the *philosophés* studied naturally analytically, the Romantics drew inspiration and awe from its mysteries and power.

> **Heads Up!** To view some of the art mentioned here, try www.artchive.com/, and for the musical selections, try www.classical.net/. You can find a clearinghouse for literature, beginning with the Romantics, at andromeda.rutgers.edu/, ~jlynch/Lit/romantic.html.

- **Nationalism**—Romanticism found a natural connection with nationalism; both emphasized change and the connection to the past.
- **Religion**—Romanticism coincided with a religious revival, particularly in Catholicism. Spirit, mysticism, and emotions were central to both.
- **The unique individual**—Romantics celebrated the individual of genius and talent, like a Beethoven or a Napoleon, rather than what was universal in all humans.

With these themes in mind, review the topics and individuals discussed next. Romanticism represents one of the most common topics for an AP essay prompt on art or cultural history.

Literature and History

Lord Byron (1788–1824)—As famous for his scandalous lifestyle as for his narrative poems, Lord Byron died from fever on his way to fight for Greek independence, a cause he supported in his writings.

Thomas Carlyle (1795–1881)—Carlyle pioneered history as the story of great men, as with his famous study of the French Revolution.

François-René de Chateaubriand (1768–1848)—In *The Genius of Christianity,* Chateaubriand glorified the mystical pull of religious faith and its connection with the beauties of nature.

Johann Wolfgang von Goethe (1749–1832)—Goethe's *Sorrows of Young Werther* recounted the tale of a passionate young man who commits suicide over an unrequited love. Along with *Faust,* in which the title character "sells his soul to the devil," Goethe's works proved enormously influential in combining a neoclassical style with the Romantic themes of intuition and emotion.

Edgar Allan Poe (1809–1849)—With his short stories, Poe demonstrates the Romantic interest in the occult and macabre.

Mary Shelley (1797–1851)—Daughter of Mary Wollstonecraft, Shelly gained fame with *Frankenstein,* a literary warning about the hubris of modern man and technology gone awry.

Sir Walter Scott (1771–1832)—Reflecting the Romantic interest in medieval history, Scott's *Ivanhoe* chronicles the conflicts between Norman and Saxon knights in England.

Percy Bysshe Shelley (1792–1822)—Shelley gained fame both from his poetry, as with his tale of rebellion against social conventions in *Prometheus Unbound,* and his lifestyle of free love and vegetarianism. He was the husband of Mary Shelley.

William Wordsworth (1770–1850)—Wordsworth's poetry glorified nature and suggested that "one impulse from a vernal wood" would teach humans more "than all the sages can."

Architecture and Painting

Eugene Delacroix (1798–1863)—Delacroix is most famous for his large canvases, bold use of color, and exotic themes. His tribute to the French revolutionary tradition, *Liberty Leading the People,* stands as his most famous work.

Caspar David Friedrich (1774–1840)—Friedrich's paintings gained notoriety for their portrayals of solitary figures confronting the immensity of nature, as with *Wanderer Above the Sea of Fog.*

Théodore Géricault (1791–1824)—His immense painting, *The Raft of Medusa,* demonstrated the Romantic fascination with nature and also the incompetence of the government in addressing a shipwreck. Gericault's works on the insane illustrate the Romantic interest in the exotic and unique.

Houses of Parliament (1830s)—The most famous architectural example of the neo-Gothic revival in Britain.

J. M. W. Turner (1775–1851)—Turner used vivid colors and atmospheric effects to depict the untamed power of nature in his *Rain, Steam, and Speed* and *Slaveship.*

Music

Ludwig von Beethoven (1770–1827)—Beethoven pushed the classical style to its limits with his sophisticated orchestral arrangements. Despite growing deafness, Beethoven helped establish the Romantic movement in music with his nine symphonies.

Hector Berlioz (1803–1869)—Berlioz developed program music in which the action of the drama parallels the motifs of the music. His famous *Symphonie Fantastique* portrays a drug-induced imagination of a witches' gathering.

Though Romantics occupied themselves primary with cultural expression, many combined their aesthetic vision with political activism. Romantics urged freer lifestyles and political systems, which explains the crossover from Romanticism to nationalism, as well as Liberalism. In fact, many historians term the first half of the nineteenth century, the Age of Romantic Nationalism. As we see in the next section, Romanticism fueled the revolutionary sentiments sweeping across Europe in the period 1815–1850.

REVOLUTIONS AND REFORM

The Restoration political settlement, designed to stop revolution, inadvertently fed the grievances of nationalism and Liberalism in the period 1815–1848. This Age of Revolutions gained fuel from industrial problems and the legacy of unfulfilled promises from the French Revolution. Among the great powers, Great Britain avoided revolutionary outbursts through the enactment of tentative Liberal reforms in this period. Revolutionary turmoil culminated with the revolutions of 1848, one of the more overlooked events in European history.

The Revolutions of 1830–1831

We have already seen how the great powers used the Concert of Europe from 1815 to 1830 to subdue revolutionary movements in Sicily and Spain. However, these successes hid the underlying force of Liberal and national movements. In 1830, the fever of revolution flared again, as usual beginning with France.

The second Bourbon king of the restoration, **Charles X** (1824–1830), reestablished the power of the Catholic clergy and favored the interests of former aristocrats. When elections repudiated the king's policies, he issued the Four Ordinances in July 1830, which curtailed voting rights and censored the press. Militant republications and middle-class moderates joined in overthrowing the king, who quickly abdicated. As a compromise, the throne went to the Duke of Orleans who, though a relative of the Bourbons, had republican credentials. The new King **Louis Philippe** (1830–1848), known as the "bourgeois king," promised to abide by the Constitution of 1814.

Events in France inspired revolts in Belgium and Poland in 1830–1831. The Belgians never fully accepted their absorption into a Dutch kingdom and, following the French example, declared their independence. Because the great powers agreed to maintain **Belgian neutrality,** the new nation was permitted to establish a new Belgian kingdom. However, this was not the case with Poland, which also revolted against Russian authority in 1831. With no outside support, the Polish revolt was brutally crushed by Nicholas I, "Congress" Poland was eliminated, and the territory was directly incorporated into Russia.

When the Christian Greeks revolted against their Islamic Turkish rulers in 1821, the event inspired an outpouring of support by European intellectuals, who praised the ancient Greeks as the founders of Western civilization. By the 1820s, the great powers had come over to the cause of Greek nationalism, even Metternich. The Turks were defeated and by the Treaty of Adrianople (1829), a new independent Greek state was created, a rare example of a successful nationalist revolt in this era.

Reform in Great Britain

Great Britain avoided revolutionary upheaval because of its ability to adapt to the challenge of Liberalism. To incorporate the new industrial bourgeoisie and provide an orderly process of representation for new cities, Parliament passed the **Reform Act of 1832,** which doubled the number of males who could vote, but retained a property requirement. Further reforms followed with the abolition of slavery in the British Empire in 1833 and the Poor Law of 1834. In reflecting the Liberal notion of self-help, the latter law actually punished the poor by making relief in government workhouses more unpleasant than any job. One of the more important principles favored by Liberals was free trade, hence their opposition to the protective Corn Laws. In the context of the Irish potato famine, Parliament in 1846 finally **repealed the Corn Laws,** initiating a century of British support for free trade. Conservative Tories supported their own notion of reform—through protective legislation. Following the Factory Act of 1833, Tories in Parliament helped pass the **Mines Act,** banning children and women from mines, and the **Ten Hours Act,** limiting hours in textile mills. In giving the middle class a "stake in society," British reformers hoped to gain their support for compromise over revolution.

The Revolutions of 1848

Sidebar: Due to France's seemingly constant political upheavals, one observer coined the expression "When France sneezes, Europe catches a cold." The quote reflects not only the potential instability inherent in French revolutionary traditions but also the continuing cultural and political influence of the nation.

Revolutions broke out all over Europe in the fateful year 1848. Though few of these revolutions achieved their stated objectives, their consequences proved significant nonetheless. Three major causes account for the stunning outburst of revolutionary activity: (1) Liberals felt profound frustration at the lack of political change toward constitutional and representative government; (2) nationalists chafed under the 1815 Vienna settlement and its blunt rejection of self-determination for ethnic minorities; and (3) the lives of the working class suffered from poor agricultural productivity (the era was known as the "hungry '40s") and jobs were lost to new industrial machinery. The combination of these factors made for an explosive compound, and once again the match was lit in France. For an overview of events, see the following chart:

Location	"Trigger"	Leaders	Events	Results
France	Discontented over the slow pace of reform and corruption in Louis Philippe's government, Liberals engage in a **"banquet campaign"** to agitate for suffrage expansion. When the government cancels the planned banquet of February 22, 1848, Paris revolts.	* **Louis Philippe**—king who abdicates under pressure of violence in Paris. * **Louis Blanc**—socialist advocate of national workshops for workers. * **Louis Napoleon**—nephew of Napoleon I who had for years attempted to overthrow the monarchy; elected president of the Second Republic in 1848.	* Following Louis's abdication, a provisional government is formed, composed of moderate and radical republicans. * To appease the working class of Paris, Blanc's **national workshops** are formed, but end up as a system of poor relief, not a means of promoting worker control of industry. * In June, radicals attack the democratically elected Constituent Assembly in hopes of creating a socialist republic. * The **"June Days"** see class violence between radical republicans and the army, which results in the deaths of 10,000 radicals and the establishment of a moderate republic.*Louis Napoleon is elected president in December by a wide majority and moves to consolidate power.	France establishes the **Second Republic,** but only after class warfare reveals the divisions in French society between the middle and working classes. Louis Napoleon exploits fears of further social conflict to establish authoritarian control of the nation.

Location	"Trigger"	Leaders	Events	Results
Prussia	Inspired by the French example, Prussian Liberals in March revolted in Berlin against the Prussian monarch, who had resisted sharing power.	* **Frederick William IV** (1840–1861)— king who agreed to the election of a Prussian assembly, refused the Frankfurt Liberals' offer of a crown of a united Germany, but granted a conservative constitution to his kingdom in 1850.	* Liberals forced the election of a Prussian Assembly, which proceeded to grant autonomy to the Polish minority. * By the end of spring, the Prussian army had reestablished control of the nation and reversed the pro-Polish legislation of the Assembly.	Prussian Liberals failed to meet their objectives of political equality and reduce the influence of traditional institutions. However, despite its three-tiered class voting system, the **1850 Constitution** did provide for representation.
Frankfurt	After the riots in Berlin, Liberals overthrew the traditional political structures of the other German states. After elections, delegates met in Frankfurt to discuss the unification of Germany.		* Deliberations divided over whether the Austrian empire, with its large non-German population, should be included in a unified Germany. The debate between advocates of a **"small" vs. "large" Germany** caused a fatal delay as conservative forces regathered their strength. * By December, the Liberals had issued a Declaration of Rights for the German people.	By the time German Liberals had completed a constitution, their moment had passed. Frederick William IV rejected the **"crown from the gutter,"** and the work of German unification would ultimately be accomplished by a conservative (see next chapter).

Location	"Trigger"	Leaders	Events	Results
Frankfurt			* In April 1849, the **Frankfurt Assembly** completed its constitution and offered the crown to Prussian King Frederick William IV.	
Austria	Workers and students rebel in March in Vienna, causing Metternich to flee to Britain.	* **Klemens von Metternich**—conservative foreign minister and creator of the Congress System, unable to withstand the revolutions of 1848. * **Franz Joseph I** (1848–1916)—became emperor in December upon his father's abdication.	* Serfdom is abolished throughout the Austrian empire. * Emperor Franz Joseph agrees to a Constitution in 1849.	After the initial nationalist revolts within the Austrian Empire, the new emperor and army reestablished control and crushed further opposition. Franz Joseph rejected the constitution in 1851 and worked toward the centralization of power, though the ethnicities issue would fester.
Prague	Seeing the turmoil in the Austrian Empire, Slavic nationalists meet in Prague to discuss the unification of all Slavs.	* **General Windischgrätz** —German army commander who succeeded in dispersing the Prague Assembly.	After initially promising autonomy to Bohemia, whose capital was Prague, the Austrian emperor reversed course and broke up the **Pan-Slav Congress.**	Though unsuccessful, Slavic nationalism remained a problem for the Austrian Empire and formed an essential cause of World War I.

Location	"Trigger"	Leaders	Events	Results
Budapest	Events in Paris inspired the Hungarian Diet in March to proclaim liberty for Magyars (another ethnic minority in Austria).	* **Louis Kossuth**—Hungarian Liberal and nationalist who led the cause of the Magyars.	* In the fall of 1848, Hungarian nationalists proclaim a new constitution that promotes the Magyar language but suppresses the rights of Slavic minorities in Hungary. * After the constitution is rejected by the Austrian emperor, Hungary declares complete independence. * Emperor Franz Joseph in 1849 asks Russian leader Nicholas I to crush the nationalist movement in Budapest.	The Austrians are able to exploit Slavic fear of Hungarian power to crush the revolt, with Russian support. However, Magyars remain the most restive of the ethnic minorities in the empire.
Italy	After the March Days in Vienna, several Italian states rise in revolt against Austrian rule.	* **Charles Albert** (r. 1831–1849)—king of Piedmont-Sardinia who urged the Italian states to resist Austrian rule. * **Pope Pius IX** (1846–1878)—began as a reformer, but when expelled from Rome by revolutionary forces, turned against modernism.	* Charles Albert of Piedmont-Sardinia grants a constitution to his people and declares war on Austria to gain territory in Italy. * Numerous other Italian states rise in revolt against Austrian rule. * When the pope is expelled from Rome, Mazzini proclaims a **Roman Republic.**	Italians experience few specific victories in 1848, other than the abolition of serfdom in some states and a constitution for Piedmont. However, the revolutions set the stage for later Italian unification under Piedmont-Sardinian leadership and its opposition by the papacy.

Location	"Trigger"	Leaders	Events	Results
Italy		* **Giuseppe Mazzini—** Italian nationalist who established the Roman Republic.	* Austrian authorities agree to abolish serfdom in Italian Habsburg lands, hoping to win over peasants. * The Austrian army defeats Charles Albert and restores authority in the other Italian states. * To win over Catholics, Louis Napoleon in 1849 sends French troops into Rome to restore Pope Pius IX.	

What began with heady enthusiasm and high hopes ended with bitter disappointment and violent suppression. In general, the Liberal and nationalist revolutions of 1848 failed to achieve their objectives, and for this three key factors are responsible: (1) Though revolutionaries boasted lofty rhetoric and inspiring visions, they lacked the institutional power of conservative forces, such as armies and bureaucracies; (2) conservatives successfully exploited middle-class fears of radical revolution after the June Days in Paris; and (3) rulers pitted ethnic minorities against one another to "divide and conquer" and reestablish authority. Despite these failures, the revolutions of 1848 may be the most underestimated event in European history. The revolutions set the stage for the rise of socialism and a growing division between the middle and working class. In addition, the Romantic age of revolution seemed dead and, philosophically, many intellectuals turned to a more hard-headed realist and materialist vision of the world. Most important, conservatives learned the lesson that they could no longer ignore nationalism, so if they wished to stay in power, they had to appeal to public opinion and sponsor movements of national unity from the top down. It is to this topic that the next chapter is devoted.

ADDITIONAL RESOURCES

Anderson, M. S., *The Ascendancy of Europe, 1815–1914*, 3rd ed. (2003)—Comprehensive overview of the nineteenth century.

Ashton, T. S., *The Industrial Revolution* (1997)—A classic account that briefly traces the process of technological change.

Chapman, Tim, *The Congress of Vienna: Origins, Processes, and Results* (1998)—Brief and focused account of the Congress of Vienna and its impact.

Daunton, Martin, *Progress and Poverty: An Economic and Social History of Britain, 1700–1850* (1995)—A volume that explores the social effects of and responses to industrialization.

Deane, Phyllis, *The First Industrial Revolution,* 2nd ed. (1979)—Good introduction to the technological changes involved.

Hobsbawm, Eric J., *The Age of Revolution: Europe, 1789–1848* (1962)—Challenging, but packed with insights, this volume is authored by a famous Marxist historian.

Kissinger, Henry, *Diplomacy* (1994)—By the former secretary of state, this book offers chapters on the Vienna settlement and beyond.

Kohn, Hans, *Nationalism: Its Meaning and History* (1982)—Slim volume analyzing an important topic.

McLellan, David, *Ideology,* 2nd ed. (1995)—A brief but helpful introduction to the concept of ideology.

Stearns, Peter, *1848: The Revolutionary Tide in Europe* (1974)—A good overview of revolutions in all the affected nations.

Stearns, Peter, *A Century for Debate: Problems in the Interpretation of European History, 1789–1914* (1969)—For those students interested in historiographical issues.

Taylor, Phillip A. M., *The Industrial Revolution in Britain: Triumph or Disaster?* (1970)—From the Problems in European Civilization Series, this volume provides both primary and secondary readings.

www.womeninworldhistory.com/lesson7.html—This site offers documents related to women's experiences during the Industrial Revolution.

www.spartacus.schoolnet.co.uk/IRchild.main.htm—This site addresses the issue of child labor, from the viewpoints of its opponents, supporters, and those who experienced it firsthand.

www.fordham.edu/halsall/mod/modsbook14.html—From the Modern Internet History Sourcebook, this site offers numerous interesting documents related to industry.

PRACTICE QUESTIONS

1. All of the following proved advantageous in Great Britain's leadership in industrialization EXCEPT:
   a. a supply of important mineral resources, such as coal and iron ore.
   b. mercantile and industrial classes represented in government.
   c. strong banking and financial institutions to provide capital.
   d. an increasing percentage of the population involved in agriculture.
   e. a strong navy to promote commerce and protect markets.
2. Which of the following can be concluded regarding industrialization of Britain in the nineteenth century from the chart on page 205?
   a. The percentage of national production from agriculture remained steady.
   b. By 1900, manufacturing had become the largest sector of Britain's economy.
   c. Britain experienced significant economic problems after midcentury.
   d. The most rapid increase in Britain's economy occurred before 1850.
   e. Britain's was the largest economy in Europe by 1850.

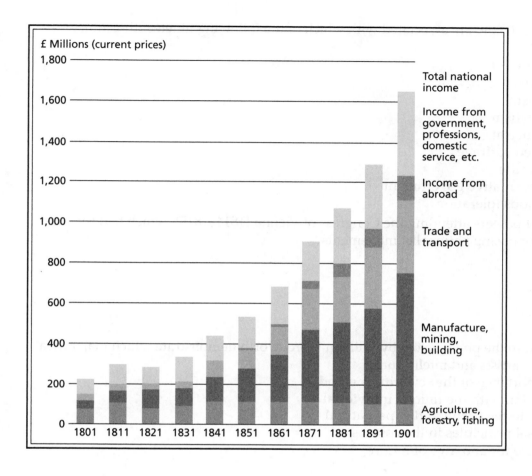

£ Millions (current prices)

Total national income

Income from government, professions, domestic service, etc.

Income from abroad

Trade and transport

Manufacture, mining, building

Agriculture, forestry, fishing

3. A key difference in the industrialization of the European continent compared with that of Great Britain in the nineteenth century was the:
   a. greater importance of technological innovation.
   b. lack of population growth attending industrialization.
   c. role played by traditional guilds in mechanization.
   d. decisive role played by government in promoting it.
   e. absence of corresponding social problems.

4. Which of the following represents an important social consequence of industrialization in the first half of the nineteenth century?
   a. increase in population and greater percentage living in cities
   b. the strengthening of families as a productive unit
   c. a decrease in social conflict because of shared wealth
   d. increasing standards in living and working conditions
   e. successful establishment of socialist states in some nations

5. The most direct rejection of mechanization in industry during the nineteenth century came from:
   a. classical economists.
   b. trade unionists.
   c. Chartists.
   d. utopian socialists.
   e. Luddites.

6. The concepts below are associated with which of the following nineteenth-century ideologies?
   a. socialism
   b. nationalism
   c. Liberalism
   d. conservatism
   e. Romanticism
      • limited suffrage
      • free trade
      • representative government
      • religious toleration

7. Of the great powers attending the Congress of Vienna (1814–1815), which had the most to gain by opposing nationalist movements?
   a. Prussia
   b. France
   c. Great Britain
   d. Austria
   e. Russia

8. The lines from the poem below by William Wordsworth demonstrate which major idea of Romantic artists and intellectuals?
   a. the importance of the scientific method
   b. fascination with the unique individual
   c. interest in the occult and supernatural
   d. universal principles in the cosmos
   e. reverence for and awe of nature

   Books! 'tis a dull and endless strife:
   Come, hear the woodland linnet,
   How sweet his music! on my life,
   There's more of wisdom in it.
   Enough of Science and of Art;
   Close up those barren leaves;
   Come forth, and bring with you a heart
   That watches and receives.

9. Which of the following best explains the motive behind the Reform Bill of 1832 passed by the British Parliament?
   a. an effort to give the middle class a stake in society
   b. belief that the excesses of industry had gone too far
   c. a concerted plan to disenfranchise the working class
   d. to fulfill the laissez-faire idea of free markets
   e. to provide for orderly immigration of the Irish

10. Which of the following resulted from revolutionary turmoil in Europe, 1848–1849?
    a. the creation of an effective means of collective security
    b. Workers established their political power in several nations.
    c. Conservatives adopted nationalism and worked for unity.
    d. Romanticism gained renewed strength in art and literature.
    e. Italy was unified under the leadership of the papacy.

Liberty Leading the People by Eugène Delacroix (French, 1798–1863)
(Giraudon/Art Resource, NY)

SAMPLE ESSAY

Using the painting above as a starting point, analyze the connection between Romanticism on one hand and Liberalism and nationalism on the other in the period 1800–1850.

This picture was painted by Delacroix during one of the French revolutions in the period 1800–1850. It shows a Romantic mindset very clearly. If you look at the painting closely, you can see a woman representing liberty and leading a group of her people revolting against unfair government. Many European citizens during the first half of the nineteenth century were attracted to different ideologies, like Liberalism and nationalism. But they also found a lot of truth in Romanticism, with its strong ideas about nature and the emotions.

In the painting, lady liberty is holding a flag; it's called the French tricolor. During the French Revolution, many people flew the tricolor to show their support of the ideals of liberty, equality, and fraternity. Though this event was later (I think in 1848), French people were still focusing on how important the French revolution was to politics. The painting is very dark and ominous, perhaps showing how liberty is threatened by governments that might not respect liberties. The men in the painting seem dressed like ordinary people. This is to show that these revolutions were about equality for the people.

Looking closer at the painting, we see some who have already been killed. During the period 1800–1850, many people died in revolutions across Europe, fighting for nationalism and Liberalism. There were revolutions everywhere in Europe in 1848: Germany, Italy, France, and Czechoslovakia. Though this painting is about France, the same idea of Liberalism and nationalism applies to all the revolutions. People were upset about backward governments with no rights and with a lack of unity for different ethnic groups. We don't see this issue in the painting, because all the people are French, but many of these revolts did attempt to create united nations without foreign influence.

So as we can see, nationalism and Liberalism were very related to Romanticism. The painting is by a Romantic painter—Delacroix—but it also shows themes related to nationalism and Liberalism. The period of 1800–1850 was rife with revolutions, and many artists wanted to show their support for different ideas. That's why Delacroix painted *Liberty Leading the People,* and that's why we study it today.

Though this student makes some relevant points about Liberalism, nationalism, and Romanticism in the period 1800–1850, his response does not address the question clearly. First of all, when you encounter an FRQ with a visual prompt, make sure that you do not get bogged down in simply describing the illustration. You should begin with the painting but quickly move into providing historical context. This response makes several historical references to the period in question; however, the essay does not clarify the content of the three ideologies in the prompt, or what possible connection they might have. In addition, the historical references are thin and in several cases erroneous (for example, the painting represents events in 1830). When you address a prompt like this one, make sure that you have an adequate understanding of the ideologies AND some specific knowledge of relevant events of the period. Unfortunately, much of this student's response is off-task or tangential to the question. Also, the references provided are too general and not linked effectively to a thesis, which is not to be found in the introduction or anywhere else in the essay. Score: 2–3.

CHAPTER 12

Realism, Nationalism, and Imperialism, 1850–1914

Failure in the revolutions of 1848 vaulted Europe into a new era. Intellectually, the Romantic temperament no longer held sway, as artists, scientists, and politicians adopted a hard-headed mindset of realism and materialism. Military power, industry, organization, electricity, commodities—these products of modern life replaced the imaginary, spiritual, emotional, idealistic, and rhetorical ideas of Romanticism. This chapter reviews the post-1848 realist and materialist ethos in the arts and ideas, its application in national unification projects, in the continuing progress of technological and industrial change, and, ultimately, how all these became tools in Europe's domination of Asia and Africa with imperialism. The events in this chapter culminate centuries-long developments and represent the zenith of European power in world history.

> **Note:** To users of Palmer, Colton, and Kramer, *A History of the Modern World*, this chapter pulls together material from Chapters 12 and 14 in combination with all of Chapters 13 and 16 for a thematic focus on Europe's advancing economic and political power.

REALISM AND MATERIALISM

If the Romantics presented a world of possibilities through the imagination, then the realists refocused their attention on the world as it really was, warts and all. For writers and artists of the second half of the nineteenth century, industrialization and technology dominated the lives of Europeans.

Art and Literature

After 1850, writers turned from Romantic themes to the lives of those directly affected by a changing material reality. Characters in realist novels struggled to understand and cope with the impersonal forces of economic and social change. British author **Charles Dickens** (1812–1870) filled his novels with compelling casts of characters thrown into a world of sooty cities, cruel orphanages, and corrupt business practices. Stories such as *Hard Times* and *Oliver Twist* revealed the underside of Britain's rapid industrialization and the crushing inequality attending material progress. Realist writers abandoned the conventions of Romantic rhetoric in favor of an unsentimental, precise style, as in **Gustave Flaubert's** (1821–1880) *Madame Bovary*. The title character becomes disillusioned with her mundane middle-class life and marriage, engages in several adulterous affairs, and ultimately commits suicide.

Realist artists turned their canvases into windows on the lives of the downtrodden. French painters led the way in revealing the difficult circumstances of landless peasants and exhausted factory workers. **Jean-François Millet** (1814–1875) highlighted, in paintings such as *The Sower* and *The Gleaners*, the backbreaking labor of culling enough from the earth to eke out survival. His paintings were echoed by those of **Gustave Courbet** (1819–1877), whose *Stonebreakers* eloquently captured the brutal work of two manual laborers crushing stones for gravel. We focus on the physical posture of the workers rather than their faces, which are covered in shadow. As photography developed throughout the century, an additional medium became available to depict difficult social problems.

Postivism

As the influence of organized religion declined in Europe, many substituted a belief in the potential of science. The power of scientific thought seemed validated by its production of immense material benefits through industry and technology. French philosopher **Auguste Comte** (1798–1857) captured this faith with his theory of positivism. Comte believed that history had progressed through three stages—the theological, metaphysical (or philosophical), and the scientific. The great revolutions of 1789–1848 faltered, according to Comte, because of their adherence to overly abstract principles. Progress must rely on a hard-nosed and empirical investigation of reality, avoiding wishful thinking and unsupported generalizations. Comte categorized all the sciences and argued for a science of society (sociology), which would become a new secular religion.

Heads Up! Marxism represents a common topic for multiple-choice and free-response questions. Make sure that you understand the conceptual framework as well as its influence as a motivating ideology in the nineteenth and twentieth centuries. Even if one rejects communism, one needs to give credit to Marx for contributing to sociology—or the notion that social forces influence individual behavior.

Marxism

Karl Marx (1818–1883) claimed the mantle of a "scientific socialism" and turned his political philosophy into one of the most important ideas in history. From a middle-class family, Marx studied philosophy and law in college and eventually fell in with German radicals. Working for a series of left-wing publications, Marx hailed the revolutions of 1848 as the beginning of the socialist age. Marx's lifelong collaborator, **Friedrich Engels** (1820–1895), was the son of a German textile owner who rebelled against his inheritance and had already published *The Condition of the Working Class in England* (1844) to highlight the inequalities generated by capitalism. Together the two produced the famous pamphlet *The Communist Manifesto* (1848), urging the working class to unite and throw off their chains. Though the revolutions of 1848 failed, the manifesto established the outlines of Marxian socialism and a program of nationalization of property, universal suffrage, and the redistribution of property. As the collaborators worked within the newly established First International—founded in 1864 to promote a union of working-class parties—Marx labored at his masterwork of political economy, *Capital,* later finished by Engels in the 1880s. Marx and Engels wove together three diverse strands into their comprehensive critique of capitalism: German philosophy, British industrialism, and French radicalism. Marxian socialism comprises the following pillars:

- **Alienation of labor**—In his early writings, Marx blamed the increasing division of labor (i.e., specialization) for alienating (or creating a feeling of separation) the worker from his product, his labor, himself, and his fellow man, who exploits him.
- **Labor theory of value**—Borrowing from the British classical economists, Marx held that the value of a product equaled the amount of labor that went into producing it. Therefore, the difference between the worker's wages and the ultimate price of the products—what the factory owner calls "profit"—represents a theft of the worker's uncompensated "**surplus labor.**"
- **Dialectical materialism**—Marx took Hegel's historical notion of the clash of opposing forces as producing change (thesis → antithesis → synthesis) and applied it to clashing systems of production. Whereas Hegel emphasized a dialectic of ideas, Marx held that antagonistic material forces produced change, often called **economic determinism.** Marxism, thus, offered a complete view of history, in keeping with German philosophy.

- **Class struggle**—Each economic system is associated with a particular dominant class that owns the **means of production**. For example, in feudalism the aristocracy owns the essential resource (land) and exercises power based on this ownership. The **bourgeoisie** who own capital (factories, banks, etc.) represent the most productive class in history, but their exploitation of the propertyless unskilled workers who are forced to sell their labor, the **proletariat,** inevitably produces the system opposing capitalism—socialism. As workers increase in number, they will develop **class consciousness** and eventually unite to overthrow those who oppress them.
- **Revolution**—Marx condemned the early utopian socialists and the anarchists of eastern and southern Europe for what he considered their unrealistic schemes. Rule by the oppressed proletariat would only result from organization, agitation, and planning, not by separate communes and assassinations. Though Marx hoped for a worldwide movement of the working class, he believed it possible, if unlikely, that the revolution might succeed through democratic means in some nations.

Marxism exercised wide influence among all working-class movements, both revolutionary and democratic. Even those who rejected Marx's critique of capitalism had to confront his powerful ideology of change. Many have claimed that the appeal of Marxism lies in its similarity to an organized religion, though Marx rejected religion as the "opiate of the masses." Marxism offers its adherents religious-like symbols: prophets (Marx and Engels), holy books (Marx's writings), a chosen race (proletariat), and an end of the world (history's culmination with **communism,** where the state "withers away"). Marxism would finally gain power in the twentieth century in some states, though some claim that these experiments represent a distortion of Marx's doctrine, suggesting that there may be "as many Marxisms as there are Marxists."

NATIONAL UNIFICATION

It seems every century experiences an earth-shattering political event that completely transforms the diplomatic landscape. In the nineteenth century, the unifications of Italy and Germany altered the entire framework of European diplomacy. European political structures proved unable to incorporate successfully the emergence of these two new powers, leading to the most destructive wars in history in the twentieth century. Italy and Germany stood disunited for centuries. What allowed for their unification in the middle of the nineteenth century? Once again, we must look to the failed outcomes of the revolutions of 1848.

The Crimean War, 1853–1856

Revolutions in 1848 undermined the Concert of Europe—the agreement of the great powers to resolve issues collectively—and paved the way for the midcentury Crimean War. The Crimean War seemed easily avoidable and was poorly fought, but ultimately proved of great importance for subsequent diplomacy.

For centuries after its last foray into central Europe in 1683, the Ottoman Empire slowly receded in power. The empire found itself prey to continual attacks by a Russian nation intent on gaining a coveted warm-weather seaport. Only the intervention of Britain, who opposed Russian expansionism into the Mediterranean, kept the "Sick Man of Europe" on life support. When Napoleon III of France in 1853 wrung concessions from the Ottoman sultan to protect Christian minorities within the empire, the Russians demanded the same treatment be accorded to them. Fearing the further growth in Russian power, the French and British encouraged the sultan to reject the ultimatum and promised aid in the event of war. When war ensued, the Russian navy shattered the archaic Ottoman fleet in the Black Sea and moved into the Turkish

Sidebar: The decline of the Ottoman Empire is also known as the Eastern Question, and it played a major role in establishing rivalry between Austria and Russia in the Balkans. This rivalry stood at the crux of events leading up to World War I.

provinces of Moldavia and Wallachia (current Romania). France and Britain demanded that the Russians evacuate the two key provinces or face war. Even though Russia complied, the two western powers declared war anyway as a result of the anti-Russian public opinion they had aroused in their nations. Austria's actions proved more controversial. Russia had aided Austria in 1849 by crushing the Hungarian revolt. Now instead of repaying the favor, Austria exploited Russia's predicament by moving into Moldavia and Wallachia. Isolated, Russia attempted to defend itself against the combined weight of France, Russia, and the Italian kingdom of Piedmont-Sardinia.

The Crimean War was the initial modern conflict, with the first use of trenches, telegraphs, and railways. Nonetheless, poor communication, strategic errors, and disease cost an inordinate number of lives. The only hero of the struggle was **Florence Nightingale** (1820–1910), who helped found the nursing profession and demonstrated how women were capable of taking on productive public roles. By 1855, Nicholas I had died and the new Russian tsar, Alexander II, realized that the war had revealed Russia's technological and economic backwardness. To end the conflict, the combatants negotiated the **Treaty of Paris (1856),** in which Russia agreed to demilitarize the Black Sea and halt its expansion into the Balkans.

Though the war was over, the issues raised by it were not. By forever destroying the Concert of Europe, the Crimean War encouraged states to pursue national interests with little regard for the effects on the international order. Napoleon III considered the war a great victory and was falsely convinced of France's strength and prominence. British leaders felt disappointed at the cost and outcome of the war and fell into "splendid isolation" for half a century, standing aside while Italy and Germany unified. With its overly subtle diplomacy, Austria had isolated itself, a fatal error as it would face two wars in the next 10 years. Before the ink was dry on the treaty, Russia was determined to reform internally and continue its expansion at the first opportunity. Finally, by its involvement, little Piedmont-Sardinia won itself a great power patron in its drive for unification.

The Unification of Italy

Background and Romantic Nationalism

The Italian peninsula had lain disunited since the time of the Roman Empire. Though Italy pioneered the Renaissance, the diverse city-states in the late fifteenth and early sixteenth centuries lost their independence as a result of foreign invasion. Since then, foreign powers dominated political life in Italy. The nationalism of the French Revolution and the policies of Napoleon revived dreams of a united Italy. The Congress of Vienna's restoration of traditional rule frustrated these aspirations. Despite failure to expel foreign rule in the revolutionary period of 1815 to 1848, Italian nationalists could now look to leadership from Piedmont-Sardinia and exploit the increasingly tenuous position of Austria, the foreign power blocking unification.

Many Italian nationalists preferred the creation of a united republic, including a takeover of the Papal States. Following the Congress of Vienna, the resurgence of Italian nationalism (*Il Risorgimento*) was fueled by two republican advocates: Giuseppe Mazzini (see Chapter 11), the founder of **Young Italy,** and Giuseppe Garibaldi, the charismatic leader of the **Red Shirts.** Both represented the spirit of Romantic nationalism. Much of the practical work for Italian unity, however, was accomplished by a bookish and wily moderate, **Camillo Benso di Cavour** (1810–1861).

The Role of Piedmont-Sardinia and Cavour

Because of Piedmont-Sardinia's anti-Austrian role in the revolutions of 1848, many Italian nationalists looked to it for leadership. In 1848–1849, King Charles Albert granted his people a constitution and then attempted to unite the other Italian states in a war of liberation against Austria. Owing to his failure, Charles Albert abdicated in 1849, turning power to his son **Victor Emmanuel II** (r. 1849–1878). In 1852, the new king appointed Cavour as prime minister. Cavour supported Liberal ideas and had urged the unification of Italy in his newspaper, *Il Risorgimento*. In addition, Cavour understood practical affairs, having made a fortune in agriculture and business. As prime minister, Cavour looked to modernize the Piedmontese state—updating the tax and budget system, building railroads, pursuing free trade, limiting the power of the Catholic Church, and building a small but strong army. Though Cavour was willing to use Romantic ideals to his advantage, he favored a realistic (*Realpolitik*) approach to Italian unity. And this required a foreign ally.

With the **Treaty of Plombières** (1858), Cavour had convinced Napoleon III of France to join Piedmont-Sardinia in a joint attack on Austria. By the treaty, Piedmont would gain the Italian states of Lombardy and Venetia, while Napoleon would reconfirm French leadership of nationalism and exercise influence in Italy. In the ensuing war, Piedmont and France defeated the Austrian army at Magenta and Solferino, setting off revolutions in the other northern Italian states. Fearing that the situation was spinning out of control and might affect French troops in Rome guarding the pope, Napoleon III signed a separate agreement with Austria that granted Piedmont only Lombardy. However, the northern Italian states in 1860 voted by plebiscites (votes related to issues not candidates) to join the Piedmontese state, which Napoleon acknowledged in exchange for Nice and Savoy from Piedmont.

Cavour now urged Garibaldi to take advantage of the revolutionary situation brewing in the Kingdom of the Two Sicilies, the backward Bourbon monarchy controlling the southern half of the peninsula. With just over a thousand of his Red Shirts, Garibaldi rallied the countryside to his cause and moved up the peninsula. Once again, concerns over the position of the papacy complicated matters. Cavour did not wish to involve French troops guarding Rome in the situation, so he and Victor Emmanuel met Garibaldi south of Rome and asked him to relinquish his conquest to Piedmont-Sardinia. Though a republican, Garibaldi consented, and plebiscites confirmed the unification of the northern and southern halves of the peninsula. In March 1861, the new Italian kingdom was proclaimed, with Victor Emmanuel as its first monarch. Two months later, Cavour died, one might say from complications of nation-birth. Thus, it has been said that the new Italian kingdom represented the "passion of Mazzini, the audacity of Garibaldi, and the cunning of Cavour."

Sidebar: Pope Pius IX (1846–1878) began as a reformer but turned conservative after the revolutions of 1848 in Italy. He actively opposed Italian unification and in 1870 found the papacy's lands reduced to the Vatican grounds of today. Pius condemned modern ideas in his *Syllabus of Errors* (1864), and at the First Vatican Council (1870–1871) declared the doctrine of papal infallibility. Pius's papacy was also the longest in the history of the Catholic Church.

Italy completed its unification by gaining Venetia in 1866 and Rome (excluding the Vatican) in 1870 when Prussia, with whom Italy was unified, defeated Austria and then France in war. Though united, Italy experienced significant problems—opposition by the papacy to the new Italian state, economic underdevelopment, a corrupt political system known as *trasformismo* (the bribing of political opponents), and the wide cultural and economic differences between northern and southern Italy (called the *Mezzagiorno*). Because it came so late to national unity, Italy often compensated by aggressively seeking colonies and attempting to regain "unredeemed" Italian-speaking territories.

The Unification of Germany

Background: German Dualism

Like Italy, Germany's limbs had lain severed in central Europe for centuries. Conflicts between the Holy Roman Emperor and papacy in the Middle Ages stymied either from unifying Germany. Due to its elective nature, the emperor never became a strong absolutist ruler like the kings of France. Religious conflict in the sixteenth and seventeenth centuries further splintered German politics, formalized with the Westphalia settlement in 1648. In the nineteenth century, the existence of two German powers—the dualism of Austria and Prussia—effectively checked either from consolidating the smaller German states into one nation unified around German language and ethnicity. When Liberals failed in 1848 at Frankfurt to act decisively for German unity, it opened the door for a different path to the same objective.

Prussia's great military tradition had decayed since the time of Frederick the Great (d. 1786). The kingdom entered the French revolutionary wars late and was decisively defeated by Napoleon in 1807. Moreover, Austria under Metternich dominated German politics after the Congress of Vienna, leaving Prussia to play second fiddle. In fact, following the revolutions of 1848, Austria imposed upon Prussia the so-called Humiliation of Olmütz (1850), whereby Prussia guaranteed not to work toward German political unity. When **William I** (r. 1861–1888) inherited the Prussian throne from his insane brother, he set out to reestablish Prussia's power.

With his first act, William introduced long-overdue reforms in the army. At the advice of his generals, William called for the expansion of the army, regular conscription (the draft), the creation of a General Staff (to devise war plans), and the introduction of modern rifled weapons, such as the breech-loading needle gun. According to the Prussian Constitution of 1850, representatives to the **Reichstag** (lower house of the parliament) were apportioned by a unique three-tiered voting system, designed to favor the wealthy Junker elite. However, as Germany industrialized, the power of middle-class **Liberal Party** grew in Prussia. These Liberals in the Reichstag resented the conservative influence of the army as well as the Junker class who dominated it and opposed the king's reforms. Neither king nor Reichstag would budge, plunging Prussia into a constitutional crisis.

The Work of Bismarck

To solve the crisis, William turned in 1862 to **Otto von Bismarck** (1815–1898), appointing him **Chancellor.** Bismarck hailed from the Junker class, but surpassed that often provincial and mediocre group with his intelligence and ambitions. A Romantic turned conservative, Bismarck gained wide diplomatic experience representing Prussia to France, Russia, and the German Confederation. As he matured, Bismarck expanded his allegiances—from Junker, to Prussian, to German, and finally to European statesman. In his political approach, Bismarck acted as the consummate practitioner of *Realpolitik.* Bismarck did not have a predetermined plan for bringing about the unification of Germany; rather, he effectively took advantage of opportunities presented to him. To deal with the political crisis in Prussia, Bismarck turned the tables on the Liberals in the Reichstag, claiming that they possessed no constitutional power to block needed reforms. He appealed to Prussian patriotism, arguing that the other German states did not look to Prussia's liberalism—that was the mistake of 1848—but to its **"iron and blood."** When the Reichstag continued to refuse the king taxes to implement the army reforms, Bismarck simply instructed the bureaucracy to collect the taxes anyway.

To unify Germany, Bismarck waged three separate wars. His opponent in each war found itself diplomatically isolated and maneuvered into appearing as the aggressor. When the Poles revolted against Russian authority in 1863, almost every great power expressed support for their national aspirations, but without any actual assistance. Bismarck calculated that he needed the future friendship of great power Russia, so he supported Russia's crushing of the Polish revolt. In 1864, Denmark formally incorporated the mainly German-speaking provinces of **Schleswig** and **Holstein** (which it had occupied since 1848) into the Danish kingdom, violating an international treaty. Nationalism flared in Germany. Rather than working through the German Confederation as Austria preferred, Bismarck suggested a joint approach by the two leading powers. Austria relented, and the two powers easily defeated their enemy in the **Danish War,** occupying the two provinces of Schleswig and Holstein.

The joint occupation of the two provinces offered ample opportunity for conflict between the two German powers. The dispute festered, as Bismarck intended, and eventually Austria turned to the German Confederation for relief. Citing a violation of the occupation agreement, Prussia went to war against Austria. Before entering the conflict, Bismarck ensured Austria's isolation—Russia was favorable after Bismarck's support for the Polish revolt, Napoleon was bought off with vague promises of French expansion, Italy hoped to gain Venetia from Austria, and Britain maintained its splendid isolation. In the ensuing **Austro-Prussian War** (or **Seven Weeks' War**) of 1866, Prussia's superior railroads, staff organization, and needle gun overwhelmed the Austrians. Despite the designs of William, Bismarck treated Austria leniently; they lost only Venetia and, more important, had to bow out of German affairs. Prussia annexed the states of north Germany, and in 1867 Bismarck created the **North German Confederation,** insisting that its Reichstag be elected by universal male suffrage. What's more, the Reichstag hailed Bismarck's achievement by retroactively approving the illegally collected taxes with the **Indemnity Bill of 1866.**

The mostly Catholic German states stood outside this union. Anticipating future conflict with France, Bismarck convinced these states to join in alliance with the North German Confederation should war break out with France. When the Spanish throne became vacant in 1870, Bismarck had his pretext. The Spanish nobles offered the throne to a Hohenzollern relative of William's, an offer that Bismarck pressed the candidate to accept. Not wishing to be surrounded by Hohenzollerns, the French vehemently objected. William relented and encouraged his cousin to drop the offer. Now Napoleon III of France overplayed his hand and demanded an apology from William via the French ambassador. Bismarck edited an account of the meeting, known as the **Ems Dispatch,** to make it seem as if the king had insulted the French ambassador. Napoleon took the bait and declared war. Once again, Bismarck's opponent was isolated; the French were easily defeated in the **Franco-Prussian War** and, embarrassingly, Napoleon himself was captured at Sedan. The resulting **Treaty of Frankfurt** imposed a 5-billion franc indemnity on the French, and, more important, they lost **Alsace-Lorraine,** which became a source of enmity between the two nations throughout the twentieth century. In January 1871, Bismarck's work was complete with the proclamation of the **German Empire** with William I as kaiser.

Though Bismarck helped engineer a federal constitution that respected the traditions of the other German states and allowed elements of democracy, power was still exercised in an

Sidebar: British Prime Minister Benjamin Disraeli recognized the significance of Germany's unification. He said, "There is not a diplomatic tradition which has not been swept away. You have a new world, new influences at work, new and unknown objects and dangers with which to cope. . . .The balance of power has been entirely destroyed." These words would prove sadly prophetic in the twentieth century.

authoritarian fashion. Government ministers reported to the **kaiser,** not the Reichstag, and Bismarck effectively concentrated key positions in his own hands (Chancellor, Prussian Minister of State), which allowed him effectively to exploit democratic mechanisms to ensure his domination of policy. This new German empire immediately upset the balance of power in Europe. Its economic and military potential threatened to dwarf its neighbors. Even though Bismarck worked to maintain peace in Europe after 1871, some historians believe that he laid the foundation for the militarism and state glorification that gave rise to the Nazis in the twentieth century.

OTHER NATION-BUILDING EFFORTS

Italy and Germany represented the best examples of the power of nationalism to unify states. However, already territorially unified states, such as France and Russia, worked toward greater internal cohesion through reform. The following states demonstrate three different models of reform.

France: Napoleon III and the Second Empire

After being elected president of the Second Republic, Louis Napoleon quickly consolidated his power. Presenting himself as a man of the people, he dissolved the Chamber of Deputies over the issue of universal male suffrage. In a coup d'etat in 1851, Napoleon rescinded the 1848 republican constitution. With popular approval through a plebiscite, Napoleon announced in 1852 the **Second Empire,** with himself as Emperor Napoleon III. Though Napoleon's foreign adventures proved disastrous—loss of control over Italian and German unification, a failed effort to create an empire in Mexico—he did modernize France internally.

Working through a professional and centrally controlled bureaucracy, Napoleon focused on France's economic development. He founded the **Credit Mobiliér** bank, built railways, promoted French industry, and in his most celebrated reform, **rebuilt the city of Paris.** Napoleon hired the talents of the architect and engineer **Baron von Haussmann** (1809–1891), who tore down the old city walls and housing, constructed a modern sanitary system, built grand boulevards, and adorned it all with a feast of opera houses, theaters, and shopping centers. As Napoleon said, "I found Paris stinking, and left it smelling sweet." Due to increasing criticism, Napoleon after 1860 allowed more legislative input, relaxed press censorship, and pursued a policy of free trade with Great Britain. But such reforms could not rescue Napoleon from his foreign policy failures, and in 1870, the emperor himself was captured by the Prussian army (see previous discussion) and the empire ended. Workers of the shiny new Paris refused to surrender, however, and established the revolutionary **Paris Commune,** which harkened back to the principles of 1793 with its socialist program. Eventually, a popularly elected Constituent Assembly crushed the Paris Commune and established the Third Republic. Another French republic thus started off with the taint of class violence and military failure.

Russia: Alexander II's Modernization

The Crimean War demonstrated Russia's weakness vis-à-vis the other great powers. Recognizing the backwardness of his nation, **Alexander II** (r. 1855–1881) embarked on a series of top-down reforms that proved ultimately too little and too late to save the Romanov dynasty.

Fearing violent peasant upheaval, Alexander **abolished serfdom** in 1861. By terms of the liberation, peasants continued to live on the village *mirs* until they paid for the land they received. Russian agriculture continued to suffer from land shortages and rural overpopulation into the twentieth century. In addition, Alexander introduced equality into the legal system, abolished corporal and capital punishment, created local assemblies known as *zemstvos,* and reformed the army. These wide-ranging reforms did not heal the growing rift in Russian society between those who emphasized Russia's unique traditions (called **Slavophiles**) and those who believed Russia must become more modern (Westernizers). Led by discontented intellectuals, such as Alexander Herzen and **Mikhail Bakunin** (1814–1876), **anarchism** gained support in the context of an autocratic and archaic Russia. Eventually, an anarchist-inspired movement known as the **People's Will** succeeded in 1881 in assassinating Alexander after numerous failed attempts.

Austria-Hungary: The Dual Monarchy

The tattered Austrian empire was until the First World War I ruled by **Franz Joseph I** (r. 1848–1916), a leader not known for his decisive action or ambitious projects. Franz Joseph attempted to hold together his diverse realm through the bureaucracy, the army, and loyalty to the Habsburg dynasty. Following the revolutions of 1848, Austria focused on internal development, building railroads and promoting industry, as well as centralization around the German language. These policies had the effect of further alienating the Slavic and Magyar ethnic minorities. Following losses in the Italian and German wars of unification, Franz Joseph allowed the creation of the **Dual Monarchy** in 1867. This new Austro-Hungarian monarchy allowed autonomy for the Magyars but maintained unity through common ministries of finance, foreign affairs, and war. However, neither of these kingdoms was democratic. In fact, the Hungarians pursued **Magyarization** in their part of the empire, suppressing Slavic languages and culture. Not until 1907 did Austria grant universal male suffrage and even then, the imperial Reichsrat so often descended into ethnic conflict that Franz Joseph was forced to rule by decree. Austria-Hungary's ethnic problems laid the powder trail that ignited into World War I.

> **Sidebar:** Most of the ethnic minorities in the Austrian empire spoke languages in the Slavic family—Czechs, Slovaks, Poles, Ruthenians, Slovenes, Serbs, Croats. The Magyars descended from the medieval "Huns" who invaded Europe in the ninth century. Hungarian represents one of the most difficult languages to master and uniquely in Europe is not part of the Indo-European language family but the Finno-Ugric, sharing common roots with Finnish.

THE SECOND INDUSTRIAL REVOLUTION

Historians point to the year 1850 as roughly dividing the initial phase of industrialization from a new one characterized by a larger scale of industrial enterprises, a further geographic expansion of industry, and a much closer relationship between theoretical science and its application in technology. This new phase we call the Second Industrial Revolution.

New Technologies and Methods

The period 1875–1900 represents arguably the greatest concentration of technological advance—including our own age—in the history of the human race. Steam engines now powered larger factories, as mechanized production became the predominant form of manufacture. American Henry Ford pioneered a new form of **mass production,** the assembly line, which allowed for increased economies of scale (i.e., reduced costs at high levels of production) and cheaper products. With the **Bessemer process,** steel replaced iron as the essential metal in construction, railways, and for military use. Reinforced concrete and steel girders allowed for the development of skyscrapers, adding a new element to modern cities.

Advances in theoretical chemistry boosted the chemical industry. Germany quickly became the dominant producer of chemicals, which had numerous industrial, pharmaceutical, and military uses. Europeans harnessed the power of **electricity** to light cities, power streetcars, and provide for a seemingly inexhaustible source of energy. After its discovery in 1859, **petroleum** grew into a mineral resource vital to the needs of the new **internal combustion engines** and to nation-states dependent on its potential power. The catalog of advances described here only scratches the surface; refrigeration, photography, elevators, kitchen appliances, motion pictures, synthetic fabrics, TNT, x-rays, and many others could also be included.

Transportation and Communication

Technological advances revolutionized transportation and communications. **Steamships** allowed for faster ocean journeys and greater geographic mobility, establishing an essential means for European control of distant empires. The completion of the **Suez Canal** (1869) and the Panama Canal (1914) reduced transoceanic travel even further. Invented in 1903, **airplanes** would not alter passenger travel for several generations, but did yield immediate military applications. New power sources also allowed for the development of city streetcars and subways, and by extension, the creation of suburbs and the further separation of home and work.

The technology of human communication had not changed much since the invention of the printing press in the 1450s. The late nineteenth century witnessed a series of inventions that made the world smaller and allowed European power a truly global reach. A transatlantic telegraph cable was laid in the 1870s to create the first instantaneous communication over continents; the invention of the **telephone** was not far behind. To facilitate railway schedules, **standardized time zones** were introduced in the 1880s. Marconi's discovery of **radio** waves translated in the early twentieth century into a new technology for governments to coordinate military power and control public opinion.

Business Cycles and Managing Markets

Despite the great wealth generated by this technological dynamo, the European economy suffered from **boom-bust cycles** during the period 1873–1896. Overproduction and unpredictable commodity prices routinely plunged Europe into recession, creating fear for governments of worker unrest and corporate bankruptcies. To manage the market, businesses became more organized. The **modern corporation,** with its complex administrative structures, accounting procedures, and stocks, dates from the late nineteenth century. Some industries informally collaborated in **cartels** to control the production and thus the prices of their manufactures. Banks pooled investment resources in **consortia** to control interest rates. More formal arrangements were termed **horizontal** and **vertical integration**—the former involved the control of several corporations by a holding company able to influence the policies of each and the latter involved a corporation controlling all stages of the production and distribution process. Though governments continued to rely on market mechanisms and the **gold standard** to ensure stable currencies, many states began to move away from free trade toward **protectionism** of national industries.

Technological advances translated into new goods. Former luxuries became necessities. To reach all consumers, corporations began to exploit communication advances for marketing purposes. Advertising in billboards, newspapers, and catalogs opened a new world of **consumerism** to European citizens. With its modernization, Paris sponsored the first department store, **Bon Marché,** in the 1870s. An increasingly sophisticated economy opened new employment opportunities in so-called white-collar areas, such as retail, marketing, communications, and services.

The Balance of Power and Global Integration

New developments in industry shifted the balance of economic power worldwide. Within Europe, Germany surpassed Britain by 1900 in steel, iron, coal mining, and chemical production. The United States arose as a competitor outside Europe, besting Britain and Germany both in steel and coal production also by 1900. European capital, however, came to dominate the world. With huge profits and sophisticated banking and investment methods, European corporations and governments came to dominate the functioning of the world economy. Imperial powers such as Britain, France, and Germany invested in Asian, African, and Latin American ventures, influencing the economic decisions of those regions, if not controlling them outright. By 1914, economic activity had become truly global, with developments in one area of the world rippling throughout.

IMPERIALISM

European control of global markets was nothing new in the nineteenth century. In fact, the period 1763–1871 saw a net decline in European colonial control, with American independence and Europe's preoccupation with revolutionary movements and internal development. Following the unification campaigns of Italy and Germany, as well as other internal nation-building programs, Europe's aspirations for national greatness turned outside the continent. With the advance of technology and organization stemming from the Second Industrial Revolution, European powers as of 1870 possessed both the means and motives for further penetration of the global market. Compared with earlier colonization, the distinguishing features of European imperialism in the period 1871–1914 were the more direct control of foreign territory and the greater emphasis placed on colonies' internal infrastructure development.

Motives and Means

Motives for European imperialism can be divided into three basic categories—economic, political, and cultural. As you might expect, Marxist historians stress the push of economic factors arising from the expansive nature of capitalism. However, other historians contend that the pursuit of even valueless colonies demonstrates the power of national prestige as a driving force, or that the cultural impulse to "civilize inferior peoples" acted as more than a cynical pretext, but as a genuine idealistic mission.

- **Economic motives**—As nations industrialized, they needed access to **raw materials,** particularly with the more sophisticated industries of the Second Industrial Revolution. Rubber, oil, bauxite, copper, diamonds—all could be found in great supply in Asia, Africa, and Latin America. With European rivalries heating up, the great powers did not wish to depend on potential enemies for supplies of strategic resources, and so **colonies** opened the door for **self-sufficiency.** In addition, with the problems of overproduction, nations looked to colonies as **markets** for finished products and outlets for **investment** of profits. However, most of the imperialist powers' capital went into more established industrialized areas, such as the United States or other European nations.
- **Political motives**—Imperialist powers coveted certain locations for their strategic value. Great Britain bought up shares in the Suez Canal Company and eventually formed a **protectorate** (a nominally independent state indirectly controlled by another state) over Egypt

in 1882 because of the strategic value of the Suez as a "lifeline to the British Empire." When the United States became an imperial power in 1898 after the Spanish-American War, it looked at the Philippines and Pacific islands as important coaling stations or military bases. Nations such as Italy pursued colonies at great cost primarily as a claim to status as one of the great powers. After 1871, the European powers carved up Africa with a **nationalistic fervor** driven by public opinion. In Germany, Bismarck disdained colonies in Africa but pursued them anyway to appease public opinion; colonies are "for elections," he said. Finally, many feared that the mushrooming European population (from 260 million in 1850 to 450 million in 1914) would lead to political discontent. Colonies might act as an **outlet for surplus population;** indeed, 30 to 50 million immigrants left Europe in this period, but most went to the United States, the Americas, or Australia.

- **Cultural motives**—Missionaries arrived first in Africa. The famous David Livingstone traveled to the Dark Continent as a medical missionary and was followed by British middle-class Victorians who believed it was their duty to civilize the supposedly inferior races. This paternalistic European attitude finds perfect expression in **Rudyard Kipling's** (1865–1936) famous poem "The White Man's Burden," which some view as an endorsement of the civilizing mission, whereas others view it as a satire. By the 1870s, the influence of Charles Darwin's ideas (see next chapter) had seeped into the consciousness of writers, businessmen, and political leaders. Many viewed history as an ongoing struggle among races for resources and territory. In this **Racial Darwinism,** war elevated the nation by calling for self-sacrifice and establishing the proper hierarchy among the victors and the defeated. Europeans often took their easy subjugation of technologically inferior tribal peoples as a moral endorsement of their imperial ambitions.

> **Heads Up!** You be the judge on this historical controversy. Access to the poem is available at the Modern Internet History Sourcebook: www.fordham.edu/halsall/mod/Kipling.html.

How was it possible for the small continent of Europe to control, directly or indirectly, almost two-thirds of the world's population by 1914? First, European control arose directly from the technological advances of the Second Industrial Revolution. Steam power, telegraphs, medical advances (e.g., the discovery of quinine to treat malaria), and railroads allowed for global trade and communication as well as penetration of the interior of Africa and Asia. Second, with the industrialization of war, Europeans gained an overwhelming military superiority. The Asian civilizations of India and China, not to mention the tribal societies of Africa, proved no match for high-powered artillery, armored battleships, and machine guns. Finally, the complex and highly organized nature of modern corporate capitalism sustained a long-term presence in colonies and provided for the systematic exploitation of resources.

The Partition of Africa

In 1870, Europe had colonized little of Africa; most areas beyond the coastline were unknown. The pursuit of African colonies got under way with the founding of the International Congo Association in 1878 by **King Leopold II** (r. 1865–1909) of Belgium. Private bankers financed Leopold's venture, which was an entirely personal rather than national concern. In response to the possible opening of Africa, Bismarck called in 1884–1885 the **Berlin Conference** among the great powers. The imperial powers agreed to create the **Congo Free State** as Leopold's personal fiefdom and also devised procedures for the orderly establishment of colonies. Leopold's rule proved to be one of the harshest in Africa, as he ignored the prohibition on slavery, plundered the nation of rubber and ivory, and did nothing while the native population was decimated by disease and overwork.

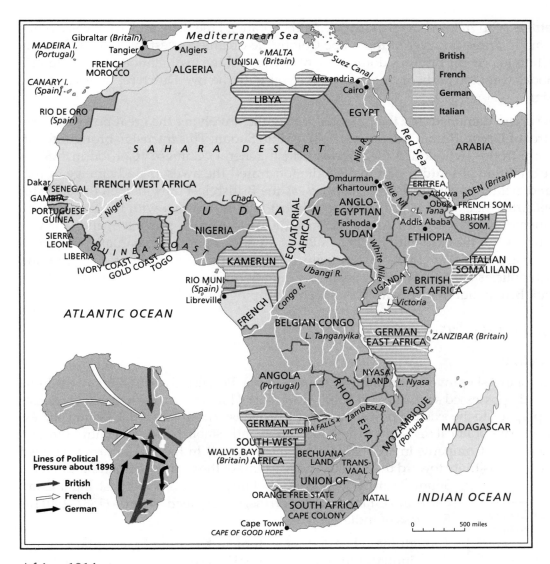

Africa, 1914

The Berlin Conference produced the opposite of the intended effect. By simply establishing coastal control, European nations could claim huge swaths of Africa's interior by drawing lines on a map, usually with no regard for linguistic or tribal divisions. Imperialists exploited Africans' lack of experience with European legal and economic concepts, with tribal leaders often casually signing away trade and resource concessions. By 1900, all except Liberia and Ethiopia had fallen under direct European rule.

To understand the nature of African imperialism, we examine the British example briefly. Early on, colonial secretary **Joseph Chamberlain** (1836–1914) favored the creation of a tariff union between Britain and its colonies. Fearing the spread of independence movements, Chamberlain wished to bind Britain's colonies together by a system of "imperial preferences." Gradually these dominions (self-governing areas such as Canada) would achieve complete self-rule but maintain strong economic ties with the mother country. Chamberlain's idea would later bear fruit with the commonwealth system after World War I. African imperialism seemed to belong to adventurers like **Cecil Rhodes** (1853–1902) rather than statesmen like Chamberlain. Britain had already established in 1815 control of the Cape of Good Hope on the southern end of Africa, dispossessing the Dutch settlers who trekked overland to create the Orange Free State and Transvaal. When Rhodes was made prime minister of this Cape Colony, he dreamed of establishing a **Cape-to-Cairo** connection to cement Britain's dominance of Africa and the exploitation of his diamond interests. Rhodes went too far by trying to provoke war with the two Dutch republics and was forced to resign.

African imperialism demonstrated the potential for conflict involving the great powers. To secure the control of Egypt, Britain extended its power into Sudan. This intrusion brought resistance by Muslim troops, who killed the famous British general "Chinese" Gordon in 1885. A subsequent expedition at **Omdurman** in 1898 demonstrated the awesome advantage of machine guns and artillery over muskets and spears, as the British lost only 48 men to 10,000 for the Sudanese. After their victory, British troops almost fell into conflict with the French, who controlled much of north and west Africa, at **Fashoda.** Cooler heads prevailed, and war was avoided. Such was not the case with the Dutch Boers. Rhodes's policies eventually embroiled Britain in the costly **Boer War** (1899–1902), in which Britain's use of concentration camps and scorched-earth policies led to its international condemnation. The potential for further conflict in Africa shook Britain out of its isolation as it went shopping for allies.

Imperialism in Asia—Three Examples

The British in India

European control in Asia proved more indirect than in Africa. Because civilizations such as India and China already possessed sophisticated political and social hierarchies, European imperialists preferred to "plug in" to the existing power structure to establish control. In India, Britain had exploited that country's political divisions to gain local allies and establish indirect control through the British East India Company. In 1857, soldiers (called sepoys) in the Indian army revolted against Britain's insensitivity toward the Hindus and Muslims of the country. Britain subdued the **Sepoy Mutiny** with great brutality, dissolved the East India Company, and established direct rule, with **Queen Victoria** (1837–1901) as Empress of India.

> **Heads Up!** For a literary take on how imperialism distorted the attitudes of the colonizer and the colonized, read the very short story by George Orwell, "Shooting an Elephant" (1936), accessible at www.online-literature.com/orwell/887/.

Though India boasted its own manufacturing base, Britain turned the country into a raw materials producer. On the other hand, Britain attempted to modernize India's culture by building railroads, instructing the population in English, and educating elites at British universities so they might become effective civil servants. Ironically, many such students imbibed Western ideas of nationalism and equality, tools that would be used by the likes of **Mahatma Gandhi** (1869–1948) and **Jawaharlal Nehru** (1889–1964) to establish Indian independence later.

The Carving of China

China disdained contact with foreigners and generally dismissed them as uncivilized. However, the weakness of the Qing Dynasty (1644–1911) allowed westerners to exploit China's growing disintegration to their advantage. Though Europeans coveted Chinese goods, the only commodity Europeans seemed able to sell in China was opium. When the Chinese government attempted to stop the import of this noxious substance, the British responded with overwhelming military force. After several such Opium Wars at midcentury, Britain and France had

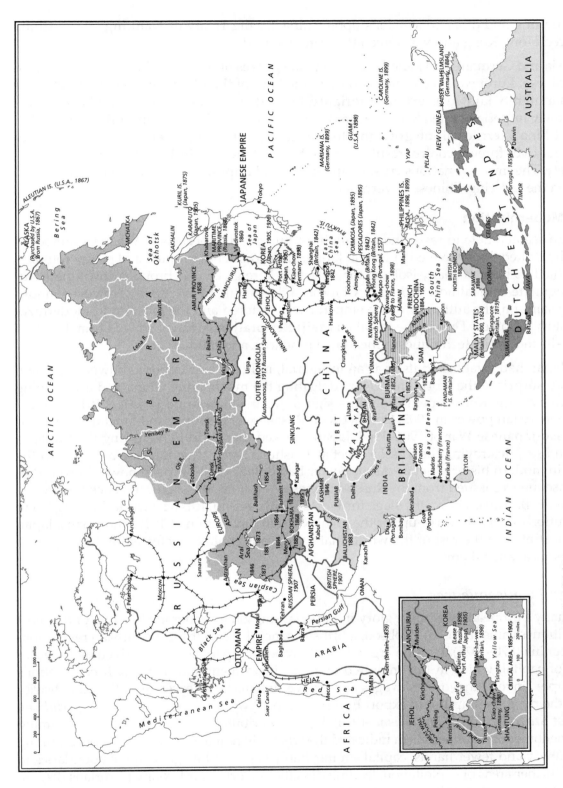

Imperialism in Asia, 1840–1914

imposed trading and other concessions upon China. By the **Treaty of Nanking** (1842), China surrendered Hong Kong and was forced to create free-trade "treaty" ports.

Soon Russia and Germany had joined in carving out **spheres of influence** in China. Even worse for the Chinese, Europeans were subject only to the laws of their home nation, not to those of China, an indignity known as **extraterritoriality.** In an attempt to keep open the Chinese market, the newly imperial United States secured agreement to the **Open Door Policy,** an effort to maintain China's territorial integrity and the free access of each power to the others' treaty ports. Anger over foreign control resulted in the **Boxer Rebellion** in 1900, led by a secret Chinese society. The imperial nations crushed the revolt and imposed even more indemnities and controls on the faltering Chinese government.

Japan's Modernization

Only Japan seemed able to resist the onslaught of European imperialism. When Commodore Perry of the United States arrived in 1853 in Japan, he encountered a united and prosperous civilization that had been virtually isolated for 300 years. Foreign contact brought down the Tokugawa Shogunate and almost led to a Chinese-style treatment of Japan. However, under reforming samurai, the authority of the emperor was restored and the most rapid modernization in history followed. During the so-called **Meiji Restoration,** Japan borrowed from the West liberally—its industrial techniques, educational practices, and military arts.

By 1890, Japan had established itself as an industrial, military, and imperial power in its own right. Japan surprised the world in 1894 by defeating the much larger China and establishing dominance over the Korean peninsula. In a sign of Japan's newfound prestige, Britain allied with the new Asian power in 1902. Conflict with Russia over resources in Manchuria soon led to the **Russo-Japanese War** of 1904–1905. Japan shocked the world by defeating the Russians on land and sea, destroying the Russian fleet at Tsushima Strait. The outcome represented the first time in modern history that an Asian power had defeated a European power in war. Profound consequences issued from the Russo-Japanese War: First, Russia turned back toward expansion in the Balkans, setting the stage for World War I; second, Russia's weak showing led to the Revolution of 1905, a warm-up for the great Russian Revolution of 1917; and finally, Japan had demonstrated to the rest of the world that Europeans could be defeated by turning their own weapons against them.

Critics and Consequences

Though many Europeans saw great glory in imperialism, some condemned it. Two of the most famous critiques came from J. A. Hobson, a British economist, and the great Russian revolutionary, **V. I. Lenin** (1870–1924). Hobson argued that European imperialism was driven by the accumulation of capital, which in turn required overseas investment and markets. If corporations would simply "invest" in workers' wages and if governments taxed excess wealth and redistributed it to the poor, the impulse to export European capital would diminish. In his *Imperialism, the Highest Stage of World Capitalism* (1916), Lenin contributed to Marxist theory by claiming that the phenomenon of imperialism indicated the crisis inherent in capitalism. By concentrating power in fewer and fewer hands, capitalism inevitably expanded its geographic boundaries in pursuit of further areas of exploitation, leading directly to World War I. Many historians dispute these assertions; the case of Italy is instructive. Italy desperately pursued colonies in Africa. In fact, at the hands of Ethiopia in 1898, Italy experienced the first major defeat by a European power in Africa. Nonetheless, Italy persisted in its ventures, risking war and diplomatic isolation, to gain, in 1911, Libya, a vast expanse of desert hardly worth the cost in men, money, and resources.

How did European imperialism change Europe and the world? There are several arguments:

- **Rise of new powers**—As a result of colonial opportunities, the United States and Japan both rose as imperial powers. After the Spanish-American War (1898), the United States acquired its first overseas possessions—Hawaii, the Philippines, and control of Cuba and the Panama Canal. The rise of these two Pacific powers would lead later to their conflict in World War II.
- **Intensification of European rivalries**—World War I did not begin in Africa or Asia, but the seeds of war were planted in colonies. To illustrate, conflicts between Russia and Britain over Persia and between Germany and France in the Moroccan Crises (1905, 1911) helped cement the mutually antagonistic alliance systems that escalated that conflict.
- **Decolonization and dependency**—Europe's hold on it colonies weakened after World War I and was severed after World War II. Today, no European nation possesses a colonial empire, yet issues of colonial dependence and resentment toward former European (and American) dominance show up in terrorism, tribal conflicts, and persistent economic underdevelopment.

Imperialism reveals a domestic connection as well. Colonial ventures acted as a laboratory for some to test the ideas of Darwinism and **eugenics** (the pseudoscience of studying racial characteristics), as well as new industrial and military technologies. The overseas drive for colonies reveals the intense domestic pressures operating at home—social, intellectual, and political. In the next chapter, we turn to these issues.

ADDITIONAL RESOURCES

Craig, Gordon, *Germany, 1866–1945* (1978)—The interested student might focus on the relevant sections for a strong narrative account of German unification.

Hamerow, T. S., *Otto von Bismarck: A Historical Assessment* (rev. 1994)—This volume provides various interpretations on a key figure of the period.

Headrick, Daniel, *The Tentacles of Progress* (1988)—The author concentrates on the important role of technology in imperialism.

Hobsbawn, Eric, *The Age of Empire, 1875–1914* (1988)—An insightful account of the period from a famous Marxist historian.

Hochschild, Adam, *King Leopold's Ghost: A Story of Greed, Terror, and Heroism in Colonial Africa* (1998)—A gripping account of one of the worst experiences under imperial rule.

Pakenham, Thomas, *The Scramble for Africa* (1991)—Strong narrative account of the partitioning of Africa.

Rich, Norman, *Great Power Diplomacy, 1814–1914* (1992)—A survey of European diplomacy in an important era.

www.postcolonialweb.org/—This site provides literature from the perspective of former British colonies.

PRACTICE QUESTIONS

1. A major feature of realism in the arts and in literature in the nineteenth century involved:
   a. an emphasis on the experiences of the upper classes.
   b. scenes of social harmony arising from reform movements.
   c. the portrayal of people trapped in economic and social forces.
   d. the glorification of national and military traditions.
   e. an abstract style requiring knowledge of the author or artist.

2. The quotation below represents an idea essential to the work of which of the following?
   a. Auguste Comte
   b. G. W. F. Hegel
   c. Napoleon III
   d. Cecil Rhodes
   e. Karl Marx

   "Freeman and slave, patrician and plebian, lord and serf, guild-master and journeyman—in a word, oppressor and oppressed, stood in constant opposition to one another, carried on an uninterrupted, now hidden, now open fight, a fight that each time ended, either in a revolutionary reconstitution of society at large, or in the common ruin of the contending classes."

3. Which of the following best explains the motives of Prime Minister Camillo Cavour for involving Piedmont-Sardinia in the Crimean War (1853–1856)?
   a. to test out Piedmont's new military technologies
   b. to block Russian expansion in the Balkans
   c. to rally the other Italian states for unity
   d. to gain the support of a great power
   e. to undermine revolutionary movements at home

4. All of the following were employed by Bismarck in the unification of Germany EXCEPT:
   a. waging war against Austria to drive it out of German affairs.
   b. collecting taxes for army reform without the Reichstag's approval.
   c. annexing German states to Prussia to form the North German Confederation.
   d. supporting the Polish rebellion against Russia to advance nationalism.
   e. goading France into war by editing the Ems Dispatch.

5. Which of the following conflicts effectively destroyed the Concert of Europe?
   a. Crimean War (1853–1856)
   b. Franco-Prussian War (1870–1871)
   c. Boer War (1899–1902)
   d. Russo-Japanese War (1904–1905)
   e. World War I (1914–1918)

6. Which of the following nation-building reforms among the great powers is INCORRECT?
   a. France—expansion of credit and transportation
   b. Great Britain—regulation of factories and public health
   c. Russia—creation of local assemblies
   d. Austria-Hungary—independence for Slavic minorities
   e. Germany—adoption of universal male suffrage

7. The Second Industrial Revolution differed from the first in that it:
   a. focused on new techniques rather than technologies.
   b. was concentrated mainly in central Europe.
   c. had little effect on the lower classes.
   d. avoided volatile economic cycles.
   e. was much larger in scale and scope.

8. Which of the following best expresses the relationship between European economic developments and imperialism in Asia and Africa?
   a. Europe's poor economy led businesses to seek profits elsewhere.
   b. Industrial processes fed demand for raw materials overseas.
   c. Fluctuating currencies promoted efforts at worldwide market control.
   d. Widespread strikes led governments to seek outlets for the discontented.
   e. Stable business conditions allowed for orderly colonial development.

9. This cartoon represents a contemporary characterization of which of the following?
   a. British designs for a Cape-to-Cairo connection in Africa
   b. an endorsement of the "White Man's Burden"
   c. German plans to dominate Africa after its unification
   d. a satire on Italy's inability to win an African colony
   e. the potential for conflict in Africa between France and Britain

10. Which of the following best explains the impact of the Russo-Japanese War (1904–1905)?
    a. The position of Russia was strengthened in the Balkans.
    b. Britain allied with Japan to check a growing Russia.
    c. It sparked nationalist movements against European imperialism.
    d. The decline of the Ottoman Empire was halted in the Balkans.
    e. China's division into spheres of influences was completed.

SAMPLE ESSAY

Efforts toward the unification of both Italy and Germany failed during the revolutions of 1848. Analyze how Cavour and Bismarck learned the "lessons of '48" and employed Realpolitik *to accomplish the unifications of their respective nations in the period 1850–1871.*

The revolutions of 1848 ambitiously attempted to undo the hated Congress of Vienna and fulfill national goals. Both Italy and Germany waged futile campaigns to unite their nations. They failed because they lacked real power. While slogans and passionate belief were useful for agitation, they were not sufficient for a successful revolution. Foreign intervention crushed these revolts. If you wanted to become unified, you needed power—armies, railroads, and bureaucracies. Also, diplomacy required getting the support of an outside power. Cavour of Italy and Bismarck of Germany proved very successful at this realistic strategy, known as *Realpolitik.*

Many Italian nationalists, like Mazzini, were passionate republicans. They created revolutionary groups and met in secret around campfires. However, it was a shrewd businessman like Cavour who actually did the hard work of Italian unification. After he became prime minister of Piedmont, Cavour built up industry, reformed the state, and built a good army. Even though it had no real interests in the Crimean War, Piedmont joined in the fighting, just so it could gain an ally. Which they did when Piedmont allied with Napoleon III of France against Austria, the nation that controlled most of Italy. After this war, Piedmont gained territory but also many states flocked to join them. Cavour did not stop there; he told the famous revolutionary Garibaldi to attack the king of southern Italy. Then when he did this, Cavour actually convinced Garibaldi to turn it over to Piedmont. The new kingdom of Italy was born, all because one man practiced Machiavellian politics like conducting a symphony.

Bismarck was even better at *Realpolitik* than Cavour. When Bismarck became Chancellor of Prussia in the 1860s, the nation was in a crisis between the king (Wilhelm) and the Reichstag, which would not approve taxes for the army. Bismarck simply collected the taxes without the approval of the legislature, and later when his policies proved successful, they voted the taxes legal. In other words, Bismarck was so good at *Realpolitik,* he got the legislature to ratify his illegal acts! After this, Bismarck put that army to use in three separate wars—against Denmark, Austria, and France. In each of these conflicts, Bismarck made sure his opponents were isolated and made them appear in the wrong, like when Napoleon declared war on Prussia because of a fake insult that Bismarck had manufactured. In some cases, Bismarck even treated the defeated nation with lenience, as with Austria in 1866. He was counting on being allies with them later and did not want to anger them too much. Bismarck was able to do what many German leaders had failed to do for centuries—unite his nation.

Both of these leaders practiced realistic politics to a tee. They certainly learned the lessons of 1848 well. They focused on real means of power; they used armies and diplomacy to unite their nations. As Bismarck said, we need "iron and blood," which also applies to economic power. And after Germany was unified, its economy really took off. We should credit these two men with a great accomplishment, though the new nations also upset the balance of power, which would lead to more wars in the next decades.

This is a model essay. Clearly the student demonstrates a mastery of the topic, as well as a strong logical structure. Though this is a two-part question, the student addresses both parts in the introduction and links them together, showing how the "lessons of 1848" translated into policies for Cavour and Bismarck. Body paragraphs show a strong connection to the thesis and ample evidence for support. Though the response does not always explicitly refer back to the terms of the questions ("lessons of 1848"), it is obvious that the student addresses the question. Finally, the conclusion brings the reader back to the thesis, but also adds a few additional examples and perspectives, including the strategy of "looking forward" to the impact of Italian and German unification. That the conclusion reads somewhat choppily need not detract from an otherwise excellent essay. Score: 9.

CHAPTER 13
The Challenges of Modern Europe, 1850–1914

By 1914, Europe had reached the zenith of its power and influence in the world. Many observers hailed this era of technological advance, scientific discovery, democratic reform, and creativity in the arts as *la belle époque,* or Europe's golden age. Optimists proclaimed the coming utopia where remaining problems would be solved by the application of the scientific method and tapping the energies of Europe's industrial and political structures. Concurrent with Europe's greatest accomplishments, modern trends toward mass politics, mass society, and mass production threatened to overwhelm classical Liberal ideas of individualism and rationality. Outsiders demanded inclusion in the political process and often used violence to liberate themselves from traditional restrictions. Intellectual trends emphasized themes of struggle and the irrational, and glorified violence and war. Art moved from the objective portrayal of reality to subjective emotional states and abstraction. Amid the power and prosperity, many sensed an impending explosion of either revolutionary violence or war. This fear provides a contrasting pessimistic perspective on this era of plenty— the *fin de siècle,* or the end of an era.

> **Note:** to users of Palmer, Colton, and Kramer, *A History of the Modern World*, this chapter combines Chapters 14 and 15 in your textbook.

MASS SOCIETY

Demographic Trends

> **Heads Up!** Try to develop a short-hand understanding for each century in the course as it relates to demographic developments. The AP Exam usually includes three or four questions on this topic, often with a chart. For example, you might describe the nineteenth century as "rapid expansion and urbanization." Then do this for the other centuries.

Industrialization and improved public health and medicine supported a rapidly expanding European population from 1850 to 1914. During the period, Europe's population soared by 75 percent, from 260 to 450 million. Much of the increase was fueled by a drop in the death rate, not a rise in the birth rate. Europe began to adopt the modern population trend of smaller family sizes with an increasing life expectancy. Long the most populous nation in Europe, France first experienced a leveling off of its population around 1830 and eventually was surpassed by Germany and Britain by 1914. In addition to the rising population, more people congregated in industrial cities. By the end of the period, Great Britain housed more than half its population in urban areas. Cities ballooned in size, taxing infrastructure and causing a myriad of problems for governments to address. This new urban context formed the breeding ground for a culture of mass leisure and mass politics.

Medicine

The late nineteenth and early twentieth centuries stand as the heroic age of medicine. Central to this breakthrough was the discovery of bacteria and the germ theory of disease. **Louis Pasteur** (1822–1895) demonstrated how microorganisms caused disease and devised a method for killing them in liquids, called pasteurization. To combat infectious diseases, Pasteur advanced the field of **vaccination,** developing a rabies vaccine, and helped to create the modern field of immunology. Using Pasteur's ideas, **Joseph Lister** (1827–1912) developed the first **antiseptic** treatment for wounds and for use by physicians before surgery. Surgery itself became safer with the development of **anesthetics** by American William T. G. Morton, who pioneered the use of ether. Improved clinical training allowed for the continuation of such discoveries. In the United States, **Johns Hopkins University** was incorporated in Baltimore along the German university model, with a focus on research; its medical program and associated hospital set the standard for a new scientific and clinical approach to medicine. Governments recognized the importance of public health in an urban setting, wishing to avoid infectious disease outbreaks and potential unrest among the working classes. The British government, for example, tracked the spread of disease, established public health boards, sponsored vaccinations, and introduced modern sewage and sanitation.

Urban Reform and Mass Leisure

By 1870, most governments recognized the need for urban reform. In the late nineteenth and early twentieth centuries, states systematically began to address problems such as pollution, working and living conditions, and transportation. Moreover, urban planners advocated the development of public parks, architectural attractions, and cultural amenities. We have already addressed how **Baron von Haussmann** (1809–1891) helped rebuild Paris to include grand boulevards, opera houses, theaters, shopping areas, and modern sewage and sanitation to make it the cultural center of France. In the process, many workers and poorer residents lost their housing to the new grandiose buildings. This Haussmannization was completed in other major European cities, notably in Vienna with its **Ringstrasse,** a famous boulevard circling the city and an attraction with its architecture, history, and shopping. New technological developments, such as electricity, provided cleaner power sources and allowed for the construction of subways and streetcars. Social reformers addressed the need for public housing for the poorer classes, and though states responded slowly, they did provide increased inspection and higher minimum standards. They also encouraged municipal and private charitable efforts. In Britain, Octavia Hill symbolized a new public spirit by championing local associations in providing "social housing" for the poor.

An increase in **leisure time** coincided with urban reform. With the recognition of unions and protective legislation by governments, workers began to realize improved wages and shorter working hours. Many reformers were concerned about the lower classes using this time for excessive drinking, crime, or revolutionary agitation. Cities created organized leisure pursuits to meet this need, such as dance halls, amusement parks, and sporting contests. With their competitive ethos, team spirit, and regimentation, **sports** teams paralleled military discipline. Rules for soccer, tennis, cricket, and others were formalized in this period to allow for orderly play and avoid violence. Nationalists created gymnastics associations to promote discipline and physical fitness. The ideas of Racial Darwinism influenced notions of national health and spurred the physical fitness ethos. Not surprisingly, the competitive nations of Europe established the modern Olympiad first held in 1896 in Athens.

Education and Literacy

Literacy rates increased markedly in the period 1850–1914, with some states in western Europe achieving nearly universal literacy. Governments came to view state-supported compulsory education as essential to their national interests. Educated citizens could handle the more complex demands of an industrial and increasingly service-oriented economy. Under the Liberal administration of William Gladstone, the Parliament passed the **Education Act of 1870,** establishing the basis for elementary education in Britain. For nations like Germany, the traditional *Gymnasia* and *Realschule* systems were expanded and extended to all classes. Literate citizens held political opinions and could read dissenting opinions; however, governments increasingly exploited nationalism and xenophobia (fear of foreigners) for purposes of national unity.

Family and Childhood

In Britain, **Queen Victoria** (1837–1901) became the model of domestic propriety; this **Victorian ideal** reflected distinct gender roles for men and women. Males were to dominate the rough-and-tumble public sphere of business, politics, and war while women managed the domestic sphere. In this model, the home was viewed as a refuge from the harsh world outside and women were viewed as its moral guardians. Isabella Beeton published her *Book of Household Management* (1859) to introduce women to this fine art of domestic engineering.

> **Heads Up!** For social history topics, such as family and child-rearing, it is useful to create brief timelines that give you the big picture, so that you can link specific historical content to more general trends.

With the decline in birth rates, European families invested increasing resources in the upbringing of their children. Enlightenment attitudes of childhood as a distinct phase of development seeped slowly down to all classes. New attitudes were reflected in governmental legislation restricting child labor and providing for compulsory schooling. Reformers and educators created special games, toys, books, clothing, and activities for children. Reflecting the trend toward mass leisure and physical fitness, the Boy Scouts and Girl Scouts were both founded in the first decade of the twentieth century.

MASS POLITICS

Historians speak of the rise of mass politics in the second half of the nineteenth century. Mass politics arose from the Dual Revolution—the ideal of representative government and public opinion as reflected in the French Revolution *and* the development of transportation and communication technologies as a product of industrialization. Three basic features characterize mass politics in the period 1850–1914:

- **Mass communication**—With telegraphs, telephones, radio, and cheap newspapers, governments both responded to and manipulated public opinion. Literate and educated citizens demonstrated awareness of political issues and expected governments to reflect national interests.
- **Democracy <u>and</u> Authoritarianism**—Despite democratic forms such as elections, representation, and constitutions, authoritarian structures (ruling dynasties, bureaucracies, the military) continued to play the decisive policy-making role in most states.
- **Increase in conflict**—Public opinion also sharpened ethnic and class conflict. "Outsiders," such as women, workers, and ethnic/religious minorities, demanded inclusion in the political process while demagogues (those who appeal to prejudice and fear) fanned popular hatreds such as anti-Semitism and extreme nationalism.

Liberal Accomplishments and Challenges

The nineteenth century marked the high tide of classical Liberalism. By 1880, Liberals had accomplished many of the items on their economic, social, political, and religious agendas. Symbols of the Liberal achievement include:

- **Constitutional government**
- **Representative assemblies**
- **Free trade**
- **Expansion of suffrage (the vote)**
- **Guarantees of rights** (though not always observed)
- **Middle-class influence in government**
- **Spread of education and literacy**
- **Weakening of established churches**
- **Self-determination for nations** (though not for all)

Most of these points reflect the Liberal concern for individual rights, representative government, economic freedom, and the expansion of opportunity. Despite these significant outward achievements, classical Liberalism was already weakening by 1880. Mass politics mobilized citizens in large groups and allowed authoritarian leaders to manipulate public sentiment; individual and minority rights were often threatened by this trend. With an increasingly complex industrial economy, it became difficult to sustain a laissez-faire approach to the side effects of industrialization—urban blight, crime, poor working conditions, and boom-and-bust cycles. Already by 1880, many governments had abandoned free trade in favor of protecting domestic markets. Many Liberal parties had by 1900 abandoned the notion of pure capitalism in favor of extending social welfare benefits to those in need. Finally, rising nationalism, imperial conflicts, and the militarization of society strengthened the hand of authoritarian interests, who seemed ready to subvert Liberal ideas and institutions in times of crisis or emergency. As you review the following discussions of nations, keep in mind these themes of mass politics and the successes of and challenges to Liberalism.

France and the Tensions of the Third Republic

Ideological differences have marked French politics since 1789, and the **Third Republic** (1870–1940) proved no different. You may recall the poor start to the Third Republic—class conflict followed the end of the Second Empire and loss in the Franco-Prussian War. Moderate republicans crushed the revolutionary government of the **Paris Commune** and either shot or exiled 30,000 of its participants. By 1878 and after exploiting divisions within the royalist camp, moderates had succeeded in establishing the basis for a parliamentary democracy. Nonetheless, important groups, such as the Catholic Church and monarchists, never reconciled themselves to the existence of republican government, which they associated with the worst excesses of the French Revolution.

Two important public scandals highlighted the divisions within the Third Republic. Bringing together conservative elements and radical republicans who wished to avenge France's recent defeat against Prussia, **General Boulanger** (1837–1891) seemed poised to take over the government and establishment military rule. However, Boulanger lost his nerve at the last minute and fled the nation. The **Dreyfus Affair** proved even more serious and divisive. In 1894, a French military court found Captain Alfred Dreyfus, a Jewish officer, guilty of treason on very thin evidence. Despite indications Dreyfus was innocent and was the victim of anti-Semitism, he was sent to Devil's Island, and the army refused to reopen the case. Republicans and even foreign governments rallied to Dreyfus's cause, which became the legal case of its day. French author **Emile Zola** (1840–1902) condemned authoritarian institutions in his pamphlet *J'Accuse* (*I Accuse*) and made the issue a test of republican strength in France. Eventually the government pardoned Dreyfus, but the fallout continued. Republicans conducted an anticlerical campaign culminating in the complete separation of church and state in 1905 and the secularization of education by the state.

Parliamentary Democracy in Britain

Britain's **Victorian Age** represented a period of prosperity, imperial greatness, and the evolution of a true parliamentary democracy. Unlike the continent, reform in Britain was driven by the competing visions of two mass political parties—the **Conservatives** and the **Liberals**—and was implemented locally rather than by a centralized bureaucracy. Parliament passed two further reform bills in 1867 and 1884, expanding the vote to almost all adult males. The brilliant though occasionally arrogant **William Gladstone** (1809–1898) led the Liberal reform effort, geared toward expanding opportunity and lifting religious and political restrictions on citizens. Under Gladstone's first prime ministry, the Parliament enacted universal schooling, the secret ballot, and legalized unions; introduced civil service exams; and lifted religious requirements for universities. Conservatives under **Benjamin Disraeli** (1804–1881) pursued a philosophy of protecting workers from the worst effects of industrialization, passing acts regulating public housing and sanitation.

By 1900, the Liberal party had abandoned its laissez-faire economic approach, and in an effort to combat support for the new Labour Party (see following discussion) moved toward the development of a social welfare state. Between 1906 and 1916, the Liberal Party initiated a wide-ranging welfare system of sickness, accident, old-age, and unemployment insurance (**National Insurance Act**—1911). To conciliate labor, restrictions on strikes and unions were lifted. To pay for these programs, Parliament passed progressive income and inheritance taxes. When the House of Lords attempted to block the legislation, its veto power was removed with the **Parliament Act of 1911**. Despite these efforts, workers continued to agitate for improved working conditions, initiating a wave of strikes in 1911 and 1912. Moreover, women's groups pushing for the vote, called **suffragettes** (see following discussion), used militant tactics to gain publicity for their cause and provoked embarrassing conflicts with police and government. Britain's most difficult issue, however, continued to be the situation in Ireland. Though Gladstone had disestablished the Anglican Church in Ireland and assisted tenant farmers there, the Catholic Irish demanded home rule. **Home Rule** split the Liberal Party and was not granted until 1914, but implementation was delayed until 1922 because of the outbreak of World War I. Though an age of greatness, the Victorian Age also saw Germany and the United States surpass Britain in industrial production and the increased tensions of mass parliamentary democracy.

Germany's Growing Pains

After its unification, German industrial, political, and military power soared. However, this rapid development placed great strains on an authoritarian political system struggling to incorporate its democratic forms. One figure dominated German imperial politics until 1890— Chancellor Otto von Bismarck (r. 1862–1890). Bismarck successfully manipulated democratic politics and the party system in the Reichstag to enact his policies. First, Bismarck allied himself with the Liberal Party, which supported his attack on the Catholic Church in Germany. The *Kulturkampf* (struggle for culture) arose from the complex situation surrounding Italian unification. Pope Pius IX (r. 1846–1878), who lost the Papal States in 1870, condemned modern ideas such as religious toleration, nationalism, and Liberalism in his *Syllabus of Errors* (1864), and in 1870 called the First Vatican Council to enunciate the doctrine of **papal infallibility** (that is, the acceptance of papal decrees on doctrine without question). In response, Bismarck pushed through the Reichstag laws restricting the powers of the clergy, expelled the Jesuits, and jailed a number of bishops. When the campaign proved unsuccessful, and after Pius died in 1878, Bismarck abandoned it and formed an alliance with the **Catholic Center Party.**

Bismarck now moved to restrict the power of the **Social Democratic Party** (SPD). Though Marxist in theory, the SPD, in fact, operated as a moderate socialist party interested in obtaining benefits for the working class through the exercise of political power. Using several assassination attempts against Kaiser William I (r. 1861–1888) as pretext, Bismarck won approval for several **Antisocialist Laws,** which restricted the ability of the SPD to meet and publish its newspaper. To win over workers, Bismarck initiated a welfare program (what he called "**state socialism**"), the first in Europe, of old age, accident, unemployment, and health benefits. Despite these efforts, support for the SPD continued to grow. To appease extreme nationalists such as the **Pan-German League** and industrialists, Bismarck moved further away from Liberalism in the 1880s with protective tariffs and the pursuit of colonies in Africa. When the young, erratic, and ambitious **Kaiser William II** (r. 1888–1918) ascended to the throne upon the unexpected death of his father, he soon dismissed Bismarck and embarked on a more conciliatory policy toward the SPD at home and a more aggressive foreign policy abroad. With immense potential power, emerging conflicts at home, and an insecure ruler, Germany was poised for entrance into World War I.

Austria-Hungary: Ethnic Tensions

Austria-Hungary continued to experience ethnic tensions after the creation of the Dual Monarchy in 1867. Within Hungary, large landholders continued to dominate, and the Magyars imposed their language and culture on the many Slavic minorities in their section of the empire. To manage the political situation in Austria, Prime Minister Edward von Taaffe (1833–1895) expanded voting rights and tried to win over the Czechs, Slovaks, and Poles by including them in the Imperial Parliament (Reichsrat) and appealing to their loyalty toward the Habsburg emperor. German nationalists resented these policies, and the resulting tensions often led to the breakdown of parliamentary function. Anti-Semitism emerged as a political force in Austrian politics with the rise of the **Christian Social Party.** From 1897 to 1910, **Karl Lueger** (1844–1910) served as mayor of Vienna and pursued policies of restriction and exclusion against Jews. It seemed that on the eve of World War I, the Habsburg Empire was fracturing along nationalist and ethnic lines.

> **Sidebar:** While Lueger was mayor, Adolph Hitler lived in Vienna as a struggling artist. It was here that Hitler first encountered members of the Jewish community and developed his anti-Semitic views, taking Lueger as a model of an uncompromising anti-Semite.

Other Areas and Developments

To develop the theme of mass politics, the nations just discussed should prove sufficient for purposes of the AP Exam. To complete the picture, we review Italy and Spain as well.

As noted in the previous chapter, Italy faced a rocky road after unification. Liberal parties in the parliament engaged in the suspect practice of *trasformismo,* whereby political leaders attempted to keep out extremist nationalists on the right and socialists on the left by use of bribery and personal alliances. As a result, Italy did not develop political parties around consistent ideas or programs but along shifting personal relationships. To illustrate, the leader most associated with the practice of *trasformismo,* Giovanni Giolitti, served as prime minister five different times between 1892 and 1922. Economically, northern Italy industrialized while the south remained mired in poverty and illiteracy. Irrational antiparliamentary ideologies and an active anarchist movement also plagued Italian political life.

Spain lingered on the periphery of European events in nineteenth century. Despite its constitutional monarchy and parliamentary democracy, Spain continued to be dominated by conservative interests, such as large landowners and the Catholic Church. Spain's defeat in 1898 in the Spanish-American War led to a loss of its empire and calls for social reform, led by a group of intellectuals known as the **Generation of 1898.** Like other less-developed nations, Spain encountered anarchist violence. In 1909, anarchists in Barcelona resisted government efforts to call up army reserves, leading to an armed clash. Because of its preoccupation with internal divisions, Spain did not enter either of the world wars in the twentieth century.

Parliamentary democracy had taken root in most European nations by 1914. All but Romania and Hungary allowed universal male suffrage prior to World War I. Political parties developed modern techniques of electioneering, communication, and institutional organization. In short, political life in many ways was more stable and democratic than it had ever been. However, many still felt excluded from the political process and agitated for change, often straining the new foundations of democratic government.

Outsiders in Mass Politics

Workers and Socialist Variants

By the late nineteenth century, workers were able to leverage their growing numbers into political influence. This influence expressed itself in a variety of ways. Early unions faced the difficulties of government opposition and small numbers. By the 1870s and 1880s, most states had recognized the rights of unions to bargain collectively for better wages and working conditions. Many trade unions supported such a "bread-and-butter" approach. Workers suffered from the boom-and-bust cycles of the period 1873–1896 and used strikes to achieve their demands. Strikes became more violent and persistent in many nations on the eve of World War I.

With the expansion of suffrage, the working classes also created political movements to agitate for change. One of the more successful efforts occurred in Germany with the Social Democratic Party (SPD), founded in the 1870s by moderate socialists. Though officially adhering to the Marxist doctrine of class warfare, the SPD in reality acted as a mass-based political party dedicated to winning seats in the German Reichstag. Despite Bismarck's efforts to eliminate their party, the SPD grew into the largest party in the Reichstag by 1912. Other socialist parties were founded in France, Italy, and Russia in the late nineteenth century. To organize for the coming socialist revolution, the leaders of these parties formed the **Second International** in 1889, which eventually broke up during the nationalism unleashed by World War I. British labor leaders and intellectuals, such as H. G. Wells (1866–1946) and George Bernard Shaw (1856–1950), advanced a more moderate, or **Fabian,** socialist movement. In 1900, Scottish worker **James Keir Hardie** (1856–1915) helped organize the movement into the **Labour Party,** which won 29 seats in 1906 and eventually became Britain's second political party.

By 1900, it was clear to many socialists that the Marxist prediction of impending revolution was a way off in the future. In addition, many believed that participation in democratic processes might better secure workers' rights than violent means. These insights led to the development of **Revisionist socialism,** or the brand of socialism represented by most of the western and central European socialist parties. In Germany, the primary voice of this evolutionary path was **Eduard Bernstein** (1850–1932), and in France, **Jean Jaurès** (1859–1914). Militant socialists condemned this "sell-out" to capitalism and worked to expel them from the International.

In less-developed nations where workers were smaller in numbers, revolutionary movements focused more on violent tactics or mass political agitation. French workers boasted a strong tradition of militant action stemming from the French revolution. Influenced by the ideas of French philosopher **Georges Sorel** (1847–1922), **anarcho-syndicalists** worked to create a single industrial union aimed at shutting down the nation through the General Strike, an act that gained a force of mythological proportions. Pure **anarchism** arose out of the Russian experience—no democratic tradition or social institutions. **Mikhail Bakunin** (1814–76) opposed all governmental systems as a corruption of human freedom and a tool of the privileged classes. Anarchists believed that assassination ("the Act") would sever the "head" of the leader from the body of the government, thus opening the way for voluntary and mutual associations of free individuals. Despite thousands of assassinations across Russia of other European leaders, anarchism seemed only to deepen government repression in the face of such "terrorism."

The "New Woman" and Feminism

During this period, feminists articulated a clear agenda for change and achieved some significant economic and political gains. Economic developments during the Second Industrial Revolution allowed women to establish a measure of autonomy. **"White-collar" jobs** in new economic sectors—telephone operators, clerks, nurses, teachers—provided many women with income and better working conditions. However, many working-class women found themselves strapped with the dual responsibility of raising children at home while aiding the family income through the assembly of simple items, known as **"sweating."** The measure of autonomy from these jobs led many women, particularly those in the middle classes, to demand economic and legal reforms.

The first area women targeted for reform was the legal system. In some western nations between 1850 and 1914, women gained the right to control property, divorce, and gain custody of their children. Most states prohibited the publication and distribution of information regarding birth control. **Annie Besant** of Britain (1847–1933) and **Margaret Sanger** of the United States (1879–1966) both championed the cause of birth control in the face of obscenity laws, believing female control of reproduction a vital element of the feminist program. Reflecting the double standard regarding sex, the British Parliament in the 1860s passed the Contagious Diseases Acts, which required prostitutes to submit to tests for venereal disease and be confined to prison hospitals if found to be infected. Due to the unyielding efforts of reformer **Josephine Butler** (1828–1906), Parliament repealed the laws in 1886.

Some women viewed suffrage as the logical culmination of the advance toward women's equality. Suffragettes, as they were called, established a transatlantic movement to push for the right to vote. These suffragettes were led in Britain by the **Pankhurst** family—**Emmeline** (1858–1928) and her daughters Christabel and **Sylvia** (1882–1960). The Pankhursts' organization, the **Women's Social and Political Union** (WSPU), participated in militant actions to gain the vote—throwing eggs at public officials, arson, chaining themselves to public buildings, hunger strikes, and in the case of Emily Davison, throwing herself in front of the king's horse at a racing event. Government officials even attempted to force-feed the jailed protestors. Eventually, many nations in western and northern Europe granted women the vote immediately after World War I, a recognition of their contributions to that conflict.

The independent figures just highlighted earned the designation of **New Women.** Though many if not most women accepted as natural the dependent and domestic role prescribed by tradition, these females articulated and lived an autonomous existence. They were not confined to an explicitly feminist agenda. Italian education reformer **Maria Montessori** (1870–1952) pioneered a child-centered elementary curriculum. **Florence Nightingale** (1820–1910) and others founded the modern nursing profession. British-born **Elizabeth Blackwell** (1821–1910) became the first women in the United States to earn an M.D. degree and established a hospital for the poor in 1857. Literature also reflected themes of independent women. In Henrik Ibsen's play "A Doll's House," his character Nora Helmer eventually leaves her traditional marriage and children to establish her own personhood; the play provoked controversy for its scathing critique of the sexual double standard inherit in the Victorian ideal.

Sidebar: Is Judaism a religion or a race? Clearly, Judaism consists primarily in a set of religious beliefs, one of the oldest such sets in the world today. Saying Jews are a race strikes many as reminiscent of Nazi ideology designed to stigmatize Jews as "alien." Because race is genetically inherited, it would seem clear that Judaism is not a race; but it does seem more than a religion. Many secular Jews still consider themselves part of the Jewish "nation" or "people," which may be the best way to think of this identity.

Jews, Anti-Semitism, and Zionism

With the Enlightenment and French Revolution, many governments liberated Jews from their segregated existence in ghettoes and from legal restrictions. Throughout the nineteenth century, this **emancipation** led to the **assimilation** of Jews into business, medicine, law, and academia. Prominent Jewish intellectuals, such as Marx, Freud, and Einstein, not only contributed significantly to developments in the period but also seemed to provoke a backlash of **anti-Semitism.** Anti-Semitism was nothing new to Europe and traditionally was based on religious discrimination. In the late nineteenth century, anti-Semitism took on a new racial tone, indirectly influenced by Charles Darwin's ideas of struggle among species. Mass politics fed the creation of popular anti-Semitic political movements, especially strong in central Europe. In response to anti-Semitism, some prominent Jews called for the creation of a Jewish homeland. Appalled by the Dreyfus Affair in France, Austrian journalist **Theodor Herzl** (1860–1904) founded **Zionism** in the 1890s, which resulted in the immigration of thousands of Jews to Palestine, then controlled by the Ottoman Empire. Some nations, such as Russia, organized persecutions against Jews, called **pogroms,** to divert popular energies away from potential antistate activities. Despite the assimilation of millions of Jews into European cultural and economic life, they remained a vulnerable religious and ethnic minority. It is not difficult to see the outlines of the future Holocaust already taking shape in the nineteenth century.

Heads Up! On the AP Exam, one FRQ is usually dedicated to a major intellectual movement, such as the Renaissance or Scientific Revolution. The period 1850–1914 forms a rich source for such questions. In terms of your studying, you are well advised to focus on the "big three" of Darwin, Freud, and Marx (addressed in the previous chapter).

MODERN IDEAS

As an intellectual framework, modernism was born in the period 1850–1914. In philosophy, the sciences, and the social sciences, many thinkers helped fulfill the Enlightenment project of using reason to discover the laws of nature in various fields. However, many cherished Enlightenment notions were called into question by the emerging trends of irrationality, subjectivity, randomness, and struggle. As you read the following discussion, attend not only to specific intellectuals and their ideas but also how their contributions represent a challenge to Enlightenment beliefs in progress, rationality, and objectivity.

New Ideas in Science

Darwinian Evolution

Evolution was not a new idea in the nineteenth century. Previous versions explained evolution by the inheritance of acquired characteristics. After studying the diversity of bird species on the Galapagos Islands (off the coast of Ecuador), **Charles Darwin** (1809–1882) concluded that the finches he observed descended from a common ancestor. Knowing his theory would be controversial, Darwin waited 25 years to work out the details before publishing *On the Origin of the Species* (1859), easily one of the most influential scientific works ever published. Darwin borrowed from Malthus's population theories to argue that species are locked in a constant struggle for resources and survival. Through **random variations** (what we would call mutations, but Darwin did not understand the mechanism that produced them), some individuals gained a survival advantage in a local environment. If an evolutionary change was "successful," the mutation would spread within a species population through reproduction, eventually producing new species. What Darwin called **natural selection,** and others later termed "**survival of the fittest,**" suggested that biological development occurred *randomly*, not through design or purpose. All of nature seemed in chaotic flux, with no role for the permanent and the "good," as defined in theological terms.

Darwin's theory caused an immediate uproar and was condemned by religious figures, particularly those committed to biblical literalism. Not only did Darwin reject the hand of God in creation, his theory suggested that the earth was millions, not thousands, of years in age. Geological developments in the nineteenth century seemed to provide confirmation for Darwin's rejection of a "young earth." Many scientists and intellectuals, such as **T. H. Huxley** (1825–1894), known as "Darwin's Bulldog," rushed to Darwin's defense. Austrian monk **Gregor Mendel** (1822–1884) later provided additional support for natural selection by articulating the gene theory of reproduction. With *The Descent of Man* (1871), Darwin applied his theory to the evolution of the human race from earlier primate species, once again undermining humanity's special place in the universe. Though some counseled dialogue between religion and science, partisans on both sides drew the cultural lines sharply between "atheistic science" and "superstitious religion."

The New Physics

Newtonian physics ruled the world of science for two centuries. In addition to providing accurate explanations of natural phenomena, Newtonian mechanics offered an appealing vision of the cosmos as orderly and predictable. Quantum mechanics and relativity theory undermined this confidence. Accepted theory held that the atom was the simplest particle and indestructible, the fundamental building block of reality. Accumulating scientific evidence proved this atomic theory incorrect. **Marie Curie** (1867–1934) demonstrated how atoms emitted radioactive energy as they disintegrated. British scientists J. J. Thomson and Ernest Rutherford elaborated a more complex view of the atom as made up mostly of empty space and comprising subatomic particles. Such discoveries provided practical applications, as with **William Röntgen's** (1845–1923) discovery of the x-ray and its ability to see within the human body.

German physicist **Max Planck** (1858–1947) in 1900 articulated the **quantum theory.** According to Planck, particles did not emit or absorb energy in constant streams but in bundles, or "packets," of energy. Further, experiments demonstrated how light acted sometimes as a particle and sometimes as a wave, depending on the circumstances of observation. More jarring to the Newtonian view, it was demonstrated that the behavior of many particles could only be expressed by probability, not with objective certainty.

It took the great physicist **Albert Einstein** (1879–1955) to transform our commonsense assumptions regarding time and space. Through a series of scholarly articles, Einstein argued that absolute time and space do not exist, but rather are relative to the observer and his or her status of motion. For example, Einstein showed how for objects that traveled at or near the speed of light, time slows down relative to a "stationary" observer. To our three-dimensional universe, Einstein's **relativity theory** thus added another dimension—**space-time.** In the presence of a massive object, such as the sun, space and time *both* curve, as was confirmed from observations of a solar eclipse in 1919. In addition, Einstein expressed how matter and energy were interconvertible in the famous formula, $e = mc^2$. This discovery suggested how the destruction of an atom might potentially liberate massive amounts of energy and/or destruction.

Advance of the Social Sciences

As European civilization became more complex, the social sciences offered further explanation for human behavior. Many of the social sciences were born during the Enlightenment but reached their modern expression during this period. Psychology, political science, anthropology, criminology, and sociology each demonstrated how human behavior resulted from impersonal economic, political, and social forces. And many of these theories radically altered Europeans' conception of human nature.

Freudian Psychology and the Irrational

Enlightenment *philosophés* fairly glorified human reason. **Sigmund Freud** (1856–1939), in contrast, revealed the instinctual and unconscious nature of human behavior. Based on his systematic clinical studies, Freud developed his theory and practice of **psychoanalysis,** wherein the therapist attempted to "unlock" the hidden desires, fears, and memories of the patient that caused his mental illness. Freud divided the psyche into the **id** (the "pleasure principle"), the **ego** (reason), and **superego** (conscience), and claimed that unresolved conflicts among these parts created neuroses. Unpleasant or painful memories might be buried in the **subconscious,** though such memories could be explored through hypnosis and analysis of the patient's dreams, a conclusion articulated in *The Interpretation of Dreams* (1900). Perhaps most controversially, Freud claimed that sexual feelings occurred early in life, with children developing through a series of stages, each marked by a conflict, such as the hidden desire to replace the parent of the same sex in the eyes of the parent of opposite sex (the **Oedipal** or **Electra complex**). Freud's ideas gained increasing currency during the twentieth century and added an entirely new psychological vocabulary to everyday experiences.

Sociology

Freud's work showed that human action often resulted from factors other than human choice. His work found additional support. Russian psychologist **Ivan Pavlov** (1849–1936) famously demonstrated how he could condition dogs to salivate automatically at a particular signal, and suggested that human behavior could also be controlled through the appropriate stimuli. Criminologists gathered statistics and performed studies to show that criminal behavior might result from genetic inheritance rather than deliberate choice, a conclusion subversive to the cherished notion of free will. Sociologists such as **Max Weber** (1864–1920) and Emile Durkheim explored the influences of impersonal bureaucratic structures and crowd mentalities on the individual. In Weber's study, he determined that only a charismatic individual could overcome the inertia of large institutions.

Social scientists borrowed the methods and ideas of science. Many recognized the power of Darwinian theory to explain cultural and historical evolution. British sociologist **Herbert Spencer** (1820–1903) applied Darwin's ideas to society to produce Social Darwinism. Spencer argued that inequalities and divisions with classes or races resulted from the same process of natural selection as applied to human affairs. Public aid and charity for the destitute would only weaken the genetic pool and cause more suffering in the long run; it was Spencer who coined the phrase "survival of the fittest." Nationalists distorted Darwinian science to advance their ideas of racial inferiority, producing a **Racial Darwinist** support for European imperialism of Africa and Asia. Francis Galton, a cousin of Darwin's, developed the pseudoscience of race, known as **eugenics,** in attempt to better the human race through selective breeding. In the context of competitive nation-states, Darwin's ideas eventually found their way into justifications for war as a natural mechanism to separate the fit from the unfit.

Philosophy: A Flight to the Irrational

Philosophy had long upheld reason, but in the late nineteenth century, the most influential philosophers showed the power of irrationality. French thinker **Henri Bergson** (1859–1941) introduced his theory of "**vitalism,**" which held that nature could not be divided into analyzable units or discrete parts, as practiced by the scientific method. According to Bergson, irreducible vital forces pervaded the natural world, suggesting that human behavior was driven by the same forces and therefore not capable of being reduced to any set of explanatory factors. Beginning with the provocative assertion "God is dead," German philosopher **Friedrich Nietzsche** (1844–1900) embraced in his thinking the chaos and flux inherent in nature. Ideas did not actually represent reality, which was inaccessible to human reason. Human systems of thought and morality represented a "**will to power,**" and constituted tools for the individual to overcome himself. Nietzsche also recognized that human nature comprised both the rational and the instinctual. Christianity twisted human nature by teaching people to suppress their natural tendencies toward domination and self-assertion. Morality, for Nietzsche, was personal and beyond common conceptions of good and evil. Ultimately, Nietzsche called on the best Europeans—not the "herdlike masses"—to create a new, more honest system of values and to make of their lives a "work of art."

Religion: The Challenge of Modernism

Modern ideas produced a crisis for Protestant and Catholic Christianity. As is clear from the previous descriptions, scientific and philosophical works stressed secular if not openly anti-Christian approaches to knowledge. Even within religious communities, some scholars attempted to update religious beliefs to reflect modern techniques of understanding. French historian Ernst Renan (1823–1892) in his *Life of Jesus* explained the origins of Christianity as if Jesus were merely human and a result of historical, not providential, forces. Being more committed to the Bible as the source of authority, Protestants found it difficult to shield members from such ideas. As a result, Protestant denominations began to split between modernists and fundamentalists, as church attendance declined in Europe or merely expressed adherence to customs.

Sidebar: The division within Protestantism between modernists and fundamentalists continues to this day; however, this conflict is primarily an American, rather than a European, phenomenon. Battles over Darwinian theory are unknown in Europe, as growing secularism and miniscule church attendance has virtually settled the issue.

The long and conservative pontificate of **Pope Pius IX** (r. 1846–1878) represented the high tide of the Catholic Church's reaction to modernism. His successor, **Leo XIII** (r. 1878–1903), attempted to tone down antimodern attacks and advance the cause of social justice. Leo ended the prohibition of Catholics' participation in Italian politics and formulated a social doctrine that combined a belief in private property with a concern for poverty and inequality. In the encyclical *Rerum Novarum* ("of modern things"), Leo suggested that much in socialism reflected Christian teachings, but he firmly rejected Marxist ideology as materialist and antireligious. Perhaps with the Galileo incident firmly in mind, the Church refrained from issuing any condemnations of Darwinian theory, adopting a wait-and-see attitude. Catholic Church attendance remained fairly stable through the period, but the Church's full reconciliation with modern trends would not occur until the second half of the twentieth century.

THE AVANT-GARDE IN THE ARTS

A diversity of cutting-edge artistic movements marked the period 1850–1914. Artists placed a premium on experimentation and self-expression within the media of paint, architecture, print, and music. For purposes of preparing for the AP Exam, it is helpful to consider art as a reflection on the economic, political, and social context in which it was created. As you review the following discussion, keep in mind the dominant themes of industrialization, nationalism, mass politics, and imperialism.

Painting: Beyond Representation

Photography altered the purpose of the artist. By 1860, the technology of picture-taking was perfected, and photography emerged as both an artistic medium and a means of photojournalism. Danish-American Jacob Riis (1849–1914) used his camera to document the underworld of New York City's slums and back alleys in his book *How the Other Half Lives*. While photography provided new tools to journalists, it seemed to undermine a traditional purpose of painting—to represent life and nature—as the camera could accomplish this more directly.

Impressionism

The first major artistic trend following the invention of photography was **Impressionism.** A self-named movement, Impressionism attempted to capture "how the eye really sees," with off-center positioning, visible brushstrokes, fleeting glimpses of street scenes, and exploration of light and shadow. **Claude Monet** (1840–1926) named the French-centered movement and became famous for his many depictions of water lilies, haystacks, and Notre Dame Cathedral at different times of day. For good depictions of the Impressionist interest in middle-class scenes of urban life and its interest in glimpses of reality, see **Pierre-Auguste Renoir's** (1841–1919) *Dance at Le Moulin de la Galette* or *Luncheon of the Boating Party*. In **Edgar Degas's** (1834–1917) paintings of ballet studios, we appreciate the Impressionist experimentation with perspective and off-centered framing. Demonstrating the international flavor of the movement, American **Mary Cassatt** (1844–1926) exhibited her works of domestic scenes, such as a mother bathing her child, with her European compatriots in Impressionism.

Postimpressionism

Postimpressionists moved away from the Impressionist fascination with light and shadow. More interested in form and structure, major postimpressionist painters included **Vincent Van Gogh** (1853–1890), **Paul Cézanne** (1839–1906), **Paul Gauguin** (1848–1903), and **George Seurat** (1859–1891). Though Van Gogh sold only one painting in his lifetime, his paintings today sell for tens of millions of dollars. Expressing his inner psychological torment, Van Gogh painted with swirling brushstrokes and, showing the influence of Japanese woodblock prints, distorted perspective and a strong palette of yellows. Van Gogh's unique style is best seen in *Starry Night* and the *Night Café*. Van Gogh's suicide in 1890 seemed to capture the archetype of the tortured artist. Cézanne incorporated a geometric approach in his paintings and with his still lifes, how depth and the passage of time might be captured if we look at an object with a binocular vision, first with one eye and then the other. Frustrated by what he considered the overly artificial nature of European painting, Paul Gauguin traveled to Tahiti and developed a primitive style of bulky figures and simple lines reminiscent of the artistic styles of the Pacific. Georges Seurat created a related movement named **pointillism,** after the small "dots" of color, which when combined formed a clear picture of shadow and light. Seurat's *Sunday Afternoon on the Island of La Grande Jatte* provides a view of the individualistic leisure of the modern city.

Expressionism

Near the turn of the century, artistic experimentation accelerated. A group of French painters known as the Fauves, or "wild beasts," emphasized strong fields of color and simple lines to convey expression over detail. When **Henri Matisse** (1869–1954) received criticism for his work *Green Stripe*, a portrait of his wife with a green stripe down the middle of her face, he replied, "I have not made a woman, I have painted a painting." Like the later **expressionists,** Matisse demonstrated that the key task of the artist was not to represent but to convey an emotional stance. To appreciate the intensity of expressionist distortion and use of color to capture the angst and alienation of modern Europe, one must view Norwegian **Edvard Munch's** (1863–1944) *The Scream,* in which a ghostly figure's silent scream wafts into an ominous red sky. Painting gradually moved toward abstraction, as with the Russian **Wassily Kandinsky's** (1866–1944) canvases exploding with color, designed to convey musical compositions in visual form—a genre known as abstract expressionism.

Cubism and Futurism

Prior to World War I, the movements of Cubism and futurism most directly show the influence of technology on artistic representation. Founded by Georges Braque and **Pablo Picasso** (1881–1973), **Cubism** broke apart scenes into analyzable parts and reassembled them in unique ways to provide the viewer with simultaneous multiple perspectives. In this way, Cubists employed the revolutionary insights of Einstein's theory of relativity to art. One of the first paintings in the Cubist style was Picasso's *Les Demoiselles d'Avignon* (1907), which stirred controversy for its unconventional depiction of female beauty by portraying a group of prostitutes with African and Oceanic masks for faces. Picasso painted in many styles, creating one of the most prolific and influential collection of works by any artist. The Italian **futurists** F. T. Marinetti and **Umberto Boccioni** (1882–1916) glorified speed and technology in art as a means to achieve political change. Not content simply with artistic creation, the futurists published manifestoes calling for the abolition of traditional aesthetics (such as nudes, religion, and historical paintings) in favor of automobiles, airplanes, and industrial plants, though many of Boccioni's works, such as *Dynamism of a Cyclist*, actually have *motion* as their subject. Futurism fizzled out in the technological nightmare that was World War I.

Modern Architecture

Modern buildings express the ideal that **"form follows function."** Instead of employing ornamentation or classical motifs, modern architects allow the functional requirements of a building to determine its shape and logic. The first modern architects were American and used the new building materials of concrete, reinforced steel, and glass. **Louis Sullivan** (1856–1924) created the first skyscrapers and designed buildings with simple, clean lines and few decorative elements. **Frank Lloyd Wright** (1867–1959) strove to create a new aesthetic for single-family homes, replacing "Victorian monstrosities" by emphasizing horizontal lines and earth tones, called the Prairie Style. After World War I, modernism emerged as the dominant architectural style.

Literary Trends

Like art, literature reflected the larger social and intellectual context of the time. Darwin's ideas influenced the literary movement of **Naturalism.** French author **Emile Zola** (1840–1902) wrote a series of novels portraying the destructive influence of heredity on the lives of his characters, as they seemed unable to determine their actions freely. Zola's frank depiction of sex, alcoholism, and violence brought him condemnation from traditionalists. This period also represents the great age of Russian literary genius, best shown in the works of **Leo Tolstoy** (1828–1910) and **Fyodor Dostoevski** (1821–1881), both of whom explored the themes of suffering and spirituality. Tolstoy's *War and Peace* presents the reader with a tapestry of events and characters designed to show how social and economic forces trump the designs of great men. In *Crime and Punishment,* Dostoevski raised the moral dilemma of whether good ends justify evil acts. Dostoevski's lifelong theme of the individual struggling to find meaning in a world of suffering and alienation helped lay the foundations for existential philosophy in the twentieth century.

Music: Romanticism and Nationalism

Romanticism did not die in music after 1848. Many composers worked to establish national styles and continued to explore national traditions. The most influential of these figures was the German **Richard Wagner** (1813–1883), who used his music to express his vision of a revolutionary and nationalist Germany. Wagner envisioned music as a *Gesamtkunstwerk,* or "total work of art," combining all artistic genres and capable of transforming national culture. Wagner synthesized music and drama through the use of leitmotifs—musical themes that coincided with particular characters or plot lines. The *Ring Cycle,* a series of four operas spanning 16 hours, represents the culmination of Wagner's grandiose vision and is one of the most ambitious pieces of music ever written. Russian **Igor Stravinsky** (1882–1971) also explored national themes in his *Rites of Spring.* When the ballet was first performed in 1913 in Paris, its theme of pagan Russian rituals, dissonant primitive music, and unorthodox dance maneuvers caused a riot in the theater.

> **Sidebar:** Wagner's music left a profound legacy, influencing many composers and artists. His rabid anti-Semitism and grandiose German nationalism made Wagner an artistic hero to the later Adolph Hitler, whose music he sponsored and adopted in public displays of propaganda.

POSTSCRIPT—THE ROAD TO WORLD WAR I

The riot following the performance of *Rites of Spring* demonstrates the divided legacy of modernism. On one hand, advances in industry, technology, ideas, and the arts demonstrate the intense dynamism of modern European civilization. On the other hand, the themes of revolutionary liberation, racial and national struggle, and the glorification of the irrational reveal the destructive potential of Europe's modern achievements. These two themes would merge tragically in World War I.

ADDITIONAL RESOURCES

Barzun, Jacques, *Darwin, Marx, Wagner: Critique of a Heritage* (rev. 1981)—The author explores how each of the figures undermined classical Liberalism.

Kern, Stephen, *The Culture of Time and Space* (1983)—This challenging but worthwhile book explores how technology altered conceptions of time and space.

Lee, Stephen J., *Imperial Germany, 1871–1918* (1999)—A slim interpretive volume with documents, from Routledge's Questions and Analysis in History series.

Stone, Norman, *Europe Transformed: 1878–1919* (rev. 1999)—Covers major trends of the era prior to World War I but also provides insightful essays on individual nations.

Tuchman, Barabara, *The Proud Tower: A Portrait of Europe Before the War, 1890–1914* (1996)—A popular historian examines the unsettled nature of European culture and politics amidst prosperity through a series of vignettes.

Wohl, Robert, *The Generation of 1914* (1981)—This book examines the experiences of the generation that came of age right before World War I.

www.artchive.com/—You can search the site by artist or movement. An essential link to the descriptions of art given in this review guide.

www.clas.ufl.edu/users/rhatch/pages/02-TeachingResources/readingwriting/darwin/05-DARWIN-PAGE.html—This site provides links to resources on Charles Darwin and related topics.

www.time.com/time/time100/scientist/profile/freud.html—This brief essay by noted biographer Peter Gay explains Freud's influence. Part of *Time* magazine's profiles of 100 famous persons—look for other relevant figures.

www.fordham.edu/Halsall/science/sciencesbook.html#New%20Science:%20Darwin,%20Freud,%20Einstein—From the Internet History of Science Sourcebook, this page is an excellent clearinghouse for documents on the intellectual life of this important period.

www.spartacus.schoolnet.co.uk/resource.htm—Comprehensive site that provides biographies of key figures in women's suffrage, women's organizations, and feminist tactics and campaigns.

PRACTICE QUESTIONS

1. Which of the following represents a major demographic trend in Europe during the period 1850–1914?
    a. a rise in the birth rate, supporting an increased population
    b. decrease in immigration abroad, due to an expanding economy
    c. increasing population, with a greater percentage living in cities
    d. stagnant population growth, due to the advent of birth control
    e. declining life expectancy, because of poor urban conditions

2. All of the following urban improvements occurred in Europe from 1850–1914 EXCEPT:
    a. development of public parks and organized sports.
    b. better standards of public health and medical care.
    c. creation of public transportation such as streetcars.
    d. government guarantee of public housing for the poor.
    e. consumer provisions such as theaters and department stores.

3. Which best characterizes the results of feminist agitation for equality prior to World War I (1914)?
    a. Women had gained the right to vote in most European states.
    b. Legal and economic rights were extended to women in several nations.
    c. Large percentages of women entered college and the professions.
    d. Several prominent women gained leadership roles in western Europe.
    e. Governments reduced economic opportunities for women in reprisal.

4. The most successful socialist party before World War I in Europe was in:
    a. Germany.
    b. Britain.
    c. France.
    d. Spain.
    e. Russia.

5. During the late nineteenth century most European governments operated in an environment of mass politics. What resulted from this trend before 1914?
    a. development of nationalist and extremist groups
    b. the establishment of several socialist governments
    c. an increase in social harmony and compromise
    d. continuous warfare among the great powers
    e. a return to absolute monarchy in some states

6. Which of the following is the most accurate characterization of anti-Semitism in the second half of the nineteenth century?
    a. Governments made strong public efforts to eliminate anti-Semitism.
    b. The Dreyfus Affair led to Kaiser Wilhelm II's dismissal of Bismarck.
    c. As Jews assimilated into European society, anti-Semitism decreased.
    d. Renewed anti-Semitism caused Britain to curtail the rights of Jews.
    e. Anti-Semitism was expressed increasingly in racial and political terms.

7. In his *Origin of the Species* (1859), Darwin argued that:
    a. humans are an inferior species compared with other primates.
    b. evolution occurs through random variations, not design.
    c. all spiritual truths are false from a biological basis.
    d. acquired traits could be inherited via reproduction.
    e. mass extinction would result unless humans stopped industry.

8. In this passage, Sigmund Freud addresses a psychological concept important to his theories. Which concept is that?
   a. superego
   b. repression
   c. Oedipal complex
   d. subconscious
   e. pleasure principle

"Dreams are not comparable to the spontaneous sounds made by a musical instrument struck by some external force rather than by the hand of a performer; they are not meaningless, not absurd. They are a completely valid psychological phenomenon, specifically the fulfillment of wishes. Dreams can be classified in the continuity of waking mental states; they are constructed through highly complicated intellectual activity."

9. Of the following sets of figures in the period 1850–1914, which are most associated with developing theories related to quantum mechanics, radioactivity, and relativity theory, respectively?
   a. Ernest Rutherford, Albert Einstein, Max Planck
   b. Marie Curie, J. J. Thomson, Albert Einstein
   c. Niels Bohr, Max Planck, Marie Curie
   d. William Röntgen, Ernest Rutherford, Niels Bohr
   e. Max Planck, Marie Curie, Albert Einstein

10. The accompanying painting is associated with which of the following modern art movements?
    a. Impressionism
    b. postimpressionism
    c. Cubism
    d. abstract expressionism
    e. futurism

Digital Image © The Museum of Modern Art/Licensed by SCALA/Art Resource, NY. © 2007 The Estate of Pablo Picasso/Artists Rights Society (ARS), New York (Les Demoiselles d'Avignon, 1907 by Pablo Picasso (1881–1973))

SAMPLE ESSAY

In what ways did feminists, workers, and Jews attempt to gain political rights and power in the period 1850–1914? To what extent did these efforts meet with success?

Mass politics dominated Europe during this period. Democracy advanced with increased voting and more representative government. As part of this development, many "outsiders" tried to be liberated from the restrictions placed on them by laws and traditions. Three of these groups were feminists, workers, and Jews. Feminists and workers used agitation, like protests and acts of violence, to gain rights. On the other hand, Jews felt more vulnerable and went about getting power in a more diplomatic and quiet way. Each group gained some power before the First World War, but workers had the most impact.

Some women did not like the restrictions placed upon them. Laws did not allow women to inherit property, divorce, and especially vote. Feminists wanted to be independent—to have careers, establish a legal personality, and exercise political power. Suffragettes in Britain like the Pankhursts marched for rights, destroyed buildings, and one even jumped in front of the king's horse to show their cause. Though women did gain some legal rights, few nations gave women voting rights before 1914.

Workers formed socialist parties and other movements, like anarchism, to gain political rights. The German Social Democratic Party ran for seats in the Reichstag and became an influential party. In fact, Chancellor Bismarck even tried to eliminate the party by outlawing their activities and introducing some welfare programs for workers. Still, this did not decrease support for the SPD. In some places, anarchists used assassinations to kill the leaders of capitalism.

During this time, anti-Semitism was on the rise, perhaps because of the ideas of Darwin. Many Jews were assimilating into European life. However, events like the Dreyfus Affair in France convinced many Jews that they needed to have their own homeland. Prominent Jews began the Zionist movement, calling for land in Palestine. Some Jews even began to move there before WWI started. Nonetheless, anti-Semitism continued and would later lead to the Holocaust.

Each of these groups shows the importance of mass politics. Feminists, workers, and Jews all struggled for power and met with different degrees of success. It just shows that if you want rights, you have to keep fighting for them with whatever you have.

Here is an example of a strong essay that might easily be improved. The student begins with a strong thesis. In fact, the introduction models an effective strategy: it gives one or two sentences of context, identifies the three groups' actions and impact, and makes a comparative conclusion regarding success. Please note that this is a two-part question, and in the body paragraphs, the student deals more directly and effectively with the first part of the question, regarding tactics. Though some attention is given to successes, the response is underdeveloped on this issue. The introduction claims that workers gained the most, but that paragraph does not address this part of the question directly. Each paragraph offers several appropriate and reasonably well-explained examples, but the support remains thin. By the end, the student seems rushed, as the conclusion adds little to the analysis in its brevity. Clearly, this student has attempted to answer the question, addressed the tasks in general but unevenly, and provides relevant evidence. However, the essay does not fulfill the promise of its strong introduction. With a few more examples and some analysis in the conclusion, this essay could easily have earned a top score. Score: 6.

CHAPTER 14
World War I and the Russian Revolution

World War I and the Russian Revolution represent the defining events of the twentieth century. For decades, intellectuals and political leaders had predicted the coming of a great war, but few expected the devastation and disillusionment that broke upon Europe in 1914. This chapter examines the complex causes of World War I—one of the most analyzed events in European history—the course and nature of the war, how various nations organized for the first total war, and how the war ended in revolution and a controversial treaty settlement at Versailles. It also explores the fall of the Romanov Dynasty in Russia—a consequence of the country's poorly organized involvement in World War I and a growing discontent with the tsarist rule. In 1917, the Bolsheviks (forerunners of the Communist Party) defeated their foes in a civil war, purging "enemies of the state" in the Red Terror and securing control of the new Union of Soviet Socialist Republics (USSR), Europe's first socialist government. The existence of the Soviet Union coincides directly with the twentieth century that helped create it, a century that began in violence and revolution.

> **Note:** To users of Palmer, Colton, and Kramer, *A History of the Modern World,* this chapter combines Chapters 17 and 18 on World War I and the Russian Revolution.

THE CAUSES OF WORLD WAR I

Who or *what* caused World War I is a hotly debated historical issue. Long-term diplomatic and political clashes building up for over a century were ignited by the assassination of the heir to the Austro-Hungarian throne, Archduke Franz Ferdinand. As you review this chapter, consider how long-term and short-term factors interacted to produce the conflict.

MAIMIN'

Students often find mnemonic devices helpful in recalling information. The standard for World War I's causes is MAIN. However, as you will see, this formula tends to overlook the importance of internal and intellectual causes, which are harder to identify precisely but are important nonetheless. Therefore, we use MAIMIN'. The following provides a bird's-eye view of these causes (and their corresponding mnemonic letter). We look more closely at these events further in the chapter.

Militarism and Military Plans—After the wars of unification in the mid-nineteenth century, armies exploded in size and firepower, driven by mass production and the dynamic Second Industrial Revolution. These technological and industrial advances rendered warfare even more efficient and deadly. Never before or since have greater percentages of populations served in their nations' military. Conscription (drafts) and regular military training militarized society by creating **mass citizen armies.** Government leaders associated national greatness with a strong military, and many adopted military dress in public ceremonies. In preparation for the upcoming conflict, nations expanded their armaments and navies.

Germany's desire to build a world-class fleet of battleships antagonized Great Britain and made an enemy out of a potential ally. *Kaiser Wilhelm II's* (r. 1888–1918) reading of American Admiral A. T. Mahan's *The Influence of Sea Power on History* (1890) convinced him that if Germany wished a "place in the sun," it must develop a commercial empire akin to Britain's. Given the Kaiser's erratic and bombastic personality, this threat to British naval dominance represented the first of many actions by Germany upsetting the balance of power after 1890. As often occurs in history, the Great War was preceded by arms and naval races.

Upon the completion of the Franco-Russian alliance in 1894, Germany began work on the **Schlieffen Plan,** designed to fight a two-front war against Russia (to the east) and France (to the west). Germany's was only the most famous of such plans; each nation developed complex blueprints involving railroad timetables, troop movements, and battle strategies that often significantly affected political decisions. These plans often limited, or were perceived to limit, the options open to policy makers and, in most cases, escalated regional clashes into an inevitable world war. For example, when Germany began mobilizing troops in 1914 in accordance with the Schlieffen Plan, all hopes of political negotiations to prevent war were lost.

Alliance System—Chancellor Otto von Bismarck worked after Germany's unification in 1871 to maintain the balance of power and prevent war through a complex system of interlocking alliances. As Bismarck put it, Germany was a "satisfied giant" that desired no additional territory. He believed a war among the great powers would be a disaster for Germany. Bismarck aimed to isolate a French nation bent on avenging the loss of Alsace-Lorraine and to stay allied with three of the five great powers. To achieve this purpose, Bismarck attempted to mediate the potential for dispute in the Balkans by forming the **Three Emperors' League** in 1873 between Germany, Austria, and Russia. This agreement proved difficult to maintain, so Bismarck formed a strong mutual defense treaty with Austria (**Austro-German Alliance**) in 1879 and the **Triple Alliance** with Italy and Austria in 1882. When Russia refused to revive the alliance with both Germany and Austria, Bismarck convinced the Russians to sign the **Reinsurance Treaty** in 1887 simply with Germany. Moreover, Bismarck maintained friendly relations with Great Britain and even avoided antagonizing France. Within the Bismarckian alliance structure, no great power could count on the support of any other should it initiate aggressive war, and might in fact trigger a hostile alliance against it.

Sidebar: World War I was also a family struggle, as most of the monarchs of Europe were related. Queen Victoria (1837–1901) of Britain acted as the matriarch, yet she also carried a recessive gene for hemophilia, a disease plaguing Tsar Nicholas's heir, Alexis. Queen Victoria was Wilhelm's grandmother, her grand-daughter Alexandra was married to Nicholas, Nicholas and Wilhelm were cousins, and the later kings of Britain Edward VII and George V were uncles to Wilhelm. In this instance, blood proved thinner than interests of state.

Kaiser Wilhelm dismissed Bismarck in 1890 and quickly undid his alliance system. Wilhelm allowed the Reinsurance Treaty with Russia to lapse, counting on his personal relation with the Russian tsar (they were cousins), which freed Russia to complete the **Franco-Russian alliance** in 1894. As it industrialized and pursued colonies more vigorously, Germany's potential military and economic might created concern among the other great powers. Wilhelm's efforts to match Britain's navy, and his militant personal style, drove France and Britain together with the **Entente Cordiale** (friendly understanding) in 1904. Soon after, in 1907, Russia, smarting from its military defeat to Japan, agreed with Britain to the **Anglo-Russian Entente** to compromise its contending interests in central Asia. These series of loose agreements among Britain, France, and Russia came to be known as the **Triple Entente,** which now opposed the Triple Alliance. Within a generation, Wilhelm had destroyed Bismarck's alliance system and caused Germany's encirclement. As of 1907, two mutually antagonistic alliances faced off, with the potential of a minor conflict between Austria and Russia dragging the whole of Europe into war. The alliance system thus acted as a chain of causation leading to an all-out war once the first trap was sprung.

Imperialism—World War I did not begin over colonial issues; however, conflicts among imperial powers increased tension and hardened the emerging alliance structure. Italy's pursuit of colonies in North Africa brought it into conflict with France and led in 1882 to its joining the Triple Alliance. To test the new alliance between France and Britain (Triple Entente), Wilhelm provoked the **Moroccan Crises of 1905 and 1911,** a dispute over French control of the North African region. His aggressive action produced the opposite of the intended effect, as the two Atlantic nations drew closer in their joint military plans. In addition, Britain's isolation during the Boer War (1899–1902) led it to approach Japan, France, and Russia in the next decade to ensure its security vis-à-vis an expansive Germany. We have already seen how Russia's imperial defeat by Japan led it to end the Anglo-Russian antagonism stretching across the nineteenth century. Finally, Italy's attack on the crumbling Ottoman Empire in pursuit of the North African colony of Libya (1911) triggered a series of crises in the Balkans culminating in World War I.

Mass Politics—By 1914, many European states faced significant internal problems—strikes, ethnic violence, extremist groups, and outsiders demanding rights. To promote unity, governments promoted imperialism and fanned nationalist sentiments. As leaders contemplated the momentous decision for war in July 1914, they may have viewed the crisis as an opportunity to solve domestic issues. When war broke out, citizens celebrated in European capitals, and political dissenters called for an end to internal disputes. Kaiser Wilhelm called for a **Burgfrieden,** or "civil peace," for the duration of the war, while in Britain, female suffrage and Irish home rule were tabled. Socialist parties, which wished to unite workers of all nations, generally supported the call to arms, in spite of their Marxist ideology. Mass politics had worked only too well in promoting popular nationalist sentiment in favor of war.

Intellectual Context—Many observers of the European scene sensed that a major war loomed on the horizon. It had been 40 years since the Franco-Prussian War, and with the advent of Darwinism and irrationality in philosophy, some glorified war as a natural product of human advance—noting how it called upon patriotism and sacrifice and separated the weak from the strong nations. For example, German writer Friedrich von Bernhardi, in *The Next War* (1912), welcomed the prospect of demonstrating Germany's national greatness and predicted that technological advances would render warfare brief and decisive. Europeans' faith in technological and scientific solutions to problems and belief in the productivity of warfare seem naïve today only because of the results of the war they produced.

Nationalism—Nationalism caused World War I in two ways: (1) by making it difficult for nations to compromise what they perceived as their national honor and (2) by feeding the ethnic tensions in the Balkans that drew Austria and Russia into conflict there.

European Diplomacy, 1871–1914

By destroying the Concert of Europe, the Crimean War not only opened the way for the unification of Italy and Germany, it effectively destroyed an international mechanism for containing conflict. Germany's defeat of France in the last of its unification wars established the perennial rivalry at the base of World War I. With this unstable diplomatic situation and intense national rivalries, all that was needed was a *casus belli* (cause of war). This proved to be the volatile situation in the Balkan peninsula, involving Austria, Russia, and the Ottoman Empire.

Like Russia, the Ottoman Empire realized its backwardness during the Crimean War. However, efforts by reformers, known as Young Turks, to introduce national citizenship, abolish religious hierarchies, and establish legal equality only provoked a conservative backlash. The "Sick Man of Europe" seemed unable to stem the disintegration of its multiethnic realm. In fact, attempts at reform led in 1876 to an unstable situation that culminated in the ethnic massacre of Christian minorities by Ottoman officials. Amid a revolutionary situation, Russia intervened, both as protector of its brother Slavs in the Balkans and in its perennial drive to gain territory at the Ottomans' expense.

The ensuing **Russo-Turkish War** (1877–1878) resulted in Russia's clear victory and the **Treaty of San Stefano,** which granted independence to Serbia, Montenegro, and Romania from the Ottoman Empire, and created a large Bulgarian state stretching from the Black Sea to the Aegean Sea. It was assumed that Russia would dominate this new **Bulgaria** and thereby gain access to the Mediterranean, threatening Britain's control of the Suez Canal. To prevent a possible Anglo-Russian conflict, Bismarck acted as an "honest broker" and called the **Congress of Berlin** (1878) to resolve the issue. The Congress decided to divide Bulgaria into varying degrees of autonomy and allowed Austria to occupy (but not annex) **Bosnia-Herzegovina,** coveted by nationalistic Serbs. Most viewed the Congress of Berlin as a defeat for Russia. The subsequent anti-German feeling in Russia led Bismarck to conclude an Austro-German alliance in 1879; however, Germany and Russia eventually reestablished friendly diplomatic relations with the Reinsurance Treaty. Nonetheless, the conflict revealed the explosive potential of the Balkans.

Beginning with the first decade of the twentieth century, the Balkans experienced a series of crises. In a rare sign of cooperation, Austria and Russia made a secret agreement in 1908 at the expense of an Ottoman Empire once again undergoing internal instability. In exchange for allowing Russia to take the strategic **Dardanelles** (straits from the Black Sea to the Mediterranean Sea), Austria was to annex Bosnia-Herzegovina, which it already occupied. Fearing the dismemberment of the Ottoman Empire, the other great powers blocked its advance into the Mediterranean. Meanwhile, Austria took Bosnia anyway, demonstrating the power of coercion over diplomacy. Russia stood humiliated, while its smaller neighbor Serbia was incensed, viewing Bosnia's Slavic population as rightfully belonging to a future greater Serbia. Soon after, Serbian pan-Slavists formed the terrorist **Black Hand,** bent on expelling Austrian influence from the Balkans.

Like a flock of vultures, the smaller Balkan nations circled the carcass of the dying Ottoman Empire. After Italy's defeat of the Turks, the smaller nations formed the Balkan League (Serbia, Bulgaria, Greece, and Montenegro) and attacked the Ottomans in the **First Balkan War** (1912–1913). Following the Balkan League's victory, Serbia stood poised to gain access to the Adriatic Sea. At the **London Conference** (1912–1913), Austria, Italy, and Germany forced upon Serbia and its protector Russia the creation of an independent Albania, designed specifically to block Serbian access to the sea. Once again, Russia had been forced to back down in its own backyard. When the victors could not agree on how to divide the conquered territory of Macedonia, Bulgaria faced off against the other Balkan nations and the Ottomans in the **Second Balkan War** (1913). Bulgaria was easily defeated. The two conflicts heightened the animosity between Serbia and Austria, convinced Russia of the need to save face in the next crisis, and set the stage for the ultimate conflict.

The July Crisis of 1914

Archduke Franz Ferdinand (1863–1914), the heir to the Austrian throne, visited the capital of Bosnia (Sarajevo) with the intention of building support for his solution to the ethnic problems in the Balkans—a Triple Monarchy. Franz Ferdinand hoped to appease the Slavic minorities in the region by granting them autonomy *within* the Habsburg empire (like the Magyars); however, the Black Hand feared the plan would undermine its goal of establishing a unified independent Serbian kingdom. To stop Ferdinand's plan and punish Austria, the Black Hand trained a group of young assassins to kill the Archduke and his wife, Sophie. On June 28, 1914, the 23-year-old **Gavrilo Princip** fulfilled his mission, plunging Europe into crisis.

Austria believed the Serbian government was behind the assassination and a month later issued it an ultimatum. Kaiser Wilhelm of Germany gave his only reliable ally a so-called **"blank check"** to settle its ethnic issue permanently, emboldening Austria to take a hard line and risk war with Serbia's ally, Russia. Fearing Germany's military plans, France in turn stood firm behind its ally Russia. Meanwhile, Britain refused to signal its intentions clearly, trying in vain to mediate the dispute. When Serbia rejected one point of Austria's ultimatum, Austria declared war against it, an action that prompted Russia's declaration of war against Austria. Russia's war plan presumed a war against *both* Germany and Austria, forcing Tsar Nicholas to mobilize his army on both nations' borders. Despite a last-minute flurry of telegrams between cousins "Willy" and "Nicky," Germany declared war on Russia, triggering the trap of the alliance system. France quickly joined the conflict, and because Germany's Schlieffen Plan had violated Belgian neutrality, Britain too declared war on Germany. Europe was now engulfed in the war for which many had planned but of a nature that few expected.

> **Heads Up!** The behavior of each nation in the July Crisis proved relevant for more than academic discussions of causation, but also to determine blame for purposes of the Treaty of Versailles. With that document, Germany was forced to accept full blame for the war, a view almost all Germans rejected. Keep this issue in mind as you consider the treaty settlement, as well as the entire postwar period.

FIGHTING ON THE FRONTS

Europe did not get the war it expected. What was supposed to be over by Christmas turned to stalemate by the end of 1914. Though the war eventually involved the nations of six continents, the hinge turned on the Western Front. It is most important for you to understand the nature of the war and its phases; do not be overly concerned with battles.

The Nature of the War

Military tactics often lag a generation behind technologies. World War I illustrates this adage in bold type. Generals of the day learned the Napoleonic tactics of rapid movement and the massed infantry assault. Military theorists assumed that the new technologies of airplanes, high-powered artillery, and machine guns would favor the traditional offensive by overwhelming a static opponent with massive firepower. The reverse turned out to be the case, as these weapons and technologies proved advantageous to entrenched defensive positions. In all, 9.2 million Europeans (almost all soldiers) were killed during World War I, largely the result of an inability to conceive of new tactics in dealing with defensive weapons.

Once the Western Front settled down to a stalemate, each side entrenched positions and fortified them with barbed wire. In between stood **"no-man's land,"** an expanse denuded of trees, houses, and crops. Generals attempted to soften up enemy positions with artillery bombardments, often lasting days, as a prelude to **"over the top,"** where infantry ran exposed through no-man's land in a vain effort to overwhelm the enemy trench. Though trenches had been used during the Crimean War and the U.S Civil War, the combatants in this war relied on them extensively. **Trench warfare** emerged as a dehumanizing and absurd symbol of the futility of World War I. Many other important technological breakthroughs occurred or were first used in World War I, but none exercised the decisive impact as hoped and only increased the body count: **tanks, airplanes,** flamethrowers, **submarines (U-boats), high-powered artillery,** grenades, **poison gas, barbed wire,** zeppelins, and aerial bombardment.

The War of Illusions: 1914

Germany gambled that its Schlieffen Plan would allow it to defeat France before Russia could mobilize. The plan called for a huge right flanking maneuver in August 1914 through Belgium to hit Paris from the back and trap the French army at Alsace-Lorraine. Violation of Belgium neutrality brought Britain in the war on the side of the Entente, and moreover, Belgium put up unexpected resistance to German forces. This resistance led to the first atrocities of the war against Belgian civilians, providing the Allies with an important propaganda weapon against their German enemy.

As the German advance toward Paris stalled, the French regrouped and hit the German flank at the Marne River. **The Miracle of the Marne** halted the German offensive. After each side unsuccessfully tried to outflank the other by racing to the English Channel, the Western Front had settled down by Christmas to a stalemate, with a string of trenches from the English Channel to the Swiss frontier—300 miles in length. On the more open and less populated Eastern Front, the Germans met with more success by capturing an entire Russian army at **Tannenberg.** This battle was the prelude to the generally poor performance of the Russian army, whose men were captured in much larger numbers than any combatant nation.

Stalemate: 1915

To break out of the stalemate, the **Central Powers** (Austria-Hungary, Germany) and the **Allied** forces (Russia, France, Britain, Belgium) expanded the war by bidding for new allies. To recapture its lost territories, Turkey joined the Central Powers in November of 1914. The Allies, meanwhile, bribed Italy, via the **Treaty of London,** with the promise of Austrian territory to join the war against the Central Powers. From 1915 to 1917, Bulgaria, Romania, and Greece all entered the conflict to achieve territorial objectives left over from the pre-1914 Balkan conflicts.

Each side engaged in probing offensives aimed at finding the enemy weak spot. To knock out the Turks and secure Europe's "soft underbelly," the British in April 1915 launched the poorly planned **Gallipoli** campaign, an amphibious assault designed to capture Constantinople and the Dardanelles. British forces found themselves pinned down on a narrow ridge and after months of futile charges withdrew in early 1916.

Germany and Great Britain both attempted to blockade the other and starve it into submission. The German navy's reliance on the submarine made blockades dangerous—the U-boat had to either surface to inspect enemy ships, making it vulnerable to enemy fire, or gamble and destroy the potential enemy craft. This problem almost brought the United States into the conflict when a German U-boat sank the British liner *Lusitania* off the coast of Ireland, killing 1,200, including 128 Americans. President Wilson was able to maintain U.S. neutrality while extracting a promise from the German government to avoid unrestricted submarine warfare. However, U.S. exports and loans to Britain and France skyrocketed as aid and trade to Germany fizzled.

Slaughter: 1916–1917

By 1916, the effects of total war were exhausting all nations involved in the conflict. To break the deadlock, Germany rolled the dice on another bold plan. In February 1916, Commander Erich von Falkenhayn launched a massive surprise attack at the key position of **Verdun** in the French line. Though the attack met with initial success, the Germans were unable to follow up their success. They did not call off the battle, however, until January 1917, making Verdun the longest battle of the war and one of the deadliest in history. In all, the French and German armies combined experienced 1.1 million casualties.

To take the pressure off the French, the British launched the **Somme** offensive in July. The battle proved a disaster for the British army, which lost 30,000 in the first three hours of the attack, known as the bloodiest day in British military history. In addition, the Russian army surprised the Austrian army with the **Brusilov Offensive,** driving their enemy back hundreds of miles before the Germans stabilized their collapsing ally. One success for the Central Powers was their victory over Serbia; this country was knocked completely out of the war, losing a greater percentage of its population than any other warring nation.

In one of the ironies of the war, the large battleships that had provoked such animosity between Britain and Germany generally stayed in port, with leaders fearful of destroying such large investments. The only major naval engagement of the war occurred in 1916 off the coast of Denmark at **Jutland.** Both sides were bloodied but survived, and the German battleships returned to port. After the armistice, the Germans scuttled (sank) their expensive fleet rather than allow it to fall into enemy hands.

Exhaustion and Revolution: 1917–1918

In 1917, the Allied forces lost a key nation: Russia. At the same time, they gained perhaps an even greater force: the United States. Russia's deteriorating economic and political situation resulted in the fall of the Romanov Dynasty, and in late 1917 the newly empowered Bolsheviks pulled Russia out of the war. Germany once again rolled the dice to end the war, betting that **unrestricted submarine warfare** around the British Isles, in violation of an earlier pledge, could knock Britain and France out of the conflict before the United States could effectively mobilize. They were wrong. The announcement of Germany's U-boat campaign, combined with the **Zimmerman Telegram**—in which the German ambassador promised Mexico the recovery of lands lost to the United States if it entered the war—drew the United States into the war in April 1917. Contrary to German plans, American involvement proved decisive.

By mid-1917, it looked as if the Central Powers might prevail. Austrian and German forces routed the Italian army at **Caporetto,** forcing the diversion of French and British forces into the difficult Alpine fighting to prop up their ally. In Belgium, British, **ANZAC** (Australian and New Zealand Army Corps), and Canadian forces worked to retake the town of **Passchendaele.** In the subsequent battle, thousands drowned in muddy shell holes, a morbid symbol of the futility of warfare. By March 1918, the Germans imposed on the Bolsheviks the severe **Treaty of Brest-Litovsk,** costing Russia significant territory and resources.

In Germany's final gamble of the war, its High Command launched one last major offensive in spring 1918 on the Western Front. Despite initial success, which brought the Germans to within 30 miles of Paris, American troops began to inject fresh manpower and morale into the Allied cause. American and French counteroffensives pushed the German lines back by early fall 1918. By this time, ethnic minorities were establishing independence from the Austrian Empire, and Germany faced a revolutionary situation at home from an exhausted populace. Though few troops stood on German soil, the German High Command asked for an armistice on November 11, 1918. The **Armistice** ended fighting, yet Europe faced a revolutionary situation in which a return to the prewar world would prove impossible.

ORGANIZING FOR TOTAL WAR

The Great War involved the full mobilization of each nation's resources and populations. Despite modern industrial, military, and bureaucratic techniques, most nations found the burdens of fighting the war an enormous strain, fueling a revolutionary mindset in 1918 and after.

Government and Economy

Pressures of total war forced the abandonment of laissez-faire practices. Governments moved quickly to oversee wartime production to ensure an adequate supply of matériel. To appreciate the demands of the Great War, you may consider that at the battle of Verdun more projectiles were dropped than in all previous warfare in human history combined. Many combatant nations managed production via bureaucratic centralization—that is, running the war effort as one large industry. In Germany, industrialist **Walter Rathenau** (1867–1922) helped Germany deal with severe shortages and maintain adequate supplies by overseeing production in the **War Ministry.** When Britain experienced a shortage of shells in 1915, future prime minister **David Lloyd George** (1863–1945) was made **Minister of Munitions** to avoid future shortfalls. Because of such policies, large businesses and labor unions benefited, as governments found it more efficient to award government contracts to and oversee large enterprises.

To pay for the war, governments exercised three options: raise taxes, depreciate currencies, and borrow money. Raising taxes could only go so far; as the war dragged on, governments grew fearful of placing any additional demands on an already strained populace. By the end of the conflict, France and Britain had borrowed significant amounts from the United States, making it a creditor for the first time in its history. All nations appealed to their citizens' patriotic duty to purchase **war bonds.** In all, the war cost the nations involved over $350 billion. Inflation acted as a hidden tax and resulted in currency depreciation, a situation that rendered a return to prewar economic stability difficult when the war finally ended.

Nationalist Unrest and Agitation

> **Sidebar:** The Allies' policies in the Middle East led directly to the current turmoil in that region. Though it is often said that tension in the Middle East involves "ancient hatreds," conflict actually resulted from the arbitrary drawing of borders and mutually exclusive promises made to various groups by the French and the British during World War I.

Almost every nation experienced internal ethnic conflicts, and their enemies attempted to exploit them. For example, the German government gave aid to Irish rebels wishing for independence from the British in the **Easter Rising** of 1916. Though British men and resources were diverted, the attempt failed. Not to be outdone, the Allies promoted the creation of independence committees for various minorities within the Austro-Hungarian empires, especially for the Poles and Czechs, an effort that yielded the dissolution of the empire by 1918. Most famously, the British sent **Colonel T. E. Lawrence** ("of Arabia," 1888–1935) to promote the cause of Arab nationalism within the Ottoman Empire. Though these efforts did not play a decisive role in the outcome of the war, they did set up future nationalist conflicts after the war.

The Home Fronts

World War I represents the culmination of the trend toward mass politics in the previous half-century. Governments called on citizens to sacrifice for the war effort by enlisting, buying war bonds, and **rationing.** Rationing went furthest in Germany. By 1916, the Kaiser had turned the government over to the famous generals **Erich Ludendorff** (1865–1937) and **Paul von Hindenburg** (1847–1934), who quietly established a military dictatorship, part of which involved allotting families ration books for a particular number of calories per day. By the end of the war, many Germans agonized over eating "sawdust bread" and shortages of essential fats and oils.

Because of the manpower shortage, many women entered the workforce outside the home for the first time. In Britain, industrialists employed women in the production of TNT and shells. Neglect of safety conditions led tragically to the poisoning and infertility of thousands of female laborers. These **"women with yellow hands"** demonstrated the potential public role of women and helped to earn women the vote in many nations after the war ended. The Provisional Government of Russia even formed a military unit, the **Women's Battalion of Death,** which saw action at the front and in defense of the state. Among other groups, skilled workers gained the most, as they won wage increases and recognition of union collaboration in production. Nonetheless, strikes did occur. Governments often responded with the promise of improved conditions *and* the threat of violence if the strike continued. By the end of the war, union discontent broke out into open rebellion, helping to bring down teetering governments in the fall of 1918. On the other hand, small business owners, those in traditional crafts, and the lower middle class often found themselves struggling with competition from large businesses favored by government officials.

Freedom is often the first casualty of war. Though states worked to build positive support for their war efforts, they were also quick to crush dissent. Early in the war, the British Parliament passed the **Defense of the Realm Act** (DORA), which in addition to regimenting the lives of British citizens also **censored the press** and allowed the government to requisition war supplies from private citizens. All states, including the United States, established stricter laws against treasonous activities and dissent against the government. Germany used spies to infiltrate radical unions, while many governments simply jailed the most outspoken opponents of the war effort.

Propaganda and Genocide

Propaganda came of age during World War I. To motivate citizens, governments employed both positive patriotic appeals with national symbols and negative attacks on the enemy, portraying the war as a battle over civilization against a brutal and inhuman foe. Demonizing the enemy seemed a logical culmination of mass political pressures in the previous half-century—anti-Semitism, xenophobia, extreme nationalism, and glorification of struggle. A tragic culmination of this logic was the first genocide of the twentieth century. In 1915, the Ottoman government feared that its Armenian Christian minority might aid the Russian war effort. Several hundred leaders of the Armenian community were executed, while thousands of Armenians were deported to camps with inadequate facilities, where between 500,000 and 1.5 million died from neglect, disease, and starvation. Even today, the Turkish government rejects the notion of an **Armenian Massacre,** though most independent scholars classify the event as an act of genocide.

> **Heads Up!** For an excellent discussion of the uses of propaganda in various nations, along with plenty of poster examples, see http://www.firstworldwar. com/ posters/index.htm.

> **Sidebar:** Peace agreements were signed with Austria (Treaty of Saint-Germain), Bulgaria (Treaty of Neuilly), Hungary (Trianon), and Turkey (Treaty of Sèvres) between 1919 and 1921. Republicans established a new Turkish government and rejected the Sèvres settlement, while fighting to prevent the dismemberment of their new state by Greece. The new Treaty of Lausanne in 1923 recognized the secular Turkish Republic. Dissatisfaction with these agreements led several nations to side with the Nazis in World War II in the hopes of regaining lost territory.

THE TREATY OF VERSAILLES AND REVOLUTION

The Treaty of Versailles ending World War I represents one of the most significant diplomatic events you will study this year and is essential to your understanding of the twentieth century. The Versailles settlement is often compared with the Congress of Vienna in 1814–1815 regarding their respective uses of collective security and the success of their decisions. Though the Allies negotiated treaties with each of the Central Powers, the settlement with Germany proved most important for future events.

Revolutionary Fallout

When the Allied victors met in the Palace of Versailles starting in January 1919, they found it nearly impossible to put "Humpty Dumpty" back together again. Revolutionary violence led to the toppling of four empires—Austro-Hungarian, German, Ottoman, and Russian. What kind of governments and states would replace these traditional diplomatic entities remained an open question. Allied leaders were prepared to confirm the **creation of new states** out of the former Habsburg Empire (Austria, Czechoslovakia, Poland, Yugoslavia, and the Baltic states of Lithuania, Latvia, and Estonia) and promote democratic governments there and in Germany. Even after the completion of treaties, revolutionary unrest continued, often fed by the existence of a new socialist government in the east, the Soviet Union.

Differing Goals for and Visions of the Peace

President Woodrow Wilson (1856–1923), the first American president to travel abroad, set foot on European soil as a hero. He authored the renowned **Fourteen Points,** his idealistic vision for reconstructing Europe and "making the world safe for democracy." He also declared that WWI should be the "war to end all wars." Wilson dreamed of a new diplomatic order guided by open diplomacy, freedom of the seas, arms reduction, national self-determination, and collective security. The last objective was to be achieved by the creation of an international governing body to mediate disputes—the **League of Nations.** Wilson knew that Germany must be punished but hoped that drastic action might be avoided to build a more secure foundation for democratic government after the war.

French Premier George Clemenceau (1841–1929), nicknamed "the Tiger," considered Wilson's vision overly idealistic and concentrated on security for France by emasculating Germany's military and economic potential. British Prime Minister David Lloyd George stood somewhere in between Wilson and Clemenceau (famously remarking, "I had God on one side and the devil on the other") in wanting to punish Germany but not utterly destroy it. And though **Prime Minister Vittorio Orlando** (1860–1952) represented Italy in negotiations, he eventually walked out in protest over Italy's territorial spoils. Importantly, Russia sat out the negotiations, as the new Bolshevik leader Lenin denounced the gathering as a capitalist plot. The Allies rejected German participation and continued the naval blockade until June 1919 when Germany signed the treaty; in all, approximately 750,000 died of starvation during and after World War I. Given these circumstances, it is not surprising that the treaty pleased no nation.

The Final Product

After months of negotiations, the reluctant German delegates signed the Versailles settlement in the palace's famous Hall of Mirrors on June 28, 1919 (five years to the day from the start of the war). By all accounts, the treaty represented a harsh peace:

- **Territorial Losses**—Germany lost 13 percent of its territory and 12 percent of its population. The important Saar industrial region was placed under League of Nations control until 1935. East Prussia was cut off from the rest of Germany to provide the new Polish state with access to the sea. Finally, Germany surrendered its overseas colonies.
- **Demilitarization**—The German army was reduced to 100,000 men, the nation's naval fleet was severely curtailed (including the banning of U-boats), and its air force was eliminated. Fearing further German aggression, the French insisted on the **demilitarization of the Rhineland,** adjacent to France.

- **War Guilt**—In perhaps the most controversial provision of the treaty, Germany was forced to accept "full responsibility" for the war via **Article 231.**
- **Reparations**—Based on the War Guilt clause, the Allies in 1921 set a reparations amount for the German government of 132 billion marks (some $33 billion), a figure most German observers considered exorbitant.
- **League of Nations**—To promote collective security, the Allies agreed to Wilson's idea of a League of Nations. However, because the U.S. Senate refused to ratify the treaty, the United States never joined, and the new Soviet Union and Germany were initially excluded.

Consequences and Conflicts

Few were fully satisfied with the Treaty of Versailles, but none less so than Germany. Germany's new postwar government, the Weimar Republic, started off with two strikes against it, being saddled with what most Germans perceived a "dictated peace." Discontent over the treaty was fed by extremists groups such as the Nazis and played a major role in bringing down Germany's short-lived experiment with democracy. Almost immediately, observers condemned the economic arrangements of the treaty. Economist **John Maynard Keynes** (1883–1946) attended the negotiations on behalf of Britain and afterward predicted in his *Economic Consequences of the Peace* (1919) the ruination of the world economy, which was not long in coming. Overall, the inability of the victors to establish a consistent diplomatic approach torpedoed their efforts at establishing a stable balance of power, but perhaps the complexity of the issues and intensity of the conflicts might have doomed any settlement. Certainly a major reason for the treaty's failure proved to be the subsequent isolation of both the United States and the Soviet Union. America's unwillingness to guarantee French security after 1920 and the fear of Soviet communism opened the way for a revival of German power. Without a full commitment to collective security and the League of Nations, Europe drifted in the next two decades toward an even more destructive conflict.

THE RUSSIAN REVOLUTION: IMPORTANCE AND CAUSES

Like World War I that sparked it, the Russian Revolution helped define the political and ideological issues of the twentieth century. Historians often compare it with the earlier French Revolution. Both revolutions proceeded through several phases, appealed to those outside their borders, and forced philosophical divisions throughout the world. One difference, however, was that France stood as Europe's leading nation in 1789 when its revolution began, whereas Russia lagged behind in 1914. Russia's revolution did prove more immediately successful, though, as the Bolsheviks secured power and held it for three quarters of a century. In France, the Old Regime returned to control in 1814, just 25 years after the struggle began. Without the Russian Revolution, the history of the twentieth century—including World War II, the Cold War, decolonization, and the nuclear arms race—would be a different story.

Long-Term Causes, 1861–1905

Throughout its history, Russia faced two perennial and irresolvable problems: (1) its technological and economic backwardness vis-à-vis the other European powers and (2) its inability to develop a form of government that successfully harnessed the will of its people. The Russian Revolution can be viewed as a drastic solution to these problems.

Following Alexander II's (r. 1855–1881) reforms, Russia seemed to be moving in the right direction. However, each top-down move by the government engendered a new set of problems.

Following the abolition of serfdom, former serfs were forced to continue living on the *mirs* (rural communities practicing subsistence agriculture) until they had paid for their lands. Moreover, large landholders (the **gentry**) garnered most of the best lands for themselves, sticking former serfs with the rest. Rural overcrowding and a shortage of land led to continual unrest in the countryside, which served as a magnet for revolutionary groups.

Russian intellectuals were divided between those who lauded the unique features of Russia's Slavic culture (called **Slavophiles**) and those who believed the nation needed to become more like the West to survive (**Westernizers**). As Russia industrialized after 1880 under the leadership of Finance Minister **Sergei Witte** (1849–1915), these divisions deepened. Many of the worst problems of industrialization previously experienced by western European nations seemed accentuated within Russia's undemocratic political system. Moreover, the rapid pace of advance proved problematic. Industry and the attending urban problems of overcrowding, pollution, and poor working/living conditions were concentrated in two cities—**Moscow** and **St. Petersburg.** Russian manufacturing enterprises tended to be large, making it easy for workers to organize politically. As such, large cities and factories emerged as centers of proletarian unrest and revolution in subsequent decades.

Reform only seemed to fuel the growth of movements that wished to take things further. Among the Slavophiles, an anarchist movement known as the **People's Will** succeeded in assassinating Alexander II in 1881, causing a brutal suppression of revolutionary groups by his successor, the reactionary **Alexander III** (r. 1881–1894). Anarchists succeeded, in fact, in assassinating thousands of Russian officials between 1870 and 1914. Less violent but also radical were the **Social Revolutionaries,** who favored a socialism led by the peasants that stressed Russia's rural tradition. Westernizers stood strongly divided between the **Constitutional Democrats** (Cadets), who favored the development of a capitalist economy and a parliamentary democracy like Britain's, and the Social Democrats, a Marxist party founded in 1898 in exile. Even within the **Social Democrats,** divisions existed; the **Mensheviks** wished to establish a mass-based political party like the SPD in Germany, and the **Bolsheviks** claimed that only a conspiratorial group of professional agitators could survive in Russia's autocratic political climate.

Revolution of 1905

The divisions in Russian society burst to the fore under the ongoing pressure of the country's repeated military defeats. Russia's poor showing in the Russo-Japanese War (1904–1905) produced an economic crisis and a breakdown of the nation's infrastructure. Revolutionary groups looked to exploit the situation for significant change. Strikes broke out in the major cities, the small number of university students rallied, and a group of peaceful protestors marched on the tsar's **Winter Palace** to request change. Troops, though unprovoked, fired on the crowd, killing hundreds, in an event known as **Bloody Sunday.** To calm the furor that followed, Tsar Nicholas II (r. 1894–1917) issued the **October Manifesto** promising the creation of a legislative assembly, known as the **Duma,** and further reforms. For the moment, these actions appeased the more moderate reform parties.

Any moderate efforts toward the evolution of a constitutional monarchy were undermined by the actions of Nicholas II. Much like Louis XVI, Nicholas seemed a well-meaning and religious family man who, while espousing divine right rule, proved incapable of upholding what this ideal entailed. Nicholas's prime minister, **Peter Stolypin** (1862–1911), offered the last chance to pull Russia through its difficult transition. Stolypin introduced a series of far-reaching reforms in the decade before WWI designed to move Russia toward a functioning parliamentary democracy and a modern economic system. Peasants were finally allowed to sell their land shares to the *mir* and move to cities; property rights were advanced; and the provincial *zemstvos* government councils) were strengthened. Unfortunately, Nicholas thwarted Stolypin's attempts to work with the Duma in creating parliamentary coalitions, exercising his royal prerogative to suspend the legislative whenever its policies annoyed him. When Stolypin was assassinated in 1911, it marked the end of Russia's chance for a peaceful transition to modernity.

THE MARCH REVOLUTION AND PROVISIONAL GOVERNMENT

World War I served as the proverbial straw that broke the camel's back of the Romanov Dynasty. Russia did not fare well in the conflict, experiencing a lack of supplies, poor morale among troops, and numerous casualties. Once again, war had exposed Russia's economic and technological weakness in comparison with the western European powers. As political divisions deepened, Tsar Nicholas II in 1915 dissolved the Duma. Following failures at the front, Nicholas took personal control of the troops, a task for which he was woefully unprepared. Many soldiers were sent to the front with inadequate clothing and weapons. Meanwhile, public opinion turned against the monarchy, as it became increasingly viewed as distant and corrupt. Discontent toward the royal family centered on the mysterious figure of **Rasputin** (1869–1916), a dissolute monk who exercised sway over the tsarina (the tsar's wife) because of his supposed ability to cure her son, Alexis, of his hemophilia. Nobles at the court decided to end Rasputin's corrupting influence by assassinating him in December 1916.

Only a crisis was needed to topple the tsarist regime. On March 8, 1917, International Women's Day, a food riot broke out over the high cost of bread in an event eerily similar to the women's march on Versailles during the French Revolution. Revolutionary agitators pushed the crowd toward a political insurrection. When nearby troops refused to fire on the crowd, the Romanov Dynasty collapsed like a house of cards. Two new governments came to the fore as a result of the March Revolution. First, the **Provisional Government** replaced the deposed tsar and was made up primarily of constitutional democrats and moderate socialists. Second, more radical groups founded councils of workers, sailors, and soldiers known as **soviets,** the most important of which was the **Petrograd Soviet** (the city of St. Petersburg had been changed to Petrograd because it sounded less German). The Petrograd Soviet played much the same role as the Paris Commune during the French Revolution, pushing the government further to the left.

> **Sidebar:** Russia's rulers clung to the old Julian calendar. This was not changed until the Bolsheviks seized power in late 1917. Thus, the March Revolution is also known as the February Revolution, and the November Revolution of the Bolsheviks as the October Revolution. To align Russia to standard European time, by the Gregorian calendar, 14 days were eliminated.

The Provisional Government elected to continue the war effort and honor its treaty commitments. Meanwhile, peasants seized land from the gentry, and discipline among troops dissolved. The Petrograd Soviet aided the latter development by passing **Army Order No. 1,** which provided for democratically elected committees to run the army, causing the breakdown of all discipline. In April 1917, the German army sent Lenin through their lines in a sealed train to Petrograd in the hope that he would further undermine the Provisional Government. He did not disappoint. Bolshevik leaders were blamed in July for trying to overthrow the Provisional Government, now led by the young and charismatic moderate socialist **Alexander Kerensky** (1881–1970). The effort failed, and top Bolsheviks were arrested. Lenin fled to Finland. Kerensky now faced in August a coup attempt from the right led by conservative general **Lavr Kornilov** (1870–1918). To defeat the coup, Kerensky released Bolshevik leaders to aid in the defense of the government, clearly a sign of weakness.

THE BOLSHEVIK REVOLUTION

The Role of Lenin

V. I. Lenin provided the intellectual and organizational energy behind the Russian Revolution. From an upper middle-class family, Lenin became radicalized when his brother was executed for indirect involvement in an assassination attempt against Tsar Alexander III. Unable to find work and arrested for his revolutionary affiliations, Lenin went into exile in Switzerland, where he joined the Social Democratic Party and urged a hard line against capitalism. Lenin's writings, such as the *April Theses* issued upon his arrival in 1917 in Russia, accommodated Marxism to the experience of Russia. His contributions to socialist ideology include:

- **Imperialism**—As noted in Chapter 12, Lenin incorporated the phenomenon of imperialism into Marx's critique of capitalism. Lenin claimed that imperialism represented the highest stage of capitalism's concentration of power into fewer and fewer hands and signaled an imminent crisis.
- **Vanguard Party**—Lenin insisted, in contrast to the Mensheviks, that only a small group of professional revolutionary conspirators could operate successfully in Russia's undemocratic political climate.
- **"Weakest link in the chain"**—Orthodox Marxism held that the revolution would occur first in the most developed capitalist nation, such as Britain or Germany. Lenin countered that because capitalism operated as a worldwide system, revolutionaries should concentrate on the weakest link—Russia—enabling the spread of revolution to the other "links."
- **Telescoping**—Many Russian socialists cooperated with the Provisional Government, believing Russia was unready to enter into a socialist phase of development before its complete industrialization. Lenin rejected this notion and claimed that the time was ripe for revolution. He further claimed that Russia's rapid industrialization could occur under the dictatorship of the proletariat.
- **Revolutionary tactics**—To stir the masses, Lenin and the Bolsheviks focused on simple slogans and uncompromising opposition to the Provisional Government. **"Peace, bread, and land" and "All power to the Soviets!"** indicated clearly the thrust of the Bolshevik message.

Bolshevik Consolidation of Power

By November 1917, Lenin judged that the hour for action had arrived. Troops in Petrograd voted to support the Bolshevik-controlled soviets. The Bolsheviks easily seized key communication, transportation, and utilities, while the Provisional Government fled for lack of support. Lenin and the Bolsheviks timed their takeover to coincide with the Congress of Soviets, which elected Lenin the head of the **Council of People's Commissars,** an executive body. Bolshevik leaders quickly moved to consolidate their power by confirming peasant seizures of land and worker control of factories. More important, the Bolsheviks in January 1918 disbanded the recently elected **Constituent Assembly,** which had produced majorities for the Social Revolutionaries and Mensheviks. This action plunged Russia into civil war. Claiming to speak on behalf of the proletariat, the Bolsheviks (now the **Communist Party**) proclaimed a dictatorship in their name.

The Treaty of Brest-Litovsk

Now preoccupied with a civil war, Lenin more desperately needed to end Russia's involvement in World War I. In March 1918, the Bolsheviks signed the draconian **Treaty of Brest-Litovsk** with Germany. By the agreement, Russia recognized the independence of the Baltic provinces,

Poland, and the Ukraine. In the process, the Bolsheviks lost the most densely populated regions of their nation, important mineral resources, and some of Russia's best farmland. Bolshevik leaders gambled that Russia would regain these lands amid the inevitable socialist revolution accompanying the collapse of the war effort all around.

Russian Civil War, 1918–1922

To fight the civil war, the Bolsheviks formed the **Red Army**. Led by the brilliant organizer and former head of the Petrograd Soviet, **Leon Trotsky** (1879–1940), the army faced a motley collection of former tsarists, Cadets, Mensheviks, and Social Revolutionaries known as the **White Army.** Organizing the war effort was accomplished through "war communism." The Bolsheviks nationalized key industries, allowing workers to run factories but dealing harshly with peasants who hoarded grain and refused to surrender their crops and livestock for the Reds' worthless paper money. Bolshevik policies, exacerbated by economic problems, produced class warfare, especially between wealthy peasants on one side and landless laborers and urban dwellers on the other. Complicating the situation, Allied governments landed armies under American, Japanese, and Czech control to aid the Whites and bring Russia back into World War I.

Despite being outnumbered, the Bolsheviks were able to survive. Several factors account for this. First, the Bolsheviks stood united in a common vision, in contrast with their enemies who could only agree that they hated the Bolsheviks. Second, intervention by foreign powers allowed the Bolsheviks to paint their opponents as traitors. Third, efforts by the White Army were hindered by exterior lines of communication, making it difficult for them to coordinate their attacks and allowing the Bolsheviks to travel on the "inside of the circle" they controlled to meet any incursion. Finally, the Bolsheviks simply exhibited a more ruthless willingness than their opponents to maintain their newly won power. Soon after their revolution, the Bolsheviks formed a **secret police,** known variously as the Cheka, NKVD, and later famously as the KGB, to infiltrate and eliminate centers of opposition.

Though the situation remained fluid, by 1922 the Bolsheviks had secured control of the nation. In fact, the Red Army recaptured some of the lands lost in the Treaty of Brest-Litovsk and from ethnic minorities that had declared independence since 1918. Once the Bolsheviks had secured power, they engaged in a **Red Terror** designed to eliminate "class enemies." Under the influence of the **Cheka,** thousands of former bourgeoisies, gentry, and White Army collaborators were shot summarily without trial. The Bolsheviks were determined not to repeat the "mistakes" of French revolutionaries who allowed supporters of the Old Regime to survive or escape. In all, estimates run over 2 million for those killed by the Bolsheviks; no Russian after 1922 would openly call for a return to traditional or even antisocialist government.

THE UNION OF SOVIET SOCIALIST REPUBLICS (USSR)

By 1922, the Bolsheviks felt secure enough in their power to create the **Union of Soviet Socialist Republics (USSR),** also known as the Soviet Union. Eventually the new nation consisted of 15 such republics. It is important to remember that only about 50 percent of the citizens in this new USSR claimed Russian ethnicity and language. In that sense, the USSR acquired an international character. During the 1920s, many communists continued to hold out hope for the imminent overthrow of capitalism. To this purpose, the Bolsheviks in 1919 created the **Third International** of communist parties, or **Comintern,** to rival the Second International, which had divided

> **Heads Up!** Russia appears frequently on the AP Exam for FRQs, often related to its unique political and geographic issues. Consider how the Russian Revolution reflects these issues and how it influenced the Soviet Union until its fall in 1991.

over entry into World War I. Supposedly an alliance of socialist parties, in actuality, the Comintern represented a Soviet effort to control the international communist movement.

Party-State Structure

The political structure of the Soviet Union expressed a unique party-state dualism. For each function of government, there existed both a party and a state organ. Because the party acted as the driving force of the revolution and direct representative of the proletariat, it played the primary policy-making role. State organs essentially worked to carry out policies. Constitutions were created in 1924 and 1936 to outline the complex workings of a strongly centralized government. Elections featured only one party, the CPSU (Communist Party of the Soviet Union), and authority worked according to the principle of "**democratic centralism,**" a significant principle of Lenin's political philosophy. Elections and discussion flowed upward to the top, where decisions were made and adhered to by all party members. At the top of this centralized structure stood the **Central Committee,** made up of several hundred top CPSU officials. Within the Central Committee, a **Politburo** (policy bureau) of a dozen individuals dominated the decision-making process. Once Stalin came to power, the position of **general secretary** took on an important role in maintaining strict discipline, electing members to key positions, and managing decision-making.

The Nationalities Issue

For centuries, the Russian tsars had unsuccessfully attempted to "Russify" the 50 different ethnic groups of their empire, in which over a hundred languages were spoken. To address the nationalities issues, the Bolsheviks adopted a federal structure of government whereby the various republics, and less important autonomous regions, could theoretically secede. In fact, the dominance of the Communist Party, many of whose officials were appointed by Russian leaders of the CPSU, prevented any movement away from the Soviet Union's centralized structure. However, the minority issue never died, and under Mikhail Gorbachev's rule (1985–1991) once again came to the fore in the form of national independence movements, leading to the disintegration of the Soviet empire.

The New Economic Policy (NEP)

As a result of the ravages of World War I, civil war, and resulting famine, the Soviet economy stood at only a small fraction of its prewar productivity. To jumpstart production, Lenin introduced the **New Economic Policy** (NEP) in 1921, a strategic retreat and compromise with capitalism. Under the NEP, peasants were allowed to sell their grain themselves, and middlemen in towns and cities began exchanging goods for profit. A new class of wealthy peasants, called **kulaks,** arose in the countryside, often resented by landless laborers. Though the NEP did help to revive production, the Soviet economy by 1928 had still only returned to its prewar level. Moreover, the policy provoked a split in the Politburo between those who favored continuing the NEP and those who wished to move further toward communism.

Social and Cultural Changes

The 1920s were a decade of experimentation in the Soviet Union. Legal changes provided women with a measure of equality—the vote in 1918, the right to divorce, and access to birth control and abortion. Such reforms did not always translate into immediate changes in the daily lives of women, especially as families struggled to rebuild after a disastrous decade of violence.

One of the more prominent women involved in the building of a socialist society was **Alexandra Kollontai** (1872–1952), appointed People's Commissar for Social Welfare. Kollontai helped found **Zhenotdel,** a women's bureau designed to fight illiteracy and educate women about the new marriage laws. Sparking controversy, Kollontai argued that as a natural instinct, sexuality should be freed from oppressive traditions, which mainly harm women. As for children, the Soviet Union created the Communist Youth League, or **Komsomol,** to promote socialist values and promote membership in the CPSU.

Artists and intellectuals eagerly assisted in the government's efforts to promote literacy. The great filmmaker Sergei Eisenstein pioneered new techniques of portraying action and political themes. Soviet leaders sponsored Eisenstein's famous film about the revolution, *Potemkin* (1925), critically acclaimed by film critics for its innovations. Radical artists incorporated the style of futurist art with a socialist message. Eventually, Stalin ended this period of experimentation, enforcing a cultural orthodoxy of "socialist realism" in the arts, celebrating factories and tractors, and reversing many of the provisions regarding women's equality.

Stalin versus Trotsky

Soon after the Russian Civil War, Lenin fell ill from a series of strokes. Behind the scenes, General Secretary Stalin and Leon Trotsky—a true intellectual force in socialism and the organizer of the Red Army—battled for control of the party. Trotsky condemned the NEP as a sell-out to capitalism, calling for **"permanent revolution"** and protesting the bureaucratization of the Communist Party. Stalin proved the more organized and ruthless. With his control of patronage in the CPSU and by wrapping himself in the mantle of Lenin, Stalin engineered Trotsky's dismissal from the party and then his exile. By 1928, Stalin had secured his absolute hold on power and moved to implement his plans to modernize the Soviet Union.

RESULTS OF WWI AND THE RUSSIAN REVOLUTION

It would be difficult to overestimate the combined impact of World War I and the Russian Revolution on European and world history. In 1914, Europe stood at its zenith of power. Less than a decade later, total war and revolution changed that. First, violent and extreme forces liberated by the war and revolution would bear full fruit with the totalitarian movements of the 1920s and 1930s. Second, laissez-faire ideas regarding the economy were abandoned under pressure of the war effort, and the Versailles settlement laid the seeds for the Great Depression. Third, World War I and the Russian Revolution both radically altered diplomatic structures and destroyed the balance of power. Fourth, prewar cultural trends toward irrationality and alienation gained currency from a decade of upheaval and dominated ideas during the interwar period. Though the Treaty of Versailles attempted to remake a stable world order, the task proved too much given the extreme circumstances facing Europe in 1919. The twentieth century achieved its violent birth amid the chaos of World War I and Russian Revolution.

ADDITIONAL RESOURCES

Fitzpatrick, Sheila, *The Russian Revolution,* 1917–1932 (1982)—Concise analysis of the founding of the Soviet Union.

Fussell, Paul, *The Great War and Modern Memory* (2000)—One of the great nonfiction books, this volume explores how British writers interpreted their war experiences.

Keegan, John, *The First World War* (1998)—By Britain's greatest military historian, this volume might be the best single overview of the war.

Mosier, John, *The Myth of the Great War: A New Military History of World War I* (2001)—The author argues that Germany really fought the most effectively, with only the United States saving the Allies. A great text for military history aficionados.

von Laue, Theodore H., *Why Lenin? Why Stalin? Why Gorbachev?: The Rise and Fall of the Soviet System* (1997)—The author analyzes the continuities and difficulties of Russian history.

Remarque, Erich Maria, *All Quiet on the Western Front* (1929)—The classic antiwar novel.

Winter, Jay, *The Experience of World War I*—Combining a wealth of text, special features, and maps, this "coffee-table" book presents the war from the perspectives of politicians, generals, soldiers, and civilians.

The Great War and the Shaping of the Twentieth Century, eight VHS tapes (1998)—An outstanding PBS documentary focusing on the psychological impact of the Great War.

http://www.firstworldwar.com/—This excellent site offers interpretive essays, primary sources, and thousands of visuals.

http://www.pitt.edu/~pugachev/greatwar/ww1.html—Good clearinghouse with links to numerous sites, many focusing on the experiences of individual nations.

http://history.acusd.edu/gen/text/versaillestreaty/vercontents.html—Contains the entire text of the Versailles settlement, in addition to visuals, chronologies, and documents.

PRACTICE QUESTIONS

1. The diplomacy of German chancellor Otto von Bismarck (1862–1890) was designed to prevent an alliance from forming between which two nations?
   a. Austria-Hungary and Russia
   b. Great Britain and France
   c. Italy and Austria-Hungary
   d. France and Russia
   e. Great Britain and Italy

2. Which of the following is true regarding the onset of World War I?
   a. Governments and populations were unprepared for the war's length and extent.
   b. The military plans and strategies of the Great Powers were largely fulfilled.
   c. The declaration of war was greeted among the public with widespread opposition.
   d. A conference among the Great Powers nearly averted the conflict.
   e. Russia remained neutral pending the outcome of Austria's campaign against Serbia.

3. This description of trench warfare on the Western Front conveys which of the following regarding the nature of the World War I?
   a. War allows for the testing of a nation's strength amid struggle.
   b. World War I surpassed other conflicts in possibilities for glory.
   c. The experiences of the combatant nations differed markedly.
   d. Military technologies rendered warfare more tedious yet safer.
   e. The war marked a generation filled with alienation and disillusionment.

"Now I look back: four years of development in the midst of a generation predestined to death, spent in caves, smoke-filled trenches, and shell-illuminated wastes; years enlivened only by the pleasures of mercenary, and nights of guard after guard in an endless perspective; in short, a monotonous calendar full of hardships and privation, divided by the red-letter days of battles."

4. The accompanying poster, titled "Fatherland, Family, and Future," demonstrates which of the following about World War I?
   a. Governments reluctantly made use of propaganda to appeal to the public.
   b. Of the combatants, Germany proved most reliant on public opinion.
   c. Governments often portrayed the war as a struggle for civilization.
   d. State power extended to propaganda but not to economic regulation.
   e. Governments permitted a wide range of opinions regarding the war effort.

akg-images

5. Which of the following is the most accurate characterization of how World War I and the Russian Revolution affected the status of women?
   a. Women gained the right to vote in many nations following 1918.
   b. The equality of women in the workplace was confirmed.
   c. Women earned top positions of leadership in many states.
   d. The status of women stayed virtually the same after both events.
   e. Segregation of gender based on "separate spheres" was ended.
6. All of the following provisions were imposed on Germany as a result of the Treaty of Versailles (1919) EXCEPT:
   a. loss of Alsace-Lorraine to France.
   b. dismemberment into three German states.
   c. reduction of Germany's military capacity.
   d. acceptance of full guilt for the war.
   e. payment of reparations as damages.
7. Following the abolition of serfdom, from 1861–1905, which of the following best characterizes the situation of the Russian peasantry?
   a. A new class of small commercial farmers dominated Russian agriculture.
   b. Most peasants moved from the village communes into urban areas.
   c. Rural overpopulation and land shortage caused continuous unrest.

    d. Peasants successfully revolted and established socialist-based communes.

    e. Peasant income rose dramatically, improving the peasant standard of living.

8. A major reason for the success of the Bolsheviks in establishing power in Russia was:
    a. their willingness to form coalitions with liberal democratic parties.
    b. Lenin's rejection of Marxism in favor of a program of anarchist violence.
    c. the Provisional Government's loss of prestige after making peace with Germany.
    d. their promotion of peaceful means for uniting all revolutionary groups.
    e. the successful use of slogans, such as "peace, bread, and land."

9. As a result of the New Economic Policy (NEP) from 1921 to 1927, the Soviet Union:
    a. moved rapidly toward the collectivization of agriculture.
    b. allowed the development of free markets and profit.
    c. completed free trade agreements with the western powers.
    d. was plunged into a widespread famine, killing millions.
    e. nationalized key industries, such as utilities and steel.

10. All of the following resulted in Europe from World War I (1914–1918) EXCEPT:
    a. increased government regulation of the economy.
    b. the entrance of large numbers of women into the workforce.
    c. reestablishment of the balance of power and diplomatic stability.
    d. the democratization of society through shared suffering.
    e. an increase in the power and prestige of labor unions.

SAMPLE ESSAY

Analyze at least THREE reasons why the assassination of Archduke Franz Ferdinand, heir to the Austro-Hungarian throne, sparked World War I (1914–1918).

World War I stands as one of the most significant events in history, basically defining everything about the 20th century. Ironically, it began with the assassination of a man nobody really liked very much—Franz Ferdinand. When the heir to the Austrian throne was killed, it set in motion of chain of events that led directly to one of the worst conflicts in European history. Without the issues of nationalism in the Balkans, domestic pressures at home, and the alliance system, "World War I" might have remained another regional war among the great powers.

The Balkans is the most complex region in Europe, consisting of many different ethnic groups and languages. Slavic languages and peoples dominate the region and had been ruled for centuries by the crumbling Ottoman Empire. As the Sick Man of Europe faded like an old photograph, the Slavic Russians moved in to lead the Slavic peoples there and seek their warm-weather port. However, the Austro-Hungarians controlled many of the Slavs and did not want them to establish strong independent nations, because then their Slavic groups, especially the Serbs, would want to join with them. This was shown clearly in 1878, when a war in the region led to the creation of a few states but also Austria's control of Bosnia, which the Serbs thought should be theirs. Later on, these new Balkan states attempted to gain more territory in the two Balkan Wars, which almost led to war when Austria and Germany stood firm in blocking Serbia's access to the sea. Russia was humiliated, as it had been in 1878, and was determined not to lose its great-power position in the Balkans.

Mass politics made governments respond more to pressures. With nationalism, leaders had to appeal to all the people and act like they represented them. This meant that many new groups wanted to get more rights, such as workers, women, and ethnic groups. Workers formed socialist parties, went on strike, and even used assassinations if they were anarchists. Suffragettes demanded the vote. With all of this chaos, governments tried to manipulate nationalism to "rally round the flag." Before 1914, this meant that states pursued colonies, like Italy and Germany, mostly to appeal to their public's demand for national glory. Urban areas grew larger and industrialization created many new problems. All of these issues placed great strain on governments. Why is this relevant? When the decision for war came, many leaders considered that a war might rally the public around the government. In fact, many citizens celebrated the declaration of war and groups, like the SPD in Germany, decided to support the war effort, even though they were supposed to be socialist.

All of these factors would not have mattered without the alliance system. Without the two opposed alliances, the crises in the Balkans probably would have stayed between Austria and Russia. When Bismarck ran Germany, he focused on keeping the balance of power and isolating France. His alliance system was really complex and few understood it. However, when Kaiser Wilhelm got rid of Bismarck in 1890, he decided to get Germany's "place in the sun" by building up the navy and getting colonies. His actions alienated Russia and Britain, who joined with France in an alliance. Though Germany was allied with Italy, their only really ally was Austria. This meant that Germany depended on a weak nation with lots of nationalism problems. Germany was encircled and feared losing its only ally, so when Austria took a hard line against Serbia in 1914, the Kaiser issued the "blank check." When Russia defended Serbia, this drew in Germany, France, and eventually Britain.

WWI is one of the most complicated events because of many background causes. Franz Ferdinand's assassination was only the tip of the iceberg. Beneath the surface, Balkan nationalism, mass politics, and the alliance system ensured that this "trigger" would explode in a European war.

This is an excellent student response, a paragon of the student being "in control" of the question. From the outset, the student demonstrates a grasp of the historical context and clearly identifies three relevant factors. Body paragraphs begin with a strong topic sentence and then proceed to explain how and why the particular causal factor is relevant. The student chooses the examples judiciously and applies them explicitly to demonstrate *how* and *why* each factor acted as a cause. In addition, the response is fully developed with balanced treatment of each topic. Finally, though the conclusion is brief, the student employs a couple of vivid metaphors to reinforce her point. Score: 9.

CHAPTER 15
Democracy, Totalitarianism, and World War II, 1919–1945

Europe struggled to return to peace after the end of World War I. Though the continent had never before boasted so many democratic governments, in the next two decades, most of these new democracies crumbled under the onslaught of the Great Depression and the rise of totalitarian ideologies, such as Fascism and communism. Nineteenth-century intellectual trends combined with the extreme circumstances of World War I produced the totalitarian movements. Dictators exploited new technologies of mass communication to mobilize their populations. At the same time, themes of alienation and disillusionment permeated high culture. Ultimately, Europe's inability to deal effectively with the dual crises of economic depression and extreme political movements culminated in the most destructive conflict in history—World War II.

> **Note:** For users of Palmer, Colton, and Kramer, *A History of the Modern World,* this chapter combines Chapters 19 and 20, along with the section on Stalinist Russia in Chapter 18, in your text.

AN UNCERTAIN PEACE: ENFORCING THE TREATY OF VERSAILLES

After World War I, France attempted to enforce the Versailles settlement vigorously. This proved difficult without the active support of Great Britain and the United States, both isolationist in sentiment, and due to the Bolshevik Revolution, which eliminated Russia as a counterweight to a revived Germany. Many in Europe preferred to rely on the new **League of Nations** to ensure collective security. The league unfortunately lacked enforcement mechanisms as well as the membership of Germany, the Soviet Union, and the United States. For security, France turned to the less satisfactory alternative of allying with those new Eastern European democracies sandwiched between Bolshevik Russia and a vengeful Germany. France's **Little Entente** with Poland, Czechoslovakia, and Romania proved no substitute for France's recent WWI allies in balancing Germany. When Germany agreed in 1922 with the **Rapallo Pact** to supply manufactures to the Soviet Union and engage in joint military maneuvers, it signaled the potential danger to France's security system and to the position of the new Eastern European democracies.

> **Heads Up!** In recent years, the Test Development Committee has worked to include more questions related to eastern Europe, particularly focused on Russia. As you review this chapter, consider the differing issues facing eastern compared with western European nations.

The Advance of Democracy in Eastern Europe

Europe enjoyed a general but short-lived trend toward democracy after World War I. Women earned the right to vote in many nations, labor unions gained power, and governments enacted social legislation to benefit their citizens. An entire new region experienced democracy for the first time. In Eastern Europe, the new states of Czechoslovakia, Yugoslavia, Austria, Hungary, Poland, and the Baltic states emerged out of the former empires. Other than Czechoslovakia, none of these new nations claimed a democratic tradition. Though these new states were formed around the notion of national self-determination, each confronted an ethnic minority problem (e.g., the presence of millions of ethnic Hungarians in Romanian Transylvania). More ominously, millions of ethnic Germans lived in Czechoslovakia and Poland.

In addition, conservative interests opposed the new democracies on one hand, while extreme socialists worked to overthrow them on the other. The specter of Bolshevism hung over Eastern Europe, as in 1919 when radical leader Béla Kun attempted to establish a Soviet regime in Hungary, before his ouster in 1920. Even the great social change in the region—**land reform**—failed to solve the problem of underdevelopment. The new democracies lacked the integrated economies they had experienced as part of former empires. Though peasants were confirmed in ownership of their small farms, the development of a middle class—the traditional basis for parliamentary democracy—lagged far behind Western Europe. Other than Czechoslovakia, the new Eastern European democracies proved thin reeds and fell over easily with the crisis of depression and the threat of dictatorship.

Germany's Failed Experiment with Democracy: The Weimar Republic

Germany's Weimar Republic began with two strikes against it. Born amidst the turmoil accompanying the end of World War I, the republic faced a myriad of economic and political problems. Many influential Germans, particularly military officials, judges, and civil servants, opposed the new government as a weak substitute for imperial Germany. Extremists groups on both the left and the right attempted to overthrow the government in the first years of its existence.

Two parties helped found the republic and draw up its constitution—the Social Democratic Party (left-center) and the **Catholic Center Party** (right-center). The former had all but abandoned its Marxist rhetoric and seemed more concerned with advancing Germany's welfare system; both wished to avoid communist and rightist takeovers. In 1919, a Soviet-inspired communist movement, known as the **Spartacists** and led by Rosa Luxembourg and Karl Liebknecht, attempted an overthrow of the Berlin city government but were captured and executed by the *Freikorps,* a right-wing paramilitary group. Then in 1920, the Freikorps itself attempted a coup d'etat against Weimar known as the **Kapp putsch.** Only the intervention of the working class saved the republic an early death. Political violence seemed to mark the short history of the republic, as when Foreign Minister Walter Rathenau was assassinated in 1922 by two conservative army officers.

According to the Weimar constitution, delegates to the Reichstag (the popular branch of the parliament) were chosen by **proportional representation,** meaning that if a party received 10 percent of the vote, it would earn approximately 10 percent of the seats in the Reichstag. Though this allowed for a diversity of views, the system also made it difficult to establish stable majority government and easier for extreme views to gain a political voice. Also, in times of "imminent danger," the president of the republic could suspend parliamentary rule and rule by decree. This so-called **suicide clause** (Article 48) provided a pretext for those who wished to undermine democratic rule.

Perhaps most damaging to Weimar was its association with the Versailles settlement. Even left-of-center Germans viewed the treaty as a *Diktat,* or "dictated peace." Demagogues such as Hitler perpetuated the myth that the German army in 1918 stood on the verge of victory when it was "stabbed in the back" by the "Jews, socialists, communists, and democrats" bent on establishing republican government at any price. No matter how untrue and unfair this charge, it allowed right-wing groups to scapegoat the Weimar Republic for Germany's problems. When this catalogue is added to the economic problems of reparations, hyperinflation, and the Great Depression, Weimar's failure is not difficult to understand.

Reparations, the Ruhr, and Hyperinflation

In 1923 the Weimar Republic fell behind on its reparations payments. Under the determined leadership of Prime Minister **Raymond Poincaré** (1860–1934), the French along with the Belgians invaded the industrial Ruhr Valley to extract the payments in the form of coal and steel. The result benefited neither France nor Germany. Weimar leaders encouraged workers to engage in a campaign of passive resistance and refuse to operate the factories and mines. This action required the Weimar Republic to pay the workers' benefits and wages in ever-increasing amounts of paper money. By November 1923, the German mark had plummeted to catastrophic levels. At the worst of this **hyperinflation,** $1 equaled 4 trillion marks. Over night, middle-class savings, pensions, insurance policies, and interest income all become worthless. Confidence in the Weimar Republic plunged, emboldening **Adolph Hitler** (1889–1945) and his Nazi Party to attempt to overthrow the Bavarian government in the **Beer Hall putsch** (1923). Though the coup failed, Hitler received only a five-year sentence from a justice system always more lenient on right-wing than left-wing violence. While in prison, Hitler wrote his political testament, *Mein Kampf* (1924), which outlined his racial ideas and goals for Germany.

> **Sidebar:** The Young Plan of 1929 extended the reparations payments further out into the 1980s. Due to the Great Depression, reparations were suspended in 1931, and Germany never made another reparations payment.

Great Britain and France criticized France for its provocative gesture. To defuse the situation, the United States intervened economically. Because America's former allies claimed that they could not pay back loans to the United States without German reparations, the United States extended loans to Germany and rescheduled the reparations payments in exchange for a French withdrawal of the Ruhr. Funds from the **Dawes Plan** aided a short-lived economic revival in Germany, while a new spirit of cooperation emerged from the French and Germans. However, the French learned an important lesson; its vigorous action brought down the Poincaré government and earned it the criticism of allies fearful of another war.

The Spirit of Locarno

The period from 1924 to 1929 produced optimistic hopes of peace and prosperity. Moderate leaders emerged in the principal nations who were dedicated to resolving disputes through negotiation and diplomacy, most important, **Gustav Streseman** (1878–1929) of Germany and **Aristide Briand** (1862–1932) of France. In 1925, these two leaders engineered the **Locarno Pact,** which contemporaries considered the true end to World War I. Germany recognized its western borders as permanent (meaning the loss of Alsace-Lorraine) and agreed to revise its eastern borders with Poland and Czechoslovakia only by common agreement. As a result, Germany was allowed to enter the League of Nations in 1926. The "spirit of Locarno" culminated with the **Kellogg-Briand Pact** of 1928, by which the 65 signatory nations condemned war as an instrument of international politics.

Like the Kellogg-Briand Pact, the League of Nations lacked the means to enforce its decisions. Collective security proved informal and not binding on any nation. When Japan invaded Manchuria in 1931 and Italy invaded Ethiopia in 1935, the league made rhetorical protests and contemplated sanctions, but took few concrete actions to punish the aggressors. Such diplomacy left underlying issues unresolved and seduced some nations into adopting isolationist policies in deference to the league. In 1930, France began work on a set of defensive fortifications along the German border known as the **Maginot Line,** a term that symbolizes a false notion of security behind an imaginary strong frontier.

THE GREAT DEPRESSION

Causes

World War I and the Treaty of Versailles sowed the seeds for the Great Depression. Before 1914, economic activity had become increasingly global, meaning that disturbance in one area transmitted quickly to other areas. During the period of international stability, 1924–1929, the world economy was marked by prosperity, especially in new sectors such as automobiles, household appliances, and communications. This prosperity proved shallow, however, and was hindered by the following factors:

- **Strong inflationary pressures**—During World War I, governments engaged in rationing and borrowed money at record rates. In addition, most states depreciated their currencies in an effort to reduce their debt. Inflation complicated the return to a peacetime economy and wreaked havoc on the world system of stable currencies existing before 1914.
- **Disrupted markets**—While Europe fought World War I, competitors moved into its worldwide markets. For example, India developed its own textile industry and was less interested in British imports following the war. North America and Australia established themselves as major exporters of grain. When the war ended, European nations found it difficult to reestablish former trade patterns.
- **Agricultural depression**—A glut of grain worldwide drove down prices and left many farmers bankrupt or destitute.
- **Economic nationalism**—To protect fragile domestic markets and head off unrest, most states enacted high tariff barriers. The United States, in particular, refused to replace Great Britain as financial world leader; rather than lower tariffs to allow Germany to accumulate capital from trade and thus pay off reparations, the United States enacted some of its highest barriers ever.
- **Reparations**—The cycle of world capital flowed from the United States to Germany, then from Germany to France and Britain, and finally back to the United States. This unnatural arrangement disrupted investment, while making world economic activity unusually reliant on American financial conditions.
- **Credit financing**—The advent of the installment plan allowed consumers to defer payment on purchases. In addition, expanding American stock market activity occurred "**on margin**," by borrowing up to 90 percent of the stock's value. Any small economic downturn threatened to burst this speculative bubble.

When the United States **stock market crashed** in October 1929, it triggered the various components of the above "trap" into place, causing a downward economic spiral.

Effects

Europe had experienced economic cycles throughout its history, but nothing compared with the Great Depression in the 1930s for length and depth of contraction. Stock values plunged from 1929 to 1932 as businesses cut back production and laid off workers. Investment and **world trade plummeted. Unemployment** reached shocking proportions, strengthening those parties who promised extreme solutions to problems. Germany and the Unites States were hardest hit; as many as 35 percent of workers stood idle in both nations. Due to the unstable credit situation, the stock market crash rippled throughout the financial world, causing global bank failures. In 1931 the failure of the leading Vienna bank, the *Creditanstalt*, sparked additional financial collapses.

Most nations experienced a drain on their treasuries to pay off debts. **Currency values depreciated** even further, wrecking the stable gold-backed system dating from the mid-nineteenth century. Investors lost confidence in the British pound, causing a massive sell-off. Long the world financial leader, Great Britain was forced **off the gold standard** in 1931, followed soon after by the United States and the rest of the industrialized world. In many cases, trade reverted to **bilateral agreements** and even barter, wherein one nation would exchange goods directly with another. Such arrangements hindered world trade and made it difficult for nations to obtain necessary products and earn income from exports.

Democratic Responses

The Great Depression created a crisis for democratic governments. Economy orthodoxy seemed impotent in addressing the downward spiral. According to Liberal economic theory, in times of depression states should pursue austerity much like individual families: cut the budget and raise taxes. However, these policies failed to stimulate production and increased the misery of the unemployed. British economist **John Maynard Keynes** (1883–1946) introduced an alternate approach to economic stimulation in his *General Theory of Employment, Interest, and Money* (1936). Contrary to accepted wisdom, Keynes argued that governments needed to "prime the pump" through deficit financing, by cutting taxes and spending on government programs to aid the needy. Though few nations consistently followed such policies before World War II, "Keynesian" economics emerged as the new orthodoxy after 1945. On the AP Exam, questions tend to focus on the general structure of the economy during this period; however, the following brief review of democratic responses illustrates the depth of the crisis.

Great Britain: Of all the industrial nations, Great Britain depended most on trade. World War I and the Great Depression both struck a blow against Britain's dominant position. Welfare legislation enacted before the war eased some of the burden on the unemployed. Despite the negative economic conditions, workers were reluctant to surrender gains made in wartime. Conflicts with industry led in 1926 to a **General Strike,** which was eventually squashed by government intervention. Politically, the Labour Party replaced the Liberal Party and, after gaining power in 1924 and again in 1929, worked to extend the rights of workers. In 1931, former Labour Prime Minister **Ramsay MacDonald** (1866–1937) joined with Conservatives in a **National Government** that attempted to reduce the budget deficit through traditional retrenchment. To address imperial issues, Britain provided autonomy for Egypt and the Irish Free State in 1922, and in 1931 formalized relations with former colonies such as Canada, Australia, New Zealand, and South Africa by granting dominion status. The combined problems of economic stagnation, diminished world status, and political tension placed Britain in a weakened position to confront Nazi aggression.

> **Sidebar:** Leon Blum became France's first socialist and first Jewish prime minister, a fact that many right-wing groups used to oppose his Popular Front government. Such ideological divisions remained after the collapse of the Third Republic with the Nazi invasion, as conservatives viewed the Vichy government as an opportunity to rid France of "alien" influences.

France: France escaped some of the worst effects of the Great Depression. Less dependent on trade than Britain, France was not as hard hit by the world downturn. In addition, Poincaré succeeded in stabilizing the *franc* at a fraction of its prewar level, making French exports cheaper on the world market. Amid the growth of right-wing and fascist groups, a coalition of left-wing parties, called the **Popular Front,** held power briefly from 1936 to 1938 and promoted a series of significant reforms—the 40-hour workweek, paid vacations, and stronger collective bargaining rights for unions. Socialist Prime Minister **Léon Blum's** (1872–1950) government eventually fell victim to heightening ideological tensions, particularly after the outbreak of the Spanish Civil War. However, France preserved its republican government for the time being and enacted legislation that still benefits French workers today.

United States: Under **President Franklin Roosevelt** (1882–1945), the United States initiated a wide-ranging but somewhat haphazard program of relief, recovery, and reform. The **New Deal** began with a flurry of legislation in 1933 providing subsidies for farmers, public works jobs in the Civilian Conservation Corps (CCC), and market regulation through the National Recovery Administration (NRA). Congress created numerous "alphabet" agencies to regulate the stock market and the banking industry, provide jobs, and address environmental issues. Later, Roosevelt turned to reform. **The Social Security Act** (1935), for example, provided unemployment, disability, and old-age insurance. Though these acts provided relief, unemployment spiked again from 1937 to 1938. It would take World War II for the United States to recover fully from the Great Depression.

Scandinavia: The Scandinavian nations of Norway, Sweden, and Denmark demonstrated that governments could effectively combine elements of socialism and democracy. These states enacted the most wide-ranging social welfare programs to curb the worst effects of the Great Depression. Additionally, Scandinavian nations most eagerly embraced creative and Keynesian approaches, such as **producers' cooperatives** to regulate the price of agricultural products and state ownership of key industries.

TOTALITARIANISM

Totalitarianism represents a phenomenon of the interwar period, yet it also claims roots in the pre-1914 period as well. Mass politics and intellectual trends after 1870 fueled the development of irrational ideologies. You may recall the growth of political anti-Semitism, anarchism's glorification of violence, and the rabid nationalism associated with imperialism. In addition, Darwinian evolution emphasized the importance of struggle, a notion taken up by racists and extremists to justify domination of the "weaker." During World War I, states grew significantly in their powers of regimentation and mobilization, employing propaganda to control public opinion. Communication advances in the interwar period, such as radio and motion pictures, provided additional means for controlling the populace.

Dictatorship was not new to Europe, so how can we distinguish totalitarianism from the absolutism of the seventeenth and early eighteenth centuries? Absolute monarchs such as Louis XIV derived their power from traditional dynastic and aristocratic institutions, and it extended to those areas deemed essential to the state's interest, such as trade, taxes, and religion. Even then, geographic and customary obstacles hindered centralization. Totalitarian dictators exploited mass media to mobilize the public to fanatical support of the "movement," not simply passive obedience, as with absolute monarchs. Twentieth-century dictators aimed at total control of society; any independent civic or social life must be subordinated to the party, movement, and leader. Modern communications allowed for such control but also increased the potential for catastrophic violence, as would be clear during World War II.

Fascism and Mussolini's Italy

Fascism represented a European and even world phenomenon in the interwar period. For many, fascism acted as a "third way" between faltering Liberal democracies and revolutionary, class-based Marxism. With its roots in nineteenth-century irrational ideologies but feeding on the unstable conditions of the 1920s and 1930s, fascism seemed a genuine threat to supplant democracy as the wave of the future. Before turning to the Italian variant of fascism, the following list may prove helpful in understanding the nature of fascist ideology:

- **Militarism**—Fascists extolled war as the proving ground of national identity and for sorting out the hierarchy of nations.
- **Glorification of the state**—Not only was the state seen as all-powerful, it also represented the culminating force in historical evolution.
- **Fuhrer principle**—German for "leader," the Fuhrer principle stated that the voice of the people reached its highest expression not in assemblies or representation but in a single person, for example, Mussolini or Hitler.
- **Antidemocracy**—Fascists scorned the weakness of democratic mechanisms of government and argued that the national spirit cannot be captured by specific institutions.
- **Anticommunism**—Though communists and fascists shared many tactics, fascists condemned class warfare and upheld the importance of racial and national identity, in contrast to communists, who condemned racism and nationalism.
- **One-party rule**—In fascist states, democratic mechanisms such as elections, multiparty systems, and the free press were suppressed.

The Rise of Fascism in Italy

Italy came out of World War I as a victor, but in name only. Right-wing nationalists condemned the Versailles settlement for not allowing Italians to recapture "unredeemed" lands from Austria and the new nation of Yugoslavia. To make matters worse, the Italian economy suffered from unemployment, inflation, and high budget deficits. Workers engaged in numerous strikes, often fanned by extremist groups hoping to institute a socialist state. Already low before the war, respect for Italy's parliamentary democracy sank further.

Into this atmosphere strode **Benito Mussolini** (1883–1945) and his fascists (after the Latin *fasces*, or bundle of sticks carried by ancient Roman officials to symbolize state power). Named for a Mexican revolutionary, Mussolini began as a revolutionary left-wing journalist but moved rightward with the outbreak of World War I. Influenced by the writings of Sorel and Nietzsche regarding the irrational, Mussolini glorified the state and violence as a means of combating Italy's perceived enemies. To gain power, Mussolini used a paramilitary group, the *squadristi* (or **Blackshirts**), to intimidate political opponents and promote the breakdown of parliamentary order. Though the fascist movement won only a small percentage of parliamentary seats in the 1921 election, Mussolini continued to gain adherents, who ironically saw him as a champion of law and order against the threat from the left. By 1922, Mussolini decided the moment had arrived for his movement to seize power. In October of that year, thousands of fascists converged on the capital to intimidate the king into appointing Mussolini as head of government. The so-called **March on Rome** convinced Victor Emmanuel III to name Mussolini as premier.

The Italian Fascist State under Mussolini

Mussolini moved quickly to exploit the emergency powers he was granted to cement his hold on the government. To ensure a functioning majority, the parliament passed the **Acerbo Law,** which granted two-thirds of the seats to the party that gained the most votes. With help from this law and the tactics of the squadristi, the fascists in 1924 gained control of the parliament.

Soon after the election, a respected socialist deputy, **Giacomo Matteotti,** was **assassinated** by fascist thugs for exposing corruption and violence within the government. Public outrage demanded the resignation of Mussolini, who, nonetheless, used the incident to secure his hold on government.

By 1926, fascism had **censored the press,** eliminated all opposition parties, and employed a **secret police,** the OVRA, to ferret out dissent. In keeping with fascist ideology, Mussolini condemned laissez-faire capitalism, democracy, and Marxist appeals to class. National solidarity and glory, symbolized by Mussolini himself, *Il Duce,* replaced a pluralistic society made up of varying groups. In economic affairs, Mussolini introduced the **corporative state,** in which the economy was run as 22 separate corporations, with representatives from business, Fascist-organized labor unions, and the state. State interest dictated actual policy and production priorities, though private property and profit were allowed.

In social and cultural life, the fascists worked to orient the lives of Italians around the state. To end the conflict with the Catholic Church, dating from 1870, Mussolini signed the **Lateran Accord** in 1929, which recognized the sovereignty of the church over the Vatican in exchange for the papacy's promise not to interfere with the functions of the state. To address Italy's declining birth rate, Mussolini provided incentives for larger families, gave awards for fertile mothers, and created holidays to honor motherhood. In a fascist state, women were clearly to play the domestic role of rearing strong children for the state. A healthy race demanded a regimen of physical fitness. Schools required calisthenics, and the government sponsored recreational and outdoor activities through the state-sponsored *Dopolavoro.*

The fascist corporative state failed to address effectively the problems of the Great Depression. Mussolini turned to a program of public works to provide jobs for Italians—swamps were cleared, roads built, and a move toward self-sufficiency in wheat and power was made. Though it was said that Mussolini "made the trains run on time," he was forced increasingly after 1935 to engage in imperialist adventures to revive support for his flagging movement. Despite fascist efforts, Italy was never able to realize the totalitarian state to the degree of Nazi Germany or Stalinist Soviet Union.

Nazi Germany

Hitler and the Rise to Power

Perhaps no political movement in history is associated more with a single person than Nazism and Adolph Hitler. Hitler came from a lower-middle-class Austrian family of unremarkable circumstances. The young Hitler moved to Vienna to pursue his artistic aspirations. After failing entrance to the Viennese art academy, Hitler attempted to live by selling his watercolors and postcards. While in Vienna, Hitler absorbed the anti-Semitism of its mayor, Karl Lueger, and grew to hate the "mongrel" Habsburg Empire with its ethnic diversity and aristocratic airs. To avoid being drafted into the Austrian army at the outset of World War I, Hitler crossed the border into Bavaria and enlisted in the German army. The young corporal served with distinction at the front as a message runner, and ended the war in a hospital, the victim of a poison gas attack, when he heard the news of the armistice. Hitler found his war experience the most significant of his life and joined a military-style political group in 1920 known as the **National Socialist German Workers' Party** (NSDAP), later known as **National Socialists,** or simply Nazis. The ragtag group of political misfits soon recognized the spellbinding quality of Hitler's oratory and made him their leader.

After the failed Beer Hall putsch of 1923, Hitler and the Nazis focused on a **"legality strategy,"** designed to take advantage of parliamentary politics to create a mass movement capable of taking power when democracy broke down. The Nazi message was simple: Weimar represented rule by the worst—democrats, socialists, Jews—and Germany needed a strong national state based on race. As Hitler had laid out in *Mein Kampf*, Germany required *Lebensraum* (living space) in the east, as part of a new European order around a hierarchy of race. At every opportunity, Hitler blamed Germany's problems on the Treaty of Versailles and pledged to restore German honor. Members of the **S.A.** (Brownshirts or Stormtroopers) provoked street fights with rival political groups and received lenient treatment from sympathetic officials and judges. Initially, the Nazis pitched their message to workers but gained little support, earning less than 3 percent of the vote in 1928. Two developments caused a turnaround in Nazi fortunes: (1) the Great Depression and (2) a switch in Nazi tactics to appeal to the middle class.

The Nazis used modern electoral tactics to gain support. Nazi party leaders gave speeches tailored to specific audiences and portrayed themselves as the party of the young and dynamic. Hitler made effective use of modern technologies, as with his **"Hitler over Germany"** campaign, during which he visited 50 cities in 15 days via airplane. By 1932, the Nazi vote total had increased to 37 percent, winning 230 seats in the Reichstag and making Nazis the largest party. As early as 1930, the Weimar Republic already subsisted on life support, with Chancellor Brüning ruling by decree. Some old-line conservatives believed Hitler represented the best hope to defeat communism and restore order in Germany. Intriguers behind President Hindenburg convinced the aged and perhaps senile leader to appoint Hitler chancellor in January 1933. It was believed that Hitler could be controlled by other members of the cabinet, certainly one of the most egregious miscalculations in political history.

> **Sidebar:** Many falsely adhere to the notion that Hitler either seized power by force in a coup d'etat or was elected by a majority of Germans. Hitler's and the Nazi's strategy of rendering democracy impotent through a mass political movement bore fruit with Hitler's *appointment* as chancellor.

The Nazi Total State

It did not take long for Hitler to consolidate his power. Soon after his appointment, the parliament building caught fire. The Nazis blamed the **Reichstag fire** on the Communist Party, which they banned as illegal, arresting its leaders. In a subsequent election carried out in an atmosphere of intimidation and violence, the Nazis still failed to earn a majority of the votes (45 percent). Nonetheless, the Nazis rammed through the Reichstag an amendment allowing Hitler to rule by decree for five years. This **Enabling Act** essentially made Hitler a dictator, and it was followed by the 1933 **Civil Service Act,** requiring all government employees to swear a personal oath of loyalty to the Fuhrer.

In 1934, Hitler removed the last obstacles to his power. First, all parties but National Socialism were declared illegal. All federal governments, such as Bavaria or Saxony, were eliminated in favor of a unitary state. To win over the army leadership, Hitler agreed in June 1934 to purge the leadership of the S.A., grown to 500,000 men and perceived as a threat to the army's monopoly of military force. With Hitler in power, the S.A. no longer seemed necessary, and its leader, **Ernst Röhm** (1887–1934), represented one of the last potential challenges to Hitler's unquestioned leadership of the party. On the night of June 30, 1934, top leaders of the Brownshirts, in addition to numerous other political opponents, were summarily executed in what became known as the **Blood Purge.** When President Hindenburg died two months later, Hitler assumed the position of president.

Terror formed an elemental weapon of Nazi rule. Internally, a secret police, the **Gestapo,** arrested real and imagined opponents, committing thousands to a constellation of **concentration camps.** Following the S.A. purge, the **S.S.** (Schutzstaffel) emerged as the primary perpetrators of terror, eventually absorbing control of the Gestapo, running the death camps, and forming the leading edge of a new "Aryan" racial elite. Another ingredient of the total state involved "**coordinating**" any independent social and civic organizations—charities, youth groups, unions—into Nazi organizations. Though not all Germans belonged to the Nazi Party, all social activity was to be geared around the state and its goals. The Nazi Party also positively promoted loyalty through propaganda, such as the annual **Nuremberg rallies,** a spectacle of pageantry and regimentation captured effectively in the film "**Triumph of the Will.**"

To solve Germany's economic problems, the Nazis engaged in "pump-priming" techniques of government spending on public works and rearmament. By 1936, the Nazis had developed a **Four-Year Plan** to promote the goal of self-sufficiency (**autarky**) in strategic commodities such as fuels and rubber. Hitler won over industrialists with the promise of government contracts for rearmament and eliminating the perceived socialist threat. In addition, the independent labor unions of the Social Democratic Party were replaced by the **National Labor Front,** a state-run union requiring each worker in good standing to carry a booklet before being able to procure a job. With projects such as the Autobahn, many Germans credited Hitler with getting Germany back to work, even if his pump priming did not represent a long-term solution to Germany's problems.

Nazi racial policy touched all areas of life. Boys were enrolled in the **Hitler Youth** and girls in the **League of German Maidens** to reinforce traditional gender roles and build a strong racial stock. Women were expected to fulfill the domestic duties of "church, kitchen, and children," while their public and economic roles were limited by the state. Anti-Semitic policies fulfilled the Nazi racial vision. At first, Jews were excluded from the civil service and army. To clarify the position of Jews in Germany, the Nazis passed the **Nuremberg Laws** of 1935, which defined who was a Jew, stripped Jews of citizenship, and prohibited sexual relations with "Aryans." Many Jews preferred to remain in Germany, hoping to ride out the Nazi tide. However, Nazi policies turned violent with the *Kristallnacht* (Night of Broken Glass) of November 1938, in which synagogues were burned, businesses destroyed, and hundreds of Jews killed or arrested. To further the goal of a pure Aryan race, the Nazis also engaged in campaigns of **sterilization** for the "mentally unfit" and euthanasia for the terminally ill, insane, and physically deformed. This **T-4 program** killed approximately 200,000 between 1939 and 1941 before protests by religious groups slowed and eventually halted it. For the attentive, the genocidal program laid out in *Mein Kampf* was apparent before the onset of World War II.

The Soviet Union under Stalin, 1928–1939

In the 10-year period 1928–1938, the Soviet Union under Stalin experienced one of the most rapid modernizations in history. After expelling Trotsky, Stalin ended the New Economic Policy (NEP; see Chapter 14) and began building **"socialism in one country."** It was clear by 1928 that world revolution was not imminent, and Stalin wished to push forward the Soviet Union's industrialization as rapidly as possible, appropriating Trotsky's ideas regarding strong central planning to accomplish it. As Stalin saw it, "We are fifty or a hundred years behind the advanced countries. We must make good this distance in ten years. Either we do it, or we shall be crushed."

To move forward, Stalin instituted the first of several **Five-Year Plans** in 1928. Its goals were to build a strong base of heavy industry, aim for self-sufficiency, and create a modern infrastructure of electricity, roads, and factories. Overseeing every intricate detail of production and resource allocation was **Gosplan,** a central government agency staffed by thousands of party bureaucrats. Because the Bolsheviks had repudiated the tsarist debt and could not draw on foreign capital, funds for industrialization had to come from the agricultural sector. During the NEP, a class of wealthy peasants developed who accumulated land and often hired labor among the landless. These **kulaks** were resented by many. To absorb the excess capital of the kulaks, Stalin forced them and all peasants onto collective farms. The kulaks resisted the **forced collectivization of agriculture,** often by destroying crops and slaughtering livestock. Though by 1932 almost all peasants lived on collective farms, the cost proved high—millions of kulaks were killed for resisting collectivization, and millions more died in the **famine** that ensued in Russia and Ukraine from the disruption in agriculture.

> **Sidebar:** Many view this artificial famine as an example of genocide, with estimates of up to 10 million Ukrainians killed. Unfortunately, such questions can become politicized, making it difficult for the impartial to separate fact from fiction. Regardless of the terms used, Stalin's policies certainly resulted in the deaths of tens of millions.

By some measures, the Five-Year Plans proved remarkably successful. The Soviet Union avoided the economic contraction of the Great Depression and soon became the world's largest producer of tractors and railway locomotives. Overall, only the United States and Germany surpassed the Soviet Union in productive capacity. Soviet authorities extolled socialist heroes such as the miner **Stakhanov,** who exceeded his quota for coal by 1300 percent. However, many Soviet manufactures were of poor quality, and consumer goods lagged far behind. The exponential growth in the Soviet economy is explained partly by its start from such a low level.

Stalin imposed a rigid totalitarian system on the Soviet Union. Independent political parties, labor unions, and free expression were eliminated. Government controlled cultural life—art, literature, film—for propaganda purposes. The cultural experimentation of the 1920s was ended; **socialist realism,** glorifying factories and workers, became the accepted standard. Huge posters of Stalin adorned factories and street corners as part of a **"cult of personality."** To rid himself of any real or potential enemies, Stalin initiated the **Great Purges.** Aimed at the **Old Bolsheviks,** the purges ultimately eliminated "leftists" who supported Trotsky, now in exile in Mexico, and "rightists" charged with supporting capitalism. During the Great Terror, from 1934 to 1938, it is estimated that almost 4 million were charged with crimes against the state, and close to 800,000 were executed. Though Soviet citizens experienced a somewhat improved basic standard of living, it came at a high cost. Women, for example, found that many of the reproductive rights gained in the 1920s were reversed as part of a campaign to increase the birth rate, forcing them to balance work and family obligations. Regimentation of Soviet social life acted as the natural by-product of its astounding economic successes.

THE CULTURE OF THE INTERWAR PERIOD

Cultural developments from 1918 to 1939 reflected two distinct trends: (1) the disillusioning effects of World War I in high culture and (2) the further development of a truly mass culture based on new communications technologies. We address both of these areas in turn.

Experimentation and Alienation in High Culture

The writers, artists, and intellectuals who came of age during World War I became known as the **Lost Generation.** Prewar trends of **irrationality, subjectivity,** and **alienation** were confirmed by the experience of the war. German historian **Oswald Spengler** (1880–1936) reflected this sense of pessimism in his book *The Decline of the West,* which argued that Europe possessed the innate tendency to engage in self-destructive acts and was doomed to decadence. Writers of fiction worked in similar themes. **Franz Kafka** (1883–1924) described characters caught up in an incomprehensible world with no capacity to alter their fate. In one of the great antiwar novels, Erich Maria Remarque's (1898–1970) *All Quiet on the Western Front* showed matter of factly how war destroys innocence and meaning. T. S. Eliot's epic poem **"The Waste Land"** (1922) captured a similar sense of decline and the absurdity of human existence.

Many writers experimented with **stream-of-consciousness** styles and unstructured works to convey the subjective nature of experience. Marcel Proust's *Remembrance of Things Past* explores the narrator's memories of childhood experiences amid a half-waking state. James Joyce's *Ulysses* stands as the masterwork of modernist literature, examining one day in the life of Dublin resident Stephen Dedalus through mental associations and word play. Virginia Woolf experimented with similar techniques but combined them with feminist themes. Expatriates (those who live outside their culture or nation) from the United States—Ernest Hemingway, F. Scott Fitzgerald, and Gertrude Stein—worked in similar styles and themes and demonstrated the growing influence of American culture as well as the profound sense of alienation in the Western world as a whole.

Modern art became incredibly diverse in the twentieth century. Weimar Germany, and Berlin in particular, became a center of experimentation in the arts; in painting, German artists such as George Grosz and Hannah Hoch employed expressionist and Dadaist techniques to critique the perceived weakness and corruption of Weimar. **Dadaism** represented an anti-art movement, using artistic media to show the absurdity of life. Examples include collages of disconnected images or distorted caricatures. Abstraction reduces reality down to its essentials—line, shape, and color. In the massive mural *Guernica* (1937), Pablo Picasso conveys the horror of a fascist atrocity during the Spanish Civil War through the spare use of symbols and Cubist multiple perspective. Furthermore, Freud's ideas regarding the unconscious began to influence painting with the artistic movement of **surrealism.** Spanish surrealist **Salvador Dali** (1904–1989) gained fame for his bizarre juxtaposition of objects and dreamy landscapes, as in his ubiquitous *The Persistence of Memory* (1931). In architecture, modernists from the **Bauhaus** school, such as **Walter Gropius** (1883–1969) and Mies van der Rohe (1886–1969) in Germany, worked with concrete, steel, and glass to design straightforward "boxes with windows." When the Nazis took power in 1933, they condemned the works of such architects and other artists as "degenerate" and intimidated them out of the country.

The sciences and the social sciences confirmed prewar trends toward the irrational and the uncertain. In *Civilization and Its Discontents* (1931), Sigmund Freud argued that aggressive human drives inevitably led to violence and war, an observation given credence by World War I. Building on Freud's ideas, Swiss psychiatrist **Carl Jung** (1875–1961) developed the notion of the **collective unconscious,** that part of a person's psyche common to all human beings and made up of archetypes, basic character types forming all experiences. Physicists continued to explore the structure of the subatomic world and time. **Werner Heisenberg** (1901–1976) demonstrated with his **uncertainty principle** how one could not observe both the position and momentum of a particle, as the act of observation itself alters the behavior of what is observed. Heisenberg's theory supported the quantum notion of probabilities over objectively determined realities.

> **Heads Up!** Many students, especially those who have taken U.S. History prior to this course, often conflate American and European experiences. In the twentieth century, much overlap and mutual influence exists, but try to avoid projecting distinctly U.S. experiences, such as Prohibition, onto Europe.

Mass Culture and Leisure

The experience of shared suffering during World War I provoked a shift in public morals. During the Roaring Twenties, displays of sexuality grew more open, women smoked in public, and dance halls gained popularity. Fashion challenged traditional gender roles, as women wore less defining and more revealing clothing. In many European states, laws against the distribution of birth control were abandoned. Germany's **cabaret culture** featured sultry **jazz** music along with frank themes of sexuality. African-American Josephine Baker took Europe by storm with exotic and erotic dance routines. These developments divided Europeans between those who celebrated the new openness as part of a general democratization and those who condemned it as a decadent feature of post-WWI society.

During the prosperous 1920s, many businesses developed **installment plans** and allowed buying on **credit. Advertising,** often using celebrities and sports figures, fed a new **consumerism** in household appliances, beauty aids, and automobiles. Governments openly encouraged the purchase of **radios** and attendance at **motion pictures.** New communication technologies offered opportunities to shape public opinion and promote propaganda. Nazi Germany ensured that all citizens owned a *Volksempfänger* (people's radio) so as to hear Hitler's speeches. Minister of Propaganda **Joseph Goebbels** (1897–1945) elevated visual spectacle to new heights in Nazi films and festivals. Democratic states also recognized the potential of mass communication; in 1927, the British Broadcasting Corporation (**BBC**) was chartered. Ironically, filmmakers such as Charlie Chaplin with *Modern Times* (1936) and Fritz Lang with Metropolis (1927) used the medium to critique the modern obsession with technology.

With increased leisure time, Europeans engaged in more air travel and tourism. Totalitarian states encouraged such activities around state-run agencies, such as *Kraft durch Freude* (Strength through Joy) in Nazi Germany, which sponsored camping, hiking, and boating trips. In tune with racial ideologies and eugenics, governments promoted a "**cult of the body**" through organized sports, such as gymnastics, soccer, and track and field. Nazi Germany held the **1936 Berlin Olympics** as a showplace for the superiority of the Aryan race. Though Germany did win the most medals, African-American track star Jesse Owens stole the show with five gold medals.

THE ROAD TO WORLD WAR II, 1933–1939: APPEASEMENT

Though historians still debate the causes of World War I, those of World War II lack controversy—the ambitions of Nazi Germany to overturn the Versailles settlement. Seemingly every year after taking power until the commencement of hostilities in 1939, Adolph Hitler provoked an international crisis related to his goals of creating a **New European Order** around race. Hitler sought first to regain those lands lost at Versailles; second, to subdue France and bring Britain to friendly terms; third, to turn east and conquer Slavic Europe as a vast granary and slave labor force; and finally, in the process, to eliminate "culture destroyers" such as Jews and Gypsies. That Hitler almost accomplished these goals demonstrates the fragility of the post-WWI diplomatic order.

To avoid another war, the western democracies engaged in **appeasement,** or an attempt to meet Hitler's demands through diplomacy. Today, the term suggests cowardice and folly, but at the time it was driven by several concerns: (1) lack of preparation for war due to budget constraints created by the Great Depression, (2) a greater fear of Soviet communism, and (3) the genuine feeling that the horrors of Verdun and the Somme must not be repeated. The following chronology serves to demonstrate the evolution of Hitler's goals and tactics, as well as the application and eventual abandonment of appeasement. Without the active diplomatic support of the Soviet Union (due to its exclusion) and the United States (due to its isolation), it seemed an almost impossible task to deter Hitler or Mussolini, not to mention the Japanese.

1931: In pursuit of natural resources, Japan invades the Chinese province of **Manchuria.** Rhetorical denunciations by the League of Nations provoke Japan's withdrawal from that body.

1933: Hitler withdraws Germany from the League of Nations and the Geneva disarmament conference, primarily to demonstrate domestically that no international institution can restrain German initiatives.

1934: An attempted Nazi overthrow of the Austrian government fails, due primarily to the intervention of Mussolini, who fears the growth of German power on his border and covets Austrian lands for himself.

1935: Hitler openly repudiates the Versailles provisions related to demilitarization. Great Britain "rewards" Germany's open rearmament with an **Anglo-German Naval Agreement,** allowing Hitler to build up his navy.

To avenge Italy's defeat in 1896, Mussolini **invades Ethiopia** without provocation. In a failure of collective security, Britain and France's half-hearted economic sanctions and military actions fail to prevent Italy's conquest of Ethiopia.

1936: Rejecting Versailles and the Locarno Pact, Hitler boldly **remilitarizes the Rhineland.** France and Britain do nothing, convincing Hitler of their weakness.

Since 1931, Spain had been ruled by a republic. The republican government moved against the entrenched power of the Catholic Church and large landowners. Elections in 1936 led to the creation of a Popular Front of leftist parties aimed against monarchists, clerical supporters, and army officers. Military officers, led by **General Francisco Franco** (1892–1975) and aided by the Fascist **Falange** movement, attempt to overthrow the republic, plunging the nation into a vicious civil war between nationalists and Loyalists. The **Spanish Civil War** (1936–1939) becomes a test of rival ideological forces—fascism vs. communism—and a **"warm-up for World War II."** Other than a few idealists from the democracies, the only nation willing to commit significant resources for the anti-fascist battle is the Soviet Union. Fascist forces launch aerial bombardments aimed at civilians in Madrid, Barcelona, and Guernica, a preview of the horrors to come. By 1939, Franco gains control of the nation, but only at the cost of 600,000 lives—Spain's deadliest conflict.

In the wake of the Spanish Civil War, Hitler signs the **Rome-Berlin Axis** with Mussolini and the **Anti-Comintern Pact** with Japan.

1937: In a secret meeting with his military advisors, Hitler outlines his future plans for the absorption of Austria, Czechoslovakia, and Poland into the German Reich. Those opposing Hitler's plans are replaced with Nazi "yes-men."

Japan launches an all-out invasion of China proper, leading to its control of China's coastal cities. Though China moves inland to continue the fight, Japanese forces capture Nanking. Japanese troops kill 250,000 civilians indiscriminately and rape thousands of women in an atrocity known as the "**rape of Nanking.**"

1938: With Mussolini's approval, Hitler marches into his native Austria, directly incorporating it into the German Reich. In a subsequent plebiscite (vote of the common people), the Austrian people overwhelmingly approve the annexation (*Anschluss*).

Hitler demands incorporation of 3 million Germans of the Czech **Sudetenland.** Czechoslovakia stands as the most democratic, industrial, and strategically vital nation of Eastern Europe. Tied to France through the Little Entente and with strong defenses, Czechoslovakia seems an ideal spot to stop Hitler's aggression. Nonetheless, British Prime Minister **Neville Chamberlain** (1869–1940) urges compromise at a four-power meeting (Britain, France, Germany, Italy) called by Hitler. The western democracies exclude the Soviet Union and Czechoslovakia itself at the **Munich Conference,** which signs over the Sudetenland to Germany. Upon arriving back in Britain, Chamberlain proclaims he has achieved "**peace in our time.**"

1939: Violating the Munich Agreement, Hitler in the spring marches into the Czech portion of Czechoslovakia, creating a protectorate, while making Slovakia a puppet government. In addition, Mussolini moves into Albania to establish a foothold for his *mare nostrum* ("our sea") project of controlling the Mediterranean. These actions cause a decisive shift in public opinion within the west against appeasement; however, France and Britain prove unable to win over a suspicious Soviet Union into a joint alliance against Nazi Germany.

Sidebar: Strategic bombing (i.e., of civilian areas) played a major role in the war, with the famous examples of Dresden, Hamburg, London, Tokyo, and Warsaw. Though these efforts hindered communication and transportation, as well as fuel supplies, they did not affect production decisively or break the will to fight, except in the case of the atomic bombs dropped on Japan.

Shocking the world, Hitler and Stalin in late August conclude the **Nazi-Soviet Non-Aggression Pact,** giving Hitler a free hand for his next project—an invasion of Poland to regain the **Danzig corridor,** which cuts off East Prussia from Germany proper. A secret protocol provides for the division of Poland, the Baltic States, and Finland between the supposedly bitter ideological enemies. A week later, Hitler invades Poland to begin World War II.

WORLD WAR II, 1939–1945

World War II stands as the most destructive conflict in history, killing an estimated 50 million people. It involved the nations of six continents and decisively altered Europe's position in the world. As with any war, new technologies—**radar,** rockets, jet airplanes, atomic weapons—played a major role. Never before had the line between soldier and civilian been so blurred, with civilians and entire ethnic groups targeted for extermination. Keeping in mind the previous caveats about military history on the AP Exam, the following chart should provide a general understanding of the nature and course of the conflict.

Phases of the Conflict

Phase	Goals and Strategy	Actions and Results	Assessment
Blitzkrieg, 1939–1941	In the early phase of the war, Hitler takes the initiative and attacks Poland. The following spring, the Nazis move against Norway, the Low Countries, and France. In its first defeat, Germany is unable to bring Britain to its knees. Without directly entering the conflict, President Franklin Roosevelt of the United States provides aid to Great Britain with the **Lend-Lease Act** and signs the **Atlantic Charter** with Winston Churchill, the new leader of Britain, outlining the Anglo-American war aims. By the end of 1941, Japan's attack on the United States and Hitler's invasion of its former ally, the USSR, cements the Grand Alliance	* With armored divisions and aerial bombers, Hitler's *blitzkrieg* ("lightning war") defeats Poland in a matter of weeks. Meanwhile, Britain and France declare war but do not attack, labeled by critics as the "phony war." * Soviet troops move into the Baltic states, eastern Poland, and attack Finland. Soviet troops perform poorly but eventually defeat Finnish forces. * In the spring of 1940, Hitler secures his northern flank vis-à-vis Britain and supplies of iron ore by taking Norway. The Nazis next defeat the Low Countries and France, as Mussolini lends a hand. German forces occupy the northern two-thirds of France, allowing the creation of the collaborationist **Vichy** government in the south. **Free French** forces under **Charles de Gaulle** (1890–1970) continue resistance. * Under the strong leadership of **Prime**	By the end of 1941, Hitler continues to hold the initiative. Nazi Germany continues to dominate Europe and works toward a joint strategy with Japan to link forces in Central Asia. Churchill and Roosevelt agree to concentrate on the war in Europe, with the Pacific theater taking a back seat. Hitler's invasion of the USSR takes Stalin by surprise and also allows for the beginning of the systematic **genocide** of Slavs, Gypsies, and Jews.

Phase	Goals and Strategy	Actions and Results	Assessment
Blitzkrieg, 1939–1941	against the Rome-Tokyo-Berlin Axis powers.	**Minister Winston Churchill** (1874–1965), Britain defeats Germany in the **Battle of Britain.** The German *Luftwaffe* (air force) loses twice the planes of the **Royal Air Force** (RAF). Bombing of cities by the Nazis only hardens British resistance. * Mussolini's attempted invasion in 1941 of Greece falters, drawing German forces into the Balkans. * In the largest land battle in history (3 million men on a 2,000-mile front), Hitler **invades** the **Soviet Union** in June 1941, capturing huge swaths of territory before stalling in front of Moscow in December. * The Japanese capture French colonies in Indochina, leading the United States to cut off oil and scrap metal shipments. In retaliation, the Japanese launch the surprise attack on **Pearl Harbor,** drawing America into the war.	
Turning of the Tide, 1942–1944	Hitler divides his armies into three groups in the Soviet Union—aimed at Leningrad (formerly St. Petersburg), Moscow, and the Caucasus oil fields. The Japanese attack on Pearl Harbor is followed by the expansion of its empire throughout the Pacific, called	* Soviet forces regroup and capture an entire German army in February 1943 at **Stalingrad.** At the tank **Battle of Kursk,** the Soviet Union decisively turns the tide and begins an inexorable advance toward Germany. * The German-Italian advance toward the Suez Canal in North Africa is stopped in July 1942 at **El Alamein.** An	By 1943, the tide had turned against the Axis powers. In late 1943, the Big Three (Churchill, Roosevelt, and Stalin) met at the **Teheran Conference** and agreed on the **unconditional surrender** of the Axis powers, and the Anglo-Americans agreed to open a second front in France. Before

Phase	Goals and Strategy	Actions and Results	Assessment
Turning of the Tide, 1942–1944	the **Greater East Asian Co-Prosperity Sphere,** reaching its height in the spring of 1942. German and Italian forces attack British forces in North Africa, threatening the Suez Canal. In a series of counterattacks, the Allies defeat the Axis in North Africa, the Soviet Union, and in the Pacific.	Anglo-American invasion pushes German forces under Erwin Rommel out of North Africa. * Anglo-American forces launch an **invasion of Sicily** and move up the peninsula of Italy. Mussolini is captured by Allied forces in 1943 but rescued by German paratroopers. The Allied drive up the peninsula stalls outside Rome as German forces take up the fight. * The American naval victory at **Midway** deals a decisive blow to Japan's naval strength. At **Guadalcanal,** the U.S. amphibious invasion blunts Japan's threat to Australia.	launching an amphibious assault, the United States needed to secure control of the seas from German submarines, largely accomplished by early 1944. In the Pacific, American forces began the strategy of **"island hopping"** to gain a base of operations directly against the Japanese home islands.
Endgame, 1944–1945	Anglo-American forces establish a second front in France and along with the advance of Soviet forces, move toward the German homeland. Soviet forces divert into the Balkans to ensure Soviet forces paused outside Warsaw in September 1944 to watch the Nazis destroy Soviet control of Eastern Europe following the war. U.S. forces close in on the Japanese home islands. Following fierce fighting, the Pacific war ends with the dropping of two **atomic bombs** on	* At the **D-Day invasion** of Normandy (June 1944), the United States and Britain establish a beachhead in France, which eventually leads to the liberation of Paris by August. * Soviet forces pursued outside Warsaw in September 1944 to watch the Nazis destroy the **Polish Home Army** during their effort to liberate the city. It was later discovered that 20,000 Polish army officers had been slaughtered under Stalin's orders in the **Katyn Massacre.** * In the Pacific, U.S. forces retake the Philippines, capture	The combined manpower and economic potential of the Allied powers exercises a decisive influence on the course of the war. In addition, strategic errors by the Axis powers as well as the unification of numerous groups opposed to the brutal rule of the Nazis eventually works in the Allies' favor. America's use of the first atomic weapons ends World War II but also marks the beginning of the Nuclear Age and the Cold War.

Phase	Goals and Strategy	Actions and Results	Assessment
Endgame, 1944–1945	Hiroshima and Nagasaki.	Iwo Jima and Okinawa after fierce fighting, and begin aerial bombing of Tokyo. * Widespread bombing of German cities begins, exemplified by the fire bombing of **Dresden** in February 1945. * A last-ditch German advance in Belgium (**Battle of the Bulge**) is eventually turned back, and Anglo-American and Soviet forces end the war in the Germany by May 1945. * After the dropping of the atomic bombs, Japan sues for peace in September 1945.	

Mobilization of the Home Fronts

World War II required an even higher level of mobilization and sacrifice among civilians than did World War I. Many governments centralized production, instituted rationing programs, and called on all citizens to contribute to the war effort in some way. The following are several examples of such mobilization:

Germany: Despite the common perception of Nazi regimentation and early invincibility, Germany did not mobilize effectively for wartime production. Hitler was reluctant to promote women in the workforce or call on German citizens to sacrifice consumer goods, recognizing the collapse of the war effort in 1917–1918. Nazi Germany relied extensively on **slave labor** from conquered and occupied territories for armaments production. It was not until 1942 that Hitler appointed a young architect, **Albert Speer** (1905–1981), to centralize production as **Minister of Armaments.** Only in 1944, when the war was nearing its end, did Germany move toward full mobilization, closing down popular amusements and rationing goods. German women never did enter the workforce in large numbers.

Soviet Union: For the Soviet Union, the conflict was known as the **Great Patriotic War,** a fight for its very survival. Over 20 million Soviet citizens perished in the war, by far the most of any combatant. Once the Nazis had captured some of the best agricultural lands and threatened key industrial cities, the Soviets moved entire factories inland, which commenced production before the walls went up. Stalin promoted **supercentralization** of the economy around the war effort and reduced the already paltry production of consumer goods, allowing the USSR to win the "battle of the machines." The city of **Leningrad** endured a 900-day **siege,** its residents often surviving on mice; spring thaws revealed thousands of corpses in the streets. Women also served in the armed forces, unique among the combatants, as with the famous "Night Witches" fighter pilots protecting Stalingrad.

Great Britain: Great Britain effectively centralized its economy for wartime production. Almost every able-bodied adult assisted the war effort—women went into armament production and older citizens joined the **Home Guard.** The government created ministries to oversee and distribute fuel, food, and war supplies. In addition, citizens were encouraged to develop self-sufficiency in food production, as with "**Dig for Victory**" gardens. Citizens received **ration books** with coupons and received only those goods assigned to them. The shared sacrifice of rationing continued even after the war, ending only in 1951.

United States: President Roosevelt urged the United States to become the "**arsenal of democracy**" for the Allied powers. On one hand, no nation was producing more tanks, planes, and ships by the end of the conflict. However, the United States never entered a complete wartime production footing. Though rationing was practiced, it did not reach the levels of European control, particularly with fuel consumption. After Pearl Harbor, thousands of **Japanese** citizens of the United States on the West Coast were forced into **internment camps** to prevent their conspiring with the Japanese Empire.

Collaboration and Resistance

Europeans of occupied nations faced stark choices—to collaborate or resist. A major reason for Nazi success militarily and with genocide involves the active cooperation or apathetic acceptance of many in occupied lands. Conservatives in many nations welcomed the Nazi takeover as a solution to indigenous political problems. To assist in ruling occupied lands, Nazi Germany created puppet governments. In Norway, Vadkun Quisling lent his name, "**quisling,**" to those who betray their nation by assisting a foreign power's conquest. Though nominally independent, the Vichy regime in France cooperated with Nazi authorities, assisting in the Nazi Final Solution (see following discussion). Reprisals against thousands of collaborators followed right after the armies of liberation. In the complex Balkans, the **Ustashe,** a nationalist and Catholic government of Croatia, assisted the Nazis in taking reprisals against Orthodox Serbs.

Anti-Nazi movements gained momentum as the war tide turned. Resistance groups engaged in acts of sabotage and assassination, hindered production, rescued ethnic minorities, and spread anti-Nazi or nationalist propaganda. Strongly organized movements arose in France under Charles de Gaulle and in Yugoslavia under **Joseph Broz Tito** (1892–1980). Due to the latter's efforts, Yugoslavia became the only nation in Eastern Europe that did not require the aid of the Soviet army to liberate itself from Nazi rule. The Polish council, **Zegota,** saved hundreds of Jews in Poland, while Denmark was able to engineer the rescue of almost all 8,000 of its Jewish population. Within Germany, a group of idealistic university students, named the **White Rose,** distributed pamphlets against the Nazis before being caught and executed. Conservative army officers attempted but failed to assassinate Hitler in July 1944, leading to the execution of thousands.

The Holocaust

Soon after taking power, the Nazis established a network of concentration camps to punish political prisoners and other "undesirables." From that point, Nazi policy moved step by step, from exclusion to concentration to extermination, or the **"Final Solution"**—the elimination of all of Europe's Jews, as well as Gypsies, Slavic intellectuals, Russian prisoners of war, Jehovah's Witnesses, and homosexuals. Mass killing began with the Nazi invasion of the Soviet Union in 1941; mobile killings squads, known as *Einsatzgruppen*, machine gunned thousands and buried them in mass graves.

In 1942, top Nazi officials met at the **Wannsee Conference.** Led by **Reinhard Heydrich** (1904–1942), the head of the S.S. security office, the meeting decided on the implementation of the Final Solution to the "Jewish problem." The Nazis erected a system of death camps in Poland—**Auschwitz**, Treblinka, Sobibor, Belzéc, and others—designed to kill thousands per day in gas chambers, their bodies destroyed in crematoria. Even as the war turned against the Nazis on the battlefield, Hitler continued to pour resources into this "race" war, stepping up the extermination as Allied armies approached. Only the participation of thousands of people, including those in the occupied nations, made such a massive and systematic process possible. By the end of the war, 6 million Jews had been killed (the Holocaust), along with another 5 million from the other categories discussed, in the Nazi genocide.

Results of World War II

By 1945, much of Europe lay in ruins; some cities, such as Warsaw, experienced complete devastation. World War II represents the lowest point for European civilization. Some of the results can be measured in numbers; others would become clear only in subsequent years.

- **40 to 50 million dead, mostly civilians**
- **Widespread destruction of infrastructure**
- **30 to 50 million displaced persons (DPs) wandering the continent**
- **Europe's hold on its colonies nearly broken**
- **Traditional values questioned in postwar Europe**
- **Economic activity breaks down**
- **Conditions laid for the Cold War**

All analyses aside, World War II stands as the single largest event in the history of the human race.

ADDITIONAL READINGS

Allen, William S., *The Nazi Seizure of Power: The Experience of a Single German Town, 1922–1945* (rev. 1989)—This local study provides strong insights into how the Nazi party operated.

Arendt, Hannah, *The Origins of Totalitarianism* (rev. 1966)—Explores the meaning and development of a major political development in the twentieth century; by a well-known political philosopher.

Baumel, Judith Tydor, and Walter Laqueur, *The Holocaust Encyclopedia* (2001)—A comprehensive and well-written resource.

Burleigh, Michael, *The Third Reich: A New History* (2000)—This volume serves as a useful resource on all things related to Nazi Germany.

Gay, Peter, *Weimar Culture: The Outsider as Insider* (rev. 2001)—A noted historian examines cultural experimentation amid a fractured political climate.

Mazower, Mark, *Dark Continent: Europe's Twentieth Century* (1999)—Portrays the era as a violent clash between democracy, Fascism, and communism.

Rosenbaum, Ron, *Explaining Hitler: The Search for the Origins of His Evil* (1999)—A psychologist pursues various theories to explain the nature of human evil.

Weinberg, Gerhard, *A World at Arms: A Global History of World War II* (rev. 2005)—Strictly for military history buffs, the most comprehensive and riveting account of the war.

www.indiana.edu/~league/—A photo archive for the League of Nations; also includes text on league organs and functions.

www.loc.gov/exhibits/archives/—This Library of Congress site features formerly secret documents from the Soviet archives.

www.russianphotographs.com/exhibitions/index.html—An excellent site for photographs from the Soviet perspective, including World War II.

www.ushmm.org/—The official site of the United States Holocaust Museum in Washington, D.C.; features a searchable encyclopedia.

PRACTICE QUESTIONS

1. Which is the best characterization of European diplomacy in the period 1919–1933?
   a. effective use of the League of Nations to deter conflict
   b. a coalition of great powers united against communism
   c. a growing partnership between France and the Unites States
   d. Germany's acceptance of the Versailles settlement
   e. inability to create a balance of power or collective security
2. The new democracies in Eastern Europe faced all of the following problems in the period 1918–1839 EXCEPT:
   a. Austrian efforts to reestablish the Habsburg Empire.
   b. disputes over contested ethnic borderlands.
   c. underdeveloped economies and lack of industry.
   d. lack of a strong democratic tradition.
   e. weak middle class and continued aristocratic influence.

3. The accompanying photograph illustrates which of the following problems faced by the German Weimar Republic, 1918–1933?
   a. corrupt practices by German industrialists
   b. right-wing efforts to overthrow the government
   c. rapid inflation that eroded the value of money
   d. interference by France in German affairs
   e. lack of support among influential Germans

akg-images

4. Experimentation in the arts and literature during the period 1918–1939 focused on themes of:
   a. violence and conflict.
   b. alienation and disillusionment.
   c. love and harmony.
   d. science and technology.
   e. order and symmetry.

5. This quote best expresses the political beliefs of:
   a. liberal democracy.
   b. Soviet communism.
   c. trade unionism.
   d. fascism.
   e. authoritarianism.

"The State represents the force of the nation's spirit in history. The individual's existence has meaning only within the collective will of State, represented by a people of pure racial characteristic. Nature has assigned some races to a superior position in the struggle for existence, a struggle given its highest tension with war. War calls up all of the noblest traits of the people and breathes life into the State."

6. To gain power in Germany, Hitler and the Nazi Party after 1923 attempted to:
   a. create a mass political movement and promote disorder.
   b. overthrow the Weimar Republic by armed force.
   c. form an alliance with the Catholic Center Party.
   d. win support by accepting the Versailles settlement.
   e. join with Soviet agitators in plotting a coup.

7. Which of the following best characterizes the Soviet economy from 1928 to 1938?
   a. continuation of the New Economic Policy and more consumer goods.
   b. rapidly declining levels of productivity due to the Great Purges.
   c. centralization involving rapid industrialization and communal agriculture.
   d. the development of a class of commercial farmers and wealthy merchants.
   e. foreign aid leading to increasing levels of trade with Western Europe.

8. This painting by Pablo Picasso portrays:
   a. a street riot in Berlin against hyperinflation.
   b. Soviet efforts to liquidate the kulaks.
   c. French resistance efforts during World War II.
   d. killing of ethnic minorities during the Holocaust.
   e. fascist bombing of civilians in the Spanish Civil War.

Guernica by Pablo Picasso (Spanish, 1881–1973)
Art Resource, NY/© 2007 The Estate of Pablo Picasso/Artists Rights Society (ARS), New York

9. The western democracies' policy of appeasement reached its height during the:
   a. Kellogg-Briand Pact.
   b. Munich Conference.
   c. *Anschluss* of Austria.
   d. Spanish Civil War.
   e. Rapallo Pact.

10. A major reason for the Nazis' ability to eliminate ethnic minorities, especially Jews, in large numbers during World War II was because:
    a. many in the occupied lands collaborated with the Nazi program.
    b. the Nazis kept the Final Solution a secret until the end of the war.
    c. the Allies failed in their efforts to rescue the threatened groups.
    d. many of the targeted groups were killed during aerial bombardment.
    e. the Nazis were able to pit the targeted groups against one another.

SAMPLE ESSAY

Explain the concept of totalitarianism and analyze its practice in TWO of the following nations.

Nazi Germany, 1933–1945
Fascist Italy, 1922–1943
Stalinist Soviet Union, 1928–1945

It was no surprise that after World War I many extreme ideologies arose. A majority of these extremes generally had some form of totalitarianism. It was also no surprise that this form of government arose because during World War I even many liberal democracies increased the power and role of the state in economic and political affairs. Mussolini is often considered the first totalitarian ruler, but he did not follow all of the practices of totalitarianism as well as his mentor Adolph Hitler in Germany. Even though Mussolini was first, Hitler was the first ruler to follow a majority of the theory of totalitarianism. Although both followed the main objective of totalitarianism, which is the active support and loyalty of the citizens, Mussolini made a few concessions and did not use the full power as the other totalitarian Hitler did. Both were totalitarian leaders but Hitler was to a greater extent.

Mussolini came to power in Italy after World War I because Italy was in need of a strong leader because Italy had economic, political, and social problems that could only be addressed by a strong leader. Mussolini was this leader, as he also was the first totalitarian leader of Europe. The main difference between a monarchy and a totalitarian leader is that a totalitarian leader such as Mussolini needed the active support of the citizens, not just a passive obedience. Another part of a totalitarian government that Mussolini had was the fear and chaos factor. Mussolini helped create chaos with his squadristi, or black shirts. By creating this chaos, Mussolini would be seen as a leader of order which is important for totalitarian leaders. Also, Mussolini followed another practice of totalitarianism which was that he shut out all other political opposition. He could and did stop other political parties from forming and he also had a hand in the assassination of the socialist leader Matteoti. To have no competition is another facet of totalitarianism. Mussolini also had a heavy control on the press which is very important to totalitarian leaders. He was able to control what his citizens read in the newspaper. But this is also beginning to show where Mussolini doesn't follow all of the practices as well as Hitler did in Germany. Although Mussolini controlled the press he did not use it for his benefit. He did not use the full advantages of propaganda which he could use to sway the mindset of his citizens. Also Mussolini did not have as great as citizen groups that Hitler did. Mussolini tried to concentrate on the Italian youth more than the adults by having Youth groups. But these groups even were not enforced as being mandatory and therefore Mussolini did not have as active of a citizenship as Hitler. Lastly Mussolini made a compromise with the Catholic Church during his rule which really doesn't follow the totalitarian ideology. In the Lateran Accords Mussolini made an agreement with the Pope that he would tell all of the Italians to be Catholic if the Pope recognized the Italian state. Some totalitarian leaders such as Stalin would not have made any concessions to anyone, let alone a person of the clergy. So although Mussolini was the first leader to practice the rule of totalitarianism, he did not follow all of the practices as well as some later leaders.

One such later leader was Hitler who was also a totalitarian leader, but followed more of the facets of totalitarianism than Mussolini. Hitler like Mussolini demanded the active support of the citizens because without this a leader is not truly totalitarian. Hitler also created fear and chaos in Germany with his Storm Troops. Once again like Mussolini, Hitler was seen as a leader of order which is important in totalitarian rulers. Also Hitler similarly to Mussolini got rid of all other political competition. Also like Mussolini, Hitler had a hand in assassinating another political leader, in this case Rohm. Also Hitler violently put down any other political parties with force and violence. This is where Hitler becomes more of a totalitarian leader than Mussolini. Not only did Hitler control the press like Mussolini, but Hitler fully used propaganda to further his cause and gain the active support of the citizens. Hitler had a whole ministry devoted to propaganda all used to change the mindset of the people. Also Hitler had more use of groups to enhance the active support of the citizens. He had youth groups which instilled the Nazi viewpoints in children as well as instilling them in school, which of course was mandatory. But Hitler also had groups and rallies for adults. The most famous and most influential of these was the Nuremberg Rallies, which gathered millions of Germans together and created a great sense of camaraderie and also produced active support for the totalitarian rule of Hitler. But not even Hitler was a perfect example of totalitarian rule, although he was the closest to it. Hitler too made a Concordat with the Catholic churches in Germany. Even though by doing this it furthered his power, making concessions to churches of religious people is not in the concept of totalitarianism. Although Hitler wasn't the first totalitarian leader, he put into play more of the theories of totalitarianism than the first, Mussolini of Italy.

The main concept behind totalitarianism is the active support of the citizens which both leaders received, although Hitler had more. Also important to totalitarian leaders is chaos, which was created by the Storm Troops and squadristi. Both leaders also eliminated all potential political competition by assassinating other leaders like Matteoti and Rohm. Having no other competition is important to totalitarian leaders. Both had control of the press, but Hitler was the only one who used it to his advantage, making him a more totalitarian leader. Also, Hitler had more rallies and groups to make his citizens more active than the Italians. But both leaders made concessions with the Church which does not truly follow the concept of totalitarianism.

This sample essay is a very strong response. From the outset, the student displays control of the question by defining the key characteristics of totalitarianism. In addition, an explicit comparison, if somewhat general, is given regarding Hitler's closer approximation to the theory than Mussolini. Both of the body paragraphs provide full treatment of each nation with several specific examples. Despite a few unclear references—e.g., Mussolini's use of propaganda—the essay offers more than enough support to show student mastery of the topic. The discussion of Hitler's propaganda techniques and policies related to the church illustrates a higher grasp of the material. Though the conclusion tends to repeat previous points, it certainly does not detract from an already strong essay. Score: 9.

CHAPTER 16

The Cold War
and European Recovery

Looking across Europe in 1945, one saw a civilization in ruins. Europeans suffered through one of the coldest winters on record in 1945–1946; Germans called this time their *Stunde Null,* or zero hour. Destruction and devastation created a power vacuum in Europe, into which rushed the new contending superpowers of the United States and the Soviet Union. Due to fundamental economic and political differences and a cycle of action-reaction by each side, by 1947 the two superpowers were locked in a Cold War that divided Western from Eastern Europe. Competition between the superpowers decisively shaped the contrasting development of the two regions: the West toward economic recovery and integration and the East under Soviet domination and ultimately rebellion. In the final analysis, Europe rose like a phoenix from the ashes after 1945, but its recovery has been marked by fits and starts, successes and failures. By 1991, a new era opened with the collapse of communism and the Soviet Union itself, an opportunity for the continent to work toward a European identity that combined East and West.

Note: To users of Palmer, Colton, and Kramer, *A History of the Modern World,* this chapter condenses material from Chapters 22 through 27 in your text.

THE COLD WAR, 1943–1991

Origins of the Conflict

Sidebar: The question of responsibility for the onset of the Cold War represents a major historiographical issue. During the 1940s and 1950s, American historians emphasized the role of Soviet expansion in driving the conflict. By the 1960s and 1970s, in the midst of Vietnam and with newly declassified documents, revisionist historians tended to blame the nature of American capitalism and U.S. atomic policy for the Cold War. By the 1980s, a postrevisionist school emerged explaining the conflict in terms of a downward spiral of misinterpretations and actions-reactions.

The Grand Alliance between the Anglo-American powers and the Soviet Union had always been a marriage of convenience; it was a relationship based on a battle against a common enemy—the Nazis. Since the Bolshevik Revolution, relations between the new Soviet Union and the west had been strained: (1) The Allies sent assistance to the White Army during the Russian Civil War; (2) the United States did not recognize the Soviet Union until 1933; (3) the western democracies excluded the Soviet Union from interwar diplomacy while appeasing Hitler; and (4) Stalin and Hitler joined in dividing Poland to initiate World War II.

During World War II, the so-called **Big Three** (Stalin, Churchill, Roosevelt) met several times to forge common policies; these meetings also revealed strains in the alliance. In February 1945 at **Yalta,** just months from victory, the Big Three met to discuss the layout of postwar Europe. Soviet armies stood within 40 miles of Berlin and dominated most of Eastern Europe. This reality determined much of the Anglo-American posture toward Stalin, though Roosevelt tended to see himself as the mediator between the more *Realpolitik*-oriented Churchill and Stalin. The parties agreed to the **Declaration on Liberated Europe,** which promised national self-determination and **free elections** in Eastern Europe. Stalin was especially concerned with controlling postwar Poland, which territorially was moved 300 miles west at the expense of Germany and to the benefit of the Soviet Union. As for Germany, the three leaders agreed it must be disarmed and de-Nazified, though they differed over Stalin's proposal for its complete dismemberment and the extraction of $20 billion in reparations. Finally, the Big Three agreed to create the **United Nations** in hopes of resolving future security issues. Despite the agreements, it soon became clear that the Anglo-Americans and Soviets interpreted their decisions differently, particularly free elections. Later critics viewed Roosevelt's position as a "sell out" of Eastern Europe in order to gain Soviet support for the continuing war against Japan.

When the Allies next met at **Potsdam** in July 1945, the war in Europe had ended. In the interim, Roosevelt had died and his successor, **Harry Truman** (1884–1972), proved more suspicious of Stalin's intentions. Also, during the conference, Labour leader Clement Attlee was voted into office as prime minister, replacing Churchill. The Allies agreed to hold war crimes **trials** of the top Nazi leaders **at Nuremberg,** divide Germany into **four occupation zones,** and provide **reparations** for the rebuilding of the Soviet Union. However, disagreements between the United States and the Soviet Union deepened over Poland and the other Eastern European states. When the United States abruptly ended aid to the Soviet Union (but not Great Britain) in the spring of 1945 and developed its monopoly on atomic weapons, Soviet suspicions of American intentions mounted. By 1947, a series of disagreements led to a fracturing of the wartime alliance and open if often restrained conflict between the former allies.

Nature of the Conflict

The Cold War played out as a complex, multipronged worldwide competition between the **superpowers** of the Untied States and the Soviet Union.

Political: The United States and the Soviet Union vied to spread their respective political influence throughout the world. Beginning in Europe, the Cold War soon spread to Asia, and eventually to the Middle East, Latin America, and Africa. In some cases, direct control was exercised, as with the Soviet sphere of influence in Eastern Europe; in others, indirect economic control, as with U.S. policy in Latin America, proved sufficient to maintain bloc solidarity. The system of Liberal democracy and free markets became known as the First World, the Soviet system of planned economies and one-party rule as the Second World, and those nonaligned nations refusing to choose sides as the **Third World,** a term now used to signify less-developed nations. Both sides developed alliances to maintain collective security in their blocs. In response to the Berlin Crisis of 1948–1949, the United States entered into its first peacetime alliance, the **North Atlantic Treaty Organization (NATO),** later followed by **CENTO** in the Middle East and **SEATO** in Southeast Asia. When the West rearmed Germany in 1955, the Soviets responded with the **Warsaw Pact** to defend the Eastern bloc.

With its expressed goal of spreading world revolution, the Soviet Union created fear among the Western capitalist and democratic nations. During the late 1940s and early 1950s, President Truman relied on the expertise of a former diplomat and historian named **George Kennan** (1904–2005) to develop the strategy of **containment.** Containment employed a variety of techniques—war, diplomacy, aid, intelligence, funding rebel groups—to halt the spread of communism around the world. To support its new international presence, the U.S. Congress passed the **National Security Act** (1947), which created the **National Security Council** (NSC, also with a National Security Advisor) and the **Central Intelligence Agency** (CIA) and reorganized the Department of Defense. Numerous novels and films have since reflected the cloak-and-dagger spy battles between the CIA and Soviet KGB to gain the upper hand.

Military: Nuclear weapons technology led to an **arms race** between the two superpowers. The Soviet Union exploded its first atomic weapon in 1949, and both nations developed the hydrogen bomb in 1952–1953. Under the leadership of Nikita Khrushchev, the Soviet Union in 1957 launched its first satellite—*Sputnik*—bringing the arms race to outer space. Fearing a so-called "missile gap," the United States hurriedly worked to develop rocket technology, culminating with **Intercontinental Ballistic Missiles (ICBMs)** capable of reaching the Soviet Union from silos in America or Europe. By the 1970s, both sides combined boasted about 25,000 long-range nuclear weapons. In addition, many of these missiles contained multiple warheads able to fire at several targets once in the air; they were known as **MIRVed weapons (Multiple Independently-Targeted Reentry Vehicles).** Moreover, each side developed nuclear submarines with the capacity to fire nuclear missiles from the depths of the ocean, forming a **"nuclear triad"**—on land, in the air, and under the sea.

An ironic consequence of the nuclear age was the doctrine of **Mutual Assured Destruction (MAD):** neither side had an incentive to launch a first strike because it was sure to incur unacceptable casualties from the opponent's missiles. Therefore, "missiles that kill people" kept the peace by precluding a nuclear strike, but "missiles that kill other missiles" **(Anti-Ballistic Missiles—ABMs)** threatened to upset the nuclear balance by providing an incentive to launch a first strike and were thus banned by the superpowers in a 1972 agreement. During the height of the Cold War, the Soviet Union may have spent as much as 25 to 30 percent of its gross domestic product on military expenditures, a massive commitment of resources for a modern society and a tremendous drain on its economy.

Economic: Perhaps never in history had one nation so dominated the world economy as did the United States at the end of World War II. Fully 80 percent of the world's trade passed through American hands, and 50 percent of the world's productive capacity was American. The United States thus stood in the unique position of helping to rebuild the world economy, which it wished to do by promoting free markets and access to American goods. To pursue this goal, the United States extended aid to Europe in the form of the **Marshall Plan** (1947), aid that the Soviet Union prohibited its Eastern European satellites from accepting, viewing the plan as a capitalist plot aimed at the Soviet sphere. In response, the Soviet Union organized the Eastern bloc around the rival **Council for Mutual Economic Assistance (COMECON),** an effort to create a specialization of production among its satellites.

As the Cold War expanded, the United States often exploited the power of its multinational corporations to control the economies of underdeveloped nations, particularly in Latin America. For example, when a socialist government was elected to power in **1954** in **Guatemala** with the intention of nationalizing U.S. fruit companies that dominated that nation's banana industry, the U.S. government engineered a CIA-backed coup deposing the government. Many such underdeveloped nations and former colonies sympathized with the Soviet critique of capitalism and adopted state planning to promote internal development and gain control of resources vis-à-vis the former colonial powers of the West. Both superpowers often extended aid in strategic regions with the goal of gaining allies.

Ideological: At its heart, the Cold War represented a battle over rival views of the world, a combat of antagonistic ideologies. Each side hoped to win hearts and minds with propaganda. In 1946, Winston Churchill fired the first salvo in the war with a speech in Fulton, Missouri, when he announced that an **"Iron Curtain"** had descended across the continent of Europe, dividing the free peoples of the West from the oppressed peoples of the East. The United States established the Voice of America and **Radio Free Europe** to broadcast messages from "free and prosperous citizens" across the Iron Curtain. Internally, the United States in the 1950s plunged into a **Red Scare,** or McCarthyism (named after Wisconsin Senator Joseph McCarthy), aimed at real and imaginary communist enemies in the upper reaches of government and in Hollywood.

Though Soviet propaganda tended to be more heavy-handed, it also aimed to control public opinion within its bloc. In 1948 the **Communist Information Bureau (Cominform)** was created to replace the old Comintern suspended during World War II. The notion that each side struggled for a cherished way of life—the future of civilization itself—added intensity to the Cold War not fully captured by traditional conceptions of geopolitical maneuvering.

Chronological Development of the Cold War

This section is designed to suggest the scope and duration of the Cold War. It is divided chronologically into phases, with brief explanations of the main areas of conflict. Consider it a supplement to the previous conceptual overview.

Beginnings, 1945–1953

The Cold War began with mutual suspicions related to Germany, control of Eastern Europe, nuclear weapons, and eventually the spread of rivalry into Asia.

Heads Up! The AP Exam almost always features an FRQ on the post-1945 period, as well as about six to eight multiple-choice questions. Though the chronology here addresses only one of the major themes of the postwar era—the Cold War—be careful of treating the post-1945 era as "current events" trivia. Continue to link specifics to themes to guide your studying and prevent getting lost amid the "forest."

1945: Germany is divided into four zones of occupation—British, American, Soviet, and French. Additionally, the city of **Berlin** (entirely within the Soviet zone) is divided into four occupation zones. Germany and, more specifically, Berlin become the epicenter of the emerging Cold War.

The United States explodes atomic bombs over Hiroshima and Nagasaki in Japan, ending the Pacific War but also initiating the nuclear age.

Soviet troops occupy all of the nations of Eastern Europe except Albania and Yugoslavia. At first, coalition governments of socialist/communist parties rule along with democratic and/or free market parties.

1946: Winston Churchill delivers his Iron Curtain speech.

1947: The United States extends Marshall Plan aid to the nations of Europe to be funneled through the **Office of European Economic Cooperation (OEEC)** rather than to each nation individually.

Fearing the spread of communist insurgencies in Greece and Turkey, President Truman offers financial assistance to any nation facing "insurgencies by armed minorities." Along with the Marshall Plan, this **Truman Doctrine** establishes the early outlines of a new interventionist approach by the United States in European affairs.

In most Eastern European nations, Western-backed parties are pushed out of power, while in Italy, elections vault the pro-U.S. **Christian Democrats** to leadership while limiting the influence of the usually strong socialist and communist Parties.

1948: Concerned over economic conditions in Germany and Soviet reparations policies, the United States, Britain, and France merge their three occupied German zones and introduce a new Deutschmark currency. In response, the Soviet Union imposes the **Berlin Blockade,** cutting the western part of the city off from rail and auto traffic, threatening to "starve it out." Rather than confront the Soviets directly, President Truman begins the **Berlin Airlift,** an almost year-long enterprise designed to supply the basic needs of West Berliners.

Noncommunists are kicked out of the **Czechoslovakian** government in a **coup.** The leader of the noncommunists, Jan Masyrk, is later found dead outside his window, either a suicide or murder.

1949: Stalin ends the Berlin Blockade, admitting the public relations defeat. The division of Germany becomes formal with the creation of the **Federal Republic of Germany (West Germany—FRG)** and the **German Democratic Republic (East Germany—GDR).** Under American leadership, Western Europe forms a mutual defense system known as NATO to defend against future Soviet provocations.

Communists under **Mao Zedong** (1890–1976) gain control of the Chinese mainland, driving the nationalists onto the island of Taiwan. In addition, the Soviet Union explodes its first atomic bomb. These two events spur the Red Scare in the United States.

1950: Communist North Korea invades the Western-backed government of South Korea. Taking advantage of the Soviet boycott of the Security Council, President Truman builds a UN coalition to combat the invasion and signify the American commitment to the policy of containment. The **Korean War** would drag on for three years and involve fighting between the United States and China.

1953: Joseph Stalin's death opens a new era in Cold War diplomacy. The Korean War ends with the division into North Korea and South Korea at the 38th parallel.

Coexistence and Confrontation, 1953–1970

This period began with an effort at "peaceful coexistence," but rivalries reheated over Berlin, control of the vital Middle East, and Soviet intrusion into America's perceived sphere of influence in Latin America, which almost brought the superpowers to nuclear war in 1962.

1954: Vietnamese resistance fighters under communist leader **Ho Chi Minh** (1890–1969) defeat French colonial forces at **Dien Bien Phu,** leading to Vietnam's division along the 17th parallel between communist North Vietnam and Western-backed South Vietnam.

The United States supports a coup against socialist Guatemalan leader Jacobo Arbenz Guzman to prevent the nationalization of land owned by U.S. fruit companies.

1955: NATO agrees to rearm West Germany, leading to the Soviet creation of the Warsaw Pact alliance in Eastern Europe.

Secretary of State John Foster Dulles announces the American policy of "massive retaliation," threatening an all-out nuclear attack in response to communist aggression anywhere in the world.

A **summit in Geneva,** Switzerland, between President Eisenhower (1890–1969) and Khrushchev leads to the evacuation of forces from Austria and its neutralization.

1956: Soviet leader **Nikita Khrushchev** (1894–1971) gives a **"secret speech"** to the 20th Party Congress of the Communist Party of the Soviet Union condemning the excesses of the Stalin period and signals his goal of **de-Stalinization.** Khrushchev also suggests the possibility of **"peaceful coexistence"** between the capitalist West and communism.

Taking their cue from Khrushchev, the leadership of the Polish and Hungarian communist parties begins a liberalization of economic and intellectual life. The **Hungarian revolt** goes too far for Khrushchev and is crushed by Soviet forces.

1957: Soviet leaders announce the launching of the first satellite into outer space—*Sputnik.* The United States follows with the creation of the **National Aeronautics and Space Agency (NASA),** indicating the beginning of the space race.

1959: Leftist forces under **Fidel Castro** (1926–) overthrow the U.S.-backed government of **Cuba.** Castro nationalizes the sugar industry, seizes American assets, and establishes strong ties with the Soviet Union.

1960: Soviet forces shoot down a **U-2 spy plane** over Russian territory, forcing the United States to recant previous statements denying such flights. The incident forces the cancellation of a planned superpower summit.

1961: A U.S.-backed invasion of Cuba by exiled Cubans ends disastrously with the capture of such forces at the **Bay of Pigs.**

Another crisis over control of the city of Berlin leads to the erection of the **Berlin Wall** by East Berlin to prevent its citizens from escaping to the West.

1962: Soviet plans to install nuclear missiles in Cuba lead to a two-week crisis, pushing the world to the brink of nuclear war. The **Cuban Missile Crisis** ends when **President Kennedy** (1917–1963) assures Khrushchev that the United States will not invade Cuba in exchange for the removal of the missiles.

1963: The superpowers agree to the creation of a **Hot Line** establishing direct contact in times of crisis. In addition, the two sides, along with Great Britain, agree to the **Limited Nuclear Test Ban Treaty,** prohibiting the testing of nuclear weapons underground, in outer space, or under water.

1964: America's commitment to fighting in Vietnam, between the communist north and U.S.-backed south, deepens with the **Gulf of Tonkin Resolution,** allowing **President Johnson** (1908–1973) greater latitude to involve American forces.

1967: Israel attacks its Arab neighbors and seizes the West Bank, Sinai Peninsula, and Golan Heights. In this **Six-Day War,** the United States backs Israel while the Soviets support Arab forces.

1968: Soviet forces crush the Czechoslovakian reform movement, known as the **"Prague Spring,"** and announce the **Brezhnev Doctrine,** whereby a perceived threat to socialism in one nation is taken as a threat to socialism everywhere.

Sidebar: The question of weapons in outer space continued throughout the Cold War with the development of ICBMs. Also, in the 1980s, President Reagan became committed to an antimissile shield, known as the Strategic Defense Initiative (SDI), which caused increased friction with the Soviet Union. In the long run, Gorbachev's concern over the high cost of this project helped end the Cold War. The United States recently abandoned the 1972 ABM treaty.

Détente, 1970–1978

A French term, détente, means an easing of tensions. During the decade, the superpowers work to normalize relations between their two rival blocs and to accept the permanent existence of the rival side.

1970: The **Treaty of Moscow** between West Germany and the Soviet Union establishes diplomatic relations between the two nations and recognizes the split between East and West Germany. Soon after, both nations are admitted to the United Nations.

1972: Soviet and American negotiators agree to the first limitations on nuclear weapons, the **Strategic Arms Limitation Talks (SALT I),** which also recognizes the nuclear parity that exists between the superpowers. In addition, both sides agree to an **Anti-Ballistic Missile (ABM) Treaty** to reduce the potential for a first-strike launch.

President Nixon (1913–1994) becomes the first U.S. president to visit the People's Republic (Communist) of China, which leads to formal diplomatic relations later in the decade.

1973: The United States removes its last major military units from fighting in Vietnam. In 1975, North Vietnam captures Saigon, the South Vietnamese capital, ending the war with Vietnam's unification under communism.

1975: Signed by all the nations of Europe, including the United States, Canada, and USSR, the **Helsinki Accords** bring a formal end to World War II by acknowledging existing national boundaries. In addition, human rights provisions open the door for dissent within the Soviet Union and in the Eastern European satellites. This represents the height of détente.

Revival and End, 1979–1991

The period of détente ended with a series of actions by both the United States and the Soviet Union that increased Cold War tensions. However, Mikhail Gorbachev's accession to leadership of the Soviet Union helped bring an end to the Cold War by the late 1980s.

1979: To prop up a communist regime on its border, the **Soviet Union invades Afghanistan,** bogging it down in a Vietnam-style quagmire until 1988. In response, the U.S. Senate refuses to ratify the SALT II agreement to limit nuclear weapons, and **President Carter** (1924–) limits grain shipments to the Soviet Union and boycotts the 1980 Olympics in Moscow. Further, the United States provides aid to Afghan freedom fighters known as the *mujahadeen.*

1983: President **Reagan** (1911–2004) denounces the Soviet Union as the **"evil empire"** and pledges to install intermediate-range nuclear weapons in Europe. World concerns grow over the proliferation of nuclear weapons and the dangers of nuclear power.

A Korean commercial jet strays into Soviet airspace and is shot down by Soviet forces, killing all 269 people aboard.

1985: Mikhail Gorbachev (1931–) becomes the new Soviet leader and works toward an internal reform of the Soviet system that requires a reduction in Cold War tensions.

1987: After several inconclusive superpower summits, Reagan and Gorbachev agree to the **Intermediate-Range Nuclear Force (INF) Treaty,** which eliminates an entire class of weapons on European soil.

1988: Gorbachev withdraws the final Soviet troops from Afghanistan.

Reagan and Gorbachev sign the **Strategic Arms Reduction Treaty (START),** which reduces the number of long-range missiles on both sides.

1989: Communist governments in Eastern Europe collapse as Gorbachev refuses to employ Soviet troops to defeat the peoples' revolutions. The **Fall of Communism** results in the end of Germany's division (by 1990) and the movement toward democracy and free markets in the former Soviet satellites.

1991: After a failed coup by communist hardliners fails, the **Soviet Union collapses** into its member national republics. Soviet President Gorbachev resigns with the official end of the USSR.

INTERNATIONAL CONFLICTS SINCE 1990

The first opportunity to test the post–Cold War diplomatic order was the **Gulf War.** In 1990, Iraqi forces under command of leader Saddam Hussein (1937–) invaded Kuwait, claiming it as a historic province of Iraq. Ironically, the United States lent support to Hussein during the brutal Iran-Iraq War (1980–1988), which followed Iran's Islamist revolution against the U.S.-backed government of the Shah and subsequent hostage crisis of U.S. embassy personnel. **President George Bush** (1924–) pledged that the aggressive action "would not stand" and secured agreement from both the Soviet Union and China on the UN Security Council for a multinational force to liberate Kuwait. With minimal casualties, the U.S. **Desert Storm Operation** of 1991 defeated Iraqi forces in Kuwait but left Saddam Hussein in power.

> **Heads Up!** Since the Test Development Committee creates the AP Exam several years before its administration, don't feel that you need to study "current events." However, topics such as the end of the Cold War, conflicts in Yugoslavia, and European unity have appeared on the exam recently.

Following World War II, the United States became more deeply involved in the Middle East, driven by securing strategic oil supplies and supporting its Israeli ally. The presence of American military bases and troops in many undemocratic Middle Eastern nations, as well as U.S. support for Israel, inspired terrorist incidents beginning in the 1970s, such as the **Palestinian Liberation Organization's (PLO)** killing of the Israeli Olympic team in 1972 in Munich and the hijacking of Western airliners. Such terrorist incidents caused concern for the U.S. government but posed no direct threat on American soil.

That changed when **al-Qaeda**—a terrorist group supported by the radical Islamist **Taliban** regime in Afghanistan—crashed hijacked commercial jets into the World Trade Center in New York City, a field in Shanksville, Pennsylvania, and the Pentagon in Washington, D.C., on **September 11, 2001,** causing the deaths of 3,000 people. In response, **President George W. Bush** (1946–) pledged a **"war on terror."** With broad international support, American forces successfully deposed the Taliban regime in Afghanistan but without capturing (at this writing) the top leadership of al-Qaeda. However, the Bush administration's subsequent **War in Iraq** (2003), based on the presumption of Saddam Hussein's possession of "weapons of mass destruction," won only limited support among its European allies and caused a rift in the alliance. These incidents remind us that the end of the Cold War has not eliminated conflict from the world, and, if anything, how a U.S.-Soviet rivalry often restrained its junior partners from initiating potential confrontations among the superpowers.

THE SOVIET UNION: FROM SUPERPOWER TO COLLAPSE

Cold War Repression under Stalin

Stalin continued repression in the Soviet Union during and especially after World War II. Rigid controls over economic, intellectual, and cultural life resulted in millions of persons being sent to forced labor camps (gulags) for deviations from the official "line." During Stalin's final years, the KGB (secret police) increased in power; right before Stalin's death, official anti-Semitism led to fabricated charges against a group of Jewish doctors accused of poisoning Kremlin officials. Fortunately for the accused, Stalin died before a new round of executions and imprisonment could commence in the so-called **"doctor's plot."**

Khrushchev's Abortive Reforms

After a short period of collective leadership in the USSR, Nikita Khrushchev emerged as the secretary general of the Communist Party of the Soviet Union (CPSU). Khrushchev secured his leadership by distancing himself from his predecessor, initiating a campaign of de-Stalinization with a 1956 speech. Soviet intellectual life opened up somewhat, as writers were encouraged to publish some of the excesses of the Stalinist period. One example is Alexander Solzhenitsyn's grim depiction of the gulag system, *One Day in the Life of Ivan Denisovich* (1962). Khrushchev dramatically stated his goal of surpassing the U.S. economy by 1980 with the phrase "We will bury you." Despite Soviet space successes like *Sputnik*, Khrushchev's **decentralization** of the economy and focus on **consumer goods** failed to come close to overtaking American productivity. More important, Khrushchev failed to fix the woeful productivity of Soviet collective farms; his so-called **"virgin lands"** project of opening Soviet Central Asian lands to cultivation did little to address the bureaucratic structure of Soviet agriculture. Khrushchev found his way blocked by party bureaucrats, known as *apparatchiki,* who feared the effect of his reforms on their power. Along with his provocative foreign policy failures over Cuba, Berlin, and the break with communist China, Khrushchev's incomplete reforms led to his downfall in 1964.

Nuclear Parity and Domestic Drift: Brezhnev

Soviet life in the era of **Leonid Brezhnev** (1907–1982) reminds one of the Potemkin villages in the era of Catherine the Great (see Chapter 9)—a glittering façade of power to the outside world that hides the rot within. Party leaders specifically selected Brezhnev for his status quo credentials; his goal was **"no experimentation,"** that is, to maintain the influence of the army, *apparatchiki,* and state-owned industrial enterprises. Brezhnev did preside over an important diplomatic achievement—nuclear parity with the United States by the 1972 SALT agreement. In addition, Soviet leaders could boast one of the most formidable space programs, scientific communities, and Olympic athletic successes. With the Brezhnev Doctrine (see previous discussion), the Soviet Union stood poised to maintain its sphere of influence on its borders without American interference. However, these successes could not compensate for the staggering Soviet economy. Successive Five-Year Plans barely met established quotas and hid the fact that in an emerging computer age, the nation continued to focus on production of heavy industry—tractors, steel, construction equipment. Economic life drifted amid a **lack of consumer goods** and productivity. Many workers failed to show up for work **(absenteeism),** and **alcoholism** became rife. Important indicators of social health, such as **infant mortality, suicide,** and **life expectancy,** experienced troubling reversals.

Gorbachev: Perestroika and Glasnost

Sidebar: Though technically Gorbachev failed in his reforms, he will likely be considered one of the key figures of the twentieth century for helping to end the Cold War. Also critical for their lifelong opposition to communism and role in the events of the 1980s are President Reagan and Pope John Paul II.

Soviet leadership in the late 1970s and early 1980s resembled a geriatric ward. Following Brezhnev, two aged leaders maintained the status quo. When Mikhail Gorbachev was chosen as general secretary of the CPSU in 1985, he came as breath of fresh air to the Soviet Union. At 54, he was the youngest member of the Politburo. Gorbachev recognized the problems within both the Soviet economy and social life; he hoped to save the Soviet system by creating **"socialism with a human face."** The centerpiece of Gorbachev's reform movement was *perestroika,* or restructuring, of the centrally planned Soviet economy. Gorbachev wished to promote production of more consumer goods and to decentralize control of the inefficient state-owned enterprises. The new Soviet leader underestimated the entrenched power of Soviet bureaucrats and soon added another fundamental principle to his reform—*glasnost,* or openness. Soviet citizens were encouraged to discuss openly the failures of the past; an underground press, *samizdat,* came out into the open, as Gorbachev allowed Soviet Jews to emigrate and promoted religious freedom. Nuclear disaster at **Chernobyl** in 1986 actually strengthened Gorbachev's hand by demonstrating the vital need for Soviet modernization and reform.

By 1988, Gorbachev found himself in an increasingly difficult position, pinched between hard-line defenders of the old system and "shock therapy" advocates of free-market capitalism. Agriculture presents a good example of the Soviet leader's dilemma. Gorbachev allowed small farmers to lease plots from the government collectives, but the state remained the sole owner of the land. As a result, commercial agriculture never developed, and productivity remained low. Politically, Gorbachev moved power from the party over to state institutions, as with the creation of a **Congress of People's Deputies,** which then elected him president. Dramatic by any standard, these reforms nonetheless proved inadequate either to save the old system or create a new one. Ironically, as approval for these measures plummeted in the Soviet Union, Gorbachev's reputation and celebrity in the West skyrocketed as the liberator of Eastern Europe and an ender of the Cold War.

Reformers and defenders of the old system both began to lose faith in Gorbachev. Many reformers turned to the newly elected maverick president of the Russian republic—**Boris Yeltsin** (1931–)—who had been expelled from the CPSU by Gorbachev in 1987. More important, *perestroika* and *glasnost* had inadvertently sparked **independence movements** by the many ethnic minorities within the Soviet empire, particularly among the Baltic republics. Gorbachev veered between threats of force and conciliation to prevent the break-up of the USSR. However, the Soviet leader worked out a **"union treaty"** with the 15 republics (except for the Baltic States and Georgia) for greater autonomy within the USSR to take effect in August 1991. Before the treaty could become operative, however, communist hard-liners attempted to overthrow Gorbachev. The **August 1991 coup** failed miserably due to lack of planning, popular resistance, and the leadership of Yeltsin, who gained in stature by courageously opposing the illegal action. Gorbachev returned to power, but not for long; Yeltsin outlawed the Communist Party in Russia, and the Soviet Union was voted out of existence by the federation council of the various republics. The entity that had coincided with and helped define the turbulent twentieth century no longer existed.

Russia since 1991

Russia's history since 1991 has been a troubled one. Following the collapse of the USSR in 1991, 12 republics agreed to form the loose **Commonwealth of Independent States (CIS).** Like Gorbachev, Yeltsin found himself pushed back and forth between bold reform and repression. Pushing for a "strong presidential republic," Yeltsin in the spring of 1993 dissolved the legislature and called for new elections. Hard-liners in the legislature refused to leave the building, leading to a violent clash that left 100 dead. Though Yeltsin won the battle and his new constitution took effect, public support for reform flagged, as shown by the return of communists and Soviet nationalists to the new Duma. In addition, Yeltsin from 1994 to 1996 bogged the now-decrepit Russian army down in an ethnic conflict with separatist **Chechnya,** a small Islamic enclave. The conflict continues to this day with terrorism and atrocities on both sides.

Before his resignation in 1999, Yeltsin sponsored the rise of his handpicked successor as president, **Vladimir Putin** (1952–). Putin has worked to advance Russia's independent position in world affairs, promote economic development, and centralize state authority. After his reelection in 2004,

Putin's presidency has been marked by an increase in state control of the media and repression of internal opponents of his regime. Some fear Putin will establish an authoritarian regime as a "good tsar" to see Russia through its political transition. By some measures, Russia has gained much since 1985, including democratic institutions, private property, and freedom of religion. However, Russia continues to face serious problems: terrorism in Chechnya, corruption in government, **inequality** between urban and rural areas, **organized crime,** a **decaying military infrastructure,** and **declining life expectancy,** just to name a few. Many of these stand as perennial themes of Russian history.

EASTERN EUROPE: IN THE SOVIET SHADOW

Stalinization

After suffering two invasions by Germany in 30 years and in keeping with its perennial expansion, Russia under Stalin was determined to create a buffer zone to its west. Disagreements over the fate of Eastern Europe helped precipitate the Cold War between the superpowers. By 1948, all but Albania and Yugoslavia lay firmly within the Soviet sphere of influence. To combat the Marshall Plan, the Soviet Union developed its own framework for integration in the East known as COMECON. Communism and socialism in Eastern Europe found wide appeal after the war anyway, but Stalin wanted to assure himself of pro-Soviet communist regimes on his western border and so forced purge trials of any independent-minded homegrown leftists. Therefore, the Soviet Union imposed Stalinist regimes on the Eastern European satellites, a trend that involved the following to greater or lesser degrees:

- **One-party police states**—Once the Cold War broke open, all political parties but the Communist Party and its direct allies were banned. Eastern European states closely controlled speech, culture, and religious expression.
- **Planned economies**—The Soviet model of centralized control via party bureaucrats was exported to Eastern Europe. Moreover, the USSR assigned specific economic roles to the various nations, with, for example, East Germany focusing on heavy industry, Romania on oil production, and Bulgaria on agricultural products.
- **Collectivization of agriculture**—During the interwar period, most Eastern European states redistributed land to peasants in smaller plots. The Soviet Union now reversed this trend by requiring its satellites to collectivize agriculture and establish communal farms; in the more Western-oriented nations such as Poland and Hungary, this process did not include all farmland.

These policies fomented discontent among key segments of the populations of Eastern Europe—small farmers, the middle class, nationalists, and intellectuals. However, the ever-present fear of Stalinist repression kept a tight seal on such discontent.

De-Stalinization, Revolt, and the Brezhnev Doctrine

Stalin's death in 1953 prompted revolts and hopes for change. East Berliners toppled statues of Stalin, but their revolt was quickly suppressed. A more momentous push for change came with Khrushchev's official policy of de-Stalinization in 1956. Several Eastern European states took the Soviet policy as their cue to liberalize their own economic and political systems.

Communist leaders in Poland and Hungary wished to establish a system more in keeping with national traditions. Polish party officials turned to reformer **Wladyslaw Gomulka** (1905–1982), who halted collectivization of agriculture, relaxed control over the economy, and improved relations with Poland's strong Catholic Church. Soviet leaders warned the Polish leaders that their reform had gone too far, but Gomulka stayed in power by promising allegiance to the Warsaw Pact and because the Soviets faced a bigger issue in Hungary.

Events in Poland sparked protests in Hungary. The Communist Party replaced hard-line leaders with the former prime minister **Imre Nagy** (1896–1958), who had previously been expelled from the party for "deviation." Nagy freed political prisoners and worked toward liberalizing Hungary's political and economic system. When Nagy announced Hungary's withdrawal from the Warsaw Pact and called on the world to recognize his nation's neutrality, the Soviets forced the Hungarian Communist Party to depose Nagy and appoint **János Kádár** (1912–1989) as the new leader. Soviet tanks now rolled in and crushed the uprising, at the cost of about 100,000 lives. Over 200,000 Hungarians fled the country, and Nagy himself was captured and hanged. The message was clear: Reform must not threaten the Soviet sphere of influence.

Despite the failed promise of de-Stalinization and the imposition of even harsher Soviet controls after 1956, many Eastern European satellites continued to desire greater autonomy. As part of a worldwide youth protest movement, Czechoslovakia attempted to liberalize its communist system during the **"Prague Spring"** of 1968. Reformers within the Communist Party replaced its Stalinist leaders with the Slovak reformer **Alexander Dubček (1921–1992).** Dubček encouraged a new spirit of openness and promised the relaxing of political controls, all in an effort to create a humane socialism. Though Dubček reassured Soviet leaders regarding his nation's commitment to the Warsaw Pact, he ultimately could not control the euphoria of the movement in Czechoslovakia and the concern of the surrounding Warsaw Pact leaders, who feared the spread of reform to their own nations. In August 1968, Soviet troops ended the reform and declared in the Brezhnev Doctrine that deviations from the socialist line would not be tolerated. As with Hungary, the United States tacitly accepted the Soviet action.

The Fall of Communism, 1989–1990

The collapse of communism during 1989–1990 stands as one of the most momentous and surprising events of the twentieth century. Reasons for the collapse divide into (1) propellant forces *toward* change and (2) the *lack* of restraining forces *against* it. By the 1980s, the economies of the Eastern European states were losing ground to more technological Western Europe. Also, **high oil prices** and **inefficient state-owned enterprises** had created huge **government debts.** Politically, the desire for national autonomy, religious freedom, and political rights lingered under the surface of passive obedience. Given these conditions, the presence of the Soviet army *and* the satellites' agreement to maintain their borders (to prevent refugees from escaping) acted as the only checks on a revolutionary situation. When these props were removed by Gorbachev and some members of the Warsaw Pact, the Berlin Wall came tumbling down.

> **Heads Up!** Episode 23 ("The Wall Comes Down") of the CNN Cold War series provides a helpful overview of the events addressed here. See the Web site for details: www.cnn.com/SPECIALS /cold.war/.

With this general context in mind, we survey developments in the major Eastern European nations leading to the collapse of communism:

Poland: Gomulka began as a reformer but eventually resorted to repression to maintain order. Price increases by the government in 1970 brought down Gomulka. His replacement, Edward Gierek, embarked on economic reforms, but his borrowing from the West forced upon the nation an austerity program. Once again, price increases in 1980 led to discontent and strikes by workers. Unique in a communist nation, workers founded an *independent* labor union called

Solidarity, led by the militant shipyard worker **Lech Walesa** (1943–), which soon boasted a membership of 10 million workers. Emboldened by the Catholic Church and a newly elected Polish pope, **John Paul II** (r. 1978–2005), workers demonstrated for free elections and a share in government. Fearing Soviet intervention, the new communist leader **General Wojciech Jaruzelski** (1923–) declared **martial law** in 1981. Walesa was arrested and Solidarity was driven underground. The situation drifted until Gorbachev embarked on his *perestroika* reforms, and then pressure on the satellites increased to liberalize their systems. By 1989, Solidarity had convinced the government to allow free elections, which resulted in a universal repudiation of communist rule, as Solidarity won all but one seat in the legislature. The following year, Nobel Peace Prize winner Walesa was elected president in a stunning reversal of fortunes.

Hungary: Following the Soviet crushing of the Hungarian revolt, Jánós Kádar maintained strong political control while allowing a more decentralized economy, called **"communism with a capitalist facelift."** By 1980s, like the other satellites, Hungary experienced economic stagnation and rising debt. Communist party leaders quietly pushed Kádar out of power in 1988 and soon opened the door to a more social democratic economy with **multiparty elections.** In an act of reconciliation with its past, Hungary rehabilitated Nagy and the other leaders of the revolt and provided a burial with honors for those who had been killed. More important for future events, Hungary removed the barbed wire "iron curtain" around its borders, triggering a flood of refugees from nearby East Germany.

East Germany: Since 1961, the aged and increasingly out-of-touch **Erich Honecker** (1912–1994) ruled East Germany strictly with the aid of the state police, the **Stasi.** East Germany possessed the strongest economy in Eastern Europe and had allowed stronger political and economy ties to West Germany as part of that nation's *Ostpolitik;* however, East Germany's leaders always felt insecure in the presence of their larger and more dynamic western sister, an insecurity that accounts for the Berlin Wall. When Hungary opened its borders, the action prompted a flood of refugees fleeing west via a circuitous route. When Gorbachev visited East Germany in 1989 to celebrate its 40th anniversary, he inadvertently sparked mass demonstrations calling for reform and open travel. Though Honecker contemplated military repression using the Stasi, the communist Politburo removed him and opened travel through the Berlin Wall. Soon after, a euphoric populace destroyed the hated symbol, and the communists were kicked out of power. Momentum became unstoppable toward the **unification of Germany.** With the approval of the four WWII Allied powers, including the Soviet Union, Germany was reunified in October 1990.

Czechoslovakia: Events in Eastern Europe began to resemble the proverbial snowball rolling down the hill. Inspired by the revolts in Poland, Hungary, and East Germany, mass demonstrations broke out in the fall of 1989 in the capital city of Prague. A group of intellectuals, Charter '77, led by the jailed playwright **Vaclav Havel** (1936–), became a rallying point against the Stalinist regime. By this point, the communist leaders had lost both their nerve and any remaining moral authority; within weeks, the communist monopoly on power evaporated to be replaced by free elections, a free press, and emergence of Havel as the president of Czechoslovakia. Observers dubbed the nonviolent change the **"Velvet Revolution."** Because of its democratic past, the nation moved quickly toward a multiparty political system and a free-market economy. In the aftermath, Slovakia pressed for independence, accomplished through the so-called **Velvet Divorce** that created the Czech Republic and Slovakia in 1993.

Romania: Since 1965, the iron-fisted **Nikolae Ceausescu** (1918– 1989) had ruled Romania. Ceausescu justified his regime by striking an independent pose in foreign policy—opposing the

Soviet invasion of Czechoslovakia in 1968 and building friendly ties with Western nations. Through rigid one-person rule, Ceausescu wished to force Romania into the modern industrial age; however, Ceausescu compromised the nation's standard of living to pay off foreign debt and support his family's extravagant lifestyle. Ceausescu brutally crushed any opposition with his **Securitate** police. Encouraged by the revolts across Eastern Europe, protests broke out in the city of **Timisoara,** which the Securitate smashed, at the cost of hundreds of lives. Violent street battles broke out among the regular army, which now supported the revolutionaries, and the Securitate. Eventually, Ceausescu's forces collapsed and the dictator, along with his wife, was captured. Both were executed on Christmas Day 1989. The **National Salvation Front** reform movement emerged to oversee the nation's difficult transition to democracy and capitalism.

Following the Velvet Revolution, new president Havel proclaimed, "Czechoslovakia is reentering Europe." If it takes two wings to fly, then Europe finally seems ready to take flight—with both East and West. Many of the former Soviet satellites have since rejoined the West by entering NATO and the European Union (EU); for some nations, such as Romania, Bulgaria, and Albania, the evolution toward parliamentary democracy and free markets has proven more painful but continues today.

Yugoslavia: The Balkans Again

The most violent break from communism occurred in multiethnic Yugoslavia. A diverse collection of Slavic ethnic groups, Yugoslavia was in many ways an artificial state. Though Croats and Serbs speak the same language, the former historically were tied more to the West religiously (Catholicism) and politically, whereas the latter were oriented more toward Russia and Orthodox Christianity. During World War II, the Nazi invasion of 1941 led to the creation of a Croat fascist movement, the Ustashe, which committed atrocities against Serbs. Communist resistance leader Marshal Tito succeeded in liberating his nation from the Nazis while also resisting Soviet domination. To maintain control of Yugoslavia, Tito experimented with a decentralized though socialist economic system and a federation of ethnic states, kept tightly together by the authority of the Communist Party.

Following Tito's death in 1980, ethnic tensions reemerged and burst into the open with the events of 1989–1991. The Western-oriented republics—**Croatia,** Slovenia, and **Bosnia**— voted in 1991 for independence. However, significant minorities of Serbs lived in each of these regions, prompting a series of violent wars between 1991 and 1999. Led by the nationalist **Slobodan Milosevic** (1941–2006), Yugoslavia (now simply Serbia and Montenegro) attacked Bosnia to recapture Serb territory; in the process, Serbian troops engaged in "ethnic cleansing" campaigns against Bosnian Muslims involving mass killing, rape, and the destruction of homes. Croatian armies responded with their own atrocities against Serb civilians. Europe stood appalled and impotent at the sight of ethnic conflict thought to be a relic of the WWII era. Finally in 1996, NATO and the United States engineered a cease-fire and with the **Dayton Peace Accord,** the parties agreed to the partition of Bosnia, enforced by UN peacekeepers. Now Milosevic turned to the historically important province of **Kosovo,** populated primarily by ethnic Albanians known as Kosovars. To halt another ethnic cleansing campaign, **President Clinton** (1946–) led a NATO bombing operation that once again led to an end of the killing and the placement of peacekeepers. By 2001, Milosevic had been voted out of office and placed on trial at The Hague, Netherlands, for crimes against humanity; however, he died in 2006 before his trial was completed.

Heads Up! Essay questions on the post-WWII period are likely to focus on thematic issues, such as Western European unity. While knowledge of internal policies and leaders of specific nations can be useful in this regard, make sure not to get mired in trivia; instead focus on the connection to the theme.

WESTERN EUROPE: PULLING BACK AND TOGETHER

Western Europe lay in ruins in 1945. By the mid-1950s, however, it had experienced a remarkable recovery. How? First, the nations of Western Europe pulled back from their imperial commitments, either surrendering or losing their colonies, thus freeing themselves from the expense of defending empires. Second, the two world wars acted as an icy bucket of water in the face of extreme nationalism. After 1945, the peoples of Western Europe, prompted by the United States, worked toward economic and political unity. The Atlantic alliance (NATO) provided collective security while economic unity produced a stunning turnaround.

Recovery and Reconstruction

Following World War II, Western Europe faced immense devastation. Important industrial areas had been bombed to oblivion, infrastructure lay in ruins, and regular economic structures such as currencies and trade had collapsed. Complicating recovery was the issue of **displaced persons (DPs)**—the 30 to 50 million refugees seeking relatives and shelter, and the ethnic minorities (mostly Germans) forcibly removed in the redrawing of postwar boundaries. What's more, harsh winters and poor harvests from 1945 to 1947 increased fears of the spread of communism.

With its dominant economy and readiness to enter decisively into European affairs, the United States offered Marshall Plan aid (totaling $12 billion) to the nations of Europe. American leaders insisted that such aid be funneled through the Office of European Economic Cooperation (OEEC) to promote unity—both for efficiency's sake and to create bloc solidarity as the Cold War heated up.

Learning lessons from the post-WWI settlement, industrial nations began creating international economic institutions even before World War II ended. The Allied nations in 1944 adopted the **Bretton Woods system,** which included an **International Monetary Fund (IMF)** for currency stabilization. Currencies were to be backed by gold and **exchange rates fixed** to ensure stability. Based on the strength of the U.S. economy, the dollar evolved into an unofficial reserve currency, at least until 1971 when President Nixon was forced to abandon the **gold standard** due to inflation, returning the industrial world to a system of "floating currencies." In addition, the **International Bank of Reconstruction and Development (World Bank)** provided loans for the modernization of infrastructure (e.g., dams, roads, and sewers). To avoid the economic nationalism of the interwar period, Western nations worked toward a system of free trade. The informal **General Agreement on Trade and Tariffs (GATT)** worked toward the reduction and elimination of trade barriers and eventually gave way to the more formal **World Trade Organization (WTO)** in 1997. In all, these institutions performed admirably in regulating the world economy and promoting growth, though they came under increasing criticism from opponents of economic globalization in the 1990s.

Western European governments accepted the need for state management of a capitalist economy. **Keynesian economics** emerged as the reigning theory; states employed tax and budget policies to promote growth and cushion recessions. In Britain, the new Labour government signaled its commitment to full employment and the social welfare state by following the recommendations of the wartime **Beveridge Report** (1942). Several states nationalized key industries, such as utilities and transport, to ensure the public welfare, but these new **mixed economies** (free markets *and* government regulation) did not approach the rigid controls of Soviet-style planned economies. European growth continued throughout the 1960s but stalled with the **oil shock** of the 1970s and 1980s. **Staglation** (combination of inflation and unemployment) forced a reappraisal of Keynesian theory and a move to reduce the welfare state and government regulation in favor of **supply-side economics.**

Decolonization

World War I shook Europe's control of its colonies, and World War II severed it. By 1945, most European nations no longer possessed the means or the inclination to continue as colonial powers. Also, the senior member of the Western alliance, the United States, generally opposed Europe's continued domination of colonial empires. Nonetheless, the road to independence proved rough in many cases both for the mother country and the colony. If you encounter this topic on the AP Exam, it is likely to be couched in a comparative framework. What follows are three approaches to decolonization.

Great Britain: The new Labour government lacked enthusiasm for the British Empire. After World War I, Britain ruled several areas of the world under **mandates,** a system of tutelage (protection and guidance) leading to independence. After World War II, Britain generally favored a strategy of "partition and run" for its colonies and mandates, encouraging the contending groups to sort out the political settlement. In the case of **Palestine,** a proposed partition in 1947 led to the founding of the **state of Israel** in 1948 and the first of several wars between Palestinians and Israelis. Both Hindus and Muslims had for decades urged Britain to leave India, led by Gandhi's campaign of nonviolent resistance. Britain's partition of the subcontinent in 1947 left Muslim East and West **Pakistan** divided between Hindu **India;** this geographic anomaly, along with dispute over the border region of **Kashmir,** has fed a succession of conflicts between Muslim Pakistan and Hindu India, both now nuclear powers.

In Africa, the push for independence accelerated after 1960 and is demonstrated by the increase in UN membership from the 51 original members to around 190 in 2000. Britain faced its most difficult situation in Egypt. After overthrowing the British-backed government in 1952, Egyptian leader **Gamal Abdul-Nasser** (1918–1970) announced the nationalization of the Suez Canal, sparking an invasion by British, French, and Israeli forces. The **Suez Crisis** of 1956 ended when the United States and the Soviet Union denounced the invasion and forced its withdrawal. This defeat is usually taken to signify the end of Britain's status as a world power. Britain's retreat from direct colonial control continued throughout the 1950s and 1960s in Asia as well, though many former colonies retained political and economic contacts with Britain through the commonwealth system.

Low Countries: During World War II, Japan "liberated" many Asian colonies of the European powers, including the Dutch East Indies. Even before the war, an Indonesian Nationalist Party under **Sukarno** (1901–1970) agitated for autonomy. After the expulsion of Japan in 1945, the movement actively sought independence. Attempts to subdue the revolt failed, and the Netherlands withdrew from the archipelago and refocused on European issues. After 1949, Indonesia faced a number of difficult transitional issues, such as a communist threat, government corruption, and political violence over East Timor (a Christian enclave among a Muslim majority). However, Indonesia has moved toward democracy and become a major economic and political power in Asia.

Belgium planned to grant independence to its African colony, the **Congo,** over a 30-year period following World War II. Faced with increasing pressures, Belgium changed its position and pulled out in 1960. Chaos ensued, due to separatist movements, rival political factions, and army mutinies. With UN support, Belgian forces returned in 1961 to restore order, but a leftist rebellion continued. Eventually, the Congo was ruled as a brutal and corrupt dictatorship by Mobuto Sese Seko. Because of the Congo's vast but untapped resources, its political problems spilled over into neighboring Burundi and **Rwanda.** The latter nation descended into ethnic violence in 1994 between rival tribes (Hutus and Tutsis); after several Belgian peacekeepers were killed, the nation pulled out of the country as the genocide continued.

France: To reestablish prestige after its poor showing in World War II, France was determined to hold onto its colonial empire. It soon faced a nationalist and communist insurgency in **Indochina** against the **Viet Minh,** led by Ho Chi Minh. The conflict represents an appropriate example of how communism and anticolonialism often became fused in the context of the Cold War. As noted earlier, the French were forced to withdraw in 1954, only to have the United States take up the battle in its own war in **Vietnam.** France's more agonizing war occurred in **Algeria.** Unlike Indochina, much of the Algerian population was French settlers, *colons,* and the postwar French government resolved to defend their interests. A militant and nationalist group, the **National Liberation Front (FLN),** waged an almost eight-year war against the French, with atrocities on both sides. The war produced a crisis for the French government, eventually bringing down the **Fourth French Republic** and leading to the reemergence of Charles de Gaulle. President de Gaulle ended the war in 1962, despite opposition from the army, and granted Algerian independence.

As these examples demonstrate, European nations came to realize the inevitability of independence at different times and with varying approaches, some of which proved violent. Before refocusing on Europe, you should keep in mind that Europe's involvement with its former colonies did not end with independence—issues of terrorism, peacekeeping, guest workers, and colonial dependence continued.

Western European Unity and Economic Integration

Putting aside the narrow nationalism that had brought them low, Western and Central Europeans moved incrementally in the postwar period toward economic and political integration. Key to this unity was the partnership between France and West Germany. In 1952, two practical men of business and politics, both from Alsace-Lorraine—**Jean Monnet** (1888–1979) and **Robert Schuman** (1886–1963)—proposed the **European Coal and Steel Community (ECSC)** involving Belgium, the Netherlands, and Luxembourg **(Benelux nations),** and France, Italy, and Germany. The six nations **("Inner Six")** eliminated tariff barriers and placed coal and steel production under a High Authority. Within five years, production had doubled. Flush with success, the Inner Six in 1957 adopted the **Treaty of Rome,** creating the **European Economic Community (EEC)** or **Common Market,** which worked toward the abolition of trade barriers, the free flow of capital, and common economic policies. In addition, the six agreed to coordinate their nonmilitary atomic research and development under the **European Atomic Community (Euratom).**

Heads Up! To learn more about the structure and activities of the EU, visit the Web site europa.eu/index-en.htm.

At first, Great Britain stood aside from the Common Market, owing to its special relationship with the United States and its commonwealth. Later in the 1960s when the British changed their minds, de Gaulle of France vetoed their entry for fear that Britain's overseas commitments would dilute European unity. Eventually, the British joined the EEC in 1973, along with Denmark and Ireland. During the 1980s and 1990s, more nations on the Mediterranean and in Eastern Europe, with the fall of communism, joined the growing community. After the passing of the oil shock of the 1970s, the European Community moved toward a stronger integration. In 1991, the member states signed the **Maastricht Treaty** aimed at creating a "single Europe." This new **European Union (EU)** was governed by an elected **European Parliament** and a centralized decision-making **European Commission** of civil servants and administrators. Recent expansion has increased the number of EU members to 25. More importantly, 12 EU members in 2000 adopted the new **euro** currency to replace their national currencies. Some have criticized the distant and bureaucratic nature of the EU—and indeed the movement toward a truly United States of Europe has moved in fits and starts and still lies a way off—but progress since the late 1940s has resulted in a trading bloc of 345 million, which accounts for 40 percent of the world's trade.

Western European National Politics

Though the themes of Western Europe as a region take precedence, the AP Exam may feature several multiple-choice questions that require knowledge of specific nations or an FRQ in which one may usefully employ such knowledge. To keep this material to manageable size, I have included it in chart format.

Nation	Issues	Leaders/Groups	Events	Analysis
Great Britain	Since 1945, Britain has faced an older and less advanced economic infrastructure than the other Western European nations. In addition, it has battled high unemployment and its adjustment to a second-tier power.	* The Labour Party and the Conservative Party have alternated control of the government, with Labour working toward the expansion of the welfare state. * **Margaret Thatcher** (1925–)—ideological ally of President Reagan, Thatcher attacked the size of the welfare system, **denationalized industries,** attacked the power of labor	* **The "Troubles"** in Northern Ireland between the Catholic **Irish Republic Army (IRA)** and Protestants led to continued violence in Northern Ireland. * Thatcher launched the **Falklands War** with Argentina in 1982 over control of an island chain off of South America. The conflict aroused British nationalism. * In 1973, Britain joined the Common	Britain continues to face decaying industrial cities and lower economic productivity than its Western European partners. However, growth has increased under the Blair government, and many believe Britain will one day join the euro.

Nation	Issues	Leaders/Groups	Events	Analysis
Great Britain		unions, and reasserted British power abroad. * **Tony Blair** (1953–)—current prime minister represents the New Labour, less union and more middle class, and has supported U.S. efforts against terrorism.	Market, but has not yet embraced the euro currency. * Britain has "devolved" political decision making to its various nations, such as Scotland and Wales. * A 1998 agreement between Protestants and Catholics in Northern Ireland has Britain poised to solve its long "Irish Question."	
France	The postwar **Fourth Republic** (1945–1958) struggled with the legacy of collaboration during the Vichy regime and political instability yet enacted important reform legislation. During the **Fifth Republic** (1958–) and under de Gaulle, France left the NATO military alliance and pursued a more independent	* Charles de Gaulle (1890–1970)—de Gaulle supported European integration but an independent foreign policy vis-à-vis the United States. * **Francois Mitterand** (1916–1996)—Socialist president from 1981 to 1995, Mitterand at first expanded the welfare state but was forced to retrench and "cohabit" with conservative	* In 1961, France pulled out of the NATO military alliance (remaining in the political alliance). * France developed independent nuclear weapons, known as the *force de frappe.* * **Student revolts** in 1968 led to violence in Paris and almost brought down the de Gaulle government. * **Colonial conflicts** in Indochina and Algeria caused	France benefited from its involvement in the EU and partnership with Germany. French assertions of political and diplomatic power have not always coincided with its economic power, which is second in Europe to Germany's.

Nation	Issues	Leaders/Groups	Events	Analysis
France	line in foreign affairs, known as **Gaullism.** The Fifth Republic features a strong presidency.	prime ministers. * Jean Monnet (1888–1979)—architect of European unity.	internal political conflict and changes.	
(West) Germany	West Germany—Germany after its **reunification** in 1990—has worked to demonstrate its allegiance to **democracy** and the Western alliance by distancing itself from the Nazi past.	* **Konrad Adenauer** (1876–1967)—known as the "founding chancellor." He led the **Christian Democratic Party (CDs),** a right-center party favoring laissez-faire economics and close ties to the United States * Ludwig Erhard (1897–1977)—economic minister and brains behind Germany's *Wirtschaftswunder* ("economic miracle"). * **Willi Brandt** (1913–1992)—Socialist chancellor whose *Ostpolik* (opening to the East") led to normalized relations between East Germany and the Soviet Union. * **Helmut Kohl** (1930–)—Christian Democratic	* In 1955, Germany rearmed and joined NATO. * Germany joined the UN in the 1970s as part of détente. * German reunification came soon after the collapse of the Berlin Wall in 1989.	Germany seems firmly established as a democracy and committed member of the Atlantic Alliance. Reunification cost trillions of marks and the eastern part of Germany still suffers from higher unemployment and environmental problems. Germany's economic strength and potential makes it the strongest member of the EU.

Nation	Issues	Leaders/Groups	Events	Analysis
(West) Germany		(CD) chancellor who oversaw German reunification.		
Italy	Following World War II, Italy **abolished** the **monarchy** and worked toward economic modernization. Leftist parties proved resilient, and Italy's parliamentary system has produced more than 60 different governments since 1945.	* **Alcide de Gaspari** (1881–1954)—Christian Democratic prime minister who helped establish Italy's new parliamentary system and membership in the Atlantic alliance. * Socialists finally gained power in 1983 but their policies differed little in practice from the CDs.	* In 1946, Italians by a small majority voted to abolish the monarchy for its involvement in fascism. * **"Eurocommunism"** became a continental movement—communist parties who rejected ties to the Soviet Union and the more radical features of Marxism-Leninism. * In 1993, Italy restructured its system of **proportional representation,** which has allowed for longer-lived governments and more stability.	Italy recovered economically after the war, but was hard hit by the **oil shock.** It continues to deal with lack of development in the south and corruption in government.

ADDITIONAL RESOURCES

Ash, Timothy Garton, *In Europe's Name: Germany and the Divided Continent* (1993)—The author examines the roots of German reunification.

Ash, Timothy Garton, *The Magic Lantern: The Revolution of '89 Witnessed in Warsaw, Budapest, Berlin, and Prague* (1993)—A gripping journalistic account of events in Eastern Europe during the fall of communism.

Gaddis, John Lewis, *The Cold War: A New History* (2005)—A noted diplomatic historian incorporates the latest interpretations of the conflict.

Holbrooke, Richard, *To End a War* (1998)—An American diplomat tells the story of the Bosnian conflict from a first-person perspective.

Huntington, Samuel, *The Clash of Civilizations and the Remaking of the World Order* (1996)—The author argues controversially that the post-Cold War world will experience rising conflicts over culture and religion.

Kennedy, Paul, *The Rise and Fall of the Great Powers: Economic Change and Military Conflict, 1500–2000* (1987)—With broad historical perspective, the author examines the importance of economic productivity and "imperial overreach" in the rise and decline of great powers.

Lewis, Flora, *Europe: The Road to Unity* (1992)—A thematic and nation-by-nation study of Europe on the verge of economic and political unity.

Matlock, Jack, *Reagan and Gorbachev: How the Cold War Ended* (2004)—The American ambassador to the Soviet Union recounts events of the final phase of the Cold War.

Mazower, Mark, *The Balkans: A Short History* (2000)—Provides a brief introduction to a complex region.

Remnick, David, *Lenin's Tomb: The Last Days of the Soviet Empire* (1993)—A journalist's account of the fall of the Soviet empire.

Sherwin, Martin, *A World Destroyed: The Atomic Bomb and the Grand Alliance* (1975)—This study examines the impact of America's atomic monopoly on the beginnings of the Cold War.

www.almaz.com/nobel/peace/1990a.html—Biographical information related to Mikhail Gorbachev, including primary sources.

www.wall-berlin.org/gb/berlin.htm—This site provides a history of the Berlin Wall, along with photographs.

www.ihf-hr.org/index.php—This site provides the latest information on the state of human rights in the world.

www7.nationalgeographic.com/ngm/data/2002/01/01/sights_n_sounds/media.1.2.html—Sponsored by National Geographic, this site offers maps, sources, and multimedia clips on European integration.

www.ibiblio.org/expo/soviet.exhibit/entrance.html—This exhibit provides a Soviet perspective on Cold War events.

www.cnn.com/SPECIALS/cold.war/—A companion Web site to the CNN series on the Cold War. The series contains 24 episodes with footage of events, interviews with participants, and commentary by historians. A valuable and user-friendly resource.

PRACTICE QUESTIONS

1. Which of the following accurately characterizes a major cause of the Cold War?
   a. the early Soviet monopoly of nuclear weapons
   b. American designs on controlling Eastern Europe
   c. disagreements over whether to de-Nazify Germany
   d. the superpowers' differing political systems
   e. Soviet offers of economic aid to Western Europe

2. The movements of populations in the map below can best be explained as:
   a. the result of expulsion and boundary changes following World War II.
   b. treaty agreements between the United States and the Soviet Union partitioning Europe.
   c. refugees fleeing to new economic opportunities in Western Europe.
   d. cultural exchanges designed to rebuild harmony following the war.
   e. invasion routes of guerilla armies that thrived in the postwar chaos.

3. The statement below is taken from which of the following Cold War agreements?
   a. Universal Declaration of Human Rights
   b. Communist Information Bureau (Cominform)
   c. North Atlantic Treaty Organization (NATO)
   d. Marshall Plan
   e. Helsinki Accords

   "The Parties reaffirm their faith in the purposes and principles of the Charter of the United Nations and their desire to live in peace with all peoples and all governments.
   They are determined to safeguard the freedom, common heritage and civilization of their peoples, founded on the principles of democracy, individual liberty and the rule of law."

4. Stalinist control of Eastern Europe involved imposition of all of the following EXCEPT:
   a. a one-party communist state.
   b. collectivization of agriculture.
   c. a command economy.
   d. adherence to Soviet foreign policy.
   e. independent development of nuclear weapons.

5. As leader of the Soviet Union, Mikhail Gorbachev's (1985–1991) primary goal was to:
   a. end the Cold War with the United States.
   b. save socialism through reform and openness.
   c. liberate the ethnic minorities of the USSR.
   d. reassert Soviet control over Eastern Europe.
   e. introduce a laissez-faire economic structure.

6. A major political development in Western Europe after World War II was:
   a. the rise of socialist parties that gained power in the 1960s.
   b. the movement toward common economic and political policies.
   c. withdrawal of Great Britain from the Atlantic alliance.
   d. the renewal of nationalism and territorial conflicts.
   e. America's increasing disengagement from European affairs.

7. Which of the following individuals played a major role in helping to bring about the collapse of communism in Eastern Europe?
   a. Nikolae Ceausescu
   b. Erich Honecker
   c. Imre Nagy
   d. Leonid Brezhnev
   e. Lech Walesa

8. How did the economic policies of Western European governments after World War II differ from those in the interwar period (1919–1939)?
   a. Emphasis was placed on regulation and management of the economy.
   b. High tariff barriers were enacted to protect domestic industries.
   c. The gold standard was abandoned in favor of fluctuating currencies.
   d. International organizations were avoided in favor of bilateral agreements.
   e. Welfare programs were reduced in an effort to reduce budget deficits.

9. Which Western European power experienced the greatest degree of conflict in its decolonization efforts after 1945?
   a. Belgium
   b. the Netherlands
   c. Great Britain
   d. France
   e. West Germany

10. The American policy of containment during the Cold War involved:
    a. extending economic aid for humanitarian relief efforts.
    b. easing tension with the Soviet Union through spheres of influence.
    c. halting the spread of communism through a variety of means.
    d. preventing the spread of Western Europe as a competing power.
    e. invading Eastern Europe to liberate that area from Soviet oppression.

SAMPLE ESSAY

Compare and contrast the impact of the Cold War on the movement toward unity within Western Europe and Eastern Europe, respectively, in the period 1945–1960.

The Cold War had a big impact on Europe after WWII. However, different parts of Europe were affected differently. Western Europe really gained a lot from being allied with the United States, but the East was dominated by the Soviet Union. In this essay, I will discuss the different policies of the superpowers and how the Cold War created blocs of countries that opposed each other over the Iron Curtain.

Western Europe was ruined in 1945. At first, the United States did not know what to do about the situation. Soon conflict with the Soviet Union broke out over Berlin and free elections in Eastern Europe. To oppose communism, the United States tried to help rebuilt Europe; American leaders knew that communism could spread if conditions continued to be bad. So the United States provided Marshall Plan aid and promoted the unity of the West. NATO was created and West Germany was admitted into it. This alliance tried to defend against the spread of communism. Also, Western Europe began to pool their resources together. They created the Coal and Steel Society and eventually the Treaty of Rome to knock down tariff barriers. These two organizations promoted an "economic miracle" and helped Europe get back on its feet. Some leaders, like de Gaulle of France, did not like U.S. domination of Europe but most in the West realized that they needed an American ally to fight the Soviet threat.

The Soviet Union wanted to dominate Eastern Europe, because the Soviets were all about world domination. It was part of their Marxist-Leninist philosophy. Communist governments were imposed on the satellite nations, called this because they revolved around the Soviet Union. Oppression reigned in the East and all the bad features of communism were imposed on these nations—gulags, no free press, and rigid bureaucratic economies. Some states rebelled against the Soviet Union like Hungary, because of their domination. This did not help the unity of the East because it was unity imposed by the Soviet Union. This is shown later when the nations of Eastern Europe revolted against the USSR with the fall of the Berlin Wall in the late 1980s.

As you can see, the West benefited a lot from their association with the United States. Western European nations like France and Germany experienced great growth in their economies from 1945–60 and banded together to oppose communism. NATO protected them against the Soviet Union. On the other hand, the East was dominated by the Soviet menace. Nations had to toe the Soviet line or face invasion. So in the long run, the West was positively unified but East was negatively unified.

This response clearly addresses the tasks of the question, though unevenly. First, though the thesis is explicit, the introductory paragraph might include a few sentences of historical context regarding the postwar period. As for the body paragraphs, the essay tends to be one-sided. It is obvious that the student offers a negative view of the Soviet Union; though this view is based partly on fact, the student does not offer much evidence to support her position. Both paragraphs, but especially the one on Eastern Europe, would benefit from several additional examples. If this student advances a negative perspective on the USSR, the conclusion offers some opportunity to examine the effects of Soviet policies on Eastern Europe in the period after 1960. However, the student simply repeats several of the negative assessments provided earlier. On the positive side, the student remained within the bounds of the question and established a coherent thesis. Score: 6.

CHAPTER 17
Contemporary European
Society and Culture

Wars not only reorder the balance of power and diplomatic structures, they also create major changes in society and culture. This truism certainly applies to the period following the end of World War II. Pent-up demand for products and the need for reconstruction fed an economic miracle, especially in Western Europe. Prosperity, in turn, promoted a population increase, consumerism, and technological advance. Most governments committed themselves to a more active role in economic regulation and ensuring a social welfare system. Renewed prosperity and the specter of the Cold War also worked a downside. Numerous groups of "outsiders"—students, feminists, environmentalists, terrorists— offered various critiques of European society in the years after 1945. Culturally, experimentation flourished in the postwar intellectual climate but also revealed divisions between traditionalists and modernists, and even postmodernists. Following World War II, Europe's problems are increasingly seen in a global context.

> **Note:** To users of Palmer, Colton, and Kramer, *A History of the Modern World,* this chapter concentrates on Chapter 27 of your text, but also includes additional material.

THE ECONOMIC MIRACLE AND ITS CONSEQUENCES

Europe's amazing recovery from the destruction of World War II produced a higher standard of living and increased life expectancy, but also resulted in negative side effects. In this section, we examine the social changes provoked by the changing European economy and the advance of technology.

The Baby Boom and After

The Great Depression and World War II had dampened European birth rates. After 1945, the Western world underwent a steady increase in the birth rate, known as the **baby boom.** Governments encouraged the trend in an effort to replace lost population from the war and also to allay a labor shortage in the period. State policies of **neonatalism** subsidized additional births, infant nutrition, and day care. Also aided by an influx of immigrants, Europe's population increased by 25 percent between 1945 and 1970. With the onset of artificial means of contraception, particularly the **birth control pill,** in the 1960s, the birth rate trended downward after the mid-1960s. The baby boomers born in this interval and who grew up amidst prosperity and consumerism benefited from the increased standard of living but also came to criticize it, along with their parents' values.

Since the 1970s, and especially since 1990, the population of many European nations, especially in the West, has stagnated. Some demographers forecast **negative population growth** for Italy and France over the next generation. This trend affects politics for two reasons. Government provision for generous retirement benefits must be funded by the taxes of the young. When these programs were first implemented, 20 workers funded the benefits of 1 retiree. That ratio has decreased to between three and five workers per retiree, creating a potential **entitlements time bomb** in the next few decades. Europe's prosperity also attracts immigrants from Asia, the Middle East, and elsewhere. Greater ethnic diversity has increased social tension and led to the growth of nationalist and **anti-immigrant political parties.** With the decline in religious observance among European Christians, it is estimated that **Muslims** will **outnumber Christians** in Europe by 2025. It is likely that this demographic shift will be attended by increased conflict, as witnessed by the clash over a Danish newspaper's publication in 2006 of cartoons satirizing Islam and Mohammed.

Growth of and Challenge to the Welfare State

Western and Eastern governments both significantly expanded welfare benefits following World War II. In the Eastern nations, this trend coincided with the establishment of Marxist governments dedicated to social equality and providing the basics for all of their citizens. In the West, the trend was driven by the dominance of Keynesian economic theory and fears about socialist exploitation of class conflict. Western nations provided **old-age pensions, unemployment, and disability insurance;** subsidized or **socialized medical care;** and redistributed income through progressive taxation. For the most part, this **"social safety net"** proved popular, though it came under increasing criticism during the stagnant 1970s and 1980s.

The late 1970s and early 1980s witnessed a resurgence of conservative political parties in several nations, such as Great Britain and the United States. Leaders like British Prime Minister Margaret Thatcher and President Reagan criticized the overregulated economy and bloated government bureaucracy as causing the high inflation and unemployment of the period. Even socialist Francois Mitterand of France was forced to abandon the more ambitious elements of his social reform program by the mid-1980s due to budget deficits and stagnating productivity. **Supply-side economists** argued that economic productivity would result from a reduction of taxes, regulation, and government spending on the welfare state. Supply-side policies did produce growth in the 1980s and early 1990s, but leftist groups believed the costs too high in poverty, inequality, and decline of organized labor.

Consumerism and Its Critics

Postwar prosperity brought a flood of new consumer goods. Pent-up demand from two decades of retrenchment during the Great Depression and WWII burst open with a spree of kitchen appliances, television sets, automobiles, and clothing fashions. **Mass marketing** techniques grew in sophistication, employing **TV spots** and **computer technology** to sell the "good life." Images and sounds of blue jeans and Coca-Cola were beamed across the Iron Curtain to demonstrate the superior abundance of Western society. Marketers often employed sexuality to sell products, a fact condemned both by religious conservatives and some feminists who decried the objectification of women. The Western economies (including the United States) began a shift away from traditional heavy industry toward services and information processing. While this **postindustrial economy** created new opportunities and wealth, it also gutted jobs from older industrial areas, such as the Midland cities of Britain—Leeds, Liverpool, Manchester, and Sheffield.

Many across the political spectrum—from traditionalists to socialists—found the new consumerism shallow and wasteful. Environmentalists objected to the waste of nonrenewable resources and levels of pollution. Socialists found confirmation of theories of Marxist alienation in Western society's high levels of crime, suicide, and social dislocation. British economist **E. F. Schumacher** (1911–1977) argued for balancing society's need for efficiency and productive centralization with humanistic values of community and the dignity of labor. In his famous work *Small Is Beautiful* (1973), Schumacher argued for sustainable development that would take into account the needs of future generations and the impact of production on the health of the planet.

Technological Advances

Postwar Europe saw continued scientific progress. Major advances in medicine and medical care almost doubled life expectancy during the twentieth century. **Antibiotics** cured formerly deadly infectious diseases. Medical personnel first used **penicillin** widely during World War II to fight infections following surgeries and amputations. In addition, vaccines also helped curtail a number of other dreaded diseases; Jonas Salk in 1955 pioneered an easily administered **vaccine against polio.** Safe and effective surgery, including **organ transplantation,** became common after the 1970s. Due to worldwide public health efforts, often sponsored by the United Nations, smallpox had been eradicated by 1975. However, the threat of global pandemics, such as **AIDS** (acquired immunodeficiency syndrome) and avian flu, has intensified with the further development of global trade and travel.

Much scientific research in the postwar period has been funded by governments. With the onset of the Cold War, both superpowers invested huge resources in obtaining a technological edge over the other—in rocket technology, nuclear power, and the space race. The space race produced the first **moon landing** by America's Apollo program in 1969. Not all applauded these advances. In his farewell address, President Eisenhower warned of the political dominance of a **"military-industrial complex,"** consisting of large, bureaucratized armed forces, arms manufacturers, and corporations, all of whom held an interest in the continuation of the arms race or even war. A new class of **technocrats**—engineers, managers, scientists—seemed to wield authority out of proportion to their numbers and outside democratic political processes. Moreover, many European nations adopted **nuclear power** as a beneficial side effect of the Cold War nuclear arms race. By 2000, France supplied almost 75 percent of its energy needs via nuclear power. Opponents feared that reliance on nuclear power would lead to environmental problems, such as waste disposal and **nuclear meltdowns,** as occurred at Chernobyl in 1986 and almost occurred at **Three Mile Island,** Pennsylvania, in 1979.

CRITICS AND OUTSIDERS IN EUROPEAN SOCIETY

Despite renewed economic prosperity, significant groups of Europeans felt either left out or alienated by postwar society. These groups offered critiques of consumerism, conformity, and inequality that often crossed the political spectrum.

> **Heads Up!** Though many post-1945 FRQs tend to focus on political and economic issues, this topic represents a potential essay question on the AP Exam. To address such a question, make sure that you provide historical context of the Cold War and the postwar economic advances.

Youth Revolts and the Generation Gap

The postwar baby boom generation was the first to attend college in large numbers. However, universities became a victim of their success in attracting students. Classes tended to be large and impersonal, and the professors distant. Students criticized living conditions in the dorms and demanded the addition of more up-to-date and relevant courses and programs in psychology, sociology, and women's studies. Youth criticisms were not unique to Europe; the years 1967–1968 saw worldwide protests against repression and bureaucratization. European protests began in Italy and Germany before spreading to France, which became the most fundamental critique of postwar society and almost brought down the government of President de Gaulle.

French students considered de Gaulle an elderly and distant figure, more interested in foreign affairs than domestic reform. In addition, many students and those sympathetic to leftist ideologies, such as Maoism and Trotskyism, opposed America's involvement in Vietnam and other Cold War colonial conflicts. Many students were attracted to the **New Left** critiques of neo-Marxist thinkers such as **Herbert Marcuse** (1898–1979), whose *One-Dimensional Man* (1964) condemned both the bureaucratic centralism of Soviet ideology and the rampant consumerism of Western society in favor of a culture of protest and rebellion.

In May 1968, the **University of Paris** exploded with student unrest. Students seized control of campus buildings and battled police, demanding better conditions but also a more open and less bureaucratic society. Workers initially supported the students with a nationwide general strike. When it looked as if de Gaulle's government would collapse, he defused the situation by co-opting the workers with wage increases and by assuring the support of the army for his government. Now isolated, the students eventually settled for concessions such as input into university governance and relief of overcrowding. Though the students' more ideological demands were not met, their actions highlighted growing divisions within European society.

Young people often conflict with parents as they establish autonomy. However, many used the **"generation gap"** to describe the widely divergent experiences of parents who grew up in the Great Depression and World War II with their children who experienced Cold War pessimism and economic prosperity. **Youth culture** embraced themes of rebellion, symbolized by the slogan **"sex, drugs, and rock 'n' roll."** Postwar European governments decriminalized homosexuality and abortion, and made birth control widely available. The resulting **sexual revolution** sought to separate sexual expression from family and commitment. Many young people embraced premarital sex and open sexuality as acts of rebellion against a society they perceived as rigid and conventional. During the 1960s, the recreational **use of drugs** such as marijuana and LSD grew as a way to experiment with new states of consciousness. Postwar music also expressed themes of rebellion. The **Beatles'** long hair, irreverent attitudes, and drug references introduced a generation to rock 'n' roll music. American **protest music** from Bob Dylan and Janis Joplin linked social consciousness with popular culture. Fittingly, the children of the baby boomers launched their own musical rebellion in the 1980s with **punk** and **alternative**.

Feminism

Militant feminism began as a transatlantic movement and coincided with the push for civil rights in the United States during the 1960s. Now that women had gained the vote in almost all European nations after World War II, they turned toward themes of economic and cultural liberation. **Women's liberation** was inspired by several key works. First, French philosopher **Simone de Beauvoir** (1908–1986), in *The Second Sex* (1949), demonstrated how gender represented a social construction of expectations and attitudes rather than a biological category. Throughout history, de Beauvoir argued, women have been treated as **"the Other,"** that is, a deviance from the default male gender, rather than beings in their own right. American **Betty Friedan's** *The Feminine Mystique* (1963) encouraged women to battle subtle oppression that limited women's entrance into leadership positions in academia, business, and government.

Indeed, women in Eastern and Western Europe entered the workforce in larger percentages than ever before. Moreover, many women attained **leadership positions** in government during the postwar era. Scandinavian legislatures boast close to 50 percent of seats held by women. Several famous women were elected for the first time in modern history as heads of government or state, such as Margaret Thatcher in Britain, Golda Meir in Israel, and Indira Gandhi in India, not to mention numerous others. Feminists believed that **"reproductive rights,"** such as access to birth control and **legalized abortion,** were essential to this progress. Worldwide, Europe led the way for the liberation of women, and European feminists have proven instrumental in pushing the United Nations to develop programs for female literacy, contraception, and universal rights in those developing regions where women often suffer the brunt of oppression and poverty.

> **Heads Up!** Because topics related to women's history often produce stereotyped responses, you may find it useful to trace the development of feminism over time—goals, tactics, and figures—to demonstrate its changing goals and variety.

Environmentalism

Postwar economic growth created a host of environmental problems, such as **pollution, acid rain,** and global warming. American zoologist Rachel Carson (1907–1964) spawned the global environmental movement with her investigation of the effects of pesticides on the food chain in *Silent Spring* (1962). Environmental groups sprung up in response and agitated for ecological protections, the more radical of which demanded a complete reassessment of the nature of global, consumerist capitalism. The fall of communist states in Eastern Europe revealed that socialist economies could despoil the environment as much as capitalist ones; in fact, much of the cost of German reunification has involved getting the former East Germany up to similar ecological standards as the rest of Germany. **Green parties** sprung in Central Europe in the 1980s, advocating for sustainable development and supporting various other leftist causes, such as social justice and pacifism. Germany's Green Party has proved most successful, having served in coalition with the Social Democratic Party from 1998 to 2005. Environmentalists often combined forces tactically and philosophically with feminists and the **antinuclear movement** in the 1980s and 1990s.

Most industrialized nations now support at least some of the environmental agenda. In 1992, 178 nations sent representatives to the first **"Earth Summit,"** held in Rio de Janeiro to address concerns over global warming. Science has essentially confirmed that humans' burning of fossil fuels has increased global temperatures and reduced the ozone layer. To address the issue further, 150 nations signed the **Kyoto Protocol** to halve so-called **greenhouse gases** by 2010; however, the largest producer of such gases, the United States, has of this date declined to ratify the agreement. Another issue of concern for the environmental movement has been **world population growth.** At the beginning of the twentieth century, the earth's population stood at 1.7 billion; as of 2006, it stands at around 7 billion. Much of this growth has occurred in the developing world, often complicating global problems of poverty, illiteracy, and lack of infrastructure. Controversy over measures to address this issue, such as promotion of birth control, often provokes controversy among differing cultural and religious traditions.

Guest Workers and Immigration

During the economic boom times of the 1950s and 1960s, Europe allayed its labor shortage by enticing immigrants from Southern Europe, Africa, and the Middle East. As in the United States today, these *Gastarbeiter* (as they are called in Germany) often performed jobs that local populations were reluctant or unwilling to assume. Moreover, governments often refused to extend citizenship or state benefits to these workers. When the European economy slowed in the 1970s and 1980s, local populations urged the guest workers to leave. When the fall of the Berlin Wall led to increased unemployment in the former East Germany, anti-immigrant parties and neo-Nazi groups urged their expulsion, or worse, attacked ethnic enclaves. In France, Jean-Marie Le Pen's **National Front Party** called for an end to immigration and supported economic nationalism; Le Pen polled enough votes in the 2002 presidential election to force a run-off before losing. Such issues highlight the growing diversity of European culture in an age of global capitalism and the challenges of successfully integrating new groups and redefining what it means to be "European."

Domestic Terrorism

Indigenous European terrorist movements took root in the 1970s and divided basically into two types of groups: leftists and nationalists. Leftist groups arose out of the violent youth movement of the late 1960s, especially among those influenced by Maoist and Trotskyite ideologies. The **Red Brigade** used armed violence to try to force Italy's withdrawal from the Western alliance. Most famously, it kidnapped and then **assassinated Prime Minister Aldo Moro** in 1978; its influence has declined since the late 1980s. Germany's **Baader-Meinhof Gang** also employed assassinations and kidnappings of public and business officials, most famously in the so-called German Autumn of 1977. Since the collapse of communism, the influence of the group has decreased.

Ethnic separatist movements in Northern Ireland and Spain have used tactics similar to leftist groups. **"The Troubles"** in British-ruled Northern Ireland began in 1968–1969 with communal clashes between Unionist Protestants wishing to remain in the United Kingdom and Catholics wishing to unite with the Republic of Ireland. The **Irish Republican Army (IRA)** campaigned against the British presence with car bombs, assassinations, and hunger strikes. Not until 1998 had the two sides worked out a power-sharing agreement; in late 2005, the IRA announced that it had abandoned all of its weapons. Similarly in Spain, the **ETA** has agitated with assassinations and bombings for a separate and socialist government representing the **Basque** people, the oldest ethnic group in Europe and one of the few not speaking an Indo-European language.

INTELLECTUAL AND CULTURAL TRENDS

The experience of the two world wars has fomented experimentation in the arts and reevaluation in the realms of philosophy and religion.

Modernism and Postmodernism

We often use the term "modern" simply to mean contemporary. Modernism, however, is associated with what might be called the "Enlightenment project," that is, the effort to discover the laws of nature and of human society, and thereby reach objective knowledge of the world. Once humans possess objective knowledge, they can harness nature for their flourishing and achieve progress. These notions define developments in ideas, economics, politics, and culture from the eighteenth into the twentieth centuries. The wrenching experiences of the two world wars and disgust over the crimes of absolutist ideologies such as Nazism and communism have produced a movement against the modern assumptions of objective knowledge, a movement known as **postmodernism.**

Postmodernism's roots lay in the nineteenth-century ideas of Friedrich Nietzsche and Danish philosopher **Søren Kierkegaard** (1813–1855), both of whom emphasized the lack of objective values in the world and the importance of **subjective experience.** In the postwar intellectual world, postmodernism has exercised a significant influence on literary criticism, philosophy, the writing of history, architecture, and film. Postmodernists aim to **"deconstruct"** texts—fiction and nonfiction—to find the underlying sociopolitical structure of gender, class, and race embedded in the authors' works. All ideas carry the baggage of the creator's biases and drive for power. As **Thomas Kuhn** (1922–1996) argued in his *The Structure of Scientific Revolutions* (1962), not even science possesses objective authority, instead representing a series of "paradigm shifts" that deal only with fact and theory, not truth. Postmodernists express interest more in how knowledge is "constructed" rather than its correspondence with "Truth," since the latter does not exist anyway. In art, postmodernists employ irony and satire and promiscuously blend traditional and modern styles.

Existentialism

As a philosophy, existentialism dominated the postwar intellectual world. Existentialism arises out of humanity's modern predicament—our feeling of **angst** amid a world of dizzying economic and technological change, the decline of traditional religious values, and the horrors revealed about humanity during the twentieth century. Most but not all existentialists began with Nietzsche's premise "God is dead." If this is so, then man must **"create himself."** As a movement, existentialism took hold among French intellectuals wrestling with the agonizing issues of resistance or collaboration during the Nazi occupation of France. **Jean-Paul Sartre** (1905–1980) was captured by the German army during World War II and later

> **Heads Up!** For a sense of existentialism, read Camus's "The Myth of Sisyphus" at www.nyu.edu/classes/keefer/hell/camus.html or Sartre's longer "Existentialism as a Humanism" at www.marxists.org/reference/archive/sartre/works/exist/sartre.htm.

founded a resistance movement. Sartre argued that for humans, **"existence precedes essence,"** meaning that we "turn up on the scene" without choosing to exist; because we have no creator, our essence must be defined by our own choices and values. As is demonstrated in **Albert Camus's** (1913–1960) novels such as *The Stranger* (1942) and *The Plague* (1947), humans must face the **absurdity** of existence by making life-defining choices alone. Human experience is thus subjective, and because no objective values exist for us to draw on, we must accept our radical human freedom and act with **authenticity**—without self-deception and by accepting responsibility for our choices. Existentialism significantly influenced the arts (see following discussion), and with its emphasis on subjectivity and criticism of modern society, helped lay the foundations for postmodernist thought.

Art, Theater, and Music

Signifying the increasingly important role of the United States in European affairs, the center of the Western art world shifted to New York City following World War II. Two styles dominated art in the contemporary era: **abstract expressionism** and **pop art.** In abstract expressionism, the artist does not "portray" anything, but instead uses the canvas and paint to express an emotional attitude or mood. American painter **Jackson Pollock** (1912–1956) popularized the style with his "drip technique" of pouring and splashing paint on immense canvases lying on the floor. Pop art is often associated with both the rise of consumerism in the postwar Western world and also the irony and satire of postmodernism. Artists such as American **Andy Warhol** (1928–1987) and **Roy Lichtenstein** (1923–1997) employed advertising, celebrities, and comic books in their art to comment ironically on the artificiality of consumer capitalism. When contemplating Warhol's Campbell's soup cans or Lichtenstein's comic strips, the line between advertising and artistic creativity becomes blurred.

> **Heads Up!** An excellent resource for postwar art is witcombe.sbc.edu/ARTH20thcentury.html.

The ideas of existentialist Albert Camus directly influenced the so-called **Theater of the Absurd** in postwar Europe. Whereas traditional drama concentrates on the development of plot and character, absurdist drama provokes the question, "What is happening now?" Along with the characters, the audience attempts to ascertain the significance of what is occurring on stage.

Perhaps the most famous absurdist drama is Irish playwright **Samuel Beckett's** *Waiting for Godot* (1954), in which two tramps arrive on stage and discuss waiting for a figure named Godot; not only does Godot never show, but the audience is never told why this person is important. In Tom Stoppard's *Rosencrantz and Guildenstern Are Dead* (1967), two characters from Shakespeare's *Hamlet* discuss their upcoming fate but seem unable to prevent their untimely deaths—a play within a play.

While popular music incorporated rebellion and consumerism, composers of avant-garde ("cutting edge") music experimented with **serialism.** Serialist composers such as **Arnold Schoenberg** (1874–1951) employed a 12-note scale and used mathematical series of "tone rows" to create a more abstract sound than standard tonal and melodic music. Pioneering American composer **John Cage** (1912–1992) experimented with "chance music," where elements of a composition occur randomly. Most famously, Cage "played" his composition "4'33"" in concert, a piece consisting of not a single note; Cage simply timed the composition and then closed the piano cover. In conclusion, perhaps many of these works strike the reader as far-fetched, ridiculous, or nonsensical; with postwar Western culture, it may very well be that the point is that "there is no point."

Religion in the Modern World

As previously noted, religious belief in Europe declined markedly in the postwar period. Nonetheless, religious developments continued to play a role in European culture after 1945. For the Catholic Church, the most important development has been the **ecumenical movement,** or the effort to reach out and establish common ground with other, particularly Christian, religions. Since the Council of Trent (1545–1563), the Church had generally been on the defensive against modern ideas and culture. When **Pope John XXIII** (r. 1958–1963) called the **Second Vatican Council** (1962–1965), it signaled the willingness of the Catholic Church to update doctrine and practice more in keeping with modern developments. John opened dialogues with different faiths and called on wealthy nations to support social justice and work toward human rights. His successor, Paul VI (1963–1978), continued the work of Vatican II but sparked controversy with his encyclical *Humanae Vitae* (1968), which condemned artificial means of birth control.

Paul's death in 1978 opened the door for a historic change in the church, the election of the first non-Italian pope since 1522 and the first Slavic pope ever. **John Paul II** (1978–2005), often considered the first postmodern pope, lived under both Nazi and Soviet oppression in his native Poland. Many commentators consider this experience to have shaped the John Paul's concern with what he later called the twentieth century's "culture of death." As pope, John Paul supported the Solidarity movement in Poland and worked toward the end of communist oppression in Eastern Europe but also condemned the nuclear arms race and the excesses of consumer capitalism. John Paul's long reign also witnessed his many efforts to reconcile the Catholic Church with its past, apologizing for the Crusades, Galileo's persecution, and the failures of the Catholic Church during the Holocaust. Though progressive on social issues, John Paul adhered to a conservative line on church dogma, upholding bans on contraception, female priests, married priests, and abortion. His supporters see him as providing a brake on the hasty changes made at Vatican II, while his detractors grew concerned with a renewed hierarchical stance.

> **Sidebar:** Further information on the life and writings of the recently deceased John Paul II can be found at the Vatican Web site, which also includes relevant information on the activities and dogma of the Catholic Church: http://www.vatican.va/holy_father/john_paul_ii/.

Most European Protestant denominations have reconciled themselves to modern biblical scholarship and have adapted their faiths in keeping with modern science. Nonetheless, Protestant theologians such as the Swiss **Karl Barth** (1886–1986) took reformed Christianity back to its roots in biblical revelation. Barth held that divine revelation stood on its own feet, without the possibility of being "judged" by human reason. The European Protestant experience has differed markedly from that of the United States since 1945. **Evangelical Christianity** along with a renewed fundamentalism has experienced widespread growth in America, trends that have not generally touched Europe. Formerly communist Eastern Europe suffered under religious persecution, which effectively killed religious belief in several nations. This "unchurched" Europe often conflicts with United States when it comes to issues such as Darwinian evolution and approaches to foreign policy.

Globalization

Since the beginning of your course, an ever-present theme has been Europe's place in the world. More than ever, the issues confronting the world today reflect those facing Europe. With global communication developments, such as faxes, cell phones, and the Internet, it is no longer possible for one region of the world to wall itself off from the rest. Some recognition of past mistakes in this regard is already apparent with postwar efforts to build a common European identity through economic and political integration. In some ways, Europe has renewed its power and prestige after the horrors of the twentieth century, yet it continues to struggle with its role and place in the world, as seen in the belated response to the Balkan conflicts of the 1990s. As confirmed by history since 1945, many Europeans seem to recognize that their continent functions increasingly within a global context.

ADDITIONAL RESOURCES

Armstrong, Karen, *The Battle for God* (2000)—A comparative and critical analysis of the growth of fundamentalism among the monotheistic faiths.

Butler, Christopher, *Postmodernism: A Very Short Introduction* (2002)—As the title suggests, this volume provides the reader with the basics regarding the recent intellectual climate.

Camus, Albert, *The Stranger* (1942) and *The Plague* (1947)—Two well-known novels that convey the existentialist ethos well and raise profound questions about the human condition.

Friedman, Thomas, *The World Is Flat: A Brief History of the Twenty-First Century* (2005)—The author examines the process of global economic and technological change.

Judt, Tony, *Postwar: A History of Europe since 1945* (2005)—A well-received history that offers powerful insights and the author's unique voice.

Kurlansky, Mark, *1968: The Year That Rocked the World* (2004)—Interesting analysis of the personalities involved in a year of upheaval.

Lacquer, Walter, *Europe since Hitler: The Rebirth of Europe* (1982)—This volume provides an overview of postwar developments in all areas.

Landes, David S., *The Wealth and Poverty of Nations* (1998)—An examination of how and why some areas of the world experience success and others difficulty in producing wealth.

www.art-for-a-change.com/Paris/paris.html—This site provides text and posters of the student revolts in 1968 Paris.

kennedy.byu.edu/partners/CSE/—Housed at Brigham Young University, this site provides a variety of resources on contemporary Europe.

www.ycsg.yale.edu/center/—Yale University sponsors this site on relevant features of globalization, including climate change and trade issues.

PRACTICE QUESTIONS

1. Following World War II, up to the 1960s, Europe's population:
   a. declined due to Cold War conflicts.
   b. fluctuated depending on the economy.
   c. rose because of an increasing birth rate.
   d. stagnated with the onset of artificial contraception.
   e. surpassed that of Asia and Africa.

2. Which of the following best describes the economic policies of Western European governments after World War II?
   a. a gradual reassertion of laissez-faire economic theory
   b. provision for welfare programs such as old-age pensions
   c. nationalization of most industries to provide full employment
   d. focus on the agricultural sector at the expense of industry
   e. movement toward the command economic model

3. Major technological developments in postwar Europe included all of the following EXCEPT:
   a. moon landings.
   b. polio vaccine.
   c. personal computers.
   d. nuclear power.
   e. cure for AIDS.

4. The quotes below represent ideas associated with:
   a. supply-side economists frustrated with government bureaucracy.
   b. feminists agitating for access to birth control and abortion.
   c. technocrats who opposed the interference of government in science.
   d. students protesting the rigidity and alienation of modern society.
   e. environmentalists concerned about pollution and species diversity.
      • "Boredom is counterrevolutionary."
      • "Don't liberate me—I'll take care of that."
      • "We want structures that serve people, not people serving structures!"

5. Compared with feminists of the late nineteenth and early twentieth centuries, feminists in the post–World War II period focused on:
   a. gaining the right to vote in all European nations.
   b. securing equality in the workforce and political power.
   c. protecting the environment from male exploitation.
   d. eliminating marriage as an institution of oppression.
   e. overturning laws banning prostitution and pornography.

6. In the postwar period, which of the following represents the most accurate characterization of the environmental movement?
   a. It led to cooperation between the superpowers in battling acid rain.
   b. It was initiated by Simone de Beauvoir's writings regarding pollution.

  c. It led to international success in reducing the amount of greenhouse gases.

  d. It led to immediate changes in government economic policies.

  e. It led to the establishment of Green parties, which gained some political power.

7. Existentialism is a post–World War II philosophy focusing on:

  a. the need for a revival of religious belief.

  b. a view of humans as determined by outside forces.

  c. the importance of human choice and responsibility.

  d. opposing the Cold War division of Europe.

  e. developing a universal code of values.

8. The painting below represents the artistic style of:

  a. pop art.

  b. postmodernism.

  c. Dadaism.

  d. abstract expressionism.

  e. Cubism.

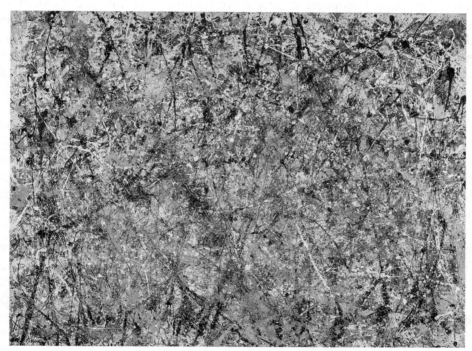

Jackson Pollock (1912–56), *Lavender Mist: Number 1, 1950.*
Bridgeman Art Library. © 2007 The Pollock-Krasner Foundation, Artists Rights Society
(ARS), New York

9. At the Second Vatican Council (1962–1965), a major goal of the Catholic Church was to:

  a. modernize the church's position on birth control.

  b. open dialogues with other faiths and modernism.

  c. elect the first non-Italian pope since the fifteenth century.

  d. seek reconciliation for the papacy's actions during the Holocaust.

  e. support the overthrow of communism in Eastern Europe.

10. All of the following represent domestic European groups employing violence for political means EXCEPT:
    a. Irish Republican Army (IRA).
    b. Baader-Meinhof Gang.
    c. Red Brigade.
    d. Palestinian Liberation Organization (PLO).
    e. Basque ETA.

SAMPLE ESSAY

Analyze critiques made of European society after World War II by any THREE of the following groups:

Feminists
Youth
Environmentalists
Existentialists

Three groups that opposed European society were feminists, youth, and existentialists. These groups varied in their criticisms of Europe. Feminists wanted women to have more power, including the vote. Young people demanded better conditions in universities and an end to Vietnam. Existentialists created a new philosophy that said "existence precedes essence," meaning that people exist before they have an essence. With their criticisms, they tried to make life better.

Feminists demanded the vote after World War II. Soon they got it in most nations, partly based on the writings of Mary Wollstonecraft. She was a French thinker, who wrote about women being the "other," which means that men have always treated them as a second-class race. Other feminists wanted women to enter the workforce and get political positions, like Margaret Thatcher of Great Britain. With these ideas, most women gained equality soon after World War II.

Young people attended universities after WWII but did not think the conditions there were acceptable. There was overcrowding and professors were out of touch with modern society. Students decided to take over many of the buildings and demand the creation of new courses, such as studying women and society. Some of these youth were called "hippies" and experimented with "sex, and drugs, and rock and roll." They listened to loud music that made their parents angry. This was part of the generation gap between them and their parents.

Existentialists came mostly from France. They tended to be atheists who said that God could not really matter in the modern world. The big idea of existentialism is "existence precedes essence." What they mean by this was that people just are here, then they have make the most of their lives. Existentialism was a big philosophy after World War II; it really influenced a lot of art and poetry.

Though WWII was over, everything in Europe was not perfect. Many groups thought Europe needed to go in a different direction. Women and youth wanted power, while existentialists wanted people to have more responsibility for their actions. These ideas played a major role in post-WWII culture.

This essay lacks appropriate historical context and makes the mistake of jumping into the three groups without giving a sense of postwar European society. To understand the critiques, we need to have a sense of what these groups found problematic in postwar society. The sample essay here indicates a mixed response. While the student demonstrates some sense of the critiques, the discussion seems general. Several more examples, with accurate explanations, would easily boost this into the stronger essay category. The reference to Mary Wollstonecraft is erroneous (Simone de Beauvoir?), while the treatment of existentialism suggests only a vague understanding. Score: 5.

CHAPTER 18
Answers and Explanations
to Chapter Practice Questions

CHAPTER 4

1. **d.** Art following the Black Death (a) focused on themes of death, though no new techniques were introduced as a result. As for the Catholic Church (b), its inability to explain the tragedy adequately undermined its influence. (c) is incorrect, for though the Black Death led to some revolts, these were invariably crushed by the state. Family bonds (e) in some instances might have been strengthened, but more generally the plague caused general social breakdown. (d) is the correct answer, as the resulting labor shortage allowed peasants to bargain for better conditions on feudal estates.

2. **a.** Yes, the Catholic Church continued to promote Scholasticism (b), but this did not constitute the greatest criticism of it after the Great Schism. If anything, the Church acted as a major patron of the arts (c). Though the papacy had traditionally attempted to exercise some diplomatic influence, it was not generally criticized for these actions (d). Christian humanist writings, by focusing the faithful's attention on original texts, did not strengthen the institutional power of the church (e). The answer is (a): to rebuild prestige, popes engaged in a misguided effort to patronize art and philosophy, while engaging in wars to consolidate control of the Papal States. Meanwhile, criticisms of corruption within the Church went unaddressed.

3. **c.** (a), (b), (d), and (e) all describe major features of Italian society that helped in promoting the Renaissance. Italy did not have a centralized monarchy (c). Note that the answer is the opposite of (e).

4. **b.** Classical architectural motifs included columns, arches, and pediments—all in geometric proportion. (a) is a better description of Gothic architecture and is not supported by the picture. Renaissance architecture tended to glorify the architect and the entity (church, state) that sponsored it, so (c) is eliminated. Though (d) is appealing because it links to a theme of the Renaissance, it takes more than one person to create such grand buildings. As the building is a chapel, choice (e) seems unwarranted. Again, make sure that your answer can be confirmed by the visual.

5. **a.** Though women may have played a role in (c), (d), and (e) during the Renaissance, it would be hard to argue that they gained most in these areas. Of course, women could become nuns (b), but the Renaissance is not associated with any particular increase in these opportunities. However, many humanists advocated education for women (a), even if it was of an inferior kind to that of men.

6. **e.** War became a major concern of the New Monarchs, which eliminates (a) as the answer. If you recall that the Spanish initiated the Inquisition during this period, (b) can be eliminated. (c) actually reverses the correct order of the situation: monarchs allied with towns to curb the influence of nobles. A major feature of the New Monarchs was their increasing desire to control religious affairs in their nations (e.g., Henry VIII, the French, Ferdinand and Isabella), eliminating (d). The correct answer is (e); the New

Monarchs focused their attention and resources on rebuilding their states, particularly through gaining central direction of warfare.

7. **c.** For this question, it may be difficult to eliminate some choices, as you may not be sure if some of the statements are true or not. The correct answer is (c); recall that Luther was a "theological revolutionary, but a social and political conservative." Though (a) might have been on Luther's mind, it was not his primary concern. Peasants did not direct their anger against Jews, and further, Luther did not generally support religious toleration (b). Because Luther encouraged the princes to use violence to crush the revolt, (d) is eliminated. Finally, you will recall that Luther's alliance with Zwingli miscarried at Marburg, so (e) is out.

8. **d.** In the early stages of the Reformation, women did play a public role in preaching and encouraging their families to adopt the new faith. This was strongest among Anabaptists (d), the group most attuned to social equality. Even this modest advance was turned back over time, but the other reformers tended to be deeply conservative when it came to the social roles of women, which eliminates the other choices. Calvinists even had men and women sit in different areas of the church during services.

9. **b.** This interpretive question requires an evaluation of the effect of the Catholic Reformation. (a) is an overstatement. The Jesuits did succeed in regaining some areas to Catholicism but certainly not most. A major feature of the Catholic Reformation was the establishment of new religious orders (c) and an increase in the power of the papacy (d). (e) is simply incorrect; though the Church was tardy in its response, it did ultimately adopt a multipronged approach. The Council of Trent did refuse to compromise with Protestants and did choose to reaffirm teachings distinctive to Catholicism (b).

10. **a.** Henry VIII wrote a treatise opposing Luther's ideas and persecuted Lutherans in England, making (b) false. As we know, Thomas More opposed Henry's policies, eliminating (c). Most nobles were aware of Henry's condemnation of Luther and did not wish to antagonize him, so they were not Protestant (d). Though Henry had designs in Europe, these did not include Italy; further, he was not excommunicated prior to his break with Rome (e). Henry's break was due to his need for a male heir; he intended to keep doctrine untouched, as with the Six Articles.

CHAPTER 5

1. **d.** All of the advancements listed in (a), (b), (c), and (e) did occur in the period of European exploration, roughly the fifteenth and sixteenth centuries. Accurate marine chronometers that could withstand the atmospheric and physical conditions of open seas voyages were not developed until the late eighteenth century (d). As a result, measuring longitude required either some lucky coincidences or educated guesswork.

2. **b.** Though Native Americans were exploited and overworked (a), enslaved (c), did suffer the breakdown of their traditional economies (d), and did commit suicide in large numbers (e), the biggest killers by far proved to be infectious diseases (b), especially smallpox, measles, diphtheria, and influenza. Not being in close proximity to large numbers of domesticated livestock, Native Americans over time developed no immunities to these killers.

3. **c.** Throughout much of Europe's history, its cultural and political center was the Mediterranean. Witness the accomplishments of Italy during the Renaissance. However, after the voyages of exploration, those nations with ready access to the Atlantic Ocean

(Portugal, Spain, England, and France) gained immensely from colonization. These nations became the leaders in commerce and in establishing colonial empires. Italy's economic greatness failed due to its political disunity and geography (a). Central Europe (b) and Scandinavia (d) did not benefit as directly as the Atlantic powers, and it would be incorrect to say England alone benefited (e).

4. **e.** Though historians often attributed the Price Revolution to the influx of specie from the New World (a), the money supply had been growing for some years before this. Guilds always restrict the supply of goods (b), but that does not account for the timing of inflation in the sixteenth century. Trade was increasing, not declining, during this period (c). Also, while governments did establish trade monopolies and this probably did cause a rise in prices (d), the limited number of these institutions by 1600 could not have produced the large-scale effect of an expanding population outrunning the supply of goods (e).

5. **a.** The illustration shows a fairly wealthy artisan family—we can tell because of the solid ceiling and brick walls. A significant feature of families during the early modern period was how they produced as a unit (a). Poverty existed in the sixteenth century and was growing, but this family clearly is not impoverished, and child labor predates the issue of poverty (b). Because the couple is laboring together, work regimens were not divided based on gender (c). The picture shows work with tools, even if they are not mechanized, but this fact does not say much about European families (d). Finally, the illustration does not depict a factory (e).

6. **c.** Mercantilism allowed private property but often restricted competition for interests of state (a). Labor was important to mercantilists, but they viewed hard money (gold and silver) as the true form of wealth (b). (d) is clearly wrong, as mercantilists actively pursued colonies as suppliers of raw materials and markets for finished products. Governments actively tried to eliminate the localism of guilds, not support them (e). Because specie was the source of value, governments attempted to bring it in their nations by promoting exports and limiting imports (c).

7. **d.** Because torture meant that anyone could be accused of witchcraft, most did not toss around accusations lightly (a). At this time, there was not an active women's rights movement in Europe (b). Though wars occurred in the period of the witchcraft accusations (1580–1720), it would be an exaggeration to say men were shielded because of this; in the days of mercenary soldiers, most men did not see military service (c). (e) is incorrect; the accusations tended to be based on a sincere belief in witches. Many were convinced that women did have special bodily powers, because of childbirth, and were weak enough to be seduced by demons (d).

8. **a.** The primary solution to France's wars of religion was simply to tolerate the minority religion of the Huguenots (a). Catholicism remained the dominant religion (b), but the Bourbon monarchy (in the person of Henry IV) now replaced the Valois (c). This new king attempted to eliminate Spanish influence in France (d) but certainly did not eliminate the involvement of the state in religion, a relationship that continued in almost all European nations (e).

9. **e.** Philip opposed English intervention in the Netherlands revolt, so did not wish to form an alliance with Protestants, who opposed his policies (a). Also, Philip had no intention of allowing independence to the Spanish colonies (b). In addition, Spain continued to depend significantly, and too much, on specie from the New World to finance its wars (c). Though Philip supported Catholicism (e), he often had a tense relationship with the papacy, which advanced its own political goals, not necessarily in tune with Philip's.

10. **b.** Though one might claim France as a victor in the Thirty Years' War, this illustration does not demonstrate that fact (a). Civilians were killed during the conflict, but the visual suggests some kind of judicial proceeding; in fact, execution of thieves (c). Germany was not unified until 1871 (d). Though the importance of religion had declined as a factor in the war, it would be an overstatement to say it played "no role" (e). A major consequence of the war was the destruction of and social breakdown in Germany, which is vividly demonstrated in the visual (b).

CHAPTER 6

1. **b.** The Peace of Utrecht ended the War of Spanish Succession. As a result, several Spanish possessions were transferred to Austria to reflect a new balance of power, making (a) incorrect. Also, (c) is wrong because the treaty specifically prohibited the union of Spanish and French crowns. Though Russia was growing in power, the treaty said nothing about its status, making (d) incorrect. The three nations listed in (e) continued to decline after the war. Therefore, the primary result of the treaty was to end Louis XIV's threat to the balance of power (b).

2. **d.** Vermeer's painting shows a domestic scene of elegant objects, pointing us toward (d). The Netherlands was not dominated by the aristocracy, nor does the painting demonstrate this, eliminating (a). During this period, the Netherlands was prosperous, so we can discount (b). We do not know if the girl in the painting is a single mother, and this was not an increasing problem in the seventeenth century (c). The Baroque style was never popular in the Netherlands, as it was not primarily Catholic and not ruled by an absolute monarchy (e).

3. **c.** Some historians believe a class element played a role in the English Civil War, but it certainly wasn't primary (a). Though the Stuarts favored a High Church Anglican structure, there were no efforts prior to 1670 to reintroduce Catholicism (b). In addition, popular riots generally did not play a role in the conflict, and the economy was in fact doing fairly well (d). Finally, the Stuart kings simply did not have the resources to "overspend," reliant as they were on indirect taxes and the approval of Parliament (e). This leaves us with the clash between the monarchy and Parliament over their respective political roles as the key cause of the English Civil War (c).

4. **e.** This EXCEPT question has four right answers, so we must find the "wrong" one. William and Mary, the new co-rulers of England, agreed to respect the sovereignty of Parliament as a condition of assuming the throne in their overthrow of James II (a). Though Protestants were treated as second-class citizens in England after 1689, they were allowed to worship freely; this did not apply, however, to Catholics (b). The Bill of Rights of 1689 stands as a major accomplishment of the Glorious Revolution and also influenced the U.S. Bill of Rights (c). By the Act of Succession in 1701, Catholics were not allowed to hold the throne, a law that continues to this day (d). This leaves us with (e): the House of Lords continued to play a legislative role in England, though its powers were periodically subject to curtailment.

5. **a.** Louis XIV's reasons for revoking Nantes appear to be primarily ideological. Though the Huguenots posed no threat to the state (b) and actually assisted the economy through their manufacturing and mercantile skills (d), Louis believed their very existence posed a threat to his goal of "one king, one faith, one law" (a). Louis often clashed with the papacy and had made no agreement with it regarding the Huguenots

(c). France had an active Jansenist movement, but its pseudo-Protestant ideas were certainly not supported by Louis (e).

6. **a.** Most of the money for Versailles came from taxes, not tariffs (b). Though Versailles may have been a wonder to foreign visitors, that was not its primary purpose (c). Certainly, many workers received income from their work at Versailles, but Louis was not an early advocate of social welfare programs for the lower classes (d). (e) is true, but is not the primary reason for building Versailles. That reason was political in nature—to keep the nobility under the watchful eye of the monarchy (a).

7. **c.** By the Peace of Utrecht, the Austrian Habsburgs had failed to unify the Spanish and Austrian crowns, eliminating (a). Though Prussia was emerging as a power, there was as yet no direct threat or conflict between the two nations; in fact, Prussia had assisted the Austrians in the recent War of Spanish Succession (b). The Austrians were anti-French, but the Pragmatic Sanction had nothing to do with this (d). In addition, serfdom would be reformed in Austria but only later in the eighteenth century (e). Charles was concerned that his daughter, Maria Theresa, maintain the unity of the empire, even though, as a woman, she could not rule as Holy Roman Emperor. The Pragmatic Sanction represented the assent of European powers to Maria's assumption of the Habsburg lands (c).

8. **a.** Though the civil service (b) and Hohenzollern monarchy (c) proved vital to the rise of Prussia, the institution most associated with its greatness is its military. After all, the state virtually formed around the army (a). Prussia was not known for either its commercial prowess or strong navy (d and e).

9. **d.** Peter's reforms never did seep down to the common person, who remained unaffected by the nation's adoption of new military and manufacturing technology (a). In fact, serfdom and its backward effects grew worse during Peter's reign, so (c) is incorrect. There was some opposition to Peter's policies, but it did not prove widespread or grow into a general effort at a revolution (b). Peter's rule was autocratic, as with most Russian tsars; thus, he did not share power with the middle class, which tended in Russia to be small in numbers and influence (e). The primary effect of Peter's policies was to make Russia a major military power, crystallized by its defeat of Sweden in the Great Northern War (d).

10. **d.** There are some appealing choices here: Poland did have a weak tax base (c) and did remain a primarily agrarian nation (b). Religious toleration was practiced in Poland in the sixteenth century, though the arrival of the Jesuits helped return the nation to Catholicism in the seventeenth century. However, it would be an overstatement to say that interdenominational conflict in religion acted as a major reason for decline (e). Poland's nobility (the szlachta) was one of the strongest in Europe and generally united in its goal of preventing a strong monarchy (a). It was Poland's weak elective monarchy, often controlled by outsiders, that left it open to invasion and control externally (d).

CHAPTER 7

1. **b.** Aquinas and Augustine were primarily theologians, not scientists, so that eliminates (a). For (c), Plato had little scientific influence prior to the Renaissance, and Copernicus introduced his ideas in the sixteenth century. Pythagoras and Plato did contribute ideas to math, but neither shaped medieval scientific views. Cicero served as a Roman statesman, so (d) is incorrect. For (e), Newton and Copernicus again promoted the New Science, so that choice is incorrect. That leaves (b)—Aristotle's ideas were synthesized into Christian

thinking by Aquinas; Ptolemy's astronomy and Galen's anatomy set the standard in science until the Scientific Revolution.

2. **c.** All but Brahe (c) made important contributions to the heliocentric theory. Copernicus (a) introduced the theory, Kepler added elliptical paths and three planetary laws (b), Galileo provided empirical support (d), and Newton synthesized the workings of the solar system with his universal law of gravitation (e). Though Brahe gathered immense data and modified the geocentric view, he never completely abandoned geocentrism (c).

3. **e.** Be careful to distinguish between Bacon's and Descartes's beliefs here. They both supported (e) but through different methods. Bacon supported (a) but Descartes thought the senses were often unreliable. Only Descartes appreciated and understood the important conceptual role of math in science (b). Neither believed that science should be based on tradition (c), which also seems to contradict (e). Bacon advocated the practical benefits of science and Descartes did so implicitly, so (d) is incorrect.

4. **a.** The understanding of infectious diseases did not occur until Pasteur's work in the late nineteenth century (b). Vesalius did produce detailed anatomical drawings, but they did not lead to the founding of new medical schools generally (c). Life expectancy did not increase and may have actually decreased in the seventeenth century due to the Age of Crisis (see Chapter 6) (d). Though the Church opposed dissection, any prohibitions would have been ineffective given the decentralized nature of European politics (e). In fact, little practical in medical care was accomplished until later in the eighteenth and certainly in the nineteenth centuries (a).

5. **d.** Spinoza did attempt to reconcile science and religion, but his ideas were difficult to understand and did not gain a mass following (a). Most scientists were, in fact, religious and saw science as supporting a better understanding of God's creation, so (b) is wrong. Of course, the Catholic Church did *try* to silence Galileo, but his ideas were published elsewhere and the Church's efforts were therefore not effective (c). Clearly, religion and science were connected—the Church sponsored astronomy and organized the calendar, so (e) is incorrect. Secularism advanced as a side effect of scientific thinking, separating matter from spirit, despite the efforts of those such as Spinoza, Pascal, Kepler, and Galileo to combine them.

6. **c.** The quote demonstrates the importance of property as a fundamental right, an idea essential to the thinking of John Locke (c). Hobbes did not believe that property rights were inalienable or that they trumped state power (a). Bossuet supported absolute monarchy, and so rejected the notion of a social contract that preceded the existence of a divine-right ruler (b). Descartes and Newton did not generally address questions of political thought and focused more on philosophy and science (d and e).

7. **a.** As we have seen, women did play a role in science, but ultimately, views toward them changed little and "science" was even used to reaffirm female inequality (a). (b) is partly true, but women did not gain any significant rights in this period, despite some minor and grudging recognition. (c) is an overstatement: Though women did face restrictions, these were never absolute. After all, fathers and husbands were free to educate their daughters and wives as they saw fit, which did occur. Most male scientists were either threatened by the entry of women into their professions or believed the female mind incapable of abstract subjects such as those inherent in science, so (d) is eliminated. Women did not generally play a major role in technological areas, as these fields tended to be dominated by men (e).

8. **e.** This painting shows Louis XIV amidst a team of scientists, seeking patronage and royal favor. There is nothing in the painting regarding openness, at least directly, to new ideas (a). This same is true of religion; there are no obvious religious references (b). National societies were founded primarily to benefit the state, even if international correspondence was involved, so (c) is out. Though some (not most) scientists were nobles, controlling the nobles was not the primary purpose of scientific societies (d). The answer, then, is (e)—a number of practical benefits are suggested by the painting and Louis's very presence suggests the importance of science to the state.

9. **c.** Though Newton believed science could not solve all philosophical riddles, he did not view the universe as an "unknowable mystery" (a). In addition, Newton did believe God was "everywhere present," but did not rely on the supernatural to explain the natural, eliminating (b). Newton did argue for the reality of motion; in fact, his notion of absolute motion was later overturned by Einstein (d). Newton did believe that natural laws possessed a reality beyond mere appearance, so (e) is wrong. That leaves us with (c), and Newton's ideas are most associated with the idea that the universe resembled a clock in its adherence to fixed laws (d).

10. **d.** Galileo had signed an agreement with the Catholic Church in 1619 to teach heliocentrism as a "mathematical supposition," so the papacy viewed his *Dialogue* (1632) as a violation of that agreement (a). Galileo's trial occurred in the midst of the Thirty Years' War (b), and even though the Church did not generally rely on biblical literalism, it did in this instance to preserve its authority (c). Though some members of the clergy, especially Jesuit astronomers, clearly thought Galileo's conclusions were wrong and unsubstantiated, this was not the major reason for Galileo's trial (e). Martin Luther did not support Copernicanism, and so any association Galileo had with the founder of Protestantism is imaginary (d).

CHAPTER 8

1. **b.** Remember that visuals are cues for important period trends. Beware of overanalyzing them. (a) may be true as a period trend, but the picture really doesn't address it; the only child in the picture is sitting by the fire while adults work. Women are working in the picture, though nothing suggests any sort of union activity, which didn't occur in this period anyway (c). Early textile mills did feature poor working conditions, but (d) is wrong because this is clearly not a factory, but a home. Poverty existed in this period, but the picture doesn't seem to address this, as the home seems comfortable and even has a few pets (e). Cottage industry advanced in the eighteenth century and is the development featured in the visual (b).

2. **c.** Here is another stimulus that requires some interpretation. Defoe argues for the importance of trade as a mechanism of advance and claims that commercial pursuits do not detract from gentlemanliness (c). Because Defoe mentions the advance of the gentry as well as nobility, (a) is incorrect. There is no mention of peasants in the passage, and they did not engage in trade generally (b). (d) might be true, but Defoe does not address that point in the quote. Though Defoe speaks of the "meanest" classes, he argues that unlike the stereotypes in other nations, trade does not attract such people in England, so (e) is wrong.

3. **e.** Louis XV was, in fact, a weak ruler who several times attempted to curb the growing power of the *parlements* but failed (a). Though the bourgeoisie could attain noble status and were increasing in numbers, their main goal seemed to be imitation of the

aristocratic lifestyle; in addition, noble privileges remained strong prior to the French Revolution (b). Taxes did increase in this period but not so much for the nobles, and the second part about private warfare is anachronistic, describing the feudal period (c). Relations between nobles and peasants were strained throughout the eighteenth century, as aristocrats tended to look down on them and would not have appealed for support (d). After Louis XIV's death, the nobles attempted to reassert their traditionally strong political position and check any further advances against absolutism. Louis XV's reign seemed the ideal time to accomplish this (e).

4. **d.** This is a straightforward identification question. Tull and Townsend made important advances during the Agricultural Revolution, not relating to children (a). Frederick William I was known for his harsh parenting style with his son, Frederick II, and though Maria Theresa was a loving mother, she did little to advocate new attitudes toward child-rearing (b). Hobbes tended toward a harsh view of human nature and Voltaire did not generally write about such issues (c). The two female figures in (e) may be appealing, and though Winkelmann was a scientist, she addressed astronomy, not children; Pompadour served as Louis XV's mistress (e). Both Locke in his *Some Thoughts Concerning Education* and Rousseau in *Emile* advocated for a new approach to education, which involved new attitudes about childhood (d).

5. **b.** All of these factors (a, c, d, and e) did occur during the eighteenth century and contributed to the increase in European population, except for (b). Though incremental improvements were made in hygiene and the professionalization of medicine, new conceptual understandings of disease would await Pasteur's germ theory of the late nineteenth century.

6. **d.** Britain was by no means a democracy or even getting close to one in the eighteenth century, so (a) is incorrect. Though landed interests did have say in government, mercantile interests did as well, so (b) is wrong, though if the distracter had read "propertied interests" it might be plausible. The reverse of (c) is in fact true, as the new Hanoverian line relied heavily on Whig leaders in Parliament to manage legislation. England did not work toward a written constitution and still employs common law as the basis of its legal system, so (e) is eliminated. That leaves us with (d), and you may recall the key role of Robert Walpole as the first prime minister and his creation of a new form of government where executive positions are held by members of Parliament who can use majorities in that body to govern.

7. **a.** All of these products became important consumer items during the eighteenth century. You may even connect tobacco (c) and cotton (d) with slavery in the American South. However, most slaves from Africa went to the Caribbean, whose societies were 90 percent African and 10 percent white, to produce sugar (a). Tea (b) and (e) spices are usually not associated with slave labor, though certainly the effort to bring them to market was strenuous.

8. **a.** Citizen armies is incorrect, as that development would await the French Revolution (b). "Private mercenaries" describes the warfare of any earlier age, perhaps the Middle Ages or early modern period (c). Civilians did suffer from warfare, but in this period, war tended to be the world of soldiers; propaganda did not play a role in warfare until the French Revolution (d). Because war was endemic to Europe, which lacked collective security mechanisms, (e) is clearly incorrect. In fact, European nations used regular standing armies of trained professional soldiers and waged frequent limited wars in pursuit of clear territorial or economic objectives (a).

9. **c.** This question takes it as given that Maria embarked on reforms but inquires about her motives. Though her son was one, Maria was not a patron of the Enlightenment and was not interested in equality for its own sake (a). Maria was a pious Catholic, but this fact had little to do with her reforms (b). (d) seems rather a stretch for a ruling monarch—to be motivated by such a thin psychological motive. (e) might strike you as appealing, but discontent in Austria was not opened by either nobles or peasants. That leaves us with (c), and, indeed, if you recall the two midcentury wars over Silesia, Maria wished to regain that land or at the least block any further Prussian gains in power.

10. **e.** France did lose territory at the Treaty of Paris, but its commerce quickly recovered and continued to expand, so (a) is false. Spain had already seen its great-power days pass it by, and though it revived slightly under the Bourbons, it certainly did not recapture predominance (b). Austria aimed to regain Silesia in the Seven Years' War but failed (c). The reverse of (d) is in fact true, as India fell further under the power of France and especially Britain. We settle on (e); the standard interpretation is that Britain won big in 1763 at Paris and was well on its way to the "sun never setting on its empire."

CHAPTER 9

1. **c.** Though monarchs did promote education in this period, universal education was still a century away (a). Most nobles either dismissed or neglected the notion of educating the masses, as this would distract them from their primarily agricultural responsibilities (b). (d) is incorrect because although women did gain in literacy, it had little to do with organized agitation. The economy was changing at this time, but not necessarily toward more skilled workers, as we can see with cottage industry (e). A major trend of the eighteenth century was the increase in the variety and amount of reading material, which promoted literacy (c).

2. **e.** The illustration shows a scene of chaos and also gives the title, "Gin Lane." None of the distracters (a, b, c, or d) provides any clues as to what is occurring in the visual. Given the title of the illustration and the scenes of calamity—a mother dropping her child, a suicide, madness, death—it seems clear that the creator condemns the moral degradation accompanying gin drinking, which plagued England during this period (e).

3. **b.** This is a straightforward identification question. All of the areas listed here occupied the interests of the *philosophés* (a, c, d, and e), but the person most associated with reform in the legal and penal system was Beccaria (b). The title of his great book on the subject was *On Crimes and Punishments* (1769).

4. **a.** Notice that this is an EXCEPT question, so we must find the false choice. A trend of enlightened monarchy was the advance of religious toleration, so (b) is true. Wesley's Methodism stands as the dominant revival movement of the century (c). Also, the eighteenth century marks the beginning of Jewish liberation from ghettoes and their assimilation into intellectual and cultural life (d). For the first time, many intellectuals openly espoused a skeptical attitude toward religion, including atheism and agnosticism (e). Most Catholics continued to attend mass and observe the externals of their faith, so (a) is the correct choice.

5. **b.** The *philosophés* understood the dark side of human nature but did not emphasize it in their writings, so (a) and (d) can be eliminated. (d), in fact, reads more like a description of Freud. "Spontaneously cooperative" ignores the criticism that writers aimed at the

inequities of the Old Regime (c). (e) may describe the views of Rousseau, but other philosophers did not share his views. That leaves us with (b), and because these terms of "reason" and "progress" are closely associated with the Enlightenment, you should gravitate to that choice.

6. **d.** As with most passages, several clues should tip off the reader. "Passions" might be a synonym for "emotions," and in this writing, the author wishes to convince us of the importance and primacy of the passions, how they instruct our reason and guide our happiness more certainly than our reason. We can thus eliminate (a), (b), (c), and (e), as none of these writers emphasized the passions as did Rousseau (d). The selection comes from his *Discourse on the Nature and Origin of Human Inequality.*

7. **e.** The religious wars horrified many Europeans and increased religious skepticism, but they did not directly affect the philosophy of deism (a). Witchcraft accusations declined in the seventeenth and eighteenth centuries but correlated with, rather than caused, the rise of deism (b). Western Europe gained economic stability in the eighteenth century, but this had little effect on deism (c). Freemasons expressed belief in a supreme being, yet their influence begins well after deism had gained a foothold (d). If you recall that deists viewed the universe as a watch with God as the watchmaker, you might remember Newton's three laws of motion and law of universal gravitation, holding all together in cosmic harmony (e).

8. **a.** These policies represent the agendas of the three key enlightened despots, except (a). Keep in mind that enlightened despots wished to strengthen and centralize the state through rational reform—(b), (c), and (d) all express this goal. Patronizing intellectual figures added to the prestige of the state as well as demonstrated the genuine interest monarchs held in the Enlightenment (e). At the same time, they were enlightened *despots,* believing that reform must be generated from the top down and imposed on the ignorant masses. Therefore, they did not patronize democratic movements at home or abroad (a).

9. **d.** This fairly straightforward question asks about the most important result of Poland's weak elective monarchy. You should recall that Poland was dismembered by Austria, Prussia, and Russia at the end of the century in three partitions (d). (a) is incorrect because the nobility remained the dominant force in society. (b) is partially true, but Poniatowski's (a lover of Catherine the Great) effort failed, leading to the second partition. Sadly, France and Britain stood aside while Poland was partitioned, eliminating (c). No doubt, Poland's economy often suffered from its political weakness (e), but (d) is clearly the most important consequence of Poland's weakness.

10. **b.** Certainly Britain's empire took a hit with the American Revolution, but it quickly recovered and remained the chief maritime power (a). Among the educated, the American Revolution was followed closely in Europe, especially as it reignited the rivalry between Britain and France, the latter which aided the colonists, so (c) is wrong. French intellectuals did participate in the American Revolution, but the characterization in (d) is overstated in suggesting a conspiracy or direct American involvement in the French Revolution. Slavery was protected in the American Constitution, and even though the antislavery movement dates from the same period, it generally was not stimulated by the success of the American Revolution (e). We are left with (b). European reformers took heart and were inspired by the example of the U.S. Declaration of Independence and Constitution (b).

CHAPTER 10

1. **a.** The clergy was negatively affected by the French Revolution, so (b) is incorrect. Though (c) has merit, it was not an intellectual struggle that directly prompted the revolution. (d) is an overstatement: Even if the bourgeoisie was more powerful than usually thought, it did not dominate the state. This is a Marxist interpretation because it emphasizes class struggle, but it is because newer research has shown the commonalities between the nobility and middle class (a), not the fall of communism (e), that the quoted interpretation seems dated.

2. **e.** France completed its first written constitution in 1791, and though it didn't last, it represents an important precedent (a). The fall of the Bastille is considered an important symbol of royal despotism's end and today stands as France's national holiday (b). The Declaration of Rights of Man represents an influential statement of enlightened principles of natural law, and so can be eliminated (c). One of the early actions of the National Assembly, after the Great Fear, was the abolition of feudalism (d). Despite the revolutionaries' efforts, France remained in debt and faced spiraling inflation by 1791, one of the major reasons the revolution turned more radical.

3. **b.** This question asks you to define a major turning point of the early phase of the revolution. (a) is wrong because just the reverse happened. It was the CCC that prompted rebellion against the revolution, so (c) reverses cause and effect. (d) is overstated; religious practice was allowed to continue, but you might be tripped up by the later de-Christianization campaign. Religious toleration was extended by Louis XVI before the CCC, and also French Protestants had experienced toleration previously under the Edict of Nantes (e). The major purpose of the CCC was to bring the Catholic Church under control of the state (b), an effort that divided the revolution and made an enemy of pious Catholics and the papacy.

4. **b.** This is another EXCEPT question, so remember to pick out the one *wrong* response. France did face invasion by Prussia and Austria; the latter wished to protect the Austrian Queen Marie Antoinette (a). Inflation continued unabated, especially with the laissez-faire policies and issuance of the paper currency, *assignats,* so (c) is correct. Counterrevolution had broken out by this time and was led by the groups mentioned in (d). As became clear with Louis's "flight to Varennes," the monarchy did not support the revolution, leading many to call for its overthrow (e). Napoleon was relatively unknown in 1792 and though a supporter of the Jacobins, he did not lead open opposition to the monarchy (b).

5. **d.** Women played a key role in the October Days, also known as the march on Versailles (d). Women were generally left out of (a), which was why Olympe de Gouges wrote her response, the *Declaration of Rights of Woman and Female Citizen.* (b) and (c) did not deal directly with issues of concern to females, nor did women play a major part in them. The Code of Napoleon, in fact, restricted the rights of women, so should be axed (e).

6. **d.** Several of these responses might seem plausible. Though some opposition to the *levee en masse* for total war was expressed, most French citizens rallied to arms (a). Price regulations proved ineffective, but were popular with the masses (b). Mercantile interests were harmed by the abolition of slavery, but those affected were few in number (c). Certainly, feminists did not appreciate their clubs being banned, but most women probably considered their class first and gender second (e). However, France still had many religious Catholics or traditionalists who thought the anti-Christian campaign was godless and pointless.

7. **c.** French generals employed new revolutionary tactics, so (a) is wrong. (b) might be a possibility, but even when anti-French nations succeeded in coordinating their attacks, they still seemed overwhelmed by the French armies, at least until the end of the wars. (d) is counterintuitive, as Louis was long dead and most soldiers believed his execution was justified. Though the French called on women to contribute, this was not as soldiers (e). Many consider the *élan*, or spirit, of the French soldier a product of the ideology of nationalism and human rights (c).

8. **a.** Though it had limitations when it came to women, Napoleon's goal with his legal code was to promote social equality (a). There may have been side benefits for Napoleon's image, but this was not the Code's main purpose (b). Anti-French German nationalism increased after 1805 but not as a result of Napoleon's Civil Code (c). Napoleon did not wish to return to principles of the Old Regime, so (d) is wrong. Though Bonaparte brooked no opposition and punished dissenters, his code did not relate to this (e).

9. **d.** If you can connect the fact of Goya's being Spanish and recall that the Peninsular Campaign occurred in Spain, you may have chosen (d). Immediately after the fall of the Bastille, counterrevolution had not developed as yet, so (a) is incorrect. Popular violence did not attend the opening of the Estates General, though it occurred later in response to events (b). Leaders of the Mountain were executed in 1794, not by royalists but by moderate republicans who feared further bloodshed (c). Britain worked to root out pro-French supporters but did not engage in mass executions, especially by soldiers, as depicted in the painting.

10. **e.** Here are the dates on the events referenced in the question: calling of Estates General (1789), storming of Bastille (1789), abolition of feudalism (1789), Civil Constitution of the Clergy (1790), Constitution of 1791 (1791), declaration of republic (1792), execution of Louis XVI (1793), Reign of Terror (1793–1794), Napoleonic Code (1801), Continental System (1807–1812), Napoleon's Russia campaign (1812–1813). Putting these in order gives us (e).

CHAPTER 11

1. **d.** This is an EXCEPT question, so look for the "wrong" answer. Great Britain used its stock of iron ore and coal to take the early lead in iron production (a). Because mercantile and industrial classes did receive representation in Parliament, they perceived policies that promoted those interests as beneficial to the nation (b). By the nineteenth century, Britain had surpassed the Dutch as Europe's financial leader (c). Most know of Britain's strong navy, which allowed it to develop a trading empire that could supply raw materials and purchase finished products (e). This leaves us with (d). In fact, the Agricultural Revolution allowed the nation to meet its food needs with *fewer* people involved in farming.

2. **b.** Remember that you must be able to draw conclusions from the charts in questions like these. Though agriculture grew larger in absolute terms, it declined significantly as a percentage of Britain's economy, so (a) is wrong. If Britain experienced economic problems after midcentury, we cannot tell from this chart, which suggests the reverse is true (c). The chart, in fact, shows that Britain experienced the largest increase in its economy *after* 1850, not before (d). Perhaps Britain's economy was the largest in Europe's by 1850, but nothing in the chart helps us determine that (e). What the chart clearly shows is that manufacturing, mining, and building had become the largest sector of Britain's economy (b).

3. **d.** Technological innovation formed a vital part of industrialization everywhere, so (a) is wrong. Continental nations also experienced population growth with early industrialization, so eliminate (b). Guilds opposed mechanization as it threatened their traditional control of crafts (c). Though social problems on the continent may not have been pronounced in the early phases of industry as in Britain, they were nonetheless important (e). The major difference between the continent and Britain was the important role of government in the former in sponsoring industrial progress (d).

4. **a.** It is generally believed that families declined as a productive unit with labor now more common outside the home, so (b) is wrong. As new classes arose and many were wrenched out of traditional productive roles, social conflict increased with early industrialization (c). Before 1850, living and working conditions in the new cities declined markedly, as can be seen by the lower life expectancies in urban areas (d). Workers were not strong enough by 1850 to overthrow any state through socialism, so eliminate (e). New productive methods did support a higher population, and more people lived in urban areas to partake in factory work (a).

5. **e.** This is an interpretive question, but one that does have a best answer. Classical economists, such as Smith and Malthus, defended the laissez-faire approach to economic policy, so accepted the system (a). Trade unionists saw problems with industry but did not reject it outright, hoping primarily to secure better working conditions (b). Chartists concerned themselves primarily with exercising political power to enhance their economic position (c). "Utopian socialists" seems possible, but remember that they did not reject industrialization per se, only the competitive capitalist spirit behind it. We are left with (e), and indeed Luddites attacked new textile machinery, perceiving it as a threat to the skilled craft tradition and livelihoods.

6. **c.** Socialists favored universal suffrage and more radical governments than simply "representative" (a). As the name suggests, nationalists addressed issues related more to national identity, such as national self-determination and linguistic commonality, so (b) is incorrect. Conservatives generally did not support free trade in the nineteenth century, and although they came to support the other three ideas, they were not associated with them at this time (d). Romanticism did hold political implications but is not generally associated with these legalistic concepts, so (e) is out. We are left with these ideas very much tied to Liberalism in the nineteenth century (c).

7. **d.** There are several choices here that may be appealing, especially Russia (e), because it did rule an empire with many ethnic minorities. We can probably eliminate Prussia (a) and France (b), as their nations were mostly homogenous (at least compared with the other states). Great Britain might be threatened by such movements in its colonies, but you might recall that Britain opposed using the Concert of Europe as a means to crush revolution. If you remember that Metternich of Austria dominated the Congress, you might also recall the tremendous diversity of the Austrian Empire and its interest in maintaining the status quo (d).

8. **e.** (a) and (d) express an interest of the Enlightenment, to which the Romantics reacted. (b) and (c) are true of Romanticism but are nowhere suggested in the poem. The poem supports the notion that wisdom is contained in nature, not simply the analytical method of reading and science (e).

9. **a.** Though there were other reforms that addressed industry (b), that was not the motive behind the Reform Bill. Many members of the working class did not receive the vote by

provision of the bill, but they were not disenfranchised because they didn't already have the vote (c). Laissez-faire ideas were an important feature of British Liberalism, but the Reform Bill did not address this issue directly (d), nor did it deal with Irish immigration (e). Many elites wished to make the middle class feel a "stake in society" by giving them the vote, and that's what the Reform Bill did—double the number of those who could vote, from the new industrial middle class (a).

10. **c.** The revolutions, in fact, caused the breakdown of the Concert of Europe with nothing to replace it, so (a) is incorrect. In no state did workers establish political power, though they did make the effort (b). Romanticism continued in music, but its ideals seemed disproved in politics and so declined after 1850 (d). Italy's disunity was confirmed by the events of 1848–1849, though the revolutions did open the door for Italian unity soon thereafter. The correct answer is (c): A new style of political conservatism arose, with leaders such as Napoleon, Cavour, and Bismarck who appreciated the power of nationalism and used it to unite their nations (c).

CHAPTER 12

1. **c.** Realist artists and authors attempted to portray life as it was actually lived, especially dealing with the negative effects of industrialization and social inequality, which gives us (c) as the answer. Given this emphasis, we can immediately exclude (a) and (b). Realists did not glorify national and military traditions; they acted more as social critics (d). Both painters and authors strove to adopt a precise and detailed "journalistic" style, which was anything but abstract (e).

2. **e.** Don't be fooled by this longish quote. Look for the central idea and pick out the key words: "revolutionary," "oppressed," and "contending classes." These notions are central to Marxism (e). Comte and Hegel also addressed historical evolution, but in terms of science and ideas (a, b). You might recall that Marx borrowed Hegel's dialectic but emphasized material conditions. Napoleon promoted nationalism, so would not glorify the class struggle (c), and Rhodes promoted imperialism, which the quote does not address directly (d).

3. **d.** (a) This might seem a possibility, for Piedmont did have a new army, but Cavour acted on more significant national motives than simply trying out new technologies. Russia's expansion was of greater concern to Britain and France in joining the conflict, not Piedmont (b). Though Cavour wished eventually to win over the support of the other Italian states, he intended to accomplish this through diplomacy not revolution, as is suggested in (c). It would be more accurate to say that Cavour wished to harness rather than thwart revolutionary movements (e). This gives us (d) as the right answer: Cavour hoped to win international recognition for Piedmont as a major player and win the favor of a foreign patron, which he did when Napoleon supported Italian unification (d).

4. **d.** For this EXCEPT question, identify the false policy of Bismarck. Bismarck's *Realpolitik* involved waging war against Austria to eliminate it as a German power (a), "illegally" collecting taxes (b), incorporating the north German states after the Austro-Prussian War (c), and, most famously, tricking Napoleon III into attacking Prussia in 1870 (e). Bismarck did not support the Polish rebellion against Russia, in order to gain the support of Russia for Bismarck's diplomacy (d).

5. **a.** The Crimean War represented the first major conflict among the great powers following the Congress of Vienna and shows the failure of the Concert to mediate disputes effectively (a). The Franco-Prussian and World War I demonstrate the *results* stemming from the Concert's breakup (b, e). The Boer War and Russo-Japanese War are colonial conflicts that had little to do with European security measures (c, d).

6. **d.** France under Napoleon modernized its credit institutions and built railroads (a), so eliminate that one. British reformers responded to the problems of industry by initiating a series of acts to protect workers from its worst effects (b). A major feature of Alexander II's reforms in Russia was the creation of the *zemstvos*, or local assemblies (c). When Germany was unified, Bismarck insisted that the new constitution allow for universal male suffrage, primarily because he believed the masses would vote for conservative policies (e). If Austria-Hungary had allowed independence for its Slavic minorities, it would have ceased to exist as a great power, so we choose (d).

7. **e.** This brief conceptual question asks you to identify a major difference between the First and Second Industrial Revolutions. Both phases emphasized new techniques and new technologies; in fact, the period 1870–1914 represents one of the greatest outbursts of technology in world history, so eliminate (a). The Second Industrial Revolution occurred all across Europe, and though Germany led the way, (b) is overstated. In addition, the second phase significantly affected the lower classes, as mass production became widespread, and produced a volatile boom-bust cycle, so (c) and (d) are incorrect. With the Second Industrial Revolution, Europeans formed the large modern corporations of today, adopted mass production, and spread industry even further geographically, giving us (e) as the answer.

8. **b.** Though Europe's economy was volatile in the second half of the nineteenth century, it would be incorrect to characterize it as "poor," with corporations making large profits at home (a). Currencies in this age of the gold standard proved remarkably stable, so eliminate (c). Strikes did occur in this period, but seeking outlets for discontented workers forms more of a political motive, and because most workers did not immigrate to colonies, (d) represents a misinterpretation. As noted earlier, Europe's economy proved less than stable, so (e) is wrong. Many imperial advocates viewed colonies primarily as a means to acquire the raw materials needed for further economic growth, such as rubber, oil, and other minerals.

9. **a.** This cartoon satirizes Cecil Rhodes's grandiose plan for Britain's creation of a Cape-to-Cairo connection in Africa (a). A subtext of the cartoon might be the attitudes satirized in the "White Man's Burden," but nothing in the cartoon clearly indicates this (b). After Germany's unification, Bismarck tended to dismiss colonies until public opinion led him to seek several in the 1880s; not until Kaiser Wilhelm (1888–1918) did Germany enthusiastically seek colonies in Africa (c). Italy did experience difficulty in obtaining an African colony, but again, the cartoon does not address this (d). It is true that Britain and France almost came to blows at Fashoda in 1898, but the cartoon only portrays one figure, and it takes two to make a war (e).

10. **c.** Russia did in fact turn again to solidify its position in the Balkans, but its weak showing in the Russo-Japanese War certainly did not enhance its position there (a). Britain and Japan did form an alliance in 1902, but this occurred before the war (b). The war had little direct effect on the Ottoman Empire, whose weakness continued with Slavic minorities continuing to demand independence in a nationalistic age (d). China's division into spheres of influence was largely completed prior to the Russo-Japanese War, though the conflict strengthened Japanese claims on its larger neighbor (e). Most

significantly, the war showed that a modernized Asian power could defeat European colonizers, and thus inspired colonial resistance movements that would bear fruit after World War I (c).

CHAPTER 13

1. **c.** Europe's population rapidly expanded in the period, but not because of a rising birth rate, rather a declining death rate, making (a) and (e) incorrect. Immigration from Europe, in fact, increased in the period, with most immigrants traveling to the western hemisphere (b). Though birth control was practiced at this time, artificial forms were not widely available; moreover, population growth was not stagnant, so eliminate (d). Europe's population expanded rapidly and more people did live in urban areas (c).

2. **d.** Urban reformers devised city plans around the goals of better health, improved functionality, and beautification. To this end, governments sponsored parks and sports (a), better medical care (b), public transportation (c), and leisure activities (e). Though governments did begin to build some public housing, no government yet considered it a duty to provide housing for every impoverished person.

3. **b.** In Europe, women had gained the right to vote only in Norway prior to 1914, making (a) incorrect. (c) is an overstatement; few men entered college prior to 1914, and the professions remained almost the exclusive preserve of men. No European nation was led by a woman prior to 1914; female queens of this era acted in more ceremonial or symbolic roles, not as actual leaders of government. Because (b) and (e) represent virtual opposites, one is most likely the correct answer; it is (b).

4. **a.** Though Britain's Labour Party included some mild socialism, it had only been established in 1900 and made few inroads before 1914 (b). French socialism was divided into a number of ideological factions, and because workers were still small in number, they were unable to translate their working-class movement into major electoral success (c). Like many underdeveloped European nations, Spain's radical movements tended more toward anarchism than socialism (d). Considering Russia's lack of democracy, even with the creation of a Duma after 1905, political parties made little headway, especially the socialists (e). Germany's SPD was one of the first socialist parties and had become the largest party in the Reichstag by 1912, prompting Bismarck's anti-Socialist legislation and welfare programs.

5. **a.** The first major nation to experience socialist rule was Russia, after its revolution in 1917, so (b) is an anachronism. Though governments showed more stability than earlier in the century, mass politics actually increased conflict among ethnic groups and between traditional powers and those left out (c). Between 1871 and World War I (1914), there were no conflicts among the great powers, so scratch (d). Governments remained responsive to public opinion before 1914, and no governments reestablished absolutism, an outmoded concept by 1900 (e). Extremist groups such as the Pan-German League or anti-Semitic parties could now participate in the political process, so (a) is the answer.

6. **e.** Though many governments extended rights to Jews in the nineteenth century, few did much to eliminate anti-Semitism from mass politics (a). The Dreyfus Affair caused tension within the Third Republic in *France*, not Germany (b). Jews did assimilate into European society in the nineteenth century, but this only seemed to sharpen the anti-Semitic attacks of those who resented Jewish influence (c). It was during this period that Britain extended rights to Jews, not the reverse (d). Due to Darwin's ideas and mass

politics, anti-Semitism became a political movement expressed in racial terms, with political parties even formed around the exclusion of Jews (e).

7. **b.** Darwin held that humans evolved from a primate ancestor, not that they were inferior to primates, and this argument was made in *Descent of Man* later, in 1871 (a). If Darwin undercut spiritual truths, it was only indirectly, and he did not hold that science could disprove "all" spiritual truths, an overstatement. The doctrine of acquired characteristics was associated with the older view of evolution; Darwin held that natural selection acted as the mechanism of producing variation of traits (d). *Origin of the Species* did not call directly for any policies related to industry, eliminating (e). Darwin believed that random variations produced advantages of survival or reproduction in a species—a process that occurred without design, a principle inherent *within* nature itself.

8. **d.** Freud's quote addresses the importance of dreams in revealing the intellectual activity of waking states. Superego or conscience (a); repression—burying unpleasant feelings (b); Oedipal complex—desiring the parent of the opposite sex (c); and pleasure principle—the id (e) are all parts of Freud's theories and could be related to dreams. However, it is the subconscious (d) that is most directly related to dreams, as they are revealed when we are not fully conscious, but when our mind is active during sleep (d).

9. **e.** At first glance, this may seem like a difficult question, especially if you don't know your physics. However, most students will know that Einstein developed the theory of relativity, so you can eliminate (a), (c), and (d). It might not be difficult to eliminate (b), since Einstein did not address radioactivity directly and we want him for relativity anyway. By process of elimination, that leaves us with (e).

10. **c.** If you recall that this painting was done by Picasso, you may associate him with Cubism, which is the answer (c). Impressionists focused on the effects of light and recognizable scenes from everyday life, so (a) is out. Postimpressionists focused on geometric structure and clean fields of color, not really shown here (b). Abstract expressionism did not involve painting specific objects, people, or events, but color and feeling (d). Futurists focused on speed and technology, clearly not the subject of this work (e).

CHAPTER 14

1. **d.** You may recall that Bismarck wished to avoid a two-front war and that France stood as Germany's main rival after the Franco-Prussian War. Consequently, Bismarck considered it vital to prevent France from joining with Germany's eastern neighbor (d). At first, Germany joined both Austria and Russia in an alliance, though Bismarck proved unable to keep that union together. Though (b) seems an appealing choice, Bismarck believed that Britain would remain a friendly neutral toward Germany, as long as Germany did not threaten the balance of power. The Triple Alliance combined Italy, Germany, and Austria together, so that choice is out (c). A combination of Britain and Italy seemed unlikely and did not preoccupy Bismarck.

2. **a.** Recall that the primary war plan was Germany's Schlieffen Plan; it didn't work (b). The reverse of (c) is actually true; most cities celebrated the declaration of war. Though Britain attempted mediation, a diplomatic conference was not held after the assassination of Franz Ferdinand (d). Russia did not remain neutral but declared war on Austria in defense of its ally, Serbia (e). Most Europeans believed the war would end by Christmas and that their supply of shells would prove sufficient. France, for example, ran out of its stock within six months. World War I stands as a testament to the unintended consequences of organized violence (a).

3. **e.** Though the quote includes some complex wording, its tone remains fairly clear—"caves," "predestined to death," "smoke-filled trenches," and "monotonous calendar" all suggest the war's disillusioning effect on the Lost Generation (e). (a) and (b) can be safely eliminated because the quote does not glorify war. Nothing in the quote suggests anything about the experiences of various nations (c). Finally, these words certainly contradict the notion of World War II as "safer" (d).

4. **c.** Because governments made extensive use of propaganda, (a) is incorrect. Though the poster is German, nothing suggests that Germany in particular relied more heavily on public opinion; all nations employed patriotic appeals (b). States intervened extensively to regulate and run the economy for wartime production, eliminating (d). Also, censorship increased and toleration of dissent decreased during wartime, contradicting (e). Posters like this one often depicted the war as a struggle either to save the home nation's way of life or defend against a brutal enemy (c).

5. **a.** Women did enter the workforce during World War I, but most returned to domestic occupations after the war ended and were never paid equal wages anyway (b). No nation boasted a female leader during or after the war (c). Overall, women did gain some rights, so (d) represents an overstatement. Some progress was made toward acceptance of women's public role as a result of both events, but (e) again represents an overstatement. In the end, women did gain the vote in many nations, including Russia, after 1918 (a).

6. **b.** The Allies forced Germany to return Alsace-Lorraine to France (a), reduce its military to 100,000 men with no air force or U-boats (c), accept the War Guilt Clause (d), and, based on this, pay reparations of $33 billion (e). Though Germany lost territory, it was NOT dismembered into several states (a).

7. **c.** Alexander II's abolition of serfdom did not solve Russia's rural problems. The hoped-for development toward commercial agriculture did not occur, as most peasants were required to live on the village *mir* (a, b). Though revolts occurred up to 1905, none were immediately successful (d). The reverse of (e) is in fact the case, as rural crowding and a shortage of land produced constant unrest, making (c) the answer.

8. **e.** Bolsheviks uncompromisingly rejected all cooperation with "capitalist" or "reactionary" parties, which cancels out (a) and (c). Like Marx, Lenin believed anarchism utopian in its belief that simple assassinations would bring about the end of capitalism; organization was needed (b). One of the criticisms of the Provisional Government was that it continued the war despite continual problems at the front and Russia's exhaustion (d). The Bolsheviks ruthlessly united their forces and conveyed simple messages that appealed to the primary discontented groups in Russia, making (e) the answer.

9. **b.** All of these developments occurred to some degree. After 1928, under Stalin, the Soviet Union did collectivize agriculture (a); the Bolsheviks signed some barter agreements with Western nations for tactical reasons (c); Stalin's later agriculture policies did produce a famine (d); and industries were nationalized (e). However, none of these related to the New Economic Policy, which acted as Lenin's temporary compromise with capitalism to jump-start the failing Russian economy.

10. **c.** Look for the "wrong" choice in this EXCEPT question. Governments strongly regulated economies to fight the war (a). Due to a labor shortage, women did enter the workforce in significant numbers (b). The war dealt a death blow to the persisting Old Regime, and the involvement of all classes in the war effort democratized fashion, manners, and customs (d). To avoid labor conflict and ease production, governments recognized union collective bargaining powers and granted skilled workers improved wages (e). In 1918, the war was over, but Europe did not turn to stability with the end of

four empires, the Russian Revolution, and dependence on the weak League of Nations for collective security (c).

CHAPTER 15

1. **e.** The League of Nations lacked enforcement mechanisms and proved unequal to the task of addressing security issues, as with Japan's invasion of Manchuria in 1931 (a). Bolshevik Russia experienced isolation in this period but not due to a formal alliance directed against it, so (b) is out. Though the United States intervened in European affairs to promote its economic interests, it refused to guarantee French security (c). After Locarno, Germany accepted its western borders but seemed intent on revising those in the east, and thus did not accept all provisions of Versailles (d). Europe seemed unable to establish a working equilibrium without the active involvement of the United States and the USSR to balance the potential for German revival; in addition, collective security arrangements, as noted earlier, failed to work effectively.

2. **a.** This is an EXCEPT question, so find the wrong answer. In the Balkans, it was impossible to draw borders that corresponded with ethnic identity, so, for example, Romania and Hungary disputed Transylvania (b). Most nations struggled to develop an independent economic existence, having recently been a coherent *part* of the Austrian empire (c). Only Czechoslovakia boasted some experience with democratic government, a major reason why it held on to its government until 1939. Lacking industry, eastern European nations did not have large cities or a strong middle class; despite land reform, nobles continued to play a major role in policy (e). Austria did NOT attempt to reestablish the empire in the interwar period (a).

3. **c.** Critics charged Weimar with corruption, but this photograph does not indicate that (a). The same is true for (b). One might claim French influence in the Ruhr occupation, but again, this is not indicated by the visual (d). Many influential Germans opposed the creation of the republic; however, those in the photograph are not of an elite class (e). However, Germany did face hyperinflation in 1923 that wiped out the savings of the middle class and rendered economic activity unpredictable, as shown by the pile of bills in this baker's shop.

4. **b.** Reflecting the fallout from World War I, artists and writers of the Lost Generation expressed themes of alienation and disillusionment (b). Violence and conflict were evident in works such as *All Quiet on the Western Front,* but that book's primary theme really is lost innocence. (c) and (e) can be dismissed fairly easily as not in keeping with the pessimism of the period. Science and technology played a major role in mass culture, but not as importantly in works of high culture (c).

5. **d.** The quote touches on race, state power, and war. These all form essential characteristics of fascism (d). The quote rejects the importance of individualism for Liberal democracy (a), equality among races in communism (b), and the importance of checking state power in trade unionism (c). Some authoritarian governments may have made similar appeals but generally did not seek the mass mobilization expressed by the quotation.

6. **a.** After the failed Beer Hall putsch in 1923, Hitler abandoned attempts to overthrow Weimar through force (b). Though Hitler took power by some backroom negotiations with the Center Party, the two were never allies (c). Hitler explicitly rejected Versailles as a humiliation to Germany (d). The Nazi Party posed as the "bulwark against Bolshevism," negating choice (e). From 1924, Hitler turned to a "legality strategy"

designed to build a mass movement that the government would be forced to employ to maintain order.

7. **c.** Stalin abandoned the NEP in 1928 to focus on heavy industry under state control, eliminating (a). Productivity increased rapidly, though it involved suffering for the average worker; the Great Purges had little effect on this (b). Stalin wished to wipe out the kulaks (wealthy peasants) and emerging merchants produced by the NEP; when the former resisted collectivization, they were killed (d). The goal of the Five-Year Plans was to produce self-sufficiency, especially given the hostility of the Western powers, eliminating (e). During this period, the Soviet Union turned to a highly centralized economy designed for rapid modernization, giving us (c).

8. **e.** A hint might be that Picasso was a Spanish painter. The scene portrays violence of some kind; *Guernica,* the title of the painting, was a Loyalist stronghold during the Spanish Civil War bombed by fascist forces, killing innocent civilians. This question represents the importance of visual literacy, as it would be difficult to eliminate choices (a) through (d) without knowing the context of the painting.

9. **b.** The 1928 Kellogg-Briand Pact attempted to outlaw war, which, though a failure, was not a part of appeasement (a). France and Britain appeased Hitler by allowing him to take Austria, but one could argue that because the two states were German, his action possessed some legitimacy (c). Western unwillingness to engage in the Spanish Civil War demonstrated weakness but, again, was not specifically an effort to appease Hitler or Mussolini (d). The 1922 Rapallo Pact created an agreement between the Weimar Republic and Soviet Union; though a source of concern to the western Allies, the treaty involved Weimar, not Hitler (e). Hitler's demands for the Sudetenland at the Munich Conference ultimately stripped France's ally of its most defensible land, especially when it was prepared to fight for it (b).

10. **a.** By 1942 or 1943, many governments and international institutions knew of the Final Solution, so (b) is out. The Allies explicitly rejected efforts at rescue, focusing their efforts squarely on the battlefield (c). Aerial bombardment would not have discriminated effectively among targeted groups and did not represent a tactic for the Final Solution (d). Many states suffered from ethnic tensions, but these did not contribute in a significant way to the Nazi "success" (e). The Holocaust constituted a massive and systematic operation requiring the involvement of thousands, many beyond Germany's borders—a sad statement of human culpability in evil (a).

CHAPTER 16

1. **d.** It was the United States, not the USSR, that possessed a nuclear monopoly at the end of World War II (a). (b) and (e) are actually reversed—the USSR wished to control Eastern Europe as a buffer, whereas the United States extended the Marshall Plan aid to Western Europe. All the Allied powers agreed to de–Nazify Germany (c). A fundamental cause of the Cold War, which predated World War II, turned on the fundamental political goals of the superpowers—capitalism vs. communism.

2. **a.** (b) is incorrect, as no formal treaty ended World War II. Western Europe's economy did not take off until after 1950, the date indicated on the map (c). (d) and (e) are not appealing choices as these events did not take place following World War II. Many Germans were expelled from the East, while several nations' borders were redrawn, namely Poland, which was moved to the West (a).

3. **c.** The best clue comes with the last phrase, which gives the answer as (c), as NATO's members were committed to these principles. (a) is not really a Cold War agreement. Clearly, communism would seem antithetical to the principles stated in the last phrase, especially individual liberty, though the socialist governments of Eastern Europe labeled themselves as "people's democracies" (b). Economic issues are not addressed in the quote, so that leaves out the Marshall Plan (d). Because communist nations signed the Helsinki Accords, we can exclude (e) for the same reason as (b).

4. **e.** As part of its control of Eastern Europe, the Soviet Union imposed its economic and political structure on its satellites. This involved choices (a) through (d). In general, the space race involved competition between the United States and the Soviet Union. Soviet leaders eventually placed nuclear weapons in Eastern Europe, but these were not under the control of the satellite nations (e).

5. **b.** (a) seems appealing, but ending the Cold War proved ancillary to Gorbachev's internal goals of restructuring the Soviet Union (b). Though ethnic minorities clamored for independence from the Soviet empire, Gorbachev discouraged this and attempted to compromise the issue through the Union treaty (c). Gorbachev explicitly rejected (d). (e) represents an overstatement; the Soviet leader wished to save, not destroy, socialism by introducing a "human face" to it.

6. **b.** Some socialist parties did gain power in the 1980s, but this trend did not apply to the 1960s (a). Great Britain did NOT withdraw from the Atlantic alliance, though France did pull out of NATO (c). (d) stands as the reverse of the correct answer (b). Though tensions have occurred in the Atlantic alliance, America has remained a firm European ally (e). European integration has been symbolized by agreements such as the ECSC, EEC, and EU.

7. **e.** (a) and (b) were communist leaders of Romania and East Germany who resisted reforms. Nagy failed to reform Hungary in 1956 and paid with his life (c). Brezhnev acted as the leader of the Soviet Union and crushed the Prague Spring of 1968 in Czechoslovakia (d). Lech Walesa helped found Solidarity, Poland's independent labor union, which undermined the authority of the Communist Party there and ultimately led to his election as president of Poland (e).

8. **a.** Governments in the West adopted a Keynesian approach of managing and fine-tuning the economy (a). Tariffs were, in fact, reduced (b), while the gold standard functioned to ensure currency stability until 1971 (c). The Bretton Woods agreements of 1944 created a number of important international organizations to oversee the global economy, so (d) is out. Right after the war, governments expanded the welfare state (e).

9. **d.** All of the nations experienced some conflicts, but France endured two difficult colonial wars in Indochina and Algeria (d). Great Britain generally surrendered its colonial commitments after partitions to divide ethnic or religious groups from one another (c). Belgium (a) and the Netherlands (b) experienced conflicts in Indonesia and the Congo, but these did not prove protracted and they soon recognized the need for colonial independence. West Germany possessed no colonies (e).

10. **c.** The United States did grant aid to nations during the Cold War, but usually to influence their policies (a). In some ways, spheres of influence evolved informally, but it did not represent an explicit policy of the United States (b). American policy encouraged Western European unity and helped lay the foundations for the EU, so (d) can be eliminated. Twice—once in Hungary (1956) and again in Czechoslovakia (1968)—the

United States avoided interfering with the Soviet Union's crushing of revolts in Eastern Europe, so the more active (e) can be ruled out. From 1947 to the end of the Cold War (1989), containment formed the basis of American foreign policy—to stop the spread of communism (c).

CHAPTER 17

1. **c.** Cold War conflicts did not involve direct fighting between the United States and the Soviet Union or actual warfare in Europe (a). Europe's economy grew steadily in the postwar period, and regardless, the population increased throughout the 1940s and 1950s anyway (b). Artificial birth control did produce stagnation in birth rates, but not until after 1970 (d). Asia's population is by far the largest of the continents, accounting for about 60 percent of world population, making (e) incorrect. This question deals with the baby boom, which is best described by (c). Recall that governments promoted a higher birth rate through neonatalist policies.

2. **b.** By 1945, almost all nations accepted the need for some degree of government regulation and oversight of the economy, making (a) an overstatement. (c) represents an overstatement; some nations, such as Britain, did nationalize some specific industries, but this action certainly did not provide full employment. Industry proved vital after WWII in getting Europe back on its feet, making (d) another overstatement. (e) is a better description of developments in Eastern Europe under Soviet domination. Western European nations recognized the importance of providing welfare benefits based on the growth of totalitarian movements in the interwar period that capitalized on economic suffering and the predominance of Keynesian economic theory after World War II.

3. **e.** After World War II, the following technological advances occurred: moon landing, 1969 (a); polio vaccine, 1955 (b); personal computers, early 1980s (c); nuclear power, early 1950s (d). Though some treatments of AIDS help prolong life, and experiments have been made with vaccines, as of 2006, no cure for the disease exists (e).

4. **d.** Several of these choices may seem appealing. The answer here is (d): Youth revolts in 1968 aimed at creating a new social order based on liberation and opposition to hierarchies, which is what the quotes demonstrate. (a) and (c) would not have employed such idealistic rhetoric, not to mention that the last quote directly contradicts the source of technocrats' power. The quotes don't seem to address the concerns of (d), leaving (b) as the most appealing choice. (b), however, makes no reference to gender, making it less viable than the correct answer, (d).

5. **b.** Soon after the war, most nations had already extended voting rights to women, making this a nonissue (a). Though feminists were involved in the environmental movement, it took a back seat to more practical female concerns (c). Some feminists criticized marriage, but (d) represents an overstatement. Certain categories of feminists did support (e), but at the same time, many feminists opposed prostitution and pornography as exploitative of women. Feminists did focus attention on equality in economic and political opportunity (b).

6. **e.** Environmental concerns did not break the logjam between the superpowers and did not lead to any type of cooperation (a). De Beauvoir's writings addressed feminist rather than environmental issues, so (b) is out. Though the Kyoto Protocol *aims* for a reduction in greenhouse gases, the world is a long way off from reaching that goal (c). Most industrialized or industrializing nations have been reluctant to cause economic problems, such as job loss, by making major changes in economic production and thus

did not immediately change policies (d). Several Green parties did compete for office and win some seats in parliaments, especially Germany, making (e) the correct answer.

7. **c.** Most existentialists gravitate toward atheism, making (a) incorrect. The philosophy emphasizes the ability of humans to transcend their circumstances through life-defining choices, contradicting (b). Many existentialists did choose sides during the Cold War, illustrating how the "facts" of one's existence force certain choices—Sartre, for example, chose socialism (d). According to existentialism, it is this very code of universal ethics that does *not* exist; each human must make her own (e). All of this leads us to (c) as the right answer—humans must define their own values by choices.

8. **d.** Because pop art employed the artifacts of modern culture (ads, comics), we can eliminate (a), as these are not featured in the painting. Postmodernism (b) influenced art but was not itself an art movement. Dadaism (c) and Cubism (e) both faded by the end of World War II; the former used art to satirize art, whereas the latter looked at objects from multiple perspectives, neither of which is conveyed here. This painting shows Jackson Pollock's "drip style," with which he popularized abstract expressionism after WWII to help make New York City the center of Western art.

9. **b.** John XXIII (1958–1963) called the council to update and modernize church dogma and practices; this included interfaith dialogues, especially with Protestants (b). However, the church's ban on birth control was later reaffirmed (a). In some sense, John Paul II (1978–2005) engaged in all the actions represented by (c), (d), and (e), but these occurred after the Second Vatican Council.

10. **d.** (b) and (c) came out of the radical movement of the 1960s. (a) and (e) both advocated ethnic separatism in Ireland and Spain, respectively. The PLO was founded to oppose Israel's policies in Palestine and win a homeland there. Though PLO actions affected Europe, the organization is not a *domestic* terrorist group (d).

Section III

Practice Exams

PRACTICE TEST 1

You are allowed 3 hours and 5 minutes for this examination—55 minutes for Section I, consisting of 80 multiple-choice questions, and 2 hours and 10 minutes for Section II, consisting of one Document-Based Question (DBQ) and two Free-Response Questions (FRQs). The first fifteen minutes of Section II consist of a mandatory 15-minute reading period during which you may not write any scorable responses, though you may plan out your responses to the essays. Each section of the exam is worth 50% of your overall score.

For the multiple-choice questions, a one-quarter point penalty will be assessed for those responses marked incorrectly. Random guessing is unlikely to improve your score, but if you can eliminate even one or two of the choices for a given question, it may be to your advantage to answer it.

Try to keep aware of the time limits and move along as quickly as you can without losing accuracy. If you encounter a difficult question, move on and come back to it if you have time.

EUROPEAN HISTORY
SECTION I
Time—55 minutes
80 questions
Percent of total grade—50

Directions: Each of the following questions or incomplete statements is followed by five suggested answers or completions. Select the one that is best in each case and then fill in the corresponding oval on the answer sheet.

"There is no point in which our adversaries are more stubborn in their opposition than that of justification: namely, as to whether we obtain it by faith or by works. On no account will they allow us to give Christ the honor of being called our righteousness, unless their works come in at the same time for a share of the merit."

1. Which of the following figures was most likely to have made this statement?
   a. Erasmus
   b. Henry VIII
   c. John Calvin
   d. Ignatius Loyola
   e. Pope Leo X

2. The enclosure movement beginning in the sixteenth century had as its aim the:
   a. replacement of communal with commercial agriculture.
   b. segregation of Jewish communities within walled ghettoes.
   c. creation of state prisons for those opposed to absolutism.
   d. consolidation of manufacturing processes under one roof.
   e. combination of various denominations into a unified reformed Church.

3. A major reason for the enslavement of millions of Africans by Europeans in the seventeenth and eighteenth centuries was:
   a. the need to remedy a labor shortage in Europe.
   b. as mercenary soldiers in continental warfare.
   c. to work in the new textile mills in Great Britain.
   d. as a by-product of European conquests in Africa.
   e. as laborers on plantations in the Americas.

4. Which of the following statements represents the most accurate characterization of the Enlightenment *philosophés'* views regarding the natural world?
   a. "Nature is an awe-inspiring spectacle that brings us closer to our spirit and to the Divine Creator."
   b. "The human capacity to understand nature is limited by irrational impulses in the human psyche."
   c. "Humans can use reason to understand the laws of nature and thus control their environment."
   d. "We must respect the complexity of nature by protecting its resources and the diversity of animal life."
   e. "Humans can never understand nature in itself but only the way it presents itself to our senses."

5. The two nations that pioneered the Agricultural Revolution of the eighteenth century were:
   a. France and Great Britain.
   b. Great Britain and the Netherlands.
   c. France and Prussia.
   d. Poland and Russia.
   e. Austria and Spain.

6. Which of the following best describes the French social structure on the eve of the French Revolution (1789)?
   a. increasing equality among classes as a result of government policies
   b. a growing rift between the clergy and nobility over tax exemptions
   c. establishment of a political alliance between peasants and bourgeoisie
   d. resentment by the Third Estate of noble and clerical privileges
   e. refusal of Louis XVI to consider any changes in the unequal tax system

7. The painting below of Napoleon was painted by Jacques Louis David to:
   a. commemorate Napoleon's agreement with the Catholic Church.
   b. condemn Napoleon's invasion of Germany and abolition of the Holy Roman Empire.
   c. honor the memory of French soldiers lost in the invasion of Russia.
   d. demonstrate the ability of the lower classes to rise in power.
   e. celebrate the heroism and military skill of Napoleon.

(*Giraudon/Art Resource, NY*)

8. Which of the following industries accounted for half of British exports by the early nineteenth century?
   a. cotton textiles
   b. railroad locomotives
   c. wheat production
   d. pig iron
   e. chemicals

9. The quote below best represents the political philosophy of:
   a. divine-right monarchy.
   b. nationalism.
   c. Liberalism.
   d. conservatism.
   e. communism.

"Nature brings forth families. The most natural state therefore is also one people, with a character of its own. A people is as much a plant of nature as is a family, except that it has more branches. Nothing therefore seems more contradictory to the true end of governments than the wild confusion of races and nations under one scepter."

10. The cartoon below, titled "Dropping the Pilot," portrays:
    a. public outrage over British military failures during World War I.
    b. German Kaiser Wilhelm II's removal of Chancellor Bismarck from office.
    c. Germany's plans to build a fleet of battleships to rival Britain's navy.
    d. an agreement between Russia and Germany limiting naval strength.
    e. an overthrow of the German constitution by Kaiser Wilhelm II.

(Getty Images)

11. Which of the following best accounts for the subject matter of the late nineteenth-century painting shown below?
    a. European conquests in Asia and Africa increased the standard of living.
    b. Socialist governments implemented policies of social equality.
    c. The end of warfare among the great powers prevented urban devastation.
    d. Women's suffrage allowed for increased social interaction between genders.
    e. Reforms provided for increased leisure time and the beautification of cities.

Georges Seurat, French, 1859–1891, A Sunday on La Grande Jatte—1884, 1884–86, oil on canvas, 81 3/4 × 121 1/4 in. (207.5 × 308.1 cm), Helen Birch Bartlett Memorial Collection, 1926.224 The Art Institute of Chicago. Photography © The Art Institute of Chicago.

12. All of the following express features of Einstein's theories in physics EXCEPT:
    a. the interconvertibility of matter and energy.
    b. that absolute time and space do not exist.
    c. nothing can travel faster than the speed of light.
    d. physical phenomena are essentially unpredictable.
    e. gravity affects time and light, not just space.

13. For most of the nations involved, the experience of World War I resulted in:
    a. the unification of political groups and social harmony.
    b. successful government efforts to combat inflation.
    c. policies of economic centralization and rationing.
    d. the use of female military units in combat situations.
    e. an improvement in the status of small business owners.

14. Which of the following acted as a major grievance against Russia's Provisional Government after the March 1917 Revolution?
    a. its compromises with the militant Bolshevik movement
    b. the inclusion of former tsarist supporters in the government
    c. vigorous policies of state centralization and taxation
    d. the decision to continue fighting in World War I
    e. its neglect of women's suffrage and equal rights

15. During negotiations at Versailles following World War I, the Allied leader who favored the most lenient treatment of a defeated Germany was:
    a. Woodrow Wilson.
    b. David Lloyd George.
    c. Georges Clemenceau.
    d. V. I. Lenin.
    e. Vittorio Orlando.

16. Which of the following allowed European women the greatest degree of personal autonomy following World War II?
    a. government policies promoting higher birth rates
    b. legislation protecting women from prostitution
    c. the advance of some women to positions in academia
    d. women's leadership in the antinuclear movement
    e. increased access to artificial means of contraception

17. The Peace of Lodi (1454) illustrates which of the following contributions of the Renaissance city-states to diplomacy?
    a. concern for balance of power politics
    b. rejection of papal influence in diplomacy
    c. use of mercenaries to enforce agreements
    d. elimination of hereditary dynasties
    e. use of collective security organizations

18. The Columbian Exchange, which followed exploration and colonization in the fifteenth and sixteenth centuries, resulted in:
    a. successful efforts to integrate European and Native American production methods.
    b. an improved European diet by the addition of crops such as tomatoes and potatoes.
    c. a revival of Native American religion under the guidance of the Jesuit order.
    d. the domination of English culture in much of North and South America.
    e. successful independence movements among the natives of South America.

19. Which of the following dynasties achieved continental domination through a series of strategic marriages in the fifteenth and sixteenth centuries?
    a. Valois
    b. Tudor
    c. Habsburg
    d. Romanov
    e. Jageillon

20. During the Dutch revolt against Spain, the Union of Utrecht (1579) functioned as:
    a. an alliance of Catholic towns supporting Spanish policies.
    b. bands of foreign soldiers aimed at weakening Dutch resistance.
    c. an economic union of merchants in all 17 Dutch provinces.
    d. a confederation of the northern provinces seeking independence.
    e. Philip II of Spain's organization of spies in the Dutch provinces.

21. With which of the following is Baroque art of the seventeenth century most closely associated?
    a. mercantilism
    b. Scientific Revolution
    c. Enlightenment
    d. Absolutism
    e. Protestant Reformation

22. This sixteenth-century illustration was used to support which of the following scientific theories?
    a. heliocentrism
    b. universal gravitation
    c. perpetual motion
    d. geocentrism
    e. Cartesian dualism

23. During the French revolutionary Reign of Terror (1793–1794), the Jacobins instituted all of the following policies EXCEPT:
    a. mobilization of people and resources for total war.
    b. promoting the equal participation of women in politics.
    c. attempting to counter inflation through price controls.
    d. launching a campaign to de-Christianize France.
    e. abolishing slavery in French colonies.

24. Which of the following describes a major social impact of industrialization in the first half of the nineteenth century in Great Britain?
    a. The number of people involved in agriculture increased.
    b. Poor living conditions caused a decline in national income.
    c. Work and home life became increasingly separated.
    d. Women gained equality from new economic opportunities.
    e. Adoption of the factory system increased aristocratic power.

25. Important new technologies first developed in the period 1850–1914 include:
    a. airplanes, petroleum, and electricity.
    b. textiles, steel, and coal mining.
    c. chemicals, railroads, and canals.
    d. telegraphs, steel, and computers.
    e. artillery, textiles, and canals.

26. The nineteenth-century Concert of Europe acted primarily as a(n):
    a. mutual defense system to protect against Russian aggression.
    b. tariff union among the German states to promote trade.
    c. international league of trading cities tied to the Americas.
    d. informal collective security arrangement of the great powers.
    e. league of Romantic poets and composers urging revolution.

27. British involvement in Egypt in the late nineteenth century was prompted primarily by the:
    a. desire to exploit its natural resources.
    b. need to stop French advances in North Africa.
    c. goal of controlling the African diamond industry.
    d. need to subdue an anticolonial Islamist movement.
    e. objective of securing control of the Suez Canal.

28. Charles Darwin's scientific theory of natural selection caused controversy primarily because it:
    a. rejected Enlightenment notions of the causal laws of nature.
    b. was based on the collection of questionable data from fossils.
    c. endorsed the notion that different races formed unique species.
    d. explicitly rejected the power of the clergy to interpret Scripture.
    e. suggested that humans were the product of chance, not design.

29. The decline of which of the following states produced conflict in the Balkans leading up to World War I?
    a. Ottoman Empire
    b. Austria-Hungary
    c. Russia
    d. Germany
    e. Serbia

30. The accompanying scene portrays which of the following events?
    a. the French evacuation at Dien Bien Phu in Indochina
    b. bombing of British cities during World War II
    c. one of the first tests of new jet aircraft in the 1930s
    d. Soviet military personnel leaving Eastern Europe in 1990
    e. American efforts to supply West Berlin during the Cold War

Hulton-Deutsch Collection/Corbis

31. Italian Renaissance artists of the fifteenth century focused primarily on:
    a. portraying the awe-inspiring spectacle of natural phenomena.
    b. employing perspective geometry to portray depth naturally.
    c. purely secular subject matter, such as portraits and still lifes.
    d. complex compositions involving symbolism and detail.
    e. small canvases that could be bought and sold easily.

32. Which of the following is the best explanation for how Germany's religious dispute evolved into the Thirty Years' War (1618–1648), which involved much of the European continent?
    a. The search for resources spread the fighting outside Germany's borders.
    b. International forces were forced to intervene to stop atrocities against civilians.
    c. It provided an opportunity for neighboring states to meet territorial ambitions.
    d. Europe's complex alliance system dragged the other powers into the conflict.
    e. The papacy called for a crusade of Catholic nations to defeat Protestantism.

33. A major reason for the decline of witchcraft persecutions by the end of the seventeenth century was:
    a. the papacy's rejection of the idea of demonic possession.
    b. a rapid increase in population, resulting in social stability.
    c. laws protecting women from unlawful prosecution.
    d. growing acceptance of witchcraft as a pagan religion.
    e. the growing belief of elites in scientific explanations.

34. Which of the following figures is most closely associated with the theory and practice of mercantilism in the seventeenth century?
    a. Adam Smith
    b. Vasco de Gama
    c. Thomas Hobbes
    d. Jean-Baptiste Colbert
    e. Johannes Kepler

35. This passage below was most likely drawn from which of the following Enlightenment works?
    a. Voltaire's *Candide*
    b. Cesare Beccaria's *On Crimes and Punishments*
    c. Montesquieu's *Spirit of the Laws*
    d. Rousseau's *Emile*
    e. Diderot's *Encyclopedia*

    "There is no liberty if the power of judging be not separated from the legislative and executive powers. Were it joined with the legislative, the life and liberty of the subject would be exposed to arbitrary control, for the judge would then be the legislator. Were it joined to the executive power, the judge might behave with all the violence of an oppressor."

36. What resulted from the British Parliament's passage of the Reform Act of 1832?
    a. Factory inspections and limits on child labor were established.
    b. Industrial cities and the middle class gained parliamentary representation.
    c. The labor of women in factories was restricted to 10 hours.
    d. Public health boards were established to promote sanitary reform.
    e. Labor unions earned the right to bargain collectively for their members.

37. Which of the following best explains the results of Western imperialist efforts in Japan after 1850?
    a. France and Britain established direct imperial control over Japan.
    b. The Tokugawa Shogunate successfully repelled foreign influence.
    c. Japan became an American protectorate because of its important naval bases.
    d. The Meiji regime modernized Japan and began its own imperial drive.
    e. China exploited Japan's weakness to set up spheres of influence there.

38. European population in the second half of the nineteenth century:
    a. increased rapidly and became more urban.
    b. declined due to availability of birth control.
    c. declined because of emigration to the Americas.
    d. stagnated as a result of economic recession.
    e. became more concentrated in eastern Europe.

39. This photograph demonstrates:
    a. the devastation of the Balkan Wars (1912–1913).
    b. British scorched-earth policies in the Boer War.
    c. trench warfare on the Western Front in World War I.
    d. Soviet resistance at Stalingrad during World War II.
    e. the defeat of French forces in the Franco-Prussian War.

Imperial War Museum, London

40. Which of the following best explains the results of elections to the Constituent Assembly during the Russian Revolution?
    a. The Bolsheviks won a clear majority of seats and established a popular government.
    b. Moderate socialists won the most seats, but the Bolsheviks annulled the results.
    c. Constitutional Democrats formed a coalition government and continued World War I.
    d. The results were inconclusive, leading to an extended period of political instability.
    e. Women's parties gained significant influence and enacted a program of social reform.

41. What is the primary criticism of the female author of this quote regarding Italian fascism?
    a. Women's opportunities in the professions have been unfairly limited.
    b. The fascist government has arbitrarily reduced freedom of dissent.
    c. Fascist economic policies have plunged Italy into a serious depression.
    d. Unfair government policies toward Italian women also harm male workers.
    e. Government guarantees for minimum wages are inadequate for survival.

"Italian fascism mouths the slogan that 'women must go back to the home' and that 'jobs should be given to the men who have to support their families.' In this campaign, fascism aims to decrease the value of female labor and cut down wages to the extreme minimum. On the other hand, the low wages for women makes it easier to attack wages in general, with employers giving new workers the same or even lower wages than the dismissed women."

42. Which of the following conflicts featured a struggle for domination in central Europe between two German states and a colonial rivalry between France and Great Britain?
    a. Nine Years' War (1689–1697)
    b. Seven Years' War (1756–1763)
    c. Napoleonic Wars (1799–1815)
    d. Franco-Prussian War (1870–1871)
    e. World War I (1914–1918)

43. Which of the following expresses a major social impact of the Protestant Reformation in the sixteenth century?
    a. Education expanded to meet the need for biblical literacy.
    b. Women gained equal access to clerical positions.
    c. Peasants successfully used religious ideals to gain increased status.
    d. The population increased because of the attack on celibacy.
    e. Ideals of religious pacifism led to a century of peace.

44. Henry IV (1589–1610) laid the foundations for royal absolutism in France by:
    a. radically reducing the number of nobles, who might oppose him.
    b. developing an equitable tax structure that tapped the nation's wealth.
    c. conquering areas of the Low Countries to add to his nation's resources.
    d. ending the French civil war with his extension of religious toleration.
    e. marrying his children into the powerful Habsburg line.

45. Which of the following rulers exemplified the theory of enlightened despotism?
    a. Louis XIV of France
    b. Peter I of Russia
    c. Frederick II of Prussia
    d. Henry VIII of England
    e. Charles V of Spain

46. Several nations founded scientific societies in the seventeenth century with the goal of:
    a. patronizing unemployed and potentially revolutionary intellectuals.
    b. building an international scientific community that would promote peace.
    c. undermining church authority through research that contradicted Scripture.
    d. improving medical understanding to address urban sanitation issues.
    e. promoting technological and military advances to increase the state's power.

47. A major difference between the industrialization of the continent in the nineteenth century compared with that of Great Britain's was:
    a. better transportation infrastructures.
    b. elites more open to the profit motive.

    c. state promotion and protection of industry.

    d. an exclusive focus on production for export.

    e. the lack of corresponding social problems.

48. The neo-Gothic style of architecture of the British Parliament buildings shown here is associated with which of the following artistic movements?

    a. Renaissance

    b. Baroque

    c. neoclassical

    d. Romanticism

    e. Realism

NEW HOUSES OF PARLIAMENT. *(Getty Images)*

49. As a result of Alexander II's (1855–1881) reforms, Russia experienced which of the following in the nineteenth century?

    a. growth of revolutionary groups demanding further change

    b. a rapid shift to a system of commercial agriculture

    c. the development of a stable constitutional monarchy

    d. successful social and economic modernization

    e. an alliance between peasants and nobles opposing change

50. Which of the following resulted from the theories of Sigmund Freud?

    a. Newtonian conceptions of physics had to be revised.

    b. Humans were shown to be irrational and instinctual.

    c. Traditional moral and religious principles were upheld.

    d. Biological change became a product of the environment.

    e. Infectious diseases were effectively prevented and treated.

51. All of the following represent policies or consequences of Joseph Stalin's (1928–1953) rule in the Soviet Union EXCEPT:

    a. the collectivization of agriculture.

    b. ending the Cold War conflict with the West.

    c. industrialization through the Five-Year Plans.

    d. the purging of the Old Bolshevik elite.

    e. joining the World War II alliance against Nazi Germany.

52. The photograph below shows the results of which of the following Nazi policies?
    a. remilitarization of Rhineland
    b. the Nuremberg rallies
    c. Beer Hall putsch
    d. *Kristallnacht*
    e. the Nuremberg Laws

akg-images

53. Which of the following proved to be a major issue for the European Union (EU) following the fall of communism (1989–1990)?
    a. the prevention of Russian aggression in Eastern Europe
    b. hostility of the United States toward the EU regarding trade
    c. growing rivalry between France and Germany over territory
    d. declining standards of living in the member states
    e. effectively incorporating the former Eastern European satellites

54. The quote below from Castiglione's *Book of the Courtier* (1527) demonstrates that in terms of their status during the Renaissance, women:
    a. made significant gains in positions of political power.
    b. gained educationally but were often treated as objects.
    c. often dominated the intellectual life of Renaissance salons.
    d. were encouraged to engage in artistic and intellectual pursuits.
    e. were the slaves of their husbands and could be bought and sold.

"Many virtues of the mind are as necessary to a woman as to a man, but I do think that beauty is more necessary to her than to the Courtier, for truly that woman lacks much who lacks beauty. In a Lady who lives at court a certain pleasing affability is becoming above all else, whereby she will be able to entertain graciously every kind of man with agreeable and attractive conversation."

55. Despite providing many of the first explorers, what prevented Italy from sponsoring its own voyages of exploration in the fifteenth and sixteenth centuries?
    a. opposition of the papacy
    b. shortage of financial resources
    c. lack of political unity
    d. interference by aristocrats
    e. preoccupation with peasant revolts

56. Which of the following accounts for the political and territorial decline of Poland during the seventeenth and eighteenth centuries?
    a. rivalries with stronger neighboring states
    b. instability caused by an autocratic monarchy
    c. internal conflicts over religious issues
    d. high taxes that sapped economic productivity
    e. lack of leadership from the Polish nobility

57. All of the following factors explain the Dutch Republic's commercial dominance in the first half of the seventeenth century EXCEPT:
    a. a powerful standing army.
    b. geographic location.
    c. strong financial institutions.
    d. elites interested in commerce.
    e. tolerance of religious diversity.

58. Eighteenth-century European society witnessed a rapid expansion in the:
    a. number of religious conflicts.
    b. rights for women.
    c. death rate due to disease.
    d. publication of books.
    e. rate of violent crimes.

59. What accounts for the involvement of peasants in counterrevolutionary movements directed against the French revolutionary government?
    a. the government's reversal of the abolition of feudalism
    b. peasants' support for persecuted high nobles of Paris
    c. opposition to de-Christianization and centralization
    d. military alliances with armies of supportive nations
    e. poor living conditions due to crop failures and famine

60. During the revolutions of 1848, which of the following cities hosted a Pan-Slav assembly to discuss the autonomy of the Slavic peoples?
    a. Frankfurt
    b. Vienna
    c. Budapest
    d. Belgrade
    e. Prague

61. The painting below, *Composition with Ace of Clubs* by Georges Braque, is associated with which of the following artistic movements?
    a. Impressionism
    b. Cubism
    c. Expressionism
    d. Dadaism
    e. Realism

Bridgeman-Giraudon/Art Resource, NY/© 2001 Artists Rights Society [ARS], New York/ADAGP, Paris

62. Which of the following represented a major diplomatic result of the Crimean War (1853–1856)?
    a. The decline of the Ottoman Empire was halted.
    b. The Concert of Europe was effectively reinstated.
    c. France withdrew in defeat from European affairs.
    d. It opened the way for German and Italian unification.
    e. Austria emerged in a strengthened political position.

63. During the interwar period (1918–1939), which of the following best characterizes the impact of mass culture on European society?
    a. Democratic governments effectively controlled the new media.
    b. New communication techniques promoted international harmony.
    c. Totalitarian movements used mass media to manipulate public opinion.
    d. Mass culture furthered the divide between eastern and western Europe.
    e. Organized sports effectively eliminated divisions between social classes.

64. A major reason for the failure of Mikhail Gorbachev's (1985–1991) efforts to reform the Soviet system was:
    a. his inability to end the Cold War and thus realize savings on defense spending.
    b. the difficulty of negotiating economic aid packages from the Western alliance.
    c. the breakdown of Soviet infrastructure, as highlighted by the Chernobyl disaster.
    d. the diversion of resources involved in maintaining control of Eastern Europe.
    e. opposition by communist hard-liners, who attempted to overthrow Gorbachev.

65. All of the following represent elements of the Western European democracies' welfare programs after World War II EXCEPT:
    a. subsidized child care and infant nutrition.
    b. guaranteed jobs of minimum annual income.
    c. unemployment and health insurance.
    d. old-age and retirement pensions.
    e. subsidized college tuition programs.

66. The expressions "form follows function" and "boxes with windows" are associated with which of the following architectural movements?
    a. Renaissance
    b. Baroque
    c. Neoclassical
    d. Modernism
    e. Rococo

67. Which of the following resulted from the Habsburg-Valois Wars (1494–1559) in Italy?
    a. Italy came under foreign rule for three centuries.
    b. Italy was unified under Habsburg leadership.
    c. The papacy was brought under French control.
    d. Russia emerged as the strongest nation in Europe.
    e. The war sparked an economic revival in Italy.

68. Which of the following can be concluded from the map below?
    a. Protestant denominations held the balance of power.
    b. Anabaptism had become the dominant faith in Germany.
    c. Calvinist influence was confined to eastern Europe.
    d. Catholicism was not the minority religion in any nation.
    e. Europe stood geographically divided along religious lines.

69. As Lord Protector of England (1653–1658), Oliver Cromwell's primary goal was to:
    a. reestablish Catholicism in Ireland.
    b. create a new royal dynasty in England.
    c. firmly establish reformed Christianity.
    d. conquer areas of France claimed by England.
    e. turn power back to Parliament.

70. Which of the following best characterizes Old Regime France based on the map below?
    a. Louis XIV (1643–1715) had effectively centralized power under absolutism.
    b. French territory had decreased throughout the eighteenth century.
    c. French administration remained divided based on geography.
    d. Louis XVI (1774–1793) refused to address the financial problems of France.
    e. Colbert's tariff union succeeded in harnessing France's wealth.

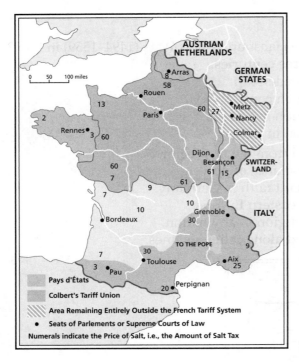

71. Prussian political economist Friedrich List (1789–1846) advocated which of the following economic institutions as the basis for German unity?
    a. Hanseatic League
    b. North German Confederation
    c. Concert of Europe
    d. *Zollverein*
    e. *Burschenshaft*

72. Which of the following represents an idea central to Marxism?
    a. "Capitalism is an unnecessary phase of economic development."
    b. "Human nature is selfish and will not change according to economic systems."
    c. "Revolution will occur first in Russia, the weakest link in the chain."
    d. "Class struggle can be avoided by social welfare programs."
    e. "History moves inevitably through economic stages, culminating in communism."

73. A major social impact of the Great Depression in the 1930s in Europe was:
    a. an increase in economic inequality and unemployment.
    b. rapid state adoption of welfare programs to allay suffering.
    c. the widespread adoption of local cooperatives to pool resources.
    d. a significant rise in the birth rate to meet the labor shortage.
    e. the movement toward extended families in western Europe.

74. What was the only Eastern European nation to retain a democratic government on the eve of World War II?
    a. Poland
    b. Czechoslovakia
    c. Russia
    d. Romania
    e. Hungary

75. The Renaissance papacy (1417–1540s) was most noted for its:
    a. success in unifying the Italian peninsula.
    b. extension of toleration to religious minorities.
    c. subordination to the French monarchy.
    d. corruption, which led to the Reformation.
    e. patronage of mysticism and lay piety movements.

76. The painting below by Jan Vermeer (1632–1675) demonstrates which of the following about Dutch society in the seventeenth century?
    a. interest in science and commerce
    b. inequality and rigid class divisions
    c. strong nobility and absolutist government
    d. lack of agriculture production
    e. dominance by foreign workers

The Geographer by Jan Vermeer (Dutch, 1632–1675)
Stadel-Museum, Frankfort am Main. Reprinted with permission.

77. With which of the following actions would the quote below most likely be associated?
    a. Popular Front governments in the 1930s in Spain and France
    b. the Bolshevik Revolution of November 1917 in Russia
    c. the assassination of Tsar Alexander II (1855–1881) of Russia
    d. King Leopold's domination of the Congo in the late nineteenth century
    e. destruction of the Paris Commune in 1871 after the Franco-Prussian War

    "On the Marxist banner is written: retention and strengthening of the State at any cost. On our banner are inscribed in fiery and bloody letters: the destruction of all States, the annihilation of bourgeois civilization, free and spontaneous organization from below upward, by means of free associations."

78. Which of the following resulted from the French occupation of the Ruhr Valley in 1923?
    a. The United States withdrew from the League of Nations in protest.
    b. International opposition led to French abandonment of strict enforcement of the Versailles settlement.
    c. German resistance to the Ruhr invasion led to increased support for the Weimar Republic.
    d. France successfully incorporated the Ruhr Valley into France, aiding its industrial production.
    e. British troops invaded the Ruhr Valley to prevent the French from seizing the region.

79. Which post–World War II conflict demonstrated Great Britain's inability to maintain its great-power status?
    a. Partition of India (1947)
    b. Arab-Israeli War (1948)
    c. Suez Canal Crisis (1956)
    d. Falklands War (1982)
    e. Gulf War (1991)

80. Which of the following best characterizes the impact of the 1968 student revolts in France on the government of President Charles de Gaulle?
    a. Political instability forced de Gaulle to withdraw France from NATO.
    b. Radical socialists used the event to overthrow the Fifth Republic.
    c. de Gaulle was forced to request American aid in subduing the revolt.
    d. de Gaulle survived the revolt, but growing unpopularity led to his resignation.
    e. The government and students reached a power-sharing agreement.

EUROPEAN HISTORY
SECTION II
Part A
(Suggested writing time—45 minutes)
Percent of Section II score—45

Directions: The prompt that follows is based on Documents 1-11 and will gauge your ability to comprehend and evaluate historical documents. Make sure in your essay that you:

- Provide an explicit thesis directly addressing all parts of the question.
- Discuss specifically a majority of the documents.
- Demonstrate a grasp of the essential meaning of a majority of the documents.
- Support your thesis with accurate interpretations of a majority of the documents.
- Analyze the sources by grouping them clearly and accurately in at least three ways.
- Take into account both the authors' points of view and biases.

You may refer to relevant historical context not addressed in the documents.

1. Analyze the effect of Charles Darwin's theory of natural selection on Europe in the period 1860–1921. To what extent did views toward the theory change over time?

Historical Background: After almost a quarter-century of research, Charles Darwin published his *Origin of the Species* in 1859. In this work, Darwin introduced the principle of "natural selection" to biological change. Species evolved, Darwin held, by random variations that provided advantages in relation to their environments. This element of randomness contradicted previous evolutionary theories of the eighteenth century, which tended to emphasize the element of design, either inherent in the organism or placed there by a higher power. Darwin applied his theory explicitly to the evolution of humans from a common ancestor with *The Descent of Man*, published in 1871. Further, geological and fossil discoveries throughout the nineteenth century seemed to give support for Darwin's theory and for the extreme age of the earth.

Document 1

> *Source*: Samuel Wilberforce, English bishop and writer, *On Darwin's* Origin of Species, 1860.
>
> Mr. Darwin declares that he applies the principle of natural selection to man himself, as well as to the animals around him. Now, we must say at once and openly, that such a notion is absolutely incompatible not only with expressions in the word of God on the subject of man's natural condition, but more importantly, with the whole representation of the moral and spiritual condition of man which is the Bible's proper subject matter. Man's supremacy over the earth; man's power of articulate speech; man's gift of reason; man's free will and responsibility; man's fall and man's redemption; the incarnation of the Eternal Son; the indwelling of the Eternal Spirit—all are equally and utterly irreconcilable with the degrading notion of the brute origin of humans who were, in fact, created in the image of God, and redeemed by the Eternal Son assuming to Himself man's nature.

Document 2

Source: "Monkeyana," *Punch,* British magazine dealing with humor and social commentary, May 1861.

MONKEYANA.

AM. I A MAN AND A BROTHER?

Am I a man and a brother?

Document 3

Source: Clémence Royer, French translator of Darwin, anthropologist, and feminist, *Preface to Origin of the Species,* 1866.

The doctrine of Mr. Darwin is the rational revelation of progress, pitting itself in logical antagonism with the irrational revelation of Man's fall*. These are two principles, two religions in struggle, a thesis and an antithesis of which I defy any who is proficient in logic to find a reconciliation. It is a categorical "yes" and "no" between which it is necessary to choose, and whoever declares himself for the one is against the other.

For myself, the choice is made: I believe in progress.

*A reference to the account of original sin given in the Old Testament.

Document 4

Source: Walter Bagehot, British journalist and economist, *The Use of Conflict,* 1872.

In every particular state of the world, those nations which are strongest tend to prevail over the others; and in certain ways the strongest tend to be the best.

Within every nation, the types of character most attractive tend to prevail; and the most attractive, though with exceptions, is what we call the best character.

These are the sort of doctrines with which, under the name of "natural selection" in physical science, we have become familiar. As every great scientific theory tends to advance its boundaries and to be of use in solving unforeseen problems, so here, what was put forward relating to animals, with a change of form, may be applied to human history.

Document 5

Source: Charles Darwin, biologist and developer of doctrine of natural selection in evolution, *Autobiography,* 1876.

Disbelief in God crept over me at very slow rate, but was at last complete. The rate was so slow that I felt no distress and have never since doubted even for a single second that my conclusion was correct. I can indeed hardly see how anyone ought to wish Christianity to be true.

The old argument of design in nature, as given by [William] Paley,* which formerly seemed to me so conclusive, fails, now that the law of natural selection has been discovered. We can no longer argue that, for instance, the beautiful hinge of a bivalve shell must have been made by an intelligent being, like the hinge of a door by man. There seems to be no more design in the variability of organic beings and in the action of natural selection, than in the course the wind blows. Everything in nature is the result of fixed laws.

The mystery of the beginning of all things is insoluble to us; and I for one must be content to remain an Agnostic.

*William Paley was an early nineteenth-century natural theologian who devised a famous argument for intelligent design.

Document 6

Source: Thomas H. Huxley, British biologist and popularizer of science, *Evolution and Ethics and Other Essays,* 1893.

The practice of what is ethically best—what we call goodness or virtue—involves conduct which is opposed to that which leads to success in the cosmic struggle for existence. In place of ruthless self-assertion it demands self-restraint; in place of thrusting aside or treading down all competitors, it requires that the individual shall not merely respect, but shall help his fellows; its influence is directed, not so much to the survival of the fittest, as to the fitting of as many as possible to survive. It repudiates the gladiatorial theory of existence.

Laws and moral precepts are directed to the end of curbing the cosmic process and reminding the individual of his duty to the community, to the protection and influence of which he owes, if not existence itself, at least the life of something better than a brutal savage.

Document 7

Source: Herbert Spencer, British philosopher and sociologist, *Social Statics,* 1896.

Pervading all nature we see at work a stern discipline which is a little cruel that it may be very kind. Meanwhile, the well-being of humanity and its unfolding into ultimate perfection are both secured by the same beneficial though severe discipline to which animals are subject.

It seems hard that a laborer, incapacitated by sickness from competing with his stronger fellows, should have to bear the resulting sufferings. It seems hard that widows and orphans should be left to struggle for life or death. Nevertheless, when regarded not separately but in connection with the interests of universal humanity, these harsh fatalities are seen to be full of beneficence—the same beneficence which brings to early graves the children of diseased parents, and singles out the intemperate and the debilitated as the victims of an epidemic.

Document 8

Source: Isabella Sidgwick, British journalist and writer, account of a debate held in 1860 at Oxford University between Samuel Wilberforce and Thomas H. Huxley on Darwinian theory, "A Grandmother's Tales," *Macmillan's Magazine,* 1898.

I was happy enough to be present on the memorable occasion at Oxford when Mr. Huxley debated Bishop Wilberforce. There were so many of us who were eager to hear that we had to adjourn to the great library of the Museum. Then the Bishop rose, and in a light scoffing tone assured us there was nothing in the idea of evolution; pigeons were what pigeons had always been. Then, turning to his antagonist with a smiling insolence, he begged to know, was it through his grandfather or his grandmother that he claimed his descent from a monkey?

Then Mr. Huxley slowly and deliberately arose. A slight, tall figure stern and pale, very quiet and very grave, he stood before us, and spoke those tremendous words—words which no one seems sure of now, nor could remember just after they were spoken, for their meaning took away our breath. Huxley avowed that he was not ashamed to have a monkey for his ancestor; but he would be ashamed to be connected with a man who used great gifts to obscure the truth. No one doubted his meaning and the effect was tremendous. One lady fainted and had to be carried out. I, for one, jumped out of my seat; and when in the evening we met, every one was eager to congratulate the hero of the day.

Document 9

Source: Karl Pearson, British mathematician and scientist, professor of eugenics,* *National Life From the Standpoint of Science,* 1900.

History shows me one way, and one way only, in which a high state of civilization has been produced, namely, the struggle of race with race, and the survival of the physically and mentally fitter race.

The struggle means suffering, intense suffering, but that struggle and that suffering have been the stages by which the white man has reached his present stage of development, and they account for the fact that he no longer lives in caves and feeds on roots and nuts. This dependence of progress on the survival of the fitter race, terribly dark as it may seem to some of you, gives the struggle for existence its redeeming features; it is the fiery crucible out of which comes the finer metal.

*Eugenics is the "science" of studying and classifying racial characteristics.

Document 10

Source: Friedrich von Bernhardi, German general and writer on military affairs, *The Next War,* 1912.

This aspiration for universal peace is directly antagonistic to the great universal laws which rule all life. War is a biological necessity of the first importance, a regulative element in the life of mankind which cannot be dispensed with, since without it an unhealthy development will follow, which excludes every advancement of the race, and therefore all real civilization. "War is the father of all things." (Heraclitus*) The sages of antiquity long before Darwin recognized this.

*Heraclitus was an ancient Greek philosopher.

Document 11

Source: Pierre Teilhard de Chardin, Catholic priest of the Jesuit order, paleontologist, philosopher, review article in a periodical, 1921.

The letter of the Bible shows us the Creator fashioning the body of man from the earth. Conscious observation of the world tends to make us perceive today that by "earth" one must understand a substance slowly elaborated by the totality of things—so that man was taken not exactly from a little bit of matter, but from the prolonged effort of the whole "Earth." In spite of the serious difficulties that still prevent us from reconciling this view completely with certain more commonly accepted versions of creation, it should not trouble us. Little by little an agreement will be reached, quite naturally, between science and dogma on the burning issue of human origins. Let us avoid, in the meantime, rejecting the slightest ray of light from any direction. Faith needs the whole truth.

EUROPEAN HISTORY
SECTION II
Part B
(Suggested planning and writing time—35 minutes)
Percent of Section II score—27.5

Directions: Answer ONE question from the three choices below. Select the question that you can answer most effectively in the time allotted. You are strongly encouraged to use about 5 minutes planning out your response before you begin writing.

Make sure that your essay:

- Offers a thesis explicitly responsive to the question.
- Deals with all parts of the question.
- Provides specific support for the thesis.
- Displays a clear organization.

2. Analyze TWO reasons for Western Europe's post–World War II economic recovery and TWO social consequences of this recovery in the period 1945 to 1970.

3. Analyze the effects of the Industrial Revolution on family life and the class structure in Great Britain from 1780 to 1850.

4. In what ways and to what extent did the Renaissance set the stage for the Protestant Reformation?

EUROPEAN HISTORY
SECTION II
Part C
(Suggested planning and writing time—35 minutes)
Percent of Section II score—27.5

Directions: Answer ONE question from the three choices below. Select the question that you can answer most effectively in the time allotted. You are strongly encouraged to use about 5 minutes planning out your response before you begin writing.

Make sure that your essay:

• Offers a thesis explicitly responsive to the question.
• Deals with all parts of the question.
• Provides specific support for the thesis.
• Displays a clear organization.

5. Identify the reasons for Russia's rise as a great power from the reign of Peter the Great (1689–1725) to the reign of Catherine the Great (1762–1796) AND analyze the consequences of Russia's rise for the European balance of power.

6. Analyze TWO causes for and TWO consequences of the Thirty Years' War (1618–1648).

7. Assess the impact of the Great Depression on any TWO European nations in the period 1929 to 1939.

ANSWERS AND SAMPLE RESPONSES
MULTIPLE CHOICE

1. **c.** The passage addresses the superiority of justification before God based on faith rather than works. The issue of justification divided Protestants and Catholics, with the former emphasizing faith alone and the Catholic Church arguing for the efficacy of both faith and works. Because Calvin is the only Protestant (Henry VIII broke from the church but did not change doctrine), he represents the correct answer.

2. **a.** Enclosure began in rural areas to close off formerly common lands that had been purchased by wealthy peasants or the gentry of England. This development led to improvements in the land, the raising of crops for cash profit, and the eventual disintegration of the village, or communal, agriculture. Jews were forced into ghettoes during this period as well (b), but this was not termed "enclosure." State prisons arose in the nineteenth century (c). Factories referred to in (d) also came later in the eighteenth century. (e) simply did not occur, accounting for the proliferation of Protestant denominations to this day.

3. **e.** The African slave trade began in the fourteenth century to allay a labor shortage brought about by the Black Death (a). However, by the sixteenth century, European population had recovered and labor tended to be abundant, accounting for perennial joblessness. European states believed Africans to be inferior fighters and did not generally employ them as soldiers (b). Textile workers tended to be European women and children (c). European states made few "conquests" of land in Africa until the late nineteenth century (d). The explosion of sugar production stimulated the slave trade in the relevant period (e).

4. **c.** Enlightenment thinkers focused on human reason as a source of knowledge and, building off the Scientific Revolution, believed that natural laws guided nature and human activity (c). (a) approximates the Romantic attitude toward nature. Irrationality gained sway later in the nineteenth century with the ideas of Freud and Nietzsche (b). The environmentalism in (d) would not occur until the twentieth century. (e) represents a summation of Immanuel Kant's ideas, who was indeed a philosopher of the Enlightenment but whose ideas are not typical of that movement.

5. **b.** As early as the seventeenth century, the Dutch protected their limited resources by creating *polders,* or land reclaimed from the sea, to maximize agricultural output. You may recall that the British pioneered new techniques, such as the hoe, terracing, fodder crops, and scientific livestock breeding, during the Enlightenment. Other nations, such as Prussia, *followed* many of these innovations.

6. **d.** The inequality of the Old Regime acted as a fundamental cause of the French Revolution, eliminating (a). Many in the First and Second Estates allied in attempting to maintain their privileges and exemptions under the old order (b). Members of the bourgeoisie often took their cultural cue from Liberal nobles and often did not see much in common with peasants (c). Louis XVI, in fact, attempted numerous reforms, but failed as a result of his political weakness (e). Choice (d) captures the issues of inequality as a cause of the French Revolution.

7. **e.** David painted *Napoleon Crossing the Alps* to celebrate the general's amazing military exploit in defeating the Austrians by following in Hanibal's footsteps in marching over the "impassable" Alps. Romantic painters such as David often glorified the heroic and unique individual; Napoleon was a favorite subject of theirs.

8. **a.** You may recall that the first industry to become mechanized in Britain was textile manufacturing. Clothing is a basic consumer good, and with Britain's productive advantage quickly became its leading export. This required, in turn, an abundant supply of cotton, often coming from the United States and reinforcing the slave system there.

9. **b.** The quote argues that natural affinities exist in politics among people with common characteristics. Combining numerous peoples under one government violates the natural order. Nineteenth-century nationalists, such as Mazzini who authored the accompanying passage, believed that traditional diplomacy corrupted a natural process toward the aggregation of common ethnic and linguistic groups in one nation.

10. **b.** We see two figures in the cartoon—a crowned man on a ship looking down on a departing "pilot." Nothing in the cartoon suggests military failures (a). Germany did build a fleet of battleships under Kaiser Wilhelm II, but the cartoon does not explicitly address this action (c). Nowhere is agreement depicted in the cartoon, also indicated by the caption (d). Because the cartoon deals with two unlabeled individuals, (b) represents a better choice than the more abstract symbolism required for (e).

11. **e.** The Georges Seurat painting *Sunday on the Island of La Grand Jatte* depicts modern bourgeoisie enjoying leisure in an urban park setting (e). This development also coincides with imperialism, but that phenomenon did not directly affect European city life (a). No socialist governments ruled Europe prior to the Russian Revolution in 1917 (b). Warfare did not end among the great powers in this period (c), and women did not receive the vote until after World War I (d).

12. **d.** This is a difficult question. Einstein's formula $E = mc^2$ expresses (a). Relativity as a theory suggests that time and space are relative, not absolute (b). Einstein also discovered

that nothing can travel faster than the speed of light (c). An eclipse in 1919 demonstrated that Einstein had been right about gravity affecting both space and time, curving the former and slowing down the latter (e). However, Einstein specifically rejected the quantum notion that physical phenomenon were unpredictable in principle, saying "God does not play dice" (d).

13. **c.** World War I began with unity but eventually led to social tensions, contradicting (a). Inflation grew worse with wartime rationing, currency depreciation, and shortages of goods (b). Only Russia employed female combatants (d). Small business owners lost (e) as governments found it more efficient to funnel government contracts through large industrial enterprises, suggesting the answer is (c).

14. **d.** Most Russians desperately wanted out of World War I because of its effects on the economy and political system (d). The Provisional Government did not compromise with the Bolsheviks, though relied on them to help defeat the Kornilov coup in August 1917 (a). Even conservative members of the Provisional Government accepted the infeasibility of Tsar Nicholas II returning to the throne in 1917 (b). If anything, many Russians would have preferred the government to take a more proactive role in addressing inflation and other social issues (c). Though women did not get the vote until the Bolsheviks granted it, this generally is not considered a major reason for the Provisional Government's downfall (e); the Bolsheviks primarily exploited class concerns and the failed war effort in gaining power.

15. **a.** Other than Lenin (d), all of these leaders did participate at Versailles. Unlike the others, President Wilson of the United States explicitly stated a goal of a peace without vengeance. Wilson compromised with Clemenceau's goal of punishing Germany in an effort to build support for his League of Nations.

16. **e.** Governments after World War II did promote a higher birth rate, but this tended to reinforce the ideal of women as homemakers (a). In some nations, prostitution became decriminalized, or at the least, was not considered any worse than it had been before (b). Undoubtedly, many women gained positions in academia, but such a development was limited to those who had access to a college education, still a minority (c). The antinuclear movement included a good share of women, but it was geared less toward women's issues (d). However, numerous women were able to limit the number of children they conceived through artificial birth control, opening possibilities other than marriage and child-rearing (e).

17. **a.** The Peace of Lodi created two equally balanced alliances among the five main powers on the peninsula, though it was not to last with foreign invasion in 1494 (a). The papacy, as one of these powers, continued to exercise influence over Italian politics (b). Italian powers did employ mercenaries, often with negative results, but other nations employed them as well (c). Hereditary dynasties, whether royal or noble, continued to play a major role in politics (d). Collective security proved only informal and, given Italy's subsequent history, not terribly effective (e).

18. **b.** One of the major effects of the exchange of goods between Europe and the Americas proved to be the improvement of the European diet, a development many historians credit with the increase of Europe's population in the eighteenth century. None of the other developments actually occurred.

19. **c.** Habsburg emperor Maximilian I (r. 1493–1519) married Mary of the important duchy of Burgundy. Their son, Philip, married Joanna, the daughter of Ferdinand and Isabella of Spain. Philip and Joanna's son, Charles I of Spain (Charles V as Holy Roman Emperor) inherited all these positions through a series of untimely deaths. Additional marriages into the Hungarian

dynasty allowed the Habsburgs to threaten continental hegemony by the mid-sixteenth century and spark the determined opposition of the French Valois monarchy.

20. **d.** The Union of Utrecht was formed in response to the shift in Spanish policies under the Duke of Parma, who attempted to subdue the burgeoning revolt against Spain by winning over the 10 southern, mostly Catholic, and French-speaking provinces into the Union of Arras. In response, the largely Calvinist and Dutch-speaking provinces declared their autonomy with the Union of Utrecht and continued opposition to Spanish rule.

21. **d.** Baroque expressed the power of absolutism, and its artistic adherents often won patronage from powerful princes, kings, and popes. Characteristic of the Baroque are the palace at Versailles and the court paintings of Diego Valezquez for the Spanish monarchs. (a), (b), and (e) did not directly inspire artistic movements, though some painters thought of themselves as promoting the Protestant cause. Several Protestant denominations, notably Calvinism, often frowned on depictions of Jesus or other holy figures as a form of idolatry. The Enlightenment of the eighteenth century promoted a more restrained neoclassical approach in direct opposition to the highly dramatic and dynamic style of the Baroque.

22. **a.** Looking closely at the illustration, we find the sun at the center of the universe with the earth orbiting it. (b) and (e) have little to do with the illustration, and perpetual motion (c) is impossible. That leaves geocentrism as an option, but such a diagram on a test would most likely focus on a depiction of *change* (d).

23. **b.** The radicalism of the Jacobins did not extend to women. Influenced by the ideals of Rousseau, those in the charge of the Terror believed the proper role of a republican woman was as mother. Female influence in politics was associated with Marie Antoinette and aristocratic intrigue. The Jacobins banned the Society for Revolutionary Republican Women, but did institute the other policies listed in the question.

24. **c.** A prerequisite for industrialization was a more productive agricultural sector, meaning that it became less labor-intensive, so eliminate (a). National income did increase during early industrialization, but it certainly was not evenly distributed (b). Before 1850, women primarily experienced factory or domestic industry, forms of labor that tended to reinforce their inferior status (d). Most factories were owned by middle-class entrepreneurs, contradicting (e). With the mechanization of labor, work and home life became separated, often considered a major consequence of industrialization (c).

25. **a.** Mechanization hit textiles well before 1850, so check off (b). Canals had been built in the ancient world, and even with the canal boom in eighteenth-century England had already been replaced by railroads by 1850 (c). Computers, of course, belong in the post–World War II period (d). All of the items in (e) predate 1850. Airplanes were invented in 1903, petroleum discovered in 1859, and electricity harnessed in the 1870s and 1880s (a).

26. **d.** Russia acted as a key member of the Concert of Europe, rendering (a) false. (b) is perhaps a reference to the Prussian-dominated *Zollverein* (c). No such entity as (c) existed. Individual Romantic revolutionaries existed, but they were not allied in a group by that name (e). Metternich's Concert of Europe operated informally to address security questions among the five great powers of Great Britain, France, Austria, Prussia, and Russia. It was destroyed by the revolutions of 1848 and the Crimean War.

27. **e.** Choices (a) through (d) represent motives for Britain's involvement in Africa generally in the nineteenth century. However, Britain's primary goal in directly intervening in Egyptian

politics in 1882 was to secure control of the Suez Canal Company and ensure access to the "lifeline to its empire," meaning India.

28. **e.** Darwin embraced the causal laws of biology, so (a) does not apply. Early critics of Darwin did not generally attack his theory on grounds of shoddy science, so (b) can be eliminated. Darwin explicitly rejected the notion that different races formed different species, though other evolutionists did advance this notion (c). Though Darwin's ideas implicitly undermined the biblical account of Genesis, he did not explicitly attack the clergy in *Origin of the Species* (d). Darwin's contemporaries, and many today, refuse to accept the notion that humans are not a special creature formed in the image of the Creator (e).

29. **a.** Political observers in the nineteenth century called the Ottoman Empire the "Sick Man of Europe," as it slowly receded in power from the Balkan Peninsula. This decline fomented nationalism among the Slavic minority and accentuated tension between the two great powers in geographic proximity—Austria-Hungary and Russia.

30. **e.** We can eliminate (a) because the on looking crowd does not appear Vietnamese, or Indochinese. Given that no bombs are falling and that the crowd simply watches the plane, (b) seems out of the question. Eliminate (c), as the plane clearly sports propellers, not jets. Soviet troops left Eastern Europe via land, and clearly the picture appears before 1990 (d). That leaves us with (e), as we see a crowd of West Berliners waiting expectantly for American supplies during the Berlin blockade of 1948–1949.

31. **b.** Italian painters did portray nature, but primarily with a realistic eye for detail (a). Though the Renaissance is often viewed as secular, 90 percent of paintings still depicted religious subject matter, making (c) an overstatement. (d) represents a better description of Northern Renaissance paintings. Italian masters often employed large frescoes in churches to complete their masterpieces, eliminating (e). Of course, one of the major innovations we associate with Renaissance art is the use of realistic three-dimensional depictions of space (b).

32. **c.** The Thirty Years' War began as an internal religious conflict among the German states, divided by religion. However, additional factors came into play as the war progressed, namely that the German powers allied with outside nations and also that those nations held territorial and political ambitions that could be met by military involvement in Central Europe. Sweden under Gustavus Adolphus represents a good example—a Lutheran king who wished to expand Sweden's Baltic holdings through intervention.

33. **e.** The papacy has never condemned the notion of demonic possession (a). Population did not recover from the seventeenth-century falloff until about 1730 (b). Nations did not pass laws protecting women until the nineteenth century, and these dealt with economic and legal rights (c). Few accepted witchcraft as a legitimate pagan religion until recently (d). Because elites ran the court system, their disbelief in witches was key in reducing and eventually abolishing the witchcraft trials (e).

34. **d.** Smith criticized mercantilism and promoted free trade and laissez-faire policies in the eighteenth century (a). De Gama sailed for Portugal in the fifteenth century (b). Hobbes wrote regarding absolute monarchy, not economic issues (c). Kepler, of course, worked in astronomy (e). Colbert acted as Louis XIV's economic advisor and constructed mercantilist policies to promote French exports, build internal markets, and pursue colonies.

35. **c.** The passage addresses the separation of powers within a constitutional form of government, a theme central to Montesquieu's *Spirit of the Laws*.

36. **b.** The Reform Act approximately doubled the number of male voters in Britain, granting the franchise to wealthy members of the middle class and to industrial cities previously unrepresented, such as Manchester and Liverpool. The other choices also represent various pieces of reform legislation passed by Parliament throughout the nineteenth century.

37. **d.** Unlike China and India, Japan successfully repelled foreign control. However, first the Tokugawa Shogunate fell and was replaced by reformist samurai, who helped restore the emperor. Emperor Meiji then embarked on a telescoped process of modernization, ultimately leading to Japan's rise as a major power in the Pacific as early as 1890, only two decades after the so-called Meiji Restoration.

38. **a.** As a result of industrialization and improved sanitation and medical care, Europe's population nearly doubled between 1850 and 1900. Additionally, many more Europeans took up residence in the new industrial cities, in search of jobs and opportunities (a). Artificial birth control was not widely available in Europe until the middle of the twentieth century (b). Many Europeans did emigrate to the Americas, yet Europe's population increased nonetheless (c). Also, population increase proved impervious to the economic cycles that dominated the era, 1873–1896 (d). All areas of Europe expanded in population, but because industrialization advanced more quickly in central and western Europe, those areas grew more quickly in population (e).

39. **c.** This photograph depicts a typical trench scene during World War I—soldiers embedded in mud, stuck out in the middle of no-man's land, awaiting enemy assault.

40. **b.** In the elections of January 1918 to Russia's Constituent Assembly—charged with creating a new constitution following the tsar's overthrow—the Social Revolutionaries and Mensheviks won a majority of the seats. The Bolsheviks finished a distant third, but charged that the election results were invalid and instead placed power in the All Russian Congress of Soviets, which they controlled. The action led to the Russian Civil War (1918–1921).

41. **d.** Italian fascism promoted a traditional role for women and encouraged a higher birth rate. To accomplish this, the fascist state "encouraged" women to turn their jobs over to male workers. However, the quote is charging that fascist rhetoric hid the additional motive of driving down wages for all workers.

42. **b.** The Nine Years' War (War of the League of Augsburg) was sparked by Louis XIV's ambitions in the Rhineland; while England opposed the French, the war did not include a struggle between German powers (a). During the Napoleonic Wars, Prussia and Austria united in their opposition to France (c). The Franco-Prussian War was fought solely between France and Prussia and did not involve colonies (d). During World War I, the two German powers of Germany and Austria were allied, as were France and Britain on the opposing side (e). The Seven Years' War featured a colonial clash between France and Britain over the Caribbean sugar trade, North America, and India, while Prussia and Austria battled it out for control of Silesia (b).

43. **a.** At first, Anabaptists allowed women to preach, but curtailed this practice under general criticism (b). Peasants attempted to use Luther's ideas of spiritual equality for social changes, but Luther condemned their effort, and their revolt was crushed (c). Population did increase during the sixteenth century, but the effect of celibacy on this trend proved negligible (d). Given the religious wars of the period, (e) seems out of the question. Both Protestant and Catholic nations promoted education during the Reformation, especially the former, due to the importance of reading the Bible (a).

44. **d.** Henry IV succeeded in driving Spanish troops, who had been assisting the ultra-Catholics, out of France. To gain the support of the French people, Henry converted to the majority faith of Catholicism but also issued the Edict of Nantes to extend toleration to French Protestants—Huguenots. Following this, Henry balanced the budget, promoted economic development, and pursued colonies. France successfully survived his assassination in 1610 and the accession of his young son, Louis XIII, to the throne. The other choices did not occur.

45. **c.** Though Peter reformed Russia, his reign was too early to be influenced by the Enlightenment. In fact, the only ruler chronologically positioned was Frederick II (1740–1786). The others came prior to the Enlightenment and/or did not espouse rational reforms.

46. **e.** Most intellectuals in the seventeenth century did not espouse revolutionary ideologies, so (a) can be dispensed with. An international scientific community did result from the societies, but this was not a major goal of governments (b). (c) may have occurred, but again, governments did not intend this result, especially as seventeenth-century monarchs tended to view religion as an important support for their rule. (d) is chronologically misplaced, better located in the nineteenth century. Most states financed science to reap the benefits of military and navigational technology within the ever-competitive European state system (e).

47. **c.** Most continental nations lagged behind Britain in industry and attempted to bridge the gap by actively promoting industrial development (c). Britain led the way with the railroad, so (a) can be eliminated. Britain's elites seemed unique in their interest in trade and industry, at least compared with most continental nations (b). Few nations would fit the description of exclusively producing for export, but Britain proved one of the most reliant on trade with its colonial empire (d). All industrializing nations experienced some degree of pollution, overcrowding, and class conflict, so (e) is false.

48. **d.** In the first half of nineteenth century, when these buildings were constructed, Romantic intellectuals promoted a revival of religion. Many looked back to the Middle Ages as a great age of faith; this led to a revival of the Gothic style shown in the picture—vertical lines, pointed arches, and elaborate ornamentation.

49. **a.** Despite Alexander's abolition of serfdom, most peasants lagged in productivity and failed to convert to commercial agriculture until much later (b). Russia never developed a stable constitutional monarchy, instead experiencing the Russian Revolution (c). Modernization did occur in Russia, but its relative success was tarnished by social conflict (d). Many peasants desired a more equal land-holding structure and staged numerous rebellions in the late nineteenth and early twentieth centuries toward this goal (e). Alexander's reforms spurred the development of anarchist and other radical groups, who succeeded in assassinating him in 1881; growth of these groups set the stage for the Russian Revolution (a).

50. **b.** As Freud criticized traditional moral standards, (c) seems out of the question. (a) deals more with developments in physics, (d) with Darwin's ideas, and (e) with the discoveries of Pasteur. Freud demonstrated how humans expressed irrational impulses and instinctual urges in his clinical studies and writings (b).

51. **b.** Stalin collectivized agriculture forcibly in the late 1920s and early 1930s (a), as well as promoted the Five-Year Plans toward industrialization (b). Stalin also eliminated his perceived enemies with the Great Purges (d). With Hitler's attack on the USSR in 1941, Stalin

joined the Grand Alliance with the United States and Britain (e). However, Stalin presided over the onset of the Cold War, a conflict still present on his death in 1953 (b).

52. **d.** A quick glance at the photograph shows broken glass on the streets of a German city. In 1938, Nazi leaders sponsored a pogrom against Jewish businesses and Jewish citizens known as the Night of Broken Glass, or *Kristallnacht,* signaling a more virulent approach to the "Jewish problem" in Germany.

53. **e.** Some Western Europeans feared a revival of Russian power after 1990, but this represented more of an issue for NATO, not the EU (a). The United States and the EU have experienced conflicts over trade, but "hostility" seems a strong word given the importance of their economic contacts (b). France and Germany seem to have moved past their historic rivalry and collaborate in EU policies for the most part (c). Living standards have noticeably increased for EU nations, contradicting (d). A major issue after 1990 has proven to be the expansion of the EU to include former Soviet satellites, such as Hungary, Poland, and the Czech Republic, a process still underway today (e).

54. **b.** Castiglione refers implicitly to women's education in their need to engage in attractive conversation with males; however, he also emphasizes the importance of women's physical appearance. Indeed, the focus in the Renaissance on objects of art, the disparity in marriage ages between men and women, and the way in which marriage was treated as a political and economic arrangement—all tended to reinforce the view of women as objects.

55. **c.** Though Italy supplied some of the great explorers, such as Columbus and the Cabots, the peninsula suffered from political division and foreign intrigue, which prevented it from sponsoring overseas voyages as in the united countries of Spain and Portugal. This fact reminds us of the need for *sustained* organization in the establishment of colonial empires.

56. **a.** Poland failed to develop a strong dynastic state in this period, eliminating (b). Poland tolerated religious diversity better than most nations (c). Polish kings proved unable to establish a strong tax base due to opposition from its strong nobility (d), which also suggests that (e) is incorrect: Polish nobles were *too* strong and effectively blocked the development of an absolutist state. This weakness allowed Poland's stronger neighbors—Russia, Austria, and Prussia—to partition it out of existence in the late eighteenth century (a).

57. **a.** As a republic, the Netherlands did not possess a strong standing army, though it did improvise a defense force in times of war, as well as employ strategies such as flooding fields to stymie invading armies. The other choices represent significant advantages accounting for the commercial strength of the Dutch in the period.

58. **d.** Religious wars ended with the Peace of Westphalia of 1648 (a). Women first began to demand equality during the Enlightenment and French Revolution but did not achieve much in this regard until the nineteenth century (b). The eighteenth century witnessed a marked increase in the population, due primarily to a lowering death rate, excluding (c). Property crimes probably increased in the eighteenth century, but violent crimes declined from the turbulent seventeenth century (e). Published materials, including books, periodicals, and newspapers, experienced a major increase (d).

59. **c.** The French revolutionary government had already abolished feudalism in the summer of 1789, so (a) can be eliminated. Though peasants joined with provincial nobles in counterrevolutionary armies, they tended to resent the privileges of the high nobles associated with Versailles (b). Peasants did not engage in formal military alliances with other nations, for obvious logistical reasons (d). By 1789, the worst of the subsistence crisis that had

acted as a cause of the French Revolution had passed, so (e) is out. Many peasants retained religious piety and resented the centralization of power in Paris during the Reign of Terror, feeding the opposition to the revolution (c).

60. **e.** The only Slavic cities are Belgrade (d) and Prague (e). Belgrade was still technically ruled by the Ottoman Empire and not affected by the revolutions of 1848. Prague hosted the Pan-Slav Congress, whose work toward independence for the Slavs within the Austrian empire was eventually crushed by conservative forces later in 1848.

61. **b.** Along with Picasso, Braque created the Cubist movement of the early twentieth century. Influenced by Einstein's ideas of relativity, Cubism portrayed reality from simultaneous multiple perspectives, accounting for the "broken up" quality of the painting.

62. **d.** The Ottoman Empire continued to decline into the twentieth century, which formed a cause of World War I (a). In fact, the Concert of Europe failed to head off the crisis and was effectively a dead letter after 1853 (b). France under Napoleon III came out of the war with a false sense of its leadership, a notion undermined by subsequent diplomatic events (c). Austria's attempt to play both the Anglo-French alliance and Russians off one another alienated both sides, leaving that nation in an isolated position in the upcoming wars of unification (e). Because of these factors, realistic leaders such as Cavour and Bismarck exploited the diplomatic "anarchy" to unify their respective nations (d).

63. **c.** Fascist and communist nations effectively mobilized their populations by employing radio, movies, automobiles, and airplanes; in fact, Nazi Minister of Propaganda Joseph Goebbels claimed that National Socialism would not have been possible without the airplane and radio (c). (b) and (d) did not occur. (a) represents an overstatement, and many sports clubs continued to organize themselves along class lines, though it could be argued that sports competitions did assist in democratizing cultural tastes during the interwar period (e).

64. **e.** Gorbachev did, in fact, help to end the Cold War, so (a) is out. It is true that the West did not offer significant aid for Gorbachev's reforms, but this did not act as a major reason for his failures (b). Soviet infrastructure was antiquated, but it would be an overstatement to peg this as a major cause of Gorbachev's fall; in fact, Chernobyl strengthened his case for reform (c). (d) is incorrect, as Gorbachev refused to crush revolts against communism in 1989–1990. Communist hard-liners attempted a coup against Gorbachev in 1991 on the eve of treaty to grant greater autonomy to the various ethnic republics of the USSR. The action ironically facilitated the disintegration of the Soviet Union and Gorbachev's fall from power (e).

65. **b.** Few societies guarantee jobs of minimum annual income, though governments may assist the unemployed or subsidize necessities such as health care or child nutrition. The other items represent the standard package of welfare commitments for Western European states after 1945.

66. **d.** Modernism embraces simplicity and austerity of design, rejecting ornamentation in favor of functionalism. These phrases capture this modernist rejection of traditional notions of beauty in favor of a stark minimalism employing glass, steel, and concrete.

67. **a.** The French invasion of Italy in 1494 to lay claims to the Duchy of Milan sparked 65 years of war with the Habsburgs. These wars brought an end to Renaissance culture in Italy, sparked the writing of Machiavelli's *The Prince,* and ultimately cost Italy self-rule until its unification in 1859.

68. **e.** This map shows the religious division of Europe as of 1560; little would change in the balance of power after this time, except for some lands in eastern Europe being reclaimed for

Catholicism with the work of the Jesuits. Catholicism remained the majority faith, though Protestants formed a strong minority, but (a) is still wrong. Anabaptism did not dominate any state territorially; it was decidedly a small movement (b). Strong pockets of Calvinism permeated all areas of Europe (c). Catholics did form the minority in the Scandinavian nations and in England (d).

69.**c.** As the leader of the Puritans, Cromwell strongly opposed Catholicism, which he associated with the deposed Stuart monarchy. Cromwell crushed a revolt by the Catholic Irish with great brutality (a). Though Cromwell ruled dictatorially, he did not wish to establish a new royal dynasty (b). Cromwell did pursue a vigorous mercantilist policy but did not lay claim to any French lands on the continent (d). Cromwell hoped one day for a republican government with a virtuous Parliament, but his casual manipulation of that body's prerogatives suggests that returning power to it was not his ultimate goal (e). Overall, Cromwell hoped to rid England of the "corruptions" of Catholicism and monarchy and establish a true reformed Christianity (c).

70. **c.** The map illustrates the administrative division of France into varying tax and tariff units, as well as the number of *parlements,* which still exercised some influence over the local power of the monarchy. Though Louis XIV claimed an absolute control over France, this did not translate into a centralized political structure. Thus when Louis died in 1715, the old provincialism and aristocratic power of France reasserted itself.

71. **d.** The *Zollverein* acted as a customs union for the member states; it created a larger trading area dominated by Prussia (d). The Hanseatic League operated similarly during the Later Middle Ages related to German trade with the rest of Europe (a). After the Austro-Prussian War (1866), Bismarck consolidated Prussian power in north Germany with the North German Confederation (b). Metternich created the Concert of Europe following the Napoleonic Wars to maintain the balance of power and crush revolution (c). The *Burschenshaft* were Liberal student unions outlawed by the Carlsbad Decrees of 1819 (e).

72. **e.** Contrary to common misperception, Marx accepted that capitalism was a necessary phase of economic development (a). Marx generally did not specify a human nature, believing human behavior and attitudes to be a product of economic systems (b). (c) represents a Leninist spin on Marx, who believed the revolution would occur in the most advanced capitalist nation, such as Britain or Germany. Marx rejected "reactionary" compromises with the capitalist order, such as trade unionism or state socialism, as Bismarck later implemented in Germany (d). For Marx, history moved inevitably toward communism, driven by the clash of opposing economic forces (e).

73. **a.** As with most economic changes, some groups were hurt more than others. The Great Depression accentuated economic inequalities, especially for industrial workers and farmers (a). Welfare programs were adopted slowly and piecemeal (b). Only Scandinavia experimented with producer cooperatives (c). Both the birth rate and average size of families (d, e) decreased during these hard economic times.

74. **b.** Among these nations, only Czechoslovakia—closely tied to the historic localism of Germany—had experienced democracy. Czechoslovakia also boasted the most industrial and diverse economy in eastern Europe, buffering some of the worst effects of the Great Depression during the 1930s, thus allowing its democratic government to survive until the nation was divided at the Munich Conference and invaded by Hitler in March 1939.

75. **d.** Some popes attempted to unify Italy but failed, so (a) is out. The papacy rejected religious toleration until much later and of course condemned the Protestant Reformation (b).

After the end of the Great Schism, the papacy was no longer under the influence of the French monarchy (c). Mysticism and lay piety aroused the suspicion of popes because they lay outside of clerical control, so they were not patronized (e). With its involvement in warfare, politics, and art, many considered the papacy too worldly and corrupt, feeding calls for reform (d).

76. **a.** The Vermeer painting is titled *The Geographer* and shows the Dutch interest in science (many intellectuals, including scientists, fled to the Netherlands for its religious toleration) and commerce, since an understanding of the globe would aid commercial activity.

77. **c.** The key words of the quote are "destruction of all states." This identifies the quote as related to anarchism. Anarchists also condemned Marxists for wishing to retain the state under control of the proletariat. Of the events listed, the assassination of Tsar Alexander II was directly inspired by the strong Russian anarchist movement of the late nineteenth century. For anarchists, assassination held mythical importance ("the Act"); with severing the "head" the destruction of the capitalist body would soon follow.

78. **b.** Because the United States never joined the League of Nations, (a) is not possible. With Germany's campaign of passive resistance toward the French occupation, hyperinflation resulted, actually undermining support for the Weimar Republic (c). France eventually withdrew, so (d) does not apply. Britain responded primarily with verbal condemnation of France's action, not militarily (e). American and British opposition to France's hard-line policy convinced the latter to abandon a strict enforcement of Versailles and work toward an understanding with Weimar leaders (b).

79. **c.** Following Egyptian leader Nasser's nationalization of the Suez Canal in 1956, the British, along with the French and Israelis, invaded to recapture the canal. United States and Soviet opposition forced an ignominious withdrawal, demonstrating that Britain could not act independently as a great power—not, that is, without the support of its stronger ally, the United States.

80. **d.** de Gaulle was able to win over sympathetic workers with promises of wage increases and appeal to public opinion for law and order. However, de Gaulle's aura of invincibility had been damaged by the events and he resigned in 1969, soon after the end of the student revolts.

DBQ COMMENTARY AND RESPONSES

Being on an abstract topic, this is a more challenging DBQ exercise. To earn the core point for the thesis, you must explicitly address both parts of the question, preferably in your introduction. Make sure you analyze the effects AND explain change over time. As for groupings, there are several possibilities—by types of authors (e.g., religious figures, biologists, social scientists), by chronology, by position (enthusiasm, reconciliation with religion, opposition). This does not exhaust the possibilities, but your groups must be logically coherent and responsive to the question. Make sure you provide at least THREE groups.

For point of view, all of the documents offer possibilities. Here are a few examples:

Document 1: Samuel Wilberforce, English bishop and writer, *On Darwin's* Origin of Species, 1860—As a leading religious figure, Wilberforce may feel threatened by Darwin's implicit challenge to the biblical account of creation in Genesis.

Document 2: "Monkeyana," *Punch,* British magazine dealing with humor and social commentary, May 1861—Visual sources can be analyzed for their purpose. Considering that this magazine uses humor for social commentary, they may have viewed Darwin's idea that humans descended from lower animals as a fitting subject of satire.

Document 3: Clémence Royer, French translator of Darwin, anthropologist, and feminist, *Preface to Origin of the Species, 1866*—This female author studies anthropology, is writing a preface to Darwin's book, and supports feminism. She may be biased by her occupation, her task of translating Darwin, or by her gender, in that she wishes to challenge the status quo.

Document 5: Charles Darwin, biologist and developer of doctrine of natural selection in evolution, *Autobiography, 1876*—Obviously Darwin will be biased toward his own theory; moreover, since this explanation of his religious beliefs appears in an autobiography, he may be engaging in some self-justification for his actions and ideas.

Document 8: Isabella Sidgwick, British journalist and writer, account of a debate held in 1860 at Oxford University between Samuel Wilberforce and Thomas H. Huxley on Darwinian theory, "A Grandmother's Tales," *Macmillan's Magazine, 1898*—Whenever you encounter a document written after the events described, you may want to consider the faulty nature of memory. This author may be idealizing the events she describes. Also, the title of her article suggests a certain degree of fabrication involved.

Document 10: Friedrich von Bernhardi, German general and writer on military affairs, *The Next War, 1912*—Bernhardi functions as a general and is writing two years before World War I. Perhaps he has been influenced by the arms build-up or spreading nationalism to advocate war as a healthy competition among races.

Document 11: Pierre Teilhard de Chardin, Catholic priest of the Jesuit order, paleontologist, and philosopher, review article in a periodical, 1921—As both a member of the clergy and a scientist, de Chardin may feel it necessary to reconcile his two occupations and suggest that science and religion need not inevitably conflict.

As you read through the documents, make sure you are capturing the full intent and meaning of the authors. Documents 6 and 11 provide more subtle views. They seem to accept Darwin's theory of biological change but wish to add additional perspectives—for Huxley in Document 6, that natural selection should NOT be applied to human affairs or ethics and for de Chardin in Document 11, that there is only one truth, so any perceived conflicts between religion and science result from misunderstandings or incomplete evidence. A major error can destroy a grouping (if you only include two documents in a group) and more than one major error will cost you the point for that core task.

DBQ Sample 1

The publication of Charles Darwin's *Origin of the Species* in 1859 and *The Descent of Man* in 1871 introduced the concepts of "natural selection" and "survival of the fittest" to explain the development of life on Earth. Darwin's theories created a tremendous controversy in Europe during the period between 1860 and 1921, polarizing people into three groups. The religious community rejected Darwin's concepts as contrary to the Bible's teachings. At the opposite extreme, progressive thinkers accepted the theory of natural selection as a rational, scientific explanation for the origin of mankind. Others applied Darwin's principles to explain social problems and justify racism and warfare. Darwin's theories gradually gained wider acceptance, but not all of his opponents were convinced, especially religious theologians.

The religious community regarded "natural selection" as incompatible with the doctrine of God's creation of man in His image. In 1860, English bishop Samuel Wilberforce preached that man's ability to speak, exercise free will, and reason proved that humans were "created in the image of God" (Doc. 1). In an 1898 debate, he stated that God made all creatures on Earth in their present form and asked his opponent to trace "his descent from a monkey" (Doc. 8). As a high-ranking representative of the church, it was not surprising that Bishop Wilberforce's comments supported creation and rejected Darwin's theories. Darwin's views also became the object of negative social commentary. The British magazine Punch in May 1861 depicted a gorilla with a sign, "Am I a man and a brother?" (Doc. 2). The provocative nature of this cartoon clearly reflected a disapproval of Darwin's ideas, and it was also a clever way of attracting readers to buy the magazine. As time passed, the hope that science could somehow be reconciled with church dogma was expressed by Catholic priest Pierre Teilhard who stated, "Faith needs the whole truth" (Doc. 11).

Progressive thinkers, primarily in the scientific community, adopted Darwin's theory of evolution over religious doctrine. In 1866, Clemence Royer argued that people had to choose between Darwin's "rational revelation of progress" and the "irrational revelation of Man's fall" (Doc. 3). As an anthropologist who wrote the preface to Darwin's 1866 book, she obviously shared his viewpoint, and she tried to influence readers by portraying Darwinism as rational and religion as irrational. In his *Autobiography*, Darwin admitted that he became an agnostic because he was convinced that "everything in nature is the result of fixed laws" and not intentional design by God (Doc. 5). Some of Darwin's followers took his theories one step further and applied them to issues involving society and government.

Darwin's scientific principles of evolution were used to justify social oppression, racial prejudice, and even war. In 1872, British journalist Walter Bagehot applied Darwin's views to the history of man, stating that "nations which are strongest tend to prevail" (Doc. 4). British philosopher Herbert Spencer wrote in 1896 that the weak must die so that the race could be propagated by the fittest (Doc. 7). However, Spencer was a sociologist and therefore emphasized the benefit to humanity over individual considerations. Eugenicist Karl Pearson stated that the highest level of civilization was produced by "survival of the physically and mentally fitter race" (Doc. 9). Since eugenics classifies racial characteristics, it's obvious that Pearson would incorporate Darwin's "survival of the fittest" into eugenics to justify racism. In 1912 on the eve of World War I, German general Friedrich von Bernhardi wrote, "War is a biological necessity" which enables the race and civilization to advance (Doc. 10). As a military leader, he used the theory of racial struggle to justify his goal of promoting war.

Darwin's theory of evolution was a revolutionary, controversial concept. It met with opposition by organized religion, was generally accepted by the scientific community, and became a tool for furthering racism and political gain. Regardless of the reason, it profoundly influenced European thinking in the period between 1860 and 1921. Darwin's work became better understood and more widely accepted with time, and it continues to be a source of debate today.

This essay addresses both parts of the question clearly and directly from the outset. It is well organized and analytical. The student seems to understand the documents and uses them effectively to support the thesis. Several examples of point of view are provided, though it would be helpful to explain them more fully. In addition, the student includes some references to outside information and skillfully integrates the documents into the essay. Though one might imagine a stronger response, this essay fully addresses the core tasks and earns 3 points in the expanded core for the strong thesis, use of documents, and additional point of view. Score: 9.

DBQ Sample 2

Darwin's ideas certainly made a splash when he introduced his theory of natural selection in the late nineteenth century. Many religious figures denounced the notion of evolution, as they believed it conflicted with biblical interpretations of how humans were created by God. Other intellectuals welcomed Darwin's ideas and quickly made use of them to justify their theories regarding race, society, and war. Some thinkers tried to reconcile the ideas of Darwin and traditional ideas of religion and ethics.

At first, religious figures and traditionalists denounced Darwin. Bishop Wilberforce of England denounced Darwin's ideas for undermining the special status of human beings. Darwin's ideas probably came as a shock to leaders of Christian churches, who may have felt that the religious beliefs of their flock would be threatened by natural selection (Doc. 1). The *Punch* cartoon pokes fun at the idea that humans could be descended from apes. Since this is a satirical magazine, they probably simply think of the issue as something to sell more copies of their publication (Doc. 2). Again we see Wilberforce debating a supporter of Darwin, Huxley, about the ideas of natural selection. The woman recounting the story seems to enjoy how Huxley made Wilberforce look like a fool, but her story might be changed because it wasn't written down until almost 40 years later (Doc. 8). Finally, a Catholic priest even says that Darwin could fit with religion, quite a change from the times of Galileo, when the church punished the heliocentric theory. Perhaps they didn't want to earn more criticism for going against Darwin (Doc. 11).

Many people thought Darwin's ideas opened up new frontiers of knowledge. Royer, apparently a female anthropologist, argues that one must choose between Darwin's way and the religious way. She says that she stands for progress, but we might expect this because she is translating Darwin and is involved in biological social sciences (Doc. 3). Documents 4 and 7, by Bagehot and Spencer, both support Social Darwinist ideas. The authors believe that competition among nations or classes is natural and helps society sort out the strong from the weak. Clearly Darwin's ideas appealed to many in these intellectual professions. Of course, Darwin himself supports his own ideas (Doc. 5), but he even explains how his investigations helped him lose his faith in God. More importantly, he seems not to find that he doesn't believe in God anymore. Some people even wanted to take Darwin's ideas to support racism and war. Document 9 by Karl Pearson shows this new study of eugenics, to improve humans by selecting racial characteristics, almost like the Nazis later. Perhaps Pearson simply wants to prove his new field true and thus exaggerates his points. Bernhardi even writes that war will be a good thing for making nations stronger and better; this is right on the eve of World War I, so maybe he is reflecting the tension of that time (Doc. 10).

Darwin's ideas of natural selection challenged people's view of the human race as unique and being a product of a special creation. The issue is still going on today with the debate over intelligent design. Many people took sides on the issue, some even tried to fit religion and science together. This may be a hard fit, but it should be tried.

This is a well-written essay that uses the documents effectively. Also, the student offers ample point-of-view analysis with strong insight into the documents. Unfortunately, the essay does not address change over time explicitly. Though the introduction hints at change, the student does not develop this part of his thesis throughout the essay. Also, as is clear from the body paragraphs, there are only two groups offered in the response, though the student referred to three groups in the introduction. As you write your response, make sure you refer back to the question and your outline to ensure you are meeting all the core tasks. The student loses the two core points for groups and a thesis that addresses both parts of the question. Score: 4.

FRQ COMMENTARY AND RESPONSES

Part B—Question 2

In this highly prescriptive question, you are asked to provide two reasons and two consequences. This charge should suggest a clear organization. Keep in mind that the prompt asks for Western Europe only and is limited to the period between 1945 and 1970. The latter year is approximately when the oil shock caused stagnation in the Western European economies. If you find yourself unable to identify two specific causes and consequences, you may be better off choosing a different question.

> After World War II, most of Europe was destroyed. It didn't look like it would ever recover. However, with some strong American aid and policies of unity, Western Europe achieved a remarkable turnaround; some even called it a "miracle." This new prosperity had two major social consequences—it helped the population increase and created a generation gap between young people and their parents.

> The United States decided to give up its isolation policies and commit to being involved in Europe. This was mostly due to the Cold War with the Soviet Union. Since President Truman was afraid of the spread of communism, he had his Secretary of State, George Marshall, come up with a plan to aid the nations of Western Europe. Overall, the U.S. gave billions of dollars to these nations. Also, Western European leaders moved toward unity. They created the ECSC and EEC, two organizations that pooled resources and promoted free trade and common policies. By the mid 1950s, Western Europe had gunned way ahead of Eastern Europe and was almost in full employment mode.

> Many people in Europe had never experienced wealth. During the bad times of the 1930s and 1940s, people simply decided not to have children because they had no money. Now they had plenty of money and started having children again. This is called the Baby Boom and it created a generation that defined the whole postwar era. Baby Boomers grew up with lots of stuff and could even go to college. Most of their parents thought they should consider themselves lucky, but they actually were rather spoiled. They did not appreciate their college educations, instead criticizing the materialism of society and the rigidity of conservative morals. Student revolts broke out and many youth experimented with "sex, drugs, and rock and roll." This was all because of the great wealth in Western Europe.

> Western Europe recovered nicely from WWII with U.S. aid and unity policies. This resulted in higher population and a generation gap between youth and parents. This just goes to show that with every good thing comes a new complication.

This essay is focused and concise. From the outset, the student establishes that she is in control of the question. Two clear causes and consequences of the economic recovery are discussed. Though the examples are spare, they are sufficient and effectively applied to the thesis. In addition, the student connects the causes and results, a sign of higher-level thinking. In all, this is a nice model of focused AP writing, though it would benefit from several additional examples and further analysis. Score: 8.

Part B—Question 3

Here we have a classic question dealing with the Industrial Revolution. Most textbooks offer a fairly extended discussion of the social effects of early industrialization. Many students who choose a question like this on the AP Exam neglect to include specific examples, instead relying on overly broad generalizations and stereotypes. Keep in mind the chronological parameters and tasks of the question as you read the sample that follows.

> The Industrial Revolution created serious negative effects on British society. Factories created negative working conditions and the growth of cities fomented urban disorder. Many reformers noted these problems; little was done about this before 1830. Family life took a turn for the worse and the class system underwent some serious changes.
>
> Traditional families tended to work together. If they lived on farms, the man would do the heavy plowing and the woman and children would do other chores around the homestead. For urban people, they often worked together doing the family craft, like making shoes or cloth. All of this changed with the factory system. Children now worked in horrible conditions, often getting maimed by moving machinery. Also, factory owners believed that women made good employees because they could be paid lower wages and were more docile. Families that used to work as a unit now rarely saw one another. Gradually reforms were introduced by Parliament to help with the situation, but this took some time.
>
> Traditionally, the nobles dominated most societies, but the Industrial Revolution was a boon for the middle class. Middle-class entrepreneurs owned the factories and made big profits. This allowed them to grow in power and challenge the position of the aristocracy in Britain. Another new class was also born, but not really for the better—the unskilled laborer. Before 1800 most manufacturing was done by guildsmen in cities. Now these skilled workers were turned into drones tied to industrial machines. So some gained because of the factory system and some lost.
>
> Industrialization soon spread to the continent and then these nations experienced many of the same problems as Great Britain.

The student responds directly to the prompts in the question. Other than some exaggeration in addressing the nature of involvement of the nobility and middle class in the Industrial Revolution, the essay provides generally accurate interpretations of the results of industrialization. The main problem with this essay is the lack of specifics. Perhaps the student might have mentioned the Factory Act of 1833 or other protective legislation passed by Parliament. For the paragraph on classes, some reference to the background of one or two early entrepreneurs may have helped him flesh out his thesis. There is certainly enough here for this essay to edge into the stronger category, but the absence of specifics limits it. Score: 6.

Part C—Question 4

Though this question addresses two mainstream topics of the course, it may present some difficulties for students in making the connection. You might begin by establishing what was common to both—a return to original texts, individualism, criticism of the Catholic Church, the role of the printing press. For the "to what extent" part of the prompt, try to avoid overly vague terms, such as "to a great extent." Aim for an interpretation. Also, simply because the question is broad needn't mean that your response be devoid of specific examples.

> The Renaissance and the Reformation were two huge events to begin the modern era in Europe. In the Renaissance, people began looking at philosophy and painting more explicitly. Also, many intellectuals revived many writings of the Greeks and Romans, like Cicero and neo-Platonism. During this period, the printing press was invented, which helped spread the Renaissance around Europe. This spread of the Renaissance helped promote the Reformation. People began to read the classics and think how the church could be better. Also, the printing press spread the ideas of the Reformation. Just think of Luther. Without the printing press, his ideas might have ended up like those of Jan Hus, who was burned at the stake earlier. One major difference between the Renaissance and the Reformation was what kinds of books they liked to read. Italian Renaissance thinkers looked at Greek and Roman ideas, even glorifying the secular ideas within them. They wanted their rewards in this world, and the ancients were going to tell them how to do that. This was not the case with the Reformation. Writers like Erasmus, a Christian humanist but not a Protestant, looked more at the Bible and early Christian leaders for their inspiration. So when you look at the situation overall, the Renaissance helped lay the foundations for the Reformation by getting people to look more at original sources and think about how things were better in ancient times—both with Greeks and Romans, as well as Church figures.

This is a deceptive essay. We may at first be inclined to score it low because of its lack of organization or an up-front thesis (the thesis seems to be the last sentence). However, within the somewhat rambling single paragraph, the student does address the terms of the question and offer a number of specific examples—Cicero, neo-Platonism, Luther, printing press, Erasmus, the Bible, etc. Clearly this essay would benefit significantly from a more systematic approach and organization. Perhaps the student was rushed for time and simply got down on paper all that was relevant to the question. This is certainly not a recommended strategy but it may be the most profitable if you find that you have only 5 to 10 minutes to write. Score: 4.

Part C—Question 5

No surprise here—a Russia question on the AP Exam. Chances are, your textbook provided fairly comprehensive treatment of Peter and Catherine, but you are not likely to remember much in between their reigns. If so, you can still answer this question effectively by dealing with several features of Russia's geography or social environment. This is an ideal essay to employ the framework mentioned previously regarding rulers and reform: Challenge → Response → Result.

> Russia occupies a unique position in Europe; for one thing, it's not even all in Europe. For centuries, Russia was hardly known to the rest of Europe undergoing the Renaissance, Reformation, and Scientific Revolution. Russia seemed more tied to Asia and lacked the technology and military might to make a name for itself. One other problem is that Russia was so big and difficult to govern—it really seemed to need a dictator. Much of this changed

with the reigns of two very important rulers: Peter and Catherine, both called "great" for reasons you will see.

Peter inherited a pretty backward country, but he was determined to lift it into greatness. Peter imposed western customs on his nation—women could leave their homes, no more beards for nobles, short coats, but most importantly, new technology. Peter traveled west and brought back with him knowledge on how to make navies, industry, and armies. When he returned, he imposed these new things on his country through the sheer force of his will. Peter also introduced a merit system into Russia and also divided it up for ease of governance. His goal in all this was to make Russia a major military and naval power, and he succeeded. Peter eventually defeated Sweden in the Great Northern War. Because of this victory, Russia became the major nation in the Baltic and Peter built a new capital city there—St. Petersburg named after him but also nicknamed the "Venice of the North."

Catherine had to deal with the fact that she was a woman, a foreigner, and the nobles had revived in power between the end of Peter's reign and the beginning of hers. Given these obstacles, she did an amazing job. First, Catherine was really into the Enlightenment and invited people like Voltaire and Diderot to her court. Both of them were fascinated with her great abilities and charm. Catherine started many projects, like primary education for girls and writing a constitution, but many of these did not get off the ground. Why? Well, Catherine had to deal with strong nobles, whom she granted a charter from state service, and also peasant revolts, like Pugachev. Despite all these obstacles, Catherine gained more territory than any Russian ruler in its history, not bad for someone with all those obstacles.

By 1800, Russia was now a major power in Europe and greatly feared. This was best shown when Russia partitioned Poland away and when Napoleon got his hat handed to him for invading Russia. People didn't make jokes about Russia anymore after 1800; Peter and Catherine made sure that Russia was now a power to be feared and involved in most of the wars of the eighteenth century. Quite an advancement . . .

This response effectively addresses the terms of the question. Throughout, it is clear that the student is in control of the essay. The introduction lays out the context of Russian politics. Both Peter and Catherine receive specific treatment, as the student effectively reviews their respective accomplishments. The response addresses the second part of the question less directly but each paragraph offers at least a sentence of analysis, and the conclusion recaps the overall results of the two rulers' policies. Several informalities do not detract from the essay, and they are more than balanced by the interesting details the student offers in support of her analysis. Score: 9.

Part C—Question 6

Here we have a classic diplomatic question that requires some specific knowledge of the Thirty Years' War. Be careful of lapsing into a narrative mode on the course of the war—your task is to *analyze* both causes and consequences. Since the chronological period for consequences is not specified, you may venture beyond 1648 in your assessment.

If you want to see violence before the two world wars, you need go no further than the Thirty Years' War of the seventeenth century. This brutal war started about religion but then became a political and territorial battle between France and Sweden over German territory.

The Thirty Years' War was caused by the Protestant Reformation. After Luther posted his 95 Theses, Europe soon became divided between Catholics and Protestants. This was especially true of Germany. Emperor Charles V tried to bring the Lutherans back into the fold of the Catholic Church, but he was always distracted by the conflict with France or the Ottoman Empire. So the Protestants survived and the empire was divided. France and Sweden joined the conflict to gain political power and territory. Cardinal Richelieu was even a cardinal of the Catholic Church but he wanted to stop the power of the Holy Roman Emperor. Sweden under Gustav Vasa, on the other hand, supported Charles to stop France from gaining too much power. Thus we have the two causes of the war—religion and politics.

Now we turn to consequences. The war destroyed much of Germany—the population went down, the countryside was plundered, and peasants were persecuted. Because of the fighting, Germany remained divided for the next 300 years, until Bismarck united her in 1870. Another major result was the very important Peace of Westphalia of 1648. By this treaty, each nation was able to focus on their own religion without interference from the outside. Also, this became the last of the religious wars. Nations turned to fighting over territory and colonies.

As you can tell, the Thirty Years' War defined an era in European religion and politics. Charles V was unable to keep the Holy Roman Empire "holy, Roman, and an empire." Instead, Germany became divided over religion. Also, this war changed Europe's power structure, as France gained and the Holy Roman Empire lost. Without this war, European politics was still about religion rather than politics, pure and simple.

This stands out as a mixed response. First, the student begins with a brief but effective introduction, laying out a fairly clear thesis, at least as it relates to causes. Then the student launches into an overview of the causes of the war, a discussion that becomes confused in its handling of the chronology and issues. The essay seems unable to get a handle on the sequence of events (e.g., Charles V ruled well before the war, 1519–1555) or the key actors involved (Gustavus Adolphus should replace Gustav Vasa). France and Sweden, it should be noted, fought on the same side against Spain and the emperor. With the second body paragraph, the student analyzes the results more effectively. Though the discussion seems brief, he does touch on the effects on Germany, the end of religious wars, and later in the conclusion, on the balance of power. With a clearer sense of the historical context and chronology, this essay would easily have slid into the stronger category. Score: 5.

Part C—Question 7
Many who take AP European History may be seniors who have already taken U.S. history. When approaching European history questions, please make sure that your responses are relevant to that course. Avoid the impulse to turn a question into a perhaps more familiar U.S. history question. The example that follows is a fair warning of the dangers of this approach.

When the American stock market crashed in 1929, the whole economy fell apart. People's savings dried up, banks failed, and no one could find work. President Roosevelt stepped in and promoted his New Deal to get the economy going again. Many nations were unsure how to deal with all of the problems created by the Great Depression, and so the responses were not very effective.

The United States dealt with the Depression pretty effectively. Though Hoover did very little to help people, Roosevelt was able to give the homeless aid or put people to work building bridges and trails. His ideas began to influence other nations, who saw that government policies might be able to help people. For example, there was an economist named Keynes who said that the economy would be better off if people just spent their money instead of saving it, like most people usually did when there was a recession. Roosevelt promoted Keynes ideas and had people spend their money.

This brings us to Great Britain. Britain had plenty of trouble with the depression—unemployment, strikes, and problems with trade. They were never able to solve these problems, despite some efforts to deal with them. Both the Labour and Conservative parties tried their hands at different policies, like tariffs, but could not seem to get the economy going. As Britain got closer to World War II, it became clearer that the economy was not ready for war. Perhaps this is a reason why Chamberlain decided to appease Hitler.

Many people who lived through the Great Depression were changed by it forever. My grandmother still talks about how when she was a girl, she was happy just to get an orange for Christmas. Can you imagine, an orange!? Nations did the best they could. Some like the United States were pretty successful with the New Deal. Britain, on the other hand, fumbled around and was not able to do much. Ironically, it seemed like the only thing that could help was war. Not until World War II did most nations get their economies going again.

Not only does this essay approach the topic in simplistic fashion, much of the discussion is off-base. The prompt clearly asks for two *European* nations—the United States does not qualify. During the course, there will be occasions—the Cold War, for example—where you will need to address American developments or policies to handle a question. In this question, the student obviously displays a weak grasp of British responses; its treatment of American responses is not much better. Finally, you are advised to avoid the kind of personal references this student included in the concluding paragraph. Nonetheless, this essay does provide several relevant examples and insights, so it is not a total loss. Score: 2.

PRACTICE TEST 2

You are allowed 3 hours and 5 minutes for this examination—55 minutes for Section I, consisting of 80 multiple-choice questions, and 2 hours and 10 minutes for Section II, consisting of one Document-Based Question (DBQ) and two Free-Response Questions (FRQs). The first fifteen minutes of Section II consist of a mandatory 15-minute reading period during which you may not write any scorable responses, though you may plan out your responses to the essays. Each section of the exam is worth 50% of your overall score.

For the multiple-choice questions, a one-quarter point penalty will be assessed for those responses marked incorrectly. Random guessing is unlikely to improve your score, but if you can eliminate even one or two of the choices for a given question, it may be to your advantage to answer it.

Try to keep aware of the time limits and move along as quickly as you can without losing accuracy. If you encounter a difficult question, move on and come back to it if you have time.

EUROPEAN HISTORY
SECTION I
(Time—55 minutes)
80 questions
Percent of total grade—50

Directions: Each of the following questions or incomplete statements is followed by five suggested answers or completions. Select the one that is best in each case and then fill in the corresponding oval on the answer sheet.

1. In *The Prince* (1513), Machiavelli promoted a secular conception of politics for the ultimate purpose of:
   a. attacking the moral authority of the Catholic Church.
   b. presenting human nature as corrupt and self-interested.
   c. liberating the Italian peninsula from foreign rule.
   d. undermining the power of the Medici family in Florence.
   e. establishing himself as dictatorial ruler of Milan.

2. The passage below by Martin Luther was written to condemn:
   a. the papacy's rejection of Luther's reform message.
   b. German peasants' use of new religious ideas to support revolt.
   c. John Calvin's creation of a rival denomination in Geneva.
   d. Charles V's edict declaring Luther an outlaw in the empire.
   e. priestly influence within the Catholic sacramental system.

   "It is right and lawful to slay at the first opportunity a rebellious person. These rebels cloak their frightful sins with the gospel, calling themselves Christian brethren, swear allegiance, and compel people to join them in such abominations. Thereby they become the greatest blasphemers of God's holy name, and serve and honor the devil under the semblance of the gospel, so that they have ten times deserved death of body and soul."

3. Which of the following state activities of the sixteenth-century New Monarchs absorbed the majority of national resources?
   a. bribing nobles and clergy to gain support
   b. sponsoring overseas voyages of exploration
   c. public works programs for unemployed peasants
   d. developing weapons and waging warfare
   e. constructing palaces and cultural attractions

4. Which of the following characterizes the early modern (1500–1700) approach to the issue of poverty?
   a. Only the "deserving poor," such as the elderly and disabled, received aid.
   b. Protestant nations set up religious groups to coordinate poor relief.
   c. Because poverty was rare in this period, private charities proved adequate.
   d. Poverty was considered a disease and treated humanely in mental institutions.
   e. Steady economic growth generally eliminated the issue of poverty in this period.

5. Frederick William, the Great Elector (1640–1688) helped raise Brandenburg-Prussia to great-power status primarily by:
    a. developing Europe's strongest industrial sector.
    b. creating Prussia's first standing army.
    c. signing a mutual defense treaty with Russia.
    d. patronizing famous scientists at his court.
    e. conquering the strategic province of Bavaria.

6. This quote highlights a principle essential to which of the following works?
    a. Thomas Hobbes's *Leviathan*
    b. Isaac Newton's *Principia*
    c. Blaise Pascal's *Pensées*
    d. Rousseau's *Social Contract*
    e. Diderot's *Encyclopedia*

    "The passage from the state of nature to the civil state produces a very remarkable change in man, by substituting justice for instinct in his conduct, and giving his actions the morality they had formerly lacked. Then only, when the voice of duty takes the place of physical impulses and appetite, does man, who before had considered only himself, finds that he is forced to consult his reasoning before listening to his inclinations."

7. Which of the following represents a major impact of Napoleon Bonaparte's conquests during the Napoleonic Wars (1799–1815)?
    a. The Continental System succeeded in bringing Britain's trade to a halt.
    b. Feudalism was reinstated in an effort to win over the aristocratic classes.
    c. A campaign of de-Christianization was imposed on Catholic nations.
    d. Civil liberties, including freedom of the press and speech, were widely extended.
    e. Nationalist sentiment, particularly in the German states, gained influence.

8. Which of the following accounts for the predominance of religious dissenters among the early inventors and entrepreneurs of the First Industrial Revolution in the late eighteenth and early nineteenth centuries in Great Britain?
    a. Religious dissenters held greater personal wealth and could draw on more capital.
    b. Persecution drove dissenters out of Britain, and they set up industries on the continent.
    c. The leadership of the state Anglican Church discouraged involvement in industry.
    d. Because state and academic positions were denied them, dissenters pursued business.
    e. Evangelical religious ideology stressed the use of science in interpreting Scripture.

9. The nineteenth-century cartoon on the following page, titled "Beating Rubber and Beating Time to the Tune of an Old Love Song," of workers in the African Congo was produced to:
    a. show that European rule of the Congo was naturally accepted by Africans there.
    b. encourage Europeans to enjoy the economic benefits of colonial settlement.
    c. celebrate African tribal rituals involving communal labor and cooperation.
    d. demonstrate the potential for international conflict produced by imperialism.
    e. condemn the excesses of European rule, such as the exploitation of labor.

© *Mary Evans Picture Library/The Image Works*

10. The women shown in the 1913 photograph below were protesting:
    a. against poor working conditions.
    b. for access to birth control.
    c. to demand the vote.
    d. British imperial policies.
    e. in favor of Irish home rule.

(Getty Images)

11. A major purpose of the German Schlieffen Plan during World War I was to:
    a. provide for an adequate supply of armaments for German soldiers.
    b. mediate the dispute between Austria and Russia in the Balkans.
    c. allow passage of Belgium troops through Germany to assist in defense.
    d. provide for Germany's economic domination of much of eastern Europe.
    e. defeat France quickly before turning to face Russia on the Eastern Front.

12. All of the following became important new technologies in interwar Europe (1919–1939) EXCEPT:
    a. nuclear power.
    b. kitchen appliances.
    c. motion pictures.
    d. radio.
    e. airplanes.

13. Which of the following resulted from the extension of American aid to Western European nations through the Marshall Plan?
    a. The Soviet Union successfully blockaded West Berlin to prevent the plan.
    b. Increased economic and political coordination occurred in Western Europe.
    c. America's economy was thrown into recession, bringing an end to the aid.
    d. Because Britain was favored, its economy came to dominate Western Europe.
    e. Despite the aid, Western Europe required decades to recover from World War II.

14. Which of the following describes a major social change in Europe after World War II?
    a. The number of workers in scientific fields decreased.
    b. The standard of living remained at wartime levels.
    c. Birth rates increased, as states encouraged population growth.
    d. Extended families became common, to pool scarce resources.
    e. Life expectancy decreased for the next several decades.

15. Most Italian city-states during the fifteenth and sixteenth centuries tended to be dominated by:
    a. political factions funded by the Holy Roman Emperor.
    b. old-line nobles tracing lineage back to medieval knights.
    c. common laborers, who controlled the production of cloth.
    d. middle-class men of professions, such as attorneys and physicians.
    e. a blend of wealthy merchants and aristocrats, who often intermarried.

16. Which best explains how the small nation of Portugal, population approximately 1 million, was able to create an overseas maritime empire in the fifteenth and early sixteenth centuries?
    a. ability to exploit its wide variety of natural resources, such as coal and iron ore
    b. use of military and navigational technologies to control key points in the Indian Ocean
    c. strategic alliances with Spain to control much of Asia and the Americas
    d. convincing indigenous rulers that Portuguese rule would bring wealth and stability
    e. exploiting the power of the Catholic Church to assist in subduing indigenous culture

17. Which of the following important dynastic families led the ultra-Catholic faction and accepted Spanish aid during the French religious wars (1562–1598)?
    a. Guise
    b. Valois
    c. Bourbon
    d. Montmorency
    e. Burgundy

18. Peter the Great's (1689–1725) primary goal with his reforms was to:
    a. liberate the serfs from oppressive regulations.
    b. allow women to contribute to Russian society.
    c. make Russia a modern military and naval power.
    d. demonstrate his commitment to the Enlightenment.
    e. secure his control of the palace guard and boyars.

19. Which of the following best describes the nature of the Commercial Revolution of the seventeenth and eighteenth centuries?
    a. the expansion of laissez-faire economic principles
    b. adoption of scientific agricultural techniques to boost production
    c. an expansion of trade involving new goods and techniques
    d. development of trading alliances among western European powers
    e. the expansion of Asian and African trading empires

20. Who is the author of the passage below?
    a. Pope Urban VIII
    b. Ignatius Loyola
    c. Martin Luther
    d. Galileo Galilei
    e. Baruch Spinoza

"In discussions of physical problems we ought to begin not from the authority of scriptural passages, but from sense-experiences and necessary demonstrations; for the holy Bible and the phenomena of nature proceed alike from the divine Word. I do not feel obliged to believe that the same God who has endowed us with senses, reason, and intellect has intended us to forgo their use . . ."

21. All of the following represent features of popular culture in eighteenth-century Europe EXCEPT:
    a. oral culture, as in the recounting of folk tales.
    b. reading material such as almanacs and chapbooks.
    c. taverns for the drinking of gin, beer, and whiskey.
    d. blood sports, such as bear-baiting and cock-fighting.
    e. a Grand Tour of European nations and cities.

22. Which of the following acted as a major intellectual cause of the French Revolution?
    a. the revival of classical art and architecture
    b. Enlightenment ideals of natural law and equality
    c. Descartes' dualism of mind and matter
    d. Hobbes's theories of human nature
    e. John Wesley's Methodist revival in religion

23. The efforts of Edwin Chadwick in the nineteenth century in Great Britain led to:
    a. women gaining equal property rights.
    b. workers gaining the right to vote.
    c. colonies being established in Africa.
    d. sanitary reforms in British cities.
    e. inspection of factory conditions.

24. Which of the following describes a territorial settlement made at the Congress of Vienna (1814–1815) as illustrated by the map below?
    a. Stronger states were created around France to check its expansion.
    b. Italy was unified in a republican confederation led by the papacy.
    c. Russia recognized a newly independent state under Polish control.
    d. The Ottoman Empire made significant territorial gains in the Balkans.
    e. Austria surrendered its leadership of the German states to Prussia.

25. The works of Sigmund Freud and Friedrich Nietzsche in the late nineteenth century stressed the importance of:
    a. laissez-faire economics.
    b. irrational impulses.
    c. religious revelation.
    d. Liberal democracy.
    e. imperial pursuits.

26. Which of the following describes the results of the Revolution of 1905 in Russia?
    a. Land was redistributed to peasants equally.
    b. The Romanov Dynasty came to an end.
    c. The Mensheviks established a socialist republic.
    d. Tsar Nicholas II agreed to create a legislative body.
    e. Traditionalists succeeded in crushing the revolt.

27. In 1916, the German High Command launched a major offensive directed against which strategically located city, prompting the longest battle of World War I?
    a. Somme
    b. Ypres
    c. Paris
    d. Brussels
    e. Verdun

28. Which of the following characterizes the Brezhnev era (1964–1982) in the Soviet Union?
    a. reaching nuclear parity with the United States
    b. allowing greater autonomy to Eastern Europe
    c. exceeding production goals in consumer goods
    d. success in launching the *Sputnik* satellite
    e. a period of ambitious domestic reform

29. Which of the following statements can be concluded from the accompanying population chart?
    a. Europe's percentage of world population decreased over time.
    b. The population of the Americas exceeded Europe's throughout the period.
    c. World population roughly doubled between 1930 and 2000.
    d. Latin America's population increased because of a rising birth rate.
    e. Only in 1950 did the rest of the world combined exceed Asia in population.

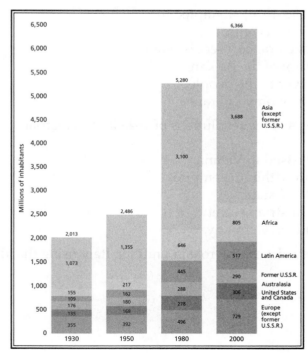

30. A major function of guilds in early modern European cities (1500–1700) was to:
    a. provide welfare benefits for unemployed tradesmen and their families.
    b. promote equality of status among its members, including women.
    c. regulate the supply of workers and quality of goods in a given craft.
    d. encourage economic specialization and mass production of goods.
    e. monitor the political activities of suspected rebels against the state.

31. Which of the following resulted from the War of Spanish Succession (1702–1713)?
    a. The Bourbon dynasties ruled Spain and France, but were not allowed to combine.
    b. Sweden emerged as the dominant power in Northern Europe.
    c. Prussia and Austria merged to create a dominant German state.
    d. Louis XIV realized his goal of expanding to France's "natural frontier."
    e. The commercial dominance of the Netherlands was confirmed.

32. All of the following ideas are associated with the work of John Locke (1632–1704) EXCEPT:
    a. socialism.
    b. education reform.
    c. state of nature.
    d. right of revolution.
    e. empiricism.

33. One could best describe Louis XVI's (1774–1793) attitude toward the French Revolution as:
    a. public acceptance, private opposition
    b. enthusiastic and material support
    c. outright condemnation of revolutionary acts
    d. skillful compromise in preserving royal absolutism
    e. joining the bourgeoisie against noble privileges

34. As emperor of France, Napoleon III (1852–1870) attempted to:
    a. conquer Italy and bring it under French control.
    b. sever ties with the Vatican and make France a secular state.
    c. compromise with Russia over control of the Balkans.
    d. liberalize France and turn power over to the people.
    e. modernize the infrastructure and economy of France.

35. One of the most important lasting effects of the revolutions of 1848 in the Austrian Empire was the:
    a. creation of a socialist government based in Vienna.
    b. abolition of feudalism and serfdom within the empire.
    c. creation of an autonomous pan-Slavic state.
    d. dominance of the middle class in Austrian society.
    e. establishment of a zone of free trade in Germany.

36. Which of the following individuals played a central role in unifying Italy using the ideas of *Realpolitik*?
    a. Guiseppe Garibaldi
    b. Pope Pius IX
    c. Victor Emmanuel III
    d. Otto von Bismarck
    e. Camillo Benso di Cavour

37. Which of the following accounts for the rise of organized sports in European society in the late nineteenth century?
    a. a return to communal values of rural cooperation
    b. royal decrees emphasizing the need for physical fitness
    c. the building of stadiums as public works projects
    d. competition among European powers and their colonies
    e. an increase in leisure time among the middle and working class

38. This event or development during World War I set the stage for the Nazi Holocaust of World War II.
    a. Battle of Somme
    b. use of poison gas
    c. rationing of food
    d. Armenian massacres
    e. sinking of the *Lusitania*

39. Due to its diplomatic isolation, which of the following nations did not attend the Munich Conference (1938), which addressed the issue of German minorities in Czechoslovakia?
    a. Italy
    b. France
    c. Britain
    d. Soviet Union
    e. Germany

40. Which of the following helped bring about the end of Renaissance culture in the sixteenth century in Italy?
    a. the takeover of Florence by the Dominican monk Savonarola
    b. the sack of Rome by Spanish troops under Charles V
    c. the spread of reformed Christianity hostile to humanism
    d. noble factionalism that led to continuous internal struggles
    e. an economic recession caused by Ottoman piracy

41. The map on page 414 portrays the diplomatic situation at the conclusion of:
    a. the Habsburg-Valois Wars (1494–1559).
    b. the Schmalkaldic Wars (1546–1555).
    c. the Thirty Years' War (1618–1648).
    d. the War of Austrian Succession (1740–1748).
    e. the Seven Years' War (1756–1763).

42. Which of the following expresses a major reason for the decline of Dutch commerce in the seventeenth century?
    a. crop failures that produced continuous famine
    b. doctrinal conflicts within the Calvinist religion
    c. the bankruptcy of the Dutch East India Company
    d. warfare with the more powerful France and Britain
    e. a disastrous alliance with the Holy Roman Emperor

43. The eighteenth-century Agricultural Revolution resulted in:
    a. greater rural equality.
    b. the end of feudal regulations.
    c. the economic rise of Russia.
    d. emigration to the countryside.
    e. an increased European population.

(Question 41)

44. In the early to mid-nineteenth century, utopian socialists emphasized:
    a. social regulation and economic equality.
    b. religious piety and traditional values.
    c. class conflict and violent revolution.
    d. free markets and nationalism.
    e. high tariffs and mass production.

45. The painting on the following page by Jean-Francois Millet, *The Gleaners*, is associated with which nineteenth-century cultural movement?
    a. Neoclassicism
    b. Romanticism
    c. Realism
    d. Impressionism
    e. Darwinism

(Art Resource, NY)

46. With which of the following political movements did women of the late nineteenth and early twentieth centuries play a significant role?
    a. Racial Darwinism
    b. socialism
    c. fascism
    d. futurism
    e. imperialism

47. All of the following represented weaknesses of the Weimar Republic (1918–1933) EXCEPT:
    a. economic problems of inflation and unemployment.
    b. a constitution that allowed authoritarian rule during emergencies.
    c. political violence, including coup attempts and assassinations.
    d. an unpopular alliance with France and the United States.
    e. association with the hated Treaty of Versailles settlement.

48. During World War II, Hitler in 1941 invaded the Soviet Union for which of the following reasons?
    a. Stalin had violated the Nazi-Soviet Non-Aggression Pact.
    b. Hitler wanted to gain domestic support with further conquests.
    c. Hitler had planned all along to gain "living space" in the east.
    d. Hitler intended to outflank a planned American invasion of the Middle East.
    e. Germany needed the Soviet stores of iron ore to continue the war.

49. Which of the following terms is related to the Balkan conflicts following the breakup of Yugoslavia in 1991?
    a. Balkanization
    b. "ethnic cleansing"
    c. Ustashe
    d. "concurrent majorities"
    e. restrained force option

50. A major impact of the development of the printing press in Europe in the fifteenth and sixteenth centuries was:
    a. the spread of ideals of religious reform.
    b. the decline of the Greek and Latin languages.
    c. a decline in artistic prestige due to copying of images.
    d. widespread unemployment in monastic scriptoria.
    e. the rise of an antihumanist movement.

51. The economic system employed by the Spanish to settle and exploit native labor in the sixteenth century in the Americas was known as which of the following?
    a. *requiremento*
    b. *audiencia*
    c. vice royalty
    d. *encomienda*
    e. Bishopric

52. Christian humanism of the sixteenth century can be characterized as which of the following?
    a. a sustained attack on the power of the Catholic Church
    b. an attack on the secularism of the Italian Renaissance
    c. a movement toward an economy based on Christian socialism
    d. an effort to promote personal spirituality through education
    e. a last stand by the papacy to stop the Protestant Reformation

53. The fundamental purpose of the Spanish Inquisition under Ferdinand and Isabella of Spain was to:
    a. reduce the number of Jews and Muslims in Spain.
    b. ensure a strict adherence to Catholic religious orthodoxy.
    c. battle the spread of a growing atheist movement.
    d. complete the *reconquista* of southern Iberia.
    e. win papal support by upholding papal infallibility.

54. The author of this quotation is mostly likely to have been which of the following?
    a. James I of England
    b. John Locke
    c. Frederick II of Prussia
    d. Niccolo Machiavelli
    e. Henry IV of France

    "Kings are not only God's lieutenants upon earth and sit upon God's throne, but even by God himself they are called gods. The head of a natural body has the power of directing all members of the body to that use which the judgment in the head thinks most convenient."

55. Both René Descartes and Francis Bacon articulated theories of the scientific method in the seventeenth century. A major difference between the theories involves:
    a. Bacon's challenging the Scholastic intellectual tradition.
    b. Descartes's continuing belief in supernatural explanations.
    c. Bacon's rejection of systematic observation of nature.
    d. Bacon's adherence to the geocentric theory in astronomy.
    e. Descartes's emphasis on the importance of mathematics.

56. This painting by Jacques Louis David portrays which of the following events during the French Revolution?
    a. publication of the "Declaration of the Rights of Man and Citizen"
    b. the Third Estate's proclamation of the National Assembly
    c. the National Assembly taking the Tennis Court Oath
    d. the abolition of serfdom and feudalism
    e. the vote to execute Louis XVI in the National Convention

(*Giraudon/Art Resource, NY*)

57. The work of the late-eighteenth-century and early-nineteenth-century classical economists—Adam Smith, David Ricardo, Thomas Malthus—emphasized which of the following?
    a. the need for government regulation of the economy
    b. the importance of tariffs to protect domestic industry
    c. economic activity operates according to natural laws
    d. labor unions check the excesses of industrial capitalism
    e. welfare programs are necessary to ensure equality

58. The architectural monument portrayed on the following page was created to celebrate which of the following?
    a. French nationalism
    b. British industry
    c. Italian fascism
    d. Dutch productivity
    e. Spanish Catholicism

Culver Pictures, Inc.

59. Which of the following scientific discoveries did Charles Darwin use in support of his theory of natural selection?
    a. Einstein's ideas regarding relative motion
    b. Lyell's ideas on uniform geological forces
    c. Marx's notions of struggle throughout history
    d. Leibniz's ideas regarding possible worlds
    e. Planck's theory of quantum mechanics

60. As a result of Kaiser Wilhelm II's (r. 1888–1918) diplomacy, which of the following occurred?
    a. The German states were unified under Prussian leadership.
    b. Germany developed a colonial empire exceeding that of the British.
    c. Germany signed a mutual defense treaty with Italy and Great Britain.
    d. Europe experienced peace and international harmony throughout his reign.
    e. France and Russia allied, presenting Germany with a possible two-front war.

61. Which of the following can be concluded from the accompanying map regarding the situation in Europe following the Treaty of Versailles settlement?
    a. The Polish state was recreated, splitting Germany in two.
    b. Russia regained the territory it had lost during World War I.
    c. Great Britain granted independence to most of its colonies.
    d. France annexed the strategic Saar and Ruhr industrial regions.
    e. Austro-Hungary was re-created as a loose confederation of Slavic states.

Europe, 1923

62. The author and context for this quotation is which of the following?
    a. Henry IV during the French religious wars
    b. Oliver Cromwell during the English Civil War
    c. Maximilien Robespierre during the French Revolution
    d. Otto von Bismarck during the German wars of unification
    e. Benito Mussolini during the fascist takeover of Italy

    "If the basis of popular government in time of peace is virtue, the basis of popular government in time of revolution is both virtue and terror: virtue without which terror is murderous, terror without which virtue is powerless. Terror is nothing else than swift, severe, indomitable justice; it flows, then, from virtue."

63. The Catholic Church responded to the Protestant Reformation in all of the following ways EXCEPT:
    a. establishing new religious orders, such as the Jesuits.
    b. reforming abuses, such as the sale of indulgences.
    c. creating the Roman Inquisition in Italy.
    d. reducing the power of the papacy.
    e. convening the Council of Trent.

64. Which of the following groups was most harmed by the Price Revolution of the sixteenth century?
    a. landowners
    b. urban craftsmen
    c. peasants
    d. aristocrats
    e. monarchs

65. This painting portrays which of the following political figures?
    a. Henry VIII of England
    b. Peter I, the Great, of Russia
    c. Gustavus Adolphus of Sweden
    d. Louis XIV of France
    e. Klemens von Metternich of Austria

(Giraudon/Art Resource, NY)

66. Which of the following events is most associated with the rise of Liberalism in nineteenth-century Europe?
    a. the Factory Act of 1833
    b. the abolition of the Corn Laws in 1846
    c. the Carlsbad Decrees of 1819
    d. the Congress of Troppau in 1820
    e. the accession of Nicholas I as tsar of Russia

67. The Second Industrial Revolution supported European imperialism of Africa and Asia by:
    a. promoting the immigration of Europeans to overseas colonies.
    b. providing the technological means for direct control of colonies.
    c. establishing the model of mass production to be used in colonies.
    d. promoting revolutionary agitation for worldwide socialist revolution.
    e. strengthening traditional cultural models of production and exchange.

68. Which of the following describes the Victorian ideal of womanhood in the second half of the nineteenth century?
    a. pursuit of independent careers in the professions
    b. accepting positions of political leadership
    c. being a virtual slave to one's husband
    d. acting as the moral guardians of the home
    e. rejecting child-care duties as reactionary

69. In this statement, V. I. Lenin advances which of the following ideas for the Bolshevik movement in Russia?
    a. Worldwide revolution and an end to World War I are closely connected.
    b. The nations of western Europe will show the way for Russia's revolution.
    c. World War I must be continued to promote the socialist revolution.
    d. The Bolsheviks should work with the Provisional Government to continue the war.
    e. An end to World War I will cause the overthrow of capitalist governments.

    "One of our immediate tasks is to put an end to the war at once. But in order to end the war, which is closely bound up with the present capitalistic system, it is necessary to overthrow capitalism itself. In this work we shall have the aid of the world labor movement, which has already begun to develop in Italy, England, and Germany."

70. This poster portrays Joseph Stalin as a:
    a. ruthless dictator.
    b. wily politician.
    c. visionary leader.
    d. radical agitator.
    e. competent bureaucrat.

71. The fall of communism in 1989–1990 in Eastern Europe was caused primarily by which of the following?
    a. an invasion of the Eastern bloc by members of NATO
    b. widespread unemployment and homelessness
    c. a loss of confidence among communist leaders of those nations
    d. Soviet leader Gorbachev's refusal to maintain communism by force
    e. a negotiated settlement of the Cold War by the United States and the Soviet Union

72. Which of the following is true of Anabaptists in the sixteenth century?
    a. Anabaptists did not establish a majority religion in any European nation.
    b. Other Protestants persecuted Anabaptists for relying exclusively on biblical authority.
    c. The Catholic Church allied with Anabaptist leaders to stop Lutheranism.
    d. Anabaptists generally employed violence to win over converts.
    e. John Calvin established a center of Anabaptism in Geneva, Switzerland.

73. Isaac Newton portrayed the universe as a clock with God as the clockmaker. With which religious movement are these concepts associated?
    a. Methodism
    b. Catholicism
    c. spiritualism
    d. pietism
    e. deism

74. All of the following policies are associated with eighteenth-century enlightened monarchy EXCEPT:
    a. patronage of well-known philosophers and intellectuals
    b. democratic procedures such as elections and constitutions
    c. codification of laws and rationalization of administration
    d. the promotion of scientific research, education, and literacy.
    e. the promotion of agricultural and industrial productivity.

75. Which of the following represents a primary reason for the establishment of municipal police forces and prisons in the nineteenth century?
    a. to investigate and punish militant agitators against the state
    b. concern among the middle class for a more ordered society
    c. state efforts to reimpose absolutist forms of government
    d. to combat a rising tide of violence involving ethnic groups
    e. to compose a reserve army force among police and prisoners

76. Life for European Jews in the nineteenth century changed in which of the following ways?
    a. Religious revival within Judaism undermined Jewish assimilation into wider culture.
    b. Many Jews established revolutionary groups aimed at gaining equal political rights.
    c. Most nations passed legislation eliminating political discrimination against Jews.
    d. The Dreyfus Affair in France led to the end of anti-Semitism in most nations.
    e. Most Jews were unaffected by industrialization and nationalism.

77. Which of the following nations during the Spanish Civil War (1936–1939) provided direct support to the Loyalist forces battling Francisco Franco's nationalists?
    a. Soviet Union
    b. Germany

    c. France
    d. United States
    e. Great Britain

78. This photograph from 1968 portrays which of the following?
    a. riots between neo-Nazis and guest workers in Berlin
    b. clashes between student protestors and police in Paris
    c. unrest related to waves of strikes in London
    d. Soviet troops battling Hungarian revolutionaries
    e. Basque separatists demanding independence from Spain

Sipa Press

79. Which of the following events caused an end to the period of détente between the United States and the Soviet Union during the Cold War?
    a. Cuban Missile Crisis
    b. Soviet invasion of Afghanistan
    c. American policy in Iran
    d. Arab-Israeli War of 1973
    e. Gorbachev's *perestroika* reforms

80. Which of the following resulted from the establishment of the European Coal and Steel Community (ECSC) in 1952?
    a. American economic influence ended in Europe.
    b. Western Europe adopted socialist economic models.
    c. Trade between Eastern and Western Europe expanded.
    d. Member states experienced a rapid increase in production.
    e. National economic borders in Europe ceased to exist.

EUROPEAN HISTORY
SECTION II
Part A
(Suggested writing time—45 minutes)
Percent of Section II score—45

Directions: The prompt that follows is based on Documents 1-12 and will gauge your ability to comprehend and evaluate historical documents. Make sure in your essay that you:

- Provide an explicit thesis directly addressing all parts of the question.
- Discuss specifically a majority of the documents.
- Demonstrate a grasp of the essential meaning of a majority of the documents.
- Support your thesis with accurate interpretations of a majority of the documents.
- Analyze the sources by grouping them clearly and accurately in at least three ways.
- Take into account both the authors' points of view and biases.

You may refer to relevant historical context not addressed in the documents.

1. Analyze the factors that affected the punishment of criminals in Europe and the extent to which views toward criminal punishment changed over the period 1750 to 1900.

Historical Background: Early modern European political institutions (1500–1700) commonly employed corporal and capital punishments, often in public ceremonies. To maintain public order and defend against criminals, municipalities and governments relied on informal forces such as night watches, local constables, or off-duty soldiers. The first penitentiaries for the rehabilitation of criminals were established in the United States in the eighteenth century and spread to Europe soon after. Great Britain established its first police force, the "Bobbies," in 1829, as did other nations in this period. Many states had also abolished corporal punishment by 1800, with Russia being the last major nation to do so in 1863.

Document 1

Source: Voltaire, French writer and philosopher, *Candide,* satirical novel recounting the adventures of young Candide and his mentor, Dr. Pangloss, 1757.

After the earthquake, which had destroyed three-fourths of the city of Lisbon, the sages of that country could think of no better means to preserve the kingdom from utter ruin than to entertain the people with an *auto da fe*,* it having been decided that the burning of a few people alive by a slow fire, and with great ceremony, is an infallible preventive of earthquakes.

Therefore, they seized on a Spaniard for marrying his godmother, and on two Portuguese for refusing to eat bacon; after dinner they came and secured Dr. Pangloss and his pupil Candide, the one for speaking his mind, and the other for seeming to approve what he had said. They were marched in procession and heard a very pathetic sermon, which was followed by an anthem, accompanied by bagpipes. Candide was flogged to some tune, while the anthem was being sung; the Spaniard and the two men who would not eat bacon were burned, and Pangloss was hanged.

That same day there was another earthquake, which made most dreadful havoc.

*An *auto da fe* is a ritual of public penance often associated with the Inquisition.

Document 2

Source: Cesare Beccaria, Italian philosopher, journalist, and legal reformer, *An Essay on Crimes and Punishments,* 1764.

It is better to prevent crimes than to punish them. This is the fundamental principle of good legislation, which is the art of bringing men to the *maximum* of happiness and to the *minimum* of misery.

Would you prevent crimes? Let the laws be clear and simple, let the entire force of the nation be united in their defense, let them be intended rather to favor every individual than any particular classes of men; let the laws be feared, and the laws only. As punishments become crueler, the minds of men grow hardened and insensible. The fear of the laws is salutary, but the fear of men is a fruitful and fatal source of crimes.

Document 3

Source: Account of a public execution on "justice day," anonymous pamphlet, published in Amsterdam, Netherlands, 1773.

Good heavens, what a frightening spectacle! Miserable man, I am indeed overwhelmed by pity for the state you are in. This one having finished his breath, is followed by six others, who have all been condemned to the rope for their wicked acts. How affected was I inside, when I saw them climb the ladder one after the other! I was cold, I trembled at every step they took. I distracted my eyes from the mortal spectacle to the endless number of spectators. I thought that I noticed in some of them the same horror at such a terrible spectacle, the same repugnance which I felt. This raised an inner joy in me; it gave me a positive view of my fellow creatures again.

Document 4

Source: Jeremy Bentham, British philosopher and founder of Utilitarianism, *Panopticon:* or the Inspection House,* plan for penitentiary, 1787, with illustration by N. Horau-Romain, French prison reformer, demonstrating a prisoner kneeling for prayer within the *"all-seeing-eye" prison, 1840.

Document 5

Source: Restif de-la-Bretonne, French author and social observer, *The Nights of Paris,* work of social criticism, 1788.

The man was broken on the wheel, as were his two companions. I could not endure the sight of that execution; I moved away. While the victims suffered, I studied the spectators. They chattered and laughed as if they were watching a farce. But what revolted me most was a very pretty young girl I saw with what appeared to be her lover. She uttered peals of laughter, she jested about the miserable men's expressions and screams. I could not believe it! Without thinking of the consequences, I said to her 'Mademoiselle, you must have the heart of a monster, and to judge by what I see of you today, I believe you capable of any crime. If I had the misfortune to be your lover, I would shun you forever.'

Document 6

Source: Maximilien Robespierre, delegate to the French revolutionary Constituent Assembly, "On the Death Penalty," speech before the assembly, June 22, 1791.

The idea of murder inspires less fear when the law itself gives the example and the spectacle. The horror of crime is diminished when it is punished by another crime. Do not confuse the effectiveness of a penalty with an excess of severity: the one is absolutely opposed to the other.

Free countries are those where the rights of man are respected and where, consequently, the laws are just. Where they offend humanity by an excess of rigor, this is a proof that the dignity of man is not known there. It is a proof that the legislator is nothing but a master who commands slaves and who pitilessly punishes them according to his whim. I thus conclude that the death penalty should be abolished.

Document 7

Source: Antoine Louis, French physician and Secretary of the Academy of Surgery, report to the French revolutionary Legislative Assembly concerning use of the guillotine for the death penalty, 1792.

Experience and reason indicate that the previous method used in decapitating criminals exposes them to capital punishment more frightful than the mere deprivation of life, which is the formal aim of the law.

It would be easy to construct an appropriate machine for the purpose of execution, whose performance would be unfailing. Decapitation would be performed instantly, according to the spirit and aim of the law. It would be easy to test it on corpses and even on live sheep. This apparatus, if found necessary, would cause no feeling and would scarcely be perceived.

Document 8

Source: Walter Venning, British Quaker and prison reformer, plans for a Russian prison system, following a visit to that nation, 1817.

Criminals are usually people controlled by their passions and who do not believe in religion and do not understand their responsibility to God. They must be taught that the all-seeing eye of God is always trained on them, and they are frightened by the righteous anger of God towards them, sinners who violate God's law. At the same time, we must inform them and persuade them that God is always ready to forgive those who come to him in sincere repentance.

Document 9

Source: Gustave de Beaumont, French public official and writer, and Alexis de Tocqueville, French historian and Liberal political philosopher, *On the Penitentiary System in the United States and Its Application in France,* 1833.

Americans believe that absolute separation of criminals can alone protect them from mutual pollution, and they have adopted the principle in all its rigor. The convict is separated from the whole world; and the penitentiaries, full of wrongdoers like himself—all entirely isolated—do not offer to him a society even in prison. If it is true that all evil originates from the interaction of the prisoners, then nowhere is this vice avoided with greater safety than at Philadelphia, where the prisoners find themselves utterly unable to communicate with each other.

However, nowhere was this system of imprisonment crowned with the hoped-for success. In general it was ruinous to the public treasury; it never effected the reformation of the prisoners. Such results seem to prove the insufficiency of the whole system; however, instead of accusing the theory itself, its implementation was attacked.

Document 10

Source: Editorial in *The Phalanx,* newspaper of the Fourierist utopian socialist movement, January 1837.

The social order is dominated by the fatality of a repressive principle and continues to kill through the executioner or through the prisons those whose natural strength rejects and scorns its regulations. These so-called criminals are too strong to remain enclosed within society's tight swaddling-clothes; they break from them and tear them to pieces, men who do not wish to be children.

Document 11

Source: Reverend John Clay, British prison reformer and chaplain, account of a visit to Pentonville Prison in France, 1840s.

A few months in the solitary cell renders a prisoner strangely impressionable. The chaplain can then make the brawny navvy* cry like a child; he can work on his feelings in almost any way he pleases; he can, so to speak, photograph his thoughts, wishes and opinions on his patient's mind, and fill his mouth with his own phrases and language.

*hard manual laborer

Document 12

Years	Death	Exile	Penal servitude*	Imprisonment	Fine, reformatory, or probation

Source: Percentage of Punishment Types for Violent Offenses against Property, analysis of data from British courts, 1834–1914, selected years.

Years	Death	Exile	Penal servitude*	Imprisonment	Fine, reformatory, or probation
1834–35	38	44	—	18	—
1836–40	17	53	—	29	—
1846–50	1	47	—	53	—
1857–60	1	5	37	58	2
1866–70	—	—	24	73	3
1886–90	—	—	12	82	6
1911–14	—	—	11	66	22

Adapted from V.A.C. Gatrell, Bruce Lenman, Geoffrey Parker, eds., *Crime and the Law: The Social History of Crime in Western Europe since 1500* (London: Europa Publications, 1980), pp. 368-369.

*With penal servitude, the inmate performs hard labor.

EUROPEAN HISTORY
SECTION II
Part B
(Suggested planning and writing time—35 minutes)
Percent of Section II score—27.5

Directions: Answer ONE question from the three choices below. Select the question that you can answer most effectively in the time allotted. You are strongly encouraged to use about 5 minutes planning out your response before you begin writing.

Make sure that your essay:

- Offers a thesis explicitly responsive to the question.
- Deals with all parts of the question.
- Provides specific support for the thesis.
- Displays a clear organization.

2. Discuss how Baroque art reflected religious and political developments in seventeenth-century Europe.

3. Account for the rise of literacy in Europe in the period 1450–1800 and evaluate the impact of this rise for European society.

4. Discuss THREE factors that explain the success of Portugal and Spain in establishing commercial empires in the sixteenth century.

EUROPEAN HISTORY
SECTION II
Part C
(Suggested planning and writing time—35 minutes)
Percent of Section II score—27.5

Directions: Answer ONE question from the three choices below. Select the question that you can answer most effectively in the time allotted. You are strongly encouraged to use about 5 minutes planning out your response before you begin writing.

Make sure that your essay:

- Offers a thesis explicitly responsive to the question.
- Deals with all parts of the question.
- Provides specific support for the thesis.
- Displays a clear organization.

5. Compare and contrast the extent to which the English Civil War (1603–1689) and French Revolution (1789–1815) destroyed the old political order in their respective nations.

6. "The primary reason for the Cold War was political miscalculation rather than an inevitable clash of ideologies between East and West." Evaluate the validity of this statement with reference to events in the period 1945–1964, focusing on Europe.

7. Compare and contrast Otto von Bismarck (1862–1890) and Adolph Hitler (1933–1945) in their views AND uses of German nationalism.

ANSWERS AND SAMPLE RESPONSES

MULTIPLE CHOICE

1. **c.** Students often forget that *The Prince* was written with a specific purpose in mind— liberate the Italian peninsula from foreign invaders and perhaps unify it (c). Machiavelli portrayed the Catholic Church as deeply involved in the political struggles in Italy and rejected the notion of divine will in politics, but he did not explicitly attack the power of the Church (a). Though Machiavelli did argue that human nature was corrupt, his goal proved larger than this—to show the need for a secular and realistic conception of politics (b). Machiavelli dedicated his book to the Medici family to get back in their good graces, so (d) is false. Milan was already ruled by a military despotism, and Machiavelli's interests focused first on Florence (e).

2. **b.** Luther often employed strong language to condemn his opponents. Here he condemns rebels for manipulating religious ideals. The only choice that fits this scenario is (b). This selection is from Luther's *Against the Robbing and Murdering Hordes of Peasants* (1525).

3. **d.** Approximately 80 percent of state revenues for early modern states went to build weapons, supply armies, and wage wars. (a), (b), and (e) also occurred but did not carry the price tag of war. States did not generally use public works to keep people employed until later in the nineteenth century (c).

4. **a.** Most Protestant states took over the dispensing of charity from previous Catholic religious orders, so (b) can be eliminated. Poverty proved a huge problem, particularly as population increased throughout the sixteenth century and the economy worsened in the seventeenth century (c) and (e). Leaders considered poverty a social blight, but not a disease; further, insane asylums were anything but "humane" (d). Attitudes stressed the distinction between the "deserving" and "undeserving" poor—the former receiving aid, the latter fending for themselves or even receiving punishments for begging (a).

5. **b.** Following the devastation of the Thirty Years' War, Frederick William created an army to protect Prussia from invasion. In fact, the entire machinery of the Prussian state coalesced around this army, which came to symbolize the regimentation, efficiency, and power of Prussia.

6. **d.** This is a difficult passage, but clues can be found in the phrases "state of nature," "substituting justice for instinct," and "morality." This is a political passage, which eliminates (b), (c), and (e). Hobbes employed the state of nature in his work but did not believe that human nature changed according to governmental systems (a). A key feature of Rousseau's *Social Contract* lies in his effort to develop a political system that would allow for the full development of human equality, justice, and morality—features suggested by the quotation (d).

7. **e.** Napoleon's Continental System failed in its objective of ruining the British economy (a). Napoleon abolished feudalism along with his conquests, winning over peasants in the process (b). Though Napoleon expressed skepticism in religion, he advocated religious toleration and even made peace with the Catholic Church, so (c) is out. Napoleon also subdued the free press and jailed opponents, so we can forget (d). Nationalism arose in Germany for two reasons—as a positive response to the example of French nationalism and as resentment against the rule of a foreign power (e).

8. **d.** Though Great Britain tolerated non-Anglicans, Protestant dissenters were not allowed to attend the state universities (Oxford and Cambridge), hold military offices, serve as public officials, or enter the paid clergy. Because dissenters were cut off from these positions, they often founded their own technical schools and excelled at invention and business ventures (d). The other items are false.

9. **a.** The title may help with this question. It suggests that Africans work happily at tasks provided them by European rulers, and that they are naturally docile and enjoy hard physical labor. Of course, Africans suffered immensely from King Leopold (of Belgium's) rule of the Congo, and if you recall this, make sure that you interpret the cartoon before jumping to conclusions.

10. **c.** All of the issues listed in the question had relevance in 1913 in Britain. Many women demanded the vote, or franchise, especially because many poor men had already won the right to vote by 1900. As the banner indicates, these women were termed suffragists, or suffragettes. The right to vote is often termed "suffrage" (c).

11. **e.** After conclusion of the Franco-Russian alliance in 1894, the Germany High Command began working on the Schlieffen Plan. This plan called for a huge flanking maneuver through neutral Belgium to approach Paris from the rear and trap the French army against Alsace-Lorraine. Then the Germans hoped to defeat the slow-to-mobilize Russian army in the east. The plan did not work as hoped and drew Great Britain into World War I because of the violation of Belgian neutrality.

12. **a.** In 1938, German physicists split the first atom. During World War II, many combatants worked to develop nuclear weapons; however, this was only accomplished at the end of the

war. Nuclear power did not become a viable source of energy until after 1945. The other items were either invented or became important consumer items in the interwar period.

13. **b.** Soviet forces did, of course, blockade West Berlin, but not in response to the Marshall Plan, and their action proved unsuccessful (a). America's postwar economy dominated world production and trade until the early 1970s, so (c) can be ruled out. Being based on older infrastructure, Britain's economy actually lagged behind the recovery of the other Western European powers (d). Western Europe recovered quickly from the war, surpassing prewar production by the early 1950s, what many called an "economic miracle" (e). The United States insisted on funneling its aid through the Organization for European Economic Cooperation (OEEC), stimulating coordination among the Western European economies and setting the stage for further efforts at integration (b).

14. **c.** The postwar increase in birth rate, known as the baby boom, lasted until the early 1960s. Governments encouraged the phenomenon to replace populations lost in World War II and resulting from the low birth rate during the Great Depression (c). Scientific fields expanded along with government investment in research, so (a) is false. Postwar economic recovery eliminates (b). Extended families have never been the norm in Western Europe (d). Life expectancy reached all-time highs after World War II (e).

15. **e.** Most European states were dominated by aristocratic landholders. As the most urban civilization in fifteenth-century Europe, Italy boasted a powerful middle class of merchants and master craftsmen. This wealthy bourgeoisie combined with the nobles to create a new class of elites based on status and wealth. These wealthy merchant-landowners were termed *seigneurs* and remained a part of the lingering feudal system, along with a segment of the mercantile elite.

16. **b.** Portugal lacked strategic natural resources, so (a) does not apply. Spain and Portugal engaged in colonial rivalry; (c) is false. The Portuguese employed diplomacy and religious conversion (d, e), but Portugal relied primarily on modern cannons, steel swords, and superior organization to control key points in the Indian Ocean to create what some historians have termed a "gunpowder empire" (b).

17. **a.** The Guise family boasted an important duke and cardinal of the Catholic Church (a). Their niece, Mary of Scotland, was married into the French royal family, the Valois (b). (c) and (d) led the Huguenot cause. Burgundy was an important province of France, not a royal house (e).

18. **c.** Peter the Great wished to make Russia a major naval and military power in the Baltic, a task he largely accomplished by the end of his reign (c). Serfdom actually grew worse during his reign (a). Though Peter did liberate women from restrictions, this did not represent a primary goal, and was more of a symbol of Russia's backwardness (b). Peter died before the Enlightenment had gotten underway, so (d) is out. Peter's reforms alienated the palace guard (*streltsy*), whose subsequent rebellion he crushed with great brutality (e).

19. **c.** Adam Smith's laissez-faire economics made little impact prior to the French Revolution (a). (b) did occur but is not considered a feature of the Commercial Revolution. Trade alliances came as a side effect of the Commercial Revolution but did not constitute it (d). European trade with Asia and Africa increased in this period, but again, this resulted from the Commercial Revolution but did not define it (e). The Commercial Revolution involved new goods, such as sugar, tea, and coffee, as well as new techniques, such as joint-stock companies and triangular trade (c).

20. **d.** This passage brought Galileo under the increased attention of the Inquisition in Rome. Though he acknowledges God in the passage, Galileo argues that our senses and reason also

represented God-given means for knowing the truth and that the Bible should not be taken literally if it conflicts with our scientific discoveries. This idea earned Galileo condemnation in 1633, as the Catholic Church came to view his ideas as a threat within the atmosphere of the Thirty Years' War and Counter-Reformation.

21. **e.** Many male aristocrats engaged in the Grand Tour of European cities to experience culture and other "diversions," often getting into trouble in the process. Members of the lower classes who participated in the popular culture activities listed in choices (a) through (d) could not afford such trips, not to mention that such cosmopolitanism did not constitute part of their worldview.

22. **b.** A century of literary and philosophical work dealing with natural rights, equality, and freedom laid the groundwork for the French Revolution. The Enlightenment is often considered *the* intellectual cause of the revolution. The others are only indirectly related or irrelevant.

23. **e.** Edwin Chadwick worked to publicize poor sanitary and living conditions in Britain with his investigations and written work. His efforts paid off with the Public Health Act of 1848 and building of a modern system of sewage and sanitation.

24. **a.** To check further French aggression and/or revolution, Metternich and the other victorious leaders at Vienna erected "buffer states" around France (a). Italy was only unified later in 1859 after a series of wars (b). Russia sought to dominate Poland at Vienna and succeeded in placing that kingdom under the direct control of the tsar (c). As a declining power, the Ottoman Empire did not make territorial additions in the Balkans (d). Austria under Metternich led the Concert of Europe, while Prussia took a back seat in central Europe (e).

25. **b.** Freud focused on the importance of subconscious thoughts and impulses, what he termed the id. Nietzsche argued that Christian morality and science both ignored the important role of the instinctual drives toward power. In that sense, both authors reflected the modern trend in ideas toward self-expression and irrationality.

26. **d.** After Bloody Sunday, public outrage led Tsar Nicholas II to issue the October Manifesto promising creation of a Duma (legislature) and providing for greater freedoms. Nicholas seemed uncommitted to political change and in subsequent years undermined the work of the Duma and reformist advisors. This failure acted as a major cause of World War I.

27. **e.** By 1916, the German leadership believed it was running out of time, so it launched a major offensive against the strategic fortress city of Verdun, also a source of French pride and history. The battle raged out of control for almost a year, yielding a decisive victory for neither side, though it did result in over 1 million casualties. The battle stands as an indelible symbol of the futility of trench warfare during World War I.

28. **a.** The Brezhnev era is characterized by domestic drift and several major foreign policy successes. During détente, the United States and Soviet Union signed several arms control agreements that recognized the rough equality between the nuclear arsenals of both powers (a). Brezhnev crushed the Czech revolt in 1968, so (b) is out. Consumer goods production lagged under Brezhnev (c). Khrushchev oversaw the launching of *Sputnik* in 1957 (d). At home, Brezhnev's slogan was "no experiments," which excludes (e).

29. **a.** Remember that conclusions from graphs must be based only on the data presented, not usually additional outside information. This would exclude (d). (b) and (e) are clearly false by some simple addition. World population much more than doubled between 1930 and 2000, so (c) is excluded. That leaves us with (a), and indeed Europe's growth rate has slowed in the twentieth century as other areas have increased their birth rates.

30. **c.** Guilds performed social functions, such as (a), but this did not represent their primary function. Many guilds, especially after 1550, did not allow female members unless it was a widow of a member (b). Guilds actually worked against specialization, as this would threaten their monopoly on skills in a particular craft (d). (e) seems to lay outside the bounds of the economic activities of guilds. Guilds operated primarily to secure a monopoly of labor and ensure quality control in a specific craft. This ensured higher wages for a guild's members and a sense of prestige as skilled craftsmen (c).

31. **a.** The War of Spanish Succession involved a conflict over the Spanish throne between Louis XIV of France and the Austrian Holy Roman Emperor. Though Louis's grandest ambitions were thwarted (d), his grandson, Philip V, did ascend to the Spanish throne, but the Peace of Utrecht prohibited the combination of the French and Spanish thrones. By 1714, Russia was defeating Sweden in the Great Northern War and replacing them as the dominant power in the north (b). (c) and (d) simply did not occur.

32. **a.** Locke's multifaceted ideas include works in philosophy, education, science, and politics. Like many British thinkers (Bacon, Hume, Smith), Locke endorsed empiricism and rejected Descartes's notion of innate ideas. This "blank slate" notion led him to suggest educational reforms in *Some Thoughts Concerning Education* Locke justified the actions of Parliament in the Glorious Revolution (1689–1690) with his *Two Treatises on Government*, in which he employed the state of nature concept to justify revolution against governments that deprive citizens of their natural rights. Socialism evolved more in response to the nineteenth-century Industrial Revolution; moreover, Locke's ideas stood firmly for private property.

33. **a.** Louis XVI acted as a well-meaning but politically ineffective king, incapable of playing "hard ball." At critical junctures, he seemed to endorse or at least accept important actions of the National Assembly during the revolution. However, he was deeply disturbed by attacks on the Catholic Church and other attacks on his royal prerogatives. Under the influence of his wife and advisors, he attempted to flee the revolution in June 1791.

34. **e.** Napoleon III involved himself in Italian unification, but his goals were less ambitious than conquest (a). For domestic support, Napoleon protected the papacy with French troops, so (b) is out. Napoleon III fought the Crimean War to inhibit Russian expansion in the Balkans (c). After 1860, Napoleon was forced to compromise on some of his authoritarian policies, but his goal was never democracy (d). Despite his foreign policy failures, Napoleon did succeed in modernizing the French economy and infrastructure (e).

35. **b.** After the heady enthusiasm of 1848, most revolutions ended in failure. In Austria, one of the few lasting reforms proved to be the abolition of serfdom and feudalism. The other developments did not occur, at least not as a result of the revolutions of 1848.

36. **e.** (a) and (c) played a role in Italian unification, but not the central role. Pius IX opposed Italian unification (b). Bismarck's policies relate to Germany, not Italy (d). Cavour used industry, diplomacy, and war to unite Italy by 1861 (e).

37. **e.** Due to increases in productivity and the power of the working class, governments reduced the working day and provided popular amusements in many cities. To ensure a well-ordered society and provide for organized recreation, with skills often translating into military uses, governments promoted sports competition.

38. **d.** The first genocide of the twentieth century involved the Armenian Christians of the Ottoman Empire (d). Though the other choices indirectly demonstrate the rise of total war and the extreme conditions of World War I, the Armenian massacres stand most directly

related to the atrocities of the Holocaust. Hitler himself cited worldwide apathy toward the Armenians in his planning for the Final Solution.

39. **d.** The western democracies systematically attempted to isolate the Bolshevik Soviet Union, fearing communism more than the rising tide of fascism. His exclusion at Munich convinced Stalin to conclude his own deal with Hitler, what became the shocking Nazi-Soviet Non-Aggression Pact of 1939, which allowed Hitler a free hand in invading Poland to begin World War II.

40. **b.** As part of the Habsburg-Valois Wars, forces under Charles V of Spain (and the Holy Roman Empire) invaded Italy. As often happened, the Spanish troops had been unpaid for months (due to Spanish financial difficulties) and took their payment in the form of looting Rome, then the center of the High Renaissance. This shocking event symbolized the political impotence of Italy and inspired a move away from ordered and symmetrical artistic compositions. Just compare Michelangelo's *Last Judgment* (1542) with his earlier work on the Sistine Chapel.

41. **c.** What clues can we use from the map to determine its chronological setting? First, the borders of France do not include Louis XIV's conquests of Franche-Comté or Alsace-Lorraine, so it must predate 1700 (excludes d and e). Germany stands divided, Italy disunited, and Russia has not gained the predominant position in the Baltic. The Dutch Republic and Switzerland are independent, so we can eliminate (a) and (b). This leads us to conclude that the map is of Europe following the Thirty Years' War (c).

42. **d.** The Netherlands lost it preeminent commercial position primarily as a result of competition with the larger and more resource-rich Britain and France. Following the Anglo-Dutch Naval Wars (fought in three stages from 1650 to 1674) and Louis XIV's wars against the Dutch (1667–1678), that smaller republic lost numerous ships and found its trading position compromised overseas. Britain soon emerged as the leading commercial power.

43. **e.** Large landholders dominated the countryside in nations such as England, due to the enclosure acts, which often drove small farmers off the land (a). Feudal regulations continued in many nations even after the French Revolution, so (b) is excluded. Russia's agricultural system lagged behind, and still does to this day (c). Cities continued to expand in the eighteenth century, mostly fed by migration from the countryside, so (d) is out. Improved food production helped support an increased European population, an important phenomenon of the eighteenth century (e).

44. **a.** Utopian socialists stressed the need to organize an ideal commune based on shared property and equality, including for women (a). Most utopian socialists came out of the French radical tradition, which rejected traditional religious values as associated with the old order (b). Unlike Marxists, utopians did not believe in violent action, but rather modeling an ideal social community (c). Early socialists rejected free-market capitalism and also criticized nationalism as a tool of the state to divide workers (d). Mass production was associated with the horrors of the factory system (e).

45. **c.** Realist painters depicted the lives of the poor and downtrodden. Millet often portrayed the backbreaking labors of rural peasants, as seen in this famous image of his. In traditional subsistence agriculture, the poor were allowed to glean the stubble from the harvest to help make ends meet.

46. **b.** Unlike the other movements, socialism stressed equality. Many socialists attacked class and gender inequalities. Many women, such as Flora Tristan, Clara Zetkin, Rosa

Luxembourg, and Sylvia Pankhurst, thus found a natural marriage between feminism and working-class radicalism.

47. **d.** Following the Versailles settlement, the Weimar Republic stood somewhat isolated in world affairs. France expressed suspicion over a revival of German power, and the United States refused to participate in the League of Nations, so (d) clearly would not apply. Germany was able to conclude a treaty—the Rapallo Pact—with the Soviet Union in 1922, another international outcast.

48. **c.** Stalin, in fact, adhered loyally to his treaty with Hitler, so (a) can be excluded. Perhaps Hitler's inability to defeat Britain in 1940 led him to turn on the Soviet Union, but this was not a prime consideration (b). The United States had already declared neutrality and no imperial designs, at least not in 1941, on the Middle East (d). Germany had secured its supply of iron ore with its invasion of Norway in the spring of 1940 (e). In *Mein Kampf*, Hitler had already indicated his ultimate goal of gaining "living space" (*Lebensraum*) for Germany in the east, at the expense of the Soviet Union. Hitler's timing proved a mistake, but the invasion seemed almost predetermined based on his ideological commitments (c).

49. **b.** After 1991, Serbian and Croatian forces accused the other of having engaged in campaigns of mass killing, systematic rape, and destruction of villages in their ethnic conflict. Many Serb leaders and military figures have been brought before the International Court of Justice in The Hague, Netherlands, for such "ethnic cleansing" in Bosnia and Kosovo.

50. **a.** Many have suggested that without the printing press, Luther would not have succeeded in his reform efforts. In 1530, almost one-third of the books published in Germany were authored by Luther (a). Greek and Latin texts increased in influence throughout the sixteenth century, as the printing press allowed for standardized versions (b). Clearly, artistic prestige continued during the Renaissance regardless of the ability to copy images (c). Unemployment for monks did not arise as an issue, as they turned to other intellectual pursuits (d). Humanism continued to spread *because* of the printing press, so (e) is out.

51. **d.** The *requiremento* was a statement read to Native Americans, promising protection if they converted to Catholicism; few understood it because it was read to them in Spanish (a). *Audiencias* were royal courts (b). The Spanish colonial empire was divided into the two vice royalties, or administrative units, of New Spain and Peru (c). Bishoprics were administrative units of the Catholic Church (e). The *encomienda* system was designed to provide for the orderly settlement of the Americas but degenerated into an exploitative system that decimated native populations (d).

52. **d.** Christian humanists such as Erasmus and Thomas More promoted a more personal and spiritual piety, but unlike Luther, they refused to break with the Catholic Church. Their criticisms of clerical corruption laid the groundwork for the Protestant Reformation, while their ideas of reform set the stage for the revival of the Catholic Church after 1540.

53. **b.** Jews and Muslims were both forced either to leave Spain or convert to Catholicism in 1492, the year the *reconquista* was completed. Ferdinand and Isabella had set up the Spanish Inquisition in 1478 to investigate adherence to religious orthodoxy by Jewish (*converses*) and Muslim (*moriscos*) converts. The Inquisition possessed no power over Muslims and Jews per se; after 1492, there technically were no Muslims and Jews in Spain. Several of these items are related, but the main goal of Spain's Catholic sovereigns was to ensure and uphold adherence to Catholic belief.

54. **a.** This passage expressed divine-right monarchy. Locke opposed divine right and absolutism (b). Frederick justified his power based on dynastic succession and being the "first

servant" of his enlightened state (c). Machiavelli's conception of politics was entirely secular (d). Henry IV helped lay the foundations for absolutism in France but is not known for his use of religious rhetoric to justify his rule (e). James I clashed with Parliament in England because he lectured that body on his God-given absolute rule. This passage comes from his book *The True Law of Free Monarchy* (1598).

55. **e.** Both thinkers challenged Scholasticism as stale and outmoded (a). Descartes accepted God but did not argue for supernatural explanations (b). Bacon championed empiricism, or systematic observation of nature (c) and accepted the heliocentric theory (d). Unlike Bacon, Descartes appreciated the power of mathematical thinking in explaining natural phenomena, thus his deductive method of reasoning, much like a geometric proof (e).

56. **c.** Eighteenth-century tennis courts tended to be indoors, as depicted here. The delegates of the National Assembly dramatically raise their hands to pledge not to disperse until they have written a new constitution for the French revolutionary state. This Tennis Court Oath is often considered one of the opening acts in the drama of the revolution.

57. **c.** The classical economists attacked mercantilism and argued for the unfettered operation of the natural laws of supply and demand. Ricardo and Malthus proved pessimistic in their assessment of wages and the conditions of the poor; though both believed any attempted solution to poverty would only create worse problems. The other options all express interferences with the "invisible hand of the marketplace."

58. **a.** The image depicts the Arc de Triomphe (Arch of Triumph) to commemorate French military exploits. It was begun during the reign of Napoleon but not completed until 1836. Clearly, it reflects French nationalism.

59. **b.** The only theory here related to evolution is (b). Lyell suggested that all of the geologic forces necessary for the evolution of life had been present since the beginning of the earth. Lyell's principle of uniformitarianism held that geologic forces operated over a long period of time, as opposed to the theory of catastrophism, which held that events such as the Great Flood brought about or eliminated life as recounted in the book of Genesis.

60. **e.** Throughout Bismarck's tenure as chancellor, he worked mightily to isolate France and prevent an alliance between France and Russia. When Kaiser Wilhelm II dismissed Bismarck in 1890, he also allowed the Reinsurance Treaty with Russia to lapse, allowing for the completion of the Franco-Russian alliance of 1894, forcing Germany into a possible two-front war.

61. **a.** The map clearly shows the recreation of the Polish state. To give Poland access to the sea, the diplomats at Versailles divided Germany in two, separating East Prussia from the rest. This division angered Germans and fed Hitler's demands for a return of the Polish Corridor, as well as the free city of Danzig, to Germany control. This issue prompted Hitler's invasion of Poland and initiated World War II.

62. **c.** Key phrases in the passage are "revolution," "virtue," and "terror." You might recall that Robespierre attempted to create what he called a "republic of virtue" in France during the revolution, but to do so, he oversaw the Reign of Terror.

63. **d.** All of these actions constitute part of the Catholic response to the Protestant Reformation, except (d). In fact, the power of the papacy was strengthened and given new tools, such as the Index of Prohibited Books and Roman Inquisition to deal with "heresy," particularly on the Italian peninsula.

64. **b.** Prices for agricultural products, and by extension, land, rose faster than manufacturing wages. Landowners, including peasants, often took advantage of the phenomenon of rising

prices to buy up new lands or convert some of their holding to "cash crops." This allowed a new class of wealthy peasants or gentry to arise in some locations. Urban workers found that they were forced to pay more for food but did not receive commensurate increases in wages for their manufactured products, a phenomenon known as the "scissors effect," for being caught between high prices and lower wages.

65. **d.** Here we have a straightforward visual identification question. This Rigaud painting is the most famous image of Louis XIV and portrays him in all his splendor as the Sun King.

66. **b.** Classic Liberals of the nineteenth century advocated laissez-faire economic principles, which differ from our modern understanding of the term "liberal." The Corn Laws protected British grain from foreign competition and thus violated the Liberal notion of free trade; their repeal in 1846 not only helped industrial workers (who could now pay less for food) but also signaled the rise of Liberal economic philosophy (b). The Factory Act of 1833 limited child labor and provided minimal education for children. Conservatives such as Disraeli supported such protective legislation for children and women (a). Choices (c) through (e) all relate to the Restoration political order in central or eastern Europe.

67. **b.** European penetration of Africa did not occur prior to 1870. New technologies made European imperialism of Asia and Africa possible—railroads, steamships, telegraphs, modern medicine, machine guns, and so on. Europeans often built modern infrastructures in colonized areas to facilitate their control, particularly with communication and transportation.

68. **d.** The Victorian ideal, or domesticity, glorified the special attributes of women—moral purity, passive love, and self-sacrifice. In this ideal, women guarded the domestic sphere from the moral pollution of the public sphere. The home acted as a refuge from the outside world, the man's world of power, politics, and business. Of course, not all women accepted this sexual division of labor and social roles.

69. **a.** (e) may also seem an appealing choice, but that puts the cart before the horse. Lenin argues that worldwide revolution and an end to World War I are related; however, he states that in order to end the war, capitalism must be overthrown (a). (c) and (d) can be excluded: Lenin and the Bolsheviks explicitly condemned World War I and sought to end it. Lenin looked to western European nations to join the working-class revolution, but of course, the revolution occurred first in Russia (b).

70. **c.** In this picture, Stalin looks off into the "future" while a hydroelectric dam rises behind him. This propaganda poster promotes the idea of Stalin's visionary leadership in modernizing Russia and building an industrial infrastructure. Though it came at great cost, Stalin promoted the electrification of and literacy in the Soviet Union.

71. **d.** The Western alliance accepted the Soviet sphere of influence in Eastern Europe, as shown by the reaction to the Hungarian revolt in 1956 and Czech revolt in 1968 (a). (b) and (c) are largely true but do not explain the timing of the fall of communism. The fall of communism did not come as part of a negotiated settlement to the Cold War; both arose indirectly from Gorbachev's policies and goals in the Soviet Union (e). Gorbachev explicitly rejected the use of force to maintain the Soviet satellites in Eastern Europe, allowing the revolutions there to succeed, unlike in 1956 and 1968 (d).

72. **a.** All Protestants placed religious authority on the Bible, so (b) is false. Catholics and Protestants both persecuted the Anabaptists, so (c) is out. Only in the city of Munster did Anabaptism turn violent; generally, Anabaptists practiced their faith peacefully, and suffered courageously under persecution (d). Calvin rejected Anabaptism and promoted his own

Calvinist reformed faith in Geneva (e). Because of their ideas regarding the separation of church and state, the Anabaptists were a minority religion wherever they existed (a).

73. **e.** Deists believed in God as the creator of the universe but rejected a personal God of divin revelation, miracles, dogmas, and priesthoods. For advocates of the Enlightenment, deism allowed for a moral foundation but without the "superstition" of rituals and doctrines. As the deist Voltaire stated, "If God did not exist, it would be necessary to invent Him."

74. **b.** Enlightened monarchs advocated "top-down" reform. Though they wished to provide for a more rational and stronger state, they did not trust the masses with power. Therefore, they did not generally promote democratic decision-making procedures.

75. **b.** With the onslaught of industrialization, urbanization, and revolutionary activity, members of the middle class came to fear disorder. Modern police forces not only combated crime but ensured domestic stability. Prison reforms during the nineteenth century also aimed to provide the missing "internal discipline" of the criminal through solitude, labor, and structure.

76. **c.** Because many nations passed legislation emancipating Jews from restrictions (c), Jews were able to assimilate into the larger culture, so (a) is out. Some Jews gained prominent roles in socialist movements, but these did not aim directly at Jewish rights (b). Few groups, including Jews, were unaffected by industrialization and nationalism (e). The Dreyfus Affair highlighted but did not eliminate anti-Semitism, as evidenced by subsequent events leading up to the Holocaust.

77. **a.** Most of the western democracies did little to aid the antifascist forces in Spain, as they seemed more fearful of socialism and communism. The Soviet Union did promote the Popular Front of leftist parties and provided military backing to the Loyalist forces in Spain. Germany and Italy, however, supported Franco's nationalist forces.

78. **b.** On the left-hand side of the picture, we have police; on the right-hand side, young people. In the background, you may recognize Paris or the French writing on the building. The only choice that fits the picture and the context is (b).

79. **b.** To prop up a tottering socialist regime on its border, the Soviet Union invaded Afghanistan in late 1979. President Carter denounced the Soviet invasion and also sponsored a boycott of the 1980 Moscow Olympics and cut back grain shipments to the Soviets. Soon after, anticommunist Ronald Reagan was elected president and turned up the rhetoric against the Soviet Union. The Cuban Missile Crisis predated détente (a). American policy in Iran did not help relations with the Soviet Union but did not threaten détente (c). The Arab-Israeli War of 1973 created tensions but did not stop the process of negotiation between the superpowers (d). And of course, Gorbachev's reforms helped bring an end to the Cold War (e).

80. **d.** Six nations (France, Germany, Italy, Belgium, Netherlands, and Luxembourg) founded the ECSC and soon realized a doubling of coal and steel production. This organization became the model for further unity, with the EEC (1957) and EU (1992). Economic coordination has benefited European output and exports.

DBQ COMMENTARY AND RESPONSES

As with any DBQ, there are a number of ways to approach this question. First, read the question carefully and try to incorporate both parts in your introductory paragraphs—"factors that affected punishment of criminals" and "extent to which views changed over time." When addressing change over time, try to use a formula in which you characterize the views at the beginning of the period and then near the end of the period. In this case, it would be appropriate to mention the continued reliance on the public spectacle of capital punishment at the outset of the period, and near the end, the focus on incarceration and rehabilitation of criminals.

For groupings, different strategies are available to you. One option is to group by type of authors—for example, reformers, observers, or politicians. A problem with this strategy is that it can often lead to simplifying more complex responses to fit them into a predetermined mode. Remember that not all observers will view the topic in the same light. Because this question calls for factors that affected changing treatment of criminals, your response may be best served by simply grouping according to those factors: humanitarianism, natural rights, rational punishments, utilitarian concerns, social order, need for discipline, religion. Within each of these groups, you will analyze how various authors perceived the punishment of criminals. Think of your body paragraphs as a brief analysis of a debate—you identify the terms of the debate, the varying positions, the reasons for these positions, and the agendas that various authors bring to their stated position. With a change-over-time question, you can always group chronologically. This strategy can often lead a student to overlook nuances in the documents in an effort to find a neat pattern. For example, in this DBQ, though many commentators had moved toward acceptance of the penitentiary systems, several documents question both the motive and effect of that system (see Documents 9 and 10).

Let's look at some examples for bias or point of view with these documents:

Document 1: Voltaire, French writer and philosopher, *Candide,* satirical novel recounting the adventures of young Candide and his mentor, Dr. Pangloss, 1757—You may recognize Voltaire as a major figure of the Enlightenment. When you encounter a well-known person, consider this an opportunity to bring in outside information that will assist with point of view. Because Voltaire was known as a satirist, he exaggerates his account of the *auto da fe* to emphasize religious fanaticism and superstition. As a fictional account, we should treat this with skepticism.

Document 3: Account of a public execution on "justice day," anonymous pamphlet, published in Amsterdam, Netherlands, 1773—We may speculate as to why this pamphlet was published anonymously. Having no information about the author, we can hypothesize that the author has an agenda against capital punishment and wishes to make the account seem like the concern of an ordinary citizen. Perhaps the author feared punishment by the state, suggesting this as a relatively truthful account. Notice how you can "spin" point of view in different ways—as long as you explain your reasoning.

Document 7: Antoine Louis, physician and Secretary of the Academy of Surgery, report to the French revolutionary Legislative Assembly concerning use of the guillotine for the death penalty, 1792—As a physician, Antoine Louis would be in a position to know the physical effects of different forms of execution. The tone of this document seems detached and impersonal. Perhaps Louis wishes to appease the Legislative Assembly with a positive report on the guillotine to enhance his own image or status.

Document 8: Walter Venning, Quaker prison reformer, plans for a Russian prison system, following a visit to that nation, 1817—As a member of the Quakers, Venning may have an interest in proving the power of religion to reform the lives of criminals. His belief that fear of God can change prisoners is not based on any scientific evidence.

Document 9: Gustave de Beaumont, French public official and writer, and Alexis de Tocqueville, French historian and Liberal political philosopher, *On the Penitentiary System in the United States and Its Application in France,* 1833—Travel writers can often view a foreign nation with fresh eyes and provide a less biased view of that nation's customs than its own inhabitants. Beaumont's and Tocqueville's ultimately negative view of the U.S. prison system may also rest on an anti-American bias.

Document 10: Editorial in *The Phalanx*, newspaper of the Fourierist utopian socialist movement, January 1837—As a socialist publication, this newspaper can be expected to look at the issue from the perspective of class and exploitation. It is in the paper's interest to portray the capitalist system as repressive, since it builds support for the socialist movement.

Document 12: Percentage of Punishment Types for Violent Offenses against Property, analysis of data from British courts, 1834–1914, selected years—With statistical data, many students often claim a higher level of reliability. This is certainly an acceptable approach. However, you may also consider whether the government wished to promote a new approach to criminal punishment by publishing this data, making it less objective.

Most of the documents in this exercise are fairly straightforward. Document 9 offers a brief explanation of the U.S. prison model with little specific commentary; in fact, it even sounds like a positive assessment. The second paragraph, however, moves to a critique of the system as ineffective and costly. As you read the documents, try to avoid simply picking out one side of them to support your thesis. Use the complexity of the documents to your advantage—show that you understand the nuances and even try to incorporate these mixed feelings into your thesis.

DBQ Sample 1

In early modern Europe, criminal punishments tended to be a brutal spectacle. The idea was to prevent crime by making an example out of violators. As we move toward the Enlightenment and French Revolution, reformers questioned the traditional punishments and favored different types, such as prison or more humane capital punishment. Different factors affected this change: humane concerns, human rights, and religion. Not all people supported the new systems of punishment, but they did seem to be an improvement on drawing and quartering.

Many writers condemned the horrible punishments of traditional Europe. Voltaire pokes fun at an execution as being part of religious superstition to prevent another earthquake. He adds humorously that there was another earthquake the next day anyway (Doc. 1). The anonymous author of Doc. 3 adds a similar perspective. He talks about how several men are executed by hanging on a special "justice day" (as if it were some kind of celebration). The author did take some solace in that several of the spectators did not approve of what they saw. De-la-Bretonne (Doc. 5) gives us another view of an execution, except he shows us a young lady who laughs at the suffering of others. Perhaps as a social observer, he wanted to highlight the issue of how barbaric punishment can ruin the souls of pretty young ladies.

Human rights became a greater concern during the Enlightenment and French Revolution. Many writers and philosophers of this period condemned the old punishments as a violation of human rights. Cesare Beccaria, a famous writer on the topic, argues that the main goal of punishment is to produce the most happiness for people; this is done by making people respect the laws, not fear other men (Doc. 2). This is a very utilitarian idea and is reflected also in Jeremy Bentham's plans for his Panopticon prison. We can even see a picture of the prisoner being seen by the "all-seeing-eye" (Doc. 4). Perhaps Bentham wanted to prove his theory of utilitarianism by building a prison that showed its ideals. Ironically,

Robespierre denounces the death penalty in the Constituent Assembly. He states that in free nations there is respect for humans and not death penalty. He must have changed his mind later, because he certainly used it later as head of the Jacobins (Doc. 6). Also during the French Revolution, Antoine Louis called for use of the guillotine. At this time, the device was viewed as a humanitarian device because it did not make the victim suffer; it would "scarcely be perceived," wrote Louis. As a physician, he would be in a good position to know its effects (Doc. 7).

Once we get into the nineteenth century, we can see a growing influence of discipline and religion for punishments. Walter Venning claims that criminals lack a fear of God, and prisons will help them repent their crimes and change their lives (Doc. 8). This is echoed by Doc. 11, where a prison chaplain shows how the criminal will "cry like a child" under the influence of a skilled mentor. Clearly, nations were using this form of punishment more, as can be seen from Doc. 12, statistics on different forms of punishment. As it moves toward the 20th century, the British government uses imprisonment and fines instead of death for property crimes. Not everyone was for the new prisons. Two French writers criticize the American system of solitary confinement as being too expensive and not very effective (Doc. 9). As French people, they may be biased against the United States. Also, the socialist newspaper *Phalanx* thinks that the system is oppressive and part of capitalism (Doc. 10).

In conclusion, punishment of criminals changed a great deal during this period. Europe seemed to get more civilized as new ideas stressed human rights and better social order, instead of a carnival-like atmosphere to execute people. Prisons are still an issue today, as Americans like a "get-tough-on-crime" approach that doesn't really rehabilitate criminals, only makes them worse when they get out.

This sample clearly addresses the six core tasks. In the introduction, the student effectively identifies three groups but also lays out her change-over-time thesis, which she also carries through the rest of the essay. Documents are used skillfully and often played off one another to show how they support or contradict. The student also employs outside information on several occasions, particularly the historical context of the Enlightenment and French Revolution. Four explicit examples of point of view are given, and the student uses all 12 documents. In several other instances, this student hints at point of view but does not follow up with explanation and analysis. If she had done this in one or two cases, her essay would have earned a top score. Score: 8.

DBQ Sample 2

At the beginning of this time, there was a tendency to inflict heinous punishments on criminals, like breaking on the wheel. As times moved closer to the nineteenth century, many reformers began to condemn such brutality. They advocated reforms to try to rehabilitate criminals or have them reflect on their sins. There are three basic periods in this question—the brutal phase, the reform phase based on the ideas of reason, and then the culmination with religious discipline.

Some writers tried to publicize the issue of brutal punishments. Many of them connected these horrible treatments with an uncivilized past that Europe needed to be beyond. In Document 1, Voltaire satirizes the treatment of his hero, Candide, by religious figures. Candide and his mentor, Dr. Pangloss were given over the Inquisition to be burned, just to avoid an earthquake. Voltaire snidely laughs at this attitude. We should keep in mind that Voltaire hated organized religion and probably wanted to show it in a bad light. One of his famous quotes was "crush the infamous thing," referring to religion. Another such account is by Restif de-la-Bretonne, who talks about a man being broken on the wheel. He shows how even women seemed to enjoy these sad displays and how changed they could become when subjected to these sights. Since he is a social critic, he might have exaggerated his account to highlight this issue or sell more of his books. People often like some good violence in their reading (Document 5).

As time went on people began to question whether these types of punishments really helped society. Part of this went along with the Enlightenment. In Document 2, Beccaria writes about how the goal of society is to prevent crimes, not punish them. To do this, the "laws should be clear and simple" and all of society should stand behind them. As a philosopher and figure of the Enlightenment, he clearly was reflecting the strong emphasis on reason in this movement. There is even a document from Robespierre (Document 6) addressing a speech before the French Assembly. In this speech, Robespierre goes against much of the opinion of the period and supports the death penalty. He was probably looking forward to the violence that was beginning to occur in France and if he got into power, he would need the death penalty to keep order.

Finally, near the end of the period, in the nineteenth century, there is a movement toward religious beliefs as a source of discipline for criminals. In Document 8, a Quaker extols the idea of an "all-seeing God" who can frighten the criminal/sinner into acting rightly. Quakers supported the anti-slavery movement and believed that all men had within them an "inner light," so we could expect them to help even condemned felons. Reverend John Clay, another religious figure, explains based on his visit to a French prison, how the chaplain can manipulate the criminal into doing good by the power of suggestion. As a chaplain himself, he would want to believe this because it is his job to feel like he is helping people. But it could be that the criminal was doing the manipulating and pretending to be reformed just to appease the chaplain. So it is clear by the end of century that reformers cared more about taking people away from a life of crimes with God rather than just hacking them to pieces.

Criminal punishment was shown to be a major issue during this time in history. Criminals went from being brutally tortured to almost being coddled by a mentor. This change seems to go along with the Enlightenment ideals of progress and optimism that humans are basically good. All that needs to happen is that society changes its institutions and crime should be abolished. This sounds very idealistic but may not actually work in practice.

This sample essay establishes a clear thesis, organizes the documents into groups, and engages in some higher-level point of view. Though the chronological format leads the student to ignore more nuanced interpretations, the essay does seem to work in its chronological organization. Unfortunately, this essay will receive a much lower score than one might expect. First, the student included only six documents (seven constitute a majority). With the new DBQ standards (see Chapter 1), students lose core points 2, 3, and 4 for not including a majority of documents. Additionally, the second body paragraph includes a major error in discussing Robespierre—his speech *condemned* the death penalty. Perhaps this student did not read the document carefully, assuming that because the author was Robespierre, it must be in support of the death penalty.

This error produces a ripple effect, as it destroys that grouping (because it includes only one other document, and two documents are minimal for a group); thus, the student loses the core point for groups. Though the response provides ample and sophisticated point of view, and therefore earns that core point, the student cannot earn points in the expanded core for this analysis because he missed other core points. Overall, this analytical essay made some fatal errors and earned core points only for thesis and point of view. Score: 2.

FRQ COMMENTARY AND RESPONSES

Part B—Question 2

Approximately once every other year, the AP Exam will feature a question like this one that requires some detailed knowledge of art. Often students will be asked to connect the style and subject matter of a particular movement to the historical context. If you choose such a question, be prepared to discuss several specific examples in some detail. General descriptions will not be adequate. Also, try to make explicit connections between the art movements and the historical context. In this case, the major religious development would be the Counter-Reformation and the major political development of the rise of absolutism.

Art often acts as a mirror on society—reflecting its interests, fears, and hopes. During the seventeenth century, the Baroque art movement in painting, architecture, and music forms a strong connection with developments in the Catholic Church and the rising absolute monarchies. Most Baroque artists gained their patronage from the Church or the state. As a result, they tended to paint, build, or compose art that glorified who patronized them. Baroque art involves a lot of movement and drama to create a strong sense of power and majesty.

After the Protestant Reformation, the Catholic Church wanted to reestablish its power and prestige. In Rome, the popes finished St. Peter's Basilica, which many artists worked on, including Michelangelo. Most famous in rebuilding Rome was Bernini. Bernini designed St. Peter's Square, the throne of St. Peter, and the "Ecstasy of St. Teresa." In all these works, he portrayed the church as a powerful institution that played a major role in people's lives. For St. Teresa, he had her levitate on a cloud with a look of rapture on her face as shafts of light from heaven fell upon the scene. Another famous artist is Caravaggio, who painted the "Calling of St. Matthew," which shows Jesus calling on Matthew to become one of his apostles. The scene is backlit for drama and makes the relationship between Jesus and Matthew seem more personal and mystical. In music, composers like Palestrina composed complex and ornate pieces for the Mass to add emotion and feeling.

Absolute monarchs, like today's politicians, needed to market themselves to the masses. They did this through building palaces, sculptures, and music. Versailles is the perfect example. In its size and grandeur, it is the perfect Baroque structure. In each room, paintings portray Louis XIV as a Roman god, connecting him to the greatness of the past. Portraits of the king in full robes and high heels (a trend Louis started) grace many parts of the building. Other monarchs imitated Louis and built palaces like Versailles. When you walk into Versailles, there is a great equestrian statue of Louis and lush gardens. Kings like to be associated with horses; horseracing has often been called the "sport of kings." Baroque gardens were very controlled and geometric to demonstrate the power of the king over nature.

Baroque art has been very influential in the art world. Its dynamic style and sense of illusion—for example, ceilings that make you look like you're staring into the heavens—show the importance of both church and state in the seventeenth century. When these institutions declined somewhat during the Enlightenment, then we see the growth of neo-classical art, which once again went back to the ancient world for greatness.

This is a very effective response. Though the student does not include numerous specific examples, those that she does include are effectively applied to the thesis. The student demonstrates a sound grasp of the historical context and makes an explicit effort to tie the art to this context. There is even some art criticism that adds to the understanding of Baroque art. Finally, the conclusion effectively adds an additional detail (about ceilings) while looking toward a subsequent art movement, which further places Baroque art in an appropriate context. Score: 9.

Part B—Question 3

Do not be intimidated by the broad chronological period in this question. First, try to pick out technological and social developments that relate to this question—printing press, Renaissance, Reformation, growth of government bureaucracies, the Enlightenment increase in printed material. Because the time period of the impact is not directly specified, you can exercise some leeway in your discussion. It would be easy for such a response to become unfocused or overly general, so make sure that you ground your analysis in a specific historical context.

Many developments affected the rise of literacy, such as the printing press and Reformation. Literacy is something we take for granted today, but it played a major role in influencing events, mostly the Enlightenment and French Revolution.

No invention affected literacy as much as the printing press. Gutenberg developed his invention in the fifteenth century. Soon after, printing presses sprung up all over Europe, selling Bibles and other classical humanist books. With more books in print and cheaper, more people could afford to read. Though the really poor people like peasants still could not afford books, the stage was set. This increase in literacy helped advance the humanist movement of the Renaissance.

Protestant reformers were pretty much obsessed with reading the Bible. They believed that even women and the poor should read the word of God. Many of them set up schools, like the Geneva Academy, to promote literacy. To respond, Catholics, like the Jesuits, set up their own schools. With both Christian groups providing schools, the literacy rate could not help but rise.

What impact did this rise in literacy have? First, it helped promote the questioning of ideas during the Enlightenment. Many people began to read philosophical works by Voltaire, Diderot, and Locke. This led them to question the Old Regime and it inequality. Public opinion could not happen without people reading newspapers and magazines about politics or other important issues.

As we can see, literacy has been very important in promoting new ideas. The printing press and Reformation helped create literacy and the Enlightenment and French Revolution put it to work.

Here we have a spare yet effective response. A brief but relevant introduction begins the essay; it certainly might be improved with one or two more sentences of historical context explaining the effects of literacy. Though the body paragraphs convey only a few examples, they prove relevant to the thesis and are focused on the question. Overall, lack of analysis and explanation keeps this essay from reaching higher into the stronger category. With a few more specifics and explanation, this response could easily have earned a higher score. Score: 6.

Part B—Question 4

This straightforward prompt requires you to account for the success of colonization efforts based on the Iberian Peninsula. For questions like this, students can often stray into narration. Keep referring back to the terms of the questions and *analyze* how the factors you identify worked to promote exploration and colonization. It may also be tempting to veer off into examining the consequences of colonization; this is really not your task.

> In 1492, Columbus "sailed the ocean blue." Many explorers followed in his footsteps and landed in the New World. They came to conquer and were able to crush the native people there. As a result of exploration and colonization, native cultures in the New World were destroyed. This essay will discuss three reasons why Spain and Portugal created empires in new lands.
>
> One major reason for the success of Spain and Portugal was new technologies. Boats were constructed better with newer woods and better sails. Maps had gotten more detailed and helped sailors find their way off the coast of Europe. Still the seafarers had to find out how to get to their destinations, so they had the compass (from China) and the astrolabe (from the Arabs). With these new devices, they got to their destinations.
>
> Getting there was one thing, conquering was another. This is where new military technologies came into play. European conquerors had machine guns and poison gas to overwhelm the native peoples. The people of India and the East Indies were no match for these powerful new technological weapons. This does not mean that the Europeans were better people, just more sophisticated with their weaponry at this time.
>
> All this colonizing had great effects. The Columbian Exchange started up where new goods, potatoes and such, were shipped to Europe. This helped Europe's standard of living and made life better for even common people. With all the wealth, Spain and Portugal became very powerful nations. In fact, with the gold and silver from the Americas, Spain emerged as the most powerful nation in Europe, especially with Charles V as Holy Roman Emperor and King of Spain. Portugal eventually was too small to keep up its great commercial power. The Dutch later stole many of their colonies. Without colonization, we would probably not be here today. In conclusion, Spain and Portugal had many new technologies to help them get across wide open oceans and then impress the people they encountered. Many of these people belonged to pretty advanced civilizations, but they had never seen such technologies before, so they could not fight back effectively.
>
> One other factor that promoted exploration was strong politics. Both Spain and Portugal possessed powerful monarchies that made them good colonizers.

Clichés do not generally make for effective openings, and this essay is no different. The quote does not start the essay off on topic and, indeed, this student can't seem to find a focus for her essay. She casts back and forth between causes and consequences. At first, we are given only two specific factors, but even here there are major errors—the reference to machine guns and poison gas may be to imperialism of the nineteenth century. Instead of a third relevant factor, the student goes on to analyze the effects of exploration. Though the discussion seems fairly accurate, it is not relevant to the question. The second-to-last body paragraph turned into a conclusion. Then, suddenly, the student seemed to remember the last factor but ran out of time in addressing it, so it adds little to the essay. Though this student did offer some relevant discussion, much of the essay is off-task, erroneous, and lacks organization. Score: 3.

Part C—Question 5

Here we have a traditional political question with two events many students will be familiar with. When dealing with a two-part question, be prepared to deal with both events. If you *only* have confidence in your knowledge of, say, the French Revolution, it may be a better idea to choose another question. For political events such as these, it will once again prove tempting to fall into a narrative. Instead, try to pick out the four or five most significant changes that occurred in each of these revolutionary movements. "Compare and contrast" simply means that you must address similarities and differences; to earn a score in the stronger category, you will need to do both, though it is acceptable to stress one more than the other in your thesis.

> Both the English Civil War and the French Revolution assaulted their old systems of government. Though the French Revolution was more violent than the English Civil War, the latter actually made more significant permanent changes in England's government, compared to France's. The French Revolution tried to create a republic, while in England all the radicals wanted to do was limit the power of the monarchy.

> With the English Civil War, the Parliament clashed with the Stuart kings. James I, the first Stuart, claimed divine right rule. This clashed with the Parliament's idea of their liberties, such as approving taxes and having trial by jury. Things came to a head with the rule of James's son, Charles I. Charles also supported an Anglican religion that seemed to the Puritans to be too close to the Catholic Church. Oliver Cromwell, the leader of the Puritans, led the Parliament forces against the king in the civil war. Charles was put on trial for treason and executed. This was a radical act and very similar to the execution of Louis XVI in the French Revolution. Cromwell ruled without a monarchy for a while, but the English brought back the Stuarts. Once again, the Parliament and king clashed over religion and the power of the monarchy. With the Glorious Revolution, the issue was finally resolved. Parliament checked the power of the kings but did not get rid of the monarchy. England kept its king but checked his power with a Bill of Rights. It would be fair to say the old order was revised, but not destroyed.

> France's revolution started out based on the Enlightenment. Leaders wanted to bring natural rights and equality. At first, positive acts occurred like the National Assembly, Tennis Court Oath, and abolition of feudalism. The revolutionaries even developed a constitution, with the king still playing some role. But then the revolution grew more radical—because of war and counterrevolution. The Jacobins were determined to completely sever themselves from the old political system. They wanted a "republic of virtue" and felt that the very existence of a king stood in the way. Louis XVI was executed, leading to the Reign of Terror and more political violence. Ultimately, the French Revolution had to turn to Napoleon to maintain order and finally, by 1815, much of the Old Regime was brought back into place. Ironically, while the French Revolution acted more radically, it actually achieved fewer long-term positive changes in the old order.

Both of these movements tried to upset the traditional political situation. England's seems like it was more in line with its traditions—the power of Parliament to approve legislation. English revolutionaries attempted to do some radical things, like kill the king, but it seemed like it was only to limit the monarch's power. On the other hand, the French revolutionaries got out of control and tried to assassinate anyone connected with France's Old Regime. The level of violence seemed to create a backlash and brought the monarchy back to power. Both revolutions seemed violent and radical but England's was less so and, therefore, more successful.

This essay is an effective model of AP writing. In both the introduction and conclusion, the student clearly lays out the issues involved in the question and addresses them directly. For the body paragraphs, sufficient detail is offered, along with analysis of the tasks in the question—similarities, differences, and an assessment of the level of radicalism. The student provides sophisticated insights into both events and places them in historical context. Noting the ironic result of a return to the old order after the radicalism of the French Revolution constitutes a nice touch. This is definitely an upper-shelf response. Score: 9.

Part C—Question 6

Questions that require response to a quote have become less common on the AP Exam but still appear. You might be inclined simply to restate the quote as part of your thesis. However, whether you agree or disagree with the statement, you should provide reasons for your conclusion. For this prompt, it will be necessary to focus on Europe, though a discussion of American policies seems almost required. Once again, be wary of transforming this into an AP U.S. History question by focusing too much on the United States. Finally, please note the dates: the prompt is not asking for an entire history of the Cold War, simply the first 20 years from its beginnings to about the Cuban Missile Crisis.

After World War II, the United States and Soviet Union clashed during the Cold War. A main battleground of this conflict was Europe, which became divided between the West (allied to the U.S.) and the East (allied to the Soviet Union). Some believe that the Cold War could have been avoided with different policy choices. However, it is clear that the Cold War was basically inevitable.

Much of Europe was in rubble in 1945, so the great powers of Europe had trouble getting back on their feet. This left the field open for the two new superpowers—the United States and Soviet Union. Both nations possessed huge resources, powerful armies, and soon nuclear weapons. There was a vacuum of power in Europe and these giants rushed in to fill it. Misunderstanding might have caused some of the conflict, but only because they already disagreed so much. Take the Marshall Plan. From the American perspective, aid to Europe was an act of generosity. For the USSR, it was a "capitalist plot" to take over Europe. Given their different ideologies, they were almost determined to view this policy differently.

One of the main battlegrounds was Germany. Once the dust settled, the U.S. wanted to get Germany running again. But that's because the U.S. did not lose 20 million people like the USSR did. Stalin wanted to disarm Germany and take away its wealth; he probably thought this was justified after what the Nazis did to his country. When Stalin and Truman disagreed over Germany, it caused the Berlin crisis, with the Soviet Union blockading the city. The U.S. responded with an airlift which saved Berlin. Soon after, the U.S. started NATO to protect Western Europe from Soviet threats. Again, this conflict was not just because of bad policies. The U.S. and USSR simply had different experiences of World War II. It was almost inevitable that they would clash.

There are other examples, like the Warsaw Pact and Cuban Missile Crisis, but the above paragraphs show how the different beliefs of the two nations almost caused them to clash. The Grand Alliance between the U.S., Britain, and Soviet Union was a hasty marriage that was bound to end in divorce. It was easy for the Americans and British to stay tied because of their similar ethnic backgrounds and political experiences. But capitalism and communism are outspoken enemies and could not long keep up their good relations once the Nazis were gone.

This sample generally stays focused on the essay prompt. Though the student addresses the issues of inevitability, this theme is not always construed in terms of ideology, as the quote suggests. The example base is limited, but the evidence is clearly applied to the thesis. When you are given a chronological period, you should attempt to use the entire stretch of time. Here the student concentrates her attention primarily on the period prior to 1950, even though the period specified ends with 1964. In addition, this stronger response would be helped by a few more specific examples and further analysis. Overall, we have a strong response but with some unevenness and a slight misinterpretation of the prompt. Score: 7.

Part C—Question 7
With "compare and contrast," we again must deal with similarities and differences. In this question, you are given two major political figures of the course, which should allow you to draw on a wide range of examples. Your specific knowledge will assist your essay, as long as you keep it focused on the issue of nationalism. Though not specifically prompted, implied in this question are the goals of Bismarck and Hitler. Try to address these as you discuss the views and uses of nationalism. When dealing with the Nazis or Hitler, it is certainly appropriate to offer negative assessments; just steer clear of chest-thumping righteousness.

Germany has often been sparked by nationalism. Two great nationalist leaders in its recent history are Otto von Bismarck and Adolph Hitler. If we look at both of these figures, we find some interesting similarities—they both wanted to make Germany a stronger nation. However, we also see some important differences—Bismarck simply wanted to unify Germany and did not seek power beyond that. Hitler, on the other hand, wanted to conquer most of Europe.

When Bismarck became Chancellor of Prussia, Germany was a collection of dozens of states with no central power. Bismarck's main task became to unify Germany under the leadership of Prussia. His nationalism was of the Realpolitik variety. He saw that Germany needed "iron and blood" to become a single nation. So in the next few years Bismarck fought a series of wars to unify Germany and make it one nation. After defeating France, the new German empire was proclaimed. Most Germans, even the Liberals who did not care much for Bismarck's philosophy, were impressed with his achievement. Even more important, Bismarck tried to keep Europe at peace for the next few decades. He did not seem like he wanted Germany to get any more territory, just stay unified.

Hitler came to power after the weak Weimar government. Many Germans wanted revenge over the Treaty of Vienna that imposed harsh conditions on Germany. Hitler skillfully used these grievances to propel the Nazis into power. Once in power, Hitler claimed that he needed to change the Vienna treaty to include all Germans, especially the Austrians and those in Hungary. Whenever he got what he wanted, Hitler kept demanding more, even though France and Britain kept trying to appease him. Hitler's mad nationalism led Europe right into WWII. Also, Hitler was so nationalistic that he was racist. Only Aryans could be part of his new Germany; all other non-Aryans were killed or sent to concentration camps. While many people rallied to Hitler's nationalism, it also had destroyed Germany by the end of 1945.

Overall, Bismarck demonstrated more skill and understanding in his use of nationalism. Hitler was basically too crazy, wanting to unify only Aryans and conquer most of Europe. Bismarck seemed to accept a reasonable amount of nationalism, at least enough to unify Germany. Hitler's nationalism led him to defeat in WWII and to commit horrible crimes in the Holocaust.

Though some simplifying creeps in related to Hitler, this response effectively addresses the tasks of the question. Explicit comparisons and contrasts are made for the two leaders. Also, this student provides sufficient historical context for the reader to understand the situation facing Germany when both leaders came to power. Each body paragraph provides several well-chosen examples that are employed effectively to develop the student's main idea. The student does repeat an error twice in her second body paragraph regarding the Treaty of Vienna—this should read "Treaty of Versailles," and the reference to Hungary should read "Czechoslovakia." Because the understanding remains on target, these factual mistakes detract only slightly from the essay. The only factors keeping this essay from a top score are the factual errors and some lack of sophistication in the characterization of Nazi policies. Score: 8.

Appendix
CHRONOLOGICAL SUPPLEMENT—TIMELINES

To assist in your chronological mastery of the course, you will find three different timelines in this section. With the first timeline, you can identify the major eras and developments by century. Next is a list of important dates. Though your understanding drives this course, it essential to have a roadmap on your journey; that is why it is strongly recommended that you commit these dates to memory as guideposts. Finally, I have provided a more detailed but still manageable timeline divided into categories. The last column for "THEMES" has been left blank for you to identify the characteristics of historical eras or simply make notes.

Timeline 1: Important Eras and Developments (by century)

Renaissance—1350–1550
Exploration—1450–1600
Protestant and Catholic Reformations—sixteenth century
Religious Wars—1520s–1650
Early Modern Society—1500–1700
Price Revolution—sixteenth century
Dutch Commercial Dominance—1550–1650
Age of Crisis—1550–1650
Witchcraft Scare—1580–1680
Scientific Revolution—1543–1687
Baroque Art—1600–1750
Conflict between Parliament and King in England—1603–1689
Age of Louis XIV—1643–1715
Absolutism—1650–1750
Commercial Wars—1650–1763
Rise of Prussia—1650–1763
Rise of Russia—1689–1815
Commercial Revolution—seventeenth and eighteenth centuries
Rococo Art—1720–1760
Rise of the Middle Class—eighteenth century
Enlightenment—eighteenth century
Agricultural Revolution—eighteenth century
Age of Revolutions—1789–1848
Feminism—1790s–1980s
Romanticism—first half of nineteenth century
Rise of Nationalism—1790s–1914
Unification and Nation-Building—1850–1875
Rise of Liberalism—1830s–1870s
Industrial Revolution—1750–1850
Realism and Materialism—1850–1870s

Second Industrial Revolution—1850–1914
Imperialism—1850–1914
Modern Ideas and Science—1850–1920s
Modern Art—1870–1920
Rise of Modern Society—second half of nineteenth century
Totalitarianism—1920s–1945
World Wars—1914–1945
Cold War—1945–1991
European Unity—1945–present

Note: A century refers to the hundred years numerically prior to the number of the century (e.g., the sixteenth century covers the 1500s).

Timeline 2: Important Dates to Commit to Memory

1348–1351—Black Death
1415–17—Council of Constance burns Hus and ends Great Schism
1453—Fall of Constantinople; end of Hundred Years' War
1455—Invention of printing press
1492—Columbus encounters America; completion of *reconquista* in Spain
1517—Luther posts 95 Theses
1519—Cortez conquers Aztecs
1534—Act of Supremacy in England creates Anglican Church
1536—Calvin establishes reformed faith in Geneva
1543—Copernicus publishes heliocentric theory
1545—Council of Trent opens
1555—Peace of Augsburg ends religious war in Germany;
   Charles V abdicates
1588—Defeat of Spanish Armada
1598—Edict of Nantes ends French religious wars
1600—Dutch East India Company founded
1603—Stuart monarchy begins in England
1648—Peace of Westphalia ends Thirty Years' War
1649—Charles I executed in England
1687—Newton publishes *Principia Mathematica*
1688–1689—Glorious Revolution; Peter the Great's reign begins in Russia
1694—Bank of England founded
1713–1715—Peace of Utrecht; death of Louis XIV
1740—War of Austrian Succession begins
1763—Treaty of Paris ends Seven Years' War
1776—American Revolution; Smith publishes *Wealth of Nations*
1789—French Revolution begins

1792—Wollstonecraft begins feminist movement with *Vindication of Rights of Women*
1799—Napoleon comes to power in France
1815—Abdication of Napoleon; Congress of Vienna
1830–1831—Revolution in France; Belgian and Greek independence
1848—Revolutions of 1848; Marx and Engels publish *Communist Manifesto*
1851—Crystal Palace Exhibition in Britain
1857—Britain establishes direct rule of India
1859—Darwin publishes *Origin of the Species*
1861—Italy unified; Russian serfs emancipated
1871—Unification of Germany; Paris Commune and Third Republic in France
1884–1885—Berlin Conference over imperialism in Africa
1900—Freud publishes *Interpretation of Dreams*
1905—Einstein publishes relativity theory; Revolution of 1905 in Russia
1914—World War I begins
1917—Bolshevik Revolution in Russia
1919—Treaty of Versailles ends World War I
1922—Fascists and Mussolini come to power in Italy
1929—Great Depression begins
1933—Hitler comes to power in Germany
1938—Munich Conference—height of appeasement
1939—World War II begins
1945—World War II ends; United Nations founded
1949—NATO formed
1951—European Coal and Steel Community (ECSC) formed
1953—Stalin dies
1956—Khrushchev's de-Stalinization speech; Hungary revolt
1957—Treaty of Rome creates European Economic Community (EEC); *Sputnik* launched
1958—Fifth Republic in France under DeGaulle
1961—Berlin Wall erected
1962—Cuban Missile Crisis
1962—Second Vatican Council begins
1968—Student revolts; Czech "Prague Spring" revolt
1975—Helsinki Accords—height of détente
1978—John Paul II elected pope
1979—Soviet Union invades Afghanistan; Thatcher elected prime minister in Britain
1980—Solidarity founded in Poland
1985—Gorbachev comes to power in Soviet Union
1989—Berlin Wall falls and collapse of communism
1991—Break-up of Soviet Union; Balkan conflicts begin in former Yugoslavia
1992—Maastricht Treaty creates European Union (EU)
1999—Euro currency introduced
2001—Terrorist attacks on United States

Timeline 3: Detailed Timeline by Topic

Date	Political/ Diplomatic	Religious	Social	Cultural/ Intellectual	Economic/ Technological	THEMES
1300		Babylonian captivity of papacy, 1307–1378 ↓	Great Famine, 1315–1317		Economic depression until mid-fifteenth century ↓	
1325						
	Hundred Years' War, 1337–1453 ↓		Black Death, 1348–1351	Early Renaissance (writings of Petrarch and paintings of Giotto) ↓		
1350						
	Golden Bull, 1356		*Jacquerie* revolt in France, 1358	Vernacular literature ↓		
					Decline of serfdom in western Europe ↓	
1375		John Wyclif's ideas of reform Great Schism, 1378–1417 ↓	Ciompi revolt in Florence, 1378			
		Conciliar movement	Wat Tyler revolt in England, 1381			
1400			Slave labor imported from Africa into Europe, until ca. 1500 ↓			
		Jan Hus burned at the stake, 1415 Council of Constance ends Great Schism, 1417			Prince Henry founds navigation school, 1415	

Date	Political/ Diplomatic	Religious	Social	Cultural/ Intellectual	Economic/ Technological	THEMES
1425			Arranged marriages in Italy, age gap between husbands and wives ↓	Florence emerges as center of Italian Renaissance ↓		
	Medicis come to power in Florence, 1430s					
1450	Constantinople captured by Turks, 1453				Economic recovery, until mid-sixteenth century	
	Peace of Lodi, 1454					
	Wars of Roses in England, 1455–1485 ↓				Gutenberg invents printing press, 1455	
	Isabella and Ferdinand unify Spain, 1469					
1475	Rise of New Monarchs, to mid-16th century ↓				Rise of Portuguese trading empire ↓	
	Isabella and Ferdinand complete *reconquista*/ Jews expelled from Spain, 1492			High Renaissance in Rome, after 1490	Columbus's voyages to the Americas, 1492	
	French invade Italy, 1494					
	Habsburg-Valois Wars, 1494–1559 ↓		Enclosure movement begins	Writings of Erasmus Christian Humanism	Price Revolution, sixteenth century ↓	
1500	Henry VIII, ruler of England (1509–1547)		Early Modern Society, 1500–1700 ↓	Machiavelli, *The Prince*, 1513		
	Charles V, ruler of Spain/HRE (1516–1556)	Luther posts 95 Theses, 1517 Protestant Reformation ↓	Population recovers to pre-plague levels		Cortez conquers Aztecs, 1519 Magellan's circum-navigation, 1519–1521	

Date	Political/Diplomatic	Religious	Social	Cultural/Intellectual	Economic/Technological	THEMES
1525	Military revolution, 1500–1650 ↓ Henry VIII creates Anglican Church, 1533–1534	Calvinism in Geneva, 1536 Jesuits founded, 1540s Catholic Counter-Reformation Council of Trent, 1545–1563 ↓	German Peasants Revolt, 1524–1525 Age of Crisis, ca. 1550–1650 ↓	Rome sacked to end Renaissance, 1527 Castiglione, *The Courtier*, 1527 Copernicus, heliocentric theory, 1543 Scientific Revolution, 1543–1687 ↓	Spanish and Portuguese colonization Rise of Netherlands as commercial power ↓	
1550	Peace of Augsburg, 1555 Elizabeth I of England (1558–1603) ↓ French religious wars, 1562–1598 ↓ Dutch Revolt vs. Spain, 1566–1648 ↓ St. Bartholomew's Day Massacre, 1572	re-Catholicization of central and eastern Europe		Baroque Art, 1550s–1720s ↓ Michelangelo dies, 1564 Shakespeare in England (1564–1616) ↓ Mannerist Art, 1560s–1600 ↓		
1575 1600	Defeat of Spanish Armada, 1588 Edict of Nantes, 1598 Time of Troubles in Russia, 1590s–1613 Stuart monarchy in England, 1603–1714 ↓		Witchcraft persecution, 1580–1700 ↓ Population peaks and then declines throughout seventeenth century ↓	Bacon advocates empirical science Galileo's *Starry Messenger*, 1610 Dutch cultural flowering, seventeenth century ↓	Commercial Revolution, seventeenth and eighteenth centuries ↓ Development of Triangular Trade	
1625	Thirty Years' War, 1618–1648 ↓		High crime rates, seventeenth century			

Date	Political/ Diplomatic	Religious	Social	Cultural/ Intellectual	Economic/ Technological	THEMES
	English Civil War, 1642–1649	Galileo before the Inquisition, 1633	Numerous revolts Wide-spread famine during "Little Ice Age"	Descartes' *Discourse on Method*, 1637		
	Age of Louis XIV, 1643–1715 ↓ Peace of Westphalia, 1648	Jansenism and Pascal in France				
1650	Cromwell and Protectorate, 1650s			Hobbes's *Leviathan*, 1651	Practice of mercantilism, to ca. 1650–1750 ↓	
	Stuart Restoration, 1660–1688			Great Age of Opera and Baroque music, 1600–1750 ↓	Commercial Wars, 1650–1763 ↓	
	Rise of absolute monarchies ↓ Rise of Prussia ↓	English Test Act, 1673				
1675						
	Ottomans besiege Vienna, 1683	Revocation of Edict of Nantes, 1685		Newton's *Principia Mathematica*, 1687		
	Peter the Great's reforms in Russia, 1689–1725 ↓	Development of deism ↓	Rise of the middle class Aristo-cratic reaction	Locke's *Second Treatise on Government* & *Essay On Human Understanding*, 1690		
	Glorious Revolution, 1688–1689	German Pietist revival in Lutheranism ↓				
1700	War of Spanish Succession, 1702–1713 (Peace of Utrecht)	Development of skepticism, atheism, and secularism			Agricultural Revolution, 18th century ↓	
	Great Northern War, 1700–1721	Wesley's Methodist revival in England, 1730s–1800 ↓			Enclosure movement in England, eighteenth century ↓	

Date	Political/ Diplomatic	Religious	Social	Cultural/ Intellectual	Economic/ Technological	THEMES
1725		Enlightened absolute monarchs extend religious toleration	Population increase begins throughout eighteenth century ↓ Concept of childhood emerges, eighteenth century ↓	Enlighten-ment, 1720s–1789 ↓ Rococo art, 1720s–1760s ↓ Montesquieu's *Spirit of the Laws*, 1748	Cottage industry system, eighteenth and early nineteenth centuries ↓ Textile innovations, 1733–1800 ↓	
	War of Austrian Succession, 1740–1748					
1750	Age of Enlightened Absolutism, 1740–1790 ↓			Diderot publishes *Encyclopedia*, 1751		
	Seven Years' War, 1756–1763	Jesuits disbanded, 1773 (until 1814)		Voltaire's *Candide*, 1759 Rousseau's *Social Contract* and *Emile*, 1762		
	Catherine the Great in Russia (r. 1762-96)					
	Partitions of Poland, 1772–1795	Jewish emancipation from restric-tions, 1780s–1918 ↓		Neoclassical art ↓		
1775	American Revolution, 1775–1783		Rise of industrial cities in Britain		Smith's *Wealth of Nations*, 1776	
	French Revolution, 1789–1799	De-Christian-ization campaign of French Revolution, 1791–1794	Population increase, nineteenth century ↓ Abolition of feudalism, 1789–1800, in western and central Europe	Wollstone-craft's *Vindication of Rights of Women*, 1792	First textile mill, 1780 Watt's steam engine, 1780s	
	Rise of Napoleon, 1796–1815					
1800		Napoleon's Concordat with Catholic Church, 1801		Romanticism, 1800–1850 ↓	Classical economists—Smith, Malthus, Ricardo	
	French Empire, 1804–1814		Rise of proletariat and labor unions	Rise of nationalism, nineteenth century ↓		
	Congress of Vienna, 1814–1815	Revival of religion during Romanticism				

Date	Political/ Diplomatic	Religious	Social	Cultural/ Intellectual	Economic/ Technological	THEMES
1825	Concert of Europe, 1815–1840s ↓ Greek/ Belgian independence, 1830–31 Revolution of 1830 in France Reform Act of 1832 in Britain Revolutions of 1848 Napoleon III in France, 1848–1870		Chartism in Britain, 1830s–1840s Potato famine in Ireland, 1840s	Utopian Socialism Marx's *Communist Manifesto*, 1848 Liberalism ascendant Positivism	Industrialization in Britain, nineteenth century ↓ First railroads, 1830s Zollverein, 1834 Reforms in Britain, 1830s–1840s List's economic nationalism, 1844 Corn Laws repealed, 1846	
1850	Crimean War, 1853–1856 Reforms of Alexander II in Russia, 1855–1881 Italian unification, 1858–1861 Bismarck as Chancellor, 1862–1890 Austro-Hungarian *Ausgleich*, 1867 German unification, 1864–1871	Pope Pius IX (r. 1846–1878) opposes modernism ↓ First Vatican Council, 1870 (papal infalli-bility) Protestant denomina-tions split between modernists and fundamen-talists	Serfdom abolished in Russia, 1861 Pasteur's germ theory, 1860s Socialist parties Urban reform movements	Realism in the arts and philosophy Darwin's *Origin of Species*, 1859 Impression-ism Nietzsche's writings, 1870s–1880s Developments in quantum physics Modern Art ↓	Second Industrial Revolution, 1850s–1914 Crystal Palace Exhibition, 1851 Sepoy Mutiny, 1857 Suez Canal, 1869 Imperialism in Africa and Asia, 1850s–1914 ↓ Business cycles, 1873–1896	
1875	Paris Commune and Third Republic, 1871 Congress of Berlin, 1878 Mass politics	Dreyfus Affair in France, 1890s			Industrialization of Russia, 1880s–1930s ↓	

Date	Political/ Diplomatic	Religious	Social	Cultural/ Intellectual	Economic/ Technological	THEMES
1900	↓ Russo-Japanese War and Revolution of 1905 in Russia World War I, 1914–1918 Russian Revolution, 1917 Treaty of Versailles, 1919	Zionism ↓	Rise of mass leisure, literacy, education Feminism Modern medical care, life expectancy increases ↓	Freud's *Interpretation of Dreams*, 1900 Einstein's relativity theory, 1905	Berlin Conference over Africa, 1885 Airplane invented, 1903	
1925	Russian Civil War, 1918–1921 Weimar Republic, 1918–1933 Mussolini in Italy, 1922–1943 Hitler comes to power, 1933–1945 Appeasement, 1930s World War II, 1939–1945 Cold War, 1945–1991 ↓ NATO, 1949	Lateran Accord between fascist Italy and Vatican, 1929 Concordat between Nazis and Catholic Church, 1933 Nuremberg Laws, 1935 Holocaust, 1939–1945	Women gain vote in many nations, 1918 Postwar baby boom Guest workers	Interwar high culture of alienation and pessimism, 1918–1939 Interwar mass culture, 1918–1939	New Economic Policy in USSR, 1921–1928 Hyperinflation in Germany, 1923 Radio and motion pictures Collectivization of agriculture in USSR, 1930s Five-Year Plans in USSR, 1928–1938 Great Depression, 1929-39 Decolonization, 1945–1970s ↓	
1950	Hungary revolt, 1956		Growth of welfare state	Postwar existentialism	ECSC, 1951 Economic recovery in Western Europe	

Date	Political/ Diplomatic	Religious	Social	Cultural/ Intellectual	Economic/ Technological	THEMES
1975	Berlin Wall, 1961 Cuban Missile Crisis, 1962 Czech revolt, 1968 Détente, 1970s	Pope John XXIII (r. 1958–1963) calls Second Vatican Council	Postwar feminism, 1960s–1980s Student revolts, 1968 Generation gap	Rock music ↓	EEC, 1957 *Sputnik,* 1957 Space race and ICBMs, 1960s Oil shock, 1970s Stagflation	
2000	Solidarity in Poland, 1980 Gorbachev in power, 1985–1991 Fall of communism and USSR, 1989–1991 German reunification, 1990 Breakup of Yugoslavia— Balkan conflicts, 1991–1999	John Paul II (r. 1978–2005) elected first Slavic pope		Pop art Post-modernism	Personal computers, 1980s Maastricht Treaty creates EU, 1991 Euro, 1999	